D0219836

EYES EVERYWHERE

In many countries camera surveillance has become commonplace, and ordinary citizens and consumers are increasingly aware that they are under surveillance in everyday life. Camera surveillance is typically perceived as the archetype of contemporary surveillance technologies and processes.

While there is sometimes fierce debate about their introduction, many others take the cameras for granted or even applaud their deployment. Yet what the presence of surveillance cameras actually achieves is still very much in question. International evidence shows that they have very little effect in deterring crime and in 'making people feel safer', but they do serve to place certain groups under greater official scrutiny and to extend the reach of today's 'surveillance society'.

Eyes Everywhere provides the first international perspective on the development of camera surveillance. It scrutinizes the quiet but massive expansion of camera surveillance around the world in recent years, focusing especially on Canada, the UK and the USA but also including less-debated but important contexts such as Brazil, China, Japan, Mexico, South Africa and Turkey. Containing both broad overviews and illuminating case studies, including cameras in taxi cabs and at mega-events such as the Olympics, the book offers a valuable oversight on the status of camera surveillance in the second decade of the twenty-first century.

The book will be fascinating reading for students and scholars of camera surveillance as well as policy-makers and practitioners from the police, chambers of commerce, private security firms and privacy- and data-protection agencies.

Aaron Doyle is Associate Professor in the Department of Sociology and Anthropology at Carleton University.

Randy Lippert is Professor of Criminology at the University of Windsor, Canada.

David Lyon is Director of the Surveillance Studies Centre and Professor of Sociology at Queen's University.

EYES EVERYWHERE

The global growth of camera surveillance

Edited by Aaron Doyle, Randy Lippert and David Lyon

Routledge
Taylor & Francis Group

LONDON AND NEW YORK

First published 2012 by Routledge
2 Park Square, Milton Park, Abingdon, Oxon, OX14 4RN

Simultaneously published in the USA and Canada
by Routledge
711 Third Avenue, New York, NY 10017

Routledge is an imprint of the Taylor & Francis Group, an informa business

British Library Cataloguing in Publication Data
A catalogue record for this book is available from the British Library

Library of Congress Cataloging in Publication Data
Eyes everywhere: the global growth of camera surveillance/
edited by Aaron Doyle, Randy Lippert and David Lyon.
    p. cm.
1. Crime prevention. 2. Video surveillance—Social aspects.
3. Closed-circuit television—Social aspects. 4. Public safety.
5. Privacy, Right of. I. Doyle, Aaron. II. Lippert, Randy K.,
1966– III. Lyon, David, 1948–
HV7431.E995 2012
364.4—dc23   2011027648

ISBN: 978–0–415–66864–4 hbk
ISBN: 978–0–415–69655–5 pbk
ISBN: 978–0–203–14162–5 ebook

Typeset in Bembo
by Swales & Willis Ltd, Exeter, Devon

MIX
Paper from
responsible sources
FSC® C004839
www.fsc.org

Printed and bound in Great Britain by
CPI Antony Rowe, Chippenham, Wiltshire

CONTENTS

Contributors   viii
Acknowledgements   xv

1 Introduction   1
   David Lyon, Aaron Doyle and Randy Lippert

PART I
Situating camera surveillance growth   **21**

2 There's no success like failure and failure's no success at all:
   some critical reflections on the global growth of CCTV
   surveillance   23
   Clive Norris

3 What goes up, must come down: on the moribundity of
   camera networks in the UK   46
   Gavin Smith

4 Seeing surveillantly: surveillance as social practice   67
   Jonathan Finn

PART II
International growth of camera surveillance   **81**

5 Cameras in context: a comparison of the place of video
   surveillance in Japan and Brazil   83
   David Murakami Wood

6 The growth and further proliferation of camera surveillance
in South Africa 100
Anthony Minnaar

7 The piecemeal development of camera surveillance in Canada 122
Emily Smith

PART III
Evolving forms and uses of camera surveillance 137

8 The electronic eye of the police: the provincial information
and security system in Istanbul 139
Alanur Çavlin Bozbeyoğlu

9 Policing in the age of information: automated number
plate recognition 156
Patrick Derby

10 Video surveillance in Vancouver: legacies of the Games 174
Micheal Vonn and Philip Boyle

11 Selling surveillance: the introduction of cameras in
Ottawa taxis 185
Aaron Doyle and Kevin Walby

12 Deploying camera surveillance images: the case of Crime
Stoppers 202
Randy Lippert and Blair Wilkinson

13 Hidden changes: from CCTV to 'smart' video surveillance 218
Joseph Ferenbok and Andrew Clement

PART IV
**Public support, media visions and the politics of
representation** 235

14 Anti-surveillance activists v. the dancing heads of terrorism:
signal crimes, media frames and camera promotion 237
Laura Huey

15 Surveillance cameras and synopticism: a case study in
   Mexico City   249
   Nelson Artaega Botello

16 Appropriation and the authoring function of surveillance in
   Manu Luksch's *Faceless*   262
   Martin Zeilinger

17 'What do *you* think?': international public opinion on
   camera surveillance   274
   Danielle Dawson

PART V
Regulating camera surveillance   **293**

18 Towards a framework of contextual integrity: legality,
   trust and compliance of CCTV signage   295
   Mark Lizar and Gary Potter

19 Mitigating asymmetic visibilities: towards a signage code
   for surveillance camera networks   309
   Andrew Clement and Joseph Ferenbok

20 Is it a 'search'? The legal context of camera surveillance in
   Canada   333
   Mathew Johnson

21 Privacy as security: comparative developments in Canada,
   the UK and the USA   355
   Christopher Burt

22 Sometimes what's public is 'private': legal rights to privacy in
   public spaces   370
   Robert Ellis Smith

Index   *380*

CONTRIBUTORS

Nelson Arteaga Botello

Nelson Arteaga Botello is a researcher of sociology in the Faculty of Political and Social Science at the Autonomous University of the State of Mexico. He received his doctorate at the University of Alicante, Spain and specializes in issues of violence, security and surveillance in Latin America. His most recent publications are 'The Merida Initiative: Security–Surveillance Harmonization in Latin America' in the *European Review of Latin American and Caribbean Studies*; 'Security Metamorphosis in Latin America' in Vida Bajc and Willem de Lint (eds), *Security and Everyday Life* (Routledge, 2011) and 'Biological and Political Identity: The Identification Systems in Mexico' in *Current Sociology*.

Philip Boyle

Philip Boyle is a Research Associate in the Global Urban Research Unit at Newcastle University, UK. His research interests are in the intersection of security, surveillance and urban governance, and his PhD research examines security provision at the Olympic Games in the post-9/11 period. He is the co-author of 'Spectacular Security: Mega-Events and the Security Complex' with K. Haggerty (*International Political Sociology* 2009: 3) and has chapters in *Security Games: Security and Control at Mega-Events* (C. Bennett and K. Haggerty, eds, 2011) and *A Handbook of Olympic Studies* (H. Lenkyj and S. Waag, eds, 2011).

Christopher Burt

Christopher Burt is currently a Master's candidate in the Department of Computer Science at Stevens Institute of Technology in Hoboken, NJ, under the advisory of Dr Susanne Wetzel. He holds a Bachelor's degree in Economics and Political Science from Boston University and has spent more than a decade in private sector banking and finance. His research interests are currently in the areas of security economics, behavioural privacy and informed consent.

Alanur Çavlin Bozbeyoğlu

Alanur Çavlin-Bozbeyoğlu is a post-doctoral fellow at the Surveillance Studies Centre, Queen's University. Her major interest is state surveillance related to data-gathering systems – namely population censuses, registration systems and identification systems – and their relationship with neo-liberal transformation and citizenship regimes. Alanur's current work includes articles on electronic ID card systems, census questionnaires, registration systems, ethnic/religious minorities' presentation and monitoring, and camera surveillance in Turkey.

Andrew Clement

Andrew Clement is a professor in the Faculty of Information at the University of Toronto, where he co-ordinates the Information Policy Research Program and is a co-founder of the Identity, Privacy and Security Initiative. He gained his PhD in Computer Science and has had long-standing research and teaching interests in the social implications of information/communication technologies and human-centred/participatory information systems development. His research has focused on public information policy, internet use in everyday life, digital identity constructions, public participation in information/communication infrastructure development and community networking. Among his recent research projects related to identity, privacy and surveillance, he is a co-investigator in the New Transparency: Surveillance and Social Sorting research collaboration, a seven-year SSHRC-funded Major Collaborative Research Initiative.

Danielle Dawson

Danielle Dawson completed her MA in Sociology at Queen's University. She specializes in the area of information and communication technology with a focus on surveillance. Involved in the Surveillance Project at Queen's University throughout her undergraduate degree, she remained a part of the Surveillance Studies Centre during her Master's. Her current research is on radio-frequency identification as a form of human surveillance.

Patrick Derby

Patrick Derby is currently a PhD candidate in the Department of Sociology at Queen's University, Canada, and a member of the Surveillance Studies Centre (SSC) and the Surveillance Camera Awareness Network (SCAN). He is interested in the marketing, use and social impact of crime control technologies broadly, and of surveillance technologies specifically. His doctoral research explores the impact of Automated Licence Plate Recognition on contemporary roads policing. Patrick is also Book Review Editor for the *Journal of Prisoners on Prisons*.

Aaron Doyle

Aaron Doyle is Associate Professor in the Department of Sociology and Anthropology at Carleton University. His research focuses on how institutions like the mass media, the criminal justice system and insurance organizations deal with risk through surveillance and other means, and the security and insecurity that result. His books include *Arresting Images: Crime and Policing in Front of the Television Camera*; three books with the late Richard Ericson, *Risk and Morality*, *Insurance as Governance* and *Uncertain Business: Risk, Insurance and the Limits of Knowledge;* and a recent collection co-edited with Dawn Moore: *Critical Criminology in Canada: New Voices, New Directions*.

Joseph Ferenbok

Joseph Ferenbok is faculty at the Institute of Communication, Culture and Information Technology at the University of Toronto. He completed a post-doctoral fellowship with the Identity, Privacy and Security Institute (IPSI) and received his PhD from the University of Toronto. His research interests focus on themes of privacy, accountability and transparency in (video) surveillance and how 'the face' may play a positive role in redressing some of the one-sided views of surveillance. His research includes the augmentation of identification documents with technologies such as radio-frequency ID (RFID) chips and biometrics like face recognition/comparison software, and how these technologies change relationships of power between individuals and institutions.

Jonathan Finn

Jonathan Finn is Associate Dean in the Faculty of Arts and Associate Professor in the Department of Communication Studies at Wilfrid Laurier University and is a member of the Editorial Board of Wilfrid Laurier University Press. He is the author of two books: *Capturing the Criminal Image: From Mug Shot to Surveillance Society* (Minnesota, 2009) and *Visual Communication and Culture: Images in Action* (OUP, 2011). He has also published numerous essays on surveillance, visual communication and visual culture. His primary area of research is the history and theory of photography, and he is currently developing a new research project on visual communication technologies and sport.

Laura Huey

Laura Huey is Assistant Professor of Sociology at the University of Western Ontario. Her areas of research are policing and surveillance issues, and she has published numerous journal articles on both topics. She is also the author of a book that combines her interests: *Negotiating Demands: The Politics of 'Skid Row' Policing in Edinburgh, San Francisco and Vancouver* (UTP, 2007).

Mathew Johnson

Mathew Johnson is Counsel with the International Assistance Group of the Department of Justice, Canada. He received his law degree and Masters of Public Administration from Queen's University.

Randy Lippert

Randy Lippert is Professor of Criminology at the University of Windsor, Canada. His research interests include urban security, governance and surveillance. He has published one book and many articles, most recently, 'Advancing Governmentality Studies: Lessons from Social Constructionism', *Theoretical Criminology*, 14(4): 473–94 (with Kevin Stenson).

Mark Lizar

Mark Lizar conducted the research for his contribution to Eyes Everywhere while enrolled on an MSc in Social Research Methods at London South Bank University. His research focused on the use of surveillance notices to regulate CCTV and identified methods for increasing social trust in London. Mark plays an active role in privacy standards internationally, focusing on the development of consent, control and the use of notices to develop security, privacy and trust in surveillance. He is particularly concerned with exploring how surveillance can be used to improve relationships between businesses and consumers to improve economic performance. Mark endeavours to contribute to the evolution of trust management and control of information in society. He is a founder of the community interest company (CIC) Surveillance Trust. Surveillance Trust is a new type of social enterprise that enables people to register and report Surveillance notices so that communities can create transparency to facilitate greater benefit and security from surveillance. http://www.SurveillanceTrust.org, http://www.cctvtrust.org/

David Lyon

David Lyon is Director of the Surveillance Studies Centre and Professor of Sociology at Queen's University: <http://www.sscqueens.org/davidlyon/>.

Anthony Minnaar

Since January 2009 Professor Anthony Minnaar has been the Programme Head: Security Management for the merged Department of Criminology & Security Science, School of Criminal Justice in the College of Law at the University of South Africa. His current research interests are in the field of criminal justice dealing with the specific issues of corruption prevention, border controls and undocumented migrants, xenophobia and refugees; use of firearms in violent crime, civilian oversight of public and private policing and private security industry issues (specifically crime prevention and private policing; and community policing and community safety initiatives); regulating and monitoring the Private Security Industry in South Africa; security at ports-of-entry; the use of CCTV surveillance systems for security; and neighbourhood safety/crime prevention.

David Murakami Wood

David Murakami Wood is Canada Research Chair (Tier II) in Surveillance Studies and Associate Professor in the Department of Sociology, Queen's University, Ontario, and a member of the Surveillance Studies Centre. He is also co-founder and Managing Editor of *Surveillance & Society*, and co-founder and trustee of the Surveillance Studies Network. He is an inter-disciplinary social scientist specializing in the study of surveillance in urban contexts worldwide, and in international cross-cultural comparative studies particularly in the UK, Japan and Brazil. He is also interested in: ubiquitous computing; resilience to disaster, war and terrorism; and science-fiction literature and films.

Clive Norris

Clive Norris is Professor of Sociology at the University of Sheffield and Head of the Department of Sociological Studies. Since 1993 he has been working on various aspects of the sociology of surveillance, first with an ESRC grant to explore the subterranean world of the police use of informers, followed by further ESRC funding to examine the social impact of CCTV surveillance. In 1998 he was awarded funding by the ESRC to run a series of seminars on surveillance. This brought together for the first time inter-disciplinary researchers concerned with the social impact of the new surveillance technologies. As a direct result he co-founded the free online journal *Surveillance & Society*. Along with colleagues from six European universities, he has worked on a comparative study of the social impact of CCTV and is currently researching the legal, ethical and social implication of 'smart' surveillance systems.

Gary Potter

Dr Gary Potter completed his PhD at Sheffield University and is now Senior Lecturer in Criminology at London South Bank University, and a Senior Researcher in the Crime Reduction and Community Safety Research Group there. His main research interests are drug use, drug-trafficking and the drugs/crime connection, but he is also interested in surveillance, privacy and environmental crime. His recent publications include *Weed, Need and Greed: A Study of Domestic Cannabis Cultivation* and (with Tom Decorte and Martin Bouchard) *World Wide Weed: Global Trends in Cannabis Cultivation and Its Control*. The common threads to these seemingly diverse interests are issues of human rights, individual freedoms and social responsibility.

Emily Smith

Emily Smith is a research associate with the Surveillance Studies Centre at Queen's University. She holds a Master's degree in Sociology from Queen's University, and has written on topics including workplace surveillance, privacy and public opinion, national identity cards and camera surveillance. She is also editorial assistant for the online journal *Surveillance & Society*.

Gavin Smith

Gavin Smith is a Lecturer in Sociology and Social Policy at The University of Sydney and an Honorary Visiting Fellow at The Centre for Law, Justice and Journalism, City University London. Gavin is principally interested in processual interplays among systems of regulation and subjects of surveillance, particularly the interpretive meanings actors attribute to surveillance encounters/exchanges and concomitant social dynamics. He is also interested in the normative assumptions structuring the surveillance studies research field. Gavin convenes The University of Sydney's 'Surveillance and Everyday Life Research Group', an interdisciplinary scholarly collective interested in intersectionalities between surveillance technologies and everyday living. He is currently writing a monograph on the labour of surveillance work – *Opening the Black Box: Surveillancein Everyday Life* (Routledge, 2012) – and a co-authored text, *Key Concepts in Social Regulation and Transparency Studies* (Sage, 2012).

Robert Ellis Smith

Robert Ellis Smith, an attorney, has published the *Privacy Journal* newsletter since 1974. It is based in Providence, Rhode Island, USA. He is author of *Ben Franklin's Web Site: Privacy and Curiosity From Plymouth Rock to the Internet* (2004), a book tracing privacy in American history.

Micheal Vonn

Micheal Vonn is a lawyer and Policy Director of the British Columbia Civil Liberties Association. She has been an Adjunct Professor at the University of British Columbia in the Faculty of Law and the School of Library, Archival and Information Studies, where she teaches civil liberties and information ethics. She is an Advisory Board member of Privacy International and has studied legal geography with Nick Blomley at Simon Fraser University.

Kevin Walby

Kevin Walby is Assistant Professor, Department of Sociology, University of Victoria. His recent journal articles have appeared in *Antipode* (2011, with Randy Lippert), *International Sociology* (2011, with Sean Hier), *Punishment & Society* (2011, with Justin Piché), *Social Movement Studies* (2011, with Jeff Monaghan), *Qualitative Research* (2010), the *British Journal of Criminology* (2010, with Justin Piché) and *Criminology and Criminal Justice* (2010, with Nicolas Carrier). He is the prisoners' struggles editor for the *Journal of Prisoners on Prisons*.

Blair Wilkinson

Blair Wilkinson is a PhD student in Sociology at the University of Victoria. He has recently published in *Crime, Media, Culture* (with Randy Lippert). His research interests include contemporary developments in public video surveillance in Canadian cities and the use of video surveillance images in policing, courts and the media. He is also interested in the development and application of public policy related to the use of video surveillance.

Martin Zeilinger

Martin Zeilinger holds a Banting Postdoctoral Fellowship in Law and Culture at York University, Toronto. His dissertation, 'Art and Politics of Appropriation' (Comparative Literature, University of Toronto 2009) is under revision for publication. With Rosemary J. Coombe and Darren Wershler, he is co-editor of the forthcoming collection *Dynamic Fair Dealing: Creating Canadian Culture Online* (2011). His research focuses on appropriation art in analogue and digital media; theories of creativity, authorship and cultural ownership; and intellectual property and the commons in socio-legal theory.

ACKNOWLEDGEMENTS

The editors wish to thank the Canadian Office of the Privacy Commissioner Contributions Program for its support of the 2010 Research Workshop from which most of the chapters in this book were drawn. The workshop was organized by SCAN, the Surveillance Cameras Awareness Network (<www.sscqueens. org/projects/scan>), under the aegis of the Surveillance Studies Centre (SSC) at Queen's University. The SSC, in turn, is mainly supported by the Social Sciences and Humanities Research Council of Canada. Within the SSC, steady and unstinting editorial support was given by Emily Smith and Sarah Cheung.

1

INTRODUCTION

David Lyon, Aaron Doyle and Randy Lippert

Today there are eyes everywhere, and it took just one generation. In thirty years camera surveillance grew from an unknown, non-issue to a frequently taken-for-granted 'necessity' on the street, in shopping malls, office buildings and factories, in transit stations and airports. Indeed, as Stephen Graham once suggested, public open-street video cameras may be considered as akin to a 'fifth utility' (Graham 1999). And while such public cameras receive much of the attention, privately owned and operated cameras are even more ubiquitous. Just how densely those cameras are distributed is a matter of some debate, of course.

Take the United Kingdom (UK), for example, often considered a leading site for camera surveillance. While earlier research projected the presence of over 4 million cameras in the UK, a more recent analysis suggests there may be 'only' 1.85 million (Gerrard and Thompson 2011). Both figures were arrived at through considerable extrapolation, but the point that the total number of cameras in the UK is in the millions is not in dispute. Even so, the UK's role as world surveillance camera leader may not last for long. While cameras have sprouted in streets, stations and stores across Europe and North America, they are also being sold as 'security solutions' in many other countries around the globe. The rationales for their adoption, and public and official opinions about their efficacy, may vary from place to place, but their widespread adoption across the globe does not appear to be slowing. Cameras have appeared on the streets and in the stores of Accra, Ghana; Kathmandu, Nepal; Tegucigalpa, Honduras; Kabul, Afghanistan; and (perhaps not inappropriately) Montevideo, Uruguay: these examples suggest there appear to be no geographical or economic limits to their use.

Meanwhile, camera surveillance also continues to multiply, intensify and evolve in the countries like the UK in which it was already well established: surveillance cameras appear in diverse new contexts such as taxi cabs (Doyle and Walby, this volume), new forms proliferate such as Automated Number Plate Recognition

(Derby, this volume), and new means of co-ordinating camera surveillance emerge, such as the MOBESE system in Istanbul (Çavlin Bozbeyoğlu, this volume), even as the move to digital technology may revolutionize the capabilities of surveillance camera systems (Ferenbok and Clement, this volume).

All that said, we need to be cautious about simply assuming a continued unidirectional march to global ubiquity of the cameras, as Gavin Smith points out in his contribution to this collection. Smith spotlights how the cost and effectiveness of CCTV schemes in the UK is increasingly coming into question, and receiving negative media attention, and some CCTV operations in that country are even closing down. Smith thus speculates about the emergence of a 'politics of retraction'. From time to time one also sees publicly expressed doubts, relating to actual analysis of the evidence, about the effectiveness of camera surveillance. Recent examples in Paris, France and Los Angeles, California, are cases in point.[1]

For the most part though, it is fair to say the spread of the cameras continues largely unchecked. Perhaps most significantly in terms of proliferation, camera surveillance has caught on in the largest countries such as China and India, where economic growth rates are high and modernization and urbanization processes are proceeding at a dizzying pace. For instance, the *Shanghai Daily* reports that the number of public space cameras is to double, in that city, to over 50,000 between 2011 and 2016, with the rationale of boosting police investigation of criminals and to track suspects.[2] China's video surveillance market was estimated to be worth over US$1.4 billion in 2009 and is likely to grow at 20 per cent per annum, reaching $3.5 billion in 2014. While camera surveillance equipment sales in China represented 17 per cent of the world market in 2009, to the US's 29 per cent, by 2014 it is estimated that 70 per cent of world video camera shipments will be to China, compared with 12 per cent in the US and 18 per cent in the rest of the world.[3]

The paradox is that for all the millions of cameras and billions spent, there is a lack of convincing evidence that they 'work'. The conundrum of the continued spread of cameras in the absence of such evidence has intrigued and puzzled social researchers, policy analysts and legal experts. It was a major theme of a January 2010 international research workshop of SCAN (Surveillance Camera Awareness Network) at the Surveillance Studies Centre at Queen's University in Kingston, Ontario, Canada (and of a report published by SCAN in 2009[4]). The workshop featured numerous scholars from the social sciences and from information and computer studies as well as policy and legal experts, and most of the chapters in this book were originally presented there.

As we discussed at length at the workshop, what the presence of surveillance cameras actually achieves is still very much in doubt. A variety of purposes is trumpeted for the cameras – deterrence, retroactive prosecution of criminals, making people feel safer – but the evidence seen throughout this volume does not support arguments that they achieve any of these purposes very effectively. In fact, international evidence in general is that they have very little effect in deterring crime (several contributors, e.g. Lizar and Potter, this volume, report that there is frequently no signage marking cameras' presence, undercutting a possible deterrent effect).

Surveillance camera footage is rarely used for prosecutions, and any possible impact in making people safer is debatable at best, and also raises questions about the ethics of a measure that may make people *feel* safer but has no effect in practice. Critics charge that the cameras may serve to place certain groups under greater official scrutiny and to extend the reach of today's 'surveillance societies', although their general failure to achieve deterrence or prosecution of offenders suggests that, as Hier (2010) notes, the panoptic effect of the cameras may currently be more dream than reality. Yet surveillance camera technologies are rapidly evolving and we must also consider their potential future functions and effectiveness, for good or ill.

The absence of evidence that the cameras 'work' immediately prompts the question: why do they continue to spread? And this is where the social sciences come in, with their attempts to understand not only a general and very rapid growth of camera surveillance, but also the particular conditions that give rise to specific developments as well as shaping responses to them in different regions and countries of the world. For example, in North America and Western Europe, growing camera surveillance is typically associated with the perception of rising crime problems (despite generally declining crime rates), increased police use of technology in general, traffic control, and of course post-9/11 preoccupations with security (Norris, McCahill and Wood 2004). In Latin American cities, arguably, urban violence is at the top of the agenda when decisions are made about installing video surveillance, while post-9/11 fears are hardly relevant (Arteaga 2009; Arteaga this volume).

Even within these regional generalizations, of course, large variations exist. There are many different countries in Latin America or Europe and even the term 'North America' covers three different countries: Canada, the US and Mexico. In the first, Canada, from which this collection originated, the situation is marked by a relative lack of cameras. While, as Sean Hier says, 'Canadian cities have not been impervious to global trends in establishing public-area CCTV surveillance systems,' he goes on, 'Canada is notable, however, for the number of cities where streetscape CCTV surveillance systems have been rejected – whether based on public and government discussion and debate, the mobilization of formal protest groups, informal networks of community resistance, short- and long-term funding concerns, or the enactment and execution of privacy laws and policy frameworks' (Hier 2010: 28). This is a reminder that the contrasting rationales must also be placed next to diverse responses to efforts to deploy camera surveillance, which may also slow growth and which also vary from place to place.

To return to the area in which camera surveillance is fastest growing, China, it appears that public responses to camera surveillance may well be muted because of the ways that dissenters may be treated. After all, one rationale among many for their deployment in China (as in some other countries) is to keep tabs on any who might question the system. But it is clear that many – especially but not only – urban Chinese have become acutely aware of the rapid deployment of public space camera systems in recent years. A 2006 international public opinion survey found a surprising 60 per cent of respondents in China claimed they were knowledgeable about surveillance cameras; Chinese focus group participants for the same study uniquely (among nine countries involved) raised the question of camera surveillance without being prompted (Dawson, this volume; Zureik et al. 2010; see also Liang and Huili 2007).

In addition to some of the 'standard' rationales for installing public space cameras, then, in some sensitive areas in China more general social order and control motifs appear, along with the monitoring of dissent and disorder. Automated Number Plate Recognition (see Derby, this volume) is in use in China, along with direct recording, such as recording the faces of those using Internet cafes. In Urumqi, where ethnic riots broke out between Han and Uighur in 2009, over 47,000 cameras have been installed (Wines 2010) and the number is set to rise to 60,000 in 2011.[5] Meanwhile in Xining, on China's remote Tibetan plateau, 4,000 cameras[6] sold by China Telecom to authorities as 'global eyes' hang over ethnically mixed areas containing high proportions of Tibetans, in an attempt to avoid a repeat of the 2008 monk-led riots there (MacKinnon 2010). Human rights activists are concerned about the targeted use of cameras in ethnically Uighur and Tibetan neighbourhoods as well as against political dissidents.

Across the country, the Ministry of Public Security says that 2.75 million cameras have already been installed in urban China,[7] although after riots in Urumqi and elsewhere, security officials also placed cameras inside mosques, monasteries and hotels (Wines 2010). At the same time, there are no national laws limiting the use of public video surveillance, although some local regulations do exist in certain places.[8] Of course, with little or no in-depth research being carried out on public space camera surveillance in that country, it is difficult to tell exactly what is happening and how it matches or contrasts with experiences elsewhere. Nonetheless, the burgeoning Chinese use of camera surveillance and the appearance in all Chinese major urban areas and 'trouble spots' of overhead camera installations is unlikely to make no impact at all.

From work in many other countries, a selection of which appears in this book, researchers have become aware of numerous issues driving and accompanying the spread of camera surveillance, but even these must be placed in context if they are to be understood. Camera surveillance is highly significant in today's world, but has to be seen against the backdrop of a more general increase in practices of organizational surveillance. Indeed, one could argue that in information-intensive environments, organizations have become dependent on surveillance. Gathering and processing personal data – of which camera images are but one kind – is now organizationally central for management of all kinds (Lyon 2007; Haggerty 2009). And especially as camera surveillance shifts from the use of celluloid film and analogue techniques towards digitized images and electronic modes of processing, storing and sharing data (see Ferenbok and Clement, this volume), so the resonances between different surveillance practices become stronger. For instance, it is only a few years since 'facial recognition' referred primarily to what the human eye could see in filmed images. Now this is thought of as something that machines can accomplish.

But not only is there an immediate context of camera surveillance as an aspect of the general growth of surveillance, the growth of modern surveillance is itself dependent on some significant ways of experiencing the world. Cameras may be thought to have some natural affinity with surveillance just because the word itself – from the French, *surveiller:* to watch over – has a visual referent at its core. Thus, especially in the Western world, one finds strong cultural emphases on the importance of visible evidence, of privileging the eye as the most accurate sense, and following from this, a belief in objective knowledge as a criterion of truth. More mundanely, as Jonathan Finn (this volume) suggests, 'seeing surveillantly' is an increasingly generalized cultural phenomenon. Yet in the same Western tradition one also finds vision denigrated and other senses elevated to a superior position (see e.g. Jay 1994). All of which suggests some profound ambiguities in the ways that vision and, by extension, surveillance may be understood (Brighenti 2010). Camera surveillance, which uses visual images but at the same time, paradoxically, reduces them to digital data, is subject to similar ambiguities.

Such matters have entered debates over camera surveillance in many countries in Europe and North America, where what was called Closed Circuit Television (CCTV) was first developed. We should note at this point that the shift towards digital images that can be circulated through the Internet and towards networked and wireless cameras means that neither 'closed circuit' nor 'television' are terms that any longer capture much of what is occurring today (see Ferenbok and Clement, this volume). As Laura Huey points out in her chapter, the Royal Academy of Engineers (2007) has argued the term 'CCTV' is increasingly no longer applicable, given the increasing number of systems using networked digital cameras, which have much greater flexibility in terms of storing, transmitting and searching for images. She quotes the Royal Academy: 'The continued use of the term is an indicator of a general lack of awareness of the nature of contemporary surveillance, and disguises the kinds of purposes, dangers and possibilities of current technologies' (Royal Academy of Engineers 2007: 33).

As camera surveillance arrives in new settings, often culturally as well as geographically remote from those sites familiar to analyses centred in the Global North, further questions arise. In countries where camera surveillance has become taken for granted, TV news use of surveillance footage may be a signal that the event 'really happened' (see Finn, this volume), but would this be true elsewhere? Equally, in countries (like Turkey) where 'privacy' is popularly thought to refer exclusively to the domestic realm, it would seem to make no sense to appeal to 'privacy' as something that ought to be protected in 'public' places (see Çavlin Bozbeyoğlu, this volume).

The approach taken here is that several important issues raised by camera surveillance now require analysis that is not only comparative between the countries of Europe and North America, but increasingly between countries in quite different and varied parts of the world. The chapters that follow explore patterns and variations across countries along the following themes: cultural, legal and political contexts of the emergence of the cameras and how these drive or inhibit their spread; 'trigger events' such as highly mediatized crimes that create a heated political climate that makes reasoned opposition to the cameras difficult; installation of cameras as a key part of security for temporary 'mega-events' such as the Olympics, with the cameras then remaining as a permanent 'legacy'; the ever-evolving technologies and systems involving the cameras, leading to new functions and uses that were not originally contemplated; the role of private business and public– private partnerships in selling and promoting the cameras and using them to attempt to secure commerce and 'safe shopping' in a broader era of globalized neo-liberalism; the role of various levels of government, police and media in promoting surveillance cameras and various factors that contribute to a 'democratic deficit' and lack of meaningful evaluation, accountability and regulation; all tied up with the central conundrum of the continued spread of the cameras in the absence of evidence of their effectiveness.

So while this book makes progress in discussing some questions that have engaged and sometimes perplexed researchers in the Global North, it also pushes the envelope to suggest that our studies are incomplete without some sense of what is happening elsewhere. The shifting tilt of the world's population, power and cultural axes may also be seen, illuminatingly, through the lens of surveillance cameras.

Situating camera surveillance growth

What are the contexts for the global growth of camera surveillance? In the first chapter, Clive Norris, one of the world's leading CCTV researchers, offers some critical reflections on its global growth. Norris says we should be careful not to treat camera surveillance as a homogenous phenomenon, but rather as continually evolving and featuring considerable variations in how it is socially organized in particular contexts. For example: is the footage simply being recorded for potential later review, or is it being monitored so events are viewed in real time? Who staffs the control room and how responsive will police be to them? Can those in the control room speak through a microphone to those being viewed? Broad variation in the socio-technical arrangements of camera surveillance also complicate generalizations about its effectiveness or lack of same.

Reviewing the history of CCTV expansion in Britain, Norris spotlights the massive publicity around the surveillance camera images from the abduction and murder of two-year-old Jamie Bulger in 1993, the seminal 'trigger event'. Norris also emphasizes the importance of the Home Office's City Challenge competition as a centralized driver funding CCTV around the nation. Certainly the absence of similar driving initiatives by national governments is one factor explaining the much slower dissemination of public open-street camera surveillance in other jurisdictions, such as Canada. Norris goes on to detail how CCTV has massively increased around the globe. Its expansion in mainland Europe has gathered pace since terrorist bombings in London and Madrid, just as it has in the United States since 9/11, although public open-street CCTV has been slower to catch on in Scandinavia. Norris next discusses evaluations of the effectiveness of CCTV as a crime- prevention and crime-fighting tool, and how these have shown mixed results at best. Indeed, he quotes one senior Metropolitan Police officer as describing CCTV as an 'utter fiasco' in solving crimes. Norris goes on to discuss the seductions of CCTV and its limits in reality. One constraint is the person-hours required to monitor fully surveillance footage when it blankets a particular scene. Norris gives the example that, after the London bombings in 2007, it took 100 police officers four days of searching to find footage of the bombers from subway cameras. Norris also explains how the supposed deterrent effects of CCTV are based on the myth of the rational offender; as criminological research shows with deterrence in general and with surveillance cameras in particular, such deterrence does not work because in practice offenders often do not approach the decision to offend in terms of a rational calculation. He also discusses a range of evidence across studies of different CCTV control rooms suggesting those behind the cameras tend to target people of visible minorities, even in the absence of any other indicators of suspicious activity. Norris concludes by suggesting that CCTV may function best simply as a way for governments and other actors to demonstrate that they are doing 'something' about the problem of crime.

Gavin Smith offers a counterpoint to Norris's narrative of the worldwide growth of camera surveillance (and indeed a counterpoint to much of the work in this volume). Smith suggests that we be careful not to assume that surveillance cameras will inevitably continue to spread and to be hailed as a panacea; Smith calls instead for more attention to the factors that may possibly contribute to the potential future retraction of CCTV. Smith details how the success of such measures is far from clear in the United Kingdom, the country that was the original fount of camera surveillance. In the UK, CCTV use is now, he argues, increasingly coming into question. Smith draws on extensive ethnographic observation from around the UK, firstly of the political processes by which CCTV gained support and was implemented locally, and secondly on extensive observation of local CCTV schemes in action. He prophesies that a 'politics of contraction' will continue to supplant the 'politics of expansion', fostered by exactly the same neo-liberal conditions that helped give birth to CCTV expansion in the first place, for example, tenuous public–private partnerships and a focus on the financial bottom line. Smith highlights how CCTV programmes in the UK are now often plagued by negative media accounts related to their cost and statistical evidence of their lack of effectiveness in actually controlling crime, and that some such CCTV programmes are now being abandoned. Of course, the public open-street cameras Smith focuses on are only one component of the expansion of camera surveillance, and evidence of cost and ineffectiveness has not stopped the entrenchment and expansion of other criminal justice measures once these measures become accepted as 'common sense'.

Jonathan Finn considers the spread of camera surveillance in terms of its broader cultural implications. As Finn argues, it is important to note that while our ways of making sense of the visual shape our views of camera surveillance, this is not a one-way process: we must also think about how the pervasiveness of such surveillance itself may feed back on and alter our ways of seeing the world. Surveillance is increasingly becoming a constitutive element of social life, Finn argues. He considers the argument that the rise of photography in the

19th century helped drive a tendency to 'see photographically'; Finn suggests that the rise of surveillance technologies and practices now leads us towards 'seeing surveillantly', as surveillance becomes woven more into the fabric of everyday life. He discusses examples of the portrayal of surveillance in commercial stock photography, which he argues demonstrate that there has been a depoliticized cultural reconception of surveillance as a banal part of everyday life. In a second case study, Finn describes the use of video surveillance in the reality television show *True Beauty* as employing a form of rhetoric that creates veracity through the crude aesthetic of the surveillance camera. Finally, he uses the example of a police shooting recorded by members of the public with cellphones and digital cameras to illustrate and discuss increasing public participation in surveillance so that camera surveillance with one's personal technology becomes a kind of civic duty.

International growth of camera surveillance

While its ubiquitous presence in the United Kingdom is well known, camera surveillance is also growing rapidly in many countries often not immediately thought of as surveillance societies. As the chapters in this section demonstrate, this growth is uneven and is characterized by different drivers depending on the country examined. Important to understanding this growth and inevitably linked to it are diverse political and cultural contexts, intertwined with and helping to shape varied perceptions of the cameras' functions and effectiveness.

David Murakami Wood compares camera surveillance growth and responses to it in Rio de Janeiro, Brazil and Tokyo, Japan. Camera surveillance has been recently introduced by Brazil's military police in Rio's densely populated *favelas*, which are already subjected to human surveillance. In some instances gangs seeking to exercise authority had already installed camera surveillance in certain neighbourhoods. Camera surveillance in Japan has been growing from the 1990s onwards, including in entertainment districts and residential areas. These systems depend on arrangements involving local authorities and volunteers. Murakami Wood elaborates how this development varies in terms of how camera surveillance is linked to other surveillance sites; its subjects; how it is regulated or resisted; and the dominant type of order in the city in which it operates. State-run camera surveillance is found to be far less systematically organized and extensive in Rio compared to Tokyo. He argues that camera surveillance is growing, under-regulated, and has become normalized in both cities due to pressures of global neo-liberalization. Murakami Wood argues that Tokyo and Rio reflect what are partially surveillance societies, but surveillance as a dominant means of social ordering is only evident in Japan.

As is the case with Japan and Brazil, the extent of camera surveillance in South Africa has previously been little researched. Anthony Minnaar addresses this gap by providing a detailed overview of the level and expansion of camera surveillance in public and private sites in that country. The proliferation of camera surveillance in South Africa was initially hampered by high cost and limited funding but more recently these systems have appeared both in public sites and in an array of private sites. South Africa now has the most multi-use camera surveillance in Africa. Drivers of the growth of camera surveillance include perceptions of increasing crime and decreasing public police services. The introduction of camera surveillance in central business districts is rarely questioned by the public on privacy or legal grounds; by mid-2010 camera surveillance was present in most urban areas.

The piecemeal development of camera surveillance in public sites in Canada is described in Emily Smith's chapter. The first public system in Canada was established in Sherbrooke, Quebec, in 1991 and by 2010 'open-street' systems had been implemented or proposed in twenty cities. Smith asserts that each site of implementation had its own drivers, advocates and detractors. As with a variety of other criminal justice measures, camera surveillance is often introduced in spaces where a well-publicized violent incident serves as a 'trigger event', with the Bulger case in Britain in the early 1990s being the paradigmatic example (see chapters by Norris, by Huey and by Doyle and Walby, this volume). Some systems have been strongly opposed, such as in Brockville, Ontario, but overall camera surveillance growth has developed despite resistance and despite the lack of evidence of effectiveness in reducing crime. Smith calls for more case studies of the introduction of camera surveillance to lend further insight into how it is being implemented.

Evolving forms and uses of camera surveillance

As camera surveillance expands to different countries, at the same time it is also intensifying in a variety of new forms and contexts within countries in which it is already established. As Alanur Çavlin Bozbeyoğlu details, Turkey has recently seen a rapid acceleration and drawing together of different forms of surveillance, including pervasive camera surveillance. The recent massive increase in the number of cameras in Istanbul has become part of a broader coordinated system of surveillance, the Mobile Electronic System Integration (MOBESE), which was instituted in 2005 as the provincial information and security system for that city.

As Çavlin Bozbeyoğlu's analysis shows, the situation in Turkey displays some similar aspects to that in other countries considered in this volume: for example, the absence of any statistical evidence that the cameras are effective in reducing crime, safe shopping as a goal and the resulting potential for urban segregation, public–private cooperation (in this case, the Turkish Textile Employers' Association donated 1,200 public cameras for Istanbul) and the permanent intensification of surveillance as a result of enhanced security for temporary events such as the Olympics (or in this case the public events held in conjunction with the European Union naming Istanbul the European Capital of Culture for 2010). There are also distinctive aspects in the Turkish context. As Çavlin Bozbeyoğlu notes in her chapter, Turkey has a long history of total state control. She describes how cameras are mounted in advance to record political demonstrations. In Turkey, there is no legal framework through which the protection of privacy might be approached, and the Turkish translation of the term privacy, *özel hayatın dokunulmazlığı*, mainly refers to privacy within the family; there is no tradition of debating expectations of privacy in 'public' spaces beyond the home and the workplace.

One element of the MOBESE surveillance system is Automated Number Plate Recognition (ANPR) technology. Here, Patrick Derby takes a more detailed look at ANPR. ANPR is a hybrid technology that represents an enhancement of camera surveillance through the use of optical character recognition technology to recognize plate numbers and match them with databases of the plates. It marks an early use of the digitization of surveillance footage – algorithms can discern licence plate numbers and letters, for the moment more effectively than they can discern faces. ANPR is just one of many emerging technologies for identifying and monitoring automobiles, which also include measures that do not rely on cameras, such as geographic positioning systems, and radio frequency identification.

ANPR is spreading to many other countries around the globe, and is used in a growing variety of contexts, including not only road tolls and traffic management but also counterterrorism. It can also be used for access control, by denying access to any vehicles for which the licence plates do not appear on a list of approved entrants. Police can use ANPR to identify vehicles or individuals of interest by comparing licence plate reads against a proliferating number of databases. With more sophisticated versions, recognition of particular licence plates can be used to trigger further surveillance of particular vehicles. Derby highlights how, as with numerous other measures discussed in this book, the spread of ANPR is fuelled largely by system developers and advocates within law enforcement, without many opportunities for public input or democratic discussion.

Micheal Vonn and Philip Boyle use the example of the Vancouver Olympics to discuss how mega-events often leave a legacy in the form of temporary surveillance cameras that become permanent. A permanent security legacy is now sold as part of the payoff of being one of the exclusive group of cities to host the games. As Vonn and Boyle note, IOC President Jacques Rogge made this point when visiting Vancouver before the 2010 Games, saying, 'Security investment always leaves a good legacy of security for the country. Whenever the Games are finished, everything that has been built, the expertise that has been acquired, the hardware that has been put in place, is serving the country and the region for decades to follow.' Such a legacy occurred with the Olympics held in Athens in 2004, when Greece spent $1.5 billion on security, including over 1,000 cameras. This also occurred in relation to events in Istanbul staged when it was designated European Capital of Culture in 2010 (Çavlin Bozbeyoğlu, this volume). Similarly, the plan is for CCTV to expand greatly in Rio de Janeiro in anticipation of the 2014 World Cup and 2016 Olympics there (Norris, this volume). Major events also provide the opportunity to pull together cameras with other surveillance and security measures. For example, preparations for the London 2012 Olympics include efforts to make London's diverse quilt of public and private cameras accessible by the Metropolitan Police.

Aaron Doyle and Kevin Walby examine the introduction of surveillance cameras into another new context: taxi cabs. Surveillance cameras in taxis have been adopted in assorted jurisdictions around the world from Glasgow to Singapore. As in other cases, the cameras are claimed to deter violence, prevent theft, and provide evidence for prosecutions. However, here again, so far there are few independent studies confirming the alleged benefits of cab cameras. Rather than assessing the effectiveness of cab cameras as such, Doyle and Walby instead consider how and why their proliferation continues in the absence of supporting evidence, using a case study of their introduction in Ottawa, Canada, where they became mandatory at drivers' expense. The taxi drivers' union refused installation, and protested vehemently. Even so, cameras were eventually installed after a series of behind-the-scenes deliberations, which Doyle and Walby examined through access to information requests.

Doyle and Walby highlight six barriers to democracy and accountability they observed in this process, all of which can also be observed in other studies in this volume: the introduction of the cameras in the aftermath of 'trigger crimes' and the constraints this context imposes on reasoned debate; the difficulties with having the introduction of cameras driven in large part by private entrepreneurs, in this case; problems with function creep or unstated additional consequences of the cameras: disconnected and uninformed stakeholders; piecemeal diffusion bit by bit, which prevents a broader debate about the cameras in general; and the point that cameras which may seem innocuous in individual contexts may coalesce with other surveillance measures into a surveillant assemblage (Haggerty and Ericson 2000) that can be drawn together on particular occasions in much more potent ways than were contemplated for any of the original, isolated measures. As camera surveillance proliferates, so too do the different kinds of uses to which that footage is put.

Lippert and Wilkinson offer another example, looking at the implications of how camera surveillance footage is increasingly used on website advertisements and YouTube by police-supported Crime Stoppers programmes in three countries, for the stated purpose of generating tips. Lippert and Wilkinson looked at a large sample of camera footage and stills used by Crime Stoppers in the province of Ontario in Canada. They found that images in Crime Stoppers advertisements often appear without masking the identity of third parties and victims, raising privacy concerns. As Crime Stoppers seems to rely more and more on surveillance camera images, this tendency also narrows the range of crimes that are publicized this way, as many types of crime are unlikely to be recorded by surveillance cameras, for example, domestic violence or white collar crimes. A particular ideology is reproduced which conflates crime to stereotypical images of 'street crime' by strangers. Lippert and Wilkinson also observe that these images have a paradoxical property in that every image of a crime committed before a camera underscores the failure of such cameras to act as a deterrent. Lippert and Wilkinson also found an over-representation of Crimestopper footage aired on Youtube showing people who were members of visible minorities.

Situating camera surveillance requires coming to terms with significant technological changes that have occurred. In the first of two chapters they have co-authored for this volume, Ferenbok and Clement describe a paradigm shift commencing in the 1990s from analogue closed circuit television (CCTV) to digital systems with 'smart' video analytic capabilities. The authors explore the selling features – such as reduced cost, wider dissemination, and higher-quality images – and the growing functions – such as live monitoring and retrospective searching – of these new systems. Video analytics is growing in scope and depth, and associated systems are being applied in various surveillance sites that include public safety, border control and retail data-mining. Ferenbok and Clement also explore new approaches to privacy protection that this move to digitization permits, including encryption and blurring techniques. The authors contemplate the implications of these significant but largely hidden technological changes that are driven by the quest for security and economic growth, for surveillance subjects and for the public interest. They argue digital growth is likely to increase concerns about privacy associated with earlier analogue systems, since the lower cost of digital systems will likely result in more persons being watched and their reduced size makes it easier to obscure their presence in given sites. Adequate policy responses to preserve privacy are lagging far behind this hidden revolution.

Public support, media visions and the politics of representation

Given the riddle of the persistent spread of cameras in the absence of evidence of their effectiveness, it is important to consider the politics of camera surveillance: how the public respond to it in various contexts and how various representations of camera surveillance are mobilized either to support or resist it, in the mass media and in the arts. In this section Danielle Dawson compares public perceptions of camera surveillance and related issues across several countries, with special focus on North America. For this she draws on the 2006 Globalization of Personal Data Project (GPD) Survey of nine countries (Canada, Brazil, China, France, Hungary, Japan, Mexico, Spain and the United States) conducted to explore issues of surveillance and privacy.

Using these data, Dawson shows what ordinary people from these countries think about camera surveillance and its effectiveness. Reported knowledge of camera surveillance is significant but it varies somewhat across the nine countries, with citizens of China reporting the greatest knowledge, followed by respondents from Canada, the United States and Spain. Persons from Mexico reported the least knowledge. A majority of those surveyed in the nine countries thought camera surveillance was at least somewhat effective in reducing crime. Dawson's analysis reveals no relationship between perceived knowledge and the perception of effectiveness but shows there is a correlation between high trust in government and strong perceptions of effectiveness of camera surveillance. Dawson argues that while the GPD provides baseline quantitative information comparable across countries, it is less revealing of the reasons why ordinary people think as they do about camera surveillance. Further ethnographic research in local contexts is suggested to complement quantitative cross-national research like the GPD.

How do different actors summon public support for their campaigns for and against surveillance cameras? Laura Huey suggests that critics of the cameras are being beaten back by the more effective communications strategies of supporters of the cameras, including police, private entrepreneurs and politicians. Indeed, she suggests the playing field may be tilted in favour of surveillance camera advocates, especially police, who hold particular advantages. Decisions to introduce cameras are often made in the aftermath of highly publicized transgressive 'signal crimes' that serve as symbolic markers of broader anxieties. Police invoke anxieties about missing children, even when there is little evidence that the cameras have helped or will help recover them. They also invoke concerns about terrorism. She gives examples of how police outshine privacy advocates in communicating their ideas in simple, punchy soundbites about crime that are more media-friendly than more complex arguments about privacy. Huey argues that public police have better access to different forms of capital in framing their messages: economic, political, cultural, social and symbolic. They have more financial resources to devote to communication, access to crime data to buttress their arguments, political influence with various levels of government, often a dominant position in relation to local news media who are dependent on police for information, and the symbolic capital associated with the cultural place of policing. Huey raises important questions about how anti-surveillance activists can and do sometimes win playing uphill.

Nelson Arteaga Botello provides a case study of a highly publicized crime in Mexico City that was used to push for enhanced camera surveillance, but this particular story has an important twist. Arteaga examines the massive media coverage of the disappearance of a young girl from a gated community and its relation to the growth of camera surveillance in Mexican municipalities and gated communities. To put this in a theoretical context, he invokes Thomas Mathiesen's concept of the 'synopticon' (Mathiesen 1997) – the notion of the many watching the few through the mass media, in an inverted apparatus of power complementary to, and reinforcing, Foucault's Panopticon.

Arteaga suggests that understanding the public demand for camera surveillance installation in Mexican gated communities and municipalities requires an exploration of the nature of media coverage of camera surveillance-related events. For example, the mother of the missing girl in this case was shown being interviewed in the girl's bedroom amid the child's toys and drawings, thus eliciting audience sympathy. The daily television coverage of the case reached unprecedented levels, among other things spawning a Facebook page for supporters devoted to finding the child. Media visibility increased even more when the case took a dramatic turn: police discovered the girl's body and the investigation shifted to considering the mother might be responsible for her death. The mother experienced massive synoptic scrutiny as television viewers assessed the interviews for clues to her guilt; psychological profiles were publicized suggesting she was the killer; and Facebook pages calling for justice and announcing her guilt appeared. The child's death was then ruled accidental, one day before the municipality and two nearby municipalities announced implementation of camera surveillance systems.

The role of camera surveillance in the episode was paradoxical. At first, the suggestion was widely made that if camera surveillance had been properly operating in the gated community in which she lived and in the particular municipality in question, those responsible for the child's disappearance would have been identified. Arteaga argues that this moment in the case, involving large segments of the population paying attention to the plight of the missing child's family, shows the synoptic process at work and that it led to pressure to introduce or properly fund public and private cameras, reinforcing the panoptic. However, once the mother became a suspect, public attention turned to mass media coverage that demonized the mother, but, peculiarly, the pressure to introduce camera surveillance was not then reduced, even though it would not have made a difference if the mother had committed the crime. The author thus argues that when cases involve those of higher social position in Mexico such as this, the bridge between surveillance cameras (panoptic) and television cameras (synoptic) may not be made. The common sense that surveillance cameras are the necessary solution remains.

Approaching this obliquely, Martin Zeilinger explores an example of artistic resistance: appropriation of camera surveillance images and resistance to surveillance culture through an analysis of Manu Luksch's ground-breaking film, *Faceless*. This widely screened film was created using camera surveillance images produced by London, England's extensive camera surveillance system. The images were appropriated via freedom of information requests provided for in the UK's Data Protection Act. Drawing from surveillance art strategies, Zeilinger investigates how the authority of camera surveillance can be resisted via its 'authoring' function. He details Luksch's approach by comparing it to 'found footage' film-making. Zeilinger argues that, by appropriating camera surveillance images as a critical project, the cameras' gaze can be turned upon itself. He argues *Faceless* appropriates the application of the UK Data Protection Act, which is not separate from – as some chapters in this volume assume – but rather an integral part of the surveillance apparatus. *Faceless* applies its own critical premise by calling into question the ethics of camera surveillance and drawing its form and content from camera surveillance.[9]

Regulating camera surveillance

The global growth of camera surveillance has also led to greater attention to how regulation of camera surveillance practices currently occurs (or does not occur), and how it might evolve, as explored by the contributors featured in the final section of this volume. Possible ways of regulating surveillance come in a number of forms, including statutory law, regulatory signage and civil law.

Mark Lizar and Gary Potter focus on the legal requirement in the UK for organizations deploying camera surveillance to notify the public. Signage is a means of obtaining informed consent from the public and it is unclear the public can trust camera surveillance. Data protection and human rights legislation address to some degree issues of privacy and trust stemming from camera surveillance: however, the mere existence of legal provisions does not equate to trustworthiness of surveillance systems. The authors report on findings of an empirical case study of 'open-street' and private camera regulatory signage on a busy street in London to demonstrate a 'compliance-scale' approach. Few signs were fully legally compliant and only one in ten systems included proper signage. Some signage was difficult to read due to positioning and some cameras were positioned in places that called legality and trust into doubt. Significantly, compared to a 2002 study of a similar London street, there was greater use of camera surveillance reflective of growth. Lizar and Potter then advocate a more elaborate four-point scale of compliance to measure contextual integrity or trustworthiness of camera surveillance. This is a valuable tool in a time of global growth of camera surveillance.

Recognizing the variability and lack of oversight of signage arrangements that the previous chapter reveals, Andrew Clement and Joseph Ferenbok take up problems with existing camera surveillance signage and seek to develop a signage code. Clement and Ferenbok argue for codifying that would ensure informed consent among those who are watched. To this end they elaborate a nation-specific, privacy-oriented, rightful-citizen scheme. Camera surveillance and its accompanying asymmetric arrangements have outgrown regulation, but a comprehensive signage system may rectify this situation by addressing governance and privacy issues. Existing signage lacks information about purposes and data storage, and often has poor positioning that contravenes fair information practices. Signage also fails to deter and is devoid of information about storage, third-party access and other vital aspects. The authors then elaborate a signage scheme designed to hail the subject of camera surveillance as a rights-bearing citizen, a scheme that attends to colour, visibility and positioning. Three innovative types of signage are described: signage posted by camera surveillance operators, regulatory enforcement agents suggesting certification, and by persons concerned about non-compliant operators.

In the US context, Christopher Burt also engages with issues of informed consent, privacy and the growth of camera surveillance. Burt draws from a case study of camera surveillance in the municipality of Hoboken, New Jersey. A major focus is informed consent in relation to public camera surveillance signage and to the uncertainty of decision-making about privacy. He argues the movement of personal information into a technological environment has produced its own security threat. His study of Hoboken shows strong public support for privacy in public places. Burt argues, however, that a shared construct of privacy is lacking; there is no universal definition of privacy. Legal protections of privacy are varied and piecemeal; signage usually fails to allow informed consent. Individuals cannot retrieve private information once released into the wider environment. This development creates an opportunity to consider privacy as a form of security in public discourse. He argues that to return to privacy in public debate may require discussing and approaching privacy as a form of security.

In a comprehensive analysis, Mathew Johnson expertly assesses the current state of the law of public camera surveillance, as well as key legal issues in Canada. Although this chapter focuses on Canadian law, legal regimes in the United States and Europe have developed in similar ways. Johnson argues that a key aspect is whether camera surveillance constitutes a legal search. The author considers the applicability and interpretation of relevant statutes, both federal and provincial, which broadly authorize and limit information-gathering, before turning to how the courts have ruled on search, privacy and surveillance questions, especially in the context of Canada's *Charter of Rights and Freedoms*. A review of these legal instruments and decisions demonstrates the absence of specific guidance on camera surveillance use. Where 'open-street' camera surveillance is concerned there is a legal vacuum. No laws have been written in Canada specifically to address camera surveillance, and no court has yet considered the substantive questions raised by their use. Johnson concludes by examining voluntary privacy commission guidelines that promise to fill the legal vacuum.

Robert Ellis Smith complements Johnson's analysis by investigating the legal landscape of camera surveillance and, in particular, the notion of privacy in public. Drawing primarily on the US legal context but also with reference to Canada, Smith critiques the conventional wisdom that the growth and current prevalence of camera surveillance in public spaces cannot be addressed legally. An element of this mistaken belief is the erroneous assumption that because conduct occurs in public there can be no protection due to an expectation of privacy. He argues federal court rulings suggest many forms of conduct in public spaces are subject to privacy protection. A key 1972 US Supreme Court ruling affirmed activities in public that should be protected and is a precedent for future protection of privacy rights. Camera surveillance includes a capacity for permanent storage of images and digital search criteria. The right to privacy is extensive and includes the right to autonomy (or 'personhood') and to anonymity.

The federal Privacy Acts in the US and Canada prohibit federal government surveillance to some degree, and in the US surveillance by private entities is covered by the common law of torts such as the 'misappropriate tort' that pertains to the 'commercial use' of camera surveillance images. Any surveillance enhanced by technology such as cameras follows the constitution standard in deciding whether the government is using techniques not in general public use. The effects of successful court challenges over the right to privacy under the constitution may be the use of mitigating technologies or the use of an independent third party to conduct searches of stored images.

Future research on camera surveillance

That camera surveillance is now in a phase of global growth is manifestly clear from the chapters of this book. They indicate some patterns and variations of rationale, usage and response across different countries, but as with all such studies, further questions are prompted by the findings. Readers of this book will come to recognize certain 'trigger events' that are often crucial catalysts for camera surveillance development, or the ways that 'megaevents' may also spawn new camera systems, often purporting to be temporary, but which turn out to be permanent. Thus 'function creep' may, in this large-scale context, quickly turn into 'mission creep' as the original task of the cameras is transformed from overseeing mega-events to simply overseeing populations that remain under the lenses. Equally notable is the general 'democratic deficit' common in many countries, in which evidence-based reasoning and workable modes of accountability and regulation seem in short supply.

Each of these issues is associated, one way or another, with the abiding puzzle of why camera surveillance continues to spread, nationally and internationally, despite the extremely flimsy evidence that they work in the ways claimed by their promoters. This in turn is linked with at least three issues discussed in this book. One, if camera surveillance does not work then why should proponents of social justice, civil liberties or privacy be concerned? Two, how long will the camera boom last (see Gavin Smith, this volume)? Three, whose cameras are they anyway? On question one, it will be clear from several chapters that despite doubts about camera surveillance success in meeting named objectives, camera surveillance is a potent tool in other ways. Automated Licence Plate Recognition, for instance, may or may not assist in the tracing of stolen vehicles but it raises serious questions about democratic practice when used for tracking political protestors en route to engaging in demonstrations.

On the second question, most chapters of this book argue that growth is still predominant, especially in the cities of Latin America, China and India. But it is an empirical question. Will new functions and capacities of camera systems, or an expanding focus on law, order and security, persuade governments and police that more cameras is better? Or will evidence-based critiques of camera surveillance effectiveness start to put the brakes on? This is not unconnected with the third question, about who owns the cameras. As noted above, the vast majority of cameras are privately owned and operated. For example, Gerrard and Thompson (2011: 11) suggest that in the camera- counting research they conducted in Cheshire, England, 96 per cent of the cameras in their sample were private (see also Leman-Langlois 2011: 540 on the Canadian context). Yet public cameras continue to receive more attention, from academics as well as from politicians, the media and others. This focus can be explained in part because spending tax money on public cameras is more obviously a public policy issue and because the very notion of privacy in nominally public spaces is more immediately controversial and contested than in privately owned and governed spaces. While this tendency is somewhat reproduced here, some chapters indicate ways to overcome it (see, among others, Lippert and Wilkinson, Johnson, and Doyle and Walby in this volume).

The question of the extent and usage of privately owned and operated surveillance cameras will continue to engage researchers for some time to come. In an era of neo-liberalism, it is clear that the task of governing is achieved by many means, well beyond the conventional wisdom about the formal operations of government and policing. The outsourcing of security and policing tasks to private corporations and, in the case of camera surveillance, the widespread use of privately acquired personal images by public police and security agencies means that the situation is very complex indeed. And while the question should rightly galvanize research in the years to come, the problems presented are of far more than merely 'academic' interest. As with all the issues raised by this book, they are questions with profound implications for democratic polity and public justice.

Notes

1 See http://insecurite.blog.lemonde.fr/2011/05/31/la-videosurveillance-un-choix-tres-couteux-et-peu-efficace/> and <http://www.latimes.com/news/local/la-me-0608-red-light-20110607,0,6393615.story>
2 See <http://www.shanghaidaily.com/nsp/Metro/2011/05/27/Spy%2Bcamera%2Bnumbers%2Bto%2Bdouble/>
3 See IMS Research <http://imsresearch.com/news-events/press-template.php?pr_id=1502/> cited in the *New York Times*, 2 August 2010 at <http://www.nytimes.com/2010/08/03/world/asia/03china.html/>
4 Surveillance Cameras Awareness Network report is at <http://www.sscqueens.org/projects/scan>
5 <http://www.chinanews.com/sh/news/2010/01-15/2075039.shtml>
6 <http://society.people.com.cn/GB/1062/10783984.html>
7 <http://www.hybbs.com/viewthread.php?tid=10063256>
8 Personal communication from JianJun Liu (then working on the regulation of camera surveillance in China at Shandong University; in 2011–12 Visiting Researcher at the Surveillance Studies Centre, Queen's University).
9 Witness (2011) 'Cameras Everywhere: Current Challenges and Opportunities at the Intersection of Human Rights, Video and Technology.' Available HTTP: <http://www.witness.org/cameras-everywhere/report-2011> (accessed 12 September 2011).

References

Arteaga Botello, N. (2010) *Sociedad de la vigilancia en el Sur Global*, Mexico: UAEM and Miguel Ángel Porrúa.

Brighenti, A.M. (2010) *Visibility in Social Theory and Social Research*, London and New York: Palgrave Macmillan.

Gerrard, G. and Thompson, R. (2011) 'Two Million Cameras in the UK', *CCTV Image*, 42, Winter: 10–12.

Graham, S. (1999) 'The eyes have it: CCTV as the "fifth utility"', *Environment and Planning B: Planning and Design*, 26(5): 639–42.

Haggerty, K.D. (2009) 'Ten Thousand Times Larger . . .: Anticipating the Expansion of Surveillance', in Daniel Neyland and Benjamin Goold (eds), *New Directions in Privacy and Surveillance*, Cullompton: Willan, 159–77.

Haggerty, K.D. and Ericson, R.V. (2000) 'The Surveillant Assemblage', *British Journal of Sociology*, 51(4): 605–22.

Hier, S.P. (2010) *Panoptic Dreams: Streetscape Video Surveillance in Canada*, Vancouver: UBC Press.

Jay, M. (1994) *Downcast Eyes: The Denigration of Vision in Twentieth Century French Thought*, Berkeley: University of California Press.

Leman-Langlois, S. (2011) 'Review of S. Hier's Panoptic Dreams: Streetscape Video Surveillance in Canada', *Surveillance & Society*, 8(4): 539–40.

Liang, G. and Huili, C. (2007) 'Surveillance and Privacy in Urban China', in *International Survey on Privacy and Surveillance* by the Globalization of Personal Data Project (2006). Online. Available HTTP: <http://www.sscqueens.org/sites/default/files/China_Report_March_07.pdf>

Lyon, D. (2007) *Surveillance Studies: An Overview*, Cambridge: Polity.

MacKinnon, M. (2010) 'Big Brother widens his watchful eye over China', *The Globe and Mail*, 13 August, A9.

Mathiesen, T. (1997) 'The Viewer Society: Michel Foucault's "Panopticon Revisited"', *Theoretical Criminology*, 1(2): 215–34.

Norris, C., McCahill, M. and Wood, D. (2004) 'The growth of CCTV: A global perspective on the international diffusion of video surveillance in publicly accessible space', *Surveillance & Society*, 2(2/3): 110–35.

Royal Academy of Engineering (2007) *Dilemmas of Privacy and Surveillance: Challenges of Technological Change.* <http://www.raeng.org.uk/policy/reports/default.htm"www.raeng.org.uk/policy/reports/default.htm>

Wines, M. (2010) 'In restive area, cameras keep watch', *New York Times*, 2 August. Online. Available HTTP: <http://www.nytimes.com/2010/08/03/world/asia/03china.html/>

Zureik, E., Harling-Stalker, L., Smith, E., Lyon, D. and Chan, Y. (eds) (2010) *Surveillance, Privacy and the Globalization of Personal Information*, Kingston and Montreal: McGill-Queen's University Press.

PART I

Situating camera surveillance growth

2

THERE'S NO SUCCESS LIKE FAILURE AND FAILURE'S NO SUCCESS AT ALL

Some critical reflections on understanding the global growth of CCTV surveillance[1]

Clive Norris

Overview

This chapter is divided into four sections. The first section describes how we should conceptualize Closed Circuit Television (CCTV). The second section documents the growth of CCTV surveillance in the UK, Europe and the rest of the world. The third section reviews the evidence from methodologically credible evaluation studies conducted around the world. In particular, it examines the evidence that CCTV leads to a reduction in crime, an increase in the detection of crime and reduction in the fear of crime. In the light of this evidence the final section argues that we need to reconceptualize how we think about the success and failure of CCTV systems.

What is CCTV?

At its simplest, Closed Circuit Television (CCTV) consists of a camera coupled by a cable to a display monitor, and it was this type of system in the early days of CCTV monitoring that was popular in many retail establishments as it was an 'affordable, do-it-yourself, self contained system' (Constant and Turnbull 1994: 3). These early systems were often extended to connect up to four cameras to the monitor, the images from which could be displayed individually or in a pre-programmed sequence. The cameras were, generally, static and had a fixed focal length. The next innovation was to add a video recorder, enabling the image displayed on the monitor to be recorded on videotape and played back at a later time. To this was added the ability to move the cameras in either the horizontal or vertical plane, usually coupled with the ability to change the focal length of the camera enabling the cameras to zoom. These fully functional cameras are often referred to as Pan, Tilt and Zoom (PTZ) cameras.

Although many, particularly larger, CCTV systems incorporate the range of more advanced technical capacities, consisting of a number of fully functional PTZ cameras coupled not just to a monitor but to a recording device as well, Gill and Spriggs have noted that while there is a 'tendency within the criminological litera-ture to discuss CCTV as if it were a single measure, CCTV systems can differ quite markedly' (Gill and Spriggs 2005: 1). Indeed, in their survey of CCTV in London, McCahill and Norris found that three-quarters of institutions had fixed cameras only, nearly one in ten (8 per cent) had no recording facility, and a third (30 per cent) did not have the capacity to multiplex the images (McCahill and Norris 2003: 60–1). The Urbaneye study of video surveillance in Europe found that the average system operating in publicly accessible space studied was 'technologically rather simple with three fixed cameras, one monitor, sequential switching between the cameras and no linkage to third parties' (Hempel and Töpfer 2004: 6).

It is not just in technical sophistication that CCTV systems differ. They also differ in their organizational arrangement. In themselves cameras do nothing. If a camera is mounted on a wall, coupled to a monitor and a video recorder, we have a CCTV system. But if no one notices the camera, and nobody looks at either the monitor or the tapes, its social and criminological impact is almost zero. It cannot be assumed that the images are being monitored. The typical situation in European countries reported in the Urbaneye study was that: 'Monitoring of images occurs only on an irregular basis by one observer who often has to fulfil other parallel tasks' (Hempel and Töpfer 2004: 7). For a CCTV camera to have an effect, at the minimum someone needs to be conscious of it and alter, or at least consider alter-ing, their behaviour because of its presence or believe that it will lead someone else to do the same.

It is therefore essential to recognize that CCTV is not merely a technical system – it is a socio-technical system. To understand its impact, as a crime prevention strategy, it is necessary to understand that it is located in a highly varied organi-zational environment, and this variation will have a significant impact as to how a system is used. Some systems have permanently staffed control rooms, in which a team of operators monitors the images from the system on a 24-hour basis, and can actively scan and track the population through the use of PTZ cameras. Other systems are unmonitored, and the tapes only reviewed if incidents come to light. In some systems control rooms are staffed by police officers, are directly linked to the command and control systems of their force and can order other police officers to attend incidents. In other systems civilians, local authority staff or private security officials monitor the cameras. Although they can relay pictures to the command and control room of their local police, they have no power to determine what the police response should be.

Finally it is worth noting that although Closed Circuit Television (CCTV) has become the accepted terminology for camera-based surveillance systems, increasingly systems are not closed but open systems. Open systems exploit digital technologies to enable surveillance images to be viewed from any location, not just the control room, via a computer connected to the internet.

The worldwide growth of CCTV surveillance

The development of CCTV in the UK

The history of the growth of CCTV surveillance in the UK has been well documented elsewhere (Norris and Armstrong 1999; Norris, Wood and McCahill 2004; Webster 2009) and as there is no space go into much detail here, a brief summary will suffice. Although the numbers of privately owned CCTV systems in the commercial and retail sectors grew steadily from the mid- 1960s, by 1991 there were no more than ten cities with open street systems in operation. What characterized these systems was that they were small scale, locally funded and set up as the result of individual entrepreneurship, often on the part of a local police officer (Ditton and Short 1998).

In 1993, two ten-year-old boys were caught on CCTV in a shopping mall abducting a toddler whom they subsequently killed. Amid high levels of public anxiety about rising crime, CCTV had been placed in the national spotlight[2] and, in reaction, the government announced a 'City Challenge Competition' to allocate £2 million of central government money for open street CCTV: 480 bids were received, and 106 schemes funded from an increased allocation of £5 million (Norris and Armstrong 1999: 37–8). The competition was repeated between 1995 and 1998, and in total £85 million was secured for the capital funding of 580 CCTV systems. By the mid-1990s CCTV dominated the government's crime prevention programme, accounting for over three-quarters of its budget (Welsh and Farrington 2004: 500).

In 1999, the new Labour administration, as part of its ambitious crime reduction programme, set aside £153 million to support the expansion of CCTV. The two rounds of the competition received 1,550 bids and around 450 of these were funded (Norris, Wood and McCahill 2004). Given that there was also substantial government investment in the CCTV surveillance of schools, hospitals and transport facilities, it is not unreasonable to estimate that between 1995 and 2005 over £500 million of central and local government funds were allocated to CCTV (see McCahill and Norris 2003). In addition, during the same period it was estimated that in total around £4.5 billion of private funds were spent on the installation of CCTV and maintenance of CCTV systems in the UK, and this excludes the monitoring costs associated with these systems (Norris, Wood and McCahill 2004).

How many cameras or systems this translates to is impossible to measure accurately, although in 1999 it was estimated that in an urban environment, on a busy day, a person could have their image captured by over 300 cameras on thirty separate CCTV systems (Norris and Armstrong 1999: chapter 3). Armitage (2002) suggests that there are 500 publicly funded open street systems deploying some 40,000 cameras. More generally, Norris and McCahill 'guesstimated' on the basis of a survey in one London borough that there may be as many as 4.2 million publicly and privately operated cameras in the UK, or one for every 14 of the population (McCahill and Norris 2003).

The development of CCTV in mainland Europe

In Europe, the proliferation of cameras in public and semi-public space was well documented by the Urbaneye project (Hempel and Töpfer 2004). The study of six European capitals found that CCTV was common in publicly accessible space such as shops, banks, restaurants, bars and transport termini. Across the sample cities, 29 per cent of such publicly accessible institutions used some form of video surveillance, although the proliferation was uneven. For instance, in London 40 per cent of publicly accessible spaces were monitored by surveillance cameras, compared with only 18 per cent in Vienna (Hempel and Töpfer 2004: 27–34).

In terms of open street, publicly operated, crime reduction systems, Urbaneye data shows that in 2003 Denmark and Austria had no open systems, that there was only one in Norway (consisting of six cameras), and that there were at least 14 systems in Budapest alone and 15 in Germany. In the UK there were over 500 systems. Thus, while in the UK there were around 40,000 open street CCTV cameras monitoring public space, there were probably fewer than 1,000 across the other European countries included in the survey (Hempel and Töpfer 2004: 27–34).

In many European countries not included in the Urbaneye survey, there was also sustained growth in open street CCTV before 2004. In France, after the laws were relaxed governing public space surveillance in 1995, there was a rapid deployment of CCTV in public space: 'between 1997 and 1999 more than 200 French cities received the approval for the installation of CCTV in high risk locations and 259 for the protection of public buildings such as town halls, public libraries, schools and museums' (Hempel and Töpfer 2002: 10). Similarly, in the Netherlands the first cameras were used in public space in 1997, but by 2003 more than 80 of the country's 550 municipalities were using CCTV in public places (Flight et al. 2003: 93). In the Republic of Ireland, the first CCTV system was installed in Dublin in the mid-1990s, and expanded in 1997. In 2004 the Minister for Justice announced a major expansion of open street CCTV throughout the country, with plans to extend to 21 different areas (PDP 2004). In Italy, in response to rising anxieties about crime, the Ministry of the Interior installed CCTV in the 'most sensitive areas' of 50 Italian cities, and in the city of Milan there are now over 600 publicly funded cameras (Calabria 2003; Fonio 2007: 6).

While some countries, particularly the Nordic countries of Norway, Denmark, Sweden and Finland, had been reluctant to install widespread open street CCTV systems for crime prevention purposes, this does not mean that they have not embraced CCTV in other settings. For instance, in 2002, although there was only one open street system in Norway and no system in Denmark, a survey of 440 publicly accessible locations in Oslo and Copenhagen found that 32 per cent had CCTV in Copenhagen and 38 per cent had CCTV in Oslo (Wiecek and Saetnan

2002). Similarly, in Stockholm, in 2000, although there was no public CCTV system there were an estimated 11,500 CCTV cameras in the city, in a variety of settings that came under the authority of the Stockholm regulatory board (Gras 2004). In 2004, in the Finnish city of Tampere, half of the city's 20 schools installed CCTV as a crime prevention measure (*Helsingin Sanomat* 2004).

As the Director-General of the Swedish National Council for Crime Prevention commented in the case of Sweden, which would be true of Scandinavia in general:

> The use of CCTV surveillance for the purposes of crime prevention has become increasingly common on public transport, in taxis and in schools. It has also become common to use CCTV surveillance in bank entrances and near cash point machines. There are, however, still few examples of the use of CCTV for crime prevention purposes in larger public spaces where large numbers of people gather and move around such as on streets, or in parks.
>
> *(Foreword to Welsh and Farrington 2007: 5)*

Since 2004, the spread of publicly funded CCTV across the European mainland has gathered pace. In the wake of the Madrid and London terrorist bombings, there has been a massive expansion of CCTV deployed in public transport infrastructures, particularly airports, railways and metro systems, of traffic monitoring, and in educational establishments.

In France, in 2007, it was announced that the government was planning to increase its estimated 340,000 CCTV cameras threefold and, in particular, to expand the number on the Paris Metro to 6,500 (Reuters 2007). Since 2004, Germany has doubled the number of cities with CCTV from 15 to 30 (Töpfer 2008), and the Republic of Ireland has increased the number of cities with either police or community-run CCTV systems from 21 to 49 (DJELR 2007). Despite the long-standing reluctance to embrace public area CCTV in Nordic countries, Finland introduced a major system in Helsinki in 2006 (*Helsingin Sanomat* 2006) and in Denmark, Copenhagen introduced a 19-camera system in 2008 (*IceNews* 2008).

In eastern Europe, the Polish capital of Warsaw launched a major citywide system with 515 cameras in 2007 (Waszkiewicz: 2009). In the Czech Republic, Prague's systems were expanded to 400 cameras (EDRI 2008), and in Croatia, Zagreb announced a new 225-camera citywide system to be introduced in 2009 (*Croatian Times* 2009). In Russia, the Moscow 'safecity' programme boasts 20,000 cameras, with 9,000 operating in the 'Central Administrative District to maintain 24/7 monitoring of city squares, street crossings, entries and yards' (Axxon 2007).

By 2009, Austria, Bulgaria, Croatia, the Czech Republic, Denmark, Finland, France, Germany, Greece, Hungary, Ireland, Italy, Lithuania, the Netherlands, Norway, Poland, Portugal, Russia, Spain, Sweden, Switzerland and the UK all boasted CCTV systems operating in public space for the purposes of crime prevention.[3]

Development of CCTV outside Europe

In the USA, the first national survey of CCTV, carried out in 1997, found only 13 police departments using CCTV to monitor public space, though by 2001 this had increased to 25 (Nieto et al. 2002: 14). However, since 2001, and the terrorist attack on the World Trade Center, billions of dollars of federal money have become available for domestic security projects, and this has fuelled a massive expansion of public area CCTV. Major cities such as Baltimore, Chicago, New Orleans, Philadelphia, San Francisco and Washington now boast extensive systems. For instance:

> Chicago has 2,250 cameras in its 'Homeland Security Grid,' which DHS helped finance with a $5.1 million grant, and will be adding cameras in the next two years with funds from another $48 million grant from Homeland Security. By 2006, Chicago will have a 900-mile fiber-optic grid. The cameras are linked to a $43 million operations center constantly monitored by police officers.
>
> *(EPIC: 2005)*

In California alone, 37 out of 131 jurisdictions now operate public space video surveillance programmes (Scholosberg and Ozer 2007: 2). In Canada, in 2009, the SCAN study reported that 30 cities had installed or were considering installing public space CCTV systems (SCAN 2009). Similarly, in Australia, Wells reported that over 30 mainland cities had installed public area CCTV systems (Wells et al. 2006: 2).

There are no systematic surveys of the deployment of CCTV in Africa, Asia or South America. However, a good sense of the inter-continental spread of CCTV can be gleaned from a brief look at some of the capital cities around the world. In Asia, the Japanese capital of Tokyo has experienced a rapid expansion over the last decade, with CCTV being deployed on the transit system and extensively at neighbourhood level (Wood 2009); the Chinese capital, Beijing, was reported to have 263,000 surveillance cameras by 2006, and was planning a massive expansion in preparation for the 2008 Olympic Games (*Express India* 2006). In contrast, Delhi, the capital city of India, has only a limited police–operated CCTV network consisting of several hundred cameras (*Hindu Times* 2010).

On the African sub-continent, in 2009 the Kenyan Inter-ministerial Committee on Nairobi Beautification announced, as part of its 'Nairobi Image and Security Project', that although CCTV coverage was to be extended in Nairobi:

> this will not be sufficient and will only cover the Central Business District and major streets . . . we are requesting that all Kenyans and especially Nairobians install CCTV cameras on their buildings or Estate Gates and streets so as to record criminal activities and recordings can be availed to police and media to identify and track criminals. CCTV and appropriate lighting are key in deterring crime.
>
> *(NISP 2009)*

In Lagos, the capital city of Nigeria, and one of the largest cities in the world with a population of 18 million people, it is planned to install 10,000 solar-powered CCTV cameras as part of the Lagos Safe City Project (African Loft 2009).

In the Middle East, Tehran, the capital of Iran, has an extensive network of police-controlled CCTV (Norris, Wood and McCahill 2006). More recently in the capital city of Saudi Arabia, Riyadh, CCTV has become a routine feature of the urban landscape, being deployed in shopping malls, on the railways and as part of the traffic management system (Alhahdar 2010).

In South America, Rio de Janeiro, Brazil's second-largest city and host to the football World Cup in 2014 and the Olympic Games in 2016, is set to see a major expansion of its CCTV network in 26 city districts, with over US$500 million set aside for developing security in the run-up to the Games (IMS Research 2010).

Public space CCTV is now truly a global phenomenon. In less than two decades it has expanded from a local initiative in a few small towns in the UK to become the international crime prevention 'success' story of the new millennium, set to penetrate every major city, in every country, on every continent. Like electricity, it appears that video surveillance will become a central part of the global urban infrastructure across the planet.[4] But how can we explain this? Such a rapid and universal take-up would suggest that the benefits in preventing and detecting crime and promoting public safety and security (the main justifications given for its deployment in any setting) are unequivocal. Let us review the evidence.

The evaluation of CCTV

In Britain in the early 1990s, the mass expansion of state-funded CCTV occurred before any systematic evaluation as to its effectiveness for preventing and detecting crime was carried out (Norris et al. 2004). The absence of evaluation seems not just to be a British malady. As Nieto et al. noted in 2002 regarding the USA:

> In general, we find that there have been very few studies of the effectiveness of the CCTV surveillance systems. Crime related statistical data are not required for use of federal grant funds, nor is there a requirement that all grantees report incidents of crime occurring where the cameras are located. Despite their increasing use, there is limited evidence that CCTV camera surveillance programs are successful crime-prevention tools.
>
> *(Nieto et al. 2002: 13)*

In Australia the story was similar, as Wilson and Sutton reported in 2003: 'To date only two evaluations of open-street CCTV are publicly available in Australia . . . However, in both cases insufficient pre-installation data was available to assess the impact of CCTV on offending' (Wilson and Sutton 2003: 2).

In the absence of systematic evaluation in the UK before widespread public funding was made available for CCTV, politicians relied on the self-interested claims of practitioners and system promoters to justify its crime reduction potential.

While a number of small-scale evaluations had been conducted during the 1990s, the results of these studies came up with mixed and often contradictory findings. In their review of 13 methodologically reliable studies conducted in the UK before 2000, Coleman and Norris concluded that in answer to the question 'Does CCTV reduce crime?', the evidence was far from straightforward and the effects neither universal nor consistent (2000: chapter 6).

The first major evaluation, funded by the Scottish Office, was of the effectiveness of CCTV in two Scottish cities, and this also produced contradictory findings. As Ditton and Short reported:

> Put at its starkest, after the installation of open-street CCTV in Airdrie, recorded crimes and offences fell to 79% of their previous recorded levels, and detections rose from 50 to 58%. Conversely after the installation of open-street CCTV in Glasgow, recorded crimes and offences rose to 109% of their previously recorded levels, and detections fell from 64% to 60%.
>
> *(Ditton and Short 1999: 212)*

A similar pattern emerges when we review the most recent key evaluations from around the world. In Los Angeles the evaluators reported that neither camera systems they studied had 'any significant effect in reducing violent or property crime rates within the target areas' (Cameron et al. 2007: 29). In Philadelphia, Ratcliffe and Taniguchi reported overall a 13 per cent reduction in crime, but this was largely made up of a reduction in less serious disorder crime. For serious crime there was no statistically significant reduction. They went on to note that: 'The introduction of CCTV was associated with considerably different inputs on each crime site. At half of the sites crime did not reduce in the target area' (Ratcliffe and Taniguchi 2008: 12).

In San Francisco, King et al. found that there was a statistically significant drop in property crime of 13 per cent. However, the rationale and justification for the system had been the reduction in violent crime: they found no evidence that cameras had an impact on violent crime (King et al. 2008: 11).

The Australian Research Council funded evaluation of the impact of CCTV in two Gold Coast suburbs and on the Queensland City Train Network concluded that overall:

> The effectiveness of CCTV as a crime prevention measure is questionable. From this research it appears CCTV is effective at detecting violent crime and/or may result in increased reporting as opposed to preventing any type of crime.
>
> *(Wells et al. 2006: iii).*

The UK Home Office funded evaluation of 14 CCTV systems, one of the largest and most systematic ever conducted, found:

> That the CCTV schemes that have been assessed had little overall effect on crime levels. Even where changes have been noted, with the exception of

those relating to car parks, very few are larger than could have been due to chance alone and all could in fact represent either a chance variation or confounding factors.

(Gill and Spriggs 2005: 43)

The findings of individual evaluation studies have, over the last decade, been systematically reviewed by a number of researchers for and on behalf of national or regional government agencies. In 2003, Deisman's review for the Royal Canadian Mounted Police concluded:

> The review shows that the effects of CCTV on crime are both quite variable and fairly unpredictable. Deterrence effects of CCTV are not constant over time and they can vary over crime categories. For example, CCTV systems appear to have the least effect upon public disorder offences. The magnitude of deterrence effects appears to depend on location: the greatest effect appears to occur in car parks.

> (Deisman 2003: 2)

Ratcliffe's 2006 review of 21 evaluation studies, as part of his *Problem Orientated Guides for Police* funded by the US Department of Justice, concluded that:

> CCTV is more effective at combating property offences than violent offences, . . . appears to work best in small, well-defined areas [and] achieving statistically significant reductions in crime can be difficult.

> *(Ratcliffe 2006: 19)*

Welsh and Farrington's 2003 UK Home Office funded meta-analysis of 22 British and American evaluations that met their minimum requirements of scientific adequacy, concluded: 'that CCTV had a significant desirable effect on crime, although the overall reduction in crime was a rather small 4%' (Welsh and Farrington 2003: 42).

While this may be seen as a partial endorsement of CCTV, it is important to note that only half of the studies included showed a positive effect, with the other half showing either negative or no effects. Moreover, CCTV had little or no effect on crime in public transport and city centre settings. The only statistically significant results were to be found in car parks (Welsh and Farrington 2003: 42–3).

In 2007, Welsh and Farrington conducted an update of their meta-evaluation, adding another 22 evaluations to the list, and concluded:

> The results suggest that CCTV caused a small (16%) but significant decrease in crime in experimental areas compared with controlled areas. However, this overall result was largely driven by the effectiveness of CCTV schemes in car parks, which caused a 51% decrease in crime. Schemes in most other settings had small and non-significant effects on crime: a 7% decrease in city and town centers and in public housing.

> *(Welsh and Farrington 2007: 8)*

Similarly, in 2008 Cameron et al., using a similar methodology, and drawing on a slightly different selection of studies, reported:

> Of the 44 evaluations included in our analysis, 43% reported the cameras had no or an uncertain effect on reducing crime, 41% reported statistically significant reduction in crime, and 15.9% reported some undesirable effect . . . Within the 19 evaluations that found no statistically significant effect on crime or were uncertain as to CCTV's effect, 36.8% (7) reported a reduction in crime, 52.6% (10) reported an increase in crime, and 10.5% (2) reported no change or a very small change in crime.
>
> *(Cameron et al. 2008: 4)*

Detecting crime and gathering evidence

Despite the fact that CCTV is often cited as being a major tool in assisting the police in the investigation of crime, as the UK Home Office's 2007 National CCTV Strategy notes:

> Little formal research has been undertaken to establish the impact CCTV has on the investigation of crime. Those examining the issue therefore have to rely on limited research and anecdotal evidence provided by operational police officers.
>
> *(Home Office 2007: 24)*

However, there is some evidence that can be derived from various studies. The evaluations of CCTV in Scotland found that, while the introduction of CCTV in Airdrie led to an increase in the clear-up rate[5] from 50 per cent to 60 per cent, in Glasgow it fell from 64 per cent to 60 per cent (Ditton and Short 1999). In their Australian evaluation, Wells et al. found that in the course of 100 hours of observation of the control rooms, 181 incidents were surveyed by the camera operators, which led to 51 arrests. However, as they go on to note:

> Although it was anticipated that most surveillance incidents would be initiated by the camera operators themselves, it was determined that approximately half resulted from the police requesting specific surveillance of a person or incident. The observational study also suggests 7 of the 51 arrests were the direct result of the camera network with the remaining arrests attributable to police communication and simultaneous detection.
>
> *(Wells et al. 2006: ii)*

In the San Francisco evaluation it was found:

> As of August 2008 the SFPD had requisitioned CSC footage 120 times, or approximately 3 times per month over the last 3 years. Since the program

began in 2005, CSC footage had assisted the SFPD in charging a suspect with a crime in 6 cases.

(King et al. 2008: 13)

The relative ineffectiveness of CCTV's contribution to prosecutions was confirmed by a senior Metropolitan Police officer who described the contribution of CCTV to cutting crime as 'an utter fiasco' since, in London, only 3 per cent of street robberies, a crime for which CCTV footage would be expected to be a particularly useful investigative tool, had been solved using CCTV footage (BBC News 2008).

CCTV and fear of crime

It is often claimed that regardless of its preventative effect or contribution to criminal arrest and prosecution, the presence of CCTV provides reassurance to the public and makes them less fearful about becoming a victim of crime. As we have seen, a number of attitude surveys have shown that people report that they would feel safer if CCTV were installed. However, while the public believe that, in general, people will feel safer when the cameras are introduced, when people are asked whether it will make them feel personally safer far fewer think it would.[6] It has also been found that knowledge of the camera watching over them had no effect on respondents' levels of fear of crime, seemingly repudiating the idea that CCTV can be justified as a measure to reduce the fear of crime.[7] The 2005 British Home Office evaluation reported:

> CCTV was found to have played no part in reducing fear of crime; indeed those who were aware of the cameras admitted higher levels of fear than those who were unaware of them.
>
> *(Gill and Spriggs 2005: 60)*

This finding is supported by studies that have attempted to explore people's actual behaviour rather than just their attitudes. These show that CCTV has a limited impact in getting people to use their town centres and high streets more.[8] As the Home Office 2005 evaluation found:

> On the whole, these findings suggest that there is no connection between worries about being a victim of crime and avoidance behaviour. They also indicate that respondents believed CCTV would have an impact on their avoidance behaviour (encouraging them to visit places they previously avoided) but in practice this rarely occurred.
>
> *(Gill and Spriggs 2005: 54–5)*

The seduction of vision

The best available evidence from evaluation studies conducted around the world suggests that CCTV has a limited impact on preventing crime, is not very effective at detecting crimes, and does not reduce the fear of crime. Why then has it become a ubiquitous part of the global urban landscape?

CCTV is seductive. It promises, from its elevated vantage point, to make visible all that is occurring in its domain and, unlike the human eye, with no capacity of creating an objective record of events, CCTV promises to capture the past in perpetuity, to be replayed at will. This seduction is underpinned by the primacy of the visual over the other senses, both in common sense and legal discourse. The epithets '*seeing is believing*' and '*a picture paints a thousand words*' point to the primacy of the visual accorded in everyday language. But this goes beyond mere belief and representation. The visual is also accredited with the status of knowledge. In English when we say '*I see*' we also mean '*I understand*'. When we are ignorant we are '*in the dark*', but become more knowledgeable when '*light has been shed upon the matter*', and have a true understanding when we have been '*enlightened*'. In the context of criminal justice, with elaborate rules of evidence, this is of particular importance. From an investigatory point of view, the problems of relying on human witnesses to recall and testify are well known. Merely locating and identifying potential witnesses can be a major part of an investigation. Even when a witness has been found, their ability to recall, and their credibility as an evidence giver, impinge on the value of their testimony. If only a camera were present. We would then be able to see: see who was there and see what happened. When we had seen, we would know what happened. And the immutable visual record could then be used as evidence.

If CCTV is seductive from an investigatory perspective, it is also seductive from a crime prevention perspective. Clearly CCTV should act as a deterrent. As a police officer might explain, 'If he's going to put a brick through a window he's not going to do it in front of the camera, is he?' And such a view is supported by classical deterrence theorists, for whom increased surveillance is often at the heart of situational crime prevention measures. The introduction of CCTV is warranted because it will influence the decision-making of the 'rational' offender who, on calculating the risks, will choose not to commit crime under the gaze of the cameras as this will increase the probability of being caught.

This seductive power of vision is constantly reinforced by a news and entertainment media hungry for images and footage. At the local level, in the UK at least, coverage of CCTV in the local printed press has tended to be highly favourable, having been enlisted by a local coalition of elites to establish and maintain support for systems (Norris and Armstrong 1999; McCahill 2002). However, the political slant of CCTV news stories is of far less importance than their discursive structure. A discursive structure that is repeated time and time again on a global level, in television news bulletins, reality crime TV shows and tabloid newspaper articles. One common story is: '*Have you seen this man?*' Here footage, or stills, are shown of a crime in progress, and then a close-up is shown of the face of the perpetrator and the public is then asked to identify him. Another common theme is '*Caught on camera*': the story tells of the successful outcome of a court case, where the cameras have filmed the misdeeds to be replayed first as evidence and then as 'infotainment'. In both cases, the discourse serves to reinforce the power of CCTV as a crime preven-tion and detection strategy: people who misbehave will be caught on camera, they will be identified, arrested and convicted. CCTV ensures that this will happen.

Of course, all of this is true. But in the particular, not the general. CCTV can be very effective in bringing a particular crime to book, yet, as we have seen from the review of the evaluation evidence, it is much less successful in leading to overall reductions in crime or increasing detections. Even so, the repeat broadcasting of success stories inevitably leads to an over-estimation of the efficacy of the cameras. It is, therefore, not surprising that, in a worldwide survey of attitudes toward sur-veillance, it was found that just over three-quarters of respondents (77 per cent) thought that CCTV was 'very' or 'somewhat' effective in reducing crime (GPDP 2008).

The promise of CCTV systems contributing to effective crime prevention and detection strategies is predicated on two seductive myths. First, that the camera is a perfect witness (or at least far better than humans) in that it is always watching, always recording and always available to criminal justice personnel to stand witness. Second, it assumes a rational offender who will be deterred by the presence of the cameras.

The myth of CCTV as the perfect witness

It is possible to imagine that in an environment such as a railway station or a seaport there could be almost total coverage of the cameras. It would require hundreds of cameras but it might enable a permanent record of what occurred. Where a system consists only of fixed cameras, this at least ensures continuous monitoring of an area; however, this makes tracking an individual difficult as a suspect will be mov-ing between cameras. If PTZ cameras are used then tracking and zooming in are enabled but at the expense of leaving other areas unmonitored. Most sophisticated systems, therefore, use a mixture of fixed and PTZ cameras. Even then, it is simply impossible, given finite resources, for the output of every camera to be monitored by a dedicated human operative. So most control rooms display the images from a multitude of cameras on banks of wall-mounted monitors, and allow an operator to draw down a particular feed onto their dedicated screen for closer inspection and dedicated high-quality recording. The result is selective and partial monitoring.

If it is not possible for each camera to be monitored, it has also not proved possible, in analogue systems, for all the images to be continuously recorded. The sheer volume of tape required to capture the images of, say, a 40-camera system recording in real time, in full quality would be overwhelming. If each camera were connected to a video recorder using three-hour tapes this would generate 6,000 tapes per month and would require a team of operatives just to manage the video recorders. The solution has typically been to 'multiplex' the monitoring and recording so that images from four or more cameras are displayed on each screen and captured on a single tape. However, it still requires the tapes to be changed every three hours. To overcome this, time-lapse recording is often used, whereby not every frame of video stream is recorded. In a five-camera system the picture rate would be updated every 0.2 seconds rather than 25 times per second. What this means is that 80 per cent of the information (images) from each camera is lost. Multiplexing and time-lapsing substantially reduce the number of tapes required, but at a considerable cost in terms of their value as evidence.

The fortuitous footage of the luckless offender, caught on camera, full face and committing the offence, may be a detective's dream but is an elusive rarity. In reality, for the investigation of a past offence, piecing together the evidence from a multitude of cameras is probably little more efficient than the trawl for witnesses by the old-fashioned method of house-to-house enquiries. Hundreds of tapes have to be assembled and then viewed frame by frame. In the investigation of the London Tube bombings on 7 July 2005, the so called 7/7 bombings, over 100 officers were assigned to the task of finding and examining the CCTV footage. It took the team four days merely to locate the bombers in the footage of King's Cross station. (*Daily Mail* 2010; *Independent* 2010).

It is not just the sheer volume of images that undermines CCTV as a witness. The quality of cameras, lenses, recording devices and tapes also varies hugely between different systems, leading to many images of dubious evidential quality. As the 2007 British Association of Chief Police Officers National Strategy Report commented in regard to quality:

> Anecdotal evidence suggests that over 80% of the CCTV footage supplied to the police is far from ideal, especially if it is being used for primary identification or identities are unknown and identification is being sought, for instance, by media release.
>
> *(Home Office 2007: 12)*

Even where footage is recovered, whether it can be used subsequently in an investigation is also far from certain, as the National Strategy Report explained:

> Police and CJS users have difficulty in playing back CCTV footage from the many proprietary recording formats. The police service is employing specialist technical staff to recover and process digital CCTV footage, but the CJS often has difficulty playing back in these formats. Currently, the measures used to overcome this are conversion to other standard formats (in most cases VHS). This is time consuming, and can result in a reduction of quality.
>
> *(ACPO 2007: 12)*

The myth of the rational offender

CCTV did not deter the 7/7 London suicide bombers. The deterrent justification for CCTV as necessitated by the terrorist threat posed by the bombing campaigns of ETA in Spain or the IRA in the UK becomes irrelevant when the bombers are prepared to die in the name of their cause. But it is not just such extreme cases where the deterrent value of the cameras has limited impact. For CCTV to act as a deterrence people have to be aware that they are being filmed. This is particularly relevant because, as studies have shown, awareness of being under surveillance cannot be assumed. Early evaluations of CCTV in the UK found that up to 60 per cent of people in city centres that had installed CCTV were unaware of its presence, and in Berlin shopping malls with cameras only 40 per cent of shoppers were aware of them (Ditton 2000; Helten and Fischer 2004: 9). Even when people are aware of the presence of cameras, given that much city centre crime and disorder is fuelled by the over-consumption of alcohol, it is unlikely that the deterrent value of the cameras will have much impact. As the evaluation by Gill and Spriggs demonstrated, crimes of disorder and violence actually increased in the areas under CCTV surveillance compared with the control groups. While this may suggest the efficacy of the cameras in discovering crime, it does not support their ability to deter (Gill and Spriggs, 2005: 35).

It is not just relatively spontaneous acts of disorder and violence that are undeterred by the presence of cameras. In Gill and Loveday's innovative study of 77 imprisoned offenders' attitudes towards CCTV, even those committing economically rational crimes, such as street robbery and shoplifting, reported being not deterred by camera surveillance:

> The presence of CCTV did not appear to be a major concern for the 19 street robbers. Only 2 reported specifically seeking out a location which did not have CCTV, and while others discussed an offence where CCTV was present, all of them said that CCTV did not affect the way the offence was committed.
>
> *(Gill and Loveday, 2003: 82)*

They go on to report:

> The shop thieves interviewed did not consider CCTV to be something that made their offence difficult to commit, but it was something they had to consider and 'work around'.
>
> *(Gill and Loveday, 2003: 85)*

The success of failure

CCTV is a failure. But it is only a failure if we judge it in line with common sense understandings of crime prevention and detection. It is of course very difficult not to judge it in these terms because that is how police, policy-makers and the media talk about it. However, it makes more sense to see CCTV as an instrument of policing, not of crime prevention and detection. As the sociological analysis of policing has made clear, policing is concerned with far more that just prevention and detection. Indeed, when the content of police work is examined, it is found that police officers spend little of their time dealing with crime or law enforcement

(Bayley 1996: 29). Rather, as Egon Bittner has argued, the primary mandate of the police is to deal with 'something-that-ought-not-to-be-happening-and-about-which-something-ought-to-be-done-now', with the aim of restoring the normative order back to the status quo (Bittner 1974). Thus as Ericson argues:

> The mandate of police patrol officers is to employ a system of rules and authoritative commands to transpose troublesome, fragile situations back into a normal or efficient state, whereby the ranks of society are preserved . . . Therefore the patrol police are essentially a vehicle in the reproduction of order.
>
> *(Ericson 1982: 7)*

If we see CCTV primarily as an instrument of policing, both of public and private space, then we can see how it may have all sorts of effects and utilities which are not captured in the simplistic notion of crime prevention and detection. CCTV is then better conceived of as primarily about the reproduction of a normative order – the normative order of the street, the mall, the shop, the metro system and so on. As a number of studies have shown, what CCTV operators focus upon is those people and behaviours that are deemed to be disruptive of the local, authoritative conceptions of order. The young child adrift from her parents, a collapsed body in the street, a car crash, a group of youths hanging around the streets, a person standing still for too long, someone running and those deemed out of place by virtue of their appearance and demeanour (Norris and Armstrong 1999; McCahill 2002). One effect of this is that CCTV surveillance becomes disproportionately targeted on minority populations and those deemed as 'other'.

In Norris and Armstrong's 1999 study it was the young, the male and the black who were systematically and disproportionately targeted, not because of their involvement in crime or disorder, but for 'no obvious reason' and on the basis of categorical suspicion alone. These British findings have been confirmed by studies in other parts of Europe.

In the Netherlands, Dubbeld's study of a railway CCTV control room described graphically the selective targeting practices of the operators:

> Operators had their own ways of categorising and classifying the objects of their surveillance. Operators identified suspicious individuals as 'Naffers' (short for North Africans, usually Moroccan or Turkish men) or called them 'cockroaches', 'crazy pancakes', 'little rats', 'nazis', 'faggots', 'annoying little men', 'mongols', or 'pancakes'.
>
> *(Dubbeld 2004: 121)*

In Milan, Fonio, on the basis of her observational study of a CCTV control room, reported:

> In particular, North Africans and East Europeans were tracked for no particular reasons but their appearance . . . Behavioural patterns did not play an

important role in determining who had been monitored. Two social categories were also targeted on the basis of their appearances: young people, in particular those who were poorly dressed, and nice-looking women.

(Fonio 2007: 14)

As von Hirsch and Shearing have noted, exclusion is frequently at the heart of situational crime prevention strategies and is 'now being extensively used in privately owned spaces that have public functions, such as shopping malls' where the local normative order is dominated by commercial rather than democratic concerns (von Hirsch and Shearing 2000: 77).

Wakefield's study of an English mall with an extensive CCTV system found, over a five-week period, that 578 people were excluded and 65 per cent of these exclusions involved 'known offenders' (Wakefield 2000: 134–5). As McCahill reported in his study of the CCTV system in a northern English mall, it was anonymous groups of teenagers who were most likely to be targeted, deployed against and ejected, not because of any past or present legal infraction but because they were, in dress and demeanour, seen to be disrupting the commercial image of the mall (McCahill 2002).

Similar results have been found in Lomell's study of the operation of three CCTV systems in the Norwegian capital:

> Summing up, one can say that in Oslo, CCTV has had its most exclusionary effects in the most privatised of public spaces, where it is used mainly as a discriminatory tool ensuring marginalised people are kept out of site of consumers. Ejections were a substantial result of video surveillance operations at two of the sites, namely the shopping mall and the transport center. In large part, these ejections were pre-emptive. That is to say, the majority of the exclusions were in response to appearances and categorical suspicions; only a minority of these ejections was in response to observed criminal or nuisance behaviours.

(Lomell 2004: 356–7)

In this sense Coleman is right when he sees CCTV as part of a strategy to 'Reclaim the Streets' in line with neo-liberal conceptions of the proper use of public space. As a result, marginal consumers such as the homeless and the poor are subject to regimes of purification (Coleman 2004: chapters 6 and 7). It is not just the neo-liberal politics of city regeneration but the post-Second World War politics of criminal justice that have also created a receptive climate for the adoption of CCTV. As Garland argues, by the 1970s there was a collapse in the social democratic consensus about the causes of crime and the efficacy of the traditional methods of controlling it. With rising affluence it could no longer be claimed that poverty was a cause of crime, and the belief in the rehabilitative power of state intervention, to transform the deviant into the law-abiding, could no longer be sustained in the wake of evaluation studies which suggested that 'Nothing Works'. Retribution, rather than rehabilitation, became the dominant justification for punishment. Rather than understanding the causes of crime, merely trying to prevent it through reducing opportunity, and increasing deterrence and detection, became the pragmatic policy.

In this context the potential of CCTV offers the promise of success. It may be a false promise, but it is highly seductive. And perhaps this is not important, because CCTV's appeal and success are less to do with its material effects and more to do with its symbolic potential. Following Garland we can argue that the rapid introduction of surveillance cameras can be seen as a form of '*acting out* – a mode that is concerned not so much with controlling crime as with expressing the anger and outrage that crime provokes' (Garland 2001: 110). CCTV is therefore best seen as a populist measure designed to send a message to the public that a government is *doing something* about the crime problem. When we are trying to understand the rise of CCTV as a global phenomenon we should not only see it as a technology but as a discursive object. A discursive object waiting to be deployed in public debate as a response to the latest perceived crisis: a school shooting, a terrorist bombing, a child abduction, a political murder, or spiralling crime rates. Will it prevent these crimes happening in the future? Probably not. But this is to miss the point, because the most important material and ideological effects of CCTV are not those that are advertised. In providing a visible, yet symbolic, response to the complex problem of crime and terror, and by privileging powerful commercial interests in the reproduction of order in public space, CCTV is very successful. In which case there is indeed 'No success like failure and failure is no success at all'!

Notes

1   With apologies to Bob Dylan. The lines 'She knows there's no success like failure, And that failure's no success at all' come from the song *Love Minus Zero/No Limit* which appeared on his album *Bringing It All Back Home*, released in 1965 by Columbia Records. There is a lively web debate as to what these enigmatic lines might mean or whether they are just nonsense.
2   These images were replayed night after night on the national news, achieving an iconic status in the subsequent moral panic about youth crime, and while CCTV had not managed to prevent the killing, the ghostly images at least held out the prospect that the culprits would be caught.
3   Austria (Töpfer 2008b); Bulgaria (Axis Communications 2008); Croatia (*Croatian Times* 2009); Czech Republic (EDRI 2008); Denmark (IceNews 2008); Finland (*Helsingin Sanomat* 2006); France (Hempel and Töpfer 2009); Germany (Hempel and Töpfer 2009); Greece (Samatas 2004); Hungary (Molnar 2003); Ireland (DJELR 2007); Italy (Calabria 2003); Lithuania (HRMI 2009); Netherlands (Flight et al. 2003); Norway (Winge and Knutsson 2003); Poland (Waszkiewic 2009); Portugal (*Euro Weekly News* 2008); Spain (Doron 2008); Sweden (Blixt 2003); Switzerland (Klauser 2007) and the UK (Norris and McCahill 2006).
4   See Graham 1999, on CCTV as the fifth utility.
5   Detections expressed as percentage of recorded crimes and offences.
6   Squires and Measor 1997 found that while 90 per cent thought CCTV would make people feel safer, only 30 per cent thought it would make *them* feel safer.

7   Ditton, J. et al. (1999) found that although 79 per cent of people thought CCTV would reduce fear of crime, before a system was introduced, answers to the post-implementation surveys show that those who were aware of the cameras 'were no more likely to say they felt safer or used the streets more often than other city centre users', as '75 per cent of those aware feel safe (as opposed to 77 per cent of the unaware), and 53 per cent of those who are aware of CCTV worry about being a victim (as opposed to 49 per cent who are unaware)'.

8   Squires and Measor (1997) found very few people, only 2 per cent in the day time and 3 per cent at night time, felt that the system had anything to do with the frequency of their visits to the town centre. Similar results were obtained in Sutton, a large majority of respondents reporting 'no influence of CCTV on their use of the high street' (Mahalingam 1996: 57).

9   All electronic sources accessed between 10 and 12 December 2010.

References[9]

AfricanLoft (2009) 'Nigeria: Safer City Project – 10,000 CCTV cameras to be installed', 15 January. Online. Available HTTP: <http://www.africanloft.com/lagos-safe-city-project-10000-surveillance-cameras-to-be-installed/>.

Alhahdar, I. (2010) *Moral Discipline, State Power and Surveillance: The rise and operation of CCTV surveillance in Riyadh*. Unpublished PhD thesis, University of Hull, September 2010.

Armitage, R. (2002) To CCTV or Not to CCTV? A Review of Current Research into the Effectiveness of CCTV Systems in Reading Crime, Nacro Community Safety Practice Briefing, London: Nacro.

Axis Communications (2008) 'The Municipality of Sliven implements Axis network cameras to provide a safer city environment', Company press release, 2008. Available HTTP: <http://www.axis.com/files/success_stories/ss_cit_sliven_31682_en_0803_lo.pdf>.

Axxon (2007) 'Moscow: SafeCity™ Now Comprises Twenty Thousand CCTV Cameras', Company Press release. Available HTTP: <http://www.axxonsoft.com/company/pressroom/news/1896/>.

Bayley, D.H. (1996) 'What do the Police Do?', in W. Saulsbury, J. Mott and T. Newburn (eds), *Themes in Contemporary Policing*. London: Policy Studies Institutes.

BBC News (2008) 'CCTV boom "failing to cut crime"' *BBC News at One*, 6 May=. Online. Available HTTP<http://news.bbc.co.uk/1/hi/uk/7384843.stm>.

Bittner, E. (1974) 'Florence Nightingale in Pursuit of Willie Sutton: A Theory of the Police', in H. Jacob (ed.), *The Potential for Reform of Criminal Justice*. Beverly Hills: Sage.

Blixt, M. (2003) *The Use of Surveillance Cameras for the Purpose of Crime Prevention*, Stockholm: National Council for Crime Prevention, Sweden.

Calabria, M. (2003) 'CCTV Closed circuit television – Italy: Industry sector analysis', *Strategis*: Industry Canada. Available HTTP: <http://strategis.ic.gc.ca/epic/internet/inimr-ri.nsf/en/gr110247e.html>.

Cameron, A., Kolodinski, E., May, H. and Williams, N. (2008) *Measuring the Effects of Video Surveillance on Crime in Los Angeles*. Prepared for the Californian Research Bureau; University of Southern California: School of Policy Planning and Development.

Coleman, C. and Norris, C. (2000) *Introducing Criminology*, Cullompton: Willan Publishing.

Coleman, R. (2004) *Reclaiming the Streets: Surveillance, Social Control and the City*, Cullompton: Willan Publishing.

Constant, M. and Turnbull, P. (1994) *The Principles and Practice of CCTV*, Hertfordshire: Paramount Publishing.

Croatian Times (2009) 'Zagreb to have 225 new video surveillance cameras', 13 February.

Available HTTP: <http://www.croatiantimes.com/index.php?id=2752>.

Daily Mail (2010) 'Families of 7/7 victims shown footage of suicide ringleader pushing supermarket trolley packed with bomb-making equipment' *Daily Mail Online*, 19 October. Online. Available HTTP: <http://www.dailymail.co.uk/news/article-1320237/7-7-INQUEST-CCTV-footage-shows-suicide-ringleader-supermarket-trolley-bomb-making-equipment.html>.

Deisman, W. (2003) *CCTV Literature Review and Bibliography*. Research and Evaluation Branch. Ottawa: Community, Contract and Aboriginal Policing Services Directorate, Royal Canadian Mounted Police.

Ditton, J. (2000) 'Public Attitudes towards Open Street CCTV in Glasgow', *British Journal of Criminology*, 40: 692–709.

Ditton, J. and Short, E. (1998) 'Evaluating Scotland's First Town Centre CCTV Scheme', in C. Norris, J. Moran and G. Armstrong (eds), *Surveillance, Closed Circuit Television and Social Control*, Aldershot: Ashgate.

Ditton, J. and Short, E. (1999) 'Yes, It Works, No, It Doesn't: Comparing the Effects of Open CCTV in Two Adjacent Scottish Town Centres', in K. Painter and N. Tilley (eds), *Crime Prevention Studies*, 10: 201–24.

Ditton, J., Short, E., Phillips S., Norris, C. and Armstrong, G. (1999) *The Effect of the Introduction of Closed Circuit Television on Recorded Crime Rates and Concern about Crime in Glasgow*, Edinburgh, SCOT: Central Research Unit, Scottish Office.

DJELR (2007) 'Major developments in provision of CCTV systems nationwide announced', press release – Department of Justice, Equality and Law Reform, Republic of Ireland. Available HTTP: <http://www.justice.ie/en/JELR/Pages/PR07000221>.

Doron, D. (2008) 'Urban Video Analytics Case Study: Madrid Suburb'. *IP Video market Info*. Online. Available HTTP: <http://ipvideomarket.info/report/urban_video_analytics_case_study_madrid_suburb>.

Dubbeld, L. (2004) *The Regulation of the Observing Gaze: Privacy Implications of Camera Surveillance*, Maastricht: Netherlands Graduate Research School of Social Science, Technology and Modern Culture, University of Maastricht.

EDRI (2008) – European Digital Rights: 'Key privacy concerns in Czech Republik 2007'. Available HTTP: <http://www.edri.org/edrigram/number6.2/privacy-czech-2007>.

Euro Weekly News (2008) 'Video surveillance system to increase safety', 27 March. Available HTTP: <http://www.euroweeklynews.com/news/6984.html>.

EPIC (2005) – Electronic Privacy Information Center – Spotlight on Surveillance <http://epic.org/privacy/surveillance/spotlight/0505/>: 'More Cities Deploy Camera Surveillance Systems with Federal Grant Money'. Available HTTP: <http://epic.org/privacy/surveillance/spotlight/0505/#footnote2>.

Ericson, R. (1982) *Reproducing Order: A Study of Police Patrol Work*, Toronto: University of Toronto Press.

Express India (2006) 'Video surveillance to cover entire Beijing', 19 May Available HTTP: <http://www.expressindia.com/news/fullstory.php?newsid=67945>.

Flight, S., van Heerwaardem, Y and van Sommeren, P. (2003) 'Does CCTV Displace Crime? An evaluation of the evidence and a case study from Amsterdam', in M. Gill (ed.), *CCTV*, Leicester: Perpetuity Press.

Fonio, C. (2007) 'Surveillance and Identity: towards a new anthropology of the person', Paper presented at the *British Sociological Association Annual Conference*, London, 13 April.

GPDP (2008) *The Globalization of Personal Data Project: An International Survey on Privacy and Surveillance, Summary of Findings November 2008*. The Surveillance Project, Kingston, Ontario: Queen's University.

Garland, D. (2001) *The Culture of Control: Crime and Social Order in Contemporary Society*, Oxford: Oxford University Press.

Gill, M. and Loveday, M. (2003) 'What do Offenders Think About CCTV?', in M. Gill (ed.), *CCTV*, Leicester: Perpetuity Press.

Gill, M. and Spriggs, A. (2005) *Assessing the Impact of CCTV*, London: Home Office Research, Development and Statistics Directorate.

Graham, S. (1999) 'The eyes have it: CCTV as the "fifth utility"', *Environment and Planning B: Planning and Design*, 26(5): 639–42.

Helten, F. and Fischer, B. (2004) *What Do People Think about CCTV: Findings from a Berlin Study*, Urbaneye Working Paper No.13. Berlin: Technical University of Berlin. Available HTTP: <http://www.urbaneye.net/results/ue_wp13.pdf>.

Helsingin Sanomat (2004) – international edition – 'Surveillance cameras reduce vandalism at Tampere schools', 7 December. AvailableHTTP: <http://www.hs.fi/english/article/Surveillance+cameras+reduce+vandalism+at+Tampere+school/1101977933528>.

Helsingin Sanomat (2006) – international edition – 'Helsinki Police Department introduces new surveillance cameras', 1 September. Available HTTP: <http://www.hs.fi/english/article/Helsinki+Police+Department+introduces+new+surveillance+cameras/1135221349513>.

Hempel, L. and Töpfer, E. (2002) *Urban Eye: Inception Report to the European Commission, 5th Framework Programme*. Berlin: Technical University of Berlin. Available HTTP: <http://www.urbaneye.net/results/ue_wp1.pdf>.

Hempel, L. and Töpfer, E. (2004) *Urban Eye: Final Report to the European Commission, 5th Framework Programme*, Berlin: Technical University of Berlin. Available HTTP: <http://www.urbaneye.net/results/ue_wp15.pdf>.

Hempel, L. and Töpfer, E. (2009) 'The Surveillance Consensus: Reviewing the Politics of CCTV in Three European Countries', *European Journal of Criminology*, 6(2): 157–77.

Home Office (2007) *National CCTV Strategy*, London: Home Office.

Ice News (2008) 'CCTV comes to Copenhagen's high street'. Online. Available HTTP: <http://www.icenews.is/index.php/2008/07/19/cctv-comes-to-copenhagens-high-street/>.

IMS Research (2009) 10 for 2010: *Top Video Surveillance Industry Predictions for the Year Ahead*. Online. AvailableHTTP: <http://www.imsresearch.com/newsletter/Security/10%20for%202010_CCTVINFO.pdf>.

Independent (2010) 'CCTV reveals calm preparations of 7/7 bombers', 13 October. Available HTTP: <http://www.independent.co.uk/news/uk/home-news/cctv-reveals-calm-preparations-of-77-bombers-2105513.html>.

Infinet (2010) 'City of Rio de Janeiro chooses Comtex and InfiNet Wireless for city-wide wireless video surveillance and security network', Company press release, 9 March. Online. Available HTTP:<http://www.infinetwireless.com/news-events/>.

King, J., Mulligan, D. and Raphael, S. (2008) *Citris Report: The San Francisco Community Safety Camera Program*, California: Berkeley School of Law. Online. Available HTTP: <http://www.citris-uc.org/files/CITRIS%20SF%20CSC%20Study%20Final%20Dec%202008.pdf>.

Klauser, F. (2007) 'Difficulties in Revitalizing Public Space by CCTV: Street Prostitution Surveillance in the Swiss City of Olten', *European Urban and Regional Studies*, 14: 337.

Lomell, H.M. (2004) 'Targeting the Unwanted: Video Surveillance and Categorical Exclusion in Oslo, Norway?', *Surveillance & Society*, 2(2/3): 347–61.

McCahill, M. (2002) *The Surveillance Web: The Rise of Visual Surveillance in an English City*, Cullompton: Willan.

McCahill, M. and Norris, C. (2003) 'Estimating the Extent, Sophistication and Legality of CCTV in London', in M. Gill (ed.), *CCTV*, Leicester: Perpetuity Press.

Mahalingham, V. (1996) 'Sutton Town Centre Public Perception Survey', in M. Bulos and

D. Grant (eds), *Towards a Safer Sutton? CCTV: One Year On*, London: London Borough of Sutton.

Molnar, L. (2003) '*Information Society as Surveillance Society*', in Monlar, L. (ed.), Information Society as Surveillance Society, Budapest: Arisztoelsz Publishers.

Nieto, M., Johnston-Dodds, K. and Simmons, C. (2002) *Public and Private Applications of Video Surveillance and Biometric Technologies*. Sacramento: Californian Research Bureau. Available HTTP: <http://www.library.ca.gov/crb/02/06/02-006.pdf>.

NISP (2009) Nairobi Image and Security Project – 'From Nairoberry to Nairobi City in the Sun'. Available HTTP: <http://www.communication.go.ke/nbp/default.asp>.

Norris, C. and Armstrong, G. (1999) *The Maximum Surveillance Society: The Rise of CCTV*, Oxford: Berg.

Norris, C. and McCahill, M. (2006) 'CCTV, Beyond Penal Modernism?', *British Journal of Criminology*, 46: 97–118.

Norris, C., Wood, D. and McCahill, M. (2004) 'The Growth of CCTV: a global perspective on the international diffusion of video surveillance in publicly accessible space', *Surveillance and Society*, 2(2/3): 110–35.

PDP (2004) – Progressive Democrat Party – 'McDowell launches Dun Laoghaire Garda', Press release from the Irish Progressive Democrat Party. Available HTTP: <http://www.progressivedemocrats.ie/local_elections_update/136/>.

Ratcliffe, J. and Taniguchi, T. (2008) *CCTV Camera Evaluation: The Crime Reduction Effects of Public CCTV Cameras in the City of Philadelphia, PA Installed During 2006*, Philadelphia: Temple University Press.

Reuters (2007) 'France to increase video surveillance', *Reuters News Agency*, 12 October.

Samatas, M. (2004) *Surveillance in Greece: From Anticommunist to Consumer Surveillance*, New York: Pella Publishing.

SCAN (2009) – Surveillance Camera Awareness Network – *A Report on Camera Surveillance in Canada*, The Surveillance Project. Queen's University, Canada. Available HTTP: <http://www.surveillanceproject.org/projects/scan>.

Scholosberg, M. and Ozer, N. (2007) *Under the Watchful Eye: The Proliferation of Video Surveillance in California*, Northern California: ACLU.

Squires, P. and Measor, L. (1997) *CCTV Surveillance and Crime Prevention in Brighton: Follow-up Analysis*, Brighton: Health and Social Policy Research Centre, University of Brighton.

The Hindu (2010) 'CCTV cameras not serving much purpose for Delhi Police', 18 October. Online. Available HTTP: <http://www.hindu.com/2010/10/18/stories/2010101860850300.htm>.

Töpfer, E. (2008a) 'From Privacy Protection Towards Affirmative Regulation: The Politics of Police Surveillance in Germany'. Paper presented at the *Workshop on 'Surveillance and Democracy'*. University of Crete, Rethymno, 2–3 June.

Töpfer, E. (2008b) 'Public Area CCTV in Europe: A Brief Discussion'. Paper given at *Crime Prevention in Urban Public Spaces*, Paris, Centre de conférences internationales, 17–18 November.

Von Hirsch, A. and Shearing, C. (2000) 'Exclusion from Public Space', in A. von Hirsch, D. Garland and A. Wakefield (eds), *Ethical and Social Perspectives on Situational Crime Prevention*, Oxford: Hart Publishing.

Wakefield, A. (2000) 'Situational Crime Prevention in Mass Private Property', in A. von Hirsch, D. Garland and A. Wakefield (eds), *Ethical and Social Perspectives on Situational Crime Prevention*, Oxford: Hart Publishing.

Waszkiewicz, P. (2009) Personal communication, March 2009, from Pavel Waszkiewicz who is evaluating the Warsaw system.

Webster, W. (2009) 'CCTV Policy in the UK: reconsidering the evidence base', *Surveillance and Society*, 6(1): 10–22.

Wells, H., Allard, T. and Wilson P. (2006) *Crime and CCTV in Australia: Understanding the Relationship.* Centre for Applied Psychology and Criminology. Australia: Bond University.

Welsh, B. and Farrington, D. (2003) *Crime Prevention Effects of Closed Circuit Television: A Systematic Review,* London: Home Office.

Welsh, B. and Farrington, D. (2007) *Closed Circuit Television Surveillance and Crime Prevention: A Systematic Review.* Report prepared for the Swedish National Council for Crime Prevention. Stockholm: Swedish Council for Crime Prevention.

Welsh, B.C. and Farrington, D.P. (2004) 'Surveillance for Crime Prevention in Public Space: Results and Police Choices in Britain and America', *Criminology and Public Policy*, 3(3): 497–526.

Wiecek, C. and Rudinow-Saetnan, A. (2002) *Restrictive? Permissive? The Contradictory Framing of Video Surveillance in Norway and Denmark,* Urbaneye, Working Paper No. 4. Centre for Technology and Society, Technical University of Berlin.

Wilson, D. and Sutton, A. (2003) *Open Street CCTV in Australia: A Comparative Study of Establishment and Operation.* A Report to the Australian Criminology Research Council (CRC Grant 26/01-02). Melbourne, Australia.

Winge, S. and Knutsson, J. (2003) 'An Evaluation of the CCTV Scheme at Oslo Central Railway Station', in M. Gill (ed.), *CCTV.* Leicester: Perpetuity Press.

Wood, D. (2009) 'At the Tokyo Metropolitan Police HQ'. Available HTTP: <http://ubi-surv.wordpress.com/2009/07/31/at-the-tokyo-metropolitan-police-hq/>.

3

WHAT GOES UP, MUST COME DOWN

On the moribundity of camera networks in the UK

Gavin Smith

Introduction

> It can be argued that CCTV looks set to follow a similar pattern of development over the next 20 years, to become a kind of 'fifth utility'. Coverage seems set to extend towards ubiquity . . . The more CCTV coverage becomes the norm, the more excluded areas will fight to gain coverage.
>
> *(Graham 2001: 239)*

> Town 'will lose CCTV coverage' due to cuts.
>
> *(Cornish Guardian 2011)*

> CCTV is 'too expensive' for council to use.
>
> *(The Wokingham Times 2010)*

An exhaustive international literature now charts the mass diffusion of video surveillance systems (CCTV hereafter) across the world's urban landscapes. Indeed, a large section of this particular collection concerns itself with documenting qualitatively and quantitatively the mass expansionary dispersal of visual monitoring devices, while also examining the plurality of socio-cultural, political and economic forces influencing this process and related social implications. Although this approach to the understanding of CCTV expansion has significant value and merit, the arguments constructed tend to overlook and mist the diverse and complex social histories in which camera schemes are nested, the everyday politics of implementation, the cultural forces and social actors shaping systemic operationalization and the ambivalent media context in which video surveillance – as discourse and as technical device – is 'representationally' embedded. This chapter takes issue with the conventional view that CCTV is inevitably destined for sustainable ubiquity (a position exemplified in the opening prologue). Instead, case study and documentary research reveals that a diversity of social, political, economic and cultural factors are collectively conspiring, as gravitational forces, to erode the electronic eye's ideological and material hegemony in the public imagination and urban landscape. Poor systemic planning and technical ineptitude at the organizational level, the introduction of a conscripted and unqualified labour force and paradoxical operating objectives and priorities, the economic recession and the relentless pursuit and framing of governmental incompetence and systemic failure by a critical news media, have, for example, created a legitimacy crisis for the future sustainability of the publicly funded CCTV scheme under observation.[1] This chapter seeks to highlight how contradictions, the result of complex neo-liberal organizational structures, managerial values and fiscal logics, are reflected in the everyday life and constitution of CCTV surveillance. Although neo-liberalism as a *productive* political economic force, cultural form and set of bureaucratic ideals/strategies gave birth to the CCTV revolution and provided a fertile contextual environment for expeditious growth, the doctrine's concomitant features – the prioritization afforded to economic capital accumulation and instrumentality, and related cultures of hyper-managerialism and auditing – can as easily (and as swiftly) instigate and prompt the decline of such politicized interventions (Davis and Monk 2007; Harvey 2005). Thus, as fiscal austerity, prudence and cost-saving increasingly become driving forces of municipal and federal authority decision-making, administration and poïesis (see BBC News 2010), medium- and large-scale public CCTV networks, with 'only' the *immaterial, imperceptible* and *transitory* commodity of order[2] to trade as justification for their continued existence, become themselves considerable financial burdens and sources of political risk. Having surpassed an organizational, cultural and temporal apex, the prophetic argument developed here is that CCTV seems set to swap its 'pole' position for eternal entombment in a graveyard of failed neo-liberal utopias. A 'politics of contraction' is fast supplanting the 'politics of expansion' emphasized in the current literature, and this empirical situation demands a fresh and innovative epistemological approach to the understanding of surveillance polity and process. In other words, where previous accounts have explored the factors encouraging growth and creep, contemporary studies need to focus attention on the factors inducing retraction. The question is less about the foregrounding of CCTV in crime control policy and application, than about the social forces inducing its contemporary moribundity.

The following three-part chapter shows how historical decisions taken in the consultation phase of CCTV construction come to influence and jeopardize not only contemporary CCTV operativity but also wider systemic sustainability and legitimacy. Part one provides context for the narrative developed, considering in brief the neo-liberal agenda underpinning the rapid diffusion of public space CCTV systems. Part two utilizes the meeting minutes from a community safety consortium, the remit of which was the introduction of a CCTV scheme in a particular UK city in the mid-1990s. The genealogical approach adopted is analytically useful for several reasons. It helps one better comprehend the rationale behind systemic inception and the everyday politics of CCTV implementation, the types of actors involved in the decision-making process and diversity of imaginations duly invested, and the wider organizational remit of the system. It also enables the implications associated with the sedimentation of historical interactivity to be identified and understood. Part three deals with 'representational politics', examining the UK media's influential role in negatively framing CCTV and reporting on CCTV erosion, and some potential implications thereof.

Context: neo-liberalism and CCTV

A number of well-rehearsed scholarly theories attempt to explain CCTV intensification in the UK, many perceiving the emergence and consolidation of neo-liberal governance and the associated cultures of risk and penality duly produced as the causal forces par excellence (Norris and Armstrong 1999; Reeve 1998; Garland 2001; Simon 2007; McCahill 2002; Coleman 2004). Neo-liberalism is both a political doctrine and a set of governmental strategies prioritizing and promoting a market (accumulative), as opposed to a welfarist (distributive), driven approach to economic and social policy. The acquisition of capital and reproduction of social stratification are key processes, with minimalist governance over traditionally administered phenomena, market de-regulation and liberalization (i.e. the privatization of key sectors, services and industry), consumerism and responsibilized individualism the basic constitutional elements (Harvey 2005). The instrumental logic and fiscal principles underpinning neo-liberalism (essentially, cost minimization and capital maximization), which collectively frame, position and organize social actors and processes in accordance with their economic worth and value, have permeated contemporary urban regeneration policy and managerial constitution at local (municipal), regional (state) and national (federal) levels. This has meant that the orchestration of urban planning and governance is now dictated by public–private sector quangos comprising a consortium of local authority members (e.g. from the emergency services, the council and civil service), business and community representatives. The 'partnerships' spawned coalesce organizationally and economically around issues of pressing community concern, such as crime, health and urban decay. The logic is that information, resources and responsibilities can be shared among agencies, so that complex social problems can be addressed from different angles and knowledge bases, and enhanced services delivered. It is this group of primary definers who have now constitutional responsibility and legislative power for *imagining* the concept city in terms of architectural design and arrangement, and for delivering key provisions and initiatives.

The regeneration protocols (i.e. securitization and renewal of the built environment) framed through 'urban renaissance' philosophy have evoked a re-ordering of the urban around commercial imperatives and resilience ideals (Atkinson and Helms 2007; Coaffee, Murakami-Wood and Rogers 2009). The acquisition of inward investment has been the major objective of those responsible for urban renewal, and this has been accomplished through spatial restructuring and through the assembly and introduction of vibrant recreational and leisure economies. Perception is a central facet of urban regeneration politics, CCTV cameras performing important symbolic functions in this wider project: they a) signify and represent (and help re-establish) state authority and power; and b) help cultivate an impression of civility and, by the same token, safety, key psychological factors in the creation of tranquil, fantasy-like shopping environments. This has prompted some to interpret CCTV as an authoritarian intervention which extends carceral disciplinary logics and 'vicarious sovereignty' into civic space, and which reflects the wider criminalization of poverty and punitive common sense espoused by the contemporary penal state (Fyfe and Bannister 1996; Wacquant 2007, 2009a, 2009b).

Having briefly articulated the neo-liberal scaffolding on which video surveillance has been hastily erected, it is now time to focus attention on the micro-politics of installation by considering the historic deliberations of a specific stakeholder group tasked with CCTV implementation. This will help us better comprehend the social forces influencing system construction and discern the core elements functioning as gravitational pulls.

The politics of CCTV implementation: from global infrastructure to glocal case study

It is easy to interpret urban video surveillance camera networks as relatively fixed, stable and self-sustaining entities. As a result of being able only to directly encounter the camera's material form upon physical structures and access secondary accounts of how systems actually function in practice (often through biased media reportage, governmental literature and industry material), there is, for many, a tendency to attribute an autonomy, independence and staticity to such schemes, and, therefore, to neglect the complex social histories in which they are entrenched. This has been a major methodological limitation of much surveillance studies research to date: the framing of surveillance systems as ahistorical structures and the de-contextualization and disembedding of these 'scopic regimes' from the messiness of their local origins and anchoring. Adopting this approach means that cultural idiosyncrasies are effectively overlooked, so too the wider comparative discontinuities existing between and among systems. In reality, surveillance nodes, when analysed as discrete units, are historically situated, symbolic structures, comprised of multiple actors, meanings, forms and objectives, and in a recurrent state of flux and dynamicism, the influence of myriad external and internal stimuli. They are both discursive formulations ('imagined structures') *and* lived realities ('social environments'), yet qualitative accounts adequately connecting the processual interplay between imagination and reality, design and actuality, are currently in short supply. As Fussey (2007: 232) notes, 'Investigations into the implementation of public surveillance cameras constitute an under-populated region in the burgeoning field of surveillance studies.' Seeking to redress such lacunae, what follows is a brief overview of the social construction of a specific public space CCTV assemblage. Thematic analysis of the 1993–6 'Rivertown'[3] City Centre Public Space CCTV Working Group's (RWG hereafter) meeting minutes, official documents, and related interview material with the Rivertown public space CCTV manager, an original operator and the RWG project's secretary helps draw attention to the major cultural forces influencing the scheme's composition and directionality, from its ideational conception and constitutional remit to its negotiated development and implementation by an assortment of structurally empowered 'primary definers'. The structural sedimentation deposited as a result of historical interactivity is later shown to exercise a considerable influence over the system's contemporary application. Ethnographic excerpts taken from an observational study of the Rivertown operations room are also selectively employed, along with citations from both local and national media. Taken together, the following sections draw attention to a range of intriguing issues: the multitude of actors, technologies and energies invested in the social construction of surveillance networks; the importance of legitimacy politics and impression management; and the processual and symbolic nature of surveillance systems as socio–historical enterprises.

Systemic inception

The original idea to inaugurate RWG to investigate the feasibility of creating a camera network in the city centre through public and private sector enterprise and collaboration was first put forward by a municipal councillor and approved at a Rivertown Regional Council Public Protection Committee (PPC) meeting in April 1993:

> My recollection was that Councillor Bob Bailey tabled a motion that Rivertown should look at the use of CCTV. I think this was following some publicity in the media that highlighted the success of what was then described as the most modern CCTV system at that time. The Councillor felt that we should not necessarily take the lead but certainly move more speedily down the avenue of exploring the usage of CCTV rather than play catch-up with the big boys at a later stage.
>
> *(RWG Secretary)*

It is evident from the meeting minutes that 'copycatting' was a major driver of the initiative, that is, a passive acceptance of pro-CCTV governmental discourse and an active desire to replicate the structural form of existing schemes and maintain a competitive edge over rival cities in terms of policing and safety policy. The group was acutely aware that system construction would require significant private revenue investment:

> *Discussion turned to how the proposed project should be funded, including the suggestion of a surcharge or supplement to non-domestic rates.*
>
> *(RWG Minutes)*

Key players and stakeholders

The group's core membership comprised carefully selected representatives from both local authority and industry. The police took the lead role, the other principal members being political officials, civil servants, the city centre manager, architectural liaison officers and redevelopers, local and national business envoys, and environmental planning and heritage staff. Most meetings were attended by around 20 invited 'members' and it is clear from discussions that the key priorities for the proposed system were community safety and the prevention and detection of crime (two registered objectives which the system still remains legally obliged to perform), public ordering, traffic management, the promotion of local trade through lower insurance premiums and attitudinal manipulation.[4] There was an obvious desire to cultivate a 'partnership' approach at the organizational level so that costs and resources could be shared and national policy strategies met. From its inception, then, the Rivertown system was heavily influenced by political economic factors and agendas, with revenue acquisition through the adoption of new technologies considered the most proficient and effective way of 'designing out' civil disorder and 'designing in' a more attractive business environment. CCTV's symbolic function is evident, the technology being interpreted as a signifier of urban renaissance and progressiveness.

Although constituted by neo-liberal logics and ideals, having members derived from both municipal government agencies and commercial industry meant that the RWG embodied a relatively diverse set of values and operating objectives. This organizational complexity created structural tensions relating to ownership and operational protocol, and also generated disquietude among system 'partners' in the wider collective, as the situated expectations and priorities of, for example, shop and bar security staff were often incongruent with the goals and frameworks of the spatially and organizationally distinct camera operators (see Smith 2007b). Although both have an interest in public order maintenance, they each possess a differing risk calculus, particularly as these relate to embodied presence and distanciated viewing.

Not only is it of key sociological interest to comprehend the types of individuals *involved* in the project's development, it is interesting, also, to identify those whose voices were *excluded* from the 'consultation' process. Systemic implementation was largely undemocratic and non-transparent, in terms of both daily decision-making protocol and wider civic engagement and community representation,[5] with no women included in the RWG, nor any representation from the voluntary sector or from groups which may have challenged the proposals on ethical or ideological grounds. This might explain the hegemonic policing narrative running through the minutes, a gendered fixation on spatial control and reconfiguration through technological – as opposed to social – intercession, and the prioritization accorded to business interests, over those of marginalized groups. It is clear from the outset that the RWG embraced a potent neo-liberal ethic and applied its power, perspicaciousness and capacity to define who would and who would not be involved in deliberations so that the initiative encountered minimal opposition.

Manufacturing consent: Legitimacy politics and systematic selling strategies

Although one tends to imagine primary definers as being equipped with consider-able structural capital and ideological power (owing to their privileged social posi-tion as municipal authorities), how the proposed CCTV plan should be represen-tationally framed and sold, both to the media (and thus the general public) and to potential business investors, was a particularly discernible and prevalent narrative. This issue dominated the majority of the group's agenda and exchanges, and it is noticeable that a range of carefully crafted information and impression management strategies were adopted by the group so that a positive image of the proposal could be duly communicated:

> Designing to manage it [the project] very carefully and as a result we had to bring in a number of personnel from organizations and agencies working within the area so they could also sell the message to their client base.
>
> *(RWG Secretary)*

> *The chairman suggested that thought be given to approaching the local television broad-caster with the request that they again highlight the project – the fact that it would be the largest in Europe – and emphasize the good experiences of other initiatives.*
>
> *(RWG Minutes)*

A separate 'publicity subgroup' was implemented early on in proceedings, with an expert 'spin doctor' appointed from each partner organization. This was initi-ated so that the information communicated was consistent, diverse queries were addressed by the relevant 'expert' entity and the system was presented positively (through carefully engineered 'sound bites'). The limited number of discussants involved, ensured that the following hegemonic accounts were reproduced: *that CCTV will lower crime and will consequently stimulate a feel-good factor within the populace; that the local authority is addressing crime concerns through the appropria-tion of vanguard technology; that the system will be operated professionally and justly; that support for the scheme is widespread; that finances are being well managed; and that imple-mentation of the scheme not only makes 'business sense' for the city of Rivertown, in terms of increased footfall and lower insurance premiums, but should also be a source of civic pride.* These emotive 'legitimacy discourses' were predominantly directed at the business sector, in order to shape attitudes and source appropriate inception funds. Indeed, two promotional letters were drafted, a pro-CCTV video utilized and a high-profile local businessman recruited in order to 'advocate' and 'incentiv-ize' the cause, and put pressure on those unwilling to contribute resources. Thus the strategical construction and tenacious promotion of a 'value for money', 'effectiveness' and 'renaissance' narrative constituted a major part of the group's activities, with positive framing of the project a key objective:

> [Sure,] there was resentment at the early stages, but again, it was working with the people saying: 'You really cannot see the value of it just now, so we need to work with you.' So it just took a little more hard work and a bit more time to bring them around to our way of thinking.
>
> *(RWG Secretary)*

> *The letter should state that there will be no significant on-cost following the installation of the scheme and highlight the benefits of reduced insurance premiums. It was agreed to continue personal approaches to organizations in addition to the letter.*
>
> *(RWG Minutes)*

It is patently evident that at the 'idea' or feasibility stage of CCTV deployment, the 'imagined Other', as comprised by reflexive actors such as the media, the public and the business community, became key collectives for artful and individualized discursive management and manipulation, with symbolism and political economy the two central heuristics drawn upon to fashion public consent and credibility, and to source the required finances. Yet this was far from a straightforward process. Indeed, for all RWG's structurally embedded power and resources, they remained largely dependent on the agency, knowledge and practices of numerous 'external' players. The wider legislative framework regulating local authority action and the reliance invested in organizationally situated actors to perform pivotal tasks, made the installation of cameras a social process defined by complexity and negotiation. The environmental and heritage bureau, for example, exercised constitutionally assigned legal powers to influence planning direction, so too numerous other actors:

> *The chairman questioned whether in law, any procedure was available for such a CCTV scheme to be implemented without planning approval. He was advised that a planning application was both essential and a legal obligation.*
>
> *(RWG Minutes)*

We had to satisfy a number of external organizations like Environmental Planning and Heritage. Quite a lot of the buildings within our catchment area were listed buildings . . . So we had to liaise with them and say: 'this is the colour of the cabling that we are using, this is the route that the cabling will take, this is the location on the building, this is the casing that we are going to be using, this is the colour we are going to be using for the camera cover itself.' All who lived, worked and used that venue for entertainment purposes had to be consulted, too, by way of the planning process so it was not a case of just turning around and saying, 'we are going to erect 53 cameras, this is where they are going to be,' there was statutory consultation that had to be done under the planning legislation itself.

(RWG Secretary)

Other social groups and organizations exercised forms of influence over the directionality of the initiative. The regional council Finance and Resource committee, for example, had discretion in determining whether requested monies would or would not be forthcoming. Individual businesses had the capacity to refrain from contributing capital. Moreover, other companies generated practical and financial problems, as illustrated in the following excerpts:

> *'Part of the increase [in cost] was as a result of having difficulties with certain parties where the work carried out may have to be repeated in order to satisfy all concerned.'* The project manager reported that difficulties had been experienced with the national rail operating company whereby a 15-week delay was inevitable in order to obtain the relevant possession order.
>
> *(RWG Minutes)*

> You had to satisfy those occupiers . . . that the camera operators were not able to view into bedroom windows or bathroom areas. Very quickly the group agreed . . . that it would have to be within the police control for the capture of the images and the usage. But you had one or two of the key players who sat around the table saying, 'Well we are contributing vast sums of money [and] we also want to derive some form of control over the cameras for our organization's purposes.' This situation caused conflict.
>
> *(RWG Secretary)*

In addition, the local media utilized their ideological and definitional power to represent the system critically and influence public and business sector opinion, a situation with consequences for the scheme's legitimacy and repute:

> I have to say that some of the media did not particularly support us because they continually referred to it [i.e. the scheme] as: 'The Spy Camera System for Rivertown', so that did not help. That went back historically to friction between the local media and Rivertown Police (RP) because of individuals within the organization, and it was taken perhaps to extremes in that respect.
>
> *(RWG Secretary)*

During the consultation process, lay individuals and collectives utilized civil powers to challenge intended camera locations and the legal legitimacy of the scheme:

> There was one particular woman who took great umbrage [to the system]. She just felt that this was Big Brother spying and she was on the community

council and she used that to good advantage, rightly or wrongly, in the consultation process to get some of the cameras moved. So there were concerns, one or two where we had just to eat humble pie and get second-best location purely and simply because we could not appease or satisfy the individual objectors.

(RWG Secretary)

Even small business owners and individual tenants had the capacity to determine whether or not their physical assets could be used as camera mounts and/or electricity supplies. Once installed, a number of agents utilized situational power to subvert the system's functionality (see Smith 2004, 2007a, 2009, 2012), with camera controllers and maintainers, those possessing definitional authority or 'expert' knowledge, capable of re-appropriating the network through the application of authoritative directives the deliverance of crippling repair invoices:

They've taken away some of our key cameras and are using them in a pointless exercise to scan moving vehicles. I mean, surely we need them more than the traffic cops do?

(Operator 9)

Deep-Sea Electronics are responsible for the maintenance of the cabling but not the connections to the cameras which are under the remit of Central Securities. A considerable degree of conflict has arisen with each suggesting the other is responsible for the maintenance.

(Rivertown Police Force CCTV Report 2004)

As the RWG Secretary insightfully put it:

When you start working with 'partner' organizations everything is great until you come to the first step; and then you suddenly realize that to get the first step achieved, there are about 20 paces in between that you have got to develop and build upon.

As we have seen, the intricate interdependency of social relations required to construct, actualize and maintain a surveillance system means that these social assemblages should need to be understood as complex, processual, negotiated and fragile. Indeed, as a result of the subjective forces constituting their historical foundation and the complex multi-actor/actant relationalities on which they depend, surveillance entities are especially vulnerable to cultural conflict and systemic rupture.

Organizational 'imprescience' as gravitational pull

It's shite and it always has been shite.

(Operator 7 commenting on the Rivertown CCTV system)

Despite having considerable resources and technocratic power the RWG contained a multitude of bureaucratic actors who had a) diminutive or no direct experience of CCTV assembly ergonomics and economics (but thought the general concept/idea was 'good'); b) a distinct scarcity of technical knowledge and expertise; and c) little inclination to invest or commit long-term resources and labour to the project's future development, and/or delegate clearly defined duties and responsibilities to operational custodians. Collectively, this meant that little consideration was given to systemic ownership or enterprise, the implication being that there was no clear or coherent blueprint for making the venture sustainable. A fixation on how revenue could be generated to *install* – not *maintain* – the system became the group's core focus. Moreover, technological reasoning (i.e. the belief that technology can mitigate any social problem regardless of its complexity) dominated the majority of discussions on system operation (how many cameras, what variety, which type of communications system, location of the operations suite, etc.), with staffing issues (e.g. recruitment, training and social integration, etc.) and broader organizational studies knowledge largely absent from the everyday agenda. When the collective did consider practical operational issues, how and where to acquire 'discounted' – not specialized – labour and exercise control over the latter's agency (through the creation of an operational code of conduct) were the main topics for contemplation. As such, little attention was paid to operational protocol, the multiple needs of camera operators and the organizational significance of these labourers, and the wider security complex, in the everyday production of surveillance (Smith 2012). These historical oversights, however, had major implications for how the system was experienced and operationalized by its 'secondary recipients', those actors who effectively inherited the structure and who now maintain and (re)define its constitutional arrangement through their everyday practices. Indeed, my argument is precisely that the sedimentation of organizational 'impresicence' and related contradictions have now come to exert considerable influence over the operability and functionality of the system, impacting heavily upon the accomplishment of institutionally derived goals and CCTV's general effectiveness as a crime-fighting tool – and hence its operational sustainability and viability. This is best illustrated by way of empirical example.

Historical sedimentation: organizational 'impresicence' and unintended sabotage

Like any social system, a CCTV network is part dependent on the historical forces which help establish a primary 'structural' (material/symbolic) form and part dependent on the energies and actions subsequently invested by those (re)constituting and influencing the system's secondary 'cultural' (lived/symbolic) form. The objective in the following section, therefore, is to connect these 'dependency' variables (i.e. historical sedimentation and lived reality), in order to demonstrate the myriad ways in which organizational impresicence exercises constraint over systemic possibilities and, in the case presented here, jeopardizes the scope of future horizons.

Discounted staff as technological plug-ins

It is evident that members of the RWG perceived the camera network in purely technical terms as an automated physical entity of control, rather than understanding it in social terms as a complex system of relational interactivity. Thus, the multiplicity of actors whose situated practices constitute the system's everyday operativity were interpreted one-dimensionally as 'plug-in' cogs within a larger machinery of control rather than as reflexive, knowledgeable and creative agents of social change. In other words, there was a preoccupation given to the mechanical ends, as opposed to human means, of surveillance systems. It was assumed that once installed and operational, the cameras would automatically and autonomously function in the desired fashion. An understanding of the intricacies of human agency and the complexities of workplace culture was decidedly absent, with technology interpreted as a social glue which would integrate and bind together a diverse assortment of organizationally situated actors and normative orders. The RWG's obsessive application of instrumental rationality and corollary desire to implement a cost-effective CCTV system is perfectly illustrated in their recruitment directive. Certain members felt it an astute idea to acquire monitoring staff from a disabled employment organization, AssistUK, as a special government subsidy for hiring registered individuals meant reduced labour costs:

> RP in an effort to reduce costs entered into a contract with AssistUK who would provide the civilian staff to operate the unit. The AssistUK employees are all Registered Disabled people requiring sheltered conditions of employment and therefore qualify for a government subsidy which currently stands at 30%.
>
> (Rivertown Police Force CCTV Review, 1997)

This decision, however, was not without operational implications. Certain recruits, for example, were unsuited physically, psychologically and socially to the multiple demands and pressures of CCTV work. Some appointees had poor eyesight, limited concentration levels, communicational difficulties, restricted mobility and long-term health problems, impairments seriously inhibiting their ability to control the system in an effective fashion:

> Operator 3 mentions how little work Operator 12 does and how the individual suffers from a medically defined 'concentration problem' – 'I mean, why oh why would you employ someone like that to monitor CCTV cameras for ten hours?' She then goes on to talk about Operator 9: 'He was another from AssistUK. I mean it's a shame and all that about his health, but the thing is that he can't speak properly because of a previous stroke and so can't communicate over the radio effectively which causes serious problems.' I find out from Operator 3 that another AssistUK recruit is off sick with a long-term illness, so this team is 'down to two for the next six months anyway.'

The majority of the initial staff appointed have visual impairments . . . I am further concerned with:

- *The lack of opportunity to rest the eyes periodically on a relatively plain surface to help reduce eye fatigue*
- *Difficulties with regard to wheelchair access*
- *The ability of individuals with physical disabilities to access cupboards and shelves*

(Letter from Force Medical Advisor, 1995)

Despite often being incompatible with the job demands, such workers were protected legally by way of their AssistUK registered status, in effect meaning that, to terminate their contract, RP had either to 'buy them out' or find other suitable employment within the organization:

Whatever happens they cannot simply terminate our contracts, unless of course we accept a voluntary redundancy offer.

(Operator 1)

Such protection enabled those with little interest in the job (but were compelled to be in work as a condition of their benefit) to 'hide' and earn 'easy money', a strategy which effectively placed further operational pressures upon other shift operators:

I'm tired all the time in here. I just can't be bothered being here. It's such a crap place to work, but it pays the bills and you can get away with doing fuck all which is quite good.

(Operator 6)

Perhaps unsurprisingly, the behaviours and (in)actions of those above created all manner of intra-organizational tensions and conflicts:

There are plenty operators who shouldn't be in here and I have told them that personally. I don't know why they [RP] are just too scared to get rid of them . . . We have known who the wasters are for years and years and years. People who are just getting paid for nothing.

(Operator 7)

Not only were operators often poorly selected, they were also inadequated trained. Thus, despite talk in the minutes of a 'comprehensive' training programme being established and administered, the reality was to prove somewhat less thorough:

We all sat round one monitor and had shots and that was our training. We went round the shopping centre to see exactly what their systems were like, but there was no basic training.

(Operator 7)

Camera positioning and inoperability

As has become evident, system designers were overwhelmingly driven by fiscal imperatives and a fervent technological consciousness. The group, however, lacked both technical and operational expertise and tacit awareness of the complexities associated with human agency and social action. Nonetheless, their social position and associated legislative power enabled them to visualize and assemble a public space camera network, operations room and set of organizational priorities. While unquestionably facilitating flows of power and control, the relative inflexibility of the system generated feelings of anger, resentment and frustration among its custodians. This exasperation specifically related to the unprofessional way in which cameras were firstly 'imagined' and then positioned. While seeming a trivial technical issue, camera placement jeopardized both systemic operability and effectiveness:

> Most of the camera positions are crap. I mean, look at cameras 9 and 10 – they're virtually touching one another; you've got to ask yourself, why on earth did they put two cameras in such close proximity to one another? It's the same as camera 47 in the multi-storey car park; we don't get any use from it as . . . it can't see out either left or right due to the wall it has been fixed to. It's such a waste of resources.
>
> *(Operator 2)*

Vision is not only impeded through the cameras' physical positioning, but also through the agency of several external actants:

> Bus shelters, buses and the 'To Let' or retail signs in the city centre are the biggest nightmare. They piss us right off as they prevent us from seeing what is going on half the time on the street when an incident takes place.
>
> *(Operator 15)*

Another technical problem exercising agency over systemic functionality concerned the camera technology itself. The RWG's inability to factor in an achievable budget for repairs and upgrades meant that certain cameras were either of limited technical sophistication or were fast becoming unfit for purpose, with camera (un)manoeuvrability and corollary image quality proving a major hindrance to daily operativity:

> Is that down to the fact that after twelve and a half years' non-stop use, it's probably obsolete equipment and it will take 'x' amount of thousands to actually upgrade it? . . . You wonder if the system is going to just crash one day and will be no longer feasible to run.
>
> *(Operator 7)*

The life of cameras and equipment is 5–10 years, therefore much of the equipment is reaching its end of the design life and the accommodation is dated. Failure of components is commonplace.

(Rivertown Police Force CCTV Review 2005)

The ergonomic design of the monitoring room also impacted significantly on the operators' ability to perform their job efficiently:

We've got about 140 cameras and three pairs of eyes for the most part, so that's one guy to watch 47 cameras, and they're talking of bringing more in. It's just a joke.

(Operator 37)

This place has been so craply set up. I don't know who the architect was but they ought to be out of a job. None of us can see over the desk so all the bottom spotter screens are lost to view, and it's virtually impossible to make out what is happening on the screens we can see, as they're just too small.

(Operator 6)

Ownership irresponsibility

Historical sedimentation is structurally deposited as much from actor activity as from actor inactivity. In the case of the RWG, a lack of economic foresight and managerial planning in the consultation period generated all manner of subsequent bureaucratic problems which, cumulatively, jeopardize the operational continuance of the current Rivertown network. Although a motion to create a CCTV Liaison Group (RLG) for both the regulation and ongoing development of the Rivertown system was agreed, this entity never materialized. Indeed, organizational management of the scheme rapidly became a police responsibility, the everyday operations being the remit of a sergeant who had little interest in the long-term viability of the scheme he had reluctantly inherited:

When I came to the post it appeared that nothing had been done to the system in ten years . . . The problem was that the post had previously been filled by a retiring sergeant who did not really have a lot of push [i.e. desire] to keep CCTV going . . . Stagnate is the word; I think the staff were managed and the maintenance was done when required but there was no forward thinking involved.

(Rivertown CCTV Manager).

An absence of legal documentation regarding who owned, and was therefore responsible for, system hardware and associated operating costs prompted the newly formed municipal authority to refuse liability:

The RWG had no real legal recourse. There was no legal document made in terms of futures. And I think that was a shortfall, that certainly was a big learning outcome as far as the project was concerned . . . Perhaps we did not appreciate how big a beast, how big a project it was going to be, and at an earlier stage we should have given thought to getting these protocol documents and agreements in place. By the time it came round to thinking about the need for them, the project was actually up and running and we had committed ourselves to the spending, to the maintenance, to the ongoing upkeep of the system without giving proper thought as to who was going to be responsible if the bubble burst.

(RWG Secretary)

An attendant lack of annual investment from the private sector (prompted by the finance sub-group's original decision to collect only a 'one-off' contribution) meant that the system was left to badly deteriorate and fragment, with no agency willing or able to part with the funds required to maintain and service ailing hardware:

There was no maintenance cost [factored in], no kind of forward planning in terms of, 'Each year we will need X amount from you', which everyone is finding throughout the UK now, because there has been no strategic planning for funding. No disrespect to them because it was a brand-new thing, but there was no foresight that we need to get each year a guarantee that they are going to contribute something towards the cameras.

(Rivertown CCTV Manager)

A liaison group was intended, [but] it kind of fell to the wayside. There was a change of heart in a number of individuals once the project was up and running because . . . they were continually putting their hands into their pockets to feed this beast and, as a result, there was a bit of friction in one or two of the organizations.

(RWG Secretary)

Hence, the failure of the RWG to craft a legally binding constitutional agreement detailing ownership rights and maintenance and operation responsibilities provoked a lengthy and heated dispute between the council and police service, a disagreement which has frosted relations between the two agencies and which has led to the system's steady fragmentation. By failing to anticipate and to identify potential risks (processes which are ironically synonymous with surveillance), the RWG unintentionally began exposing the system to icy winds generated by economic recession.

Representational politics: From technological panacea to organizational burden

The decline of CCTV has not only occurred as a result of situated socio–cultural and mechanical processes. Indeed, the legitimacy and utility of this technology has been challenged at the politico-ideological level by a prolonged spate of negative media coverage.[6] Despite previous research noting the UK media's pivotal role in 'selling' the idea of CCTV to the public and justifying its introduction through positively framed and 'technofetishistic' articulations of effectiveness and social need (Norris and Armstrong 1999; McCahill 2002), I wish to suggest that journalists have now developed a more ambivalent and critical understanding of the technology's every-day value and application. The current political and economic climate in the UK and changing media practices (i.e. the increasing prevalence of investigative and sensationalist reportage) help explain this change of attitude and representational framing. Indeed, the austerity measures and public sector spending cuts introduced in response to the global financial crisis and related economic recession are now a major focus of coverage, journalists of both libertarian and conservative persuasion being keen to identify and expose the personal inadequacies of high-profile state figures and public servants and costly/failing/liberty-reducing government initiatives, so as to both coalesce with and cajole public opinion (Greer and McLaughlin 2011). Entrepreneurial sensationalism sells programmes and papers, and this journalistic strategy constitutes what is now a competitive and covetous media industry. Given that immense resources were (and still are) ploughed into the funding of CCTV schemes and that the technology is embedded within and reflects a multitude of discredited political and authoritative relations and intentions, it has an automatic (and significant) newsworthiness, becoming an easy target for antagonistic report-age. This situation is captured perfectly in the following news excerpts:

> Ahead of G20 summit, council told to switch off illegal £15m CCTV network.
>
> (The Guardian *30 March 2009*)

> Peeping tom CCTV workers jailed.
>
> (BBC News *13 January 2006*)

> Lords: rise of CCTV is threat to freedom: World's most pervasive surveil-lance undermines basic liberties, say peers.
>
> (The Guardian *6 February 2009*)

CCTV's illegitimacy has been further confounded through the media's adoption and appropriation of a panoply of governmental reports, official statistics, court documents, media texts, and critical activist and academic research, which collectively call into question both the effectiveness and legality of the technology (in the context of associated maintenance and running costs), particularly in an epoch where the investment of public funds and civil rights/liberties/justice are under such close 'observational' scrutiny:

1,000 cameras 'solve one crime'.
(<http://news.bbc.co.uk/2/hi/8219022.stm> accessed 7 February 2011)

CCTV cost councils £300m in 3 years – with one city spending more than £10m.
(The Daily Mail 30 November 2010)

Britain's wasteful mania for CCTV: Video surveillance drains crime-fighting budgets. A new report shows how widely – and haphazardly – it has been implemented.
(The Guardian 18 December 2009)

A report by a House of Lords committee also said that £500million was spent on new cameras in the 10 years to 2006, money which could have been spent on street lighting or neighbourhood crime prevention initiatives . . . This suggests that each crime has cost £20,000 to detect.
(The Telegraph 25 August 2009)

How such reportage affects popular consciousness and whether it stimulates collective social action in the form of activism, are important methodological questions which demand urgent scholarly inquiry.

By attacking the value and implications of CCTV provision, the media have, in the process, indirectly drawn attention to failing or dysfunctional schemes and the subsequent retraction of several CCTV networks. Not only do these reports afford insight into the contemporary politics of surveillance at the representational or ideological level, they also provide evidence to suggest that CCTV systems face an uncertain operational future in a cynical and critical media-saturated environment and in volatile political economic times:

CCTV cameras to be switched off as part of £2.6m savings.
(Lincolnshire Echo, 27 January 2011)

North Kesteven to turn off all 12 CCTV cameras to cut costs.
(Grantham Journal, 11 January 2011)

Evidence-based decision-making has come to the forefront of municipal authority administration, with local partnerships finding it increasingly difficult to justify expenditure on projects which are not efficiently delivering any substantive or measurable service/commodity (Webster 2009). The 'social order' commodity is a particularly challenging (unrealistic) product to manufacture (see Smith 2012) and 'sell', particularly in the context of multiple reality shows and reports which focus on the prevalence and impact of crime and criminality. The reality of CCTV fragmentation was brought home to me in the reflexive and enlightening comments of a CCTV Manager I encountered at a recent CCTV User Group conference:

The wheels are coming off this thing. I've been going to night school at my local college the past few months to get some extra training and qualifications so that when things fold, I'm not stuck for other lines of work.

(CCTV Manager 2)

Conclusion

Drawing on empirical evidence from fieldwork carried out in and across the UK, this chapter has critically considered the social and historical origins of public space CCTV design and implementation and pointed to some contemporary implications. Focusing attention on the complex organizational configurations responsible for the installation of CCTV networks and analysing their mundane reasoning and situated practices, has enabled previously distinct nodes to be connected. The organizational messiness engendered in the group's technological incompetence, goal conflicts, recruitment policies and systemic myopticism was shown to spawn 'lived' operating cultures which are structurally incoherent and socially dysfunctional. With the passage of time, trivial faults begin degenerating into more serious failings, which media actors are then able to identify and represent in a negative and politically loaded fashion.

A major objective of this chapter has been to present surveillance systems in a holistic and longitudinal light as interconnected social systems, processual material and symbolic resources which rely on the everyday imaginations, meanings and agency (sedimented and current) invested by those performing a variety of organizational roles. Thus, CCTV surveillance need be interpreted not as some fixed, autonomous and durable entity, but as a negotiated and contested social reality, a reality reliant as much upon the historical interactivity deposited by systemic 'primary definers' in processes of construction as the situational politics and activities of those 'secondary recipients' who materially inherit and shape the everyday structure (camera operators) and who semiotically and semantically depict its representational and discursive form (journalists). In the case study presented here, structural deficiencies as deposited by the primary definers were shown ultimately to limit the accomplishment of historically derived institutional goals, thereby undermining social integration and systemic sustainability.

With growing numbers of official documents illustrating the high maintenance and operating costs of camera networks and their general ineffectiveness in reducing criminality, and with media actors keen to expose such facts in their pursuit of state incompetence, public space CCTV in the UK now faces a precarious future. The politics of CCTV still revolves around legitimacy, but these days in relation to 'contractional' drives as opposed to 'expansionary' desires. CCTV provision is now defended by a dwindling number of advocates (albeit the industry behind this technology remains something of a global superpower), many of whom have lost their structural authority and/or credibility. The genealogy and agency of the 'wired camera' is a truly remarkable social phenomenon, with so many interconnected actors and forces involved in the definitional politics constituting the technology's everyday material and symbolic positioning. A concluding irony is that the very political-economic and socio-cultural forces which propelled CCTV's rapid rise are the same ones inducing its imminent downfall. The recycling industry is likely to be the real winner of the CCTV revolution.

Notes

1   While mindful of camera network 'particularity' in terms of cultural history, organizational logic and social form, visiting a multitude of schemes during the research period permitted the identification of several shared thematic commonalities and consistencies. Thus, although not necessarily generalizable, the findings presented here almost certainly have comparative validity, as the structural composition and cultural heritage of most public space observation systems are broadly similar.
2   Social order, of course, is a precarious and transitory condition in the everyday urban metropolis (see Smith 2012; Winlow and Hall 2006).
3   To protect the anonymity of those studied, it should be stated that any research names, locations or identities employed here are entirely fictitious. The city of Rivertown is a medium-sized cosmopolitan metropolis, with a comparable spatial organization and post-industrial economy to many other UK conurbations. It therefore functioned as an excellent research laboratory.
4   Political economic imperatives underpinned the system's introduction, the RWG believing that the cameras would automatically cultivate perceptions of safety and a 'feel-good factor'. This, in turn, would enhance consumption activities while also valorizing the regime's interventionist ethic with respect to crime management and citizenry wellbeing. There was also a general belief that installing such a large network of cameras (the second-largest scheme in Europe at the time) would infuse civic pride.
5   Only one opinion poll was administered by the group and this was heavily biased in its framing of the issue. Moreover, there was no external consultancy to ascertain public attitudes on the scheme's constitutional and longitudinal directives.
6   This coverage, of course, has implicitly picked up on many of the situated bureaucratic and operational failings of CCTV schemes described above.

References

Atkinson, R. and Helms, G. (eds) (2007) *Securing an Urban Renaissance: Crime, Community and British Urban Policy*, Bristol: The Policy Press.
BBC News (2010) BBC News Spending Review. Online. Available HTTP: <http://www.bbc.co.uk/news/special_reports/spending_review/> (accessed 25 November 2010).
Coaffee, J., Murakami-Wood, D.M. and Rogers, P. (2009) *The Everyday Resilience of the City: How Cities Respond to Terrorism and Disaster*, London: Palgrave Macmillan.
Coleman, R. (2004) *Reclaiming the Streets: Surveillance, Social Control and the City*, Cullompton: Willan.
Davis, M. and Monk, D.M. (eds) (2007) *Evil Paradises: Dreamworlds of Neoliberalism*, New York: The New Press.
Fussey, P. (2007) 'An interrupted transmission? Processes of CCTV implementation and the impact of human agency', *Surveillance & Society*, 4(3): 229–56.
Fyfe, N.R. and Bannister, J. (1996) 'City watching: Closed circuit television surveillance in public spaces', *Area*, 28(1): 37–46.
Garland, D. (2001) *The Culture of Control: Crime and Social Order in Contemporary Society*, Oxford: Oxford University Press.

Graham, S. (2001) 'CCTV: The stealthy emergence of a fifth utility?', *Planning Theory and Practice*, 3(2): 237–41.

Greer, C. and McLaughlin, E. (2011) '"Trial by Media": Policing, the 24–7 News Media-sphere and the "Politics of Outrage"', *Theoretical Criminology*, 15(1): 123–46.

Harvey, D. (2005) *A Brief History of Neo-liberalism*, Oxford: Oxford University Press.

McCahill, M. (2002) *The Surveillance Web: The Rise of Visual Surveillance in an English City*, Cullompton: Willan.

Norris, C. and Armstrong, G. (1999) *The Maximum Surveillance Society: The Rise of CCTV*, Oxford: Berg.

Reeve, A. (1998) 'The Panopticisation of Shopping: CCTV and Leisure Consumption', in C. Norris, J. Moran and G. Armstrong (eds), *Surveillance, Closed Circuit Television and Social Control*, Aldershot: Ashgate.

Simon, J. (2007) *Governing Through Crime: How the War on Crime Transformed American Democracy and Created a Culture of Fear*, Oxford: Oxford University Press.

Smith, G.J.D. (2004) 'Behind the Screens: examining constructions of deviance and informal practices among CCTV control room operators in the UK', *Surveillance & Society*, 2(2/3): 376–95.

Smith, G.J.D. (2007a) 'Exploring Relations Between Watchers and Watched in Control(led) Systems: Strategies and Tactics', *Surveillance & Society*, 4(4): 280–313.

Smith, G.J.D. (2007b) 'The night-time economy: exploring tensions between agents of control', in R. Atkinson and G. Helms (eds), *Securing an Urban Renaissance: Crime, Community and British Urban Policy*, Bristol: The Policy Press.

Smith, G.J.D. (2009) 'Empowered Watchers or Disempowered Workers? The ambiguities of power within technologies of security', in K.F. Aas, H.O. Gundhus and H.M. Lomell (eds), *Technologies of Insecurity: The Surveillance of Everyday Life*, London: Routledge–Cavendish.

Smith, G.J.D. (2012) *Opening the Black Box: Surveillance in Everyday Life*, London: Routledge.

Wacquant, L. (2007) *Urban Outcasts: A Comparative Sociology of Advanced Marginality*, Cambridge: Polity Press.

Wacquant, L. (2009a) *Prisons of Poverty, Minneapolis*, MN: University of Minnesota Press.

Wacquant, L. (2009b) *Punishing the Poor: The Neoliberal Government of Social Insecurity*, Durham: Duke University Press.

Webster, C.W.R. (2009) 'CCTV policy in the UK: Reconsidering the evidence base', *Surveillance & Society*, 6(1): 10–22.

Winlow, S. and Hall, S. (2006) *Violent Night: Urban Leisure and Contemporary Culture*, Oxford: Berg.

4

SEEING SURVEILLANTLY

Surveillance as social practice

Jonathan Finn

The steady rise of camera surveillance over the twentieth and early twenty-first centuries has resulted in the now common assertion that we live in a surveillance society. As the essays in this collection emphasize, an increasing array of social spaces from taxicabs (Doyle and Walby, this volume) to university campuses (Ferenbok and Clement, this volume) are subject to the surveillance camera's gaze. Within such an environment, bodies and objects are continuously tracked and recorded by a diverse and disparate array of surveillance cameras. In addition to the rise in camera and other forms of surveillance practice, surveillance increasingly appears as a subject in film, television, video games, social networking sites, advertising and art (see Lippert and Wilkinson in this book for a discussion of Crime Stoppers advertising). In this way, surveillance has become a key feature of contemporary visual culture and of life more generally.

The prevalence of surveillance as a concept and subject in advertising, art and entertainment is not simply a reflection of the increased prominence of surveillance in society. Rather, as I argue in this chapter, it suggests a shift in the understanding or conception of surveillance. Where surveillance traditionally calls to mind police and state monitoring of individuals and groups, surveillance in the contemporary context exists more as a constitutive element of social life. More than a material or technical apparatus – more than a camera – surveillance has become a way of seeing.

In this chapter I develop the notion of seeing surveillantly. I argue that, within the contemporary Western world, surveillance is increasingly a social practice. I borrow the notion of seeing photographically as it developed in the work of photographic historians, theorists and practitioners of the twentieth century, to propose the notion of seeing surveillantly. I argue that surveillance is not simply a technology or apparatus employed in state-sanctioned programmes of social control, but that it has become a social practice: a way of seeing, understanding and engaging with the world around us.

Seeing photographically

In his 1949 essay, 'Seeing Photographically', Edward Weston instructed would-be photographers not just how to become better image-makers but also on the very nature of photography. For Weston, 'each medium of expression imposes its own limitations on the artist – limitations inherent in the tools, materials, or processes he employs' (1980: 170). Weston lamented what he saw as the dominant 'photo-painting standard' of photography from the late nineteenth through to the mid-twentieth century. Put simply, in an effort to position their work as artistic, photographers of the period adopted the conventions of painting and did every-thing possible to deny the mechanistic aspects of photographic reproduction. They used filters, blurred focus, painted or otherwise manipulated negatives so that the products more closely resembled paintings.

Weston argued that the photo-painting standard betrayed the true nature of photography which, for him, was based in the nature of the recording process and the nature of the photographic image. In the former, photography was unique because of its instantaneous recording process – once the shutter is released, there is no room for mediation or manipulation. In the latter, Weston points to the 'precision of definition' and the 'unbroken sequence of infinitely subtle gradations from black to white' (1980: 172) that are unique to the photograph. As these constitute the nature of the photo-mechanical image, Weston argues, any intervention in these (i.e. hand manipulation) negates the integrity of the image (1980: 172).

The net result of Weston's discussion is his emphasis that photographers need to see photographically. He writes:

> Hence the photographer's most important and likewise most difficult task is not learning to manage his camera, or to develop, or to print. It is learning to *see photographically* – that is, learning to see his subject matter in terms of the capacities of his tools and processes, so that he can instantaneously translate the elements and values in a scene before him into the photograph he wants to make.
>
> *(1980: 177)*

Weston's essay is indicative of an understanding of photography that lasted from its development in the 1830s through to the mid-twentieth century. This work emphasizes the unique material features of photo-mechanical reproduction. Key to this position is the separation of photograph and subject. As outlined by Weston, the camera and its operator are mutually exclusive: one is a mechanical device, the other its human operator. The ability to 'see photographically' in the Weston sense is predicated on the fact that photographs are the product of a distinct technological apparatus, one that is free from human intervention.

In his 1953 book, *Prints and Visual Communication*, William M. Ivins Jr. described photography in a way that was markedly different from that of his predecessors and contemporaries, including Weston. While Ivins too praised the unique material features of photography, he also stressed the impact of the medium on lived experience. Photography's ability to produce pictorial statements that were exactly repeatable fundamentally changed humans' experience with the live world. As Ivins notes, following the development of photography and the half-tone printing process, our understanding and engagement with objects in the world increasingly came through experience of their representation and not the things themselves. The camera brought far-away objects and spaces into our classrooms, offices and homes, making possible new forms of knowledge but also altering our very ways of seeing.

Ivins' remarks are echoed in a 1964 essay on photography by Marshall McLuhan, but it was not until the 'critical turn' in academic work of the 1960s and 1970s that photography's supposed nature (as a chemical and mechanical technology) was continually called into question. Scholars such as John Berger (1972), Roland Barthes (1977, 1981) and Susan Sontag (1977) relocated the importance of the photograph to its context of production and interpretation. That is, the photograph was no longer treated purely as the product of a photo-chemical process, but as something that emerged from an historically specific network of human and non-human actors. The result of this transition from a modern (or formal or materialist) perspective to a post-modern perspective is exemplified in John Tagg's now famous assertion that 'photography as such has no identity' (1988: 63).

Rather than recount this transition here, I want to suggest a new notion of seeing photographically that has emerged from the post-modern discourse on photography. Specifically, work by authors such as Susan Sontag (1977, 2004), Geoffrey Batchen (1997) and Lev Manovich (2003) has opened up an understanding of photography that stresses its relationship with lived experience. I refer to this latter formulation as situating photography as a social practice.

In the opening page of her 1977 text, *On Photography*, Susan Sontag writes: 'In teaching us a new visual code, photographs alter and enlarge our notions of what is worth looking at and what we have a right to observe. They are a grammar and, even more importantly, an ethics of seeing.' She continues, 'finally, the most grandiose result of the photographic enterprise is to give us the sense that we can hold the whole world in our heads – as an anthology of images' (1977: 3). Here and throughout the text, Sontag positions photography as something that is synonymous with lived experience. Photography is not simply a means to represent the world but is a practice that informs our very understanding of and action in it. For Sontag, photography gave rise not just to more pictures of the world but of a new way of seeing. She writes: 'cameras did not simply make it possible to apprehend more by seeing (through microphotography and teledetection). They changed seeing itself, by fostering the idea of seeing for seeing's sake' (1977: 93).

This particular facet of Sontag's argument is present throughout her extensive work on photography but reaches its zenith in her 2004 *New York Times Magazine* essay, 'Regarding the Torture of Others'. Commenting on the Abu Ghraib prison torture images, she writes 'there would be something missing if, after stacking the naked men, you couldn't take a picture of them' (2004: 28). For Sontag, the atrocities at Abu Ghraib were deeply informed by photography, to the extent that certain scenes – such as the stacking of naked men – were created precisely to be photographed.

Where Sontag stresses the influence of photography on lived experience, Geoffrey Batchen (1997) positions photography as part of a historically and culturally specific desire. In *Burning with Desire*, he critiques the usual origin stories of photography to argue that the practice emerged as the product of a particular Western desire in the late eighteenth and early nineteenth century. Batchen examines the experiments, documents and conversations of what he calls the 'proto-photographers' – a group of individuals in the eighteenth century who shared a concern in the process that would come to be known as photography – to argue that photography emerged as a desire to engage and exist in a culture in which dominant binaries of nature and culture, transience and fixity, space and time, subject and object were increasingly unstable. For Batchen, 'at issue was not just the theorization and depiction of nature, landscape, reflection, or the passage of time but, more fundamentally, the nature of representation and the constitution of existence itself' (1997: 100).

In developing his argument, Batchen makes an important distinction between photography as a material technology and as what I am calling a social practice. He notes:

> even if we continue to identify photography with certain archaic technologies, such as camera and film, those technologies themselves embody the idea of photography or, more accurately, a persistent economy of photographic desires and concepts. The concepts inscribed within this economy include things like nature, knowledge, representation, time, space, observing subject, and observed object.
>
> *(1997: 213)*

This leads Batchen to a working definition for photography as a 'desire, conscious or not, to orchestrate a particular set of relationships between these various concepts' (1997: 213). In Batchen's formulation, photography is less camera and film than it is a practice through which one engages with the world.

As with Batchen, Lev Manovich (2003) distinguishes carefully between the material aspect of photography and its function as a practice. In an essay on the paradoxes of digital photography, Manovich makes a compelling and concise claim: 'The digital image annihilates photography while solidifying, glorifying and immortalizing the photographic' (2003: 241). For Manovich, digital imagery is fundamentally different from photo-chemical imagery in material and technical form but remarkably similar in practice. In other words, rather than seizing on their unique capabilities, highly advanced digital technologies are often used in ways that mimic earlier, non-digital media. This is exemplified when we use a digital camera for traditional photographic endeavours, such as taking portraits of loved ones or documenting birthday parties, vacations or other important life events.

Underpinning Manovich's argument is the notion of photo-reality. The author argues that the dominance of photography as a means of representation over the past 150 years has led to it being treated as synonymous with reality. To illustrate his point, Manovich points to the continued critique of digital imagery which employs terms such as 'fake' or 'real'. Such terminology refers not to an actual, physical reality, but instead to its photographic counterpart. He writes: 'what computer graphics has (almost) achieved is not realism but only photorealism – the ability to fake not our perceptual and bodily experience of reality but only its photographic image' (2003: 246). In this way, Manovich's discussion echoes that of Ivins, specifically the latter author's assertion that our understanding of the world comes through our engagement with its visual representation. And, like Sontag, Manovich stresses that the ubiquity and dominance of photography as a means of representation has had a lasting impact on lived experience to the extent that the two are inextricably bound.

Despite their idiosyncrasies, the arguments of Sontag, Batchen and Manovich are united by the way in which they open up an understanding of photography that moves beyond its materiality. For the three, photography was so central to life in the twentieth century that it became more than a means of representation – it became a way of seeing, understanding and engaging with the world. In contrast to the view articulated by Weston decades earlier, photography is less a technology than a social practice. And where for Weston, seeing photographically was based in an acknowledgement of the particular material features of the photographic image, for Sontag, Batchen and Manovich, the phrase signals a historically and culturally specific desire to represent and to be represented – with all the complexities that those terms imply.

Surveillance as a social practice

I want to borrow the notion of seeing photographically, as developed above, to propose another, increasingly prominent way of seeing in the twenty-first century: surveillantly. It is now commonplace to refer to the contemporary world as a surveillance society. Whether in the form of driver's licences, passports, mug shots, CCTV, e-mail monitoring, commercial transactions, satellite imagery and GPS, surveillance is ubiquitous in contemporary life.

The study of surveillance has developed in tandem with the increase in its practice. Surveillance Studies has emerged as a distinct academic field complete with a dedicated journal, *Surveillance & Society*, and with introductory texts and advanced readers on the topic. The bulk of this work references a familiar trajectory from Foucault's (1977) discussion of the Panopticon through the growth of a surveillance society in the work of Kenneth Laudon (1986), Gary Marx (1988) and David Lyon (1994) to more contemporary forms of surveillance such as that by CCTV (Norris and Armstrong 1999; McCahill 2002), satellite (Monmonier 2002) and biometrics and border security programmes (Zureik and Salter 2005). Throughout this work surveillance is typically positioned as a material, technological apparatus and/or as a function of the state in the control of populations.

A developing body of work has begun to challenge and critique this traditional understanding of surveillance (Lyon 2006a; Haggerty and Ericson 2006). Of particular interest here is work that seeks to address surveillance less as a material apparatus than as an essential part of the social fabric. For example, Clay Calvert (2000) argues for the construction of a 'voyeur nation' through the mediation of surveillance imagery in television news and entertainment programming. John E. McGrath (2004) highlights the cultural fascination with surveillance as manifest in reality television shows such as *Big Brother* to argue for the productive potential of artists, performers and other cultural workers to engage with and critique forms of surveillance. And David Lyon (2006b) borrows from Thomas Mathiesen's notion of the 'viewer society' to stress the underlying human desire to watch and be watched that is at the heart of contemporary surveillance. Unlike more traditional understandings of surveillance, these authors locate it as a constitutive element of life and as something that is woven into the social fabric.

In arguing for the notion of seeing surveillantly I want to complement the work being done by Calvert, McGrath, Lyon and others, to suggest that we can open up an understanding of surveillance that moves beyond its usual treatment both as a technology and as a state-sanctioned mode of social control. In doing so, we can begin to address the complexity of surveillance in contemporary life and to raise new questions about the myriad forms of camera surveillance and their implications on lived experience.

Technologies such as Closed Circuit Television (CCTV), biometrics, satellite imaging, bar-coded passports and other forms of identification dominate the literature on surveillance. While keeping with this book's theme of camera surveillance, I want to offer three examples of surveillance from outside the usual suspects – examples from what might loosely be called the visual culture of camera surveillance. The examples point to three key features of contemporary surveillance and underscore what it might mean to see surveillantly: surveillance as an aesthetic concept; surveillance as rhetoric; and surveillance as participation in public life.

Surveillance as aesthetic concept

My first example comes from the world of commercial photography and specifically image archives such as Corbis and Getty Images which are leaders in the world's billion-dollar-a-year 'visual content industry' (Frosh 2003). As repositories of images of art, news events, important places and faces, as well as stock photography, these archives play a significant role in mediating the circulation of images throughout educational, professional, governmental, commercial and non-profit sectors. A 16 March 2010 search of Corbis and Getty image archives using the keyword 'surveillance' yields 3,092 and 47,200 images respectively. Many of these images are concrete examples of surveillance drawn from news events, as well as images of surveillance technologies, CCTV being the most prominent. Of particular interest here is the large number of creative images – images designed explicitly for sale to be used as visual content in a diversity of communicative acts. Corbis houses 1,308 creative images with the keyword 'surveillance' and Getty houses 6,948, with those numbers growing by the day.

Despite its ubiquity, stock imagery has received relatively little critical attention. There is a wealth of material addressing the practical side of stock photography but little which examines its cultural import. The work of Paul Frosh (2003) and David Machin (2004) are notable exceptions. In his extensive study of the visual content industry, Frosh argues that it is precisely this invisibility that yields stock imagery significant power within contemporary visual culture. He refers to stock imagery as 'the wallpaper of consumer culture' (2003: 1) and notes that the ideological, economic and political conditions of the visual content industry have been shielded from view (2003: 7). Thus the diverse power relations, cultural influences and impacts of stock imagery remain unseen: instead, the images are generally perceived to be banal parts of everyday life. Like Frosh, I want to stress that, despite their appearance to the contrary, stock images are anything but mundane.

Stock photographs must be generic and timeless. In order to be of use to the greatest number of clients, they must represent broad categories and concepts rather than specific places, times and faces. This is exemplified in David Machin's analysis of the representation of women in Getty Image stock archives. Machin finds recurring formal features in the images and offers a typology of stock imagery. He notes that windows, outdoor settings and bright, natural light dominate the scenes , as do blurred backgrounds and relatively simple or minimal compositions. The settings and models are generic, eliding any reference to a specific time or place. In sum, the images are relatively devoid of meaning in and of themselves; instead, their meaning is produced as they are allied with text, colour, layout and other design elements in the communication of a specific message. Frosh summarizes this feature of stock imagery, by reversing Barthes's famous proclamation to suggest that stock images are 'a code without a message' (2003: 74).

While individual stock images may lack a message, their prominence within contemporary visual culture carries significant meaning. Machin argues that the ubiquity of stock imagery functions in the production of a new visual language and that this language is increasingly the domain of large corporations such as Getty Images and its chief rival, Corbis. For Machin, this new visual language constitutes a shift in the use made of pictures from that of witness to a 'symbolic system' (2004: 317). Within such a system the image is valued less for its referentiality and documentary capability – long touted to be the defining features of photographic imagery – than for its 'meaning potential', or the range of possible meanings it affords.

That corporations such as Getty and Corbis are leading forces in the visual communication market is clear and well documented. And it is here that Frosh and Machin as well as photographic historian Geoffrey Batchen (2003) are decidedly worried. Machin stresses that the formal conventions and content of images within the new visual language are not arbitrary but that 'they are actively and intentionally created by powerful global corporations, and [that] the way in which they are created is driven by the needs and interests of these corporations' (2004: 317).

This leads him to conclude that stock images 'show a stylized, harmonized corporate world of work, commodified leisure and individualism, which is abstracted from politics and society' (2004: 318). Batchen is similarly critical in his analysis of Bill Gates's Corbis. Batchen suggests that, within that visual space, 'a world normally animated by abrasive differences is blithely reduced to a single, homogenous *National Geographic* way of seeing' (2003: 231).

The representation of surveillance in the creative image archives of Getty and Corbis follows exactly the stock aesthetic that is identified and critiqued by Frosh, Machin and Batchen. The images position surveillance as a banal, commercial concept: it exists as a generic category to be used in the construction of visual content. The images are timeless. They are non-specific scenes to be purchased and used as visual content in any number of publications from annual reports to advertisements for beauty products. They are de-politicized, de-historicized, and convey nothing of the problems and tensions associated with the practice of surveillance.

Within the organizational structure of image archives such as Corbis and Getty, surveillance becomes an abstract, aesthetic concept. Like love, happiness and freedom, it becomes a commercial category to be called up using keyword searches. Importantly, the existence of surveillance as an aesthetic concept and the prevalence of surveillance images in creative image archives is not simply a reflection of the ubiquity of surveillance in contemporary life; rather it functions in a larger, cultural reconceptualization of surveillance as a banal part of daily life – as common and as symbolic as the windows, flowers and sunshine that dominate stock imagery.

Surveillance as rhetoric

My second example is the 2009 reality TV series *True Beauty* co-produced by Tyra Banks and Ashton Kucher. In the show, six females and four males are brought to a house in Los Angeles under the auspices that they are part of a competition to find the most beautiful person in America. To this end, contestants perform in weekly challenges designed to test their outward beauty, such as the ability to perform well in a photo shoot. However, and unbeknown to the contestants, they are also being led through a series of weekly morality tests designed to show their 'inner beauty', such as the level of respect for one's elders. These informal tests are captured by a series of hidden cameras placed throughout the house. Feeds from the cameras are viewed by the show's host, Vanessa Minnillo, and its two judges, Cheryl Tiegs and Nole Marin, in a hyper-aestheticized CCTV control room. Within this space, the judges evaluate a character's 'true beauty' through recourse to the surveillance image.

While surveillance has been a central theme of film and television for decades – *The Conversation*, *Rear Window*, *Get Smart* and *The Prisoner* (recently remade into a six-part series for AMC) – it has become increasingly prominent and taken on new parameters in contemporary work. *The Truman Show*, *Enemy of the State*, *Minority Report*, the *Bourne* trilogy and *The Panic Room* are all films that are structured by surveillance (Lyon 2007). Television shows such as the *CSI* and *Law & Order* franchises routinely emphasize surveillance as an important and necessary part of daily life. But surveillance has risen to prominence in the reality TV genre. Shows such as *The Real World*, *Big Brother*, *Temptation Island* and *True Beauty* do not just employ surveillance as a tool or treat it as subject matter; rather, it is a fundamental part of the shows' narrative structure. Within these shows, surveillance serves as a rhetorical device to guarantee the veracity of the events depicted. This is nowhere more clear than in *True Beauty*. As the title of the show implies, the truth can only be found through recourse to the continuous feed of the surveillance camera.

Using surveillance as rhetoric is neither new nor limited to television. Karin Becker (2003) and Carol Squiers (1999) have each shown the use of surveillance – or what might be more appropriately called a surveillance camera aesthetic – as a rhetorical tool in photojournalism and, specifically, tabloids. Both authors highlight the extent to which tabloids developed a particular style that was directly dependent on the formal conventions of standard print media. Where traditional news media displayed images that were clear and orderly in equally clear and orderly layouts, tabloids disrupted this space, using grainy, blurry and asymmetrical images in layouts where images overlapped with each other and with text. Becker writes, 'technical "flaws" like extreme graininess and underexposure have actually become conventions of the tabloids' style, visually stating the technical compromises the newspaper will accept in its commitment to presenting the "real" story'. She continues, 'the techniques work to enhance the appearance of candour, lending additional support to the construction of these photographs as authentic' (2003: 301). Though not exclusively relying on surveillance imagery, tabloids used, and continue to use, a surveillance camera aesthetic in their claims to truth. A clean, professionally produced image of a celebrity is too easily dismissed as the product of a public relations campaign; however, the blurry and imperfect image of the telephoto lens or CCTV camera suggests the immediacy and accuracy of a moment captured in time. It is precisely this aesthetic that is adopted in reality TV shows such as *True Beauty*. In the case of *True Beauty*, the hidden, amateurish quality of the surveillance aesthetic is further pronounced as it is set against the highly aestheticized control room in which the judges search for the truth.

In his essay, 'Rhetoric of the Temporal Index', Thomas Levin (2002) has argued that a similar type of surveillance aesthetic is increasingly at work in contemporary cinema. For Levin, the moving image of the CCTV camera has replaced the still photographic image as the indexical authority of film. More specifically, he argues that the spatial indexicality of the photographic image – which had served as the basis for film in the twentieth century – is being replaced by the temporal indexicality of the real-time surveillance image in the twenty-first century. In other words, for Levin, the 'always-on' and hidden eye of the surveillance camera is used rhetorically to guarantee the reality of the scene depicted. Levin points to scenes from films such as *Menace II Society*, *Thelma and Louise*, *Sliver*, *Snake Eyes*, *The Truman Show* and *Wag the Dog* to show the extent to which real-time footage, like that produced by CCTV cameras, is increasingly being employed as a rhetorical tool in film.

While I do not support Levin's assertion that spatial indexicality has been fully supplanted by its temporal counterpart, his larger argument about the increasing prominence of surveillance as rhetoric in film is compelling and has parallels with the arguments of Becker and Squiers. In film and tabloids as well as in television and print media, surveillance camera imagery is continuously employed in truth-making claims. Combined with the popularization of surveillance imagery in contemporary mass media, its use as a rhetorical tool offers a particular authoritative weight to the surveillance camera, where its seemingly automated, anonymous and omnipresent gaze functions as a harbinger of truth.

Surveillance as participation in public life

My third and final example is the shooting of 22-year-old Oscar Grant by Bay Area Rapid Transit Police on 1 January 2009. The shooting was captured on numerous cell-phone and digital cameras, with several of the clips being posted to YouTube. The visual and auditory recording of Grant's shooting and the subsequent posting of that material online are indicative of a pervasive cultural trend of citizens documenting police activity. A 16 March 2010 search for 'police brutality' on YouTube yields over 12,000 results. Of this vast and ever-increasing amount of visual material, it is the shooting of Oscar Grant – or, more specifically, its representation – that is of particular interest here.

A YouTube posting by desertfae shows the scene in alarming clarity as an officer shoots Grant point blank. This video and others like it also reveal the tremendous presence of video recording devices on scene: arms holding cell-phones and digital cameras frequently protrude into the frame of the image, resulting in a video of a video documenting the scene. Another post, by the observateurs group, on 6 January 2009 runs a full 3:53 and shows a much more chaotic scene. The uncut video includes lengthy segments of indecipherable content as the cell-phone or camera sways randomly throughout the scene. There is laughter, talk and shouting throughout the clip, all of which serve to foreground the normalcy and reality of the scene depicted. The blurry, saccadic nature of the video further attests to the reality of the events through recourse to the surveillance camera aesthetic discussed previously. The actual shooting of Grant is barely visible and audible in this clip. What is most revealing and of particular interest here are the words of the camera operator as she realizes that Grant has been shot and as she simultaneously boards a train to leave the scene. She yells, 'Get on the train. They just shot him, they just shot that guy.' She then directs her voice away from her fellow citizens and to the police, yelling, 'I got you mother fuckers.'

The camera operator's challenge to police – 'I got you mother fuckers' – underscores the participatory nature of much contemporary surveillance.[1] The camera and its operator are not so much witness as agent, actively participating in the events that they simultaneously record. This is an important distinction and one that warrants further consideration. The uniqueness of the observateurs video, particularly as it exemplifies the larger category of citizen video documenting police activity, is best illustrated by comparison to an earlier and seminal case: the 1991 beating of Rodney King by Los Angeles Police. During that event, several officers beat King using tasers, kicks and baton strikes. Hearing the commotion outside his apartment window, George Holliday filmed the scene with a newly acquired camcorder. From approximately nine minutes of video, just over one minute was released to the public via the local news, launching a large-scale public controversy surrounding police brutality and race relations in the United States.

Rather than rehearsing the particulars of the King case, my interest here is in the visual representation of that event as it compares with the video of the Oscar Grant shooting. The video of King's beating is technically and formally amateur. It is blurry, grainy and falls in and out of focus as the operator follows the scene. The noise of a helicopter overhead and the muffled voices of the officers dominate the footage. Save perhaps for the efforts to focus the camera, there is no discernable presence of Holliday in the video. Indeed, watching the tape one feels as if one is engaged in covert surveillance – peering out from the privy of one's room to watch secretly the action unfold. This is in direct contrast to the video of the Oscar Grant shooting. While the Grant video is also amateur in quality, the presence of the camera operator dominates the scene. In fact, the actions of the officers and Grant are virtually absent from the video. What one sees and hears in this video – and in others like it – is the overt presence of the public as they literally monitor and record police activity. This is not passive or hidden observation as in the King video – this is a conscious and overt decision to record events for public distribution. In this sense, camera surveillance is employed as a form of civic engagement or duty.

The video of Oscar Grant's shooting is based in a central assumption that guides participation in public life: that the world is inherently risky and dangerous. Within such a space, we employ cell-phones, digital cameras and other devices to defend and protect ourselves and others. Over three minutes of the 3:53 video clip of the shooting of Oscar Grant is preamble – the camera swerves and records a continuous stream of data – none of it particularly important. Ultimately, what is important is that the camera is on – so that if and when an event does happen, it will be recorded visually. In a world perceived as inherently risky and dangerous, individuals are compelled to be continuously on the lookout for the next event – to be able to recognize and, most importantly, record the (presumably deviant) actions of others. In other words, individuals are compelled to see surveillantly.

Seeing surveillantly

The three examples offered above are necessarily brief and are intended to stand in as types of larger categories of practice. They highlight ways in which surveillance exists as an aesthetic concept, a rhetorical tool and as a form of participation in social life. In so doing they attest to the changing face of surveillance in contemporary society. Surveillance is no longer to be conceived as a technology employed by the state in the control of dangerous populations or a tool used by corporations to serve the interests of global capital, but is something that we encounter in advertisements and corporate communication, in video footage for news broad-casts and in our favourite (and least favourite) television programmes and films. Importantly, it is not just something we see – but is something that we do when we post photos and videos to the myriad websites that call for our participation. In this latter sense, camera surveillance takes a new form as we equip ourselves with cell-phones and compact, digital cameras, ready to record the actions of ourselves and others.

I do not want to suggest that traditional forms of surveillance – such as that used by the state in the control of populations – are absent or that they are less significant than the forms I have discussed above. On the contrary, I have argued elsewhere (Finn 2009) that the very real dangers and threats of state-sanctioned surveillance in the contemporary world must not be overlooked. Indeed, the essays in this book attest to the prevalence of state-sanctioned surveillance in contemporary life. My point is that, combined with these more traditional forms, the manifestation of camera surveillance in advertising, on television, film and on-line suggests a shift in the understanding, function and existence of surveillance in public life. Surveillance is less something that bodies are subject to than it is a constitutive part of those bod-ies. It is not just that we are complicit with surveillance or that we willingly trade private information for a perceived benefit (Lyon 1994; Andrejevic 2004, 2007; Niedzviecki 2009); but we are also willing, conscious producers of surveillance. We actively participate in the surveillance of ourselves and others to the extent that surveillance is fully enmeshed in our daily lives.

Discussing the social practice of photography, Batchen writes:

> Photography will cease to be a dominant element of modern life only when the desire to photograph, and the peculiar arrangement of knowledges and investments that that desire represents, is refigured as another social and cul-tural formation. Photography's passing must necessarily entail the inscription of another way of seeing – and of being.
>
> *(1997: 216)*

I do not want to be as presumptuous to suggest that surveillance has become the dominant metaphor for vision or life in the twenty-first century (although I suspect it has); rather, I want to suggest that, like photography, surveillance has morphed from a technology to a way of seeing and a way of being.

The essays in this book point to key recurring issues and features of contempo-rary camera surveillance, including the triggers prompting surveillance programmes, the lack of evidentiary support for the effectiveness of camera surveillance, and the murky legal waters in which surveillance operates. Seeing surveillantly is a useful complement to this discussion as it opens up a series of important questions sur-rounding surveillance in the twenty-first century. To what extent does the prolif-eration of camera surveillance and its representation in mass media obfuscate the power relations inherent in the act of watching others? How are cultural concepts of self, other, normal and deviant being defined in this aggregate field of practice?

What are the moral and ethical imperatives involved in seeing surveillantly? What are the avenues for legislation and policy-making? What are the impacts on social relations in a culture that actively promotes and rewards citizens surveilling each other? What, if any, are the opportunities for resistance? To address these and related questions, it is incumbent on us to recognize that surveillance is no longer the purview of police, the state and corporations but that it is a constitutive element of life. As producers and consumers of camera surveillance – in all its myriad forms – a critical examination of this social practice requires a self-reflexive look at our own willingness and desire to watch, record and display our lives and the lives of others.

Notes

1   The presence of the operator also dominates the desertfae video. In that document, continued conversation between individuals is brought to an end when the operator assures her friends, 'I'm fine, I'm just recording.'

References

Andrejevic, M. (2004) *Reality TV: The Work of Being Watched*, Oxford: Rowman and Littlefield.

Andrejevic, M. (2007) *iSpy: Surveillance and Power in the Interactive Era*, Lawrence: University Press of Kansas.

Barthes, R. (1977) *Image – Music – Text*. Trans. Stephen Heath. New York: Hill and Wang.

Barthes, R. (1981) *Camera Lucida: Reflections on Photography*. Trans. Richard Howard. New York: Hill and Wang.

Batchen, G. (1997) *Burning with Desire: The Conception of Photography*, Cambridge, MA: MIT Press.

Batchen, G. (2003) 'Photogenics', in Liz Wells (ed.), *The Photography Reader*, London: Routledge, 228–39.

Becker, K.E. (2003) 'Photojournalism and the Tabloid Press', in L. Wells (ed.), *The Photography Reader*, London: Routledge, 291–308.

Berger, J. (1972) *Ways of Seeing*, Middlesex: BBC and Penguin Books.

Calvert, C. (2004) *Voyeur Nation: Media, Privacy, and Peering in Modern Culture*, Boulder: Westview.

Desertfae (2009) Viewer Discretion – Full Footage of Oakland Man Killed By BART Cop. Available HTTP: <http://www.youtube.com/watch?v=eZTbJH6BNaU> .

Finn, J. (2009) *Capturing the Criminal Image: From Mug Shot to Surveillance Society*, Minneapolis: University of Minnesota Press.

Foucault, M. (1977) *Discipline and Punish: The Birth of the Prison*. Trans. Alan Sheridan. New York: Vintage.

Frosh, P. (2003) *The Image Factory: Consumer Culture, Photography and the Visual Content Industry*, Oxford: Berg.

Haggerty, K.D. and Ericson, R.V. (eds) (2006) *The New Politics of Surveillance and Visibility*, Toronto: University of Toronto Press.

Ivins, W.M. Jr. (1953) *Prints and Visual Communication*, Cambridge: MIT Press.

Laudon, K.C. (1986) *Dossier Society: Value Choices in the Design of National Information Systems*, New York: Columbia University Press.

Levin, T.Y. (2002) 'Rhetoric of the Temporal Index: Surveillant Narration and the Cinema of "Real Time"', in T.Y. Levin, U. Frohne and P. Weibel (eds), *CTRL [SPACE]: Rhetorics of Surveillance from Bentham to Big Brother*, Cambridge: MIT Press, 578–93.

Lyon, D. (1994) *The Electronic Eye: The Rise of Surveillance Society*, Minneapolis: University of Minnesota Press.

Lyon, D. (2003) *Surveillance as Social Sorting: Privacy, Risk and Digital Discrimination*, London: Routledge.

Lyon, D. (2006) *Theorizing Surveillance: The Panopticon and Beyond*, Devon, UK: Willan.

Lyon, D. (2007) 'Surveillance, Visibility and Popular Culture', in *Surveillance Studies: An Overview*, Cambridge: Polity, 139–58.

Machin, D. (2004) 'Building the world's visual language: the increasing global importance of image banks in corporate media', *Visual Communication*, 3(3): 316–36.

Manovich, L. (2003) 'The Paradoxes of Digital Photography', in L. Wells (ed.), *The Photography Reader*, London: Routledge, 240–9.

Marx, G.T. (1988) *Undercover: Police Surveillance in America*, Berkeley: University of California Press.

Matheisen, T. (1997) 'The Viewer Society: Michel Foucault's "Panopticon" Revisited', *Theoretical Criminology*, 1(2): 215–34.

McCahill, M. (2002) *The Surveillance Web: The Rise of Surveillance in an English City*, Cullompton: Willan.

McGrath, J.E. (2004) *Loving Big Brother: Performance, Privacy and Surveillance Space*, New York: Routledge.

McLuhan, M. (1964) 'The Photograph: The Brothel-without-Walls', in *Understanding Media: The Extensions of Man*, New York: McGraw Hill.

Monmonier, M. (2002) *Spying with Maps: Surveillance Technologies and the Future of Privacy*, Chicago: University of Chicago Press.

Niedzviecki, H. (2009) *The Peep Diaries: How We're Learning to Love Watching Ourselves and Our Neighbors*, San Francisco: City Lights.

Norris, C. and Gary A. (1999) *The Maximum Surveillance Society: The Rise of CCTV*, Oxford: Berg.

Observateurs (2009) '22-year-old unarmed Oscar Grant shot by BART police'. Available HTTP:<http://www.youtube.com/watch?v=caG7hG5utGM.>.

Squiers, C. (1999) 'Class Struggle: The Invention of Paparazzi Photography and the Death of Diana, Princess of Wales', in C. Squiers (ed.), *Over Exposed: Essays on Contemporary Photography*, New York: The New Press, 269–304.

Sontag, S.(1977) *On Photography*, New York: Anchor Books.

Sontag, S. (2004) 'Regarding the Torture of Others', *New York Times Magazine*, 23 May.

Tagg, J. (1988) *The Burden of Representation: Essays on Photographies and Histories*, Basingstoke: Macmillan.

Weston, E. (1980) 'Seeing Photographically', in Alan Trachtenberg (ed.), *Classic Essays on Photography*, Stony Creek, CT: Leete's Island Books, 169–75.

Zureik, E. and Salter, M.B.(2005) *Global Surveillance and Policing: Borders, Security, Identity*, Cullompton: Willan.

PART II

International growth
of camera surveillance

5

CAMERAS IN CONTEXT

A comparison of the place of video surveillance in Japan and Brazil*

David Murakami Wood

Introduction

It is being increasingly recognized that there are major differences in the character, scope and reception of surveillance in specific places (Hier and Lyon 2004; Norris et al. 2004; Bennett and Lyon 2008; Arteaga Botello 2009; Murakami Wood 2009; Zureik et al. 2010). However, we still know relatively little about the interaction of global processes of risk and security with existing historical cultural trajectories in particular places, or how the forms, operation, understanding and interactions of surveillance are mediated or moderated by the contexts of reception.

This chapter compares and contrasts camera surveillance in two very different 'global' or 'world' cities, Tokyo and Rio de Janeiro, in order to make some preliminary assessment of the kinds of surveillance society that can be seen in such world cities in the midst of their encounters with globalization. The chapter argues that globalization carries with it not just neo-liberal economic imperatives, but also new forms of governmentality, which I term here 'technocratic surveillant governmentality'. Tokyo and Rio de Janeiro are both on the path to adopting such a form of governmentality, but the current situations are very different and only in Tokyo can one see this form as becoming predominant.

Other recent transnational comparative work on surveillance, particularly the huge Globalization of Personal Data (GPD) study (Zureik et al. 2010), has been based on the national level. This research is both less ambitious and at a smaller scale. It was based on multi-method case studies of particular areas within these cities. It relied primarily on interviews with activists, community representatives, and police and government officials at various levels, as well as site visits and mapping exercises. These sought to contextualize quantitative data (e.g. numbers of cameras) by re-placing them in real urban social, spatial and political settings.

The approach here is first of all descriptive, to present the situation and development of camera surveillance in each city in broad terms. However, the description is then analysed through five lenses: the level of organization of camera surveillance; the connection of camera surveillance to other domains of surveillance; the identity of the subjects of surveillance; the reaction to camera surveillance (both regulation and resistance); and finally, the mode of order in each city.

Rio de Janeiro

In order to understand state camera surveillance in Rio, one first needs to consider the structure of Brazilian government and policing. Brazil is a federal state, and Rio de Janeiro is subject to a multi-level governance regime: it is part of Brazil (and was once the capital), and the state of Rio de Janeiro, which is headed by the Governor and the state parliament; and it also has a municipal government, headed by the Mayor. Under this level, there are various community organizations, which do not have any formal legal status but are nevertheless an important instrument for the channelling of local opinion upwards.

There are also several different agencies responsible for aspects of social order. In terms of conventional police, Brazil operates a divided system similar to many continental European countries, with a *Polícia Militar* (Military Police, PM – for public order), and a *Polícia Civil* (Civil Police, PC – for investigation of crime). Both of these forces are based in individual states. At the federal level, there is now a *Polícia Federal* (Federal Police, PF – the 'Brazilian FBI'), and many cities, including Rio, now have a *Guarda Municipal* (Municipal Guard, GM – a force more like local police forces in Britain or Canada). Rio's security landscape is also complicated by the existence of the *Batalhão de Operações Policiais Especiais* (Special Police Operations Battalion or BOPE), ostensibly a specialist unit of the PM but largely operationally independent.

The state of Rio de Janeiro operates video cameras in several municipalities, and had a total of 260 cameras in 2009. This system is managed by a special office of the Secretary of State for Public Safety. The headquarters and control room are located in the old 'Centro do Brasil' railway station in the heart of the city. The Superintendent is a senior officer of the PM, and all those who monitor the cameras are also PM officers with specialist training. These cameras are sparsely distributed, but as they are wirelessly connected, they can be moved in response to need. They also have full pan, tilt and zoom (PTZ) capability. The locations of the cameras are not published and since they are moveable, any such list would be of limited utility. The motivations for their installation have been various: for example, the cameras along the Copacabana beach are supposed to reassure tourists and visitors over petty thievery; however, during a visit to the control room, I was shown one particular example of cameras capturing an incident of child abuse.

There is also a small citywide network of 88 traffic-monitoring cameras, operated by CET Rio for the municipal government. These are fixed cameras at major intersections without PTZ. Only if traffic engineers notice a particular problem in traffic circulation or an accident will they even be checked. However, they can be accessed openly through an interactive map at the city's transport website, <http://transito.rio.rj.gov.br//>.

Many private camera systems cover public space, but these do not generally integrate with those of the state at any level, particularly those on bridges, such as the main bridge between Rio and Niteroi, the municipality across the bay. There was a special event-specific agreement that allowed access by police during the Pan-American Games in 2007,[1] and the Deputy Director of the PC, a force strongly in favour of more 'intelligence-led' and surveillance-based solutions, argued that with forthcoming mega-events such as the World Military Games in 2011, the FIFA World Cup in 2014 and the Olympics in 2016, pressure for a lasting agreement on access, information-sharing and perhaps management.

The Superintendent of Video Surveillance claimed that there was already greater centralization, co-ordination and professionalization of video surveillance operations taking place through his office. However, there was some disagreement with the GM. The GM Commander (also a senior PM officer) argued that their control room, which co-ordinated emergency response in Rio, was being upgraded and would be the natural place for co-ordination of camera surveillance, in conjunction with neighbourhood control rooms.[2] The Superintendent also expressed nostalgia for a surveillance airship hired by the Pan-American Games of 2007. According to him, the airship had been highly effective; however, its high cost and lack of measurable impact have been questioned by Marta Kanashiro (2009).

The growing use of camera surveillance was challenged by others in the police and government, and it was noticeable how indifferent were senior PM and BOPE officers. The Director of the Institute for Public Security, for example, saw them only as a useful supplement to conventional policing.[3] The office of the State Secretary for Public Safety was dismissive too, particularly on grounds of expense.[4] However, developments since these interviews appear to be favouring advocates of surveillance (see below).

Rio's multi-level governance can give rise to contradictory policy directions, if the Governor and the Mayor come from different political parties or have divergent priorities. However, at present the politics of the two levels are aligned. The Governor, Sergio Cabral, and the Mayor, Eduardo Paes, are both on the political right and draw their support from the growing middle classes. They have reversed the socially progressive policies of the previous administration, including the effective *Favela Bairro* (Favela Neighbourhood) programme, which sought to normalize the *favelas*, the more than 150 informal settlements which occupy much of the marginal land on steep hillsides or floodplains in the city. In its place they have instituted *Choque de Ordem* (shock of order).

The *Choque* policy is also targeted at *favelados* (favela residents) but favours policing and public order solutions over social ones. It has involved three main components: the demolition of new illegal constructions and the restriction of growth by building walls around some favelas; a crack-down on unlicensed street vending and the shadow economy; and finally, the occupation of some favelas by new police

'Unidades Pacificadores' (Pacification Units, UP), PM rebadged as 'Community Police'. Three favelas had been occupied by the time of the research visit in 2009 – Santa Marta, Cidade de Deus and Batan – but the number has since expanded to seven.

Until 2009, camera surveillance had not formed part of these occupations and the Superintendent of Video Surveillance explained that there were no plans for its expansion into the favelas. Captain Pricilla, commander of the UP in Santa Marta, agreed that surveillance could damage the trust that was being built up between herself and residents.[5] Representatives of the Community Association confirmed in interviews that *traficante* (drug-trafficking) gangs had been expelled and some trust was emerging between them and Captain Pricilla. However, in late 2009, a video surveillance system of nine networked cameras *was* installed in Santa Marta, and the PM announced that similar systems would be installed in other favelas occupied by UPs (*O Globo* 2009). Around the same time, a wall was built along one side of the favela.

The PM hierarchy clearly see themselves in competition with the gangs for control of the favelas, and it is equally true that the gangs have their own methods of surveillance. Gangs have co-opted many Community Associations (see Arias, 2006) and have themselves been installing camera surveillance systems. In September 2008, it was reported that the PM had found a whole clandestine CCTV system of 12 cameras, and a control room hidden behind a false wall, in Parada de Lucas, a favela in the Zona Norte of the city,[6] and in late 2009, another such control room was apparently discovered in Morro dos Macacos in the wake of a raid.[7] It therefore seems clear that it was the gangs who were first to install video surveillance in the favelas to help maintain their authority, and provide advance warning of PM raids. These control rooms and cameras, despite their cost and technical advancement, were clearly regarded as disposable.

However, by following the same tactics, and installing a video surveillance system in Santa Marta without local consent, the PM is open to the accusation that it is operating in a similar manner to the gangs. Indeed, this accusation was quite frequently put to us by community representatives of different social classes in several areas. Camera surveillance in such a context can be seen as a sign of insecurity and weakness: if the disposable gang systems showed a loss of certainty and the need for an escape route, the cameras, wall and ongoing occupation in Santa Marta by the UP have also been interpreted by residents as indicating a lack of faith in what has been achieved.

This one small case of PM surveillance and enclosure is not isolated. There are plans to build other walls, particularly along the major highway from the international airport into the city. In addition, the recent flood disasters in the area, which killed many people, prompted not an outpouring of sympathy and promises of rebuilding, but instead for the Governor to suggest that affected areas be razed and the people moved elsewhere (a tactic that has a long and controversial history in the previous authoritarian regimes in Brazil: see Fischer 2008). This process is likely to accelerate with forthcoming sports mega-events, which have been shown to be drivers of intensified surveillance and security (Samatas 2004; Coaffee et al. 2009; Bennett et al. 2011). This hypothesis is supported by the appointment as Security Advisor in late 2009 of the architect of Zero Tolerance policing and the inspiration for *Choque de Ordem*, ex-New York Mayor, Rudy Giuliani.[8]

However, for much of middle-class Rio, such measures are not 'too much' but 'too little, too late'. Near Santa Marta is the wealthy, bohemian area of Santa Teresa. Here villas have long been walled and gated; however, there are new moves to close off entire streets. So far this has been restricted to cul-de-sacs. Private security guards are employed to staff gate-posts, also monitored by cameras, to check the identity and purpose of any person attempting to pass. Residents claim that it is entirely lawful, but the Chair of the local Community Association argued that there is no legal basis for the closures.[9] He claimed that such gating was one outcome of the gentrification of the previously mixed neighbourhood, which had generated a segregated class demanding 'protection' from surrounding favelas.

The securitization of Santa Teresa is thus of a piece with the walling and surveilling of Santa Marta. In Santa Teresa the wealthier inhabitants shut out dangerous 'others', but in Santa Marta the poorer residents are subjected to multiple disciplinary tactics from an occupying police force initially installed to protect the community from outside gangs.

Tokyo

Tokyo has a simpler formal system of government than Rio de Janeiro. Japan has a bicameral parliamentary system, and Tokyo is the seat of the national government. However, the city itself is run by the unified Tokyo Metropolitan Government (TMG), with an elected council and headed by the Governor. Beneath this are the *ku* (wards), which are local governments equivalent to London boroughs or Parisian *arrondissements*. However, Tokyo has a plethora of community organizations beneath this level, in particular *choukai* (neighbourhood associations) and *shoutenkai* (shopkeepers' associations). While they may be less official than they once were, they still wield influence.

Formal policing is divided between the *keisatsuchou* (National Police Agency, NPA) and the *keishicho* (Tokyo Metropolitan Police Authority, TMPA). Although, unlike the Brazilian police, the TMPA is a single agency, it has various different departments which have differing tasks and priorities.

Video surveillance systems in Japan have been expanding since the 1990s. There are just 363 NPA cameras in Japan; however, there are more owned by local municipal authorities, particularly in Tokyo, and thousands more operated by transport networks, private companies, *choukai* and *shoutenkai*. However, the NPA also operate one of the most long-standing systems of Automatic Licence (or Number) Plate Recognition (ALPR/ANPR) systems in the world. The *N-System* has been operating since 1986 – in comparison, London's ANPR system dates to 1993 (Coaffee 2004) – and has day and night (infra-red) fixed cameras on freeways around major cities as well as throughout central Tokyo. An independent lawyer who has followed the growth of the system estimated that in 1997, after a programme of expansion, there were over 80 *N-System* locations in Tokyo, and over 400 nationally.[10]

Camera surveillance systems on public transport in Tokyo can be traced back to the Aum Shinrikyo sarin gas attacks on the Tokyo underground in 1996. However, *keishicho* officers interviewed in August 2009 claimed that neither these attacks nor the 9/11 attacks on the USA (which have been held responsible for an intensification of surveillance on a global scale) prompted a shift to state public space camera surveillance, but instead the influence of discussions of security at G8 meetings was vital.[11]

However, the direct trigger for a concerted state video surveillance strategy was another mega-event: the 2002 FIFA World Cup. The World Cup produced a combined government, police and media campaign with two main themes, both of which were based on fear of foreigners: firstly, the threat from the 'football hooligan'; and secondly, a flood of illegal vendors (Murakami Wood and Abe 2011). To counter the first, the NPA placed 190 cameras in host cities for the event (Goold 2002; Murakami Wood et al. 2007), and for the second, face-recognition was also secretly installed at the two principal international airports, Tokyo's Narita and Osaka's Kansai (Murakami Wood and Abe 2011). Since the so-called Bubble Economy of the 1980s when Tokyo came to dominate global banking and financial flows, Japan had seen a new wave of immigration of those looking for work in factories and service industries, from South America, mainland Asia and for the first time from India, the Middle East and Africa (see Clammer 2001). In the post-Bubble period a rapidly ageing Japanese population and a casualization of labour in many sectors have combined to favour the growth of low-paid, insecure employment that marginal migrants have little choice but to tolerate.

However, in Tokyo in particular, the expansion of camera surveillance was facilitated by the *Anzen anshin machizukuri jourei* (Community Security and Safety Development Ordinance) of 2003. The main reason given by the *keishicho* is that recorded crimes had reached a record high in the city in 2002. Everyone interviewed agreed that the ordinance was a direct product of the dominant personality of the Tokyo Governor, Ishihara Shintaro, an independent populist who presents himself as tough on crime and tough on the increasingly visible supposed cause of crime: foreigners.

However, the method employed by the ordinance is one of responsibilization of Tokyo's local community organizations rather than centralization. The 2003 ordinance made community safety the responsibility of the *choukai*, and increasingly Parent-Teachers' Associations (PTAs), with co-ordination, information and encouragement from the *ku* administration's *Seikatsu Anzen Bu* (Everyday Safety Divisions, SAB). A SAB consists of a mixture of local officials and officers seconded from the TMPA. Rather like the GM in Rio, their primary role had been responding to natural disasters and emergencies.

Three areas were chosen as case studies: the central commercial and administrative ward of Shinjuku; the wealthy residential ward of Suginami; and the relatively impoverished ward of Arikawa. All three SABs claimed to be practising *anzen anshin machizukuri* (AAM) but had very different emphases.

Suginami prioritizes time-intensive citizen community safety patrols, organized through the local PTAs, *shoutenkai* and *choukai*. There are 140 groups with 9,600 people actively involved in one way or another in community safety just in Suginami. They also have 15 community *ao patoka* (blue patrol cars), miniature police-style cars and bikes driven mainly by retired police officers. These have started to replace the traditional *koban* (neighourhood police boxes), which are increasingly being withdrawn by the TMPA.

Suginami also has an experimental camera surveillance system introduced by the Tokyo Metropolitan Police after 2002: the *supa bohan kamera* (super security cameras) are help points where people press a button if they feel in danger and speak to someone from the police. They have both CCTV and an alarm/red flashing light for signalling an emergency. However, the Suginami SAB officers said that these cameras have not proved effective and cause problems because children often press the buttons for fun and run away, meaning that there are many false alarms.[12]

Suginami was the first Local Authority in Japan to introduce a special *bohan kamera jourei* (security camera ordinance) in 2004, which is based partly on principles of data protection and privacy. The ordinance followed public consultation which showed that although CCTV was generally believed effective (95 per cent), a significant minority (34 per cent) were concerned about privacy, and 72 per cent thought regulation was needed. Until neighbouring Setegaya-ku introduced their own ordinance in 2008, this was the only one in Japan.

Shinjuku's Kabukicho entertainment/red-light district was also the subject of a camera surveillance experiment, being a pilot area for video surveillance, with over 50 cameras operated by the city police. The *keishicho* claimed that this was in response to a particular foreign threat: the alleged increase in violence by Chinese Triad gangs. Cameras were also introduced in four other areas of Tokyo: Ikebukuro, Shibuya, Roppongi and Ueno. There is a central control room for these cameras, but I was told that it was strictly forbidden to outsiders, even researchers, as everyone who enters has to be pre-enrolled in the police iris-scan security database.

The Shinjuku SAB has no access to this system and instead has a strategy to co-ordinate *shoutenkai* video systems. At present these systems are generally not monitored, i.e. there is no control room and images are recorded and stored for seven days before being overwritten. Both *shoutenkai* and *choukai* are being encouraged to install CCTV systems, and there are grant systems in place – approximately one-third comes from the city, one-third from the *ku* and one-third from the organization itself. This means coverage is very uneven and tends to be restricted to wealthy and/or particularly committed groups and wards. Shinjuku has many wealthy *shoutenkai* with extensive video surveillance systems.

Arakawa, in contrast, has only a handful of cameras and no camera surveillance strategy, although the police do consult with the developers of large new buildings on its installation. There is a certain degree of 'CCTV envy' of places able to afford the latest high-tech gadgets, but Arakawa SAB is also realistic about the limitations and appropriateness of camera surveillance. Instead they concentrate on using and enhancing the natural surveillance capacities of local communities. They use volunteers, retired police officers and ordinary local people, including *wan-wan* ('woof-woof') patrols which involve mainly older female residents and their dogs. Participation in the various community initiatives is encouraged through techniques like professional *rakugo* (traditional comic monologue).

Like Suginami, they also have community *ao patoka*, but they have gone further with small *anzen anshin sutashion* (security and safety stations), reopened community versions of police *koban*, often called *minkan koban* ('people's *koban*'). These small help stations, staffed mainly by ex-police, do not just provide 'security' information, they also deal with security in a broader sense, offering help for older people with social benefits, for example. Crime is not a major issue in Arakawa, which has consistently had the second- or third-lowest crime rates of all the 23 Tokyo wards. But even since the introduction of these initiatives, we were told that crime has fallen still further from the relative high point it reached a few years ago.

One could argue that the local authority is being forced to provide services once provided by the police, and give work (in some cases paid) to ex-police officers at the same time that it is losing frontline police services. The *Seikatsu Anzen Bu* of the *Keishicho* itself is a separate division that was created as a result of the 2003 *Seikatsu Anzen Jourei* and is separate from the *Chiki Bu* (the community division) responsible for the *koban* system. So, effectively a new parallel structure is emerging, prioritizing volunteeristic surveillance, to replace the previous professional community policing system.

Police and local officials in Tokyo consistently claimed they were not even doing 'surveillance', but rather that they were simply responding to local concerns over public safety and were supported by local community groups and businesses. However, controversy over a further expansion of the NPA's national surveillance camera network suggests that this should not be taken for granted. The NPA is extending its cameras into 15 residential areas starting January 2010 (two, Higashi-yamato and Musashimurayama, are suburbs of Tokyo) at a cost of 597 million Yen (around US$6.3 million). The underlying rationale is the supposed threat to children. The small camera systems (around 25 cameras each) are being installed on streets used by children going to and from school, and will be operated by local 'volunteers'. However, one of the Tokyo authorities selected said that they had not been consulted.[13]

Discussion: surveillance societies?

Academics in both Brazil (Kanashiro 2008; Bruno et al. 2010) and Japan (Ogura 2001, 2003, 2005) have discussed each as a 'surveillance society', a term that describes a highly bureaucratized nation-state in which surveillance practices constitute the predominant mode of social ordering. This label has until recently been the product of a largely northern/western interdisciplinary field (surveillance studies), which has been dependent on a particular understanding of the development of modern (and post-modern) societies in that same area of the world. In order to interrogate this concept and to contribute to the growing body of literature that recognizes the need to engage with a variety of surveillance societies, in this chapter I outlined the extent and functioning of camera surveillance in two very different world cities. In this discussion, I will ask five questions:

What is the level and form of organization of camera surveillance?

Does extant or proposed camera surveillance link to other domains of surveillance?

Who are the subjects of surveillance?

What is the reaction to camera surveillance?

How can one characterize the mode of order in each city?

Organization

It was clear that in Rio de Janeiro, state camera surveillance was limited in its systematic organization and co-ordination, whereas there was more evidence of formal organization in Tokyo. Where surveillance cameras had been installed in Rio, their placement was far from providing blanket coverage, indeed most cameras were moveable, whereas in Tokyo, by 2006, in Shinjuku, Ikebukuro and Shibuya, coverage was virtually 100 per cent for those areas where state camera surveillance had been concentrated. In addition, while the 2003 *anshin anzen machizukuri jourei* has provided the Tokyo *ku* with the legal tools to integrate public and private systems, in Rio such arrangements have been temporary and ad-hoc. However, this is recognized by police and local government, and forthcoming mega-events are providing a spur to greater co-ordination of currently disparate and disconnected systems.

Both the systems of government and the morphology of each city make blanket city-wide coverage diffcult. In Tokyo, as Murakami Wood et al. (2007) noted, the complex pattern of narrow alleys mitigates against more substantial coverage, and the different *ku*, while they may have the potential for co-ordination of camera surveillance, are not necessarily either financially able or politically willing to effect it. However, major commercial redevelopments like Times Square in Shinjuku or Roppongi Hills in Minowa-ku can create a 'tabula rasa' where surveillance can be built into new constructions. In Rio de Janeiro the extremely hilly topography, coupled with the density and the 'off-limits' character of most of the favelas, make even the currently co-ordinated local government policy of *choque de ordem*, predicated on coercive security and the introduction of more widespread camera surveillance to some of those favelas, little more than an ambition or a public relations project.

Context and connection

The second question to ask then is one of context and connection. In information societies, camera surveillance can be part of a wider strategy aiming at a broader sense of control through data collection and analysis, and might tend over time to be linked to other domains of government, like identification or health, or welfare. In less democratic societies, a great deal of formal connection between domains might indicate a more panoptic or totalitarian 'surveillance state'. A large number of mostly disconnected systems of surveillance might still add up to a sense of the normalization of surveillance as social organization, or as a channel of information between individuals, groups and organizations – a 'surveillance society'. However, camera surveillance systems can also serve discreet purposes that do not necessarily overlap or 'add up'; they can be what Bruno Latour (2005) has termed 'oligoptic', a gaze that sees very intensely but is limited in time and/or space.

In Japan, despite the introduction of the controversial local government information system, *juki-net* (Tajima et al. 2003; Ogasawara 2008) and other state databases, there is no formal connection between the *anshin anzen machi-zukuri* agenda and the *i-Japan* information society agenda driving *juki-net*, for most people, most of the time. This may be due to the lack of a more obvious threat like that of terrorism in the UK or the USA, around which such co-ordination could occur. The aggressive and isolationist neighbouring state of North Korea, the rise of China, and the long-term internal issue of an 'ageing society' are concerns and are all invoked to justify proposed policy changes, but do not generate the existential anxiety that comes from the invocation of 'terrorism' elsewhere.

For Rio de Janeiro, the complex multi-level structure of Brazilian federal government, in which different authorities at different levels frequently have entirely different ideologies and goals, mitigates against any kind of a more totalitarian surveillance state. Brazil has been through several periods of authoritarian rule, the last ending only in 1985, but its authoritarianism was of the arbitrary, military form rather than the nightmare of total knowledge and order that characterized the former East Germany. I would argue, contrary to Kanashiro (2008), that Brazil is nothing like a total surveillance society and the changes that it would take to become one would be almost inconceivable in scale and cost.

Rio's problem in some ways is one of a lack of surveillance rather than a surfeit. The state is only now introducing the kinds of protective and caring state information-gathering that can be seen in the reception of Brazilian ID cards or in the progressive and popular model of the new social welfare *Programa Bolsa Familia* (Family Grant Programme, PBF), which makes sure that children go to school if their parents are to receive benefits (Murakami Wood and Firmino 2010). At the same time, however, just as in Tokyo, there is an increasing influence of techno-cratic surveillance practices in policing, as seen with the introduction of camera surveillance in Santa Marta.

The subjects of surveillance

It is important to consider who are the subjects of camera surveillance (Smith 2007). In both cities, the predominant identity of these subjects was obvious but obviously different. While the targets were both members of groups one might label as being in 'advancedmarginality' (Wacquant 2008), the nature of surveilled marginality in each city is not the same.

In the case of Tokyo, in Shinjuku, where the systematic organization of camera surveillance was greatest, a very clear picture of who was being targeted became visible through the interviews. Both organizations working for the welfare of immigrants[14] and the Kabukicho Town Manager, who runs the day-to-day operations of the body trying to improve Kabukicho's image, *Kabukicho Renaissance*,[15] confirmed that the video surveillance system in this area of Shinjuku and the accompanying police crackdowns were now used largely to curb illegal migrant workers in the night economy, particularly South-east Asian women. So far, this effort has been disjointed at a national level. But from 2012, all foreigners will be included on the *jyuminhyo* (residents' registry), digitized and networked through *juki-net*. Residency information for foreigners will be linked to the *Houmusho* (Ministry of Justice) databases of entry records, fingerprints and facial photos. So while it may not be true across the whole population, in this case, and for these people – the most marginal in contemporary Tokyo – connections are indeed being forged between camera surveillance and other domains of state surveillance.

If in Tokyo the question of who is being secured and from whom is easily answered as the Japanese from certain categories of outsider, in Rio de Janeiro questions of wealth and class predominate over those of immigration. The poor, and in particular the *favelados*, function as the source of nightmares for wealthier inhabitants. However, the predominance of class does not mean the absence of race: for example, Vera Malaguti (2003) has identified also a suppressed racialized character to Brazilian class structure and a long-standing fear of the 'Africanization' of Rio.

Japan's increasing openness to the neo-liberal global economy without the powerful defensive economic shield it had in the 1980s has also meant a more unequal society: there is a growing gap between rich and poor, and the rich increasingly separate themselves behind gates and walls, just as in Brazil. This politically and economically dominant class, which appears to be developing transnational characteristics (Van der Pijl 1998), plays a key role in the normalization of surveillance (Murakami Wood and Webster 2009) by submitting to surveillance for its own security, but demanding that the state forces the same measures on those in advanced marginality perceived as the source of threat.

Reaction, regulation and resistance

Camera surveillance is increasingly normalized in both cities. For example, in Japan, in an editorial, the left-leaning *Asahi Shimbun* newspaper, in arguing that there should be increasing regulation of camera surveillance,[16] did not question the need for cameras in public spaces even though it admitted that evidence of their effectiveness was equivocal. And in general, compared to western nations, relatively little attention is paid to data protection and human rights around surveillance in Japan. There is no regulatory watchdog, only weak volunteeristic laws, and the principles of data protection did not appear to be understood or taken seriously by those responsible for developing new databases and surveillance systems.

There is some small organized opposition. The Campaign Against Surveillance Society (*Kanshi-No!*) argues that camera surveillance is the product of Japan's neo-liberal turn and has thus been some time in the making.[17] *Puraibashi* (privacy) was mentioned, but not as much as one would expect in western contexts. Instead the dominant socio-cultural concern was that video surveillance cameras and other surveillance measures were being used to fill a hole where real community and social trust might once have been.

Kanshi-No! claimed that the same forms of everyday 'community action' in the name of *anzen anshin* (safety) or *bohan* (security) are now being employed as anti-terrorism in Japan; however, I saw no evidence of this. They also see very little difference between the *mini-patoka* and *wan-wan* patrol initiatives in Arakawa-ku and the expansion of camera surveillance in Shinjuku. Their argument, like that of academic critics (c.f. Igarashi 2004; Ogura 2001, 2003, 2005; Tajima 2003), is a political economic one, more related to the critique of Roy Coleman (2004) in Britain or Marta Kanashiro (2008) in Brazil, which links urban regeneration or redevelopment and the introduction of camera surveillance. This argument was supported by observation of some of the most recent video surveillance schemes, for example that in the Nippori *ekimae* (station front) development in Arakawa-ku, installed as part of the social and spatial restructuring of this previously working-class entertainment area. Here camera surveillance is an essential part of a new commercial image, with signs celebrating the cameras as much as the area's overall rebranding.

In Rio, contrary to what Arteaga Botello (2010) asserts about Brazil, data protection is even more limited (Doneda 2006), and this is also exacerbated, according to human rights groups interviewed, by the fact that 'human rights' are actively unpopular with the middle and upper classes, with the perception that human rights advocates are simply defending criminals.[18] Representatives claimed that they regularly receive hate mail and threatening telephone calls, and most of their income comes from the European Union and USA. In this context, surveillance has not generally been even as much a social or political issue as it has been in Japan. Here the groups we interviewed admitted they were small and largely ignored but were not the subject of hate campaigns.[19]

In the Rio favelas, where one might expect greater concern, where cameras were not present, they were seen as a frippery of the rich unrelated to the lives of the ordinary people. However, the reaction of Santa Marta to the installation of cameras there shows that indifference can transform very quickly into resistance. With the wall along the west side of the favela described as turning Santa Marta into 'a ghetto' by one member of the Community Association,[20] the reaction to the installation of cameras was shocked and immediate. Posters appeared from the Community Association and other civil society groups calling Santa Marta 'the most watched place in Rio' and asking, 'we are a pacified favela, so why do they keep treating us as dangerous?' and 'walls, three kinds of police, 120 soldiers, cameras – this is no exaggeration. When will we be treated as ordinary citizens instead of being seen as suspects?' They also contrast the costs of the wall and cameras with the minimal amount being spent on sewage and water works in the favela. The material from the groups also claims that the Community Association was completely cut out of this decision, and this claim is supported by local contacts.[21]

Modes of order

In a recent article, Kiyoshi Abe and I argue that traditional forms of Japanese mutual surveillance were reinforced by what US historian Sheldon Garron (1997) called 'moral suasion', the persistent and pervasive promotion of a particular kind of social good by the state and its agents. We termed the resulting mode of order a 'suasive surveillance society' (Murakami Wood and Abe 2011). We claimed that the continuance of this traditional suasive surveillance society beyond its origins was dependent on the generalized benefits of economic success of Japan. Now that this can no longer be taken for granted, this mode of order is in decline.

Some we interviewed, like the Arakawa and Suginami SABs, seem to be attempting to revitalize the old mode. In Arakawa's case this has been without much success, but there has been more in Suginami, which has paid attention to privacy and boundaries between domains of government, and resisted a turn to the technologically mediated video surveillance infrastructure that is one of the key characteristics of contemporary globalized urbanity. Others, as in Shinjuku, were enthusiastic for what camera surveillance represented.

A preliminary classification would be to consider Tokyo as a city in transition between a traditional 'suasive surveillance society' and a more 'global technocratic surveillance society', albeit one, like all aspects of globalization, that is unevenly distributed and applied.

Because the predominant social fear is around everyday personal security, surveillance in Brazil is not a dominant form of social order, but secondary to security. Surveillance serves security, it does not (yet) function much in its own right. However, Brazil is not a 'security state' and the concentration on security is largely private. One report for a US state export agency[22] indicated that the security industry is growing at rates of between 10 and 15 per cent. The main trend is not towards public space video surveillance but fortification (especially the upsurge in the building of secure condominiums and communities) and the increasing numbers of private security operatives.

It is easy to see this as part of a trend towards privatization, and another facet of globalization: the growth of individualized and class-based responses, and new transnational class formation, as posited above. However, there are also several factors that point inwards and backwards in time to the immediate post-colonial period when local policing was delegated to large landowners (Holston 2008). The conflation of private interest and the law was built into the governance of Brazil, and since there has been an ongoing struggle to bring what was private into the public sphere, to create a genuine Brazilian 'public'. Yet, as Botello (2010) argues, security in Brazil is very closely connected to the safeguarding of family and privacy, a tendency which is always working in the contrary direction to that of the creation of the notion of a shared public, especially when expressed through gates and walls.

Both positive, caring state surveillance and movement to technocratic forms hasten Rio's progress towards a 'surveillance society', but the exact nature of this surveillance society will depend on whether socially progressive politics can moderate the protectionist reflex of the growing middle class. And until weaknesses in the state's understanding of personal data are addressed, there remain, as Doneda and Kanashiro (2010) argue, real risks to any project of government information collection and collation.

Conclusion

Both Tokyo and Rio de Janeiro show signs of the emergence of a globalizing form of technocratic surveillance, including the spread of camera surveillance, driven in part by the demands of a trans-national class of increasingly separated wealthy willing to submit themselves to surveillance for their own security. But globalization does not mean homogenous local reception. The particular histories, emphases, prejudices and concerns are different in each place, and there are other contradictory trajectories. Tokyo and Rio both have aspects of their governmentality that make them partially surveillance societies, but only in Japan could one argue that 'surveillance' is approaching being a 'dominant' mode of social order. Tokyo's particular form of surveillance society is undergoing an uncertain transition in the ongoing encounter with global neo-liberal capitalism, and in Rio it is security that forms the basis of contemporary order, not surveillance, with surveillance remaining a means to this end.

Notes

* This chapter draws on research conducted for the UK Economic and Social Research Council (ESRC) Fellowship, Cultures of Urban Surveillance. I am indebted to the ESRC for their support. I would like to thank my interviewees and contacts in both Japan and Brazil, in particular, in Brazil: Rodrigo Firmino, Paola Barreto Leblanc, Marta Kanashiro, Fernanda Bruno, and the Pontifical Catholic University of Parana; and in Japan: Abe Kiyoshi, Hijikata Masao, Ogasawara Midori, Murakami Kayo and Ryu Yuki.
1 Interview with the Superintendent of Video Surveillance, Rio de Janeiro, April 2009.
2 Interview with the Commander of the Guarda Municipal, Rio de Janeiro, April 2009.
3 Interview with the Director of the Institute for Public Security, Rio de Janeiro, March 2009.
4 Interview with representative of the Secretary of State for Public Security, Rio de Janeiro, March 2009.
5 Interview with Captain Pricilla, UP Santa Marta, Rio de Janeiro, April 2009.
6 UOL.com.br, 12 September 2008, 'Polícia estoura central clandestina de monitoramento de TV no RJ', <http://noticias.uol.com.br/cotidiano/2008/09/12/ult5772u806.jhtm>.
7 'Mandante da invasão ao Morro dos Macacos utiliza câmeras para controlar favelas'
8 Globo.com, 03 December 2009, 'Governo do Rio contrata ex-prefeito de Nova York para ajudar na segurança', <http://g1.globo.com/Noticias/Rio/0,,MUL1402463-5606,00.html>.

9 Interview with the Chair of the Santa Teresa Community Association, Rio de Janeiro, April 2009.
10 Sakuragaoka Law Office (nd), 'N-System Total Guide', <http://www.sakuragaoka. gr.jp/html2/nsys/index.html> [accessed 1 July 2010].
11 Interview with representatives of the TMPA Community Safety Division, Tokyo, August 2009.
12 Interview with representatives of the Sugunami SAB, Tokyo, August 2009.
13 They would also not give an on-the-record interview.
14 Joint interview with representatives of the Solidarity Network with Migrants, and Japan Civil Liberties Union, Tokyo, August 2009.
15 Interview with the Kabukicho Town Manager, Tokyo, August 2009.
16 Asahi Shimbun, July 2009, 'Editorial', <http://www.asahi.com/english/Herald-asahi/ TKY200907070062.html>.
17 Interview with representatives of the Campaign Against Surveillance Society, Tokyo, August 2009.
18 Interviews with representatives of human rights groups, Artigo 1 and Instituto Pro Bono, São Paulo, March 2009; interview with the Chair of the Parliamentary Human Rights Group, Brasilia, March 2009.
19 Interviews with representatives of the Campaign Against Surveillance Society, The Consumer's Association of Japan and the Solidarity Network with Migrants, and Japan Civil Liberties Union, Tokyo, August 2009.
20 Interview with Dona Sonia, member of the board of the Santa Marta Community Association, Rio de Janeiro, April 2009.
21 Personal communication.
22 See e.g. Massachusetts South America Office (2008) *The Brazilian Security Industry*, <http://www.moiti.org/pdf/Brazil Security Industry.pdf>.

References

Abe, K. (2001) 'The information society without others: A critique of "informatization" in Japan', *Kwansei Gakuin University Social Sciences Review*, 5: 53–74.
Abe, K. (2004) 'Everyday policing in Japan: Surveillance, media, government and public opinion', *International Sociology*, 19: 215–31.
Abe, K. (2009) 'The Myth of Media Interactivity: Technology, Communications and Surveillance in Japan', *Theory, Culture & Society*, 26(2–3): 73–88.
Arteaga Botello, N. (2009) *Sociedad de la vigilancia en el Sur-Global: Mirando America Latina/Surveillance Society in the Global South: Looking at Latin America*, Porrula Miguel Angel S a.
Arteaga Botello, N. (2010) 'Privacy and Surveillance in Mexico and Brazil: A Cross-National Analysis', in Zureik et al. (eds), 212–29.
Bennett, C.J. and Lyon, D. (eds) (2008) *Playing the Identity Card: Surveillance, Security and Identification Regimes in Global Perspective*, London: Routledge.
Bruno, F., Kanashiro, M. and Firmino, R. (eds) (2010) *Vigilância e Visibilidade: Espaço, Tecnologia e Identificação*, Porto Alegre: Editora Sulina.
Caldeira, T.P.R. (2000) *City of Walls: Crime, Segregation, and Citizenship in São Paulo*, Berkeley: University of California Press.
Castro, R.B. and Pedro, R.M.L.R. (2010) 'Redes de vigilância: a experiência da segurança e da visibilidade articuladas as câmeras de monitoramento urbano', in F. Bruno, M. Kanashiro and R. Firmino (eds), *Vigilância e Visibilidade: Espaço, Tecnologia e Identificação*, Porto Alegre: Editora Sulina, 36–60.
Clammer, J. (2001) *Japan and Its Others: Globalization, Difference and the Critique of Modernity*, Melbourne: Trans Pacific Press.
Coleman, R. (2004) *Reclaiming the Streets*, Cullompton: Willan.

Deleuze, G. (1990) 'Postscriptum sûr les sociétés de contrôle', *L'autre journal*.

Doneda, D. (2006) 'Pessoa e privacidade na sociedade da informação', *Da privacidade à proteção de dados pessoais*, Rio de Janeiro: Renovar.

Doneda, D. and Kanashiro, M. (2010) 'A transformação da identificação e a construção de bancos de dados: o caso do documento único no Brasil', in F. Bruno, M. Kanashiro and R. Firmino (eds), *Vigilância e Visibilidade: Espaço, Tecnologia e Identificação*, Porto Alegre: Editora Sulina, 272–96.

Fischer, B. (2008) *A Poverty of Rights: Citizenship and Inequality in Twentieth-Century Rio de Janeiro*, Stanford, CA: Stanford University Press.

Garon, S. (1997) *Molding Japanese Minds: The State in Everyday Life*, New Jersey: Princeton University Press.

Gilliom, J. (2001) *Overseers of the Poor*, Chicago: University of Chicago Press.

Hier, S.P. and Lyon, D. (2004) 'Introduction: International Perspectives on Surveillance, Technology and the Management of Risk', *International Sociology*, 19(2): 131-4.

Holston, J. (2008) *Insurgent Citizenship: Disjunctions of Democracy and Modernity in Brazil*, Princeton: Princeton University Press.

Igarashi, T. (2004) *Kabōbi Toshi (The Over-protected City)*, Tokyo: Chuokoron Shinsha.

Kanashiro, M.M. (2008) 'Surveillance Cameras in Brazil: exclusion, mobility, regulation, and the new meanings of security', *Surveillance & Society*, 5(3): 270–89.

Kanashiro, M.M. (2009) Presentation given at the Surveillance, Security and Social Control in Latin America symposium, Curitiba, Brazil, 4–6 March 2009.

Latour, B. (2005) *Reassembling the Social: An Introduction to Actor-Network Theory*, Oxford and New York: Oxford University Press.

Lyon, D. (2001) *Surveillance Society: Monitoring Everyday Life*, Buckingham: Open University Press.

Lyon, D. (2007) *Surveillance Studies: An Overview*, Cambridge: Polity.

Lyon, D. (2009) *Identifying Citizens: ID Cards as Surveillance*, Cambridge: Polity.

Malaguti Batista, V. (2003) *O Medo na Cidade do Rio de Janeiro: Dois Tempos de Uma História*, Rio de Janeiro: Editora Revan.

Murakami Wood, D. (2009) 'The Surveillance Society: Questions of History, Place and Culture', *European Journal of Criminology*, 6(2): 179–94.

Murakami Wood, D. and Abe, K. (2011) 'The Spectacle of Fear: Anxious Events and Foreign Threats in Japan', in C. Bennett and K. Haggerty (eds), *The Security Games*, London: Routledge, 72–86.

Murakami Wood, D. and Firmino, R. (2010) 'Empowerment or Repression? Opening up Identification and Surveillance in Brazil though a case of "Identification Fraud"', *Identity in the Information Society*, 2(3): 297–317.

Murakami Wood, D. and Webster, W. (2009) 'Living in Surveillance Societies: the Normalisation of Surveillance in Europe', *Journal of Contemporary European Research*, 5(2): 259–73.

Murakami Wood, D., Lyon, D. and Abe, K. (2007) 'Surveillance in Urban Japan: A Critical Introduction', *Urban Studies*, 44(3): 551–68.

Norris, C., McCahill, M. and Wood, D. (2004) 'Editorial. The growth of CCTV: a global perspective on the international diffusion of video surveillance in publicly accessible space', *Surveillance & Society*, 2(2/3): 110–35.

Ogasawara, M. (2008) 'A tale of the colonial age or the banner of a new tyranny? National identification card systems in Japan, in C. Bennett and D. Lyon (eds), *Playing the Identity Card: Surveillance, Security and Identification Regimes in Global Perspective*, London: Routledge, 93–111.

Ogura, T. (ed.) (2001) *Kanshi Shakai to Puraibashi (Surveillance Society and Privacy)*, Tokyo: Impact Shutsupankai.

Ogura, T. (ed.) (2003) *Rojō ni Jiyu o (Freedom in the Streets!),* Tokyo: Impact Shutsupankai.

Ogura,T. (ed.) (2005) *Gurōbaluka to Kanshi Keisatsu Kotsuka eno Teiko (Resistance against Globalization and the Surveillance/Police state),* Tokyo: Kinohanasha.

Smith, G.J.D. (2007) 'Exploring Relations between Watchers and Watched in Control(led) Systems: Strategies and Tactics', *Surveillance & Society,* 4(4): 280–313.

Tajima, Y., Saito, T. and Yamamoto, H. (eds) (2003) *Juki-net to Kanshi Shakai (Juki-net and Surveillance Society),* Tokyo: Akashi Shoten.

Van der Pijl, K. (1998) *Transnational Classes and International Relations,* London: Routledge.

Wacquent, L. (2008) *Urban Outcasts: A Comparative Sociology of Advanced Marginality,* Cambridge: Polity Press.

Zureik, E., Harling Stalker, L.L., Smith, E., Lyon, D. and Chan, Y.E. (eds) (2010) *Surveillance, Privacy, and the Globalization of Personal Information: International Comparisons,* Montreal: McGill-Queen's University Press.

6

THE GROWTH AND FURTHER PROLIFERATION OF CAMERA SURVEILLANCE IN SOUTH AFRICA

Anthony Minnaar

Introduction

Closed circuit television (CCTV) camera surveillance systems in central business districts (CBDs) in South Africa are largely used for the purpose of crime prevention, deterrence and control.[1] However, many issues such as privacy, impact, effectiveness in preventing crime, public buy-in of installation and operational and policing imperatives are largely under-researched in South Africa. While information regarding CCTV control room operations training, installation specifications and operational and training requirements is available, this is largely in the private security sector domain and has not been academically researched.[2]

This chapter is not intended to review or compare research results from international jurisdictions on all these issues or topics, but rather to give an overview of the size, extent and penetration of CCTV camera surveillance systems countrywide in South Africa. In particular, it looks at the multi-use and multiple site locations of such surveillance systems both in the public domain and private sectors.

At the time of the implementation in the late 1990s and early 2000s of CCTV camera surveillance systems in South African CBDs, the use of CCTV as a prevention, surveillance and detection measure was nothing new. This usage was largely in the private sector and fell under the label of 'security camera' surveillance. In South Africa in the mid-1970s, use of CCTV had been implemented by the mining industry on diamond mines and at gold/precious metals refineries, largely to prevent the smuggling and pilfering of diamonds and precious metals from these facilities and mines (Van Zyl 2010). The gambling industry (casinos) in South Africa was also one of the first to use CCTV for surveillance purposes of gamblers and patrons in their establishments.[3] These uses were largely 'in-house' and on private property. At a later stage the benefits of such 'security cameras' were recognized by the private security industry, which utilized them for the provision of surveillance and access control largely at commercial, retail and business premises or private residences (Rogers 2010). More recently these are also used at the so-called 'security villages/estates'.

In the early years of the start-up of CCTV camera surveillance in South Africa, one of the drawbacks to more widespread use and implementation of CCTV camera surveillance in public areas, such as central business districts, was the high cost and the inability of government departments and municipalities to fund its installation and operational costs. This was particularly the case of the South African Police Service (SAPS) in the light of more pressing priorities in combating high levels of crime and other demands on its finances and resources. In recent years, expansion has occurred not only for such publicly funded systems, but has extended to residential neighbourhoods, warehousing, sports stadiums and shopping centre malls. This includes in-house systems in supermarkets and large department stores, and along major highways and railways. While such 'roll-out' has certainly not been on the same level or extent as in many developed countries, it is without a doubt gaining ground in most major South African urban areas. Moreover, South Africa is way ahead of all other countries in Africa in the use of CCTV camera surveillance systems in its multi-use and implementation.

The initial inability to fund the installation of public open street CCTV by the national SAPS, in effect led to an 'outsourcing by default' in terms of the provision of CCTV surveillance in a number of CBDs in South Africa. Originally, the initiative to start implementing and linking CCTV camera surveillance systems in CBDs in the major metropolitan cities of South Africa was left to the local police services as a crime prevention measure. But the practical planning and funding initiative for the first such formal CBD system, emanating from the Security Plan of the Cape Town Olympic Bid, was taken in the mid-1990s by Business Against Crime of South Africa (BACSA) (see Penberthy 2001). In other cases funding was left to the city councils or local government structures. However, such outsourcing and the funding of installation and maintenance costs has been a boon to the SAPS, in that while they do not impinge on policing functions they do provide an additional support service for them without requiring any financial outlay or expensive infrastructure. The police have also encouraged such anti-crime CCTV camera surveillance and monitoring services without outsourcing or losing any purely policing functions.

Such implementation, over the last ten years, was largely premised on perceptions regarding the exceptionally high crime levels, an increase in public fears about safety and a declining service delivery from the public police. They in turn were battling with cuts in funding, staff shortages and lack of resources (inter alia vehicles and equipment) compounded by poor training or shortened training periods and an excessive workload. Many people and organizations in South Africa, i.e. private security industry, municipal authorities, businesses, the public and even the police themselves, in some form or another utilized and made use of the resources offered by the private security industry in the fight against crime. One of these has been, in its initial stages, the outsourcing and private funding of CCTV camera surveillance systems.

The roll-out in the late 1990s and early 2000s of each CCTV system in the CBDs of the major metropolitan centres of South Africa was largely couched in very similar terms, namely of being a 'major anti-crime initiative' (Smith 2001) with 'technology catching crooks doing crime' (Boyd 2004). However, it was envisaged that the CCTV systems in the major metropolitan CBDs would play a crucial role in, firstly, monitoring theft or any other criminal acts. Secondly, they would record offences and transgressions, i.e. allowing for the visual verification of events in and around properties and premises and, in the case of public space CCTV activity, in the streets and on sidewalks. Thirdly, they would assist officers on the ground not only to respond but to respond more quickly to incidents (thereby cutting down response times). Fourthly, they would assist in the identification of transgressors, thereby enhancing the success rate in the arrest and convictions of offenders, and act as visual evidence in court. Fifthly, they would act as a 'visible' deterrent in preventing the commission of these crimes. Finally, the presence of the CCTV cameras would ultimately reduce crime. An ancillary aim was to reduce manpower costs to police and security companies; and improve crime prevention efficiencies. In other words, with 'the help of the cameras, a small group of Metro police officers could be "everywhere all the time"' (the deterrence factor) (Hlahla 2005). However, it was also acknowledged that such a system 'cannot on its own stem the rising crime nor help [South Africa's] overburdened criminal justice system' (Own Correspondent 1999).

The extensions of the various metropolitan CCTV crime control and prevention programmes were based not only on the achieved successes of reducing crimes and increasing arrests but also on the identification of additional 'crime hotspot' areas, i.e. high-level occurrence of incidents of crime, outside of the CBDs where the initial systems were introduced.

When the tender to manage the implementation of the Johannesburg CCTV system in the CBD was issued in 1997, it was punted not only as part of the Gauteng Provincial Government's Department for Community Safety's crime-combating strategy, but also in terms of the urban and business renewal plans for the city. It became a central pillar in local and provincial government authorities' plans – the so-called 'Safety Lung' Project of the Department for Community Safety and the City Council's Safer Cities Programme – to attract business and residents back to the city centre after years of decline and rising crime levels. At the time, according to the Gauteng provincial Department of Community Safety's Deputy Director-General, Sylvester Rakgoadi, the use of CCTV as part of the Safety Lung Project and Safer Cities Programme would 'assist in the prevention and detection of crime, help maintain public order, enhance the sense of security of the public and reduce vandalism' (Own Correspondent 1997). In August 2001, at the formal opening of the control centre in the Carlton Centre building for the newly installed and expanded Central Johannesburg CCTV system, Johannesburg's Executive Mayor, Amos Masondo, had punted the system's uses not only for 'crime prevention and deterrence, but also to assist city management in traffic control, fire detection, emergency services alerts, and even refuse collection' (management by identifying refuse pile-ups in streets) (Own Correspondent 2001).

Other aspects of good civic governance were also emphasized. According to Neville Huxham,[4] in addition to the incident-reporting track-and-trace capabilities of the BAC-installed system in Johannesburg, by monitoring the built environment of the city it could also assist with the 'proactive management of the city . . . through [their] macro-area surveillance and facilities management' (Balancing Act News 2005).

By endeavouring to be proactive with a quick response time, not only to crime but also to such things as broken traffic lights and burst water pipes, the system would thereby subtly hold the Metro Council accountable if they did not respond quickly enough to such urban management issues, since 'unmanaged space can be chaotic so crime flourishes' (Balancing Act News 2005). In other words, a well-managed CBD would close down the space for crime to exist.

Besides better civic management of services and the freeing up of manpower, other economic benefits of the installation of such public crime control of CCTVs in CBDs were also put forward in the Johannesburg project. For instance, the control room operators would also be able to 'issue parking tickets so our [BAC(SA)'s] cameras become revenue generators for the city' (Balancing Act News 2005).

All of these CBD-sited CCTV surveillance systems are geared towards providing 'safer and crime-free CBDs' by preventing, deterring as well as 'catching criminals in-the-act'. Underlying this is the economic motive of providing encouragement to economic activity and urban rejuvenation of thecentral business districts. All have largely been accepted as a primary necessity in the national 'fight against crime'. Members of the public rarely question this motivation, and questions of privacy, legality, let alone public approval for installation and funding – obtained via public consultation or public awareness campaigns – are hardly ever raised (see Minnaar 2008).[5]

So, all in all, the CBD CCTV systems in South African metropolitan areas with their initial implementation were promoted as solving or assisting the management of many inner-city problems other than just crime control, crime prevention and the deterrence and reduction of crimes overall.

These CBD CCTV surveillance security systems also increasingly offered or linked their services to other 'stand-alone' services or extended their footprints to other public facilities such as parks, sports facilities or other recreational areas. For instance, the major banking groups in South Africa made communication links from their own surveillance systems inside their bank sites to the particular CBD Central Control Room and sometimes also funded (or paid a monthly monitoring fee) the siting of CBD cameras at the street entrances to their banks. Furthermore, increasing utilization was made of the surveillance capabilities of these CBD surveillance systems by the SAPS during their Special Operations. When such operations were being implemented, extra monitoring personnel were on duty and control rooms were directly linked to the police operation commanders on the ground. Such assistance helped the police to track down and assist in the arrest of wanted criminals in such specific operational areas. Instances of the usage of video footage collected by these surveillance cameras being submitted as evidence in criminal cases and resulting in successful prosecutions – often as the clinching factor – were regularly reported in the press (Peters 2006).

By mid-2010 the CBD CCTV camera surveillance systems in South Africa were installed in most of the major urban centres,[6] even though various management and funding sources had changed since their initial installations, the first being the Cape Town system in December 1998 (see Minnaar 2007).

These CBD systems were all operational by the end of 2004. With their claimed crime prevention and reduction successes, and reported so publicly through the media, their implementation was copied and followed by systems installation at other multiple-use sites.

CCTV camera surveillance on public access property

Public access property refers to sites such as parking areas, commercial business sites such as shopping centres and malls, as well as airports, railway stations and government department service sites (e.g. municipalities and departmental buildings, for instance Home Affairs).

From 2005 onwards, a number of operators/owners/managers of such sites, becoming aware of the apparent effectiveness of the CBD CCTV surveillance systems in the major South African cities, began installing their own systems, particularly in car parks, usually at entrance fee payment sites. The installation of these surveillance systems was again primarily to combat theft from car parks and parking garages, which had long been a problem in South African cities. As a result, all major public parking facilities, such as those at business/shopping complexes and airports, installed state-of-the-art parking control and CCTV surveillance systems to reduce such crime levels. A number of these CCTV camera surveillance systems have also been linked to vehicle registration number plate recognition technology, so that every single vehicle entering and exiting would have its registration number recorded and databased. In order to improve the overall site security and provide control of vehicle entry and exit, some systems have integrated the CCTV surveillance and control room monitoring system (number plate recognition as well as colour of vehicle) with a parking ticket by logging and tying the actual vehicle to the ticket transaction (Coetzer 2005).

Shopping centres' and malls' use of CCTV camera surveillance

For many years individual shops and the larger department chain stores have made use of in-house CCTV camera surveillance systems. While most of these systems were largely simple systems aimed at deterring shoplifting and theft from stores, the bigger stores usually had a small on-site control room with operators monitoring a bank of screens. However, these systems were not always run on a professional basis, being undermanned, having poorly trained operators, i.e. not trained to identify suspicious behaviour, working long shifts (12 hours) and often with camera placements only covering shelves of high-value goods or only over the cashiers and till points. These systems were also only operational during business hours and therefore not linked via motion sensors to the alarm system in order to record any break-ins.[8]

With the increase in business robberies and armed robberies at stores inside shopping centres countrywide, the Consumer Goods Council of South Africa, at the end of 2008, developed guidelines for target hardening at shopping centres. These encouraged shopping centre management/owners to install security CCTV camera surveillance systems throughout their shopping centres and malls, i.e. in the passages, hallways and in the adjacent car park areas, as part of overall integrated security measures at shopping centres. While many shopping centres objected to the costs involved, the festive season (November/December/January) in both 2008 and 2009 saw a high number of armed robberies occurring at shopping malls (Visser 2010; see also Coetzer 2007, 2008). As a consequence, shopping centre owners and managing companies had no alternative but to look for security solutions to protect not only their investments, but also ensuring the safety of retailers, consumers and their respective employees. By mid-2010 all of the major shopping centres had either upgraded existing systems (Visser 2010), or had installed or were installing such integrated security measures. The operational management of such on-site control rooms linked to the CCTV cameras was largely outsourced by centre management/owners to various private security companies[9] (see also Hosken 2008; Hosken 2009; Bailey 2009; Visser 2010).

CCTV surveillance in the private residential domain

While the public open street CCTV surveillance systems in CBDs in South Africa were slowly getting off the ground and becoming operational from the late 1990s and early 2000s onwards, their private property urban residential space CCTV surveillance systems counterparts have been a more recent phenomenon. They are linked to the exponential growth in security estate/village housing complexes and gated neighbourhood enclosures as well as the rollout of Sector Policing and the new Community Safety Initiatives from the end of 2008 onwards (Minnaar 2009, 2010a). Initially CCTV surveillance systems were not part of the general security arrangements for secured private property housing complexes or even gated neighbourhoods. The provision of electric fencing on top of walls/barricades encircling private estates or gated neighbourhoods backed up by inner patrols and guards at boom gate/barrier access control entrance gates was deemed a sufficient level of private security (see Landman 2002, 2003, 2004; and Kruger and Landman 2003 for detail).

In the past, CCTV camera surveillance was largely confined to shopping complexes, car parks at such public access commercial sites and individual private residences. The use of CCTV at sites such as security villages and gated neighbourhoods was largely limited, if used at all, to single camera placements at an entrance gate merely assisting in the identification of people/vehicles wanting to come in.

However, a continued high level of crimes, such as burglaries, house robberies and vehicle hijackings, occurring even inside these walled security estate areas, has seen in the last three years the placement and siting of CCTV cameras not only on perimeter walls or at entrance gates but along the streets (i.e. outside of homes) inside these secure areas.[11]

The development of more sophisticated CCTV surveillance at security estates was largely the result of the continuing development and aggressive marketing of the 'lifestyle security' aspect of security villages, where security becomes an integral factor in providing residents/buyers with 'a safer and more secure area to live in'. An ancillary 'selling' point is the likely increase in property values in a 'secured area'. This approach was tied into the concept of 'total security' – with CCTV camera surveillance being only a part of an overall integrated security system – in order to gain acceptance of the implementation of strict security measures (Landman 2002: 14–18, 21).

If the developers of the security estate houses had not from the outset installed such integrated security systems, body corporates (governing bodies mandated to manage the affairs of such private property secure housing estates) have more recently taken the initiative for such CCTV installations. By the end of 2009, 80 per cent of the 35 security estates in the Greater Tshwane area making up part of an ongoing research project[12] indicated that they had installed some sort of CCTV camera surveillance systems at the specific security estate. The smaller security estates tended to only have one camera at the access control gate entry. This is usually with vehicle licence number plate recognition (LPR) recording capabilities. The larger security estates have a more comprehensive system in place comprising of not only a number plate recognition programmed camera but also a second camera with facial recognition (focused on the driver's face). These systems are equipped with 24/7 recording capabilities on a wireless network (fibre optic being too expensive) and sent through by radio signal to a central control room operated by the private security company contracted to manage all the security at the security estate. Often the same company services a number of estates together as a competitive cost-saving measure. Besides placement of the dual-system cameras at the entry access control boom gate point, some of the bigger security estates have also installed cameras at vulnerable points (perimeter wall corners) and/or at intersections of the streets inside the estates. The smaller systems not linked to a company's central control room or monitored (live) 24/7 would operate a movement/motion sensor system with digital recording of any incident. Recorded incidents could then be downloaded and put on a DVD for evidence purposes (Butler 2010).

This level of proliferation of CCTV surveillance cameras at security estates in Gauteng Province (as at the estates looked at in the study mentioned above) is assumed to be as prevalent at security estates/villages countrywide.

Installation of CCTV cameras in open (i.e. non-security estate type of housing developments) neighbourhoods has also grown apace over the last two years. This development was hastened by the moratorium placed in 2004 on any new road closures and neighborhood gatings in the Gauteng Province (see Minnaar 2010b).

As an alternative to a road closure/boom gate at an entry street to secure or 'gate' a neighbourhood, and what also proved to be more cost-effective in the provision of a more secure area, a number of residents' associations or their representatives through their Community Police Forum (CPF) Sector Committee and the so-called Community Safety Initiatives,[13] usually in co-operation with the national rollout at the beginning of 2009 of the Sector Policing component of the Community Policing Programme, initiated projects to install CCTV cameras at each neighbourhood entry street.

Typically such neighbourhoods have installed a CCTV camera surveillance system[14] comprising of tall pole (mast)-sited cameras[15] at entry points (streets) to the specific neighbourhood.[16] Such monitoring is based on the development of a database of information of movement in and out of specific neighbourhoods by identifying out-of-neighbourhood traffic, and linked to any criminal incident that does occur inside such monitored neighbourhoods. The effectiveness of such a monitoring system is enhanced if there is full commitment of all residents to input all the relevant information of each household onto the database. In other words, the suspicious activity or incident information management is made more effective if such information as the registration of each vehicle, a photo of each household's occupants, details of the street address, etc., is placed on the database. This is done so that movement of such persons and their vehicles is immediately confirmed and then excluded from the analysis of suspicious and incident activity trends which is then typically risk assessed for more effective crime prevention application by either residents' patrols or those of the contracted security company.

CCTV camera surveillance systems implemented at alternative sites

Campus security

All 23 of the state universities[17] in South Africa have implemented CCTV camera surveillance systems on their campuses for the protection of students and staff. These systems have camera footprints that in some cases extend not only across campus grounds but also inside faculty buildings, as well as park-and-ride sites off campus. These systems are typically monitored 24/7 as well as recorded and linked to central control rooms on campus. All of the universities have a Protection Services Unit employed by the university and these operations are funded and managed by the universities themselves (i.e. not outsourced to an outside contract security company). One of the biggest residential universities, the University of Pretoria (UP), with more than 46,000 students, opened a new state-of-the art security surveillance and response centre/control room on their main campus at the end of August 2009, to monitor and provide campus security to staff, students and visitors. Their system consisted of 500 CCTV cameras dotted around the campus – all linked to the control room with 24/7 monitoring and incident recording. While most of these cameras were installed inside the UP premises, others monitored activity around residences and areas just off/adjacent to the campus (Bateman 2009). It would appear that private universities (e.g. Damelin and Varsity College) have also begun instituting campus security CCTV surveillance systems on their campuses.[18]

CCTV at schools

In South African schools, particularly high schools (Grades 7–12), there is a growing trend towards the use of CCTV camera surveillance systems. These are not only on perimeter fences (for the prevention of theft and break-ins[19]) but also as a form of control and discipline by the placement of cameras in corridors, on the playgrounds/sports facilities and in ablution facilities, i.e. used for the surveillance of areas that are not openly watched by staff members. Such systems also serve the purpose of protecting the school after hours and during holidays and to prevent incidents of vandalism. Typically, these systems are only on a motion sensor activating recording system. In other words, incidents are only recorded as they happen (no 24/7 monitoring by a control room operator which is usually too expensive for schools to afford). While such systems are being installed, they are only at those schools that can afford them since no such systems are or have been funded by either the National Department of Education or the provincial education departments. Accordingly they have largely been installed only at the so-called Model C Schools.[20] Video footage so obtained of incidents (of violence, even of stabbings and shootings) has been used not only in disciplinary hearings of scholars but also in the conviction of various crimes. The use of the video footage as evidence in these cases appears now to be readily accepted by staff, parents and scholars as part of the overall management of such schools operations and become part of the Code of Conduct for these schools (see Van Jaarsveld 2010).

Automatic Teller Machine (ATM) CCTV protection

With the high level of ATM bombings occurring in South Africa,[21] the four major banks in South Africa were forced to 'harden' ATMs and implement a range of security measures at ATM sites. One of these measures was the installation of CCTV cameras. This was done mostly at so-called 'high risk sites', which are commonly at petrol stations and inside small convenience stores. ATMs at banks or at the large shopping centres are covered by the banks' own in-bank CCTV systems. The costs of this installation are carried by the banks themselves and/or shared with the banks by the petrol station site owner/franchisee or convenience store owner. Currently there are an estimated 15,000 ATMs, of which an estimated 30 per cent are considered to be 'high risk'.

To assist the banks' own ATM surveillance systems, the Gauteng provincial government began in November 2008 with the installation of 195 cameras watching over 40 high-risk ATM spots in the province. The planning for this additional surveillance was done jointly by the Gauteng provincial Department for Community Safety, the SAPS, the South African Banking Risk Information Centre

(SABRIC) and the South African Banking Council. The banks paid for part of the system. Each of these sites has at least four CCTV cameras, which run a feed to a central monitoring station (the provincial emergency/disaster recovery control room) in Midrand (Flanagan 2010).

While video footage from the CCTV cameras at the high-risk sites has been used to determine such aspects as modus operandi, duration of the bombing, explosives used, getaway transport, numbers of perpetrators in bombing gang and firearms carried by them, such video footage has not always been able to positively identify the criminals in order to prosecute and convict them. This is because the majority of perpetrators caught on the video evidence wore balaclavas (hence the low level of successful convictions) (see Sewpersad 2010).

However, CCTV camera surveillance at ATMs has become an integral cog in the police investigations not only of ATM bombings, but also of bank robberies and cash-in-transit heists[22] in South Africa. While it is believed that such systems do not deter armed robbers/bombers per se, the surveillance videos from ATMs, inside banks and incash-in-transit armoured vehicles have assisted the special police task team on ATM bombings, bank robberies and cash-in-transit heists in the identification of the perpetrators and the building up of an images database of perpetrators for future use (in court and possible linking to multiple bank robberies, cash-in-transit heists and ATM bombings by the same gangs). A number of robberies/muggings has also occurred in the vicinity of ATMs where members of the public have been robbed of their cash withdrawals. In a number of these cases the video footage has assisted in the apprehension of the perpetrators (since they do not wear balaclavas while robbing as such camouflage would obviously alert an ATM client of the impending robbery). These successes have re-assured members of the public that such surveilled ATMs are 'secure and safe' and such security measures are there for the ultimate safety of the users and serve the purpose of crime prevention and deterrence.

Petrol (gasoline) stations

CCTV camera surveillance systems have also been installed at many of the petrol stations[23] in South Africa, not only in response to ATM bombings (if such ATMs were on their premises) but also in response to such crimes as 'drive-offs',[24] petrol card fraud, in-store[25] theft and robberies and even assaults on premises. Such CCTV camera surveillance systems are therefore not only a crime prevention/deterrence tool but also for the safety and protection of staff and customers, particularly of the on-site convenience stores. In research conducted by Kole (2010: 57), 72 per cent of the petrol stations surveyed had a CCTV system in place, and 78 per cent of these systems covered the whole forecourt of the petrol station premises (Kole 2010: 58). The existence of such CCTV camera surveillance systems at petrol stations (unless the cameras are conspicuously sited on the premises) is generally not known by the on-site convenience store customers or the motorists filling up with fuel (Kole 2010: 39). Video footage obtained from these cameras has also been used by the police when investigating all these crimes, although much of the pre-2010 footage was of a poor quality or there were problems with the operations (cameras out of order, not being maintained and serviced). The SAPS make frequent requests to petrol station owners/operators to upgrade their existing systems or install more modern cameras with better capabilities (e.g. colour and night-time recording, etc.) (see Kole 2010).

The FIFA Soccer World Cup 2010, South Africa

The hosting of the FIFA Soccer World Cup (SWC) in South Africa (June–July 2010) gave a further boost to the national footprint of CCTV camera surveillance systems (see Vonn, this volume, on mega-events and surveillance cameras). All the host cities increased the number of cameras installed, not only around the soccer stadium venues, but also at potential high-risk areas such as railway stations, and recreational clubs and restaurant areas in the suburbs. Pretoria, for instance, installed an additional 100 cameras at various crime 'hotspots' in a number of policing precincts (Staff Reporter 2010a). The Security Plan for the SWC 2010 (see Minaar and Van Jaarsveld 2010) required that CCTV cameras be placed in every one of the ten match stadiums in order for crowd control and to record any incident. In addition, cameras were installed at all the pedestrian approaches and entry points to the stadium precinct areas and in the stadium car parks. These cameras and the CBD surveillance network systems were, on match days, linked to the National SWC Joint Operations Centre Control Room, where they were monitored. This blanket surveillance system was also in direct communications contact with all the extra police officers and security officers deployed on the ground for their rapid and immediate response to any crime situation or incident developing or occurring in the camera footprint areas.

Into Africa

While South Africa has been the African contintental leader in the extensive implementation of CCTV camera surveillance systems, limited use of such systems has occurred elsewhere in Africa. However, such use has been constrained by the inability of most African states/governments to fund any public CCTV camera surveillance systems on any large scale (with the exception of Egypt). Those systems that are in place (and there are very few of these across the continent) have largely been installed and funded by the private sector or in private/public partnerships. Systems in place are often linked to the provision of protection or security at such sites as mines, oilfields and refineries (e.g. a number of mines in the Democratic Republic of the Congo (DRC), as part of the security services provided by the contracted security company installing CCTV cameras linked to an on-site control room and monitored and with recordings 24/7) (Van Niekerk 2010).

In a few African countries there are single or at best a few such systems operational in selected cities that have been either privately funded or the installation costs have been funded by the local city council. Operating and maintenance costs are funded by levies on local businesses in the surveilled city centres. Examples here are Lagos in Nigeria, Nairobi in Kenya and Dar es Salaam in Tanzania where, on the initiative of South African banks with branches in these cities, the local city councils were encouraged to implement some sort of limited CBD CCTV camera surveillance systems. The installation costs are funded by city councils but operational costs via levies on big business, and management and maintenance are outsourced to private security companies. There are, however, more extensive networks of private security systems, inter alia incorporating CCTV cameras that have been installed to protect the private residences of the wealthy and of politicians in many of the capital cities of African countries (e.g. Abuja in Nigeria, Luanda in Angola, and the cities mentioned above).

In Lagos, in 2008/9 under the Lagos State Government-funded Private/Public Partnership Initiative, an international IT firm, CISCO, installed surveillance cameras at 'strategic' locations around the city (for security reasons these were never made public but were largely at identified crime 'hotspots') (Affe 2008). The CCTV camera surveillance system was manned by 'trained security personnel' monitoring it on a 24/7 basis to 'capture images and identities of suspects and people indulging in other forms of crimes' (Bassey 2008). The Lagos CCTV project was part of the Lagos state-wide inter-connectivity network and e-payment system. This was for toll roads and traffic ticketing purposes, as well as linked to the proposed Lagos State centralised social security database, inaugurated in September 2008 by the Lagos State Governor, Babatunde Fashola (Affe 2008). This system was also designed to video and track various traffic offences (by having Licence Plate Recognition (LPR) capabilities), especially on the new Bus Rapid Transit (BRT) corridor in the city. This technology enabled the Lagos State Traffic Management Authority (LASTMA) to apprehend culprits at their leisure, i.e. not immediately after the offence occurred (Bassey 2008). However, there were bureaucratic, funding and installation delays, and by the beginning of 2010 only parts of the Lagos system were operational.

In Windhoek, the capital city of Namibia, the local municipality council towards the end of 2008 went out on tender for the installation and management of a CBD and other public spaces CCTV camera surveillance system. This small system (an initial 16 cameras installed in the CBD) was implemented in late 2009. This system was operated and managed by the Windhoek City Police,[26] and based on a crime prevention surveillance system using a computerized crime register and mapping system focused on the identification and monitoring of crime 'hotspots'. This Windhoek City Police surveillance monitoring is further backed up by co-operation with local security companies and neighbourhood watches to increase the reporting of criminal activities in the various areas of Windhoek (Isaacs 2009a, 2009b).[27] This was the first and only such publicly funded surveillance system in Namibia.

In Gabon (west coast of Africa) only three CCTV camera surveillance systems have to date been implemented in the whole of the country. All of them are state-funded but installed and operated by a South African private security company[28] – namely in Libreville, Franceville and Port Gentil (the three biggest cities in Gabon). The Libreville system has 96 cameras operational, covering the city centre, with another 16 cameras in the suburbs (covering government ministers' residences). In Franceville there are 16 CBD cameras in place, while in Port Gentil there are 32 cameras. However, all three systems appear to have been motivated by government fears of civil/political unrest or a military coup, since the cameras have been sited to cover strategic buildings and ministerial residences and places where crowds traditionally gather for political protests (Le Grange and De Koker 2010).

The situation in Egypt would appear slightly different to that in other African countries (excluding South Africa). For instance in the capital city of Cairo[29] extensive government funded and operated (police/military/intelligence departments) CCTV camera surveillance systems have been implemented. These systems are security focused in that almost every government departmental building and state/ministerial/politician's official residence – the latter of which are largely concentrated only in one of the more upmarket areas of Cairo – is covered by an integrated centralized system of CCTV camera monitoring. This system has also been extended to cover the main arterial street routes into the city centre of Cairo from the international airport on the outskirts to the main highways/streets, for instance from the Pyramids at Giza. These street cameras are more for the use of traffic control than security (Hamoda 2010).[30]

However, other than these surveillance systems there appears to be no public open street CCTV camera systems in place in Egypt. This is largely due to the fact that in all other areas (Cairo and other major Egyptian cities such as Alexandria, Luxor and Aswan), especially the tourist areas and hotels, there is the constant presence, either on patrol or in guard huts, of members of the Tourist Protection and Antiquities Police of the Egyptian police (Hamoda 2010).[31]

Some concluding remarks

The above examples of the use of CCTV camera surveillance technology and systems are by no means the only areas of use. For instance, the South African National Roads Agency Limited (SANRAL), with all the road and transport upgrades associated with the hosting of the FIFA World Cup in South Africa in 2010, also began the installation of CCTV camera systems along all the major highways in urban centres. While the primary function of these highway camera surveillance systems is traffic control and vehicle accident monitoring, other functions are linked to their operation. For instance, the new electronic tolling systems currently being built on Gauteng Province's main routes, linking Johannesburg with Pretoria, are being incorporated into the surveillance systems. This system, when operational, will automatically toll every vehicle based on a LPR registration system linked to each vehicle owner's bank account (e-tag) (Hosken 2010). Obviously the system can also serve as a crime control measure for stolen vehicles and other traffic offences, and is mooted to assist police, for instance in tracking vehicle chases of suspects who might have perpetrated any crime and are making their getaway on the highways. Cameras have also been installed along the new high-speed Gautrain rail line, while all of the international airport sites also have CCTV camera surveillance security systems in place.

The management, installation, operation and maintenance of CCTV camera surveillance systems in major prisons (by numbers of inmates and physical size) in South Africa was outsourced two years ago to a private security company as part of integrated physical security measures. They were also linked to the in-house prison tracking and management of incarcerated prisoners (Kriel 2010).

In October 2009, after a number of road accidents involving the long-distance buses of one particular company, SARoadlink, the company instituted a system of on-board CCTV cameras. Four CCTV cameras were installed on each bus, one focused on the driver, another on the road and two on the passengers. This allowed the control room centre at the company's central depot at City Deep, Johannesburg to monitor each trip and communicate directly with the driver should a problem arise (Barbeau 2009).

An interesting new field/development in the use of CCTV camera surveillance has been its use for the protection of wildlife on private game farms/reserves and in the national game parks (other than normal access control usage at entry gates) from poachers. The 'trigger' for the installation of surveillance cameras at strategic points along game farm/reserve perimeter fences came from the huge increase in poaching generally, but more specifically the shooting of rhinoceroses for their horns.[32] This is to supply the lucrative 'aphrodisiac/health medicine' Asian market. By October 2010 a number of the more upmarket game farms/reserves had installed such systems. The control and management of these are off-site and done by private security companies. This monitoring has been made possible by modern technology where such central control rooms are sited hundreds of kilometres away in a city, e.g. Pretoria (Malan 2010). A more recent development in this war against poachers has been the experimentation of using a camera mounted on a drone robotic model helicopter[33] controlled by an operator in the control room. Individual rhinos can be monitored and tracked from the air throughout such a game park. Rhinos tend to graze in one small preferred area. They are not like some other game, wandering over large areas while feeding. This has allowed them to be fitted with radio transmitters. If sudden movement is detected, an alarm is activated and the operator can then launch the drone in the area (off a platform in the bush) to put an 'eye in the sky' immediately. This drone can then track and 'see' whether the sudden rhino movement has been precipitated by the presence of poachers. A reaction team is then despatched by helicopter to try to catch the poachers while the drone continues to track any activity.

The South African experience in the increased proliferation of surveillance camera CCTV systems appears to track the growth and usage in the developed world, inclusive of the utilization of advanced technology in support of such surveillance systems. However, the lead funding would appear to be from the private sector or in private–public partnerships. Furthermore, its ready acceptance as a crime deterrent, prevention and combating tool within integrated security measures systems is strongly predicated on perceptions of high crime levels and feelings of insecurity by communities themselves. This acceptance has been built on public claims of its effectiveness in reducing crime in communities, open public spaces and at commercial sites such as car parks and shopping centres. This in turn has led to its increased installation to protect private residences/neighbourhoods funded by residents themselves. Many are also specialized, customized and site- specific, such as at ATMs and petrol stations. In other words, use is focused and specialized. Images are consistently handed over to police investigators for use in crime investigation of specific incidents.

While generally lagging behind developed countries in terms of numbers and size, as well as studies on impact, effectiveness, crime combating capabilities and even privacy issues, South Africa has been way ahead of the rest of Africa in its use and implementation of surveillance camera systems. But African countries, taking their lead from South Africa and often using service provider companies based in South Africa, are also starting to implement private–public funded surveillance camera systems.

In its major urban areas, South Africa is fast becoming a blanket surveilled country, with cameras literally all over private and public spaces. CCTV camera surveillance as a security and crime combating measure has been identified by government, police, municipal authorities as well as business and residential sectors as a key aspect of modern crime prevention systems, and is no longer predominantly the realm of the retail and gambling sectors as it once was. Today it is found in all areas where it has become a crime prevention and protection system of choice. While the basic technology has been around for many years, cutting-edge technology is now allowing it to be incorporated into integrated building management systems that also offer other desired services such as fire and other emergency management and access control. In addition, it is increasingly being used by authorities to monitor and control traffic flow and enhance road safety. This, along with the ability to run these systems from centralized off-site monitoring control rooms manned by trained professionals, is where its appeal lies today (see Griffiths-Reid 2007).

Many companies in South Africa have embraced CCTV camera surveillance primarily as a crime deterrent within a total crime prevention package. It is also used as a vital tool to aid not only the detection of crime but also to assist in arrests and prosecutions with the use of video/DVR recorded images (for evidence in building a case against suspects). CCTV camera surveillance as a crime reduction measure is only of value where it is installed as part of overall security measures. While perceptions from communities abound about its efficacy in reducing crime, in actual fact this has not been definitively linked to such reductions that have occurred. However, its prime value is linked more to perceptions and feelings of increased safety in those neighbourhoods installing them as part of overall Community Safety Initiatives (see Minnaar 2010a) and in its increasing use of recorded images to track movements of suspects in the perpetration of crimes. It also serves as a strong deterrent to the actual commission of crimes. In South Africa it is currently also being widely used as part of integrated safety and security management systems that offer accident, fire and other emergency response capabilities.

This growth and installation of blanket-type camera footprints will, in the foreseeable future, predictably continue apace in South Africa in line with worldwide trends.

Notes

1 See Minnaar 2007.
2 An exception has been the work on CCTV and control room operators' training and operations by the internationally recognized expert, Dr Craig Donald.
3 The first legal casinos in South Africa were only allowed to open in the former 'independent homelands/Bantustans' in the early 1980s, with the first one opening at Sun City in the former Bophuthatswana in the current North West Province of South Africa. These all made use of CCTV camera surveillance in their gambling areas.
4 Marketing and Communications Manager of Cueincident, the commercial company set up out of the BAC(SA)'s Surveillance Technology division.
5 In responses to street surveys administered in the four CBDs of Cape Town, Durban, Johannesburg and Pretoria during February 2007, the main reason given for why CCTV surveillance was installed in their respective CBDs was in the line of crime reduction/ crime control/crime investigation (prevention of hijackings, theft, muggings, selling of drugs, gang activity, etc.) in those areas. A further response to the question 'What improvements can you suggest?' was that many said 'Install more cameras' (Minnaar 2008).
6 Number of CBD network cameras: Cape Town: 178; Johannesburg: 231; Pretoria: 168 (expansions into outlying CBDs: Hatfield: 28; Laudium: 15); Durban (eThekweni Metropolitan Council) 220; Pietermaritzburg: 96; Port-Elizabeth: 14; Kimberley: 24; Bloemfontein: 14; Ekurhuleni Metropolitan Municipality (East Rand): 36; Mohale City (West Rand): Krugersdorp: 12); Randfontein: 10; two cameras in Westonaria. This number excludes additions made for the FIFA Soccer World Cup in 2010.
7 The Johannesburg system reported an 80 per cent drop in reported crime and boasted of a response time of only 60 seconds to any incident with 'hundreds of successful arrests . . . been made as a result of video footage which has been presented in court as evidence' (Cox 2006).
8 This information was obtained while the author and a colleague (F.C. Rogers) undertook a risk assessment of security measures at the stores for a major supermarket/retail chain in South Africa.
9 This information emanates from a work-in-progress study for a masters by N. Lutchminarain, titled 'An examination of current security measures at shopping malls: Case studies from Gauteng'.
10 In Landman's research on the spatial manifestation of neighbourhood gating and road enclosures there is little emphasis or mention of electronic camera (CCTV) surveillance systems, largely because, at the time of the research (2001–3) they were not a part of overall gated community security systems. A security risk audit conducted at a security golf estate in Pretoria by Butler (2003) found that no CCTV at all was being used as part of any security measures.
11 These surveillance systems have become technically sophisticated, based on multi-zone perimeter intrusion detection systems using CCTV camera surveillance that utilizes motion detection and video analytics, wireless streaming, fixed and high-speed pan-tilt-zoom cameras; fibre optic motion detection systems based on an intelligent electrified wall/palisade/fence with vibration detection for under-dig, break-through and climb-over of perimeter barricades (walls/fences/palisades) – all linked to a central control room (Impro technologies 2009).

12 This information emanates from preliminary findings from a Programme: Security Management, UNISA Research Project titled: 'An assessment of the crime prevention impact of security measures/strategies at gated communities (security residential estates & enclosed neighbourhoods) in Gauteng'.

13 See Minnaar 2010a for more detail on this.

14 The information in this section emanates from an ongoing research project by the author titled Community Policing and Community Safety Initiatives, and is centred on five policing precincts comprising of 25 sectors in the Pretoria East area of the Tshwane Metropolitan Council region in Gauteng Province.

15 The initial installed system made use only of one camera for licence number plate recognition (LPR) but the most advanced system (currently operational in the Val de Grace area of Pretoria East) has eight cameras mounted at the neighbourhood entrance – two cameras dedicated for vehicle licence number recognition; two for facial recognition (in vehicle); two for pedestrian movement; one for an overview at site; one covering guard hut at camera site. Such a comprehensive system using all the available surveillance camera technology is more cost-effective than the old boomgate access control labour-intensive systems previously used for enclosed or gated neighbourhoods (Malan 2010).

16 One of the longest-running (three years) of such systems in the Pretoria East area (Faerie Glen suburb) has cameras mounted on poles at three entry points, but this system (one camera for LPR and one for an overview at each entry point) – monitored 24/7 with digital recording and wireless operated – has also been linked to the current 90 cameras placed on private residences(clients of the security company). These cameras on private property are motion activated and the control room operators can link each camera to the main surveillance system so that any movement past such private residences can be tracked in a continuous real-time line of observation. Each of the separate 'private' 90 cameras can also be monitored individually off-site at the company's control room (Kniep 2010).

17 This includes the one non-residential but open distance-learning institution, the University of South Africa, whose campuses are frequented by students, i.e. although non-residential campus security is there also for staff members.

18 Information from an ongoing work-in-progress departmental research project by L. Van Jaarsveld and S. Sewpersad titled: 'Campus Security in South Africa'.

19 Typically computers/laptops and video and sound system equipment have become a target for criminals in these night-time break-ins.

20 These are public government-funded schools that have established School Governing Boards elected from the parent body and have been allowed by the government to charge annual school fees and thereby been able to fund the building of extra facilities, additional teachers, and projects like CCTV cameras – all of which the State has been unable to fund.

21 Between January 2006 and March 2009, the total number of ATM bombings in South Africa was 873, with the highest number of incidents (527) occurring in the Gauteng Province (Sewpersad 2010: 3).

22 Cameras have been placed inside and at the back of armoured cash-in-transit vehicles by the three main security companies involved in the transport of cash, not only to allow the driver and guards inside the vehicle to view what is happening around them, e.g. a heist in progress if approached from the rear, but also to record any such heist in progress. These measures were in response to the high level of C-I-T heists. In the 2006/7 reporting year, a high of 467 C-I-T heists occurred, dropping marginally to 395 in 2007/8; 386 in 2008/9 and 358 in 2009/10 (SAPS 2010).

23 There are an estimated (2008) 6,500 petrol stations operating in South Africa (Kole 2010).

24 Where a motorist drives off without paying the petrol attendant for the purchase of petrol.

25 Many petrol stations in South Africa, to become more economically viable since the petrol price and profit margin are strictly controlled by the government, have installed

small convenience stores on their premises, most of them operating 24/7 (i.e. all night as well).

26 The Windhoek City Police included the Emergency Management Division, of which the Windhoek Fire Brigade formed a part. Accordingly the CCTV system was also intended for the monitoring of emergencies and the possible outbreak of fires.

27 The author was approached to be a consultant by one of the private companies tendering for this project.

28 Coincidentally, the same South African security company is in a far-advanced stage of implementing a purely security/crime-prevention CBD public system in Gaberone, the capital city of Botswana (a neighbour country to South Africa).

29 The largest city in Africa with an estimated 27 million inhabitants (out of a current estimate of 83 million total population).

30 While most of the big tourist resort holiday complexes (particularly along the Red Sea and Sinai Peninsula coastlines) have good security measures – one access point with boom gate, perimeter walls and patrolling guards – in place for the protection of tourist guests, very few of them have installed CCTV surveillance cameras since they base their security on 24/7 patrolling guards linked to a two-way radio local network. This system has been opted for by the resort in-house security as the most cost-effective security measure for the protection of guests (security personnel are a relatively cheaper option than CCTV camera surveillance systems with central control rooms and costs of operations and maintenance) (Hamoda 2010).

31 This was confirmed by observations by the author on a trip to Egypt, 7–17 September 2010. In 2008, 83 rhinos were killed; in 2009 this figure was 122, and up to the end of October 2010 a total of 227 had been shot and killed (Staff Reporter 2010b).

32 This offer to assist the SANParks anti-poaching efforts came from the South African National Defence Force (SANDF), where one of their suppliers, Denel (a subsidiary of ARSMCOR), had developed an 'unmanned aerial vehicle (UAV)' or 'drone' for reconnaissance purposes (SAPA 2010).

References

Affe, M. (2008) 'Lagos CCTV project faces delay', *The Punch*, 19 November. Online. Available HTTP: <http://www.punchng.com> (accessed 24 August 2010).

Balancing Act (2005) Cue incident uses CDMA for crime reduction surveillance. In: CDMA special – cost and tech advantages but can it break into Africa's GSM markets. *Balancing Act News Update*, Issue No. 248. Online. Available HTTP: <http://www.balancingact-africa.com/news/back/balancing-act%20248.html> (accessed 26 July 2005).

Bailey, C. (2009) 'Experts slam security at malls after bloody heists', *Pretoria News*, 16 August: 3.

Barbeau, N. (2009) 'How we're making our buses safer – SA Roadlink', *Pretoria News*, 20 October. Online. Available HTTP: <http://www.pretorianews.co.za/general/print_article.php?fArticleId=5210636> (accessed 6 June 2010).

Bassey, J. (2008) 'New dawn in crime detection as Lagos plans CCTV', *Business Day*, 3 October. Online. Available HTTP: <http://www.businessdayonline.com/index.php?option=com_content&view=article&id=510:new-dawn-in-crime-detection-as-lagos-plans-cctv&catid=85:national&Itemid=340> (accessed 11 October 2010).

Bateman, B. (2009) 'Lights, cameras, action! Tuks tightens security', *Pretoria News*, 26 August. Online. Available HTTP: <http://www.pretorianews.co.za/general/print_article.php?fArticleId=5140547> (accessed 3 September 2010).

Botha, C. (2010) Policing and the FIFA World Cup: What lessons can be learned for policing in the future? Presentation to the Institute for Security Studies Conference: Policing in South Africa: 2010 and beyond, Kloofzicht Lodge, Muldersdrift. 30 September–1 October 2010.

Boyd, D. (2004) 'Big brother is watching you', *Business Day* (Technology Top 100 Business Directory). Online. Available HTTP: <http://www.196.4.91.173/toptech_2004/DisplayStory.asp?StoriesID%20%20=41> (accessed 26 July 2005).

Butler, O. (2003) *Woodhill Residential Estate Country Club Security Manual.* Unpublished report. UNISA, Department of Security Risk Management. Pretoria.

Coetzer, B. (2005) 'Park safe', *Hi-Tech Security Solutions,* 11(1), January. Online. Available HTTP: <http://securitysa.com> (accessed 22 September 2010).

Coetzer, B. (2007) 'Control room integration platform the key to effective shopping centre and street security', *Hi-Tech Security Solutions,* 13(4). Online. Available HTTP: <http://securitysa.com> (accessed 22 September 2010).

Coetzer, B. (2008) 'Command and control for shopping centres', *Hi-Tech Security Solutions,* 14(4). Online. Available HTTP: <http://securitysa.com> (accessed 22 September 2010).

Consumer Goods Council of South Africa (CGCSA) (2008?) *Armed Robberies: Protection for Shopping Centres.* Online. Available HTTP: <http://www.cgccrime.org.za/archive/bestpractices/BP%20Target%20Hardening.pdf> (accessed 6 June 2010).

Cox, A. (2006) 'Cameras ensure inner Joburg is safer, cleaner', *The Star,* 31 January.

Donald, C. (2004) 'How many monitors should a CCTV operator view?', *Hi-Tech Security Solutions: The Industry Journal for Security & Business Professionals.* Technews. 10(12). Online. Available HTTP: <http://securitysa.com/article.aspx?pklArticleid=3313&pklCategoryID=3>(accessed 7 June 2009).

Donald, C. (2007) 'CCTV control room design considerations', *Hi-Tech Security Solutions: The Industry Journal for Security & Business Professionals.* Technews. April. 13(4). Online. Available HTTP: <http://securitysa.com/regular.aspx?pklRegularid=2916&pklCategoryID=3> (accessed 7 June 2009).

Donald, C. (2009) 'Optimising camera viewing in control rooms', *Hi-Tech Security Solutions: The Industry Journal for Security & Business Professionals.* Technews. May: 15(5). Online. Available HTTP: <http://securitysa.com/article.aspx?pklArticleid=5627&pklCategoryID=3> (accessed 7 June 2009).

Ekurhuleni Metropolitan Municipality (2009) *Annual Report for 2008/2009.* Online. Available HTTP: <http://www.ekurhuleni.com> (accessed 27 July 2010).

Ethekwini Municipality (2008) *Annual Report 2007/2008.* Online. Available HTTP: <http://www.dbncc.co.za> (accessed 27 July 2010).

Flanagan, L. (2010) Website reveals bank secrets to ATM bombers, *Pretoria News,* 13 July. Online. Available HTTP: <http://www.pretorianews.co.za/general/print_article.php?fArticleId=5554707> (accessed 11 October 2010).

Griffiths-Reid Associates (2007) *White Paper on CCTV Operators.* May. Online. Available HTTP: <http://www.griffithsreid.co.za> (accessed 27 June 2008).

Hlahla, P. (2005) 'Street cameras cut city crime', *Pretoria News,* 6 January.

Hlahla, P. (2010) 'CCTV for Laudium crime hot spots', *Pretoria News,* 7 July. Online. Available HTTP: <http://www.pretorianews.co.za/general/print_article.php?fArticleId=5546729> (accessed 8 August 2010).

Hosken, G. (2008) 'City malls among SA's most dangerous', *Pretoria News,* 18 September: 3.

Hosken, G. (2009) 'You are not safe!', *Pretoria News,* 1 October: 1.

Hosken, G. (2010) 'Hi-tech bid to curb woes of motorists: New toll plan to cost 50c/km', *Pretoria News,* 5 July. Online. Available HTTP: <http://www.pretorianews.co.za/general/print_article.php?fArticleId=5542409> (accessed 27 July 2010).

Impro Technologies (2009) 'A power development for Serengeti', *Hi-Tech Security Solutions*, 15(5), May. Online. Available HTTP: <http://securitysa.com/regular.aspx?pklregularid=4027> (accessed 22 September 2010).

Isaacs, D. (2009a) 'Namibia: Big Brother will be watching you in Windhoek – soon', *The Namibian*, 20 May.

Isaacs, D. (2009b) 'CCTV cameras coming soon', *The Namibian,* 3 July. Online. Available: <http://www.namibian.com.na/index.php?id=28&tx_ttnews%5btt_news%5d=57033&no_cache=1> (accessed 22 September 2010).

Kole, O.J. (2010) *An Examination of Security Measures for the Protection of Petrol Stations: An Analysis of Case Studies in Gauteng*. Unpublished MTech: Security Management dissertation. Department of Criminology & Security Science, University of South Africa, Pretoria.

Kruger, T. and Landman, K. (2003) Living in an enclaved society: Practical implications of environmental design. Paper delivered to the Institute for Municipal Law Enforcement of Southern Africa (IMLE) Conference: *The Reality of Law Enforcement: Facing Common Challenges to Ensure Local Governance*, Pretoria, South Africa, 30–31 October.

Landman, K. (2002) Gated communities in South Africa: Building bridges or barriers? Paper presented to the *International Conference on Private Urban Governance*, Mainz, Germany, 6–9 June.

Landman, K. (2003) Alley-gating and neighbourhood gating: Are they two sides of the same face? Paper delivered at the conference, *Gated Communities: Building Social Division or Safer Communities?*, Glasgow, Scotland, 18–19 September.

Landman, K. (2004) Who owns the roads? Privatising public space in South African cities through neighbourhood enclosures. Paper delivered at the conference, *Privatisation of Urban Space*, New Orleans, USA, 26–27 February.

Minnaar, A. (2007) 'The implementation and impact of crime prevention/crime control open street Closed-Circuit Television surveillance in South African Central Business Districts', *Surveillance & Society*, 4(3): 174–207.

Minnaar, A. (2008) Closed-circuit television (CCTV) surveillance in central business districts (CBDs): Street surveys from four South African cities. Paper presented to the XVth World Congress of the International Society of Criminology: *Crime and Criminology – Research and Action*, Barcelona, Spain, 20–25 July.

Minnaar, A. (2009) 'Community policing in a high crime transitional state: The case of South Africa since democratization in 1994', in D. Wisler and I.D. Onwudiwe (eds), *Community Policing: International Patterns and Comparative Perspectives*, Boca Raton: CRC Press/Taylor & Francis Group, 19–57.

Minnaar, A. (2010a) 'The changing face of "Community Policing" in South Africa, post-1994?', *Acta Criminologica: Southern African Journal of Criminology*. CRIMSA 2009 Conference Special Edition 2 2010, 189–210.

Minnaar, A. (2010b) 'Balancing public safety & security demands with civil liberties in a new constitutional democracy: The case of post-1994 South Africa and the growth of residential security and surveillance measures', in K. Haggerty and M. Samatas (eds), *Surveillance and Democracy*, London: Routledge, 195–212.

Minnaar, A. and Van Jaarsveld, L. (2010) *International Event Security: The Case of the Security Plan for the FIFA Soccer World Cup, South Africa 2010*. Keynote paper presented to the 17th Annual International Police Executive Symposium: *Tourism, Strategic Locations & Major Events – Policing in an Age of Mobility, Mass Movement and Migration*, Valletta, Malta,14–19 March.

Own Correspondent (1997) 'UK engineer to manage Jo'Burg CCTV', *Business Day*, 9 August.

Own Correspondent (1999) 'Cape Town walks without fear', *Business Day*, 12 April.

Own Correspondent (2001) 'Joburg launches CCTV', *News24*, 3 August. Online. Available HTTP: <www.news24.com/News24/Archives/0,,2-1659_1061669,00.html> (accessed 21 June 2005).

Penberthy, J. (2001) *Surveillance Technology: International Best Practice and Securing a Standard: A National Priority.* Presentation to the 2nd World Conference on Modern Criminal Investigation, Organized Crime and Human Rights, ICC, Durban, 3–7 December.

Peters, S. (2006) 'Surveillance camera evidence shows killing', *Daily News*, 3 March.

SAPA (2010) 'SANDF to use drones to catch poachers', *IOL Online*, 25 November. Online. Available HTTP: <http://www.iol.co.za/news/science/sandf-to-use-drone-to-catch-poachers-1.877162> (accessed 25 November 2010).

Sewpersad, S. (2010) *An Investigation of the Bombing of Automated Teller Machines (ATMs) with Intent to Steal Cash Contents: Case Study from Gauteng.* MTech: Security Management dissertation. Unpublished. Department of Criminology & Security Science, University of South Africa, Pretoria.

Smith, A. (2001) 'Cape Town takes stand against holiday crime', *Cape Times*, 10 December. Online. Available HTTP: <http://www.iol.co.za/general/news/newsprint.php?art_id=ct2001121025150434444A25> (accessed 8 July 2005).

South African Police Service (SAPS) (2010) *Annual Report 2009/10.* Online. Available HTTP: <http://www.saps.co.za/saps.profile/strategic_framework/annual_report/2009_2010" www.saps.co.za/saps.profile/strategic_framework/annual_report/2009_2010> (accessed 15 December 2010).

Staff Reporter (2010a) 'Less than a month to go, and city is ready for the Cup', *Pretoria News*, 11 May. Online. Available HTTP: <http://www.pretorianews.co.za/general/print_article.php?fArticleId=5466456> (accessed 6 June 2010).

Staff Reporter (2010b) 'A strategy to get to grips with poachers', *Pretoria News*, 29 October: 26.

Van Jaarsveld, L. (2010) *Securing our Schools: An Investigation on Safety and Security Measures at Secondary Schools in Tshwane, South Africa.* MTech: Security Management dissertation. Department of Criminology & Security Science, University of South Africa, Pretoria.

Visser, W. (2010) 'Liberty Properties enhances mall security', *Hi-Tech Security Solutions*, 16(6): 71, June. Online. Available HTTP: <http://securitysa.com> (accessed 22 September 2010).

West Rand District Municipality (Mohale City) (2009) *Annual Report 2008/2009.* Online. Available HTTP: <http://www.linkedin.com/redirect?url=http%3A%2F%2Fwww%2Ewrdm%2Egov%2Eza&urlhash=Ut4i> (accessed 27 July 2010).

Interviews

Butler, O.S. (2010) Director: IQ Security. Pretoria. Telephone interview. 27 July.

De Koker, M. (2010) Operational Manager: Johannesburg CBD Control Room, Omega Risk Solutions (SA), Johannesburg. Telephone interview. 16 October.

Le Grange, T. (2010) Director: Technical, Omega Risk Solutions (SA), Johannesburg. Telephone interview. 16 October.

Hamoda, A. (2010) Security Manager: Serenity Makadi Heights, Makadi Bay, Hurghada, Egypt (former General (retired), Egyptian Police, Cairo). Interview, 15 September, Hurghada, Egypt.

Malan, J. (Mr) (2010) CEO: Safety Net, Pretoria, 14 October.

Kniep, H. (Mrs) (2010) CCTV Operations Manager: Ross Security (formerly Garsfontein Community Patrols), 9 October.

Rogers, C. (Mr) (2004) Senior Lecturer: Department of Security Risk Management, School of Justice, College of Law, UNISA (1997–2008)(ret.), Roodepoort, 25 June 2004 and 15 December 2010.

Van Zyl, K. (Mr) (2010) Senior Manager: Security Risk Management, Centre of Excellence, Lonrho Mining (LonMin), Rustenburg. Telephone interview, 15 December 2010 (MTech student in Department of Criminology & Security Science, UNISA with title: *An examination of the required surveillance control room operator skills: A case study from the refining and mining industry in South Africa).*

7

THE PIECEMEAL DEVELOPMENT OF CAMERA SURVEILLANCE IN CANADA

Emily Smith

Introduction

It is well known that camera surveillance is extensive in the United Kingdom, much of Europe and increasingly the United States. A popularly cited statistic that was estimated by Norris and McCahill is that the UK may have 4.2 million surveillance cameras and that there may be one camera for every 14 people in the UK (Norris and McCahill 2006: 102).[1] These cameras are operated by police, private security firms, local governments, schools, hospitals, parking lots and businesses. They monitor locations such as public streets, intersections, transportation areas, symbolic and other government buildings, entrances to pubs and apartment buildings. Norris and McCahill also estimated the Home Office spent over £250 million of public funds on open-street CCTV between 1992 and 2002 (McCahill and Norris 2002: 22). The EU-funded UrbanEye project tracked the social and political impacts of Closed Circuit Television (CCTV) in public spaces in seven European countries (including Austria, Denmark, Germany, Hungary, Norway, Spain and the UK) from its development in the 1990s to 2004. In their study of 1,400 publicly accessible spaces (such as shops, transport stations, cinemas and banks) in the capitals of these countries[2] in 2002, they found that one-third (29 per cent) operated CCTV systems (Hempel and Töpfer 2004: 3). This trend has also expanded to the United States, with cameras spreading in major city centres from Los Angeles to Chicago. Video surveillance is a rapidly growing segment of the security industry in the US, with projected sales at US$21 billion by 2010 (Bennett 2006, 18; c.f. Willey 2008). As an example of this, it is estimated that US$25 million has been spent on cameras in buses and subway stations in New York City, $5 million in Chicago on 2,000 cameras throughout the city centre and more than $10 million in Baltimore (Associated Press 2006a, 2006b; McCarthy 2007; c.f. Welsh and Farrington 2009). Cameras are not as prolific in Canada, or as studied (though see Hier 2010), but the question remains: how extensive is surveillance camera development across this country?

The answer is difficult to determine, as there is no federal government sponsored system that allocates money for cameras and no central database containing this information. Moreover, cameras are operated in public and private areas as well as workplaces and transportation systems and these are constantly changing. However, camera surveillance is growing in Canadian public streets, shopping areas, bar districts, transportation hubs and taxi cabs to name a few, with no overall planned agenda, but rather a piecemeal development influenced by local police, business interests, private organizations, public groups, activists and privacy commissions. Each specific site brings its own story of implementation, from drivers, advocates and detractors. This chapter will seek to provide a summary of what we know about where camera surveillance is taking place based on research in Canada. This information has been collected using research results from the Surveillance Camera Awareness Network (SCAN)[3] reports, previous research findings on the topic, newspaper articles, as well as freedom of information requests carried out during the summer of 2009.[4]

Development of camera surveillance in Canada

Camera surveillance, commonly referred to as CCTV (Closed Circuit Television),[5] is used to describe cameras that capture high-resolution images that are transmitted electronically to several destinations either wirelessly or through fibre optic cables to remote locations to be recorded by devices and observed by operators. There is a great deal of variability in system equipment and operation (see Ferenbok and Clement, this volume). Camera surveillance is a socio-technical system involving a combination of technological systems and the people that interact with them. It is implemented for myriad purposes and has very diverse technological system capabilities, operating systems and staffing procedures (Fonio and Derby 2009).

Most of the recorded growth of camera surveillance in Canada has been in public open-street systems in the past decade in downtown urban areas. The first known public surveillance camera was installed in 1991 in Sherbrooke, Quebec in the downtown bar district by local police to prevent delinquent behaviour (Whitson, Doyle and Walby 2009). This was removed after it was ruled to violate Quebec's privacy legislation (Superle 2003). Privately operated camera surveillance systems monitoring business and institutional settings have been in existence longer than public systems, and include spaces like shopping malls, banks, convenience stores and universities. However, less is known about the extent of these systems, as it is more difficult for researchers to gain access to information about these private sites (Whitson, Doyle and Walby 2009). The number of privately run camera surveillance systems is thought to far exceed that of public open-street systems in Canada, but it remains unknown. Public transportation systems are another area where camera surveillance is greatly increasing, in buses, subways and airports (ibid).

Various rationales are used to promote implementation of camera surveillance in Canada. It is often introduced as an instrument of crime control to keep away those seen as undesirable, such as drug dealers, prostitutes, panhandlers and the homeless, that threaten safety and economic activity. Public open street cameras are most commonly championed as an effective deterrent to crime, or to aid in investigations through detection and evidence after the fact (Whitson, Doyle and Walby 2009). These rationales are used despite the fact that there is little evidence to support these claims in Canada (Cavoukian 2008).

Increased perceptions of public safety are also a driver of camera implementation in the Canadian context. Public opinion polling on camera surveillance continually shows strong support for public and private cameras in Canada and abroad (Leman-Langlois 2009). As Danielle Dawson notes, Canadians are mostly in support of camera surveillance; however, they are not always knowledgeable about what the systems actually entail (2009). In a 2006 study on privacy and surveillance carried out by the Surveillance Project, one-half of Canadians indicated that camera surveillance is 'somewhat effective' in reducing crime in both community (public CCTV systems) and in-store (private systems). However, only about one-third of those polled claimed to be even 'somewhat familiar' with CCTV as a surveillance technology (GPD 2008). Cameras may be implemented to increase feelings of public safety, which is important to using public areas, transport and commerce.

Broader social and political forces also affect decisions about implementing camera surveillance. National security and the threat of terrorism affect policy decisions in this regard. Prominent global events have caused national security concerns to be at the top of the public safety agenda, which influences decision-making by police and security agencies about the proliferation of camera surveillance in Canada (Deisman 2009). National security rationales are especially relevant to the installation of cameras in transportation systems seen as under threat; the number of cameras in this area has grown substantially since 9/11. The top-secret nature of national security makes it difficult to obtain information about the extent of camera surveillance implementation in these domains.

Another undeniable influence is the widespread use of CCTV systems in the UK. Kevin Walby argues that 'open-street CCTV schemes in Canada are often based on schemes in the UK, or based on other "successful" Canadian schemes based on UK camera monitoring systems' (Walby 2006a: 30). An early example of this is from 1994, when after visiting Scotland, Sudbury's police chief wanted to replicate Glasgow's downtown CCTV. Five cameras were installed in the downtown area called the 'Lion's Eye in the Sky', becoming one of the earliest known adopters of the cameras in Canada (Superle 2003). This was funded by the Lion's Club, a community volunteer organization, and many other local businesses and organizations. It is the longest-running public camera surveillance system in Canada and is used as a model for other places, such as London and Vancouver (Whitson, Doyle and Walby 2009).

Mapping the trends in camera surveillance research in Canada

Research on the development of camera surveillance in Canada is limited and concentrates largely on who has influenced these initiatives, and the importance of many actors in this process (see Hier 2010, 2004; Hier, Greenberg, Walby and Lett 2007; Walby 2006a). Each site has a unique set of circumstances that has led to camera surveillance proposals, implementation or withdrawal. Taking into account the many complex factors that are involved in prompting camera surveillance installation, the gathered information has been plotted geographically across the country in map form.[6] The entries are categorized into four different areas. Red are public open-street camera surveillance that monitor public locations such as city streets. These are often run by local police departments. Yellow are privately owned systems, such as those in convenience stores, shopping malls and banks, that are often implemented by business organizations and private companies to monitor buildings. Green are transportation systems such as busses, subways, road traffic, taxis, etc. And finally brown are places where camera surveillance has been considered. Each pin contains a brief explanation of what has happened at that site, along with sources of the research.

Overall, there are currently about 75 entries: 34 public, 5 private, 22 transportation and 14 where cameras have been considered. With the danger of reporting on this early data gathering, in that it is incomplete, there is an overall estimate of over 21,000 cameras cited here, the majority being used for transportation (17,747), followed by public cameras (2,709). However, this represents only a small fraction of the cameras in actual existence, as these are only the places that have been studied, and certain areas such as private systems are largely under-represented. What follows is an overview of trends based on the information contained in the map.

Provoked by violent incidents

Many of these systems have been implemented in response to a violent incident or major event that provoked them. For example, the 1999 murder of Michael Goldie-Ryder outside a bar in the downtown core of London, Ontario, led to the creation of the community group 'Friends Against Senseless Endings' (FASE), a community-based organization dedicated to resisting community violence through education and awareness. The anti-violence campaign of FASE involving political and communications activities was influential in raising the funds from numerous donors to help launch London's surveillance camera initiative (Hier, Greenberg, Walby and Lett 2007). This public initiative led to 16 cameras being implemented by the London Police and Commissioners at City Hall at York and Richmond St, and Dundas and Richmond St in order to deter crime and anti-social behaviour, improve the ability of police to respond to crime, increase feelings of safety, increase economic activity and identify suspects (FOI 2009). Hier et al. argue that the role of FASE in establishing CCTV surveillance in London demonstrates that the implementation of cameras is not always based on top-down initiatives by business partnerships and elite networks, but can also occur through citizen-led groups from the ground up (2007).

In 2004, the mugging of Canadian figure skater Alexandre Hamel led to a news series in *The Hamilton Spectator* and police report on the 'crisis' in Hamilton's downtown core with drug use, prostitution, public intoxication and panhandling (Walby 2006a). Camera surveillance was initiated in consultation with businesses and entrepreneurs who feared that crime was hampering economic activity and attendance at the city's semi-pro hockey team games at the rink located in the downtown core (ibid). Cameras were purchased in 2001, but not activated until 2003, due to the controversy about perceived lack of public consultation about the initiative. Five cameras were installed by the Hamilton Police Services in the downtown core to deter high crime rates and anti-social behaviour, for economic benefits, for displacement and evidence gathering, but mainly to increase feelings of safety (Superle 2003; Whitson, Doyle, Walby 2009; Hier 2004). In this instance, Walby claims that this open-street CCTV was implemented as a top-down regulatory project by the Hamilton Police Service, with the support of local business through the Downtown Hamilton Business Improvement Area (2006a).

Other violent incidents provoking camera surveillance implementation from various organizations include: in 2005 a Boxing Day shooting of 15-year-old Jane Creba in Toronto resulted in a pilot project installing cameras in the same downtown location where the shooting occurred (Whitson, Doyle and Walby 2009). Cameras were also introduced on Jasper Avenue near 109th St in Edmonton, Alberta, after two police officers were attacked when intervening in a fight outside several nightclubs in this area. The cameras now operate around the clock, but are unmonitored and footage is kept for three days before being destroyed, unless it is required for evidence in court (Lyon 2009). And finally, eight Vancouver taxi drivers were killed in 12 years, resulting in a Report to the Minister of Transportation and Highways in 1999 requesting all taxi cabs in BC must have a miniature taxi-cam mounted on taxi dashboards to take pictures of customers upon entering the cab and every few seconds afterwards and co-ordinated with dispatch. This led to the installation of 500 privately run cameras produced by VerifEye Technologies (Doyle and Walby 2009). Similarly, 635 cameras were installed in cabs in Mississauga, Ontario, mostly by VerifEye Technologies, at a cost of $850 per unit (ibid). In each instance, a multiplicity of stakeholders is involved in ultimately installing the cameras.

Vancouver and the Olympic Games

Major events such as the recent Vancouver Olympic Games have led to secretive multi-million dollar security budgets involving hundreds of cameras at Olympic venues, transportation and tourist sites. Even before the Vancouver Olympic Games in February and March 2010, Vancouver was thought to have the highest concentration of government-controlled cameras in Canada. The province of BC targeted $1 million in funding for cameras in downtown Vancouver, the Vancouver suburb of Surrey, and the city of Kelowna in 2008 (Whitson, Doyle and Walby 2009). The city of Vancouver reports in our FoI request that there are four portable CCTV systems available for emergency management purposes during large-scale special events since 1999 (with the first use being the Prime Minister's visit to the Hyatt

Regency Hotel). They report that these are used for crowd control and traffic management during major events or at critical incident sites, and that the information can be used for citywide special projects, such as traffic flow surveys to enhance the ability of the city to respond in the event of a major incident. Requests have also been made by the Director of Risk and Emergency Management, endorsed by the General Manager of Corporate Services, to seek approval for the expansion of the use of portable CCTVs for event/incident management at a cost of approximately $100,000 to be achieved through the reallocation of resources (SCAN FoI 2009).

A high concentration of private cameras also exists in Vancouver's downtown area with cameras in bank machines, retail shops, bar areas, malls, SkyTrain stations, gas stations parking garages, heavily used intersections and on bridges (Mulgrew 2010). Although the exact number of cameras is unknown, 50 volunteers from the Vancouver Public Space Network in collaboration with the Simon Fraser University Surveillance Project walked every street and alleyway in the downtown and counted and recorded the location of cameras in August 2009 to raise awareness about the existing video surveillance in public space. Over 2,000 security cameras were mapped in downtown Vancouver in the central business district, Yaletown, Coal Harbour and the Downtown Eastside prior to the installation of extra cameras for the Olympic Games (see <http://www.vancouverpublicspace. ca/index.php?page=cctv>). The majority of these cameras are privately owned by stores, businesses and condominiums and monitor public spaces outside of these buildings.

The total security budget for the Vancouver Games was around $1 billion, with the total cost of installing Closed Circuit Television Systems (CCTV) estimated at about $2.5 million. The Vancouver 2010-Integrated Security Unit (V210-ISU) was set to pay $2.1 million, with the province contributing another $435,000 (Galasso 2010). In total, 970 cameras were installed for the Games in urban areas at approximately 100 Olympic venues and tourist sites. Plans included cameras with facial recognition technology to track visitors, 24-hour CCTV surveillance within designated live sites, such as public gathering and entertainment spaces, including 1,400,000 square feet of public space subject to camera surveillance monitoring (Huey 2009; Boyle and Haggerty 2009; Haggerty, Huey and Ericson 2008).

Many fear that the camera surveillance at Olympic venues will be left behind after the Games (Huey 2009). Philip Boyle and Kevin Haggerty claim, 'Public officials occasionally use the pretext of the Olympics to introduce forms of surveillance that the public might oppose in any other context, capitalizing on the fact that in anticipation of the Games citizens tend to be more tolerant of intrusive security measures' (Boyle and Haggerty 2009: 4). Previous Olympic sites, including Athens, Turin and Beijing, have retained the surveillance cameras after the Games. The International Olympic Committee President Jacques Rogge told media in February 2009, 'Security investment always leaves a good legacy of security for the country' (Galasso 2010). The City of Vancouver has admitted that $435,000 worth of cameras will not be temporary, but part of a 'redeployable unit' (Galasso 2010).

However, this remains to be seen as it has recently be reported that 1,000 cameras are being taken down after the Games, but many groups want to keep them because they believe cameras will benefit law-enforcement and public feelings of safety (Mulgrew 2010) (see Vonn and Boyle's chapter in this volume for a continued discussion of the legacy of Olympic cameras in Vancouver).

Resistance to camera implementation: citizen groups, media, privacy commissioners

Many camera surveillance systems have been strongly resisted by the public, privacy advocates and activists, which has often led to the cameras ultimately being taken down. Vancouver BC's Downtown Eastside (DTES) is one such location, which is notorious for high rates of crime, drugs and poor living conditions. Vancouver Police installed a test camera on the roof of a bank on the corner of Main and Hastings in the DTES without public knowledge in 1999 to address the drug market and crime. This caused a media relations disaster and resulted in successful resistance by local residents and activists to a larger proposal to install 16 domed cameras in 1999 and 2001 (Huey 2008). The police board recommended that the proposal be returned to the Vancouver Police Department for further study. However, the Vancouver Police continued the search for other neighborhoods to install the cameras in 2005, such as the Granville St pedestrian mall entertainment district, due to the high concentration of bars (over 5,000 liquor-licensed establishments) and high rates of crime in this area. Over 100 privately run cameras were proposed here at ATM machines, bars, retail stores and restaurants. This proposal was also successfully resisted by privacy activists and protestors in 2008 (Haggerty, Huey and Ericson 2008; Walby 2006a).

In Kelowna BC in 2001 a camera was installed above the Queensway loop near City Hall to control drug activity and prostitution, funded by the RCMP, the Downtown Kelowna Association and the City of Kelowna. The then Federal Privacy Commissioner George Radwanski was asked to rule whether the camera complied with the *Privacy Act*. He found that the camera system's recording capabilities were in violation of section 4 of the Act, which states 'No personal information shall be collected by a government institution unless it relates directly to an operating program or activity of the institution' (Radwanski 2002). In response to this the RCMP and the Solicitor-General did not take down the cameras, but stopped continuous recording, only recording when a violation of law was detected (for more on this case and the application of the *Privacy Act* and the *Personal Information Protection and Electronic Documents Act (PIPEDA)* to camera surveillance in Canada, see Johnson, this volume). In 2007, a study looked at public reactions to surveillance cameras and perceptions of safety and security. This study found that people had little knowledge about the use of camera surveillance and the scope of its operation. Generally, the public supported the use of cameras for crime detection and prevention, especially after a violent incident. However, the cameras have little impact on perceptions of safety, as there is a lack of knowledge about local surveillance systems (Superle 2001; Lett 2007).

In Brockville, Ontario, eight cameras were proposed in 1999 by Police Chief Barry King to the city's Community Services Committee to deter crime, vandalism and rowdy behaviour on 15 city blocks in the downtown core. The proposal had unanimous support of local businesses (Walby 2006a). Hier et al. argue that a series of critical news articles in the local newspaper, the *Recorder and Times*, called for greater police presence in the downtown core instead of camera surveillance, as well as using the discourse of 'Big Brother policing' against small-town community living (2007). The week before the city council was to vote on the camera surveillance proposal, citizens flooded the city council with calls voicing concerns about the increasing levels of state surveillance, which resulted in a unanimous 'no' vote against the cameras (Hier, Greenberg, Walby and Lett 2007). Thus, in this instance a combination of local media and civic resistance prevented the cameras from being implemented.

Organized resistance to camera surveillance was also demonstrated in the City of Peterborough, Ontario. Camera surveillance was implemented in 2001, with 12 cameras monitoring the local marina, museum, library and the city's Millennium Park. In December 2003, the Peterborough Restaurant and Bar Association along with the Peterborough Downtown Business Improvement Association made a proposal to city council to expand camera surveillance in the downtown core in line with their 'zero tolerance policy' towards anti-social behaviour (Hier et al. 2007). City councillors commissioned public consultations and a report to assess the expansion of the cameras. During this time, the local press, the *Peterborough Examiner*, reported on concerns about privacy, effectiveness, cost and motive. Heir et al. point out that the consultation process in Peterborough gave local interest groups the time to mount an effective resistance campaign to the expansion of camera surveillance (2007). This resistance was primarily from the Stop the Cameras Coalition (STCC), who mounted a communications campaign using community forums, data- gathering and a research report that ultimately led to the camera proposal being turned down by council. Additionally, in June 2004, 20 complaints were registered with the Information and Privacy Commissioner of Ontario, resulting in a review of the system's compliance with provincial guidelines (ibid).

Little evidence to support their effectiveness

Despite the growth of camera surveillance, very few of these sites present evidence that camera surveillance aids in deterring and detecting crime. The Greater Sudbury Police Service (GSPS) hired a consulting firm, KPMG, to review their Lion's Eye in the Sky project. The audit revealed that 'at least 300, and as many as 500 robberies, assaults, thefts and other criminal offenses have been deterred by the Lion's Eye in the Sky Project, saving as much as $800,000 in direct monetary losses' (KPMG 2000). And the police claimed a 40 per cent drop in crime. This report is often used to justify plans in other cities (Superle 2003; Whitson, Doyle and Walby 2009). However, an RCMP report by Wade Deisman in 2003 found that 'the effects of CCTV on crime are both quite variable and fairly unpredictable' (Deisman 2003:2). In a study of

Montreal Police installing cameras to reduce drug-dealing in 2008, Stephan Leman-Langlois found that instead of deterring dealers, the illegal activity was simply shifted to other areas that were not as heavily monitored (Leman-Langlois 2008).

In some cases cameras have been removed because they are not found useful. In 2003 the Edmonton Police Service (EPS) installed cameras on Whyte Avenue to deter crime, assist in investigation and provide a safer environment (Whitson, Doyle and Walby 2009). An in-house investigation by EPS found that there was not sufficient evidence to conclude that there was any deterrent effect on crime or that they assisted in any investigations. The project was abandoned in 2005 because of this, cost considerations, and some residential complaints to the Privacy Commissioner. Despite this, public support for the project rose from 39 per cent to 61 per cent over the course of the project (ibid). Civil liberties groups and residents objected to the cameras and a complaint was filed to Alberta's Privacy Commissioner, who concluded that 'placing cameras in public places is an extraordinary measure to be used only when the need for and the effectiveness of the cameras are clear' (CBC News 2006).

Transportation systems

In terms of transportation cameras, some of the most extensive systems exist in the largest urban centres, including Toronto, Edmonton and Vancouver. Toronto's transportation network of buses, streetcars and subways had 12,000 cameras installed by the Toronto Transit Commission (TTC) in 2007 at a cost of $18 million. UK-based Privacy International filed a complaint in Toronto that the cameras violated the Municipal Freedom of Information and Protection of Privacy Act, which prompted the Information and Privacy Commissioner of Ontario to review the project. Although the Commissioner found that there was a lack of public consultation of the project, they found the TTC was not in violation of the Privacy Act and the project continued (Cavoukian 2008; Whitson, Doyle and Walby 2009). Edmonton had 1,819 cameras installed on buses and another 619 at Edmonton Transit System stations and Light Rail Transit and bus stations (SCAN FoI 2009). Vancouver has 800 cameras on the Sky train route to monitor commuter activity, 24 road traffic cameras at the Cassier Connector in the east side of the city, and 12 cameras on the west side of the city at the Lion's Gate Bridge to monitor traffic coming in and out, all introduced in the last couple of years (Haggerty, Huey and Ericson 2008; Whitson, Doyle and Walby 2009). The Provincial Government of BC introduced an additional 110 red-light traffic cameras for Olympic security at a cost of CAN$20 million (Johnson 2009).

Proposals

Cameras have also been proposed in over 20 more cities such as: Surrey, Nanaimo and Victoria (British Columbia); Calgary, Lethbridge, St Albert and Medicine Hat (Alberta); Fort Qu'Appelle (Saskatchewan); Dauphin and Selkirk (Manitoba);

Thunder Bay, areas of Toronto, Sturgeon Falls, Midland, Guelph, Orillia and Ottawa (Ontario); Drummondville, Baie-Comeau and Hull (Quebec); Antigonish (Nova Scotia); and Charlottetown (Prince Edward Island) (Lett 2007; Walby 2005, 2006a). Complex issues exist in all of these locations as to why they are being considered and not yet implemented, with an often cited reason being cost. Camera systems can cost millions for such things as recording and duplication equipment, storage facilities, training, monitoring manpower and ongoing operating expenses.

Conclusions

The development of camera surveillance in Canada is not always a one-sided, top-down model of implementation. However, national security and private business rationales often lead to their initial installation, making it difficult to obtain information about how this process occurs. By examining each of the specific geographic sites of camera implementation, a more complex picture emerges where police, media coverage, business interests, legal oversight by privacy commissioners, citizen and activist groups participate in where cameras are installed before and after the fact. In some cases these individuals and groups can be drivers of the technology, while in others they can be the toughest opponents. Camera systems are increasing nonetheless, not in a straightforward open-street government and police-funded model, but rather by numerous public and private stakeholders and organizations. Limits to growth include regulations, lack of funding, few owned or funded by police, public opinion, timing, technical capabilities and lack of evidence to support effectiveness.

This overview is intended as a starting point for evidence-based awareness about where the cameras are in Canada, as well as what has led to their being considered, implemented or rejected in each case. Complex factors and stakeholders are involved in each site. Further research and analysis of their social, ethical, political and financial implications is needed. More detailed case study research will be useful in uncovering the strength of drivers in each particular area, especially of private systems which are not well represented in the research to date, and the role of technology companies in their development which is understudied here. This map will be posted on the Surveillance Camera Awareness Network (SCAN) website and a call will be made for further contributions to its content, so that we can construct a better picture of what is happening with camera surveillance in Canada. This will contribute to making the cameras visible.

Notes

1   The BBC now reports this number to be 1 million less based on estimates by a consultancy company called IMS Research. However, they report that the number of cameras in the UK are still much higher in comparison to other countries (BBC News 2009a, 2009b).

2   Their sample includes Vienna, Copenhagen, Berlin, Budapest, Oslo and London, with

only partial representation in Madrid. For more detailed analysis of results, see pp. 27–8 in Hempel and Töpfer 2004.

3   <http://www.sscqueens.org/projects/scan>, supported by the Contributions Program of the Office of the Privacy Commissioner, Ottawa, and by the Social Sciences and Humanities Research Council of Canada.

4   Freedom of information requests were carried out by Danielle Dawson on behalf of the Surveillance Studies Centre and sent to 26 of Canada's largest cities in July 2009. By December 2009, there were responses from half of these, including Edmonton, Halifax, London, Mississauga, Oakville, Richmond Hill, Saskatoon, St John's, Vancouver, Victoria, Windsor, Winnipeg and the York Region. Of these, all reported using camera surveillance, except for Cape Breton and St Catherines. Saskatoon and the York Region claimed use is only for public transit, while Vancouver reported cameras were only used for special events. Responses were not received from Barrie, Burnaby, Hamilton, Kelowna, Montreal, Oshawa, Peterborough, Sudbury, Toronto and Ville de Gatineau, while Ottawa requested additional money to provide research and Calgary did not respond, but provided information on its website.

5   CCTV usually represents low-resolution stationary cameras that send images to a central location.

6   Map will be available online at HTTP: <http://www.sscqueens.org/projects/scan>.

Bibliography

Associated Press (2006a) 'NYC to put cameras on buses', *New York Times*, 24 May. Online. Available HTTP: <http://www.nytimes.com/apoline/us/AP-NYC-Transit-Surveillance.html> (accessed 25 March 2010).

Associated Press (2006b) 'NYPD deploys first of 500 cameras', *New York Times*, 17 April. Online. Available HTTP: <http://www.nytimes.com/aponline/us/AP-Eyes-on-the-City.html> (accessed 25 March 2010).

BBC News Online (2009a) 'The statistics of CCTV', 20 July. Online. Available HTTP: <http://bbc.ca.uk/2/hi/uk_news/8159141.stm> (accessed 10 December 2009).

BBC News Online (2009b) 'Police not using CCTV properly', 20 July. Online. Available HTTP: <http://bbc.ca.uk/2/hi/uk_news/8158942.stm> (accessed 10 December 2009).

Bennett, J. (2006) 'Tech: Surveillance Cameras Become Big Business', *Newsweek On-Line*, 15 March. Online. Available HTTP: <http://www.msnbc.msn.com/id/11832024/site/newsweek> (accessed 25 March 2010).

Boyle, P.J. and Haggerty, K.D. (2009) 'Privacy Games: The Vancouver Olympics, Privacy, and Surveillance.' Prepared for the Office of the Privacy Commissioner of Canada Under the Contributions Program, March. Online. Available HTTP: <http://www.sscqueens.org/news/privacy-and-surveillance-at-the-vancouver-2010-olympic-games> (accessed 3 January 2011).

Cavoukian, A. (2001) *Guidelines for Using Video Surveillance Cameras in Public Places*, Information and Privacy Commissioner of Ontario. Online. Available HTTP: <http://www.ipc.on.ca/images/Resources/video-e.pdf>.

Cavoukian, A. (2008) *Privacy and Video Surveillance in Mass Transit Systems: A Special Investigation Report*, Information and Privacy Commissioner of Ontario. Online. Available HTTP: <http://www.ipc.on.ca/images/Findings/mc07-68-ttc.pdf>.

CBC News (2006) 'Whyte Avenue businesses want police cameras back', 18 December, HTTP: <http://www.cbc.ca/news/canada/edmonton/story/2006/12/28/police-cameras.html>.

Dawson, D. (2009) 'Understanding Public Perceptions of Camera Surveillance in Canada', in *A Report on Camera Surveillance in Canada: Part Two*, December, Surveillance Studies Centre, Queen's University. Online. Available HTTP: <http://www.sscqueens.org/projects/scan>.

Deisman, W. (2003) CCTV: Literature Review and Bibliography, Royal Canadian Mounted Police. HTTP: <http://dsp_psd.pwgsc.gc.ca/Collection/JS62_108_2003E.pdf>.

Deisman, W. (2009) 'Factors Behind the Implementation of Camera Surveillance', in *A Report on Camera Surveillance in Canada: Part One*, January, Surveillance Studies Centre, Queen's University. Online. Available HTTP: <http://www.sscqueens.org/projects/scan>.

Derby, P. (2009) 'Views from Behind the Camera's Lens', in *A Report on Camera Surveillance in Canada: Part Two*, December, Surveillance Studies Centre, Queen's University. Online. Available HTTP: <http://www.sscqueens.org/projects/scan>.

Fonio, C. and Derby P. (2009) 'The Technical Context of Camera Surveillance in Canada', in *A Report on Camera Surveillance in Canada: Part Two*, December, Surveillance Studies Centre, Queen's University. Online. Available HTTP: <http://www.sscqueens.org/projects/scan>.

Galasso, F. (2010), 'Smile, Vancouver!', *The Dominion*, 21 February. Online. Available HTTP: <http://www.dominionpaper.ca/articles/2951> (accessed 24 March 2010).

Globalization of Personal Data (2008) An International Survey on Privacy and Surveillance: SummaryReport, The Surveillance Project. Online. Available HTTP: <http://www.surveillanceproject.org/research/intl_survey> (accessed 10 January 2011).

Haggerty, K.D., Huey L. and Ericson R. (2010) 'The politics of sight/site: Locating cameras in Vancouver's public spaces', in M. Samatas and K. Haggerty (eds), *Surveillance and Democracy*, Rethymnon: Crete.

Hempel, L. and Töpfer, E. (2004) *CCTV in Europe: Final Report*, Working Paper No. 15, August, UrbanEye RTD Project, 5th Framework Programme of the European Commission, Centre for Technology and Society, Technical University Berlin, Germany. Online. Available HTTP: <http://www.urbaneye.net/results/ue_wp15.pdf>(accessed 25 March 2010).

Hier, S. (2004) 'Risky spaces and dangerous faces: Urban surveillance, social disorder and CCTV', *Social and Legal Studies*, 13 (4): 541–54.

Hier, S. (2010) *Panoptic Dreams: Streetscape Video Surveillance in Canada*, Vancouver: University of British Columbia Press.

Hier, S., Greenberg, J., Walby, K. and Lett, D. (2007) 'Media, communication and the establishment of public camera surveillance programmes in Canada', *Media, Culture & Society*, 29 (5): 727–51.

Huey, L. (2009) 'The Surveillance Legacy', in *A Report on Camera Surveillance in Canada: Part Two*, December, Surveillance Studies Centre, Queen's University. Online. Available HTTP: <http://www.sscqueens.org/projects/scan>

Information and Privacy Commissioner of Alberta (2003) *Investigation Report F2003-IR-005: Summary*. Online. Available HTTP: <http://foipuat.gov.ab.ca/commissioners_decisions/reports/summary/2003/2003- IR-005summary.cfm>.

Johnson, M. (2009) 'The "Legality" of Camera Surveillance in Canada', in *A Report on Camera Surveillance in Canada: Part Two*, December, Surveillance Studies Centre, Queen's University.

KPMG (2000) *Evaluation of the Lion's Eye in the Sky Video Monitoring Project*, Sudbury, Ontario. Online. Available HTTP: <http://popcenter.org/library/scp/pdf/100- KPMG.pdf>.

Leman-Langlois, S. (2008) 'The local impact of police video surveillance on the social construction of security', in S. Leman-Langlois (ed.), *Technocrime: Technology, Crime and Social Control*, Cullompton: Willan.

Leman-Langlois, S. (2009) 'Public Perceptions of Camera Surveillance', in *A Report on*

Camera Surveillance in Canada: Part One, January, Surveillance Studies Centre, Queen's University.

Leman-Langlois, S. and Pratt, A.M. (2009) 'Camera Surveillance in the Shopping City', in *A Report on Camera Surveillance in Canada: Part Two*, December, Surveillance Studies Centre, Queen's University.

Lett, D. (2007) *Bringing into Focus the Experience of Public Camera Surveillance*, Master Thesis, Department of Sociology, University of Victoria, Victoria. Online. Available HTTP: <https://dspace.library.uvic.ca:8443/dspace/bitstream/1828/232/1/dplett%20thesis%20v14Sep2007.pdf>.

Lippert, R. (2007a) 'Open-street CCTV Canadian style', *Criminal Justice Matters*, 68(1): 31–2.

Lippert, R. (2007b) 'Urban revitalization, security and knowledge transfer: The case of broken windows and kiddie bars', *Canadian Journal of Law and Society*, 22(2): 29–54.

Lippert, R. (2009) 'Camera Surveillance, Privacy Regulation, and "Informed Consent"', in *A Report on Camera Surveillance in Canada: Part One*, January, Surveillance Studies Centre, Queen's University. Online. Available HTTP: <http://www.sscqueens.org/projects/scan>.

Lippert, R. and Wilkinson, B. (2009) 'The Transfer and Use of Camera Surveillance Images', in *A Report on Camera Surveillance in Canada: Part Two*, December, Surveillance Studies Centre, Queen's University. Online. Available HTTP: <http://www.sscqueens.org/projects/scan>

Malanowski, J. (2009) 'Big Brother: How a million surveillance cameras in London are proving George Orwell wrong.' Online. Available HTTP: <http://www.washingtonmonthly.com/features/2009/0911.malanowski.html> (accessed 10 December 2009).

McCahill, M. and Norris, C. (2002) 'CCTV in Britain', Working Paper No. 3, Urban-Eye RTD Project, 5th Framework Programme of the European Commission, Centre for Technology and Society, Technical University Berlin, Germany. Online. Available HTTP: <http://www.urbaneye.net/ne_wp3.pdf> (accessed 25 March 2010).

McCarthy, B. (2007) 'Crime-fighting cameras are the wrong focus, some say', *Times-Picayune*, 26 March. Online. Available HTTP: <http://www.nola.com/news/t-p/frontpage/index.ssf?/base/news-7/117488685823720.xml&coll=1> (accessed 25 March 2010).

Mopas, M. (2005) 'Policing in Vancouver's downtown eastside: A case study', in D. Cooley (ed.), *Re-Imagining Policing in Canada*, Toronto: University of Toronto Press.

Mulgrew, I. (2010) 'Good riddance to Olympic security cameras', *Vancouver Sun*, 10 March. Online. Available HTTP: <http://www.vancouversun.com/sports/2010wintergames/Good+riddance+Olympic+security+cameras/2665631/story.html> (accessed 24 March 2010).

Norris, C. (2003) 'From personal to digital: CCTV, the panopticon and the technological mediation of suspicion and social control', in D. Lyon (ed.), *Surveillance and Social Sorting: Privacy, Risk, and Digital Discrimination*, London: Routledge.

Norris, C. and McCahill, M. (2006) 'CCTV: Beyond penal modernism?', *The British Journal of Criminology*, 46(1): 97–118.

Norris, C., McCahill, M. and Wood, D. (2004) 'The growth of CCTV: A global perspective on the international diffusion of video surveillance in publicly accessible space', *Surveillance & Society*, 2(2/3): 110–35. Online. Available HTTP: <http://www.surveillance-and-society.org/articles2(2)/editorial.pdf>.

SCAN FoI (2009) Freedom of information requests carried out by Danielle Dawson on behalf of the Surveillance Camera Awareness Network under the guise of the

Surveillance Studies Centre and sent to 26 of Canada's largest cities in July 2009. <http://www.sscqueens.org/projects/scan>.

Superle, T. (2003) 'Cameras in the city: video surveillance in public places', Master's Thesis, Queen's University, Kingston.

Taylor, N. (2010) 'Who's watching?', *The Packet & Times*, 26 February. Online. Available HTTP: <http://www.orilliapacket.com/ArticleDisplay.aspx?e=2465623> (accessed 25 March 2010).

Vancouver Public Space Network (2009) 'VPSN Surveillance Map', Online. Available HTTP: <http://www.vancouverpublicspace.ca/index.php?page=cctv> (accessed 21 July 2010).

Walby, K. (2005) 'How closed-circuit television surveillance organizes the social: An institutional ethnography', *Canadian Journal of Sociology*, 30(2): 189–214.

Walby, K. (2006a) 'Little England? The rise of open-street closed-circuit television surveillance in Canada', *Surveillance & Society*, 4(1/2): 29–51. Online. Available HTTP: <http://www.surveillance-and-society.org/Articles4(1)/littleengland.pdf>.

Walby, K. (2006b) 'Locating televisual and non-televisual textual sequences with institutional ethnography: A study of campus and apartment CCTV security work', *Culture and Organization*, 12(2): 153–68.

Walby, K. and Doyle, A. (2009) 'Camera Surveillance in Ottawa Taxicabs', in *A Report on Camera Surveillance in Canada: Part Two*, December, Surveillance Studies Centre, Queen's University. Online. Available HTTP: <http://www.sscqueens.org/projects/scan>.

Welsh, B.C. and Farrington, D.P. (2009) 'Public Area CCTV and Crime Prevention: An Updated Systematic Review and Meta-Analysis', *Justice Quarterly*, 26(4): 716–45.

Whitson, J., Doyle, A. and Walby, K. (2009) 'Camera Surveillance in Canada', in *A Report on Camera Surveillance in Canada: Part One*, January, Surveillance Studies Centre, Queen's University. Online. Available HTTP: <http://www.sscqueens.org/projects/scan>.

Willey, J.R. (2008) 'The Presence and Perceived Impact of Video Surveillance Technology in Indiana Public Schools as Reported by Building Principals', PhD Dissertation, Ball State University, Muncie, Indiana.

PART III

Evolving forms and uses of camera surveillance

8

THE ELECTRONIC EYE OF THE POLICE

The provincial information and security system in Istanbul

Alanur Çavlin Bozbeyoğlu

Camera surveillance is becoming a normal part of everyday life in Turkey. Closed Circuit Television (CCTV) cameras first became visible in the private sphere during the 1990s, primarily in banks, retail stores and shopping malls. Since 2000, camera surveillance has been expanded to institutional, semi-public and public spheres, such as government buildings and schools (particularly private schools), as well as common areas of public transportation, particularly railway, bus and subway stations. Cameras also became noticeable in residential areas, firstly in the gated residential communities of larger cities, then in ordinary housing areas and even at the entrance of each unit in apartment blocks (Baycan-Levent and Gülümser 2007: 5).

The monitoring of city streets using cameras has a shorter history compared to other forms of surveillance in Turkey. The key step in the institutionalization and expansion of state CCTV surveillance in town centres and city streets was the launch of the Mobile Electronic System Integration (MOBESE) in 2005 as the provincial information and security system for Istanbul. Since then, this system has become a model for other provinces' open street camera systems and MOBESE has become the publicly accepted name of CCTV surveillance in Turkey.

Open street camera surveillance in Turkey can be understood using a holistic approach that takes into consideration the general expansion of state surveillance. Turkey is on its way to achieving a surveillance society. Since 2000, the identification system has been modified through the introduction of identification numbers, the deployment of the biometric ID card, and the launch of the biometric passport. Moreover, the registration system was centralized, digitized and merged with residential registration and identification systems, based on identification number. This process can be conceptualized with the term *dataveillance*, which was introduced by Clarke (1988) to refer to systematic surveillance using personal data. State dataveillance of its citizens is not limited simply to identification; the ID number further allows each individual's personal data web to be followed, including health, financial, educational and criminal records. Visual monitoring thus represents an intensification of state surveillance in Turkey; central camera surveillance systems were launched or proposed in all provinces of the country between 2005 and 2010.

This chapter examines state-run, open street camera surveillance in Istanbul with a specific emphasis on the understanding of security and the role of surveillance within the neo-liberal context in Turkey. The issues are discussed in three dimensions: local attitudes towards global security concerns; private sector support; and Turkey's accession into the European Union. The chapter is based on the case of the provincial information and security systems in Istanbul. Two recent events are employed for the analytical discussion of this work. The first is the declaration of Istanbul as the European Capital of Culture (ECoC) in 2010 and the second is donations of CCTV cameras and PDAs (Personal Digital Assistants) by the Turkish Textile Employers' Association to the MOBESE in Istanbul, as a part of their social responsibility project. In contemporary Turkish politics and lifestyle, neo-liberal ideology is overwhelmingly dominant. Therefore, power relations between the state, private sector and citizens are also dominated by neo-liberal ideologies. Corresponding to this structure, issues related to camera surveillance in Istanbul are conceptualized by a neo-liberal critique in this chapter.

Approaches to camera surveillance

Camera surveillance, as well as other forms of surveillance, is often conceptualized using the framework of Orwell's Big Brother and the Foucauldian Panopticon in the fields of sociology and criminology. The Panopticon model, based on Bentham's (1785) architectural model of prison, conceptualizes the hierarchical relationship between unseen watchers and the watched. CCTV monitoring better fits the literal form of 'watching' more than other forms of surveillance. However, in contemporary approaches, the predominant influence of the Panopticon model is often criticized, modified or rejected (Haggerty 2006: 29). Hence, Bogard's emphasis on *hypercontrol* (2006), Lyon's notion of social sorting (2003), Haggerty and Ericson's model of surveillant assemblage (2000) and Foucault's notion of governance and governmentality (1991) are proposed as some alternative approaches that bring awareness to the extensive and dynamic characteristics of everyday surveillance.

In this study, the model of surveillant assemblage is used to analyse the open street surveillance system in Istanbul. This model was introduced by Haggerty and Ericson based on the works of Deleuze and Guattari (1987). In this conceptualization, individuals are not necessarily fixed and monitored in a particular territorial setting, but rather abstracted from their territorial settings. They are then reconstructed by widespread information flows coming from different locations through state and extra-state surveillance systems. The tendency to combine all surveillance systems together expresses a desire for control, governance, security, profit and entertainment (Haggerty and Ericson 2000: 616). Haggerty and Ericson apply Deleuze and Guattari's metaphor of *rhizome* in order to describe the expansion of contemporary surveillance. Rhizomes spread out with interconnected and multiple roots; therefore, even though some roots or some parts are destroyed, they can continue to grow and expand. Such multilevel and multipurpose expansion of surveillance is described by Haggerty and Ericson as *rhizomatic surveillance* (2000: 614).

In order properly to understand the role of CCTV monitoring in current social settings, the issue should be considered in a holistic approach that takes into account the social, political and economic contexts in which CCTV monitoring occurs. It is clear that technological developments have changed the face of visual surveillance. Camera surveillance is no longer simply closed-circuit, but is now linked with other systems of surveillance and shared through TV and the internet. However, the extended usage of CCTV monitoring and differentiation of the features of surveillance systems are not consequences of technological advancement, but rather of social, political and economic transformation (Hempel and Töpfer 2004: 7). Due to the unlimited expansion of all forms of camera surveillance and the worldwide web of surveillance (Lyon 2001), Koskela (2003: 16) calls the present period 'the cam era'.

Neo-liberalism, as the driving force behind the contemporary, predominant governing and lifestyle, is based on the idea of self-responsibility and entrepreneurship (Coleman 2003: 21). The tendency to replace welfare state ideology with neo-liberal understanding has resulted in the erosion of social rights, globally. On the other hand, during this process national security became a high political priority. Whereas welfare state ideology and its presentation as social policy for production relations of Fordism play a significant role in accommodating industry's need for human labour, neo-liberal economic relations and post-Fordist production relations do not need the work of the entire population. There is, therefore, no longer a need to keep the whole population at a minimum standard of living. During neo-liberal transformation, the role of the state as welfare distributor is reduced and the distance between the private and public sphere is blurred. One of the long-term consequences of such neo-liberal transformation is a decline of social rights. With the neo-liberal transformation, states leave the concern of welfare to the mechanisms of the private market. Thus, welfare is no longer considered for and universally provided to individuals as an *ipso facto* right of citizenship.

Neo-liberal transformation has resulted in the restructuring of social services and supports; thus the responsibilities of states have been diverted to the private sector and non-governmental organizations (Harvey 2005: 65). This process also mirrors the understanding of security. In the neo-liberal understanding, security is not being conceptualized as the structural outcome of the social, political and economic formation of society. Yet, security is presented as an independent and apolitical process which can be achieved by advanced forms of control, mainly through the employment of several forms of surveillance. As a consequence of this conceptualization, CCTV monitoring in urban centres and streets has been promoted as a panacea in order to prevent urban crime, regardless of any structural transformation in social and economic inequalities. Moreover, economically marginalized groups are the target of monitoring to a greater extent than other groups. Therefore, policing capacity of CCTV surveillance of marginalized groups is emphasized by some authors (Coleman 2009: 67; Fussey 2004: 255).

Increasing concerns about security have resulted in privacy problems. Similar to the erosion in social rights, privacy has lost its significance as a fundamental human right in the name of security in the neo-liberal era. However, the protection of human rights is equally crucial for the effective protection of citizenship rights (Isin and Turner 2007: 13).

The neo-liberal influence started in Turkey in the late 1970s; however, the institutionalization of neo-liberal discourse came with the economic agenda of the successor governments of the 1980 military coup. This neo-liberal discourse is obvious in Turkey's current economy and politics. The leading political party in Turkey, the Justice and Development Party (AKP), has been in power since 2002. The AKP is a neo-liberal party with a self-constructed moderate and con-servative image, and it played a supportive role in Turkey's accession into the European Union. The party has realized significant privatization of government assets in the fields of telecommunication, health, steel manufacturing, energy and transportation. Throughout this process, private enterprises have become the key actors in the social sector, particularly in the arenas of health, education, childcare and security.

Camera surveillance in Turkey

Like many other countries, CCTV monitoring in Turkey began in the field of commerce (Norris et al. 2004). Privately owned surveillance cameras, primarily in banks, retail stores and shopping malls, gradually started to appear in the last 15 years. Most of these systems were not capable of 24-hour recording or real-time monitoring, and footage was recorded only in cases of necessity. Currently, CCTV cameras in shopping zones have become an unavoidable part of daily life in big cities, particularly in locations frequented by the upper or upper-middle classes. Camera surveillance in workplaces, residential areas, governmental institutions and on public transportation was followed by open street camera systems in city centres and roadways. Although there is currently no data to quantify the general diffusion of camera surveillance in Turkey, it is worth mentioning that these systems can be found almost universally in both public and private spaces.

The first state-run open street surveillance camera system was implemented in Istanbul in 2005 as part of the provincial information and security system under the name of the Mobile Electronic System Integration (MOBESE). The system is operated by the Istanbul Directorate of Security with support from the Governor-ship of Istanbul (GIS). As stated previously, MOBESE is a provincial-level central system that employs an automatic licence plate recognition system (ALPR), a GIS-supported vehicle tracking system and mobile inquiry vehicles, as well as open street camera monitoring. With the launch of the system, 570 CCTV cameras were installed around the city with 24-hour monitoring. A central monitoring office provides real-time screening which is run by the Istanbul Directorate of Security.

CCTV operators are police officers who work for the Istanbul Directorate of Security. The system is operationally closed and linked to other features of MOBESE. The Minister of Interior, in his speech for Police Day 2010, calls the surveillance cameras 'the electronic eye of our police' (Atalay 2010b: 42).

The system is spreading quickly. As of January 2010, there were 4,016 cameras at 1,179 different points throughout the city. The Istanbul Directorate of Security does not report the exact locations of the cameras, but states that the cameras are placed at strategic locations around the city. However, the Directorate does release information about the number of cameras and number of monitoring points, upon request. Each camera is demarcated by signage and is given a visible identification number. At present, the technological features of MOBESE cameras are not enabled for facial recognition; however, the nature of the system allows for this facility, following future technological improvements. The UrbanEye Project shows that CCTV systems in European countries are often linked with other means of surveillance (Hempel and Töpfer 2004: 7). As previously mentioned, Turkey is experiencing an overall expansion in terms of both dataveillance and visual surveillance. Moreover, data-sharing, especially between governmental institutions, is accelerated in the name of e-governmentalization. Both the identification system, with its novel biometric electronic ID card, and the open street surveillance system are operated by branches of the Ministry of Interior, which thus has the largest web of surveillance in Turkey.

Based on the findings of the UrbanEye Project (Hempel and Töpfer 2004: 27–34), open street CCTV systems in many European countries such as the UK, France, Holland, Hungary and Germany have been in use far longer than that in Turkey; however, the expansion of the system in Turkey is occurring at a much faster rate. By 2010, the capacity, in terms of number of cameras, of the open street camera system in Istanbul was the second-highest in Europe, following London's system. In the last five years, the open street camera system in Istanbul has not only extended its coverage, but has also become a model for the other provinces in Turkey. Similar systems were established in almost all provinces[1] under the same title: MOBESE. Istanbul has the leading system in terms of its capacity and expansion capabilities. Moreover, camera surveillance is connected to other means of surveillance through MOBESE. In addition to the moderate capacity of the many cities' systems, metropolises such as Ankara and Diyarbakir have their own systems with hundreds of cameras.[2]

The Turkish government and civil administrators have presented e-governmentalization as a magical solution for a variety of the country's administrative problems. Turkey participated in the EU's 'e-Europe+ Programme' in June 2001. E-governmentalization has been touted as the primary justification for different levels of centralization and digitization processes over the last decade. In 2005, MOBESE Istanbul was selected as the best e-government project and the Istanbul Directorate of Security was awarded by Informatics Foundation of Turkey (TBV) and the Turkish Industrialists' and Businessmen's Association (TUSIAD). It is worth restating that MOBESE is not limited to open street camera surveillance systems; rather it is a combination of several levels of police control in the city. Moreover, the system is open to future interconnectivity through data-sharing acts between governmental institutions.

Taking these practices into account, one can see that e-governmentalization has given Turkish police powerful technological control. Istanbul, like other global cities such as New York and London, never sleeps. Thanks to MOBESE, 24-hour consumption, 24-hour transportation and 24-hour communication are available in Istanbul, accompanied by 24-hour monitoring capacity by police. The open street system in Istanbul has strong Panoptic disciplinary potential since screening is done by the police force from a central location. But the system is more than just visual monitoring bodies which are geographically fixed. The open street camera system allows for the monitoring of individuals and retention of visual information from different territorial settings, with the aid of more than 4,000 cameras. Furthermore, this system has the potential to be merged with other personal information. Images can be used to identify individuals, identity information can be transferred to codes by ID numbers, ID number can be linked with a plate licence, then all movements of the corresponding individual can be followed through APLR and the closest police officers can be directed for face-to-face control using GIS-supported vehicle tracking within the same system. In addition, other modes of informational, governmental or commercial flows can be attached to these conduits. From this point of view, the web of surveillance in the system is similar to Deleuze and Guattari's (1987: 9–10) *rhizome* metaphor or, more obviously, *rhizomatic surveillance* with Haggerty and Ericson's term (2000: 614).

Although camera systems are visible at the global level, the frame of surveillance differs based on the social, political and economic context of each country. This differentiation can be seen with the justification of, and legislation for, camera surveillance, which varies in different countries or according to regional contexts. While fear of crime is cited as the primary justification for the deployment of open street camera systems in the US and Northern European countries, strengthening police control, rather than crime prevention, is highlighted in Russian, Eastern European, Chinese and Middle Eastern contexts (Norris et al. 2004: 115–16). The level of privacy protection in each region determines the legal framework for open street camera surveillance. Practically, the basic points of legislation regarding open street camera surveillance are concerned with the method of informing the public about the reasons monitoring is taking place, the method by which footage is stored, the location and duration of that storage, and the reason for and level of sharing of footage with third parties.

Globally, we live in an era where privacy can be easily sacrificed in the name of security. The situation is even more likely to become volatile in Turkey due to the unquestioned power of the state and the lack of privacy protection. Historically, Turkey's citizens have been faced with various forms of complete state control. It is worth noting that privacy has not been universally defined with regard to state surveillance in Turkey. The Turkish translation of the term privacy, *özel hayatın dokunulmazlığı*, mainly refers to privacy in the private sphere and, more particularly, within family relations. The foundations of legislation surrounding camera surveillance are also related to a local understanding of privacy. Even though MOBESE has a well-structured implementation and operation procedure, there is no specific legislation related to open street camera surveillance in Turkey. The basic rationalization for the operation of the system, regardless of any legal framework, is that MOBESE cameras do not carry any risk against privacy since they are monitoring public places, not the private sphere, such as houses or workplaces (Karakehya 2009: 345). Legislation in terms of storage of footage, sharing of this footage with public or private institutions, and dissemination of footage through TV or the internet have neither been discussed nor documented properly yet in Turkey.

Images from MOBESE, particularly images from traffic accidents and robberies, are played every night on the national news, or on a number of websites. The general feature of these 'news stories' is that they overwhelmingly acknowledge the existence of cameras; however, the camera itself does not play any role in solving the main problem in most of the issues presented.[3] This populist, globally prevalent strategy of governance helps politicians to be seen to be doing something about social problems (Norris et al. 2004: 125). Even though there is no scientific research to evaluate the effects of MOBESE, politicians and administrative officers routinely defend the system's efficacy in preventing crime (Atalay 2010b: 42; MOBESE n.d.). Notably, there has been no scientific evidence of a reduction in crime rates in Istanbul, nor generally in Turkey, since the implementation of the open street camera systems. In fact, there are no accurate crime statistics in Turkey, at all. The General Directorate of Security is responsible for crime statistics and is currently working to produce complete and accurate data. The only official statistical data to estimate crime are those of criminal convictions. According to these numbers, there is no trend and only minor fluctuations in the number of convicts between 2005 and 2008, both at the national level and for Istanbul, yet the number of convicts has increased from 52,716 to 76,607 in Turkey and from 9,227 to 11,908 in Istanbul (Turkish Statistical Institute n.d.). However, in the progress report of the General Directorate of Security, MOBESE is presented as one of the essential tools for combating crime, although there is no empirical evidence for its effectiveness (Tasdelen et al. 2010: 75).

In fact, there is no evidence of CCTV's role in reducing crime in other countries, either. Only a few states, such as Norway, have taken the evaluations of surveillance systems into consideration when determining their policies and have limited or stopped the deployment of the system based on these results (Görgün 2009; Norris et al. 2004:125).

Both the presentation of the system through the media and through political propaganda may have an effect in increasing public acceptance of camera surveillance. Moreover, the successful promotion of CCTV created a demand for monitoring public places in Turkey (Karakehya 2009: 345). The neo-liberal ideology acknowledges responsible citizens who are not only passive subjects, but active participants at every level of governing including monitoring public space. Similarly, in Turkey, the citizens not only accept surveillance, but even demand to be monitored in public places. The campaign of a local TV channel in Eskisehir (a province with 669,500 residents) in 2007, and another campaign run by the Directorate of Security of Aksehir (a town with 62,000 residents) in 2009 in favour of implementing an open street camera system through public donation, are only two examples of the creation of public demand for MOBESE (Iki Eylül 2008; Akşehir Emniyet Müdürlüğü n.d.).

Support of the private sector

The responsibilities of welfare-oriented states have shifted to the private sector gradually since the 1990s with the rise of neo-liberal programmes in Turkey. Neo-liberal economic policies have resulted in an erosion of both welfare benefits and institutions that the state previously provided to maintain the economic and social well-being of its citizens, not only at the national level in Turkey, but also at the global level (Bugra 2007: 34; Isin and Turner 2007: 8). The idea of social responsibility has developed in this ideological context, with the support of civil bodies, in order to force private companies to be integrated into social and environmental concerns.

Social responsibility has a short history in the agenda of private companies of Turkey compared with the global West and North. A recent report from the Corporate Social Responsibility Association of Turkey (Göcenoğlu and Onan 2008: 38) underlines the general confusion in the definition of the concept in Turkey. Social responsibility has not been well-institutionalized in Turkey and its internationally adopted definition is still perceived as a continuation of philanthropic activity. In Turkey, the most common social responsibility activities are in the field of education. One of the country's largest employers' associations, the Turkish Textile Employers' Association, donated 1,200 CCTV cameras and 2,000 PDAs to the Istanbul Directorate of Security for MOBESE in 2008, as part of its social responsibility project. With this donation, the CCTV monitoring system in Istanbul expanded significantly and a leading business association in the country manifested its social responsibility for security concerns.

The textile industry has contributed greatly to the Turkish economy, both in terms of employment volume and export revenue. According to the report of the Turkish Textile Employers' Association (2001), the textile industry accounts for the employment of more than two million people, one-third of export revenue, and 11 per cent of gross national income (GNI). Istanbul is one of the main centres of textile production, along with two other provinces, Bursa and Denizli. It is almost impossible to estimate the exact number of workers in this sector since a significant amount of the labour force participation is informal. Recent statistics show that, in non-agricultural sectors, 28 per cent of labourers have no social security (Turkish Statistical Institute 2010b). Furthermore, the post-production stage of the textile industry is primarily performed by home-based women and child workers (Keyder 2005: 129). The donation of CCTV cameras by the Association is significant because it represents private sector support for surveillance and presents this support within the frame of the new production relations of neo-liberal terminology by citing 'social responsibility'. Private and public sector co-operation for the initiation and expansion of CCTV systems is not unique to the Turkish case.[4] Another example of this type of co-operation is one of the biggest systems of the UK: the Liverpool open street surveillance system, which was implemented by public and private funds (Coleman 2004: 299).

In the neo-liberal era, urban centres are designed for easy consumption and convenient shopping areas. Freedom and safety in this context, apparently, means the freedom and safety to shop (Coleman 2003: 29). In the last two decades, shopping areas in city centres have been replaced with shopping malls. While city centres have lost their commercial importance, they have become central locations for a visible underclass. In order to re-establish the importance of city centres for commercial purposes, urban places were redesigned and gentrified, including CCTV surveillance facilities.[5]

CCTV monitoring does not only allow a 'secure' space for consumption, but moreover, creates a significant area for commerce. The CCTV market is one of the few business areas which have continued to grow in spite of the recent global economic crisis. Therefore, universal deployment of open street camera surveillance has become the concern of both the national and international market. The 'culture of fear' plays an important role in the rise of surveillance systems (Coaffee et al. 2009: 81). Most state security services have deployed private firms, and here the state takes on the task of controlling such security companies. The General Directorate of Security trains and certifies private security guards. As of 2009, there were 513,134 certified security guards in Turkey (Tasdelen et al. 2010: 91). Moreover, politicians themselves, or their family members, have received some business in return. According to a national newspaper, daughters of the former Minister of Finance extended the scope of their trade interests for their companies in order to include commerce in all kinds of surveillance systems. They were contracted to implement open street surveillance systems for a number of provinces in 2009 (<http://www.internethaber.com> Internethaber 2010).

The meaning of security and security threats in Turkey

Istanbul is the most populated city not only in Turkey, but also within Europe, with 12,915,158 inhabitants as of December 2009 (Turkish Statistical Institute 2010a). The city is Turkey's hub of business, commerce, industry, art, education, migration and social movements, and also the centre of conflicts, inequality and crime.

The Ministry of Interior mentioned two reasons for the deployment of camera surveillance in public places in Istanbul; the prevention of crime and the prevention of anti-social behaviour. CCTV monitoring was launched as a dependable and indispensable precaution to mitigate the security risks of a megacity like Istanbul. Even though Istanbul has much lower crime estimates compared to other megacities of the world, it has the highest crime rate of the country (European Commission Eurostat n.d.). Types of crime in Istanbul vary like in other metropolises, and include robbery, domestic violence, traffic crime, killing, drug and human trafficking, unknown assault and bombing attacks. Furthermore, other than crime, Istanbul is the centre of social and political resistance. Maintaining security means not only preventing crime, but also averting social resistance in Turkey. Historically, the police and military have had strong powers and the MOBESE system (not only due to its CCTV monitoring aspects) has strengthened and centralized police control in Turkey.

City centres have a significant capacity as collection points for social resistance. Although Turkey has a democratic parliamentary regime which is under legislation to allow public events, there are several anti-liberal limitations, especially concerning demonstrations, meetings and protests. The general impetus behind limitations in Turkey is the desire of the state to be fully informed about events beforehand and to have full right to halt them. Therefore, camera surveillance has a further aim, beyond monitoring crime; the state can monitor a wide variety of public events through open street camera surveillance. Before reported or expected demonstrations, it is customary to see newly installed cameras appear in the area. For example, International Workers' Day demonstrations have been an important conflict between the state and labour unions since 1977.[6] In 2009, just three days before the International Workers' Day celebration, three cameras, one of them with 360 degree monitoring capability, were installed across from the headquarters of the Revolutionary Labour Unions' Confederation in Istanbul (Yorganci 2009).

The neo-liberal transformation of urban places has not only reconstructed space, but has also recreated inclusionary and exclusionary criteria for individuals based on post-Fordist production and consumption relations. The 'ideal bodies' of urban spaces are individuals with the strong desire and ability to consume; 'deviant bodies' are individuals with particular demographic and behavioural characteristics. Young people, especially young males, unemployed people, university students, street children, beggars and street peddlers are faced with segregation, particularly in semi-public places such as shopping malls, bars, libraries and museums. These places are under the monitoring of CCTV and face-to-face surveillance. Many restaurants have signs that read 'for families', many bars and night clubs have notices that state men are 'not allowed without being accompanied by a female partner', and many other public places have signs that declare: 'Street children, beggars and street peddlers not allowed'. With the deployment of open street surveillance systems, Istanbul's streets and squares, the only spaces for the whole population, are under 24-hour monitoring.

Although open street surveillance systems function to maintain police control over public places, there has been no strong resistance to the system. However, a group called *Gözetleme Kamerası Oyuncuları* (Surveillance Camera Players)[7] was founded and a number of public events were organized following the launch of MOBESE in Istanbul. This group is connected to the global organization of Surveillance Camera Players[8] which first formed in New York City in 1996. Even though the group is not currently active, it has a website which chronicles previous anti-surveillance events, keeps a record of related documents and aims to create better public awareness about surveillance concerns.

Globalization of security concerns

Population growth in Istanbul is higher than the national level of growth, primarily due to internal and international migration. In addition to the buying power of its increasing number of residents, tourists are important consumers in Istanbul. Istanbul was named as the European Capital of Culture 2010, giving the city official recognition as a cultural capital and lending credence to the idea that it qualifies as a European city (Göktürk et al. 2010: 5). The ECoC designation has led to an increase in cultural and tourist events, and in the number of visitors in the city. On the other hand, this particular event has increased security concerns in Istanbul. Since open street surveillance systems are presented as a major part of the e-governmentalization process of the country and e-governmentalization is necessarily linked with Turkey's accession into the European Union, the rise of CCTV has accelerated with the ECoC event. Similarly to other cities that have been the ECoC previously, security measures have become a more universal concern for Istanbul and camera surveillance has turned into an indispensable tool for maintaining security in this global city. From a neo-liberal perspective, culture does not necessarily mean the accumulation of social distinctiveness of a group or people, nor does it mean that cultural exchange is a profitable consequence of the relations between people of different cultural backgrounds; rather, it is something that can be bought and sold. Furthermore, commerce is presented as the principal way of distribution and consumption of the culture. Market relations determine the distribution of culture, therefore it is measurable in terms of quantity and quality, and its value depends on these measurable criteria. The neo-liberal era is a time of perfecting standardization. The capital value of culture is also determined within market dynamics and becomes tangible with the commoditization of culture (Keyder 2010: 27; Coleman 2004: 298; O'Callaghan and Linehan 2007: 319).

The European Capital of Culture programme started in 1985 and is co-ordinated by the European Union. Istanbul was named the ECoC for the year 2010 along with two other cities, namely Pécs (Hungary) and Essen (Germany) (Göktürk et. al 2010: 5–6). Previous examples of big cultural and sports events demonstrate that mega-events can be easily used by governments to adopt and extend various systems of surveillance and apply reconstruction projects without strong public resistance. Sports events such as the Olympic Games and the FIFA World Cup are known to include intense security measures, as well as previous ECoC events (Bennett and Haggerty forthcoming; Boyle and Haggerty 2009: 257; Coleman 2003; Hitters 2000; Samatas 2007). Following the announcement of Liverpool as the ECoC for the year 2008, that city's council restricted particular 'anti-social behaviours' in streets. Selling and advertising in the streets, drinking, and wearing baseball caps or hoodies were prohibited (Coleman 2003: 31–2). Examples illustrate that 'anti-social behaviours' are not natural, but generally fit some certain social groups (Coleman 2009: 67). Therefore, restriction of some particular behaviour was a kind of indirect restriction for unemployed people, secondary economy workers and young people from the city centre. The Istanbul 2010 ECoC Agency, which was charged with the general organization of the event, hired 413 security personnel for their operations, of which 82 were armed (Istanbul 2010 Avrupa Kültür Başkenti 2009).

There are several urban-renewal projects running in Istanbul and, similar to the previous ECoC events, ECoC Istanbul 2010 has accelerated those projects (Gunay 2010: 1174; Ünsal and Kuyucu 2010: 52; O'Callaghan and Linehan 2007: 314). During the preparation process of Istanbul 2010, a reconstruction project in *Sulukule*, a traditional Romani neighbourhood on a historic peninsula, received special attention. A villa town residential project was started in the area and the inhabitants were moved to apartment buildings, 40 km outside city centre (Göktürk 2010: 194). The project was carried out and the area is going to be gentrified, despite questions raised regarding its commercial value, central location, and the inherent cultural value of the area which has a long history as a residential centre of a tightly knit minority group. Briefly, it is worth mentioning that the ECoC Istanbul 2010 event has not altered the way of governing crime and urban landscape in the city, but rather creates a further rationalization for the ongoing extension of surveillance, social exclusion and urban renewal in Istanbul.

Conclusion

Istanbul has a centralized open street camera surveillance system which has been operated by the Istanbul Directorate of Security since 2005. It is one of the world's leading systems, both in its capacity, with over 4,000 cameras, and its connection to other means of surveillance in the city. The camera system is part of a provincial-level centralized system, the Mobile Electronic System Integration (MOBESE), and it is connected to other features; namely the ALPR, GIS-supported vehicle-tracking system, and mobile inquiry system. Despite the institutional and operational advancements of the system, there is no specific legal framework for the protection of privacy related to camera surveillance in Turkey.

The population of Istanbul has increased more than tenfold since 1950, while the total population of the country has increased 3.5 times in the same period. This rapid population change in Istanbul is primarily due to migration. Turkey has experienced massive internal migration since the 1950s, as the population moves from rural to urban areas. During the first decades of this movement, migrants were accepted as the locomotive of industrialization and urbanization and served as the workers of Fordist production relations. However, following the neo-liberal transformation and post-Fordist production relations since the 1980s, migrants in Istanbul were held responsible for all kinds of problems in the city such as unemployment, housing, traffic and pollution, as well as crime. Moreover, the 35-year-long armed conflict between the Turkish army and the Kurdish Communist Party (PKK) has resulted in a massive forced migration from the southeast of the country. Istanbul is a popular destination for these forced migrants (Keyder 2005: 131). New migrants, especially Kurds, are marginalized groups in Istanbul who are largely blamed for a variety of urban issues, including crime. Since newcomers are usually employed in the informal market in central locations of the city, they also become targets of open street monitoring.

Norris et al (2004: 126) underline the role of CCTV systems for politicians 'to be seen to be doing something' to promote security, and recent presentations of MOBESE are one of the best examples of this pretense. The government in Turkey has not employed structural projects to combat crime, but has increased the number and the scope of open street surveillance. Moreover, the launch of the system in every city is a big attraction for the press, with promising speeches being offered up by the Ministry of Interior. These speeches proclaim the effectiveness of camera surveillance without any scientific reference or evaluation. Previous studies in various countries show that there is no measurable effect of the CCTV surveillance in crime reduction. However, like most countries, Turkey is continuing to extend its open street camera systems.

Although open street surveillance systems are presented as an inevitable step of e-governmentalization within the framework of the European Union negotiation process, the recommendations[9] of the Union in terms of privacy protection are officially ignored.

Other countries' experiences demonstrate that the number and coverage of cameras grows especially following periods of economic and social instability and during the rule of conservative governments. In the UK and Hungary, countries that have, respectively, the highest and the second- highest reliance on open street camera surveillance in Europe, deployment of the systems accelerated in the period of Thatcherism and after the collapse of the Soviet Bloc (Norris et al. 2004: 121). Correspondingly, the neo-liberal and conservative tones of current governance in Turkey provide a convenient social, economic and political environment for strong police control, and support of the private sector for a wide web of surveillance, as well as the erosion of social, human and privacy rights.

Acknowledgements

I would like to thank all the participants at the Camera Surveillance in Canada Workshop for their fruitful presentations and discussions which helped me to frame this chapter. An earlier version of this chapter was presented at the XVII International Sociological Association World Congress of Sociology in Gothenburg, July 2010. I wish to thank David Lyon for the organization of the session, as well as for his helpful comments on my chapter. I would also like to thank Emily Smith and Sarah Cheung for their comments on earlier drafts of this chapter.

Notes

1 Through notice of the Office of Prime Ministry in January 2008, all governors were charged to put their street camera surveillance systems into operation. According to a press statement by the Minister of Interior of 10 April 2010, implementations of their camera surveillance systems have been completed in 53 provinces and 17 towns. The implementation processes are continuing in 17 provinces and seven towns, with an aim of fast completion.

2 Six gateways to the city are under 24-hour monitoring, as well as the 206 cameras that monitor the city centre in Diyarbakir. Footage is kept for 20 days by the city's

Directorate of Security (Diyarbakır Emniyet Müdürlüğü 2010); as of October 2010, there are 825 cameras in Ankara and 83 of them are connected to ALPRS. Footage is kept for 30 days by the Directorate of Security (Ankara Directorate of Security's report).

3 For instance, one of the articles details how a woman fell asleep while begging and her infant child crept away on the street. Thanks to MOBESE cameras, the baby was rescued by police from street traffic before being injured and the mother received a penalty for abuse and neglect (Mobese Kameralar 2010). The state, as this event demonstrates, does not relate social problems to the general issue of poverty, but rather focuses on the consequences of urban poverty using romanticized media events, and therefore exaggerates the necessity and success of camera surveillance. However, other examples show that even though criminals are captured using surveillance footage, problems in the judicial system create obstacles for justice. For example, just after the January 2007 assassination of Hrant Dink, a well-known Turkish-Armenian journalist, the assassin was identified by MOBESE cameras and arrested. However, almost four years after the assassination, the court decision has not yet been set and the juridical investigation has turned into a scandal (*Hürriyet Daily News* 2010; Wikipedia n.d.).

4 After the G20 protests in Toronto in June 2010, Toronto Police used the Canadian Banking Association facial recognition software to identify some of the protesters (Csanady 2010).

5 During the International Workers' Day demonstration in Taksim Square on 1 May 1977, 36 persons were killed and around 150 persons injured. Since then, Taksim Squared had been closed for May Day demonstrations. On 1 May 2010, the Unions' Confederation organized the first legal May Day demonstration in Taksim Square.

6 For more details about the group and its activities, visit <http://www.izleniyoruz. net>(accessed 11 November 2010).

7 For more details about the group and its international connections, visit <http://www. notbored.org/the-scp.html> (accessed 22 July 2010).

8 The Data Protection Directive in the Convention of Human rights and Fundamental Freedoms and the Automated Processing of Personal Data of the Council of Europe.

References

Akşehir Emniyet Müdürlüğü (n.d.) 'Akşehir MOBESE Çalışmaları Devam Ediyor'. Online. Available HTTP: <http://www.aksehiremniyet.gov.tr/default.asp?part=duyuru&gorev =oku&id=2> (accessed 22 July 2010).

Ararat, M. and Göcenoğlu, C. (n.d.) 'Drivers for Sustainable Corporate Responsibility, Case of Turkey'. Online. Available HTTP: <http://www.csrturkey.org/dl/CSRTurkeyMDF5.pdf> (accessed 2 July 2010).

Atalay, B. (2010a) İçişleri Bakanlığı Basın ve Halkla İlişkiler Müşavirliği, Basın Açıklaması, NO: 2010/27 Online. Available HTTP: <http://www.icisleri.gov.tr/default.icisleri_ 2.aspx?id=4556> (accessed 19 May 2010).

Atalay, B. (2010b) '10 Nisan 2010 Polis Günü Dolayısıyla İçişleri Bakanı Prof. Dr. Beşir Atalay Tarafından Yapılan Konuşma', *Çağın Polisi Dergisi* 101: 42. Online. Available HTTP: <http://www.caginpolisi.com.tr/101/42-43-44-45-46-47-48.htm (accessed 12 June 2010).

Baycan-Levent, T. and Gülümser, A. A. (2007) 'Gated Communities in Istanbul: The New Walls of the City', *EURODIV PAPER* 51.2007. Online. Available HTTP: <http:// www.susdiv.org/uploadfiles/ED2007-051.pdf> (accessed 12 July 2010).

Bennett, C. and Haggerty, K. (2011) *Surveillance and Control at Mega-Events Security Games*, London: Routledge.

Bogard, W. (2006) 'Welcome to the Society of Control: The Simulation of Surveillance

Revisited', in K.D. Haggerty and R. Ericson (eds), *The New Politics of Surveillance and Visibility*, Toronto: University of Toronto Press.

Boyle, P. and Haggerty K.D. (2009) 'Spectacular Security: Mega-Events and the Security Complex', *International Political Sociology*, 3: 257–74.

Bugra, A. (2007) 'Poverty and Citizenship: an Overview of the Social-Policy Environment in Republican Turkey', *International Journal of Middle Eastern Studies*, 39: 33–52.

Clarke, R. (1988) 'Information Technology and Dataveillance', *Communications of the ACM*, 31(5): 498–512.

Coaffee, J., Murakami Wood, D. and Rogers, P. (2009) *The Everyday Resilience of the City: How Cities Respond to Terrorism and Disaster*, New York: Palgrave Macmillan.

Coleman, R, (2009) 'Policing the Working Class in the city of Renewal: the state and social surveillance', in R. Coleman, J. Sim, S. Tombs and D. Whyte (eds), *State Power Crime*, London: Sage.

Coleman, R. (2003) 'Images from a Neoliberal City: the state, surveillance and social control', *Critical Criminology*, 12: 21–42.

Coleman, R. (2004) 'Reclaiming the Streets: closed circuit television, neoliberalism and mystification of social divisions in Liverpool, UK', *Surveillance & Society*, 2(2/3): 293–309.

Csanady, A. (2010) 'Police using facial recognition software to help ID G20 suspects', *National Post*, 15 July. Online. Available HTTP: <http://news.nationalpost.com/2010/07/15/police-using-facial-recognition-software-to-help-id-g20-suspects/> (accessed 28 October 2010).

Deleuze, G. and Guattari, F. (1987) *A Thousand Plateaus*, Minneapolis: University of Minnesota Press.

Diyarbakır Emniyet Müdürlüğü (2010) 4 April. Online. Available HTTP: <http://www.diyarbakir.pol.tr/ver2.0/video_haber.asp?id=677> (accessed 4 October 2010).

European Commission Eurostat (n.d.) 'Crime and Criminal Justice Database'. Online. Available HTTP: <http://epp.eurostat.ec.europa.eu/portal/page/portal/crime/data/database> (accessed 7 October 2010).

Foucault, M. (1991) 'Governmentality', in G. Burchell, C. Gordon and P. Miller (eds), *The Foucault Effect*, Hertfordshire: Harvester Wheatsheaf.

Fussey, P. (2004) 'New Labour and New Surveillance: theoretical and political ramifications of CCTV implementation in UK', *Surveillance & Society*, 2(2/3): 251–69.

Gunay, Z. (2010) 'Conservation versus Regeneration? Case of European Capital of Culture 2010 Istanbul', *European Planning Studies*, 18(8): 1173–86.

Göktürk, D., Sosyal, L. and Türeli, I. (2010) 'Introduction: Orienting Istanbul', in D. Göktürk, L. Sosyal, and I. Türeli (eds), *Orienting Istanbul Cultural Capital of Europe?*, Routledge: London and New York.

Görgün, I. (2009) *Denetim Toplumlarındaki Gözetleyen Gözetlenen İlişkisi Bağlamında MOBESE ve NOBESE Projeleri*. Online. Available HTTP: <http://izleniyoruz.net/php/makale/ipek_gorgun_mobese_ve_nobese_iliskisi_pdf.pdf"> (accessed 12 December 2009).

Haggerty, K.D. and Ericson, R.V. (2000) 'The Surveillant Assemblage', *British Journal of Sociology*, 51(4): 605–22.

Haggerty, K.D. (2006) 'Tear down the walls: on demolishing the Panopticon', in D. Lyon (ed.), *Theorizing Surveillance The Panopticon and Beyond*, Devon: Willan Publishing.

Harvey, D. (2005) *A Brief History of Neoliberalism*, Oxford: Oxford University Press.

Hempel, L. and Töpfer, E. (2004) *On the Threshold to Urban Panopticon? Analysing the Employment of CCTV in European Cities and Assessing its Social and Political Impacts*. Final report to European Union, Technical University of Berlin. Online. Available HTTP: <http://www.urbaneye.net> (accessed 12 July 2010).

Hürriyet Daily News (2010) 'Hrant Dink's friends demand answers from Turkish president'. Online. Available HTTP: <http://www.hurriyetdailynews.com/n.php?n=8216hrant-dink8217s-friends8217-ask-other-8216friends8217-to-join-in-for-questions-to-the-state-2010-09-01> (accessed 7 October 2010).

Iki Eylül (2008) 'Teşekkürler Eskişehir,' *Iki Eylül*, 15 January. Online Available HTTP: http://www.ikieylul.com.tr/yazar_goster.asp?ne=y48&sira=4312 (accessed 22 July 2010).

Internethaber (2010) 'Unakıtanlar'ın yeni favorisi', 8 June. Online. Available HTTP: <http://www.internethaber.com/unakitanlarin-yeni-favorisi-mobese--259114h.htm> (accessed 12 June 2010).

Isin, E., Brodie, J., Juteau, D. and Stasiulis D. (2008) 'Recasting the Social Citizenship', in E. Isin (ed.), *Recasting the Social in Citizenship*, Toronto: University of Toronto Press.

Isin, E. and Turner, S.B. (2007) 'Investigating Citizenship: an agenda for citizenship studies', *Citizenship Studies*, 11(1): 5–17.

Istanbul 2010 Avrupa Kültür Başkenti (2009) 'Ihale Ilanı'. Online. Available HTTP: <http://www.istanbul2010.org/GENERIC/GP_598453?WebsiteSearch=true> (accessed 22 July 2010).

Karakehya, H. (2009) 'Gözetim ve Suçla Mücadele: gözetimin tarihsel gelişimi ile yakın dönemde gerçekleşen hukuki düzenleme ve uygulamalar bağlamında bir değerlendirme', *Ankara Üniversitesi Hukuk Fakültesi Dergisi*, 58(2): 319–57.

Keyder, Ç. (2005) 'Globalization and Social Exclusion in Istanbul', *International Journal of Urban and Regional Research*, 29(1): 124–34.

Keyder, Ç. (2010) 'Istanbul into the Twenty-First Century', in D. Göktürk, L. Sosyal, and I. Türeli (eds), *Orienting Istanbul Cultural Capital of Europe?*, London and New York: Routledge.

Koskela, H. (2003) 'Cam Era: the contemporary urban Panopticon', *Surveillance & Society*, 1(3): 292–13.

Lyon, D. (2001) *Surveillance Society: Monitoring Everyday Life*, Buckingham: Open University Press.

Lyon, D. (2003) *Surveillance as Social Sorting: Privacy, Risk and Digital Discrimination*, London and New York: Routledge.

MOBESE (n.d.) Online. Available HTTP: <http://mobese.iem.gov.tr/> (accessed 22 July 2010).

Mobese Kameralar (2010) <http://www.mobese.gen.tr/antalyada-mobese-kameralar-bebe-gin-hayatini-kurtardi/" \o "Antalya'da Mobese Kameralar Bebeğin Hayatını Kurtardı yazısına git" Antalya'da Mobese Kameralar Bebeğin Hayatını Kurtardı', 4 October. Online. Available HTTP: <http://www.mobese.gen.tr/page/5/> (accessed 25 October 2010).

Norris, C. and Armstrong, G. (1999) *The Maximum Surveillance Society: The Rise of CCTV*, Oxford and New York: Berg.

Norris, C., McCahill, M. and Wood, D. (2004) 'The Growth of CCTV: a global perspective on the international diffusion of video surveillance in publicly accessible space', *Surveillance & Society*, 2 (2/3): 110–35.

O'Callaghan, C. and Linehan, D. (2007) 'Identity, Politics and Conflict in Dockland development in Cork, Ireland: European Capital of Culture 2005', *Cities*, 24(4): 311–23.

Samatas, M. (2007) 'Security and Surveillance in the Athens 2004 Olympics: Some Lessons from a Troubled Story', *International Criminal Justice Review*, 17(3): 220–38.

Taşdelen, S., Özcan, A. and Doğanyiğit, G. (2010) TC Emniyet Genel Müdürlüğü 2009 Faaliyet Raporu, Ankara: Emniyet Genel Müdürlüğü.

Turkish Textile Employers' Association (2001) 'Turkish Textile and Apparel Industry

Position For EU – Turkey Customs Union and EU – Third Country Trade Relations'. Online. Available HTTP:<http://www.tekstilisveren.org.tr/english/rep2001. htm (accessed 11 November 2010).

Turkish Statistical Institute (2010a) 'Address Based Population Registration System Population Census Results, 2009', Press Release, 25 January. Online. Available HTTP: <http://www.turkstat.gov.tr/PreHaberBultenleri.do?id=61788> (accessed 26 May 2010).

Turkish Statistical Institute (2010b) 'Household Labour Force Survey for the Period of February 2010', Press Release, 17 May. Online. Available HTTP: <http://tuik.gov. tr/PreHaberBultenleri.do?id=6247 (accessed 20 May 2010).

Turkish Statistical Institute (n.d.) 'Statistical Tables'. Online. Available HTTP: <http://www.turkstat.gov.tr/VeriBilgi.do?tb_id=1&ust_id=12> (accessed 22 July 2010).

Ünsal, O. and Kuyucu, T. (2010) 'Challenging the Neoliberal Urban Regime: Regeneration and Resistance in Başıbüyük and Tarlabaşı', in D. Göktürk, L. Sosyal and I. Türeli (eds), *Orienting Istanbul Cultural Capital of Europe?*, London and New York: Routledge.

Wikipedia (n.d.) 'Hrant Dink Assassination'. Online. Available HTTP: <http://en.wikipedia. org/wiki/Hrant_Dink_assassination> (accessed 7 October 2010).

Yorganci, S. (2009) 'Birileri DISK'i Gözetliyor', *Habervesaire*. Online. Available HTTP: <http://www.habervesaire.com/haber/1409/> (accessed 22 July 2010).

9

POLICING IN THE AGE OF INFORMATION

Automated number plate recognition

Patrick Derby

Introduction

Recent advances in camera, database and optical character recognition technologies have contributed to the emergence of a new hybrid surveillance technology – Automated Number Plate Recognition (ANPR), also referred to as Automated Licence Plate Recognition (ALPR). Since its inception, ANPR has been used in a variety of applications, from road-tolling and traffic management to access control, counter-terrorism and, more recently, mainstream policing. To date, the use of vehicle licence plate recognition as a police technology has received scant attention from surveillance scholars and criminologists alike. This chapter addresses this lacuna, providing an overview of the emergence and current state of ANPR within law enforcement in the UK, USA and Canada. Some of the arguments and rationalities that underpin support for the proliferation of this policing technology are also examined, and issues of privacy, data security/accuracy and discrimination are discussed in the hope of generating awareness and debate about the spread of this emerging surveillance technology.

What is Automated Number Plate Recognition?

ANPR is just one of many existing and emerging automated vehicle identification (AVI) and monitoring (AVM) technologies, which also include geographic positioning systems (GPS), radio frequency identification (RFID) and electronic vehicle identification (EVI). Over the last decade ANPR has become the dominant technology employed in private and state AVI/AVM applications, spawning a competitive niche market. While there is variation between ANPR systems, the following provides a general overview of how these systems function.

From the exterior, ANPR cameras appear no different from any of the other surveillance cameras that have become ubiquitous in contemporary life. They consist of a lens, and some plastic and electronic materials, and are housed in a ruggedized casing. However, hidden dimensions, made possible through digitization, are what make ANPR stand out from basic camera surveillance systems. ANPR comprises a complex assemblage of technologies and processes that begins with the digital capturing of a vehicle's registration plate with a surveillance camera. Algorithms are then employed to analyse each frame of a video feed in search of a vehicle's licence plate. Once a licence plate is located, its image is isolated and optical character recognition (OCR) software is used to locate, segment and convert its alphanumeric characters into editable digital text. How this digital text is then used depends on the specific ANPR application. In some situations this data may be immediately cross-referenced against other databases. For instance, ANPR, when used for access control, compares captured licence plate data against a database of authorized vehicles, denying access to any that do not appear on the list. In other cases, data may simply be stored for record- keeping or used for future analyses. For example, post hoc analyses of the elapsed time between ANPR camera reads can be used to determine such things as parking fees or travel speeds.

To facilitate innumerable applications, ANPR has been developed on various platforms. Fixed systems, consisting of ANPR cameras affixed to gantries or street posts, are used for such things as traffic management, tolling and congestion-charging. ANPR may be integrated with already established CCTV or camera surveillance networks; however, older schemes may require upgrading to a digital IT infrastructure and the installation of high-resolution cameras. ANPR is also available in portable and mobile models. Portable models comprise tripod-mounted surveillance cameras used in conjunction with a laptop computer for the purpose of covert surveillance, or a handheld system that can be used for such things as parking enforcement. Finally, a mobile, vehicle-mounted platform has been developed specifically for law and parking enforcement applications. This mobile variant consists of cameras mounted to a vehicle's exterior, which are linked to a digital signal processor, typically installed in the trunk, as well as to a data terminal, serving as a user interface, inside the cab of the automobile. While any of these ANPR platforms can be, and in many cases are, utilized by police, mobile ANPR has been the fastest growing among North American law enforcement agencies. 'ALPR in every car' is the trademarked slogan of PlateScan, Inc., a USA- based company specializing in the development of ANPR for the law enforcement community.

Despite its rapid emergence, ANPR has received little scholarly attention. In their groundbreaking study, Norris and Armstrong (1999) argue that the panoptic potential of CCTV is strengthened through computerized automation. For them, facial recognition and ANPR are an extension and intensification of closed-circuit camera surveillance, made possible by the camera's integration with the storage and processing powers of the computer. However, it is technologically inaccurate and conceptually misleading to refer to ANPR either as *closed circuit* or *camera* surveillance. Properly used, the term CCTV refers to a closed (non-broadcast) proprietary network of surveillance cameras. But this is the technology of yesteryear. The digitization of camera surveillance technologies has permitted video images to be transmitted globally over the internet, even wirelessly, to any computer along the cyber network, including mobile devices (Fonio and Derby 2009; see also Kruegle 2007). In the case of ANPR, collected images and data ebb and flow through cyberspace, from the remote camera site to digital servers and networked digital recorders, and from databases back to live system users.

Furthermore, while the camera is a necessary component of current ANPR systems, capturing the image of a vehicle's licence plate with a surveillance camera is just the beginning of the process. Once the alphanumeric characters of a licence plate are converted into digital text, ANPR takes on characteristics of dataveillance. On the one hand, most ANPR systems include, at a minimum, an overall photograph of the vehicle, which may include an image of the driver. More sophisticated systems, however, allow for pre- or post-event recording, whereby licence plate hits are utilized to trigger the recording of video images, which may include surveillance footage captured before and/or after the trigger. This allows for automated visual surveillance and tracking of a vehicle of interest. On the other hand, the database is crucial to the functioning of ANPR, in terms of the storage, retrieval and categorization of information. While ANPR databases may be used simply to log licence plate reads, recording the comings and goings of vehicles, they may also be used for post hoc data analysis, as well as allow for the mining of data from disparate databases or personal information systems, creating a data-double that serves to represent an embodied person (Haggerty and Ericson 2000). In addition to creating this digital representation, ANPR systems can make this virtual identity 'visible' to interested individuals or agencies through a user interface. Employed by law enforcement, ANPR is used to make 'visible' the identity and character of a vehicle's registered owner, and to sort out the innocent from the guilty or the suspicious. In sum, ANPR is a hybrid camera-surveillance-dataveillance system that makes vehicles, and by extension, persons, of interest visible in both a literal and a figurative sense.

The emergence of ANPR as a law enforcement tool

The potential of automated vehicle identification (AVI) and monitoring (AVM) technologies for law enforcement was first highlighted in the 1967 President Commission on Law Enforcement and Administration of Justice (Larson et al. 1977). Early on, AVM was said to enable police units to reduce response time and to increase operational efficiency by allowing dispatchers to deploy and direct resources, and to control traffic based on patrol vehicle location (Fenton 1980; Roth 1977). These technologies were also thought to enhance police officer safety by automatically providing location information in emergency situations (Roth 1977).

The introduction of computer-aided dispatch (CAD) into police work allows the whereabouts of officers to be made visible to dispatchers and supervisors. While most early systems required the manual inputting of location data, in the mid-1970s the St Louis Police Department (SLPD) became the first policing agency to automate the tracking of its patrol resources (Larson et al. 1977). The SLPD employed computer-assisted dead-reckoning technology, which operated by estimating a patrol vehicle's location based on interval readings of distance and heading data. By the 1990s, CAD was commonplace (Ericson and Haggerty 1997); however, imprecise dead- reckoning technology has been supplanted by more accurate GPS systems.

In addition to tracking law enforcement vehicles, AVI/AVM was offered as a solution to transport truck theft and hijackings. It was believed that the installation of AVI/AVM in commercial fleets enabled police to rapidly locate commercial vehicles reported stolen or missing, as well as function as a deterrent to would-be criminals (Fenton 1980; Hauslen 1977). In 1970, the Chicago Transit Authority, responding to a series of bus robberies, installed an alarm system which, when engaged, automatically provided law enforcement with the vehicle co-ordinates (Roth 1977). The system was purported to be an effective deterrent to crime on, and against, the city's buses (ibid.). Finally, early proponents suggested that the universal implementation of AVI/AVM in privately owned vehicles would enhance the ability to trace citizens in need of emergency services, as well as to locate and/or to identify vehicles and persons of interest to police, acknowledging that it would be several years before all vehicles would be equipped with AVI/AVM transponders (Hauslen 1977).

Today, the automatic identification and monitoring of every vehicle is a real possibility. After-market GPS systems are readily and cheaply available, and many vehicles come fully loaded with convenience services, such as OnStar, which provide precise vehicle location data to emergency services in the case of a collision. More significantly, ANPR has emerged as a dominant method of AVI/AVM. Since every vehicle is required to have an affixed registration plate, containing a unique identifying alphanumeric character combination, ANPR provides an inexpensive alternative to other AVI/AVM methods. While the evolving nature of technology makes the lifespan of any specific AVI/AVM system finite, ANPR is currently the only AVI/AVM technology to be used specifically by law enforcement agencies, for applications beyond fleet management and CAD. Still in its infancy, the emergence and proliferation of ANPR as a general law enforcement tool has gone largely unnoticed, allowing the technology to creep into use with little public awareness or debate. The remainder of this section maps the emergence and current state of ANPR-enabled policing globally, placing particular emphasis on its evolution in the UK, USA and Canada.

United Kingdom

The UK leads the way in the proliferation and use of ANPR. The technology was developed at Cambridge University (UK) in response to domestic terrorism, and for more than a decade it has been used as a counter-terrorism measure at strategic sites in London. Following IRA bombings, the City of London implemented a network of CCTV cameras to record traffic movement in and out of the city centre, creating what is referred to as the 'Ring of Steel' (Coaffee 2004). ANPR capabilities were later introduced to the network of surveillance cameras, allowing police to compare the registration plates of vehicles entering the city centre against databases of suspect, stolen or wanted vehicles. The system also generates a database of vehicle plates entering and exiting the centre; vehicles that do not exit within a specified timeframe trigger an alarm, alerting the operators to the presence of a suspect vehicle (Norris and Armstrong 1999: 215). Despite counter-terrorism roots, the use of ANPR in the city centre was presented to Londoners as a traffic management tool (Coaffee 2004).

After several years of use for counter-terrorism and traffic management, the use of ANPR has been expanded. In 2002, the UK Home Office's Police Standards Unit (PSU) and the Association of Chief Police Officers (ACPO), with assistance from PA Consulting Group, pursued ANPR as a general policing technology. Playing a significant role in the promotion and proliferation of ANPR in the UK, PA Consulting Group, a UK-based IT consulting firm, not only approached the Home Office and ACPO with the ANPR concept, but was subsequently tasked with practical implementation, national roll-out and evaluation of the programme. PA Consulting Group, the PSU and ACPO launched a five-year, multi-phased programme titled Project Laser. The first phase of the project, operating from September 2002 to March 2003, saw nine police forces test the use of ANPR with designated police intercept teams. It should come as little surprise that PA Consulting Group declared ANPR a promising policing tool, crediting it with increasing arrests and automobile seizures, as well as improving stolen vehicle recovery rates. Over the next several years ANPR was rolled out across England and Wales, with funding assistance provided through the Home Office's Crime Reduction Programme.

ANPR is now used nationwide for policing and intelligence purposes. In addition to supporting local traffic and law enforcement needs, the development of a national ANPR infrastructure supports the UK's National Intelligence Model and its intelligence-led policing initiatives by storing data on millions of vehicle journeys for up to five years (Lewis 2008). This nationwide proliferation of ANPR, with more than 3,000 ANPR-enabled cameras (Gaumont and Babineau 2008), is facilitated in part by piggybacking on the already existing CCTV networks and is producing what has been referred to as one of the most valuable reserves of data imaginable (Lewis 2008).

United States of America

In the fall of 2006, the International Association of Chiefs of Police (IACP) adopted a resolution supporting the use of ANPR, outlining its benefits and encouraging its use for general law enforcement. In addition, the resolution prompts the US Congress to offer funding opportunities for law enforcement agencies interested in deploying ANPR. While it is difficult to obtain precise data, in 2008 it was estimated that at least 400 of the 1,800 policing agencies in the USA have at minimum one licence plate reader in operation, a number which is expected to grow as the price of the technology continues to fall and the word of its potential spreads (McKay 2008). A perusal of the 'in the news' sections of websites for major ALPR providers reveals that the technology is coming online at a rapid pace across numerous police jurisdictions in the USA.

Despite several ANPR formats being deployed by US law enforcement agencies, the mobile (in-car) design appears to be most common. The extent of the technology's deployment varies by jurisdiction, with large police agencies, such as the Los Angeles Police Department (LAPD), equipping multiple vehicles in their fleets with plate readers and smaller police departments limiting their capabilities to one patrol vehicle (McKay 2008). Also, the complexity of ANPR systems varies widely. At one end of the spectrum, the small thoroughfare town, Georgetown, South Carolina, uses two ANPR-enabled cameras to monitor vehicles travelling through the town, to and from larger urban areas (Altman et al. 2009). At the other end, in 2008, New York City officials introduced ANPR cameras in conjunction with other 'domain awareness technologies' as part of the Lower Manhattan Security Initiative; the city's very own London-inspired 'Ring of Steel' (Bloomberg et al. 2009).

ANPR propagates in the US as policing organizations that test the technology often look to expand its use. For example, based on perceived successes in addressing vehicle theft, police agencies in San Diego, California, seek to expand the use of ANPR throughout San Diego County (Shumate 2009), while city officials of Rancho Palos Verdes, California, consider whether to purchase additional ANPR units on their own or to enter into a co-purchasing agreement with neighbouring regional police organizations (Petru 2009). The modular nature of ANPR and its ability to integrate various police-relevant databases also underpins the technology's proliferation in the USA. First introduced predominantly within specialized policing units, such as auto theft task forces (McKay 2008), ANPR is currently being used for law enforcement tasks as diverse as tracking the movement of gang members, drug traffickers and sexual predators, and executing warrants. The technology is also used for geo-tagging vehicles, and for enforcing traffic and vehicle documentation offences, as well as for catching parking scofflaws (Shumate 2009).

Despite endorsement from the IACP, the expansion of ANPR in the USA is not co-ordinated at a national level, as is the case in the UK. Rather, most police agencies have established ANPR capabilities on their own, creating islands of ANPR data that, at least presently, cannot be easily shared across jurisdictions (Shumate 2009). While police agencies on the East Coast have begun networking their ANPR systems, few agencies on the West Coast have done the same (ibid.). At the moment, the existence of numerous ANPR developers, and a lack of technological standardization, as well as incompatible IT infrastructure between many police agencies, pose challenges for the widespread interoperability of ANPR systems in the USA. However, this may all soon change as other agencies, such as insurance companies and the US intelligence community, become cognizant of how ANPR, in the hands of law enforcement agencies, may benefit them.

PlateScan Inc., a US leader in ANPR, recently entered into a strategic invest-ment and development agreement with In-Q-Tel. As an 'independent' entity, In-Q-Tel is tasked with establishing partnerships with companies, and fostering the development of cutting-edge technologies of interest to the Central Intelligence Agency (CIA) and the wider intelligence community. In addition to the CIA's interest in the intelligence possibilities of ANPR data, individual state departments of insurance are attracted to its potential for addressing vehicle theft and insur-ance fraud, making monies available to law enforcement to tackle these issues. In 2009, the Louisiana Department of Insurance provided the Baton Rouge Police Department with a grant to install ANPR into its fleet, and the state's Commis-sioner of Insurance hopes to extend ANPR capabilities to all major cities. Indeed, third-party *interest* in the police use of ANPR helps fuel its expansion through the infusion of capital for the purchase of new equipment; however, their *interests* also help shape how ANPR is subsequently used by the law enforcement agencies that benefit from such grants. Understanding these interests is crucial to understanding and forecasting how ANPR, implemented for one purpose, can be enrolled into initially unintended uses – what surveillance scholars refer to as *function creep* (Win-ner 1977).

Canada

Canada has been slower than the UK and USA at adopting ANPR, which was first introduced in the country for highway tolling purposes in the Greater Toronto Area (GTA) and security along the Canada/US border (Gaumont and Babineau 2008). ANPR first hit Canadian streets as a law enforcement tool in 2003, when the Toronto Police Service (TPS) deployed the technology to fight vehicle theft (Project Street Sweeper), under then Chief of Police Julian Fantino (TPS 2003). The list of Canadian municipal police organizations currently utilizing ANPR includes two police services in the GTA, as well as police in the cities of Calgary and Winnipeg. In addition, the provincial police services in Québec and Ontario are currently employing ANPR. In 2008, Québec provincial police, the Sûreté du Québec, deployed eight ANPR-enabled police cruisers along the province's highways (Wyatt 2008), while the Ontario Provincial Police (OPP) launched their own three-vehicle ANPR test-project in December 2009 (OPP 2009). The OPP's ANPR programme was initiated at the request of the former OPP Commissioner, Julian Fantino, who was impressed by what the technology achieved while he was commanding the TPS.

The Royal Canadian Mounted Police (RCMP) in the province of British Columbia has undertaken Canada's largest deployment and evaluation of ANPR. Seeing the technology at a European conference inspired the RCMP to test ANPR in BC's lower mainland (Lysecki 2007) in conjunction with the Integrated Munici-pal Provincial Auto Crime Team (IMPACT) and the Integrated Road Safety Unit (IRSU). Nine ANPR-enabled police vehicles were deployed across the Greater Vancouver Area in 2006 to explore its potential (Gaumont and Babineau 2008).

After the RCMP completed a Privacy Impact Assessment, they expanded the use of the technology to Vancouver Island, where it is currently being tested by police in the cities of Victoria and Nanaimo, BC (Cordery 2009). In November 2009, the RCMP released a Notice of Proposed Procurement (NPP) wherein, in addition to hinting at plans for the procurement of ANPR systems in time for the 2010 Olympic and Paralympic Games, it is estimated that the organization will purchase approximately 40 mobile ANPR systems and 20 portable systems over the next three years, to be deployed throughout British Columbia (PWGSC 2009).

While use of ANPR among Canadian law enforcement agencies is growing, exploitation of the technology's potential remains limited, as there is currently no cross-jurisdiction integration of systems. Nor do ANPR-equipped police organizations in Canada have real-time access to relevant policing databases. Rather, vehicle licence plates of interest to police are downloaded daily from the RCMP-managed Canadian Police Information Centre (CPIC) (i.e. warrants, stolen vehicles) along with relevant, provincially run, Ministry of Transportation (MTO) data (i.e. vehicle registration, suspended drivers), creating an ANPR 'hotlist'. At present, ANPR 'hotlists' are used to identify unregistered vehicles and vehicles associated with individuals wanted on warrant, as well as prohibited, uninsured or unlicenced drivers, among other offences. In addition to downloading 'hotlists' from CPIC and the Insurance Corporation of British Columbia (ICBC), the RCMP are also able to manually generate their own list of licence plates associated with vehicles or individuals of interest, a feature available to most police agencies with ANPR capabilities.

It must be noted that not all police agencies have access to the same data sources and information. For instance, vehicular insurance policies are provincially operated in the provinces of British Columbia and Québec, making insurance data available to police in those provinces. Many police organizations in Canada's other provinces, on the other hand, cannot or will not access insurance data via their ANPR systems. At the moment the OPP is not interested in integrating ANPR with insurance bureau data. This fact notwithstanding, the Canadian Association of Mutual Insurance Companies (CAMIC) is very interested in ANPR's potential and its benefits for the insurance industry (CAMIC 2009).

The Canadian insurance industry has helped push the use of ANPR within law enforcement in North America. The Insurance Bureau of Canada donated the first two patrol vehicles used in Toronto's ANPR-equipped 'Project Street Sweeper' (TPS 2003), while AutoVu Technologies, a Montreal-based ANPR provider, donated their wares. This project is said to have been the first ANPR law enforcement initiative implemented in Canada. 'Project Street Sweeper' was also used to showcase ANPR to police agencies across North America (ibid). Unquestionably ANPR can be profitable for the insurance industry, both in terms of increasing the rate and speed with which stolen vehicles are recovered and returned to their owners, and its potential for identifying vehicles being driven without valid insurance policies. Thus it would not be surprising if the spread of ANPR use by Canadian law enforcement agencies continues to be driven, in part, by the insurance industry.

Across the globe

ANPR is currently being used across the globe. While a detailed account of the technology's emergence internationally is beyond the scope of this chapter, a brief survey is provided here as an indication of ANPR's expansive proliferation. Internationally, Australia stands out for its extensive use of ANPR for a variety of purposes. In Australia ANPR is used in conjunction with traffic management and congestion applications, as well as for governing the commercial trucking industry. Additionally, most police agencies across the nation employ ANPR toward traffic and law enforcement ends. In 2006, CrimTrac, an Australian Government agency with a mandate for providing national information-sharing solutions in support of law enforcement, received a 'proceeds of crime' grant in order to carry out a scoping study on the feasibility of implementing a national ANPR strategy (CrimTrac 2010). While a final report was delivered to federal and state- level governments and police stakeholders early in 2009, no final decision regarding a national system has yet been rendered.

Other nations employing ANPR for general law enforcement and/or homeland security purposes include the United Arab Emirates, France, Ireland, Italy, Mexico, New Zealand and South Africa. ANPR is being used for security purposes at border checkpoints by nations such as Bulgaria, Cyprus, Finland, Mozambique, Serbia and Singapore. The technology is also deployed to secure Vatican City, to provide security at gas pipelines in Algeria, and for the purposes of parking and airport security in Qatar. Furthermore, ANPR is currently deployed alongside coalition soldiers in Iraq and Afghanistan as part of DARPA's 'Combat Zones That See' project, which utilizes algorithmic camera surveillance technology to assist in predicting and pre-empting security threats from vehicles in the theatre of war (Packer 2006). Including countries using ANPR as part of intelligent transportation systems (ITS) (i.e. electronic tolling, congestion-charging, traffic management and electronic vehicle registration schemes), the list grows further still to include Austria, Germany, Norway, Romania, Switzerland and Thailand.

A few caveats must be borne in mind when considering the above list of nations employing ANPR. First, this is neither an exhaustive enumeration of all the states currently making use of the technology, nor does it include the multitude of private ANPR applications presently in operation. Second, many of the countries listed above utilize the technology to multiple ends. For instance, like Australia and the UK, France employs ANPR for both law enforcement and traffic management. Finally, a note must be made regarding ANPR's possibilities for integration and interoperability, as well as the potential for non-related ANPR schemes to be enrolled or even hijacked for the purposes of law enforcement or national security. As stated briefly above, the modular nature of ANPR allows for the easy integration of additional cameras, databases and software-based analyses, and each added layer has potential implications for ANPR's reach, scope and social consequences. The addition of speed-enforcement software to traffic management cameras to automatically generate speeding fines may have significant ramifications for police–citizen relations and citizen perceptions of justice (Wells 2008). Similarly, 'law–abiding' citizens may accept the use of ANPR to trawl public roads for known 'criminals'; however, in a democratic state this acceptance might not extend to the police use of the technology to harass activists (Lewis and Evans 2009) or target minority groups. Furthermore, while ITS operators draw a clear line between their systems and the use of ANPR by law enforcement, these lines have begun to blur in a post-9/11 world as highways are (re)conceptualized as critical infrastructure, falling under the jurisdiction of national or homeland security (Monahan 2007). While Monahan (2007) warns of the potential for transportation control centres to become 'war rooms' in future emergency operations, it is also foreseeable – and perhaps more likely – that law enforcement agencies will seek to enrol ITS camera surveillance footage and ANPR data for more general criminal investigative purposes.

Supporting rationalities for ANPR within law enforcement

The emergence of ANPR as a policing technology has sparked excitement in the law enforcement community, leading some to label the technology 'revolution-ary' (Ward 2006). Whether this is really the case remains an open question and will depend on how the technology is deployed in the long term. Rather than try to assess the veracity of such a claim, this section undertakes the more modest task of highlighting some of the current rationales and justifications given to support ANPR-enabled policing.

In everyday life there are an abundance of (quasi) legal violations that evade enforcement. These form what criminologists refer to as the dark figure of crime. One, though certainly not the only, explanation for the disparity between laws violated and laws enforced is a lack of police resources. Technological solutions to the problem of crime are increasingly being sought to make up for limited, and expensive, human resources (McKay 2008). ANPR is perceived as one such tech-nological solution, being marketed to the policing community as a force multiplier. It is argued that ANPR-enabled officers in the UK have an arrest rate ten times the national average (PA Consulting Group 2003). Furthermore, ANPR is pitched as providing an immediate return on investment. The authors of an article highlight-ing the benefits of ANPR indicate that police in Georgetown, South Carolina, made their first ANPR-associated arrest within hours of installing the technol-ogy, when a camera, still being configured by the technicians, registered a hit for a stolen vehicle (Altman et al. 2009). It seems that every news story about recent ANPR deployments contains a similar anecdotal tale, along with some variation of a statement by a police spokesperson suggesting that in a very short time ANPR 'has proved its worth'.

It is also argued that ANPR improves officer efficiency. Indeed, recovery rate statistics are often offered as a demonstration of ANPR's potential for combating vehicle theft. Statistics from the LAPD suggest that ANPR-enabled police officers recover approximately five times the number of stolen vehicles when compared to officers not utilizing ANPR (McKay 2008), and statistics from 2008 indicate that the Toronto police's parking enforcement unit recovered 1,539 stolen vehicles, of which 884 recoveries are credited to ANPR (City of Toronto 2009). In addition to improving the recovery rate for stolen vehicles, proponents also point out that, because vehicles are recovered more quickly using ANPR, they are in much better condition than those found by traditional means (Altman et al. 2009), reducing losses for the insurance industry. In addition to improving profits for insurance companies, the use of ANPR is said to produce spin-off benefits to consumers through stable or decreased insurance premiums. The technology is also marketed as a mechanism for generating government revenue through the efficient enforcement of tax avoiders or parking scofflaws. In short, ANPR is sold on the ground that it will pay for itself in a short period of time through improving efficiency, revenue generation, and savings to consumers and taxpayers.

ANPR's perceived success in combating auto theft is believed to be merely the tip of the iceberg with respect to the technology's applicability to general law enforcement. A spokesperson for the Royal Canadian Mounted Police (RCMP) indicates that auto theft and traffic enforcement merely scratch the surface of the technology's potential (Duncan 2008). It is increasingly being used by police organizations for the purposes of investigation and general crime detection, as vehicle documentation offences and other minor traffic offences are viewed as being symptomatic of more significant criminality. Analysing RCMP ANPR data, researchers found that 'one-third of people who illegally parked in disabled parking spots has a previous criminal record . . . and one-fifth were of immediate police interest or were known or suspected of having involvement with other criminal activities' (quoted in Ross 2008). Furthermore, police view auto theft as a conduit to further criminality, as many crimes, such as robbery and drug trafficking, are believed to be committed using stolen vehicles. When viewed through this lens it is not surprising that the strategic intent of ANPR use in the UK is to prevent crime by 'denying criminals use of the roads' (PA Consulting Group 2003), an aim that has been imported to North America.

While ANPR systems in Canada do not allow for the same level of intelligence-led policing that the national-level system in the UK does, the RCMP are nonetheless using the technology to deny criminals use of the road. For instance, the RCMP is using ANPR at sobriety checkpoints, resulting in the recovery of stolen vehicles and property, the execution of warrants and the apprehension of unlicenced and prohibited drivers (Gaumont and Babineau 2008). The ability of ANPR systems to scan automatically thousands of licence plates increases the number of 'hits' obtained over manually inputting licence plates in police databases. Ironically, however, the increased number of licence plate matches means that use of ANPR requires more resources than initially anticipated if all alerts are to be intercepted. According to statistics available on the RCMP website, limited resources only allowed for police to respond to 16 per cent of ANPR hits between winter 2007 and fall 2009. Similar resource issues have limited ANPR's potential in the UK, leading to the use of designated intercept teams, a model also considered by police in some jurisdictions in Canada and the USA. Further, proponents of ANPR in the UK are calling for policy direction to guide the prioritization of ANPR hits (PA Consulting Group 2007), an approach also being recommended in Canada (Gaumont and Babineau 2008).

Another argument in support of employing ANPR within law enforcement is its presumed ability to ensure the safety of both the public and police officers. Proponents of ANPR indicate that drivers who let their insurance policies or vehicle registration lapse are also more likely to be involved in serious crime and traffic collisions (Gaventa 2005; PA Consulting Group 2005). The technology is also offered as a method for enforcing vehicle safety and emissions testing requirements, ensuring the security of other road users and the protection of air quality. As well, the use of ANPR is said to limit the need for police vehicle chases as, properly deployed, ANPR allows police surveillance teams effectively to track vehicles of interest. The limiting of police pursuits would reduce collateral damage to property, as well as prevent injury or death from collisions (Gaumont and Babineau 2008). Finally, ANPR may be used to ensure police officer safety by allowing police officers to concentrate on operating their vehicle rather than inputting licence plate data while driving, decreasing potential injury from a vehicle collision. The technology is also thought to improve an officer's situational awareness by providing relevant and timely information about a vehicle or an associated individual.

Privacy, data security/accuracy and discrimination

From the perspective of the law enforcement community, ANPR is believed to be a valuable tool as it serves to extend the reach of police. However, use of the technology by police also raises significant concern. Some have compared policing with ANPR to 'fishing with a net versus a line' (McKay 2008). Because of its ability to facilitate drag-net policing, ANPR has attracted criticism beyond simple cries of 'Big Brotherism', from privacy advocates and civil libertarians. This section explores some of the risks associated with ANPR-enabled policing.

Jeff Gamso, legal director of the American Civil Liberties Union of Ohio, has argued that the use of ANPR infringes the privacy rights of innocent drivers whose licence plates get captured by the plate-reading technology. Such claims have been brushed aside by ANPR proponents who suggest that the technology simply acquires and processes information in a manner similar to a police officer manually inputting the plate data into her or his in-car data terminal. Furthermore, ANPR provides an example where privacy controls are incorporated into technological design. In most instances, the personal information of a vehicle's registered owner remains unknown to the police unless the vehicle is on a hotlist; only then will the personal information of the owner, or an associated driver, be made visible to the ANPR user. In short, these 'designed-in' technical features make privacy claims and challenges somewhat more easily dismissible as the majority of vehicles that pass through ANPR checkpoints remain anonymous to law enforcement officials.

There are significant disparities in data retention between countries, perhaps most notably between Canada and the UK. While the national ANPR programme in the UK retains collected data for up to five years, more stringent privacy guidelines in Canada mean that law enforcement agencies cannot retain data as freely. The ANPR system employed by the RCMP stores 'hit' information for two years, and licence plate data that did not result in a 'hit' are automatically purged from the RCMP's secure server after three months (Ministry of Public Safety and Solicitor General 2006). Other police agencies have self-imposed stricter controls on data retention. By design some systems used by Canadian police agencies immediately purge image data, only storing information when a 'hit' is achieved. In other instances the system automatically overwrites itself after a designated time period, with each new licence plate scan replacing the oldest (IPCO 2003). The fact that privacy features are being designed into some contemporary digital surveillance technologies, such as ANPR, speaks to the successes of privacy advocates in shaping surveillance futures. However, variability in the use of the technology, and data retention, across jurisdictions and applications means that privacy challenges will remain an important aspect to the regulation of ANPR. This will be especially pertinent should the law enforcement or intelligence communities push for the expansion and interoperability of currently disparate ANPR networks, or should cross-jurisdictional ANPR data-sharing become common practice.

More pertinent than privacy regulation per se is the need for guidelines on data security. In the UK, where the stored data is reaching peta byte levels (Evans-Pughe 2006) and can be used for speculative data-mining, national debate is urgently needed to address how ANPR data is to be used and secured. In Canada, despite urging from the Information and Privacy Commissioner of British Columbia for the creation of guidelines regarding the handling of ANPR data, limiting access and ensuring data security, no such protocols currently exist. Indeed, ANPR in Canada and the USA cannot – at least as of yet – systematically track the movement of vehicles the same way that is possible in the UK; however, pro-active public debate is still needed to set limits on how the technology is employed now and in the future. While ANPR use in Canada is currently limited, for the most part only used to identify and recover stolen vehicles and enforce vehicle documentation offences, its use can easily be expanded to target particular offences and groups, such as suspected terrorists, sex offenders or parolees. The technology can also be adapted to target, monitor and even harass political protesters, as has occurred in the UK (Lewis and Evans 2009). For whatever future end ANPR is to be potentially deployed, experience demonstrates that it is difficult – though not impossible – to have surveillance systems dismantled after their implementation. It is for this reason that, in democratic societies, the use of ANPR by police agencies must not precede public consultation and informed debate. Unfortunately, few police agencies using ANPR, or considering its use, have engaged in public consultation. Recent controversy surrounding a cameras surveillance scheme in Birmingham, UK, demonstrates both the lack of, and need for, public consultation prior to the implementation of camera surveillance in public space. In June 2010, it was revealed that 'Project Champion', comprising 218 surveillance cameras (106 of which were ANPR cameras, with 72 operating covertly), sited in areas of Birmingham with significant Muslim populations, was funded through the 'Terrorism and Allied Matters' fund, administered by the Association of Chief Police Officers (ACPO). A considerable outcry sparked a public meeting, at which an apology was offered to the affected communities along with an announcement that the 72 hidden cameras would be removed pending public consultation. It was also announced that an inquiry into the police use of covert surveillance cameras would be conducted in order to learn from past mistakes. While police and Home Office personnel are taking steps to try to address public concerns, this matter has undoubtedly further damaged already strained relations between the police and Muslim communities in the UK.

ANPR law enforcement applications rely heavily on databases maintained by government and/or private entities, whether they are police records systems, ministry of transportation (MTO) data or insurance information, to name just the most common. While many citizens would likely be uncomfortable knowing the extent to which ANPR could be used to mine personal data, they are often assured that only the 'guilty' need to worry about ANPR, as only the licence plate data of persons/vehicles of interest to the police or in poor standing with the MTO are uploaded to the police's ANPR system. However, a recent UK study reveals that a large portion of information held within police-relevant databases is inaccurate (PA Consulting Group 2006). The most common error reported by police forces across England and Wales is the failure to remove a 'stolen vehicle' tag when a vehicle is recovered, resulting in the vehicle's proper owner being intercepted for possessing a stolen vehicle. While, to my knowledge, there has been no comparable study conducted regarding the accuracy of police-relevant databases in Canada and the USA, no system that relies on multiple databases will be error free. Thus, the very real possibility of database inaccuracies is itself something to be fearful of (Evans-Pughe 2006).

Finally, the issue of discrimination requires some discussion. It has been suggested that ANPR does not discriminate, that it cannot distinguish the colour of a driver's skin or the condition of their vehicle. Miriam Lips and her collaborators (2009: 726) opine that ANPR results in fairer, more equitable law enforcement, based on ANPR-mediated 'evidence' rather than postulations that may be the consequence of human prejudice. Such a suggestion assumes, of course, that use of ANPR is equitably distributed, and ignores the politics of its deployment. In the name of effective resource exploitation, the placement of ANPR cameras and the deployment of ANPR intercept teams in the UK takes into consideration such things as 'hotspots', 'known offender locations' and 'area demographics' (PA Consulting Group 2007), which may themselves be based on subjective biases and prejudices. Take again, for instance, the example of Birmingham's 'Project Champion'. Officials insist that while the funds for the surveillance camera scheme were secured under ACPO's counter-terrorism fund, the cameras were sited based on general crime data – not just counter-terrorism intelligence. It is not yet clear whether the siting of this camera surveillance network was rationalized based on known crime 'hotspots' or the collection of counter-terrorism intelligence – perhaps both. However, what is known from this case is that ANPR surveillance is not universal. Fixed and mobile ANPR networks, more than 3,000 cameras strong, reach across England and Wales, in a nationalized way not currently found in other jurisdictions, such as Canada or the USA, where the technology tends to be deployed more narrowly within specialized mobile police units. As is common in US urban areas, the use of ANPR in conjunction with anti-vehicle theft task forces or anti-gang police units likely does more to reinforce the policing of marginalized areas and populations than it does to make policing more equitable. As such, claims regarding the unbiased nature of ANPR-enabled policing need to be treated as suspect, and empirically scrutinized within the specific contexts of the technology's deployment.

Conclusion

While the law enforcement potential for automated vehicle identification (AVI) and monitoring (AVM) technologies was recognized over three decades ago, this possibility did not become a practical reality until relatively recently. Today, ANPR is proliferating globally in a growing number of applications. Since the turn of the millennium it has emerged as a significant security and policing technology, increasingly being used in Europe and North America. How ANPR is used by police varies by jurisdiction. Most police agencies utilize the technology to identify vehicles or individuals of interest by comparing licence plate reads against a growing number of police-relevant databases. In most cases, ANPR systems are introduced within police organizations on a limited trial basis and are then expanded quantitatively, in terms of procuring additional ANPR units, and/or qualitatively through function creep, increasing the scope and purpose for its deployment. The addition of new cameras, databases, software algorithms, as well as the increased interoperability of divergent ANPR initiatives, create new possibilities for ANPR-based policing. However, the modular nature of ANPR facilitates its rapid spread, which will bring about practical and political challenges. ANPR-enabled policing has undoubtedly given, and will continue to give, rise to a number of social consequences that we are yet to understand fully or appreciate.

Despite no known rigorous, independently published evaluations of ANPR, the technology has received acclaim within the law enforcement community for its force-multiplying capabilities, its investigative and intelligence-gathering abilities, as well as its potential for enhancing public and officer safety. This potential, whether real or perceived, then serves to justify the further expansion of ANPR in policing. This proliferation is occurring without much by way of citizen consultation or public debate. 'Project Champion' in Birmingham, UK, provides merely one example of an ANPR network going up without public consultation and citizen input. Indeed, 'Project Champion' may be an extreme case; however, similar stories play out worldwide. Police agencies across the global north are acquiring ANPR, yet citizens are only advised that the technology is in use through tightly scripted media releases that underplay the social consequences of the technology, overstate its effectiveness and efficiency, and seek quickly to alleviate public concern with a 'those with nothing to hide have nothing to fear' discourse.

So on what fronts can we challenge the proliferation of ANPR? While privacy concerns have been raised over ANPR, privacy enhancement features are increasingly designed into digital surveillance systems, which may serve to quiet privacy proponents. The privacy features designed into many law enforcement ANPR applications are a testament to the effectiveness of privacy advocates; however, there may be much more work to be done should ANPR systems become interoperable and data-sharing across jurisdictions and/or ANPR networks become the norm. There are, of course, other grounds on which ANPR systems may be challenged, including issues of data security and database accuracy. Use of the technology by police also raises questions regarding discrimination and social sorting that beg further exploration.

This chapter sheds some light on ANPR as an emerging technology of policing; however, more empirical, conceptual and critical work is necessary, as currently the discourse around ANPR is largely being shaped by system developers and proponents within the law enforcement community, hardly a recipe for critically informed public debate. As someone who currently does not drive, it could be argued that I have nothing to fear from ANPR-enabled policing. But alas I am fearful. Some law enforcement proponents for ANPR herald the technology as 'revolutionary'. Notwithstanding the questionable strength of such a claim, it seems clear that ANPR represents a change-step in law enforcement practice, facilitating some degree of 'dragnet' policing. The ability of police agencies in liberal democracies to implement such a significant shift in police tactics without public consultation or debate – hence without informed public consent – is frightening indeed.

References

Altman, D., Heater, D. and Besco, M. (2009) 'Georgetown (S.C.) Police Department uses LPR to Combat Crime', *Law Officer Magazine*, 5(4). Available HTTP: <http://www.lawofficer.com>.

Bloomberg, M., Kelly, R. and Falkenrath, R. (2009) *Engineering Security: Protective Design for High Risk Buildings*, New York: New York Police Department.

Canadian Association of Mutual Insurance Companies (2009) *Newsletter*, Winter 2009. Ottawa.

City of Toronto (2009) *Toronto Police Service: 2008 Annual Report on Parking Tag Issuance*, Toronto.

Coaffee, J. (2004) 'Rings of steel, rings of concrete and rings of confidence: Designing out terrorism in Central London pre and post September 11', *International Journal of Urban and Regional Research*, 28(1): 201–11.

Cordery, W. (2009) 'Keen-eyed cameras will be added soon to RCMP arsenal: Devices scan licence plates while officers are on patrol', *The Daily News* (Nanaimo), 6 October. Available HTTP: <http://www.chtv.com/ch/cheknews/story.html?id=2b158f49-84aa-48c0-bfe7-bc57d7f50175>.

Duncan, J. (2008) 'Peek-a-boo . . . I see you!', *Tech Talk. The British Columbia Institute of Technology*, Spring: 7–8.

Ericson, R.V. and Haggerty, K.D. (1997) *Policing the Risk Society*, Toronto: University of Toronto Press.

Evans-Pughe, C. (2006) 'Road Watch', *Engineering & Technology*, July.

Fenton, R. (1980) 'On future traffic control: Advanced systems hardware', *IEEE Transactions on Vehicular Technology*, 29(2): 200–7.

Fonio, C. and Derby, P. (2009) 'The technical context of camera surveillance in Canada', in *A Report on Camera Surveillance in Canada: Part Two*, Surveillance Camera Awareness Network, Kingston: Queen's University.

Gaumont, N. and Babineau, D. (2008) 'The role of automatic license plate recognition technology in policing: Results from the lower mainland of British Columbia', *The Police Chief*, 75(11). Available HTTP: <http://policechiefmagazine.org>.

Gaventa, J. (2005) 'Policing Road Risk: New Technologies, Road Traffic Enforcement and Road Safety.' Paper presented at RoSPA Road Safety Congress, March.

Haggerty, K.D. and Ericson, R.V. (2000) 'The surveillant assemblage', *British Journal of Sociology*, 51(4): 605–22.

Hauslen, R. (1977) 'The promise of automatic vehicle identification', *IEEE Transactions of Vehicular Technology*, 26(1): 30–8.

Information and Privacy Commissioner of Ontario (2003) 'Privacy Investigation: The Toronto Police Service's Use of Mobile Licence Plate Recognition Technology to Find Stolen Vehicles.' Toronto.

Kruegle, H. (2007) *CCTV Surveillance: Analogue and Digital Video Practices and Technology*, New York: Elsevier.

Larson, R., Colton, K. and Larson, G. (1977) 'Evaluating a police-implemented AVM system: The St Louis Experience (Phase 1)', *IEEE Transactions on Vehicular Research*, 26(1): 60–70.

Lewis, P. (2008) 'Fears over privacy as police expand surveillance project', *The Guardian*, 15 September. Available HTTP: <http://www.guardian.co.uk/uk/2008/sep/15/civil-liberties.police>.

Lewis, P. and Evans, R. (2009) 'Activists repeatedly stopped and searched as police officers "mark" cars', *The Guardian*, 25 October. Available HTTP: <http://www.guardian.co.uk/uk/2009/oct/25/surveillance-police-number-plate-recognition>.

Lips, M., Taylor, J. and Organ, J. (2009) 'Identity management, administrative sorting and citizenship in new modes of government', *Information, Communication & Society*, 12(5): 715–34.

Lysecki, S. (2007) 'Licence plate recognition tool used for auto theft recovery and border security', *Canadian Security Magazine*, 27 June.

McKay, J. (2008) 'License plate recognition systems extend the reach of patrol officers', *Government Technology*.

Ministry of Public Safety and Solicitor General (2006) 'Government and police launch new crime-fighting tool', News Release. November. Available HTTP: <http://www2.news.gov.bc.ca/news_releases_2005-2009/2006PSSG0054-001342.htm>.

Monahan, T. (2007) '"War rooms" of the street: Surveillance practices in transportation control centers', *The Communication Review*, 10(4): 367–89.

Norris, C. and Armstrong, G. (1999) *The Maximum Surveillance Society: The Rise of CCTV*, Oxford: Berg.

Ontario Provincial Police (2009) 'OPP licence plate recognition project means traffic offenders more easily detected on roads and highways', News Release. 3 December. Available HTTP: <http://www.opp.ca/ecms/index.php?id=405&nid=94>.

PA Consulting Group (2003) 'Engaging Criminality – Denying Criminals Use of the Road.' London.

PA Consulting Group (2005) 'ACPO and Home Office Police Standards Unit: Denying criminals use of the roads through "joined up" application of number-plate recognition technology.' London.

PA Consulting Group (2006) 'Police Standards Unit: Thematic Review of the Use of Automatic Number Plate Recognition Within Police Forces.' London.

PA Consulting Group (2007) 'Police Standards Unit: Evaluation of Automatic Number Plate Recognition 2006/2007.' London.

Petru, C. (2009) 'Memorandum – Pilot Program Status Report on the Automatic License Plated Recognition (ANPR) System.' Rancho Palos Verdes.

Public Works and Government Service Canada (2009) 'Notice of Proposed Procurement – Automated License Plate Recognition.' Available HTTP: <http://www.merx.com>.

Ross, C. (2008) 'Plate scanner help nab traffic offenders', *The Gazette*, 70(2). Available HTTP: <http://www.rcmp-grc.gc.ca/gazette/vol70n2/news-nuvelles1-eng.htm>.

Roth, S. (1977) 'History of Automatic Vehicle Monitoring (AVM)', *IEEE Transactions on Vehicular Technology*, 26(1): 2–6.

Shumate, D. (2009) 'License plate readers in San Diego County', *The Police Chief*, 76(5). Available HTTP: <http://policechiefmagazine.org>.

Toronto Police Service (2003) 'Toronto Police Service Annual Report 2003.' Toronto.

Ward, D. (2006) 'High-tech "street-sweeper" sorts licence plates', *Vancouver Sun*, 10 Novemeber. Available HTTP: <http://www.canada.com/vancouversun/news/story.html?id=7bb1cf15-ed06-4a1f-9ec8-52d709346e0b>.

Wells, H. (2008) 'The techno-fix versus the fair cop: Procedural (in)justice and automated speed limit enforcement', *British Journal of Criminology*, 48: 798–817.

Wyatt, N. (2008) 'Que. Police using cameras to snare motorist', *The Canadian Press*.

10

VIDEO SURVEILLANCE IN VANCOUVER

Legacies of the Games

Micheal Vonn and Philip Boyle

In February 2010, Canada hosted the Winter Olympics in Vancouver, BC. With a budget of CAN$900 million and involving 5,700 police officers, 4,000 members of the armed forces and 4,800 private security personnel, authorities and critics alike described this event as the largest security operation in Canada's history. Surveillance cameras were an integral part of these efforts. Public authorities used nearly 1,000 surveillance cameras to monitor event venues and perimeters, two outdoor 'live sites', major transportation hubs and corridors, and various other locations around Vancouver during the course of the Games. In what has become a recurring pattern for the host cities of the Olympic Games and other major events, some of these cameras were retained for post-event use. As such, the Vancouver Games are a recent example of the role of major events in driving the proliferation of surveillance cameras in urban space.

The local politics of public surveillance in Vancouver

The role of the 2010 Winter Games in boosting the number of cameras in the city needs to be seen against the backdrop of the local politics of public surveillance in the city.[1] There have been at least two concerted efforts to establish public surveillance cameras in Vancouver prior to the Olympics. The first was in 1996 when the Vancouver Police Department (VPD) proposed installing 16 cameras in the city's Downtown Eastside, a zone of deeply impacted poverty where drugs, alcoholism and property crime are part of daily life. This initiative was put forward as a way to monitor the street-level trade and use of drugs in the community but was derailed after encountering significant and unexpected community opposition to the idea (Haggerty, Huey and Ericson 2008). The second attempt came in 2006 when the VPD proposed establishing surveillance cameras along Granville Street in downtown Vancouver. Once a thriving commercial corridor home to a number of decadent theatres, Granville Street experienced significant decline in the 1970s and 1980s, and became populated by gritty hotels, pawnshops, homeless people, and the centre of a swift drug trade. Part of Granville Street was rezoned in the 1980s as a pedestrian mall in an effort to compete with a newly opened indoor mall nearby, but revitalization remained slow, difficult and highly uneven (Lees 1998). In 1997, municipal authorities tried a different tack by designating a three-block stretch of Granville the 'Theatre Row Entertainment District' and allowing greater densities of liquor seats in the area. The number of drinking establishments swiftly increased: prior to 1997 the area had 1,175 licenced liquor seats, which grew to an estimated 6,700 by 2007 (COV 2007: 3).

This revitalization effort predictably generated its own problems. As the Entertainment District became a popular night-time destination for people from across the region, it also became a chief problem area for the police, where assaults, gang-related activity, and high levels of noise, drinking and vandalism are weekly routines, particularly during the summer months. After a number of high-profile incidents, the Entertainment District became the next candidate site for video surveillance in the city, with a proposal coming before the Vancouver Police Board in early 2006 to study the issue. Unlike the previous attempt, this proposal accentuated problems associated with the night-time economy, high call loads and officer safety, previous instances of civil unrest (the 1994 Stanley Cup riot and 2002 Guns & Roses riot are specifically cited as occurrences when video surveillance could have helped to maintain public order), their anticipated use during the 'heightened security around the Olympic domain' (VPB 2006: 3), and their potential counter-terrorism uses. The proposal distanced itself from the 1996 plan by assuring the board and members of the public in attendance that 'the cameras would not be focused on the DTES' (VPB 2006: 3). A subsequent examination of the utility of cameras in the Entertainment District also included the endorsement of a senior UK police constable who states, 'this is exactly the kind of area where we would install CCTV in England' (Sullivan 2006).

The proposal initially planned to have 'Phase One' operational sometime in 2008, but no further discussion of the matter came before the police board after December 2006, leaving privacy advocates to wonder what had occurred (Huey 2009). In hindsight it appears that the VPD may have been aware of developments occurring elsewhere related to the Olympics and dropped the proposal in a strategic move to take advantage of those developments in the future.

Surveillance cameras as a spatial tactic

Surveillance cameras were an integral element of the overall security plan for the 2010 Olympics. The RCMP's Integrated Security Unit (ISU), the federal-level policing unit with overall responsibility for security for the Games, deployed approximately 900 surveillance cameras to monitor event venues, perimeters and other Olympic sites directly under their jurisdiction. These cameras were joined by approximately 70 video cameras operated by municipal authorities to monitor two outdoor 'live sites' in downtown Vancouver where patrons could view events on large video screens, the Robson and Granville corridors where much of the Olympic revelry was located, and a mobile surveillance unit 'essential for ensuring effective emergency management in key areas' during the Games (COV 2009: 1).

We suggest that it is useful to see these cameras as one element in a complex of tactics that aimed to establish territorial control during the event (Vonn 2010; Zick 2006). The most striking examples of tactics of spatial control can be found in the evolving craft of policing at major political summits, which relies in large part on controlling space with tactics such as partitioning, dispersing or containing ('kettling') protesters, barricading leaders within highly fortified island sites, or simply hosting the event in remote locations (Warren 2002; Waddington 2008). These tactics often interlock with legal provisions that are spatial in nature, such as laws that restrict or exclude activities to and from defined zones or suspend the normal principles of due process. One contentious example of this sort comes from the 2010 G20 meeting in Toronto, where provincial authorities defined the perimeter fencing around the meeting zone as a 'public work' and thus subject to the provisions of the obscure Protection of Public Works Act, which grants police officers enhanced search and arrest powers in the immediate vicinity of these areas.[2]

Security for the Olympics is less overtly militarized than for major political summits but is no less about establishing territorial control. In Vancouver, the overall security plan for the Games was predicated on the spatial distinction between the 'Olympic domain' and the 'urban domain', with the ISU responsible for the former and local authorities for the latter. Approximately two-dozen Olympic domain sites were identified at the early stages of planning for the Games, which grew to nearly 200 by 2010 as further locations were added to the list. This designation did not set these sites apart in a legal sense, but risk assessments were performed on an ongoing basis for all Olympic domain sites, with the most at-risk locations subject to intensive security before and during the 17-day period of the Games. The venues themselves were the most tightly controlled, with fenced perimeters set well back from the structures and airport-style security checks required for access. Prominently regulated areas in the urban domain included the two live sites in downtown Vancouver, the Robson/Granville area, and hotels where officials and diplomats were lodged. Concerns were also raised that a number of existing or proposed legal provisions would be selectively enforced in order to displace people and activities deemed incongruous with the Olympic ideal. These concerns stemmed in part from the trademark protection laws – otherwise known as ambush marketing laws – required by the IOC and adopted at both the federal and municipal levels, which critics said left too much discretion for authorities to confiscate material critical of the Olympics (signs, pamphlets, artwork) on the basis of trademark infringements.[3] Concerns were also raised that the police planned to aggressively enforce the province's Safe Streets Act and Assistance to Shelter Act in order to keep Vancouver's homeless population away from the festivities. The most contentious proposal had to do with safe assembly sites for protesters, which appears to have been briefly considered by the ISU before being dropped. These security measures in and around Vancouver were joined by the reinforcement of existing security measures at key transportation locations such as the regional ferry network, international airport, and US border 50 km to the south, all of which took place under the regional perimeters established by the Canadian Forces and NORAD's early warning radar system.

As the Vancouver instance suggests, security for these global events is less of a bubble of absolute security as it is an elaborate archipelago of secured island sites, nested perimeters and fortified corridors that produce a complex geography of security that can span entire metropolitan regions. Video surveillance is integral to this geography. The sheer concentration of surveillance cameras during the Games serves to highlight its role in establishing spatial control over populations by defining a carefully monitored 'security space' of perimeters, corridors and points of passage. This in turn can be seen as part of the wider embrace of a 'resilient' mindset in which exercising 'command and control' by attaining 'full situational awareness' during times of heightened uncertainty has become a key governmental objective (Lakoff 2007; Coaffee, Murakami Wood and Rogers 2009).

This element of territorial control was most evident during the protests that occurred in Vancouver during the first two days of the Games. As touched on above, the ISU ultimately abandoned the proposal to establish safe assembly sites for the Games, presumably due to a mix of negative public response and questionable constitutionality of the practice (Pue and Diab 2009). Instead, protesters were 'allowed' to assemble in front of the Vancouver Art Gallery, a site that has been traditionally used for public demonstrations in the city (which was arguably a more effective strategy on the part of authorities to concentrate protests than safe assembly sites would have been anyway). Being squarely in the heart of the festivities in downtown Vancouver, this area was densely monitored by surveillance cameras. Surveillance of the protest went mobile as it moved from the art gallery towards the venue of the opening ceremonies, where it was recorded by a moving cordon of officers from ground level, nearby rooftops, and above by a police helicopter. The march eventually came to a halt at the venue itself when it met a heavy line of officers that formed at an intersection near the venue. Police videotaped the protest from behind the line, and protesters reciprocated the gaze by recording the police in turn.

This situation was repeated the following day in a more frantic manner when a smaller group of protesters attempted to march upon a West End hotel where IOC executives were lodged. Crowd control police channelled the bulk of the protest away from the hotel and partitioned the group into smaller and smaller crowds, many of whom dispersed as a result of further tactics such as bluff charges or simply because of the sheer number of officers that converged on the area.[4] The core of the protest was eventually contained on a major West End street where police once again filmed protesters, who in turn filmed the police for approximately two hours before being tightly corralled along a sidewalk and convinced to leave – an agreement recorded, of course, on camera. Viewing footage from the protests that was widely available online after the event, it seems clear that video surveillance was one element in a 'turf war' at play between protesters and the police in which each attempted to claim and control space at the expense of the other.

Surveillance legacies

There was much debate in Vancouver over whether the surveillance cameras used during the Games would be retained after the event. ISU representatives repeatedly stated that the cameras were not permanent and would be removed after the Games, but these assurances did not allay concerns among those trying to keep up with developments. Gaining even rudimentary details about preparations for the Games was extremely difficult given the wider constellation of agencies involved in the Games, which was compounded by deliberate efforts on the part of authorities to remain opaque to outside observers. For example, approximately a year before the Games the ISU bluntly stated that it would not continue, or seriously slow down, the processing of Freedom of Information Requests because the number of requests was becoming too onerous for ISU labour to keep up (see also Huey 2009).

But looking back on the Games with the benefit of a year's hindsight, it appears safe to say that the more sinister visions of a post-Games police state in Vancouver were not realized. That said, the Olympics did auger developments that made the retention of some surveillance cameras a foregone conclusion even before the opening ceremonies. As noted above, municipal authorities deployed approximately 70 cameras to monitor sites in the urban domain during the Games. These cameras were obtained in part by funds granted through a provincial initiative to study the use of video surveillance in high-crime areas of the province (BC 2008). Vancouver received approximately half of the CAN$1 million made available to BC municipalities through this programme. The city also received over CAN$2 million from the Integrated Security Unit specifically for monitoring sites outside the ISU's jurisdiction. This came before city council in early 2009 when Vancouver's Office of Emergency Management (OEM) asked council to accept the combined CAN$2.5 million of funding in order to provide 'rapidly deployable temporary monitoring capabilities at large public events or in response to hazards, emergencies and other unforeseen eventualities' (COV 2009). Though these cameras were described as temporary, critics were quick to note that the funds from the province were specifically earmarked for the construction of a permanent monitoring station in the city's OEM building. Pressed to explain the discrepancy, city officials suggested there had been a miscommunication, saying when they used the term 'temporary', they had actually meant 're-deployable' (Hasiuk 2009). This confirmed for many that authorities had not only been shopping for a suitable neighbourhood in which to establish surveillance cameras (Haggerty et al. 2008: 48) but had found an opportune moment to implement them as well.

The monitoring station is of additional significance because of its technical architecture, which has been configured to open standards so that future expansion or linkages with other systems (such as to the regional transportation authority) are possible in the future. As an OEM official explained to one of us in an interview,

In the system design and work that we are doing in terms of the network infrastructure and technology infrastructure we have kept future interoperability in mind. We wanted to make sure that the technical piece was capable of doing that, but those linkages haven't been made yet.

How exactly the cameras purchased and owned by the OEM will be used in the future or what linkages between the OEM and other systems might be forged remains an open question at this point, but previous official statements indicate they will be used for mobile monitoring capabilities for the city's annual Festival of Lights, other large-scale gatherings (such as major hockey games) and public emergencies. Official interest from the VPD in having cameras in the Entertainment District remains high, however; indeed, the VPD expressed their interest in being consulted on the use of the cameras almost as soon as the Paralympic Games concluded in early March 2010 (Lupick 2010).[5] Given the long-standing interest in having cameras in this area, widespread support in the media, lack of local opposition to the idea, and technical capability to grow the system, it seems it may only be a matter of time before surveillance cameras creep into the Entertainment District.

The Vancouver Games are but one expression of how lasting security transformations, including the retention of surveillance cameras, have become predictable outcomes of hosting major events. Indeed, such transformations are now explicitly encouraged alongside investments in transportation infrastructures, sporting facilities and hospitality amenities as yet another upshot of being among the select few cities to host the Games (Boyle and Haggerty 2009a, 2009b; Giulianotti and Klauser 2010). Peter Ryan, former top law enforcement officer during the 2000 Sydney Games and now one of the IOC's foremost security consultants, clearly articulates this kind of opportunism when he states, 'The preparations for the Games and the investment in security infrastructure will be an enormous legacy for the country and its national security capability after the Games are over. This opportunity should not be wasted' (Ryan 2002: 26). IOC President Jacques Rogge made a similar point when visiting Vancouver before the 2010 Games, saying, 'Security investment always leaves a good legacy of security for the country. Whenever the Games are finished, everything that has been built, the expertise that has been acquired, the hardware that has been put in place, is serving the country and the region for decades to follow' (Simpson 2009).

In Greece, for example, security preparations for the 2004 Games took place within the broader modernization of the country's national security apparatus that had been ongoing for at least a decade (Samatas 2004). It was in this context that Greece spent an estimated US$1.5 billion on security for the Olympics, which was timed to coincide with the Games but linked to the long-term policy objectives of the state. Greece's Minister of Public Safety said this of Greece's unprecedented security budget: 'This great expenditure is not concerned only with the duration of the Olympics. It is an investment for the future. The special training, technical know-how, and ultramodern equipment will turn the Hellenic Police into one of the best and most professional in the world, for the benefit of the Greek people' (Floridis 2004: 4). The centrepiece of this 'ultramodern equipment' was a large-scale communications and data transmission system designed to integrate all security-related sub-systems, including up to 1,600 surveillance cameras during the Games, into a single network that was designed and delivered as a lasting legacy of the Games (Samatas 2007). Likewise, security for the 2008 Beijing Games was nested within the broader modernization of Beijing's policing and surveillance capabilities. Official reports from China state that US$350 million was spent on security for the 2008 Games (Thompson 2008), but the Security Industry Association (2007) estimates that China spent US$6.5 billion on security projects as part of the 'Grand Beijing Safeguard Sphere', one of nearly 300 'Safe Cities' programmes being rolled out across the country in the last decade, the legacy of which prompts cultural critic Naomi Klein to refer to post-Games Beijing as 'Police State 2.0' (Dickinson 2008).

The long-term outcomes of the Games will obviously differ in each case due to a wide variety of factors; Vancouver is not Beijing or Athens, and London is not Sochi or Rio de Janeiro. Nonetheless, these examples underscore how the Games can justify surveillance 'surges' involving the rapid introduction of new measures with less public debate than usual because they are deemed necessary responses to a given situation (Ball and Webster 2003: 141). Importantly, these measures can endure long after the events are over as host governments try to obtain a return on what is now an immense financial investment for a one-off event or capitalize on weakened public opposition to introduce new measures that would otherwise encounter stiff resistance. A glimpse of this latter dynamic is gained from a leaked memo from the 'No. 10 Policy Working Group on Security, Crime and Justice, Technological Advances' in the UK, which deals with the implementation of a number of proposed surveillance measures, including the expansion of a DNA database for suspected terrorists and their families. In anticipating the public disapproval that such measures might encounter, the memo concludes, 'Increasing [public] support could be possible through the piloting of certain approaches in high-profile ways such as the London Olympics' (in Hennessy and Leapman 2007, insertion in original).

Furthermore, the legacies of Athens and Beijing highlight the governmental ambition to 'bring systems together, to combine practices and technologies and integrate them into a larger whole [. . .] with such combinations providing for exponential increases in the degree of surveillance capacity'(Haggerty and Ericson 2000: 610). If surveillance assemblages are 'all about linking, cross-referencing, [and] pulling threads together that previously were separate' (Lyon 2003: 647), then major events provide the need and opportunity for the 'pulling together' of assemblages with the power of scrutiny that is significantly greater than the sum of its parts. In the UK, for example, preparations for the Games include efforts towards making London's patchwork of surveillance cameras spread among other public agencies and the private sector accessible by the Metropolitan Police, which if successful would boost the Met's monitoring capabilities exponentially. The legacies of the Vancouver Games are not as sweeping as those of recent Olympics but they are fully in keeping with their overall dynamics.

Conclusion

In this chapter we have outlined how video surveillance was one element in a repertoire of tactics used to control space during the Games. We also touched on some of the lasting outcomes of this event, namely the retention of video surveillance cameras for use in public space, against the backdrop of the local politics of public surveillance in Vancouver. As we have outlined, the rationale for implementing video surveillance in Vancouver has undergone a discernable shift over the years from one that underscored urban decay and victimization to one that emphasizes the need for enhanced crowd control and emergency response capabilities that grew out of the inherently chaotic and liquor-fuelled nature of the Entertainment District. Given the immense public support for the idea and lack of community-based opposition in the area, the use of video surveillance in the Entertainment District was already looking probable even without the additional impetus of the Olympics (Haggerty, Huey and Ericson 2008; Huey 2009). The Games did, however, greatly accentuate these concerns, making the need for cameras even more pressing and self-evident while further marginalizing any remaining opposition. Furthermore, the city merely had to accept funds for the cameras from higher levels of government rather than allocate funds from other budgets or circulate proposals through the police board as with previous practice, making the retention of the cameras after the Games a foregone conclusion (Huey 2009). Again, it remains an open question as to whether they will be used in the Entertainment District, but the combination of free money from other levels of government, pre-existing official interest in video surveillance in the city, their 'proven' utility as a tactic of spatial control to manage large crowds and emergencies, and technical capability to expand the system strongly suggests this is a possibility in the future. These developments in Vancouver are but one instance of a recurring pattern wherein surveillance measures introduced for temporary major events are retained for post-event use and become embedded features of the urban landscape.

While the retention of cameras in Vancouver is a notable development, we should also avoid letting this single issue detract from the wider panoply of surveillance-related developments associated with hosting the Games. In Vancouver, the 70-odd cameras retained by the OEM are also joined by those that accompanied major projects such as the city's new convention centre, rail link to the airport, and highway to Whistler. BC Ferries alone added over 800 cameras and refurbished its central monitoring station with security upgrades timed to coincide with the Games. A full and accurate inventory of this wider proliferation of cameras is probably impossible to ascertain, but at the same time it probably dwarfs those owned and operated directly by the city. And cameras, of course, are not the only – or even primary – method of monitoring people. Surveillance is the collection and analysis of information in order to govern people and processes (Haggerty and Ericson 2006: 3). Thousands of individuals were entered into government databases that may remain today as part of accreditation requirements for the Games or because they were caught in the dragnet of pre-Games surveillance that focused on protesters from across Canada. Advance preparations for the Games included the high-resolution aerial mapping of the lower mainland region to provide a 'common operating picture' for agencies involved in the Games, as well as 'all future emergency and public safety events' (Inwood 2008). The Games were also taken as a need and opportunity to accelerate the implementation of enhanced drivers' licences in BC and the state of Washington in order to meet the needs of the Western Hemisphere Travel Initiative. At other Games we have witnessed attempts to make RFID- and biometrically enhanced tickets workable on a large scale, the piloting of surveillance cameras augmented with various recognition capabilities, and, in Greece, a phone-tapping scandal that threatened the highest levels of government (Samatas 2007). Non-security related problems such as doping in sport and the epidemiological dimension of mass gatherings produce substantial informational requirements around which surveillance has grown exponentially (Park 2005; Lombardo et al. 2008).

As these examples suggest, surveillance cameras are the most visible tip of myriad surveillance measures that coalesce around the Games to make these events visible and governable, the legacies of which can extend far beyond the events themselves as they sharpen the perception of need or provide the opportunity to advance institutional agendas. Perhaps the wider significance of these global events that happen in intensely local sites is that they highlight the ongoing deepening of security and surveillance into the fabric of urban life (Coaffee and Wood 2006; Coaffee et al. 2009; Graham 2010). Technologically, these events are showcases for developments in surveillance and security products before they are promoted as 'proven' security solutions for a range of security anxieties within the global homeland security market. Epistemologically, these events are key locations in the production and globalization of security expertise pertaining to 'joined-up' governance and crisis management, the lessons from which are carried forward to other events and drawn upon as models of 'secure and resilient' cities in general (Boyle 2011). And culturally, they are fertile grounds for concerns about catastrophic terrorism that reinforce the refrain that we are living in a world of unpredictable, high-consequence risk in which ever-greater levels of security are necessary, desirable and of unquestionable legitimacy. Being microcosms of developments in surveillance today and laboratories for surveillance tomorrow, the ultimate legacy of the Games may be that they provide glimpses of a more heavily monitored urban future.

Notes

1   Like many cities, surveillance cameras are ubiquitous in private and quasi-private space in Vancouver. The Vancouver Public Space Network has mapped up to 2,000 privately owned cameras in central Vancouver (see <http://www.vancouverpublicspace.ca>). Our discussion in this chapter is limited primarily to cameras owned and operated by public agencies.
2   Authorities failed to clarify until after the G20 that these provisions only applied to certain buildings *within* the security perimeter, not the perimeter itself, even though police had enforced the law as if it applied to the perimeter during the event.

3   The municipal bylaw, which authorized the *immediate* confiscation of trademarked material, was not in effect during the Games, having been repealed by the City after a constitutional legal challenge was launched. The federal legislation, which did not authorize immediate confiscation and included specific exemptions for the use of trademarks for 'criticism or parody', was in effect during the Games and expired at the end of 2010.
4   During the march around the West End on Day One of the Olympics the police would form lines to partition the diffuse crowd into smaller groups, then 'charge' at the stragglers in formation while blowing whistles and yelling. The VPD employed this tactic on numerous occasions on this day.
5   In a similar development, Toronto's police chief expressed interest in retaining approximately two-thirds of the 77 cameras leased by the city for the G20 in order to expand surveillance coverage of Toronto's Entertainment District on the basis of their 'proven' utility during the G20 (Paperny 2010).

References

Ball, K. and Webster, F. (2003) 'The Intensification of Surveillance', in K. Ball and F. Webster (eds), *The Intensification of Surveillance: Crime, Terrorism and Warfare in the Information Age*, London: Pluto Press, 1–15.

BC (2008) *Province Announces Pilot to Monitor High-crime Areas*, Victoria: Ministry of Public Safety and Solicitor General and Ministry of the Attorney General.

Boyle, P. (2011) 'Knowledge networks: mega-events and security expertise', in K.D. Haggerty and C. Bennett (eds), *Security Games: Surveillance and Control at Mega-Events*, London: Routledge, 169–184.

Boyle, P. and Haggerty, K.D. (2009a) 'Spectacular Security: Mega-Events and the Security Complex', *International Political Sociology*, 3(3): 257–74.

Boyle, P. and Haggerty, K.D. (2009b) *Privacy Games: The Vancouver Olympics, Privacy, and Surveillance*, Ottawa: Privacy Commissioner of Canada.

Coaffee, J. and Murakami Wood, D. (2006) 'Security is Coming Home: Rethinking Scale and Constructing Resilience in the Global Urban Response to Terrorist Risk', *International Relations*, 20(4): 503–17.

Coaffee, J., Murakami Wood, D. and Rogers, P. (2009) *The Everyday Resilience of the City: How Cities Respond to Terrorism and Disaster*, London and New York: Palgrave MacMillan.

COV (2007) *Administrative Report from the VPD Chief Constable, VPD and Chief Licence Official and General Manager of Engineering Services Re: Granville Entertainment District*. Vancouver: Vancouver City Hall.

COV (2009) *Minutes of the Mar. 29 Standing Committee on City Services and Budgets Report re: Acceptance of Funding for Temporary CCTV*, Vancouver: Vancouver City Hall.

Dickinson, T. (2008) *Under surveillance: Q + A with Naomi Klein,'*29 May. Online. Available HTTP: <http://www.rollingstone.com > (accessed 27 August 27 2008)

Floridis, G. (2004) 'Security for the 2004 Athens Olympic Games', *Mediterranean Quarterly*, 15(2): 1–5.

Giulianotti, R. and Klauser, F. (2010) 'Security governance and sports mega-events: towards an interdisciplinary research agenda', *Journal of Sport and Social Issues*, 34(1): 49–61.

Graham, S. (2010) *Cities Under Siege: The New Military Urbanism*, London and New York: Verso.

Haggerty, K.D. and Ericson, R.V. (2006) 'The New Politics of Surveillance and Visibility,' in K.D. Haggerty and R.V. Ericson (eds), *The New Politics of Surveillance and Visibility*, Toronto: University of Toronto Press, 3–25.

Haggerty, K.D., Huey, L. and Ericson, R.V. (2008) 'The Politics of Sight/Site: Locating Cameras in Vancouver's Public Space', *Sociology of Crime, Law and Governance*, 10: 35–55.

Hennessy, P. and Leapman, B. (2007) *Ministers Plan 'Big Brother' Police Powers*, 2 April. Online. Available HTTP: <http://www.telegraph.co.uk> (accessed 12 February 2007).

Huey, L. (2009) *The Surveillance Legacy: What Happens to Vancouver's Camera Surveillance Systems After the 2010 Olympics?*, Kingston, Ontario: The Surveillance Project.

Inwood, D. (2008) 'HD aerial pics aim to bolster 2010 security', *The Vancouver Sun*, 14 December, A23.

Lakoff, A. (2007) 'Preparing for the next emergency', *Public Culture*, 19(2): 247–71.

Lees, L. (1998) 'Urban Renaissance and the Street: Spaces of Control and Contestation', in N. Fyfe (ed.), *Images of the Street: Planning, Identity, and Control in Public Space*, London: Routledge.

Lombardo, J., Sniegoski, C., Loschen, W., Westercamp, M., Wade, M., Dearth, S. and Zhang, G. (2008) 'Public health surveillance for mass gatherings', *John Hopkins Technical Digest*, 27(4): 347–55.

Lupick, T. (2010) 'Vancouver police want say in future of Olympic surveillance cameras', *Straight.com*, 3 March 2010. Online. Available HTTP: <http://www.straight.com/article-296373/vancouver/vancouver-police-want-say-future-olympic-surveillance-cameras>

Paperny, A. (2010) 'Police aim to keep G20 cameras, sound cannons', *The Globe and Mail*, November 15, A13.

Park, J. (2005) 'Governing doping bodies: the world anti-doping agency and the global culture of surveillance', *Cultural Studies*, 5(2): 174–88.

Pue, W. and Diab, R. (2009) 'Security for the Olympics: British Columbia needs a public order policing act', *The Advocate*, 67(5): 595–602.

Ryan, P. (2002) *Olympic Security: The Relevance to Homeland Security*, Salt Lake City: The Oquirrh Institute.

Samatas, M. (2004) *Surveillance in Greece: From Anticommunist to Consumer Surveillance*, New York: Athens Printing Company.

Samatas, M. (2007) 'Security and Surveillance in the Athens 2004 Olympics: Some Lessons From a Troubled Story', *International Criminal Justice Review*, 17(3): 220–38.

SIA (2007) *China Security Market Report Special Supplement: Olympic Update*, Alexandria, VA: Security Industry Association.

Simpson, S. (2009) 'Greater industrial security expected at 2010 Games', *The Vancouver Sun*, 13 October, C4.

Sullivan, S. (2006) *Closed Circuit Television Project*, Vancouver: Vancouver Police Board.

Thompson, D. (2008) 'Olympic security collaboration', *China Security Review*, 4(2): 46–58.

Vonn, M. (2010) 'CCTV and the 2010 Vancouver Games: spatial tactics and political strategies', *Case Western Reserve Journal of International Law*, 42: 505–605.

VPB (2006) *Minutes of the May 17 Vancouver Police Board regular meeting*, Vancouver: Vancouver Police Board.

Waddington, D. (2008) *Public Order Policing: Theory and Practice*, Portland, OR: Willan Publishing.

Warren, R. (2002) 'Situating the City and September 11th: Military Urban Doctrine, "Pop-Up" Armies and Spatial Chess', *International Journal of Urban and Regional Research*, 26(3): 614–19.

Yu, Y., Klauser, F. and Chan, G. (2009) 'Governing security at the 2008 Beijing Olympics', *International Journal of the History of Sport*, 26(3): 390–405.

Zick, T. (2006) 'Speech and spatial tactics', *Texas Law Review*, 84(3): 581.

11

SELLING SURVEILLANCE

The introduction of cameras in Ottawa taxis

Aaron Doyle and Kevin Walby

Introduction

Surveillance cameras in taxicabs (hereafter simply referred to as 'cabs') are touted by those inside and outside the taxi industry as keeping drivers and passengers safe. What we will call 'taxi-cams' are a seemingly innocuous form of surveillance in which tiny cameras are mounted inside cabs – often near the rear-view mirrors – that record what goes on inside the cab so it can be downloaded later by police or others if need be. Cameras in cabs are said by their advocates to deter violence, prevent theft and provide evidence that facilitates prosecutions.

Whether the cameras actually work in reducing crime against drivers is a difficult question to answer. There are so far no independent studies confirming the benefits of cab cameras, reflecting a broader situation in which there is a lack of evidence regarding the effectiveness of surveillance cameras more generally (see Norris, this volume). Nevertheless, cameras in taxis have become more prevalent over the last dozen years or so. The number of jurisdictions mandating surveillance cameras in taxis in Western countries continues to grow. One cab camera company called VerifEye Technologies boasts on its website that it had installed 74,000 cameras globally in cabs, limousines and buses as of January 2009. And VerifEye is only one of numerous companies.

We became interested in another kind of question: understanding the *process* by which the cameras have been introduced, as part of a consideration of patterns in the introduction of surveillance cameras, and implications of these patterns. Rather than assessing the effectiveness of cab cameras as such, this chapter instead considers how and under what terms the taxi cameras continue to proliferate, despite the lack so far of definitive evidence of any benefit.

After providing some context regarding introduction of taxi-cams, briefly describing their diffusion across Canada and elsewhere, and reviewing the arguments and evidence about effectiveness, this chapter presents a case study of the debate over cab cameras in Ottawa between 2006 and 2009, ending in their eventual installation. The City of Ottawa proposed installing cameras in Ottawa taxis at drivers' expense. The taxi drivers' union refused installation, and organized three protests at City Hall to demonstrate frustration over proposed terms. Even so, cameras were eventually installed after a series of behind-the-scenes deliberations. We draw in part on access to information (ATI) requests to examine the exchanges that occurred between VerifEye Technologies and the City of Ottawa regarding the cameras. Responsible for cameras in over 70 cities and 20 countries, VerifEye is a proficient marketer of its cameras. We examine how the cameras were ultimately sold to different constituencies: the councillors and staff of the City of Ottawa, the drivers and their union, and the public. We use these data to suggest that the process regarding Ottawa taxis illustrates broader concerns about surveillance, democracy and accountability. We consider what lessons can be learned from these events about the spread of cameras in taxis and in other contexts, and about the spread of surveillance more generally. This chapter thus contributes to building the literature on how, when and why camera surveillance gains political and public support (see e.g. Webster 1996; Norris and Armstrong 1999; Coleman 2004; Hier 2010). It helps build towards a theory of the processes by which surveillance is introduced, something that Gary Marx calls for in his article 'Desperately Seeking Surveillance Studies' (see Marx 2007).

Methods

The empirical research that this chapter is based on has to do with the introduction of taxi-cams across Canada and the specific case of Ottawa. Our exploration began when we interviewed 31 female and male taxi drivers in Ottawa, Toronto and Winnipeg as part of a larger research project on risk and work. While these interviews are not central to our chapter, we draw selectively from them. Because of the nature of the sample,[1] these 31 interviews should be treated as exploratory, rather than representing the views of all drivers.

While the interviews were underway, we became interested in the process by which surveillance cameras were being considered for Ottawa cabs. As a result of this interest, the second author attended two days of protest by taxi drivers at Ottawa City Hall in February 2008 and made field notes. We also collected newspaper articles and material from assorted websites concerning taxi drivers, victimization and camera surveillance, both regarding the particular case of Ottawa and concerning other jurisdictions. Finally, we filed an access to information request with the City of Ottawa concerning their correspondence with the VerifEye cab camera company. Several of the requested documents were redacted under the Municipal Freedom of Information and Protection of Privacy Act for the following reasons: 'prejudices significantly the competitive position or interferes significantly with contractual or other negotiations of a person, group of persons, or organization; could reasonably be expected to be injurious to the financial interests of the

City; could reasonably be expected to prejudice the economic interests of an institution', and others. Nevertheless, we were fortunate to obtain revealing data from the access request. It is rare to be able to access third-party business information through such requests.

Between these various sources of data, we were able to gain insights both into the situations that led to the call for the cameras in Ottawa and into the process by which cameras were introduced.

Assault and robbery of cab drivers

Criminal victimization of cab drivers is a serious concern. According to 2006 figures from Statistics Canada, there were at that time 47,185 Canadians who worked in the taxi, limousine and chauffeur industry. More than 38,000 of these people drove taxis. While many people may think of taxi work as simply driving around in a car all day, it is one of the most risky occupations in terms of criminal victimization. Drivers are highly vulnerable to assault and robbery as they are awkwardly immobile in the front seat of the taxi with their back to the passengers. When making decisions about whom to pick up, drivers must quickly assess passengers' trustworthiness (Toiskallio 1998; Hamill and Gambetta 2006). The driver must evaluate whether passengers' words and gestures signal a person who is risky (Gambetta and Hamill 2005). Picking up a 'bad fare' can result in violence or even death. A study by Stenning (1996) found that Canadian taxi drivers are victimized twenty times more than the average citizen, and that taxi drivers face occupational homicide at a rate four times higher than police. Eighty-five per cent of drivers in Stenning's study had experienced some form of victimization other than fare-jumping (fleeing the cab without paying). One-third had been robbed. Fifteen per cent reported a weapon being used against them. Gilbert's (2005) research on taxi-driving in the USA suggested that the occupational homicide rate for taxi drivers was actually six times higher than that of police. One report from the National Institute of Occupational Safety and Health (1996) suggests that taxi drivers in the USA face an occupational homicide rate 60 times higher than the national average. Elzinga (1996) found similar patterns in the Netherlands, showing that likelihood of victimization for taxi drivers increases with city size and frequency of night shift work. Many factors explain these high levels of driver victimization: for example, working alone, working in a confined space dealing with a continual turnover of strangers, handling cash, pressure to pick up fares to cover costs, having to drive passengers to dimly lit and out-of-the-way places, and working at night. Seventy-five per cent of taxi homicides occur at night (Knestaunt 1997). Ninety-five per cent of robberies and 89 per cent of assaults occur at night (Seattle Taxi Report 2004).[2]

The spread of cab cameras

Are surveillance cameras in taxis the answer to victimization of cab drivers? Everywhere in North America from Little Rock to San Francisco, Winnipeg to New

York and Chicago and Los Angeles, industry representatives have pursued cab cameras with the idea of trying to provide safety to drivers and security to customers.

Having surveillance cameras in cabs is not only a North American trend; there is a global diffusion of cab cameras. Cameras were installed in Beijing taxis before the 2008 summer Olympics. Cabs in Singapore had cameras in 2007. In the UK, Sheffield also added cab cameras in 2007. Glasgow added cab cameras in 2009. Cab cameras are not compulsory in New Zealand, although in 2009 and 2010 cab cameras were in use in many cities after violence against several drivers. Cab cameras became compulsory across Australia as of November 2010, particularly in response to violence against Indian cab drivers in major cities such as Brisbane. The government in the Northern Territory of Australia was offering drivers $3,000 each to outfit their vehicles.

Below we look at the camera company VerifEye, which has several offices on every continent. We zero in on one particular city in Canada and the process through which cameras were implemented.

Cab cameras record a series of images, usually one per second, which are accessible after an incident. Some cities start out permitting but not mandating cab cameras; others adopt cameras for the whole fleet straight away, making them mandatory for all licenced taxis. Some cab company owners adopt cameras to attract drivers to their fleet. But not any camera will do. Software must be compatible with police computers. Hardware must prevent unsolicited access to images. Lighting can impact the image quality. Camera technology companies thus specialize in providing not only the technology but also installation training, software, signage and more.

As part of our research we have documented the diffusion of the taxi cameras across Canada. This diffusion has occurred in piecemeal fashion, one small site or jurisdiction at a time, as has been the case in Canada and elsewhere with surveillance cameras (Whitson, Doyle and Walby 2009; Hier 2010) and surveillance more generally.

Within Canada, taxi-cams are perhaps most widespread in British Columbia. In February 2005, 700 cab cameras were installed by VerifEye Technologies in North Delta, British Columbia. The Vancouver Taxi Association installed Honeywell FareView and VerifEye cameras in over 500 taxis in 2006. Eight Vancouver drivers had been killed in the previous twelve years. A provincial 'Report to the Minister of Transportation and Highways' (1999) had called for cab cameras years earlier. As of 31 March 2009, all taxicabs in Victoria, British Columbia and surrounding area must have a camera. The two largest cab companies in Prince George and Williams Lake, British Columbia use cameras. The camera contracts in Victoria, Prince George and Williams Lake are with VerifEye. Cabs in British Columbia are subject to province-wide regulation (see Passenger Transportation Board ruling 2008), whereas it is more common elsewhere in Canada for municipalities to regulate such matters. This may help explain the widespread adoption of cab cameras in the province of British Columbia, relative to other Canadian jurisdictions. There was a protocol in place for their adoption, simplifying the process of introducing them.

The cameras have also been considered or adopted in a number of other Canadian jurisdictions. In Saskatoon, United Blueline decided to mount digital cameras in 115 cabs in July 2008. Gary Dickson, Saskatchewan's Information and Privacy Commissioner, questioned the initiative. But according to the City Treasurer's office, there were no cab cameras in Saskatoon as of March 2009. There has been discussion regarding whether shields between the driver and the passenger should be mandatory, but it has been left to individual cab owners to decide.

In January 2008, cab drivers in Edmonton faced public complaints (Diotee 2008) regarding poor service and being available at night. Edmonton taxi drivers said more of them would be working if cameras and/or shields were installed for protection (Ruttan 2008). The Edmonton cab commission previously considered making shields and cameras mandatory in 2005 but faced resistance from cab officials concerning cost of installation. The Chief Livery Officer for the City of Edmonton said that as of March 2009, cab cameras in Edmonton taxis are permitted but not mandated. There are only about 15 cameras in Edmonton's fleet of 1,185 regular taxi cabs. All 35 of Edmonton's Accessible Taxi vehicles have mandated operational digital video recording devices. There have been no instances where the camera images were used to help solve a crime or similar incident. The City of Edmonton passed a regulation making it mandatory to have safety shields installed in all taxis by 31 May 2009.[3]

Cabs in Mississauga, Ontario were mandated to install cameras as of October 2005. Six hundred and twenty cameras were installed by VerifEye Technologies; however, there were about 15 operators that opted for the Honeywell FareView cameras. The cost at that time was $850 per unit. The City of Mississauga started retraining all drivers for robbery prevention.[4]

In London, Ontario the City Council's environment and transportation committee accepted a proposal to make cab cameras mandatory on 11 December 2007. 'It's a good day for cabbies in London,' said Councillor Steven Orser, a former taxi driver, and 'it's a bad day for the criminals that want to rob cabs' (Maloney 2007). London's Taxicab and Limousine Licensing by-law L-126-256 stated that each cab must be equipped with a fully operational security camera satisfactory to the City Clerk by 31 October 2009. Access to the data from the camera will be limited to the London Police Services for law enforcement purposes. However, at the time of writing, no camera technology had been approved, and no contract had been struck.

An intense debate about the benefits and drawbacks of cab cameras played out in Windsor, Ontario in summer 2008, with the Windsor Licensing Commission arguing that cameras prevent violent attacks and independent cab drivers arguing instead that cameras would increase job stress in various ways.

The City of Moncton in New Brunswick has considered cab cameras, but there is no planned date for installation. Cab cameras have also been considered several times in Halifax, Nova Scotia. The Halifax Regional Municipality, Taxi and Limousine Advisory Committee consulted with Jerry Kozubal of the Manitoba Taxicab Board in March 2006 about safety and surveillance issues, Kozubal being one of the foremost proponents of cab cameras in Canada (see below regarding the Winnipeg case). In winter 2006 the Halifax Taxi and Limousine Advisory Committee requested that Gary Jollymore, member of the Halifax Taxi Drivers' Association, conduct a survey regarding cameras and shields in taxi cabs. Two hundred and fourteen taxi drivers responded. Drivers suggested they did not want cameras or shields to be made mandatory, but would like financial assistance to cover the cost of the safety equipment/installation if a driver decided to install a shield or camera (Halifax Regional Municipality, Taxi and Limousine Advisory Committee minutes, 11 May 2006). As of March 2009, the move to introduce cab cameras was stalled in Halifax.

Do the cameras work?

Do the cameras work in protecting drivers and passengers? We could find no independent research concerning the effectiveness of taxi-cams. Advocates of the cameras and camera technology companies produce dramatic statistics saying they work. We think it is quite possible that the cameras could work in helping reduce victimization but we also know from general experience with surveillance cameras to approach such claims with some scepticism.

Advocates claim the cameras do three things. Two of these claims are commonly made about many kinds of surveillance cameras: that the cameras deter crime, and also that they are useful after the fact, in arresting and prosecuting people. Previous research on surveillance cameras indicates we should exercise caution with the deterrence argument (Gill 2003; Waples and Gill 2006; Welsh and Farrington 2009; Webster 2009). For example, a report for the Home Office by researchers from the University of Leicester (Gill and Spriggs 2005: 115) examining the effectiveness of 14 British CCTV systems found that 'the majority of the schemes evaluated did not reduce crime and even where there was a reduction this was mostly not due to CCTV'. The authors of the report found that there was a 'lack of realism about what could be expected from CCTV' and that it was oversold as the answer or 'magic bullet' to the crime problem (ibid: 116). As is the situation with surveillance cameras situated in malls and other spaces, there is often little or no notification to passengers that they are under surveillance, even though such notification would aid in possible deterrence (see Lizar and Potter, this volume and Clement and Ferenbok, this volume). Signage is a product of privacy legislation and guidelines, and not all countries where cameras are in cabs have such legislation and guidelines. In Canada, legislation and guidelines call for notification through signage, and the same goes in Australia and New Zealand. Future research should explore the issue of signage in countries where cab cameras are being implemented but no privacy legislation and guidelines exist, and where notions of individual privacy are far different.

Lippert and Wilkinson (this volume) suggest that the Crime Stoppers images they discuss actually show the absence of a deterrent effect of the cameras – with many crimes taking place with little apparent regard for the cameras. We in Surveillance Studies could probably draw more on the criminological literature about how and why deterrence often does not work. It is well established that certainty is more important than severity in terms of a deterrent effect of criminal sanctions (see for example, Agnew 2005). It remains to be seen how much the presence of a camera in a cab indicates to a potential offender the certainty of punishment. Deterrence measures often do not tend to work very well because they are premised on a notion of criminal as rational actor that may not apply to a lot of crime (including, often, the assault and robbery of drivers). Such crime is often committed by people at their worst in moments of desperation or rage, and often under the influence of alcohol or drugs.

Though there has never been a definitive study published, one set of figures concerning reduction of victimization due to cab cameras comes from advocates of the cameras in Winnipeg, Manitoba. The murder of driver Pritam Deol on 17 July 2001 led to a campaign to make shields and cameras mandatory. Advocates of the cameras state that Winnipeg Police Service crime statistics indicate that there were 20 fewer reported taxicab robberies in 2002 compared to 2001, a reduction of 71 per cent, and that Winnipeg Police Service crime statistics in 2003 indicated a further 8 per cent reduction in taxicab robberies. Meanwhile, during 2003, reported crime in Winnipeg actually increased by 10 per cent: 'although crime in general has increased in Winnipeg and other major cities in Canada, taxicab crime and taxicab driver risk has been reduced significantly due to the use of the in-cab camera' (Harries and Kozubal 2004: 2). Advocates said Winnipeg police also reported an increase in arrest rates with respect to taxicab robberies and assaults, the arrest rate being 35 per cent in 2001 and 66 per cent in 2003 after camera installation. Over 86 per cent of Winnipeg taxicab drivers reported in a survey that they felt much safer because of the cab camera (see Mundy 2009). The Manitoba Ombudsman found the cameras and police protocol for accessing stored information did not violate privacy legislation.

The third kind of claim made about taxi cameras is more unique. The claim is that they are useful during an incident – the driver can point out the camera to the assailant, and say something like 'Look – everything you are doing is being recorded!' This sounds plausible, although during this study we read many accounts of cameras in cabs and did not come across a single example of an incident where this occurred.

While the cameras could be a considerable benefit if they did work, the history of surveillance cameras suggests caution about their potential. In addition, not all cab drivers favour camera installation, especially when they must bear camera costs. Some drivers point out they can still be robbed from outside the car or at the driver's window in the camera's blind spot. The Cab Drivers Welfare Association of Hamilton formed in January 2008 under the banner 'shields not cameras': the word 'shields' refers to plastic partitions between driver and passengers that can prevent some attacks. Though shields prevent through-the-seat stabbings, passengers can still reach around the shield unless it is a full partition. But the full partition prevents drivers from communicating with passengers; shields were rejected for this reason in Vancouver because drivers argued such partitions are not 'tourist friendly'

(Seattle Taxi Report 2004) and limit the ability of drivers to earn tips that comprise part of their income.

Some drivers believe the cameras would do little in case of a serious attack: 'Cameras are not going to stop our heads from being blown away,' said one Edmonton driver (Landry 2008). A Windsor cab driver said he would resist camera installation: 'I'm not putting one in . . . If someone is going to attack me or rob me, the camera just gives them another job to do – get rid of the camera' (Puzic 2008). And there is no guarantee the camera will function the way it is designed to. In December 2007, the San Francisco Police Department Taxi Detail admitted that they were unable to pull images from the cab cameras 80 per cent of the time.

The Ottawa case

The Ottawa example suggests there are a number of barriers to good democratic decision-making around the introduction of the cameras. In the remainder of the chapter, we weave a narrative of the Ottawa case into a discussion of six barriers.

1. Introduction of cameras after high-profile crimes

The first difficulty we identified is that taxi cameras, like other kinds of surveillance cameras and other anti-crime measures, tend to be introduced in the aftermath of high-profile 'trigger events' or 'signal crimes' (Innes 2004; Hier 2004; Hier et al. 2007; Doyle 2006; Huey, this volume), making it difficult to have a reasoned debate. Many readers will be familiar with the massive impetus given to CCTV in Britain after the James Bulger case in Britain (Young 1996) and then the explosion of camera surveillance after 9/11 (Lyon 2003), but on a smaller scale, this is a recurring motif that cross-cuts the introduction of surveillance cameras in Canadian cities and elsewhere. One interpretation is that authorities want to be seen to be doing something about the crime problem, and the introduction of cameras is a politically viable response. As Whitson, Doyle and Walby (2009) point out, high-profile crimes have been instrumental in legitimating the implementation of open-street CCTV in several Canadian cities. In addition to the Winnipeg example just mentioned, there are others. The murder of Michael Goldie-Ryder in London, Ontario's downtown core in 1999 led to intense media coverage followed by the formation of 'Friends Against Senseless Endings' (FASE), a citizen's group that helped raise over $200,000 for London's CCTV initiative (Hier 2010). A similar high-profile crime in Hamilton, the mugging of figure skater Alexandre Hamel, led to a news series reporting a 'crisis' in Hamilton's downtown core. This was followed by the eventual establishment of Hamilton's CCTV project in 2004 (Hier, Greenberg, Walby and Lett 2007). In Toronto, the Boxing Day 2005 shooting of 15-year-old Jane Creba led to a drive for public surveillance cameras. Soon, cameras were introduced as a pilot project in the same downtown area where the Creba shooting had occurred.

Signal crimes have also figured in claims in favour of cab cameras. On New Year's Eve 2000, two taxi drivers were murdered in Toronto, and there was a push for cameras to be installed in all cabs there. In November 2002, Toronto police for the first time posted photos from cab cameras on the Toronto Crime Stoppers website, part of their 'Rob a Cab – You will be Nabbed' programme. Following in the footsteps of Toronto, the Ottawa Blue Line drivers' union, Ottawa's largest taxicab drivers' union at the time, called on the city to require cameras in taxis. Stabbings of taxi drivers in 2004 in Cornwall likewise prompted Ottawa's taxi drivers to press again for safety initiatives, including cameras. At this time, there was an amalgamation of disparate Ottawa taxi unions into Local 1688 of the Canadian Auto Workers' Union. An Ottawa woman died in November 2005 after being dragged more than a kilometre by a taxi. Although this was not a crime but more of a tragic accident, the high-profile incident resulted in calls for more surveillance of taxis. Demanding an inquest into the death, her family requested that cameras become mandatory for Ottawa taxis. In 2007, an Ottawa cab driver was robbed at gunpoint and forced into the trunk of his cab.

2. Camera marketers drive the process

A second problem is that the implementation process often seems to be largely driven by the companies that market the cameras. With open-street camera surveillance, one approach is that security companies will give away hardware as a sample, trying to entice local government to purchase a more elaborate system. There are similar entrepreneurial strategies with cab camera companies. In Ottawa, the key player in the introduction of cameras was the Toronto-based company discussed above, VerifEye Inc. VerifEye is pro-active in marketing the cameras, focusing on municipal governments and taxi boards. One difficulty in Surveillance Studies is knowing just how the camera industry promotes itself and strikes up partnerships with municipal governments – there are barriers to knowing about the practices of private companies. We were lucky to get at some of the correspondence between VerifEye and the City of Ottawa using access to information (ATI) requests, shedding partial light on the entrepreneurial strategies at work with this particular case. Through access requests, we were able to unearth data showing that VerifEye made a deal with the city to sell the cameras *before* any consultation by the City with taxi drivers.

While government has increasingly moved to a focus on the bottom line through such interactions with business, how best to provide accountability in government tendering and procurement is often an on-going challenge (see for example, Arrowsmith et al. 2000). The active role played here by the company can also be situated as part of a broader trend towards criminal justice being increasingly driven by the private sector in different ways (for assorted criminological analyses, see Johnston 1992; O'Malley 1992; Braithwaite 2000; Christie 2000).

A lot of the promotion of the taxi-cam technology was going on behind the scenes through communications between the camera company and the City of Ottawa. What we learned is that the approach for the City of Ottawa was to sign a deal first and then enlist support from drivers after the fact. How do we know this? The results of our access to information request allowed us to look at a lot of the email correspondence between VerifEye and the City of Ottawa as well as internal memos for the City. These revealed the following sequence. Before any correspondence with the taxi union or drivers, two camera companies came to Ottawa in summer 2007 for equipment demonstrations: one of these was Verif-Eye; the other was Eagle Eye Technology. The invitation for an in-vehicle camera demonstration was sent by the City on 18 May 2007. The City decided upon VerifEye because the company provided an installer training plan. VerifEye was alerted on 14 September 2007 that they had been awarded the contract. Orders for 1,106 VerifEye camera units and GPS trigger devices were being processed on 26 October 2007. The City was already trying to schedule the training for camera installation technicians on 6 November 2007. Drivers did not become aware of this process until February 2008. When they did find out, there were major protests at City Hall, as we will discuss. Not only did the City go ahead before consulting drivers, they had already devised a plan to recuperate the costs by charging more money to cab licence owners. The City, as they put it in one budget communiqué, 'donated' $100,000 to itself to offset the shortfall by taking monies from 'excess projected revenues'. But plans to recuperate the funds included creating a $35 sur-charge on taxi driver and plate holder fees, increasing plate transfer fees, as well as introducing stiffer taxi broker licence fees.

3. Surveillance creep

A third kind of problem also emerged which is a broader theme concerning democracy and accountability in the introduction of surveillance measures: 'func-tion creep' (Winner 1977) or more specifically 'surveillance creep' (Lyon 2007). Particular kinds of surveillance sneak in without much public debate because they are unstated and sometimes unanticipated additional consequences of the introduc-tion of new technologies (see Greenberg and Hier 2009). The way the camera technology was originally set up meant the Ottawa taxi drivers felt they would not know when the drivers themselves were being monitored by the cameras. The drivers feared the cameras would be used by the companies or by the City to spy on them. One driver we interviewed said 'they will be tracking your every move, 24 hours a day'. This was not an unfounded concern – the particular global posi-tioning system (GPS) technology linked to the camera and proposed by VerifEye would have allowed the taxi company to monitor the location of the cab in real time, although no live feed of the camera was planned to be delivered to the taxi company via satellite. A taxi union rep said, 'I don't believe it is about driver safety . . . I believe it is going to be used as a witch-hunt and they're going to use it to discipline drivers for minor infractions.'

Studies show taxi drivers are a tightly knit group and taxi work involves a high level of worker solidarity (Hoffman 2006; Mathew 2005). This solidarity among cab drivers emerged front and centre in debates concerning surveillance cameras in Ottawa cabs. In 2007–8, the City of Ottawa proposed to install cameras in Ottawa taxis, at the drivers' expense. Taxi drivers refused installation, and staged protests at City Hall to demonstrate their frustration. Did the drivers feel the cameras would violate their privacy or the privacy of customers? Not so. In fact, various taxi driver unions in Ottawa had been calling for cameras since 1997. Cab drivers in Ottawa are not overwhelmingly for or against camera surveillance in their vehicles. Some cab drivers we spoke to describe the cameras as useless (e.g. 'real' thieves know how to find the blind spots) while other drivers argue that cameras protect them against claims by passengers regarding sexual assault. The Ottawa cab camera protests instead erupted simply over the process through which the particular technology was selected and purchased. It seems from this example that worker perception of autonomy, control over work conditions and control over decision-making about technology is important. In other words, it is key to consult with the drivers before any decision to implement cab cameras.

Between the cost and the idea they would be spied on, this became too much for the drivers. Almost 600 taxi drivers crowded City Hall in Ottawa to protest. 'I've been doing this now for about 24 years and I haven't seen our people so angry before', one driver said. Due to pressure from the union, and the protests, the City of Ottawa had to back down and make a compromise deal in May 2008. This compromise resulted in the City itself absorbing a lot of the cost of the cameras and also a switch to a technology which gave the drivers more control over when the cameras would be running. There was an agreement that cab camera pictures would only be downloadable by the police.

The cameras were eventually introduced in 1,100 Ottawa taxis in 2008. There was consultation with drivers in the end, because the drivers forced it with protest.

4. Disconnected and uninformed stakeholders

Another, fourth, barrier to democratic process which was also illustrated by these events is the fragmented nature of the 'publics' affected by particular surveillance measures – disconnected and unaware stakeholders. In the Ottawa case, the drivers successfully resisted the introduction of surveillance cameras and eventually negotiated their introduction on terms more favourable to themselves. However, there was no representation of passengers in the process. Do the passengers care? The question is complicated somewhat by the difficulty of defining the interior of a taxi as either a public or a private space, and identifying what reasonable expectations of privacy might be in such a space. This is especially true in a broader social context where expectations of privacy are shifting rapidly. Research in Norway suggests taxi passengers generally approve of the cameras there; 47 per cent in favour, 25 neutral, 28 against (Hempel and Töpfer 2004). Why could it be a problem for passengers? One reason is that a lot of people take taxis when they are drunk. The privacy commissioner of the state of Victoria in Australia has raised concerns about footage from taxi-cams there showing the backseat antics of impaired passengers winding up on the Internet and reality TV (Privacy Victoria 2006). Such speculations are not entirely far-fetched (see Doyle 2006). The HBO network's hidden camera documentary series, *Taxicab Confessions*, ran from 1995 to 2006. Passengers were recorded secretly without their permission and then later asked to sign releases so the footage could be aired.

5. Piecemeal diffusion

As illustrated by these data above, a fifth kind of barrier to democracy is the piece-meal diffusion of the cameras. A surveillance technology like this is gradually intro-duced in local contexts, and little by little becomes the norm without being consid-ered on a grand scale by bodies of government with resources to investigate. This chapter, like others in this volume, fits with other accounts of the diffusion of cam-era surveillance (in the Canadian context, see Walby 2005 and Hier 2010). Norris, McCahill and Wood (2004) have previously discussed the diffusion of open-street camera surveillance on a global scale. One commonality with most of these cases of diffusion is a lack of public debate before cameras are installed. With the Ottawa case, there are repeated gestures by authorities towards consulting the public after measures are largely in place. Taxi drivers reported feeling like second-class citizens due to the lack of transparency and consultation. Ottawa city council minutes from February 2008 repeatedly claim that extensive public consultation had gone on, with the Ontario Privacy Commissioner, with the taxi company and the technol-ogy companies competing for the contract, but this consultation did not extend to drivers until after the protests.

6. The whole as more than the sum of the parts

Finally, seeing this as one of a whole range of surveillance measures, there is the character of surveillant assemblages as a threat to democracy and accountability. As Kevin Haggerty and Richard Ericson (2000) have argued, there is a gradual introduction of a set of individual surveillance measures like taxi-cams such that each seems relatively innocuous on its own. But together they make a whole that when it is drawn together is much more than the sum of its parts. The assemblage model is based on the idea that discrete surveillance technologies start to commu-nicate with one another, sharing data across former boundaries, leading to more information- sharing. Data captured in some realms of social life starts to have an impact in others. As Hier (2004) argues, this sharing of data tends to have a more negative impact on people lower in social hierarchies. There has already been talk in the United States of outfitting taxis with surveillance technologies such as mobile sensors for road surface monitoring and detectors for nuclear threat monitoring. If the GPS technology part of a cab camera system produces data that starts to be consolidated with other databases or is shared more widely with other organiza-tions, this assemblage of data flows could have serious consequences for drivers. Or if surveillance technologies are attached to cabs for other purposes, it might end up further controlling the labour process of cab drivers. Taxi-cams become part of a much broader assemblage of surveillance and data flows that are mostly latent but, when drawn together, moves us towards a kind of total surveillance with serious political and social ramifications.

Conclusion

We have argued that the example of the introduction of cameras in cabs illustrates a number of important social processes involved in the diffusion and implementation of surveillance cameras. We have sought to highlight the barriers to democracy and accountability inherent in these processes.

We end on a brief methodological note. This chapter has illustrated that use of access to information (ATI) laws can contribute to Surveillance Studies. Marx (2007) has argued that Surveillance Studies is still searching for theoretical and methodological clarity. ATI can help researchers get at what Marx (1984) called 'dirty data' produced behind closed doors of governmental and policing agencies (also see Walby and Monaghan 2010; E. Smith, this volume). Researchers should explore the extent to which access to information can be used in various countries for studies of surveillance.

Notes

1   Twelve of the drivers were from Ottawa, four of the drivers were from Toronto, and 15 of the drivers were from Winnipeg. Sixteen of the drivers we initially interviewed were male, and 15 of the drivers were women. Our interviews greatly over-represented women cab drivers, as women constitute less than 5 per cent of the total number of taxi drivers in North America, but we were interested in their experience in particular as part of the larger study. However, as the concern is sometimes expressed that taxi driving is particularly unsafe for women, it may be appropriate to pay particular attention to the views of women drivers in a study of a taxi security measures. In Ottawa, interviewees were contacted through the taxi union as well as through a local eatery where many of the male drivers eat lunch. In Winnipeg, the interviewees were contacted through the taxi licensing board. Interviews typically lasted between 40 and 70 minutes. Taxi drivers are a tough group to interview given that time off the road costs them money.
2   It is difficult to know whether these figures are deflated since police do not always identify victims as cab drivers. Sometimes two or more crimes are recorded in one category. Taxi drivers do not often report victimization because they feel the police will do nothing. The time it takes to file a complaint is time off the road, which means less income.
3   This information is based on personal correspondence with the Edmonton Chief Livery Officer in November 2009.
4   This information is based on personal correspondence with the Mississauga Office of the City Manager in November 2009.

References

Agnew, R. (2005) *Why Do Criminals Offend? A General Theory of Crime and Delinquency*, Los Angeles: Roxbury.
Arrowsmith, S., Linarelli, J. and Wallace, D. (2000) *Regulating Public Procurement: National and International Perspectives*, The Hague: Kluwer Law International.

Bird, J. (2008) 'Cabbies to top hectic day at City Hall; Drivers angry about in-car cameras just one of three hornet's nests facing council today', *Ottawa Citizen*, 13 February: C1.

Braithwaite, J. (2000) 'The New Regulatory State and the Transformation of Criminology', *British Journal of Criminology*, 40: 222–38.

Christie, N. (2000) *Crime Control as Industry: Towards Gulags Western Style*, London: Routledge.

Coleman, R. (2004) 'Reclaiming the Streets: Closed Circuit Television, Neoliberalism and the Mystification of Social Division in Liverpool, UK', *Surveillance and Society*, 2(2/3): 293–309.

Dare, P. (2006) 'Taxis to install in-car cameras', *Ottawa Citizen*, 19 April: C7.

DeRosa, K. (2007) 'Blue Line, West-Way taxis to have cameras installed within year; Dangerous customers pose risk to drivers, company head says', *Ottawa Citizen*, 21 April: E3.

Diotee, K. (2008) 'Tackle the Taxi Problem: Citizens Can No Longer Hack Bad Service', *Edmonton Sun*, 20 January. Online. Available HTTP: <http://www.edmontonsun.com/Comment/2008/01/20/pf-4783307>

Doyle, A. (2006) 'An Alternative Current in Surveillance and Control: Broadcasting Surveillance Footage of Crimes', in K.H. Haggerty and R.V. Ericson (eds), *The New Politics of Surveillance and Visibility*, Toronto: University of Toronto Press.

Elzinga, A. (1996) 'Security of Taxi Drivers in the Netherlands: Fear of Crime, Actual Victimization and Recommended Security Measures', *Security Journal*, 7/2: 205–10.

Gambetta, D. and Hamill, H. (2005) *Streetwise: How Taxi Drivers Establish their Customers' Trustworthiness*, New York: Russell Sage.

Gilbert, E. (2005) *Understanding Violence Against Taxi Cab Drivers*. PhD dissertation. University of Washington.

Gill, M. (2003) *CCTV*, Leicester: Perpetuity.

Gill, M. and Spriggs, A. (2005) *Assessing the Impact of CCTV*, Home Office Research Study 292. Available HTTP: <http://www.homeoffice.gov.uk/rds/pdfs05/hors292.pdf>.

Greenberg, J. and Hier, S. (2009) 'CCTV Surveillance and Poverty of Media Discourse: A Content Analysis of Canadian Newspaper Coverage', *Canadian Journal of Communication*, 34(3): 461–86.

Haggerty, K.H. and Ericson, R.V. (2000) 'The Surveillant Assemblage', *British Journal of Sociology*, 51(4): 605–22.

Halifax Regional Municipality, Taxi and Limousine Advisory Committee meeting minutes, 11 May 2006.

Hamill, H. and Gambetta, D. (2006) 'Who Do Taxi Drivers Trust?', *Contexts*, 5/3: 29–33.

Harries, L. and Kozubal, J. (2004) Manitoba Taxicab Board. 'Camera effective in reducing taxicab crime'. Paper submitted to the 17th Annual International Conference of the International Association of Transportation Regulators.

Hempel, L. and Töpfer, E. (2004) 'CCTV in Europe: Final Report'. The UrbanEye Project. Online. Available HTTP: <http://www.urbaneye.net/results/ue_wp15.pdf> (accessed 10 June 2010)

Hier, S.P. (2003) 'Probing the Surveillant Assemblage: on the Dialectics of Surveillance Practices as Processes of Social Control', *Surveillance & Society*, 1(3): 399–411.

Hier, S.P. (2004) 'Risky Spaces and Dangerous Faces: Surveillance, Social Disorder, and CCTV', *Social & Legal Studies*, 13(4): 541–54.

Hier, S.P. (2010) *Panoptic Dreams: Streetscape Video Surveillance in Canada*, Vancouver: University of British Columbia Press.

Hier, S., Greenberg, J., Walby, K. and Lett, D. (2007) 'Media, Communication, and the Establishment of Public Camera Surveillance Programs in Canada', *Media, Culture, and Society*, 29(5): 727–51.

Hoffman, E. (2006) 'Driving Street Justice: The Taxicab Driver as the Last American Cowboy', *Labour Studies Journal*, 31/2: 31–48.

Innes, M. (2004) 'Signal Crimes and Signal Disorders: Notes on Deviance as Communicative Action', *British Journal of Sociology*, 55(3): 335–55.

Johnston, L. (1992) *The Rebirth of Private Policing*, London: Routledge.

Kent, G. (2005) 'Survey prompts commission to focus on taxicab safety', *Edmonton Journal*, 23 July: B4.

Knestaunt, A. (1997) 'Fatalities and Injuries among Truck and Taxicab Drivers', *Compensation and Working Conditions*, Fall: 55–60.

Landry, F. (2008) 'Cabbies Calling for Shields in Wake of Positive Winnipeg Report: Violence Cut Dramatically in that City', *Edmonton Sun*, 17 January. Online. Available HTTP: <http://www.edmontonsun.com/News/Edmonton/2008/01/17/pf-4778620.html>

LaRocque, J. (2008) 'Invasion of privacy', *Ottawa Citizen*, 21 February: C4.

Lyon, D. (2003) *Surveillance After September 11*, Cambridge: Polity.

Lyon, D. (2007) *Surveillance Studies: An Overview*, Cambridge: Polity.

Maloney, P. (2007) 'Individual taxi owners would have to pay $1,000 to $1,200 for the security cameras, Cab cameras go to council', *London Free Press*, 11 December.

Marx, G. (1984) 'Notes on the Discovery, Collection, and Assessment of Hidden and Dirty Data', in J. Schneider and J. Kitsuse (eds), *Studies in the Sociology of Social Problems*, Norwood, NJ: Ablex.

Marx, G. (2007) 'Desperately Seeking Surveillance Studies: Players in Search of a Field', *Contemporary Sociology*, 35(2): 125–30.

Mathew, B. (2005) *Taxi! Cabs and Capitalism in New York City*, New York: The New Press.

McCarthy, P. and McCarthy, S. (2007) 'Please don't oversimplify taxi incident', *Ottawa Citizen*, 26 May: B5.

McCooey, P. (2004) 'Cornwall cabbies demand security after stabbings: Drivers want city to enact safety bylaw', *Ottawa Citizen*, 13 April: B3.

Mundy, R. (2009) 'Winnipeg Taxi Study – Volume One'. Tennessee Transportation & Logistics Foundation.

National Institute of Occupational Safety and Health (1996) *Violence in the Workplace*, Publication Number 96–100.

Nickel, R. (2008) 'Taxi firm installs cabbie cams, United Blueline believes cameras will improve safety', *The Star Phoenix*, 5 July.

Norris, C. and Armstrong, G. (1999) *The Maximum Surveillance Society. The Rise of CCTV*, Oxford: Berg.

Norris, C., McCahill, M. and Wood, D. (2004) 'The Growth of CCTV: a Global Perspective on the International Diffusion of Video Surveillance in Publicly Accessible Space', *Surveillance and Society*, 2(2/3): 110–35.

O'Malley, P. (1992) 'Risk, Power and Crime Prevention', *Economy and Society*, 21: 252–75.

Passenger Transportation Board ruling (2008) 'BC Taxi Camera Programs, Standards & Requirements.' Online. Available HTTP: <http://www.th.gov.bc.ca/ptb/documents/rule_BC_Taxi_Camera.pdf>.

Privacy Victoria (2006) *Surveillance Cameras in Taxis. Report on Findings*, Melbourne: Office of the Victorian Privacy Commissioner.

Proudfoot, S. (2006) 'Petition seeks coroner inquest for "justice" in dragging death', *Ottawa Citizen*, 19 February: A11.

Puzic, Sonja (2008) 'Surveillance cameras to keep eye on taxis', *Windsor Star*, 20 March.

Rogers, D. (1997) 'Taxi union suggests plan to curb attacks: High-tech idea links cameras, satellite tracking and in-cab ads', *Ottawa Citizen*, 9 July: B3.

Ruttan, S. (2008) 'Taxi commission to study mandatory shields', *Edmonton Journal*, 21 January 21.

Rupert, J. and Bird, J. (2008) 'Ensure cameras aren't used to "spy" on us or we're walking off the job, cab drivers say', *Ottawa Citizen*, 15 February: F1.

Rupert, J. (2008) 'Contentious day at City Hall', *Ottawa Citizen*, 14 February: B1.

Rupert, J. (2007) 'Ms. McCarthy's family maintains justice wasn't served. Committee endorses inquest suggestions', *Ottawa Citizen*, 6 July: D2.

Schick, S. (2002) 'Cab Company gets Smart on Security', *Computing Canada*, 13 December: 20.

Seattle Taxi Report (2004) 'Taxicab Driver Personal Safety in Seattle and King County: Final Report and Recommendations'. Report of the Taxicab Advisory Group Committee on Driver Safety to the Director of the Department of Executive Administration for the City of Seattle.

Seymour, A. (2008) 'Third Ottawa taxi robbed in two days; Cabbies still have concerns about in-car cameras', *Ottawa Citizen*, 16 February: E2.

Skok, W. and Baird, S. (2005) 'Strategic Use of Emerging Technology: The London Taxi Cab Industry', *Strategic Change*, 14: 295–306.

Stenning, P. (1996) *Fare Game, Fare Cop: Victimization of, and Policing By, Taxi Drivers in Three Canadian Cities – Report of a Preliminary Study*, Department of Justice Canada: Research, Statistics and Evaluation Directorate.

Taxi Study Panel (1999) 'A Study of the Taxi Industry in British Columbia'. Report to the Honourable Harry Lali, Minister of Transportation and Highways.

Toiskallio, K. (1998) 'Simmel Hails a Cab: Fleeting Sociability in the Urban Taxi', *Space and Culture*, 1/6: 4–20.

van Straaten, T. (1998) 'Digital camera helps cabbies fight crime: A Toronto-based company is helping taxi drivers around the world feel more at ease', *Ottawa Citizen*, 2 November: D9.

Walby, K. (2005) 'Open-Street Camera Surveillance and Governance in Canada', *Canadian Journal of Criminology and Criminal Justice*, 47(4): 655–83.

Walby, K. and Monaghan, J. (2010) 'Policing Proliferation: on the Militarization of Police and Atomic Energy Canada Limited's Nuclear Response Forces', *Canadian Journal of Criminology and Criminal Justice*, 52(2): 117–45.

Waples, S. and Gill, M. (2006) 'Effectiveness of Redeployable CCTV', *Crime Prevention and Community Safety*, 8(1): 1–16.

Welsh, B. and Farrington, D. (2009) *Making Public Places Safer: Surveillance and Crime Prevention*, Oxford: Oxford University Press.

Webster, W. (2009) 'CCTV Policy in the UK: Reconsidering The Evidence Base', *Surveillance and Society*, 6(1): 10–22.

Webster, W. (1996) 'Closed Circuit Television and Governance: The Eve of a Surveillance Age', *Information Infrastructure and Policy*, 5(4): 253–63.

Weeks, C. (2005a) 'Tracking systems would let dispatchers know where their cabbies are', *Ottawa Citizen*, 21 July: B1.

Weeks, C. (2005b) 'Plan to retrain cabbies leaves them steamed', *Ottawa Citizen*, 10 August: B1.

Weeks, C. (2005c) 'No decision on taxi re-zoning', *Ottawa Citizen*, 9 September: F10.

Whitson, J., Doyle, A. and Walby, K. (2009) 'Camera Surveillance in Canada', in *A Report on Camera Surveillance in Canada, Volume I*, Surveillance Cameras Awareness Network.

Winner, L. (1977) *Autonomous Technology: Technics-out-of-Control as a Theme in Political Thought*, Cambridge, MA: MIT Press.

Young, A. (1996) *Imagining Crime: Textual Outlaws and Criminal Conversations*, London, Thousand Oaks, CA, and New Delhi: Sage.

12

DEPLOYING CAMERA SURVEILLANCE IMAGES

The case of Crime Stoppers

Randy Lippert and Blair Wilkinson

A neglected aspect of the global growth of camera surveillance is what is done with its products. Some visual information produced as recorded camera surveillance images undoubtedly remains in perpetual storage, never to be activated; other images are periodically deleted due to technological limits or legal restrictions; still other images are extracted from storage because they later become useful information for institutions. This chapter explores how much and how surveillance images[1] are used by police-supported Crime Stoppers programmes in several countries through a case study of Crime Stoppers advertisements.[2] Privacy and other implications related to the use of surveillance images are discussed, in particular the transfer of images from private surveillance sources to police, and then to Crime Stoppers programmes that post the images in website advertisements and to the video-sharing website YouTube.[3] This chapter also discusses who benefits from the transfer and use of camera surveillance images by Crime Stoppers, and who may be potentially harmed by this practice.

Crime Stoppers programmes

Like camera surveillance, Crime Stoppers has undergone rapid growth in Canada, the United States and globally since appearing in 1976 in New Mexico. It is now arguably the most well-known and established police-supported crime prevention programme in existence and operates in 20 countries, including India, the Netherlands and South Africa (Crime Stoppers International 2009). In North America each programme covers a specific geographical area, such as a city or county. In Canada there are more than 100 such programmes and more than 1,000 in the US (Crime Stoppers International 2009). As well, the original Crime Stoppers programme has spawned programmatic offspring specially designed for school children, college and university campuses and seniors (Lippert 2002). Symbolic of Crime Stoppers' prominence and widespread acceptance by local governments and communities, motorists on major roadways entering most cities and towns in the Canadian province of Ontario now encounter near-billboard-size 'Crime Stoppers' signs displaying a toll-free telephone number at their base through which to submit 'tips'.

Crime Stoppers purports to be a 'partnership of the public, police and media that provides the community with a proactive programme for people to assist the police anonymously to solve crimes' (Toronto Crime Stoppers 2009). Significantly, Crime Stoppers representatives consistently assert that the programme is independent of particular police services: 'Ours, like other programmes, is not a police programme . . . It is a public programme that is run by a Board of Directors . . . ordinary concerned citizens who live in York Region and volunteer their time' (Crime Stoppers of York Region 2009).

Crime Stoppers seeks to generate information about crime by advertising through various media outlets and formats, including radio, print, television and the internet. These marketing efforts are designed to encourage persons to anonymously submit information (a 'tip') about criminal activity to Crime Stoppers, where it is then screened and, if deemed appropriate, passed to police. If information is provided that leads to an arrest or seizure of property or illegal drugs, the 'tipster' is offered a monetary reward (Lippert 2002). From the inception of these programmes, advertisements have often adopted the form of a 'Crime of the Week'. Such a format tends to consist of a narrative describing a particular incident of criminal activity. By 2000 such advertisements were appearing on local Crime Stoppers websites (Lippert 2002). More recently, camera surveillance images (primarily 'stills') have begun to be a regular feature of these advertisements. The latest development is for camera surveillance footage to be transferred by Crime Stoppers to websites such as YouTube for the same purpose. Below is a typical example of a 'Crime of the Week' advertisement:

Locker Theft and Frauds

February 7, 2008

The Ottawa Police Service needs your help in the investigation of a theft from a locker in an East End gym and the subsequent fraudulent use of the victim's credit card.

On December 11th 2007 at about 1pm the victim attended the Newbody Dimensions Gym located at 1800 St Laurent Blvd. She entered the women's locker room and she began to place her belongings in an empty locker. While she was doing this a female in the locker room placed herself directly behind the victim and began to stare at her. The victim feeling uncomfortable placed her belongings in the locker and she walked to the mirrors to comb her hair. Again the female suspect followed the victim and this led to the victim leaving the locker room.

When the victim returned to her locker, she was unable to open her combination lock. After the gym staff cut the lock the victim noticed that her purse was missing from the locker.

A subsequent police investigation revealed that the female suspect was not a registered member of the gym and that she had purchased a day pass to work out. The victim's credit card was used in several stores near the gym shortly after the theft.

Surveillance video at the gym and in the targeted stores identified 3 female suspects. They are described as:

1– Olive skinned female (who was in the gym), heavy set, long dark hair tied in a bun, in her twenties, red shorts and a white t-shirt.

2– Black female, slim, early twenties, long black wavy hair wearing a grey 3/4-length coat.

3– Black female, slim, early twenties, long black straight hair, dark coat, wearing glasses.

The 2 black females were not seen in the gym and are suspected of being accomplices.

(Three Camera Surveillance Images Redacted)

If you have any information regarding this incident, or any other criminal activity, call Crime Stoppers at 613–233-TIPS or toll free at 1–800–222–8477. Crime Stoppers does not subscribe to call display, we will not record your call and you are not required to testify in court. If your information leads to an arrest or a charge, you could qualify for a cash reward of up to $2000.

(National Capital Area Crime Stoppers 2008)

Previous research

Despite its long-standing presence and consistent expansion since the late 1970s, Crime Stoppers has received little empirical scrutiny internationally (on Canada and the United Kingdom, see Carriere and Ericson 1989; Lippert 2002; Gresham et al. 2003). Claims of programme success, which are prominently displayed on Crime Stoppers websites and other materials, have never been subjected to careful study using controls to determine whether the programme is more effective in reducing crime than police appeals to the public for information about an incident (see Lippert 2002). More important for present purposes, existing studies looking into its workings, including its advertising practices, largely predate the increased use of camera surveillance by private and public institutions, as well as private citizens. Given its international presence and popularity, Crime Stoppers will serve as a clear window into police-related transfer and use of images produced by camera surveillance for crime reduction purposes and into the issues this raises. New developments and issues identified in this context undoubtedly have broader relevance.

Method

For this case study we first examined 1,056 'Crime of the Week' or equivalent (e.g. 'crime file') advertisements from Crime Stoppers programmes in three countries

– Canada (Ontario), Australia and the United Kingdom – from early 2004 through early 2008 to determine the extent of surveillance image use internationally. Many advertisements in this sample were found to contain surveillance images (either stills or footage) (N = 307) from which we then selected Ontario Crime Stoppers programme advertisements. This resulted in 130 Crime Stoppers advertisements comprising surveillance images and adjacent text available for analysis. We also drew on an existing 2000–1 data set of 640 Crime Stoppers advertisements from ten Ontario programmes (see Lippert 2002: 478) to compare with this new sample to determine the changing extent of surveillance image use. As well, at least two Ontario Crime Stoppers programmes have begun to take advantage of YouTube as a means of uploading camera footage and crime re-enactments as 'Crimes of the Week' or equivalent for display. To explore this more recent development, 27 instances of the use of surveillance camera footage on YouTube from 2007 and 2008 associated with these two Ontario Crime Stoppers programmes were selected. Key features such as type of crime and apparent camera surveillance image source were identified for both the Crime Stoppers website advertisements and YouTube surveillance footage. The image analysis also entailed determining whether the image displayed features (such as a figure holding a visible weapon or wearing a mask or other disguise) that were strongly indicative of a crime (e.g. robbery) being committed, as well as whether the images displayed personal information about a victim, third party or suspect. In three cases, where image sources were identified, the notification arrangements (i.e., camera surveillance signage) were investigated.

Privacy issues

Potential privacy issues stem from the use and transfer of camera surveillance images. These are: (1) transfer of images of alleged criminal activity held by third parties (e.g. a retail business) to police and the subsequent transfer of images to Crime Stoppers and then YouTube; and (2) inclusion of identifiable third parties in images released publicly in advertisements (either with co-operation of news media or another website) on the Crime Stoppers or YouTube websites.

Crime Stoppers is a non-profit organization with charitable status. As noted above, Crime Stoppers claims to be independent of police, in order to generate information from those unwilling to testify in court and who wish to remain anonymous (see Lippert 2002). Thus, the transfer of the surveillance image from police to Crime Stoppers is itself tantamount to transfer to a third party. Once posted to a Crime Stoppers website, images can be transferred to anyone with internet access and with an inexpensive storage device (e.g. hard-drive). Their transfer and subsequent uses then become unlimited. It can be argued that camera surveillance images are more accurate than mere sketches and physical descriptions in some cases, and thus are justifiably used in attempts to solve crimes. A counterpoint is the problem that when third parties are included in such images, these persons can also be better identified and inadvertently associated with criminal incidents in ways that could be detrimental to their reputations and livelihoods.

Transfer of surveillance images from third parties to police raises issues of notification. Potential subjects of surveillance should be made aware their personal information (i.e. their image) is being collected, stored and potentially transferred to police, Crime Stoppers and beyond. Section 7(1)(b) of *PIPEDA* (see Johnson, this volume) states that a lack of notification is acceptable when the 'collection is reasonable for purposes related to investigating a breach of an agreement or a contravention of the laws of Canada or a province'.[4] Yet this information is also gathered and transferred for other ends. These include 'general demographic or traffic flow analysis' (Future Shop 2009) to devise retail marketing strategies based on the types and consumption behaviour of in-store customers, and the Crime Stoppers' marketing (i.e. advertisements) discussed in this chapter. Furthermore, guidelines for private organizations using camera surveillance recently have been made available through the Office of the Federal Privacy Commissioner; one guideline indicates such organizations should erect signage to communicate the presence of camera surveillance (OPC 2008) (see Ferenbok and Clement, this volume). Many businesses deploy camera surveillance systems, but do not erect signs notifying persons of the presence and purpose(s) of surveillance cameras. Although some have signs in place that inform persons entering the premises of the presence of cameras and state the purposes for which personal information is collected, typically this signage is vague and aimed only at deterring certain behaviour. Thus, signage typically attempts to communicate to customers entering the business that they are being watched should they decide to engage in theft, robbery or vandalism, or that the camera surveillance in place will prevent their own victimization while on the premises. However, even signs erected solely to deter behaviour do not preclude the possibility that customers who read the signs assume lesser transgressions (e.g. theft and vandalism) will be handled by 'in-house' security and informal measures (e.g. a warning, a store ban) and not brought to the attention of police and Crime Stoppers. It is well known that many private businesses seek to avoid bad publicity associated with arresting and prosecuting customers caught shoplifting or engaging in vandalism. Thus, even where signage is in place, it is not self-evident from signage that police will be given direct access to camera surveillance images as a matter of course or that these images may later be transferred to Crime Stoppers and YouTube websites should an incident deemed to be criminal in nature occur.

Where images of third parties were captured by the researchers and where an organization or business housing the cameras could be identified, the notification efforts of the organization or business franchise or chain were sought. Three highly recognizable Canadian chains (a supermarket, a gasoline station and an electronics retail outlet) (see Lizar and Potter, this volume) were present in Crime Stoppers advertisements. While the outlets of these chains that we subsequently examined to assess notification practices were not those particular outlets depicted in the footage, it is reasonable to assume the signage policy for surveillance, like signage for merchandise, is uniform across a retail chain. In the first instance, a national grocery chain was examined. At one store a sign was present on both automatic doors at each entrance. The sign read 'PLEASE BE ADVISED our store has video surveillance for both our customer protection and to help keep prices low' (emphasis in original). These signs were found on the entry doors below eye level. They disappear behind the doorframe as the customer approaches and the doors slide open. The gas station featured signs on the pumps at waist level that read: 'This area is under video surveillance'. In the third instance, a national electronics retail outlet was visited. No signage was detected. The only evidence of surveillance cameras was the somewhat ominous globes, presumably containing cameras, hanging from the ceiling more than a metre overhead immediately inside the entrance and throughout the store. Thus, while the grocery store and gas station chains sought to notify the customer of surveillance, this was not true for the electronics store. In all three cases legislative authority for the collection of personal data was not indicated. The lack of signage at the electronics retail outlet may mean this private retail chain assumes that those entering their establishments understand that surveillance cameras will be present and understand their purposes. Alternatively it may mean that the corporation lacks knowledge of privacy guidelines consistent with federal privacy legislation (OPC 2008).

The transfer of the camera surveillance image from a private business to police and then to Crime Stoppers raises the possibility of errors with harmful effects. This became a reality in 2002 when a Canadian chartered bank in Winnipeg erroneously transferred two images of a customer thought to have cashed stolen cheques. The images were then transferred by police to Crime Stoppers and included in one newspaper advertisement. The person identified as engaged in this crime then launched a complaint with the Federal Privacy Commissioner (OPC 2002). Once the error was recognized, Crime Stoppers, with the newspaper's co-operation, arranged for a printed retraction a week later:

> However, in the meantime, many people had recognized the complainant's image from the first article. Several friends and family members had called to inquire about her trouble with police, and she also became aware that other acquaintances had begun to entertain suspicions about her character. Believing her good name to be integral to her ability to secure work in clients' homes and workplaces, the complainant was very worried that the incident might adversely affect her reputation and her business and was most upset that suspicions about her had been allowed to gather for a full week.
>
> *(OPC 2002)*

The complaint was judged to be well-founded following the investigation. The Commissioner stated: 'The decision caused the complainant embarrassment and worry about her reputation and her livelihood' and that 'the bank should have taken due care to ensure that the information was accurate so as to minimize the possibility of a wrong decision with adverse consequences' (OPC 2002). It is unknown if, or how many, others have become the victims of such errors. This is in part because not everyone whose reputation is damaged in this way may become aware of it. Those individuals who become aware that their image has been displayed in error may not want to, or know how to, complain to the Privacy Commissioner. It remains unclear whether and how organizations that use sur- veillance cameras and store their images exercise 'due care' in transferring images to police before they are transferred to Crime Stoppers and beyond. It is vital to recognize that, had the surveillance images also been posted on the Crime Stoppers or YouTube websites, many more persons may have viewed or copied the images, thus making a 'retraction' impossible. As well, the increasingly short time between image capture and its use in a website advertisement (due to digitization) poten- tially reduces time to identify errors (in comparison to staging crime re-enactments by Crime Stoppers – see below). Furthermore, while most people would not seek these images through internet back doors, they can remain archived on the internet indefinitely even after intentional removal from the Crime Stoppers website. Using the Internet Archive, we were able to retrieve camera surveillance images related to crimes as far back as 10 June 2004 from the archived website of one Ontario Crime Stoppers programme (Internet Archive 2009). This is the case even though those persons depicted may have been long ago acquitted of the crimes they are alleged to have committed, or even when the cases are no longer prosecutable due to their summary offence status.

The police themselves may not have the means to know whether the image actually recorded a criminal act. If it is an organization's policy to forward all images to police for prosecution purposes, customers should be notified of this, and of the possibility that their personal information will be transferred in error. The distribu- tion and display via Crime Stoppers, whose personnel undoubtedly take images' accuracy at face value if transferred from police, and then to YouTube and beyond, raises the potential for serious harm. This is why third-party transfer – especially without proper notification – is a serious issue.

YouTube and website advertisements

Increased use of camera surveillance images

An examination of camera surveillance images in advertisements reveals that there is currently significant use of such images within 'Crime of the Week' or equivalent advertisements. Crime Stoppers is also increasingly using YouTube (and related formats) to display surveillance camera images under the Crime Stoppers banner to encourage 'tips' from the public. Though such images may have been sparingly used by at least one Crime Stoppers programme in advertisements in the late 1980s to encourage 'tips', there since has been a marked increase. Camera surveillance images are only mentioned once in a previous study on Crime Stoppers from this period, and not as a central feature of advertisements (Carriere and Ericson 1989: 69). In a previously drawn sample from 2000–1 (see Lippert 2002), surveillance camera images were present in a small portion of 'Crime of the Week' advertise- ments in some Ontario programmes and absent in others. But this current analysis reveals that such images now figure more largely in programmes. It was found that

21.6 per cent of advertisements from Ontario Crime Stoppers programmes currently use surveillance camera images. The Crime Stoppers programmes covering the largest urban regions of York, Peel and Toronto elicited over 25 per cent image saturation. This is undoubtedly due to greater availability of surveillance camera images in urban areas. While only four of 48 Toronto Regional Crime Stoppers advertisements (8.33 per cent) used camera surveillance images based on the 2000–1 sample, by 2007–8, 30 of 116 (25.9 per cent) of Toronto Crime Stoppers advertisements used images from surveillance cameras. Previously Toronto Crime Stoppers advertisements for television featured re-enactments (see Carriere and Ericson 1989; Lippert 2002) but now the programme's website states that a 'televised re-enactment *or surveillance video of the crime* is shown on television' (Toronto Crime Stoppers 2009; emphasis added) rather than relying exclusively on re-enactments. Crime Stoppers of York Region includes surveillance images in 72.1 per cent of its advertisements. Although we have no data on the number of times the website and television advertisements were viewed, our snapshot of YouTube data shows an average of over 9,000 views with a range of 18 views, for a new release, to 130,005, for a year-and-a-half-old murder case.

As significant a change as this might be across programmes, it is interesting to note that so far Ontario lags behind Crime Stoppers operations in other countries. In the United Kingdom the percentage of advertisements using camera surveillance images is 28 per cent (n = 59) and in Australia it is 48 per cent (n = 118).

This flow of surveillance camera images from point of capture to police to Crime Stoppers has been accelerated by the move to digitization of camera surveillance technologies, such that the products of surveillance cameras are now easily transferred to a Crime Stoppers website where they are displayed with or without an accompanying narrative. While perhaps unsurprising at first glance, the increased use of camera surveillance images is significant for several reasons. There is evidence from empirical research that persons place more stock in television news coverage (YouTube is televisual) than radio or print media (Ericson et al. 1991). Some advertisements were posted to the Crime Stoppers websites as 'news releases', and in some cases the made-for-television advertisement was present on the website. Audiences often tend to understand that 'seeing is believing' (Doyle 2006; see Ericson et al. 1991: 23) or that 'the camera never lies'. This means surveillance images can make a criminal incident described in an advertisement seem more believable to many audience members than accounts without images. One

TABLE 12.1 International Crime Stopper advertisements

Crime Stoppers programme (by country)	Advertisements	Advertisements with camera surveillance images present	Camera surveillance image saturation
Canada (Ontario)	603	130	21.6%
Australia	244	118	48.4%
United Kingdom	209	59	28.2%
Total	1056	307	29.1%

issue raised by Crime Stoppers' posting of camera surveillance footage on YouTube is their 'authentic' depiction of violence, as seen in five of the 27 (18.5 per cent) instances. Interestingly, this contravenes YouTube's 'Terms of Use' which forbids such depictions (YouTube 2009b).

In many advertisements camera surveillance images were found dominating accompanying text, and in other instances displacing text entirely, leaving only an oral description of the image and the 'crime'. Of the 27 instances of Crime Stoppers displaying surveillance camera footage on YouTube, nine lacked a written narrative in the information sidebar of the webpage. The narrative in all but one of the nine instances was incorporated as a voice-over into the footage.

The surveillance image is plainly becoming the focal point or centrepiece of advertised incidents. Put differently, the camera surveillance image is increasingly shouldering more of the work of generating 'tips' than before. This is significant for a number of reasons, not the least of which is that this helps limit the kinds of crimes displayed as advertisements to a narrow range of activities that can be captured by surveillance cameras. It may be that Crime Stoppers' increasing dependence on the surveillance image for advertisement content solidifies the practice identified in previous research of promoting only a narrow range of 'street crimes' (see Carriere and Ericson 1989; Lippert 2002) to the neglect of other types (practices elaborated later in this chapter). This is also significant because it ignores the unreliability of identification based upon camera surveillance images (see Davis and Valentine 2008).

Moreover, it is important to note that camera surveillance images only provide the most obvious information, that is, an often murky image of what a particular subject looked like in a certain location at a given time, while all 'other information needs to be coaxed out of them – or read into them' (Phillips 1997: 29). In the one case in which no textual or audio narrative was present, the surveillance footage, had it not appeared in a Crime Stoppers context, could be best described as depicting a transaction between a gas station cashier and customer. Indeed, 13 of the 27 (48.1 per cent) instances of Crime Stoppers surveillance footage on YouTube, and 100 of 130 (76.9 per cent) images in advertisements displayed on Crime Stoppers websites revealed no actions that were obviously criminal in nature. Moreover, most of the Crime Stoppers advertisements deployed the image with a narrative that implied guilt rather than stating the criminal act was alleged. While the police and Crime Stoppers have an interest in avoiding false arrests, it is possible that others may use images that have been assigned a criminal meaning through Crime Stoppers in nefarious ways. The anonymity of the internet could allow for the subsequent posting of surveillance footage to damage the reputation or livelihood of another by associating them with criminal activity.

Crime Stoppers expansion

As revealed in a Toronto Crime Stoppers YouTube video, Crime Stoppers advertising using camera surveillance images is permeating other public areas. In 2007, Toronto Crime Stoppers started the 'Underground Alert' programme in Toronto

Transit Commission (TTC) subway stations, entailing the display of 'crime files' on LCD television screens in the subway stations. According to the press release displayed on the YouTube page, 'Underground Alert enables authorities to message millions of commuters immediately following a crime in an attempt to catch the suspect' (YouTube 2009a). With the potential for millions of commuters to view the footage, this new Crime Stoppers programme underscores the importance of protecting privacy rights. Moreover, the unintended transfer of images to the Internet Archive and the intentional transfer to YouTube present privacy implications well beyond those related to Canadian legislation as these web-servers are based in California, USA and thus governed by other legislation.

Privacy and third parties

What privacy and related issues are raised by the release of this personal information to third parties? Crime Stoppers is a third party to which camera surveillance images are systematically transferred. While the province of Ontario Municipal Freedom of Information and Protection of Privacy Act (MFIPPA) contains provisions that allow for the disclosure of personal information to third parties, in doing so the dignity and rights of individuals whose personal information is being released is supposed to be safeguarded. Care is supposed to be taken when distributing this information. More specifically concerning camera surveillance images, the identifying features of victims or third parties could be removed through digital techniques such as blurring faces.

Deterrence

Ironically, each use of surveillance camera images in Crime Stoppers advertisements that seek 'tips' supports previous research that fails to find conclusive evidence that camera surveillance systems are an effective deterrent. Thus, the inclusion of each surveillance image in a Crime Stoppers advertisement is a growing testament to the failure of surveillance cameras to deter or to 'stop crime' on their own. This assumed lack of deterrence was acknowledged during an interview with a Business Improvement Association representative responding to the prospect of establishing 'open-street' closed circuit television cameras (CCTV) in the area: 'People commit bank robberies all the time. Everyone knows that almost every bank has camera surveillance and yet people go in there without even a ski mask; it's not a guarantee at all that stuff won't happen' (Interview 1). The effectiveness of surveillance cameras in reducing crime or securing criminal convictions is currently unknown, though there is reason to doubt their effectiveness. Consider a recent high-profile murder case in Ontario in relation to the use of surveillance camera images to solve the crime. The Crown withdrew the first-degree murder and five attempted murder charges in 2009 against Owen Smith and Wendell Cuff, allegedly depicted in surveillance footage posted to YouTube by Toronto Police (Dimanno 2009). The footage showed an individual shooting into a crowd at a Toronto housing complex in March 2008 while another individual was approaching the scene in the background. The footage of the shooting was viewed some 10,000 times (ibid.). Despite violating YouTube's 'Terms of Use' (YouTube 2009c) due to its depiction of violence, this footage may have been downloaded by individual users (including via programmes such as GetTube and KeepVid), potentially preserving the image that allegedly depicts a criminal act and that associates those persons depicted with it. The reproduction of the surveillance image is evident given that an internet search displays several other websites where this video is duplicated or to which it is linked. This is particularly important in the case of the second accused individual whom – even if near the scene – based on the footage may have had no knowledge of the shootings about to happen. Despite the charges being dropped, the duplication of this footage may be publicly available forever, potentially detrimentally affecting their life chances (e.g. employment, personal relationships).

In another piece of camera surveillance footage on YouTube, the suspect was apparently careful to avoid identification by robbing a convenience store while wearing his jeans inside out, a pillowcase over his head, and no shoes. Instead of being deterred, this person simply innovated to avoid subsequent identification. The use of these images in Crime Stoppers systematically calls into doubt one of the commonly stated justifications for using surveillance cameras to collect personal information in the first instance (on studies showing a lack of deterrent effect of camera surveillance, see Doyle and Walby, this volume).

Who benefits and whom is potentially harmed?

As noted earlier, one consequence of the increased use of and reliance upon surveillance camera images is that only certain types of crime are advertised. Camera surveillance systems are increasingly present in everyday life, but they are not everywhere; they are typically not in private offices and homes capturing everyday work or domestic practices. This systematically decreases the possibility of including types of crimes (of the powerful) occurring in these sites. With re-enactments, places that cameras typically do not or legally cannot record (e.g. bathrooms, private residences, workplaces) can still be depicted, thus encouraging 'tips' about incidents from such places. Thus, the types of crime depicted in 'Crime of the Week' using surveillance images frequently benefit powerful groups because the types of crimes they tend to commit are systematically left out.

In this way, the results of the analysis mirror earlier findings (see, for example, Doyle 2006: 208). For example, no Crime Stoppers advertisements in the sample portrayed domestic violence, corporate malfeasance, or crimes by police. Compared to the advertisements deploying still surveillance images, the YouTube advertisements contained a greater percentage of violent acts, in particular homicide. The homicides were caught by cameras apparently located on private property, although the events they captured occurred in public space. The lack of advertisements detailing domestic violence, corporate malfeasance, and crimes by police is also problematic as it conveys that certain types of crime are more prevalent, for example, robbery, while implying other crimes with harmful impacts on victims are less prevalent. These selective depictions may well promote a regressive 'law and order' ideology that imagines crime to be the result of rational actors and its control – in this instance through an attempt to locate the perpetrator of a crime – therefore translating into increased punitiveness or incapacitation by state authorities (see Carriere and Ericson 1989; Doyle 2003: 66–9; Doyle 2006: 208).

Moreover, to the extent that advertisements increasingly use and depend on camera surveillance images, the fact that most cameras (i.e. private and 'open-street' surveillance camera systems) are operated by businesses, the police and other government interests means that these other serious crimes are likely increasingly to be ignored. It is unlikely, for example, that a business will voluntarily (i.e. without a search warrant) turn over surveillance images that may implicate itself in malfeasance.

Table 12.2 shows the types of crimes reported as 'Crime of the Week' or equivalent. Of the 130 advertisements from Ontario programmes, 93 (over 70 per cent) depicted crimes committed against businesses (Property Crimes against Business).[5] The YouTube data from Ontario programmes had a greater (compared to the website advertisements) number of non-business related crimes, and an equal number of homicides and crimes against business (11 each, see Table 12.3). However, none

TABLE 12.2 Crime types in advertisements on Ontario Crime Stoppers websites

Crime	Number	Percent
Property (business/violent)	69	53.1
Property (business/non-violent)	24	18.5
Property (citizen/non-violent)	9	6.9
Sexual assault/other sex related crime	8	6.2
Property (citizen/violent)	6	4.6
Credit card fraud	5	3.8
Physical assault	5	3.8
Property (public/non-violent)	2	1.5
Child abduction	1	0.8
Firearms offence	1	0.8

TABLE 12.3 Crime types depicted on YouTube

Crime	Number	Percent
Homicide	11	40.7
Property (business/non-violent)	7	25.9
Property (business/violent)	4	14.8
Property (citizen/non-violent)	2	7.4
Physical assault	1	3.7
Property (citizen/violent)	1	3.7
Sexual assault/other sex related crime	1	3.7

of the images appeared to be taken from 'open-street' or public surveillance cameras. While this may be due in part to the limited number of 'open-street' camera surveillance systems in Canada, it is significant that businesses are the immediate beneficiaries of using camera surveillance images in Crime Stoppers advertising.

Given the increasing credence given to the authenticity of ('seeing is believing') camera surveillance images, if victims are unaware of the possible existence of these images (the presence of surveillance cameras) in a given context they may decide not to report a particular crime. A lack of notification may thus lead to crimes against persons not being reported too. Citizens, unaware that the images produced by surveillance cameras are being recorded, may feel they have no corroborating evidence to support reports of being victimized. While it is important to notify the public of surveillance cameras to gain 'informed consent', this notification is also required to make individuals aware that their victimization or the victimization of others may have been witnessed and recorded by cameras, assisting them in reporting such incidents.

The use of camera surveillance images on the Crime Stoppers and YouTube websites raises additional privacy concerns in relation to victims. Of the 130 advertisements, 32 (24.6 per cent) contained images with a visible third party or victim. In only two of these 32 images (6.3 per cent) was intentional distortion or digital editing used. In eight of the 32 images (25 per cent) the victim or third party is clearly identifiable. Since these advertisements provided a description of the suspect, the reader may distinguish between suspect and victim/third party. However, the inclusion of third parties and victims may elicit other concerns. While it may be that third parties are included because they are also wanted for questioning about the incident, none of the advertisements appeals to these other persons to come forward to police or Crime Stoppers, and it can be reasonably assumed that victims would have already provided a statement to police. Compared to the advertisements on Crime Stoppers websites, the YouTube camera footage sought to hide the identities of third parties and victims to a greater extent. However, of the files displaying third parties or victims, nine of 20 (45 per cent) did not use some form of intentional distortion. It is possible that, if apprehended, the suspect may seek retribution against one of the third parties believing they were the 'tipster'. This failure to render third parties anonymous starkly conflicts with Crime Stoppers' stated focus on anonymization (see Lippert 2002).

Of the 44 suspects identified in the YouTube surveillance footage, 13 suspects (29.5 per cent) were apparently White, 20 (45.5 per cent) were Black,[6] five (11.4 per cent) were other visible minorities, and the 'race' of six (13.6 per cent) was unidentifiable (due to disguise or poor video quality). The high percentage of camera surveillance footage selected for display that depicts visible minorities committing criminal acts (56 per cent) is potentially harmful to these already disadvantaged groups. Previous research has found racism in camera surveillance monitoring (see, for example, Norris and Armstrong 1999) and in selection of reality television footage such as in programmes like *Cops* (Oliver 1994). Such depictions can fuel racist sentiments, as seen in comments left by YouTube users in relation to this footage. The racist tone of comments posted on the Toronto Crime Stoppers YouTube page prompted Toronto Crime Stoppers to make the following statement on the website:

> We had a retired educator write to us about the racist remarks on some of the comments . . . we don't support racism in any way – we do support free speech . . . and we would like to use this comment section to educate as much as possible . . . and generate tips to solve this crime and many others . . . please be responsible in your postings . . . racist comments *can come back to haunt you* at times of job interviews etc. . . . be tolerant of all . . . stand up for the good, and correct the wrong.
>
> *(YouTube 2009c; emphasis added).*

That Crime Stoppers points out that posting racist comment on websites can later haunt individuals is laudable. However, there is no similar mention or apparent recognition that selective depictions of visible minorities in surveillance images in Crime Stoppers advertisements can also 'haunt' identifiable innocent individuals and other members of visible minority groups whom – as noted above – may be completely unaware that their images were collected and posted by associating them with criminal activity.

Conclusion

This chapter explored the deployment of camera surveillance images by police-supported Crime Stoppers programmes in three countries. Since 2001 there has been a significant increase in the volume of surveillance camera images used by Crime Stoppers in its advertisements. More recently Crime Stoppers in at least one country – Canada – has increasingly posted camera surveillance footage on the video-sharing website YouTube. This increased use raises privacy and other issues. Such images have been erroneously shared with police and have made their way into Crime Stoppers advertisements. Such occurrences have the potential to detrimentally affect a person's reputation and livelihood. There is now less delay between the capture of video footage and its subsequent release in advertisements, and thus less opportunity to identify error. Also, images in Crime Stoppers advertisements often appear without masking the identity of third parties and victims, presenting serious privacy and ethical concerns as these individuals become implicated in a criminal incident. Questions about appropriate notification are also raised by such arrangements. Individuals should have the option of avoiding situations where their image may be captured and potentially posted to the internet.

Crime Stoppers' use of surveillance camera images also casts doubt on claims that camera surveillance has a deterrent effect. Evident are many instances where crime was committed despite the camera's presence. Finally, an increased dependence on surveillance camera images over traditional re-enactments has the potential to narrow the range of crimes portrayed in Crime Stoppers advertisements. Such a narrowing of crime types will tend to benefit mostly private business rather than the general public and promotes the spread of 'law and order' ideology. Finally, this research revealed that camera surveillance images posted on YouTube by Crime Stoppers disproportionately portray visible minorities as engaged in criminal activity. This is another troubling practice that is potentially harmful to the well-being of the specific racial or ethnic groups depicted.

Notes

1 We use 'image' to refer to both CCTV footage and stills.
2 We use 'advertisements' rather than, for example, 'news releases' or 'appeals' since there is evidence (see Carriere and Ericson 1989; Lippert 2002) their intent is as much promoting or marketing Crime Stoppers (and its sponsors) in an attempt to generate 'tips' generally or about certain types of crime (e.g. drug-related crime) than to generate tactical information to solve a particular crime or capture specific criminals depicted. To illustrate this point, only three of the 130 advertisements in this study claimed a suspect had been apprehended.
3 YouTube appeared in 2005 partially as a result of a shift in video technology comprising inexpensive camcorders and easier-to-use video software coupled with the rapid proliferation of the availability of high-speed internet connections and dramatically increased memory storage capacity.
4 This section seems to refer only to reactionary surveillance in response to specific criminal incidents in an area, rather than to continuous surveillance of premises.
5 The proportions were slightly less for Australia (57.6 per cent) and the United Kingdom (55.9 per cent).
6 'Black' was used by Crime Stoppers rather than 'person of colour' or 'African-Canadian' and so was reproduced here. Although these categories are contested and 'race' is to be understood as a social construction, Crime Stoppers advertisements often use these categories to describe suspects.

References

Carriere, K. and Ericson, R. (1989) *Crime Stoppers: A Study in the Organization of Community Policing*, Toronto: Centre of Criminology, University of Toronto.

Crime Stoppers International (2009) *Programs*, Crime Stoppers International. Online. Available HTTP:<http://www.c-s-i.org/Programs.aspx>.

Crime Stoppers of York Region (2009) *Crime Stoppers in York Region*, Crime Stoppers of York Region. Online. Available HTTP: http://www.crimestoppersyr.ca/aboutus/about_csyr.html>.

Davis, J.P. and Valentine, T. (2008) 'CCTV on Trial: Matching Video Images with the Defendant in the Dock', *Applied Cognitive Psychology*, 23/4: 482–505.

Dimanno, R. (2009) 'Video of killing reveals no secrets', *Toronto Star*, 27 February. Online. Available HTTP: <http://www.thestar.com/News/Columnist/article/593931>.

Doyle, A. (2003) *Arresting Images: Crime and Policing in Front of the Television Camera*, Toronto: University of Toronto Press.

Doyle, A. (2006) 'An Alternative Current in Surveillance and Control: Broadcasting Surveillance Footage of Crimes', in K. Haggerty and E. Ericson (eds), *The New Politics of Surveillance and Visibility*, Toronto: University of Toronto Press.

Ericson, R., Baranek, P. and Chan, J. (1991) *Representing Order: Crime, Law, and Justice in the News Media*, Toronto: University of Toronto Press.

Future Shop (2009) Privacy Policy. Online. Available HTTP: <http://www.futureshop.

ca/informationcentre/EN/privacypolicy.asp?logon=&langid=EN> (accessed 2 December 2009).

Gresham, P., Stockdale, J. and Bartholomew, I. (2003) *Evaluating the Impact of Crime Stoppers*, Home Office Online Report. 22/03.

Internet Archive (2009) 'Internet Archive Way Back Machine'. Online. Available HTTP: <http://web.archive.org/web/20061103091303/www.222tips.com/index.php?pt=content&sec=5&sub=34>.

Lippert, R. (2002) 'Policing Property and Moral Risk Through Promotions, Anonymization and Rewards: Crime Stoppers Revisited', *Social Legal Studies: An International Journal*, 11(4): 475–502.

Lippert, R. (2009) 'Signs of the Surveillant Assemblage: Privacy Regulation, Urban CCTV and Governmentality', *Social and Legal Studies: An International Journal*, 18(4): 505–22.

National Capital Area Crime Stoppers (2008) 'February 2008 Archives', National Capital Area Crime Stoppers. Online. Available HTTP: <http://crimestoppers.ca/2008/02/>.

Norris, C. and Armstrong, G. (1999) *The Maximum Surveillance Society*, Oxford, UK: Berg.

Office of the Privacy Commissioner of Canada (2002) PIPED Act Case Summary #53. Ottawa. Online. Available HTTP: <http://www.canlii.org/en/ca/pcc/doc/2002/2002canlii42356/2002canlii42356.html>.

Office of the Privacy Commissioner of Canada (2008) Guidelines for Overt Video Surveillance in the Private Sector. Ottawa. Online. Available HTTP: <http://www.privcom.gc.ca/information/guide/2008/gl_vs_080306.asp>.

Oliver, M. (1994) 'Portrayals of Crime, Race and Aggression in "Reality-Based" Police Shows: A Content Analysis', *Journal of Broadcasting and Electronic Media*, 38(2): 179–92.

Phillips, S. (1997) 'Identifying the Criminal', in S. Phillips, M. Harworth-Booth and C. Squires (eds), *Police Pictures: The Photograph as Evidence*, San Francisco: Chronicle Books, 11–31.

Toronto Crime Stoppers (2009) *About Toronto Crime Stoppers*, Toronto Crime Stoppers. Online. Available HTTP: <http://www.222tips.com/aboutus.php>.

YouTube (2009a) *UNDERGROUND ALERT Media Launch*. Toronto Crime Stoppers. Online. Available HTTP: <http://www.youtube.com/watch?v=KZtQnDf2m2g&feature=channel_page>.

YouTube (2009b) 'Terms of Use'. Online. Available HTTP: <http://www.youtube.com/t/terms>.

YouTube (2009c) *Appeal for Info – Violent Mac's Store Robbery 1800222tips*, Toronto Crime Stoppers. Online. Available HTTP: <http:/www.youtube.comwatchv>.

Legislation

Personal Information Protection and Electronic Documents Act, S.C., 2000, c. 5.

Privacy Act, R.S.C., 1985, c. P-21.

Municipal Freedom of Information and Protection of Privacy Act, R.S.O. 1990, c. M.56 (Ontario).

13

HIDDEN CHANGES

From CCTV to 'smart' video surveillance

Joseph Ferenbok and Andrew Clement

Introduction

Behind the familiar camera housings and lenses, and hidden from their surveilled subjects, video surveillance systems are becoming much 'smarter'. Though many people still associate video surveillance with analogue CCTV (closed-circuit television), these new digital systems differ significantly. Behind the scenes, video analytics – computer-assisted video monitoring, analysis and indexing – is changing what can be 'seen' using surveillance camera networks. Video analytics (VA) is software that uses signal processing and pattern recognition techniques to automatically generate meaningful or semantic data from video images. Video analytics marks a paradigmatic shift in visual surveillance practices – in how information is purposed and repurposed – and in the potential consequences for surveillance subjects.

How video surveillance systems are being networked and augmented remains largely out of public view. This obscured deployment contributes to 'a lack of realism about what could be expected from CCTV systems' (Deisman et al. 2009: 15). The covert data flows and undisclosed algorithmic practices also marginalize public debate and hinder informed policy-making. To help open these technological changes (and informational exchanges) to scrutiny, this chapter looks at how CCTV technologies are being transformed and integrated with information communication technologies (ICT) and signal processing algorithms to expand the scope and nature of video surveillance well beyond CCTV.

We begin by highlighting the central features of the conventional CCTV model and then show how 'smart' or 'intelligent' digital video surveillance aims to overcome the limitations of this model. We review the enhanced functionalities of digital video techniques, especially video analytics, and how they are being applied in a growing range of surveillance settings. This chapter seeks to contribute to the broader discussion of what is at stake at a time of intensifying surveillance regimes both in North America and around the globe (see this volume). We are particularly interested to understand how camera surveillance augmented by video analytics is being deployed and what this deployment may generally mean for individual citizens and the public interest. The resulting better understanding of the implications for civil liberties and public policy of the new generation of video surveillance techniques may help redress the growing imbalance between the watched and the watchers, especially in 'open-street' public surveillance in retail contexts.

The CCTV paradigm

CCTV represents the first generation of visual surveillance. It was first used by German scientists in 1942 for remote monitoring of rocket launches (Reuter 2000). At its most basic, a CCTV system is a camera linked to a monitor. Connected by a continuous or closed electronic circuit, the camera captures images that are then transmitted to the monitor. In this model the information flow is uninterrupted and unidirectional. The closed path from camera to monitor implies an indexical relationship between the surveyed space and the image – a visual truth that hides the mediation imposed by the technology of the medium, and the viewer from the viewed. This visual, photographic truth (Tagg 1988), combined with the inherent one-way flow of information, supports institutional infrastructures of knowledge production that reinforce dominant social power.

The one-camera one-monitor closed-circuit model was readily adapted for surveillance of multiple spaces or for multiple camera viewpoints. The first 'open-street' deployment came in 1969, when the London Metropolitan Police used two temporary cameras in Trafalgar Square to monitor Guy Fawkes Day Activities (Norris and Armstrong 1999). Over the next two decades CCTV systems evolved to include more than just cameras and monitors. To facilitate multiple camera inputs and viewing options, additional devices such as switchers, controllers and recorders were integrated. Figure 13.1 presents a typical CCTV system model including multiple cameras, a switcher/controller and a video recording device.

This conventional CCTV model has one or more cameras that feed into a switcher or controller. Controllers may be used to direct PTZ (pan, tilt and zoom) cameras, allowing operators to change the field of view remotely. Information then flows from the switcher to a monitor for real-time remote viewing and a recorder for future viewing. The two key features of the system are that it is closed, so that no information is broadcast elsewhere, and that it represents images using analogue signals. Analogue signals or information means that image elements are coded by continuously varying properties of the physical medium, such as voltage in the transmission circuit and magnetic field strength in the case of recording tape. Analogue signals also mean that images often have low resolution and quality, and are prone to various technological errors. Compared to current technologies, analogue signals are also relatively hard to process, so that doing more than sequential viewing and storing involves complex customized hardware. So another limitation becomes the difficulty in handling the flood of visual information generated.

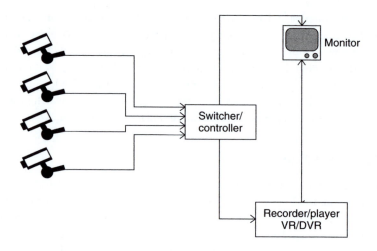

FIGURE 13.1   The classic CCTV model.

Human operators have limited attention spans: the more cameras, the more information is produced, the more the switcher moves between channels, and the more information remains unseen and unrecorded.

Beyond analogue CCTV

Since the 1990s the adoption of digital techniques for handling visual data has facilitated the transition from analogue cameras and closed networks towards digital image capture, transmission, storage, analysis and encoding. Digital recording of multiple cameras on hard drives greatly reduces the costs associated with recording and storage. A contemporary video surveillance network model can receive signals from various camera types: analogue or digital, with fixed views or pan, tilt and zoom capabilities. Surveillance networks may also incorporate multiple compression, transmission and encryption standards; incorporate local or networked video recording (NVR) and storage; incorporate digital signal processing (DSP); and employ computer-mediated real-time analytics. As internet protocol (IP) standards are increasingly adopted, individual components and entire networks can be readily linked together to aggregate, exchange or repurpose information over the Internet. Figure 13.2 demonstrates some variations on information-processing associated with more sophisticated digital video surveillance systems.

Although a wired CCTV camera is by no means obsolete, increasingly cameras are digital and information is at some point transmitted using wireless networks and/or over the Internet. The switch to digital sensors provides the foundation for 'smart' security – that is, security augmented by computer-mediated processing. Contemporary digital sensors are typically in the range of several megapixels, but surveillance cameras with 50 megapixel resolution and higher are commercially available. The imaging technology is improving rapidly: in 2010 the Department

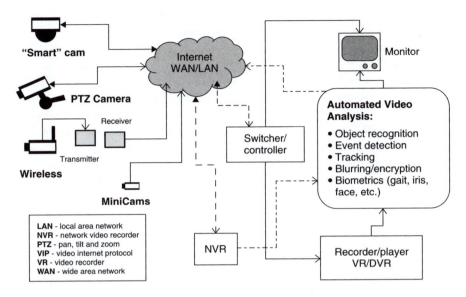

FIGURE 13.2 Video internet protocol (VIP) surveillance network.

of Homeland Security announced development of a 100 megapixel camera with a specialized fish-eye lens for 360 degree surveillance (HSNW 2010). The potential resolution or amount of information gathered using these digital sensors is significantly greater than analogue cameras. To make this point more clear, consider a face recognition system that uses images as small as 'an average face size of 75 pixels between the centers of the eyes' (Phillips et al. 2007) for identification. For analogue CCTV images, this represents roughly a fifth of a standard TV image. With digital images, where the resolution is measured in megapixels, a 75 pixel average distance between pupils can represent a much smaller fraction of the information captured in a single image. So a face in a digital frame with high-resolution imaging has more possibilities for cataloguing, analysis and identification than an analogue image with the same field of view. The amount of data is not all that has changed: the quality of that data too has seen significant improvements.

Digital video signals also tend to have better and more consistent image quality than analogue CCTV. Digital capture and recording eliminates many of the errors characteristic of analogue video recording. Time-based errors occur because of the mechanical instability of video recording devices– for example, the slight difference in tape speed between the beginning of a cassette and the end of one – making mixing or comparison of video difficult without correction. Dropout errors derived from the recording device produce blurred, skewed or blotchy images when using analogue video recordings. In contrast, digital video recorders, although they present new challenges, virtually eliminate time-based and dropout errors. Finally, digital video eliminates generation loss (Watkinson 1994). With magnetic tape-based analogue video recorders, each copy – or each generation – introduces noise that degrades the original signal. Since digital recordings may be reproduced without generation loss, digital surveillance video does not fall prey to the same types of information degradation from being copied and distributed multiple times for multiple viewings at multiple sites.

The transition to digital technologies represents a significant change in the development of video surveillance – a kind of renaissance in quality and a movement away from strictly closed-circuit systems. The move to digital means information can exist in multiple archives and in multiple formats over multiple networks – allowing for unprecedented distribution, manipulation, aggregation and sharing. This movement towards more open, networked, heterogenous infrastructures of surveillance marks a notable shift in how visual information is exchanged, stored, indexed and analysed. At the extreme end, PTZ cameras are being controlled and monitored by geographically distributed people, either with access permissions, or via interactive broadcasts entirely open to all visitors. An example of this is the Texas Sheriff's strategy for border control (Reay 2008). Roaming video surveillance cameras were deployed so that the public could voluntarily monitor the Texas border for illegal migration from an online site. Not all open video surveillance feeds are advertised, but many are openly broadcasting, some unwittingly – a search for '"ViewerFrame?Mode="' produces a horde of IP addresses openly streaming surveillance images that often include offices and commercial spaces. These examples of video surveillance, encoded into packets and accessible either by password-protected sites or as open video, can no longer be understood as CCTV. With commercially available cameras increasingly 'internet ready', this decoupling of camera from monitor and from storage or recording device means that visual information can travel across the globe for analysis or retention. This shift in information flow is typically understated when CCTV cameras are discussed and has significant implications for privacy, security and democratic rights of all surveilled subjects.

As challenging to privacy and public policy as these changes in the flow of visual information represent, they only pave the way for more and different challenges that algorithmic processing of that information will likely bring. The ability to integrate video analysis software into multiple nodes of a surveillance network represents a shift towards what its promoters refer to as 'smart' visual surveillance. If analogue CCTV represents the first generation, then the so-called 'smart' surveillance 'solutions' that integrate video analytics with digital storage and networking are clearly a new generation of video surveillance.

Hidden processing

Increasingly, surveillance systems integrate one or more layers of analytics that mediate the flow of information between the operator(s) and the camera(s). This intermediate video processing is most commonly referred to as Video Analytics (VA), though vendors also use terms such as smart video surveillance, Intelligent Video Analytics (IVA), Intelligent Analytics (IA), Video Content Analysis (VCA) to describe a range of video image processing techniques. Video Analytics incorporate a range of functionality 'from systems that classify and store simple data, through more complex systems that compare the captured data to other data and provide matches, to systems that attempt to predict events based on the captured data' (Norris and McCahill 2006). This digital processing enables a form of algorithmic surveillance (Introna and Wood 2004) that is hidden from even the most observant surveillance subject.

Programming computers to detect, classify, code and semantically label temporal and spatial patterns of pixels in a video stream is a complex problem. Video analytic architectures tend to be modular – that is, a series of software modules strung together – where outputs of one module are used as inputs for the next. Modules are typically independent but use common protocols throughout a processing chain. There are distinct algorithms for detecting, classifying and identifying objects and their trajectories as well as for initiating responses. Generally an early processing stage includes a module that attempts to distinguish and track objects across successive video images. Differences between frames can help demarcate moving objects in the foreground from the background. Once detected, the background is subtracted, or discarded, so subsequent object and event detection modules can process the pixels that remain, for instance by comparing them with patterns in earlier frames or pre-defined reference models.

The image information can then pass on to object and event classification modules where patterns are classified and alerts triggered automatically. The criteria for alerts are based on predefined or user-specified models for various types of objects and events, such as the presence of a gun, a person running or an unexpected package. In the classification stages, video analytic engines produce meta-data that both guides the visual processing and provides semantic descriptions of the video inputs. This classification of objects and events can also produce an index of objects and recognized events, which in turn can be used as meta-data for future search and retrieval and as data for further processing. For example, objects recognized as humans can be characterized, measured, compared and slotted into generalized categories (male/female, white/asian/. . . etc.), and profiled to assess risk in both security and retail domains, and opportunities in forms of targeted marketing and other forms of intervention. Cisco Systems Inc. encourages their retail store customers to monitor shoppers based on a range of demographic criteria, potentially influencing how customers are sorted and treated. In a pamphlet aimed at retailers, Cisco advertises that 'cameras can also identify gender and age, and send out real-time alerts [and] . . . when combined with an IP network, video . . . can be easily retrieved, shared, integrated, and analyzed within the store and across the enterprise' (Cisco Systems Inc. 2009).

Based on the class of object recognized – e.g. a vehicle, body or face – other algorithms may be employed to identify objects individually and track them between frames and across different video streams. If an object is classified as a licence plate, for example, automatic number plate recognition (ANPR) (also known as automatic licence plate recognition (ALPR)) software can then be used to correct any distortion and apply optical character recognition (OCR) to identify the registration.

An object determined to be a body can be analysed for individual identity or behavioural pattern (e.g. 'loitering'). Though perhaps further off than ALPR in terms of routine adoption, but at least as challenging with respect to policy and individual rights, are the analytic techniques for behavioural analysis and biometrics such as gait or face recognition. Tracking and identifying people in video is an active area of research, development and commercialization (Cai et al. 2009; Bojkovic and Samcovic 2006; Gorodnichy 2006; Shaokang et al. 2008; Suman 2008; Goffredo et al. 2008). It is driven by the hope that video analytics will enable video surveillance networks to follow individuals, detect anomalies, anticipate potential danger and take appropriate action, all in real-time. This convergence of biometric identification infrastructures, notably those based on facial images, and VA represents a new horizontal integration of contemporary video surveillance systems (see Figure 13.3). High-resolution surveillance cameras supported by digital processing linked to private, public or government biometric databases may significantly extend our already extensive data shadows into public spaces and subject us to profiling, risk assessment and pro-active interventions.

Video Analytics (VA) addresses at least two major limitations of the conventional analogue CCTV model: live monitoring and retrospective searching. Watching video surveillance can be tedious and boring. Often there can be hours or days of video from multiple sources where very little of interest actually happens. The

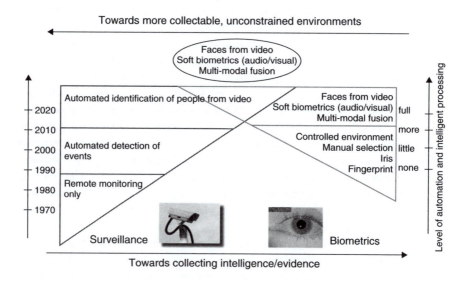

FIGURE 13.3   Towards 'smart' surveillance: merging of biometrics and surveillance techniques (Gorodnichy 2009).

volume of information produced by multiple cameras running 24 hours, seven days a week means much information captured by analogue CCTV cameras is not viewed in real-time or retained, and if recorded, is not viewed. Bosch Security Systems presents the problem this way:

> No matter how few or how many cameras your system uses, monitoring everything effectively presents a serious challenge. Even observing just a single screen for long periods pushes concentration to the limit – after only 20 minutes, an operator can miss as much as 90% of the activity in a scene.
>
> *(2009)*

Video Analytics is presented as a promising solution. Processing the video input can help prioritize information in real-time and bring significant events to the foreground for human agents that require intervention or further monitoring. Bosch Security Systems offers Intelligent Video Analysis (IVA) to help 'operators focus by introducing a new level of automation to CCTV monitoring' (2009a). They bill their system as an extra set of unblinking eyes that help operators to stay focused and on top of the action. Video analytics introduces '. . . a new level of automation to CCTV monitoring. Edge-based, real-time processing identifies alert conditions, giving your security team the information it needs to react swiftly and take action' (2009).

Video Analytics also potentially addresses another significant limitation with conventional CCTV surveillance: sequential, time-based information access, requiring linear searches through recordings. With standard recording equipment, video information could not generally be accessed in other than a linear fashion, say by event type. This makes reviewing CCTV footage time-consuming and labour-intensive. Video analytics tools can recognize and catalogue objects and events to produce a semantic index of visual data, which facilitates more advanced processing and analysis, e.g. enabling searches by object, gender, age, habit, predefined event, etc. This more sophisticated video search technique has multiple applications across many domains.

This shift to 'smart' video surveillance is being made almost entirely out of public view. The transition is hidden in the sense that existing infrastructures can be upgraded with video image processing software without any overt or visible change to existing cameras. In fact, this is a selling point. IBM's Smart Surveillance Solution is designed to be interoperable and 'integrate with existing video and capture systems to provide video/sensor analytic capabilities' (Sullivan 2008). So once the visual images are captured they can be remotely stored, indexed and analysed for what IBM refers to as 'valuable business information'.

Applying video analytics

VA is being applied in a variety of surveillance contexts, including such broadly defined domains as: public safety, security, border control, finance and retail data-mining. For public safety and security VA may be used to identify and report people who need emergency medical attention: a person who collapses in a parking lot for instance. For border control, video analytics are being employed at airports to 'detect' abandoned or suspicious items.

The business opportunities that come from applying computer vision techniques in everyday settings have attracted the interest of hundreds of companies. There are large integrators like IBM, Bosch and Cisco who offer comprehensive 'solutions' to surveillance, security and visual data-mining; and smaller companies like IQeye, Smart Camera Systems, VideoIQ Inc. and 3VR that specialize in specific areas of video analytics. The variety of vendors means that there is a broad range of customizable systems designed to trigger automatic and, often, user-defined alerts. As a result, the application of VA in video surveillance can vary widely, including counting the number of cars that use a roadway, as part of traffic safety (Coleshill et al. 2007; Pflugfelder et al. 2005), investigating banking fraud and conducting market research.

In financial institutions 'smart' cameras are used to assist forensics investigations. Automated analysis of ATM video images can provide legal evidence while reducing investigation costs (Russo 2008). In retail spaces, cameras pointed at employees may be looking for transaction fraud; while the cameras pointed at customers may help analyse shopping habits through digital signage networks (DSN) (Dixon 2010). DSN are a growing phenomenon where stores employ cameras embedded in digital signage to record potentially useful behavioural information. Video analytics can report how long a customer interacts with the sign and demographic information about the customer to establish customer profiles. These cameras can be hidden behind video screens, and retailers generally provide little notice about whether they employ this form of video capture and analysis (Dixon 2010). With digital video surveillance infrastructures in place, and as the utility of mining visual information increases, the temptation to gain valuable insights into customer patterns will likely lead to this becoming increasingly commonplace.

As a vendor of integrated systems, IBM claims benefits to their customers can include: cross-agency sharing; remote access; reduced security overheads; reduced need for guards; and non-linear search capabilities. Facilitated by video analytics, non-linear search capabilities allow for 'queries based on color, object, size and other attributes' (Sullivan 2008). According to IBM, this type of fine-grained analytics will help its clients benefit by 'getting business information out of security-related data' (Sullivan 2008). Repurposing security surveillance video data by means of video analytics allows retailers potentially to mine and capitalize on the behaviours and patterns of both clients and staff. It also threatens to erode the principles of purpose specification, use limitation and data minimization that underpin all privacy regulation.

The events of 9/11 provided a brief but important impetus to the development of video analytics. Promoters of the latest generation of video surveillance were quick to promote its virtues in stopping future terrorist attacks. One of the most prominent of these was Dr Joseph Atick, co-founder of Visionics Corporation (CNN 2001), but despite his confident claims, his Face-it technology proved much less than ready for deployment during tests at Logan International Airport a year later (Murphy and Bray 2003). Failures at other sites like Tampa, Florida (Stanley and Steinhardt 2002) contributed to the reading of automated systems as expensive, prone to false alarms, hard to configure, unreliable and easy to fool. For example, researchers demonstrated multiple ways to circumvent face recognition technologies (Alexander and Smith 2003). However, although the initial roll-out of video analytic systems following 9/11 fell prey to over-stated claims and poor system performance (BSIA 2010), video analytics has developed apace. With modest (or at least less easily refutable) claims and expanded capabilities, video analytics is finding wider markets.

As research continues to improve real-time video signal processing and analysis, images captured by video surveillance may increasingly serve as gateways to our identities. At a time when visual information is becoming increasingly personal, linkable, mobile, searchable and thereby valuable, images caught on surveillance cameras pose an increasing threat to privacy and identity integrity. Collectors and custodians of visual information should adhere to fair information practices. They should understand the capacities and limitations of their systems, keep to justifiable purposes, and provide information on their information practice policies involving any form of automated processing, storage or transmission of personal information. This ideal remains elusive.

Hidden alternatives

The digital techniques for video image capture, storage, networking and algorithmic analysis discussed so far are aimed at enhancing the discriminatory capabilities of surveillant authorities, but with no corresponding reciprocal visibility or accountability. In this way such techniques contribute to further imbalance established relationships of power away from surveillance subjects and towards those deploying the video surveillance. But while the asymmetric 'big brother', panoptic and one-way metaphors that dominate the discussion of the social implications of video surveillance have a valid basis and help inform resistance to the more egregious forms of surveillance, they also tend to obscure the possibilities that digitalization can offer for opening up alternative forms of surveillance that might help mitigate some systemic imbalance. Can the techniques of digital signal processing, object coding and video analytics that surveillance operators deploy for their advantage also be used on behalf of surveillance subjects? Can alternate forms of surveillance be used to demonstrate privacy enhancing surveillance strategies? At least technically, and under favourable conditions, the answer appears to be 'yes' – they can help protect personal privacy and enable greater public accountability and oversight of legitimate surveillance operations.

An obvious approach to privacy protection offered by video analytics is through the anonymization of personal image data. Most straightforward technically is encryption, or the systematic mathematical scrambling of the digital data. Only with the appropriate key can the encrypted images be viewed. This is currently routine in many uses of wireless cameras to prevent surreptitious eavesdropping of the transmission from the camera to its base station. However, once the video signals reach the more protected wired circuits and storage devices, typically they are de-encrypted and from then on appear in plain form. Where video surveillance is used exclusively for forensic purposes, the stored images could remain encrypted until law enforcement authorities obtain an authorized key to decrypt the specific time period when a serious incident is strongly suspected to have occurred. The keys could be held by the judiciary, and only provided upon legitimate formal request, such as a search warrant submitted to a judge. The computer system hosting the video image database could also automatically log and regularly report on such key release authorizations and decryptions, including such details as the date, time, rationale and authorizing body. Even when there is a need for viewing the live video stream, all subsequent storage and viewing could be regulated in this fashion.

Another approach to anonymization is through the blurring of specified video objects. The same techniques for detecting objects, such as faces, bodies and licence plates, in the video stream for subsequent analysis and recognition can also be used to blur them. Once spotted, these objects can be permanently smudged by randomizing the visual information. The software for accomplishing this is simpler than that required for the enhancement and analysis techniques mentioned above. The best known example is Google Blur, the software used by the search engine giant to smudge the faces and licence plates in Google Street View images. Of course, the success of this technique depends on the accuracy of the underlying object recognition algorithms – and mistakes have been well documented in the media. Also, if the blurring is not performed in the camera, but later in the process, it would be possible to retrieve the un-blurred images.

Encryption can be combined with object detection to produce a broader range of anonymization options. Researchers at the University of Toronto have developed a technique they refer to as secure visual object coding. The technique selectively encrypts particular types of objects, such as faces, and treats them separately from the rest of the video stream (Martin and Plataniotis 2008). In normal live viewing the background would appear as usual, but with the protected objects appearing in outline form with a randomized texture (see Figure 13.4).

Once the images are encrypted in this way, it is very difficult for anyone without proper authorization to view the full video image. This could enable live monitoring, say of subway platforms or public places, but without revealing individual identities. Access to personal information can then be controlled through a rigorous administrative and technical regime. Secure visual object coding is still in experimental development and testing, but it already illustrates the potential for approaches that exploit digital characteristics for privacy protection. In particular, it can help reinforce the data minimization principle by setting the standard for the amount of personal data used for security and other purposes at a much lower level. However, it is unlikely that this or other similar techniques will be adopted and implemented without strong policy, regulatory or other forms of external pressure.

FIGURE 13.4   Demonstration of secure visual object coding technique, showing original surveillance frame and with encrypted object texture (Martin and
Plataniotis 2008).

Furthermore, even if 'improved' privacy-protective surveillance techniques
become prevalent, they alone cannot address all risks posed by the shift to digital
video surveillance. The following section explores the implications of this asymmetric and differential visibility in terms of everyday identification and surveillance. This
analysis highlights the need to mitigate this asymmetry and the challenge of making
the surveillance infrastructure and the propagation of faces and other personal visual
information collected through it more visible and hence more accountable.

Social implications for surveillance subjects

To this point we have concentrated on how capabilities of video surveillance
technologies have grown since the 1990s, mainly in response to the demands for
enhancing security and the increased availability of flexible, inexpensive, interoperable digital hardware and software. We turn now to address issues of what these
changes mean for surveilled subjects' well-being and civil rights.

It hardly can be claimed the central challenges posed by video surveillance, even
in its simpler CCTV form, have been adequately addressed. Lingering questions
remain: is video surveillance effective, and under what circumstances? For what
purposes is it, or should it, be used? Who is looking at my live and recorded images?
Who is doing what, and why, with my personal information and how will this
affect me? All remain largely unanswered. The on-going transformation of video
surveillance technologies and practices generally make these questions even harder
to answer. This further suggests that the well-founded concerns for civil liberties
associated with conventional CCTV are likely to be exacerbated rather than mitigated by digital growth. Concerns over reasonable expectations of privacy in public
spaces, already an issue identified by the results of the Urbaneye project (Hempel
and Töpfer 2004), will likely be exacerbated by digital repurposing of security
information for other forms of visual data mining.

Technological changes alone never produce specific social outcomes. Organizational, cultural and other factors also play important roles. However, it is useful
to consider how the adoption of digital video surveillance techniques creates new,

socially significant affordances and constraints. Digital technologies typically greatly reduce the component costs for the capture, transmission, storage and display of video surveillance images. Even if the conventional CCTV model remained un-changed, this would encourage the wider adoption of video surveillance for its original security purposes and make it more attractive for other purposes, such as observing consumer behaviour. At the very least these lower costs mean more people would be subject to its potentially intrusive, chilling and privacy-invasive effects.

Conventional CCTV cameras, with their recognizable housings and prominent public placement, are becoming almost invisible through their ubiquity in contemporary urban landscapes. The much-reduced size of digital cameras makes video surveillance easier to hide and further obscures it from public view. But even when the cameras appear in their familiar bulky form, they are only one part of a much larger surveillance assemblage, in which the growing number and variety of actors, human and otherwise, remain unseen. We have noted that digital technologies now make it possible to connect large arrays of cameras together in wide area networks, to disseminate the signals widely, and to archive unprecedented volumes of video material in multiple remote locations for later analysis and viewing. This enlarges the potential number of viewers and distributes them across space and time. With conventional CCTV systems it was hard enough for a determined person to find out who was watching her, where her personal images were stored and for how long. This basic openness requirement for privacy protection and democratic accountability more generally is now decidedly more difficult to achieve with networked systems – unless surveillance operators become more forthcoming than previously. So far there is no sign of this.

But the most significant social challenges that digital, analytic surveillance pose come from the enhanced capabilities that digitalization offers for automated image analysis and subsequent decision-making. The step of transforming the visual image stream into data that can be processed algorithmically opens a vast new array of surveillance possibilities. Some are relatively simple and benign, such as detecting litter so cleaners can be dispatched to remove it. When people become the subject of algorithmic gaze, the risks magnify. The more rudimentary forms of detection rely on comparison to 'normal' appearance and behaviours, so deviations from the norm invite scrutiny. Walking too slowly may be interpreted as loitering, walking too quickly as fleeing. Carrying or wearing something unusual can be treated as suspicious. Some techniques are aimed at classifying surveillance subjects – particularly ethno-racially and socio-economically – based on visual data. Introna and Wood (2004) in particular highlight the ethnic biases of algorithmic surveillance and face recognition technologies. They further note that face recognition systems are a 'particularly good example of a silent technology' (Introna and Wood 2004) – a technology whose significance and application are often hidden within existing infrastructures, such as ID card schemes and CCTV networks.

It is this potential to connect live video surveillance with existing digital records about individuals which raises the greatest long-term societal concerns because of the potential for continuous, ubiquitous, surreptitious, fine-grained surveillance of whole populations. The hitherto separate surveillance infrastructures of video and administrative data are now on the verge of being brought together via the recent growth of facial image databases running facial recognition software for managing ID documents such as driver's licences, health cards and passports. As these databases go on-line, it will be increasingly tempting for law enforcement and other agencies to search them using visual images captured in the field. There are already signs of this in the call by Ontario's police chiefs 'to give officers access to a database of driver's licence photographs to help instantly verify the identity of suspects and traffic accident victims' (*Globe and Mail* 2010). In this case the images would be stills, but if they are successful with this request, can the next step of pulling images from live video feeds be far behind?

The failures of the face recognition field trials following 9/11 illustrate the immaturity of the video analytics field. While progress has been made in improving the performance of video analytic software, there are some inherent technical limitations, especially in the area of facial recognition, that are likely to persist. The complexity of the algorithms and the overall inscrutability of the increasingly complex networked configurations make it difficult even for technical experts, familiar with the systems, to assess whether they are functioning reliably and effectively. In the face of the obvious shortcomings of conventional CCTV, and promise of video analytics to overcome them, the incentive to install sophisticated albeit faulty systems, before they are field-proven, could be irresistible. As long as the failures remain out of public scrutiny, the allure of 'smart' new techniques will remain bright and their deployment will multiply with unknown consequences.

The deviations, classifications and identifications produced by correctly functioning automated surveillance schemes are typically of little consequence, but sometimes can fit threat profiles that trigger discriminatory, and sometimes forceful, responses. In forensic applications, automated techniques can be a boon for investigators searching through large volumes of recordings for particular patterns. In such situations there will be usually the opportunity for competent investigators to probe more deeply, and discard the 'false positives' before any harm is done. However, in real-time monitoring settings, especially when there is strong pressure to intervene pro-actively to preserve public safety, there will be little such opportunity for reflection, possibly resulting in injurious over-reaction. While the widely reported cases of police killing innocent people based on mis-interpreting visual and other cues (e.g. the Robert Dziekański Taser incident (Wikipedia 2010a) in Vancouver airport and the London shooting of Jean Charles de Menezes (Wikipedia 2010b) following the 7 July 2005 bombings) are extreme examples and so far appear not to involve video analytics, they illustrate the possible severity of outcomes when relying on automated threat profiling in security operations.

Conclusion

In the four decades since video surveillance techniques have been deployed in public settings, the key technologies have undergone a revolution – a paradigm shift from analogue remote viewing to computer-mediated content analysis. As part of the wider digital transformation of information and communications technologies, video surveillance capabilities have expanded enormously in terms of accuracy, speed, storage capacity, image analysis, database linkage and identity recognition. While these developments are largely invisible to surveillance subjects, the behind-the-scenes changes are so significant that they call into question the assumptions based on the 'classic' CCTV model – about who or what is watching, for what purposes and with what consequences. Driven by an apparently insatiable demand for more detailed personal information in the pursuit of 'security' and economic growth, the scope and intensity of video surveillance activities are raising qualitatively new challenges, far outstripping our understanding of its effectiveness, limitations and implications for civil liberties. Lagging further still is the institutional policy response, which is inadequate for regulating even the old-style CCTV deployments.

The growing scope and depth of digital video analytics needs to be considered thoroughly as the technologies develop and their applications ramify. We need new understandings and attitudes towards how visual data are or should be stored, transmitted, analysed and acted upon. Under most privacy law, images captured by organizations of identifiable individuals, whether actually identified or not, constitutes personal information and should therefore come under some level of legal protection. So far, there is little sign that current measures are effective in this regard. When individuals become routinely identified through biometric techniques such as iris, gait or face recognition and without their knowledge, the privacy stakes are much higher. But how will the organizations responsible be brought to account? Who is in a position to comprehend and intervene appropriately in overseeing this emerging phenomenon?

If the current lax to non-existent oversight of video surveillance prevails during the current phase of rapid but largely hidden digitalization, then the civil liberties risks will continue to grow while becoming harder to rectify.

Acknowledgements

We appreciate the support of the Identity, Privacy and Security Institute, University of Toronto.

References

Alexander, J. and Smith, J. (2003) 'Engineering privacy in public: Confounding face recognition', *Privacy Enhancing Technologies*.

Bojkovic, Z. and Samcovic, A. (2006) 'Face Detection Approach in Neural Network Based Method for Video Surveillance', *Neural Network Applications in Electrical Engineering, 2006. NEUREL 2006. 8th Seminar.*

Bosch Security Systems (2009) 'CCTV – Bosch Security Systems The Americas'.

BSIA (2010) 'BSIA reports an increase in the use of Video Content Analysis'.

Cai, Y., Kaufer, D., Hart, E. and Solomon, E. (2009) 'Semantic Visual Abstraction for Face Recognition' in G. Allen, J. Nabrzyski, E. Seidel, J. Dongarra, G.D. Vanalbada and P.M.A. Sloot (eds), *Computational Science – ICCS 2009, Part I.*

Cisco Systems Inc. (2009) 'Video Analytics: Enabling Retailers and Casinos To Build Brand Loyalty, Increase Competitive Advantage, and Improve Customer Service', Cisco IBSG.

CNN (2001) 'How the facial recognition security system works'. Online. Available HTTP: <http://articles.cnn.com/2001-10-01/us/atick_1_facial-recognition-visionics-corporation-joseph-atick?_s=PM:COMMUNITY> (accessed 25 January 2011).

Coleshill, E., Ferworn, A. and Stacey, D. (2007) 'Traffic Safety using Frame Extraction Through Time', *System of Systems Engineering, 2007. SoSE '07. IEEE International Conference on*.

Deisman, W., Derby, P., Doyle, A., Leman Langlois, S., Lippert, R., Lyon, D., Pridmore, J., Smith, E., Walby, K. and Whitson, J. (2009) *A Report on Camera Surveillance in Canada: Part One*, Surveillance Camera Awareness Network (SCAN)

Dixon, P. (2010) *The One-Way-Mirror Society: Privacy Implications of the new Digital Signage Networks*, World Privacy Forum.

Globe and Mail (2010) 'Ontario police forces seek access to driver's-licence photos'. Online. Available HTTP: <http://www.theglobeandmail.com/news/national/ontario-police-forces-seek-access-to-drivers-licence-photos/article1564150/> (accessed 10 May 2010).

Goffredo, M., Carter, J.N., Nixon, M.S. and IEEE (2008) *Front-view Gait Recognition*.

Gorodnichy, D. (2006) 'Editorial: Seeing Faces in Video by Computers', *Image and Vision Computing*, 551–6.

Gorodnichy, D. (2009) 'Merge of Biometrics and Surveillance', *PowerPoint*, Toronto: IPSI.

Hempel, L. and Töpfer, E. (2004) 'Working Paper No. 15: CCTV in Europe Final Report', Berlin: Centre for Technology and Society, Technical University Berlin.

Homeland Security News Wire (HSNW) (2010) 'New video camera offers very high resolution from afar – and up close'. Online. Available HTTP: <http://homelandsecuritynewswire.com/new-video-camera-offers-very-high-resolution-afar-and-close> (accessed 25 January 2011).

Introna, L.D. and Wood, D. (2004) 'Picturing Algorithmic Surveillance: The Politics of Face Recognition Systems', *Surveillance & Society*, 2: 177–98.

Martin, K. and Plataniotis, K.N. (2008) 'Privacy Protected Surveillance Using Secure Visual Object Coding', Toronto: Multimedia Laboratory.

Murphy, S. and Bray, H. (2003) 'Face recognition devices failed in test at Logan', *Boston Globe*.

Norris, C. and Armstrong, G. (1999) *The Maximum Surveillance Society: The Rise of CCTV*, Oxford: Berg.

Norris, C. and McCahill, M. (2006) 'CCTV: Beyond penal modernism?', *British Journal of Criminology*, 46: 97–118.

Pflugfelder, R., Bischof, H., Dominguez, G.F., Nolle, M. and Schwabach, H. (2005) 'Influence of camera properties on image analysis in visual tunnel surveillance', *Intelligent Transportation Systems, 2005. Proceedings. 2005 IEEE*.

Phillips, J., Scruggs, T., O'Toole, A.J., Flynn, P.J., Bowyer, K.W., Schott, C.L. and Sharpe, M. (2007) 'FRVT 2006 and ICE 2006 Large-Scale Results', Gaithersburg: National Institute of Standards and Technology.

Reay, D.L. (2008) 'Texas Border Sheriff's Coalition institute border surveillance cameras', *Sheriffs News*.

Reuter, C. (2000) *The V2 and the German, Russian and American Rocket Program*, New York: S.R. Research and Publishing.

Russo, S. (2008) 'Digital Video Surveillance: enhancing physical security with analytic capabilities', IBM Corporation.

Shaokang, C., Berglund, E., Bigdeli, A., Sanderson, C. and Lovell, B.C. (2008) 'Experimental Analysis of Face Recognition on Still and CCTV Images', *Advanced Video and Signal Based Surveillance, 2008. AVSS '08. IEEE Fifth International Conference on.*

Stanley, J. and Steinhardt, B. (2002) *Drawing a Blank: The Failure of Facial Recognition Technology in Tampa, Florida* AN ACLU SPECIAL REPORT. American Civil Liberties Union.

Sullivan, F. (2008) 'Leveraging security data for business intelligence: IBM Smart Surveillance Solution', Frost & Sullivan.

Suman, A. (2008) 'Using 3D pose alignment tools in forensic applications of Face Recognition', *2008 IEEE Second International Conference on Biometrics: Theory, Applications and Systems*, Washington, DC: IEEE Xplore.

Tagg, J. (1988) *The Burden of Representation: Essays on Photographies and Histories*, Massachusetts: University of Massachusetts.

Watkinson, J. (1994) 'The future of digital video recorders', *International Conference on Storage and Recording Systems, 1994.*

Wikipedia (2010) 'Robert Dzieański Taser Incident', in *Wikipedia, the free encyclopedia.* Online. Available HTTP: <http://en.wikipedia.org/wiki/Robert_Dzieka%C5%84ski_Taser_incident> (accessed 7 July 2010).

Wikipedia (2010) 'Jean Charles de Menezes'', in *Wikipedia, the free encyclopedia.* Online. Available HTTP: <http://en.wikipedia.org/wiki/Jean_Charles_de_Menezes> (accessed 7 July 2010).

PART IV

Public support, media visions and the politics of representation

14

ANTI-SURVEILLANCE ACTIVISTS V. THE DANCING HEADS OF TERRORISM

Signal crimes, media frames and camera promotion

Laura Huey

Recently I was invited to give a talk on the subject of resistance at a conference on national security and surveillance issues. The focus of my presentation was the question of why anti-surveillance activists, privacy advocates and other individuals and groups with a stake in resisting surveillance had yet to mobilize into a social movement in the face of an ever-increasing panoply of surveillance forms. While the process of critically working through this question produced a number of answers from which I could draw some preliminary conclusions, other answers were provided to me courtesy of an entirely unexpected source: a presentation at this same conference by a former US Department of Homeland Security official during the Bush administration.

His talk began with a PowerPoint slide containing what has now become a fairly iconic image: the destruction of New York's twin towers. The image was quickly replaced with another: a slide containing cropped head shots[1] of 19 people, the alleged 9/11 terrorists. Using his mouse to point to the head of Khalid al-Midhar, who had been flagged in an INS database on 21 August 2001, we were told that al-Midhar could be linked to another 9/11 terrorist through an address that each provided when they made their fatal airline reservations. Still other suspects could be added to inter-linking chains through shared phone numbers found in public records and commercial databases. In essence, this gentleman's argument was simple: with access to each of these databases and complex sorting routines to cross-reference names and other identifiers, with seven mere clicks, US security intelligence would have been able to identify these suspects and thus prevent the events of 11 September 2001.

During this talk, I found myself in an uncomfortable position: as each slide built on its predecessor, guiding the audience to a penultimate conclusion, I found myself nodding my head in agreement. Linking databases to provide officials with the intelligence necessary to find would-be terrorists, what a great concept! Then something dawned on me: in order for those seven clicks to draw each link in the chain, millions and millions of pieces of data – including such otherwise innocuous bits and bytes as Frequent Flyer points – would have to be made accessible to law enforcement. Further, to produce the web that would link these 19 men, the number of potential false positives produced could be staggering. Something else also occurred to me. I leaned over to a well–known privacy advocate sitting next to me and said, 'I think I see your problem. They have better PowerPoint slides.'

Along with the proliferation of forms of public and private surveillance across the West, we have also seen the field of surveillance become an increasingly contested political terrain upon which public and private actors variously attempt to 'influence the volume or configuration of surveillance' (Haggerty and Ericson 2006: 7). Typically we find among those actors and institutions arrayed in favour of a surveillance scheme, police, business and resident groups and politicians of various stripes. Mounting a vigorous defence against specific proposals or against surveillance creep more generally, we find a number of professional privacy advocates, as well as volunteer and/or ad hoc civil libertarian coalitions, community groups and so on. While their respective goals may diverge widely, to the extent that success requires public support for their respective positions, both sides seek to sway public opinion. Thus, both sets of actors engage in the art of persuasion, shaping their message so as to find what they hope will be a sympathetic audience. As an example, whether one is referring to the desire to build mega-databases for national security purposes or local plans to install public CCTV systems, we can see that surveillance schemes are actively promoted through the use of powerful imagery that taps into public fears, careful framing of issues for wider audiences, and with easily digestible media bites that render the complex simple, among other strategies. As I discuss in what follows, when it comes to the marketing of public surveillance systems, of these groups, the police, who are usually the principal proponents of such plans, hold distinct advantages in comparison to the anti-surveillance activists and other groups typically arrayed in opposition.

Although my focus here is on the advantageous use of signal crimes, media frames and symbolic politics by Canadian police agencies in their quest for public support for surveillance schemes, it is worth noting that Canadian law enforcement is hardly alone when it comes to the strategic framing of their message. Indeed, similar use of iconic fear-provoking imagery and rousing media sound bites can be seen in relation to the framing of messages by American pro-surveillance advocates (as can be seen in the story that begins this chapter), in the UK (notably the images of Jamie Bulger or the 2005 London tube bombings) and elsewhere. In short, although this chapter is based on research into the politics of surveillance in Canada, given the rapid proliferation of public surveillance in countries across the globe, it is rather likely that strategic marketing of pro-surveillance messages is not unique to Canada or even solely a North American phenomenon. To illustrate how these advantages play out in the marketing of public camera systems in Canada, within the sections that follow I draw on a variety of documents on public CCTV schemes produced by Canadian law enforcement for external audiences. These documents include: CCTV proposals, media releases, evaluation reports, and 'blurbs' on web pages belonging to various police departments. I am also including, where relevant, similar material produced by anti-surveillance activists and/or privacy advocacy groups. Some material was already in my collection, having been previously provided to me for other projects; other documents were collected through internet searches or through personal contacts. Document data is supplemented here with newspaper articles of CCTV-related stories acquired through searches of the Canadian newsstand database for the period 1996 to 2009. Where relevant, I also include data from interviews conducted with privacy advocates and anti-surveillance activists from previous studies on resistance to surveillance (Huey 2009; Haggerty, Huey and Ericson 2008) and from a study that I am currently working on that examines the interest group work of voluntary police organizations (Huey 2010c).

Signal crimes: Jamie Bulger as a marketing tool

In 2006 the Vancouver Police Department (VPD) put forward a proposal to City Council to implement a public CCTV system with cameras located throughout the City's Granville Mall pedestrian zone. Previous attempts by the VPD to have cameras installed in public spaces throughout an adjacent downtown area had been resoundingly defeated by local activists. In 2007, when it seemed as though this proposal might be successful, I made contact with various sources to begin fieldwork on a new study of the site, set up interviews and began collecting data (Haggerty, Huey and Ericson 2008). Among the material collected was a softcopy version of a Power-Point presentation put together by the VPD's Planning and Research Department. Clearly designed as a communication tool to market the VPD CCTV proposal, in many respects the presentation slides contained are not particularly noteworthy, being the type of thing that one routinely sees at business meetings, academic conferences and so on. However, one particular slide proved to be the exception.

In their analysis of Crime Stoppers (this volume), Lippert and Wilkinson contend that, to date, a relatively neglected area of surveillance studies is the question of what becomes of the products of various surveillance schemes. One answer is that the images captured are sometimes used to promote new surveillance projects. Such use can be seen in various promotional materials for CCTV schemes. For example, in attempting to make their case for a public CCTV system in Vancouver, the VPD planners sought to communicate as clearly as possible what the perceived benefits of such a scheme would be for police and the general public. After slides discussing the scope of the project and how crime has purportedly been reduced in the UK as a result of CCTV, a slide appears that details a number of ways in which CCTV can serve as an investigational aid to police. This slide is followed by two more that are clearly intended not only to illustrate the investigational utility of CCTV, but more importantly to resonate in a meaningful way with the viewing audience. The first slide reads 'Jamie Bulger case – 1993' and shows the now famous image, captured by a CCTV lens, of the young boy being led away by one of his murderers (VPD 2006).

It is not coincident that the image chosen functions as a 'signal crime'. Martin Innes (2004: 336) defines this concept in the following terms:

> some crime and disorder incidents matter more than others to people in terms of shaping their risk perceptions. This is because some crimes and some disorders (but not other ostensibly similar incidents) are especially 'visible' to people and are interpreted by them as 'warning signals' about the risky people, places and events that they either do, or might, encounter in their lives.

While Innes does not explicitly draw a similar conclusion, I would add to his contention that signal crimes provide a means of helping people to 'articulate and give form to the rather more inchoate, existential and pervasive anxiety that seems to be characteristic of late-modernity', that they are characteristically those acts that are viewed as the most transgressive (ibid: 336). The violent destruction of a child – the ultimate symbol of innocence and purity – would certainly rank as not only transgressive, but as constituting a significant source of public anxieties over crime and the perceived threat of social decay. For such reasons, the image of little Jamie Bulger being led to his death is not merely every parent's worst nightmare, but has come to 'stand in for the horrors of contemporary society; his image speaks of a reality that includes all of us' (Young 1996: 114).

The Vancouver Police are hardly alone in employing references to signal crimes in order to tap into public anxieties about crime and disorder (see Doyle and Walby, this volume). Fears related to missing children and the possibility that CCTV might prevent or assist in the investigation of such cases, have similarly been invoked by other police agencies. On its web page detailing the 'Lions Eye in the Sky' programme, the Greater Sudbury Police Service (2009) claim that 'public safety has also been enhanced as the project allows the Service to locate missing children'. I note that no specific claim is made that the programme *has* actually assisted in the locating of missing or abducted children, just the statement that it *could* possibly do so.

In the game of symbolic politics, not only do privacy advocates not have an easily comparable image with which to try to wrest the upper hand, they are frequently forced into the position of being seen as those whose dangerous message potentially imperils children. As it happens, I have some insight into how this can play out. I was once invited by a local news programme to discuss surveillance-related issues. After giving what I thought was a fairly reasoned critique of the proliferation of CCTV cameras throughout the West, I was asked to watch a video clip on a monitor in the studio and offer comments in response. The footage was from a CCTV camera in a parking lot and showed a man walking off with a young child. The voice-over provided by the programme host alerted me as to what was to come: the police, we were told, were able to locate the abductor and save the child because of this tape. 'Dr Huey, what do you say to parents who see this tape and feel that the presence of a camera is a small price to pay for the life of a child?' I can say from experience that my standard response – pointing out that very few

Canadian children are abducted by strangers each year – is not typically seen as satisfactory.

Media frames: 'They're going to try and sell it'[2]

The marketing of a public CCTV system, whether in proposal, implementation or post-implementation phase, can be a complex, tricky process. Proponents of such systems must not only convince local police boards and city councils of a project's merits, but must win over local stakeholder groups and area residents. In order to do so, they need to be able to communicate effectively, first, that there is a problem and, second, that CCTV represents a viable solution. Of critical importance then is the matter of how a given problem is defined by police. As Nisbet and Huge (2006: 10) suggest, 'problem definition has important implications for how much attention an issue receives'. Thus actors attempt to use 'frames' as means of 'packaging complex issues in persuasive ways' (ibid: 10).

In 2006, when the VPD sought to convince the public that a CCTV system should be implemented throughout Granville Mall, its members cited various actual and potential problems as issues that needed immediate address. In media releases the police repeatedly referenced the fact that the Mall's entertainment zone – with some 5,000 liquor licence seats concentrated within a few short blocks – created a heavy call burden on police who were repeatedly having to deal with drunken fights, vandalism, public disorder and so on (Haggerty et al. 2008). Privacy advocates interviewed at the time noted with some scepticism that

> all of a sudden Granville Street is this site of carnage and horror, and then it seems to disappear. Coincidentally, the last time they decided Granville St. was horrible was right around St. Patrick's Day, a bit of an exceptional situation where they have a major festival, parade and all sorts of stuff happening. They tried to build a little bit of that fear up around the Canucks recently with the hockey playoffs.

Referencing crime and disorder in relation to the City's night-time economy was only one framing device used. Police officials also publicly raised the spectre of terrorism. Indeed, former Chief Jamie Graham made the link between terrorism and CCTV as its solution explicit in the comments offered in an interview to promote the VPD's CCTV proposal: 'There are people in the world and there are situations unfolding in different parts of the globe and there are people who want to do us harm' (Mason 2006: S1). I note with some interest that this comment is highly reminiscent of much of the rhetoric that was then being employed in the US and elsewhere in relation to the 'global war on terror'. The trope of a hidden enemy waiting to strike civilian targets on North American soil is a dominant frame repeatedly found in sources ranging from Presidential speeches to mainstream media reporting to pundit blogs found throughout the Internet.[3]

It is not simply the case, however, that the police propose a plan, convince various authorities that CCTV is an excellent solution to a given problem, and then go off to implement it. Rather, such proposals frequently serve as political battlefields upon which various stakeholder groups attempt to stop, alter or win decision-makers' acceptance of the scheme (Haggerty and Ericson 2006). Public opinion serves a vital function in this process by serving as a mechanism to garner decision-makers' votes. Thus, stakeholder groups will attempt to take their message to media outlets in the hope of influencing public opinion. Typically, those arrayed against a public camera system will cite privacy concerns, attempting to convince the public that their privacy is imperilled, whereas stakeholder groups in favour of a CCTV proposal will attempt to trump the 'privacy card' through resort to public safety issues that they hope will resonate with a given audience.

As media scholars have noted, when framing an issue for an audience, journalists tend to select quotations that are short, simple and convey powerful or appealing messages (Brewer and Sigelman 2002). In reviewing various articles that quote police officials, it would appear that the 'public safety card' can be a fairly effective rhetorical strategy, particularly in relation to media framing which lends itself to short, punchy 'media bites'. For instance, in 2001 the Calgary Police sought to implement cameras in the City's downtown core. In response to potential privacy concerns around CCTV usage, then–Chief Jack Beaton stated, 'If you don't get stabbed as much in the downtown core because we are using technology that's available, I'm not so sure people will be upset by it' (Wilton and Dumont 2001: A1).

While there is a certain level of skill involved in restructuring complex ideas into 'media bites', and most police organizations today send officers who may be called upon to do media work for appropriate training, it is also the case that some messages are easier to recast than others. As I have argued elsewhere (Huey 2010b), privacy is a subjective concept with variable meaning that frequently appears as amorphous or unconnected to individual concerns. The complexities of the issue can thus render pro-privacy messages difficult to parse down to a snappy sentence or two, which cannot always be said about pro-CCTV messages. For example, the following is from a web page produced by the Winnipeg Police Service (2009) in support of implementing a trial public CCTV system in that city:

> The Winnipeg Police Service endorses the opportunity to apply technology to effectively address three aspects of street-level crime in an effort to:
>
> Reduce victimization
> Create a safer environment
> Establish a tool for investigation.

In contrast, when we look at some of the informational material produced by anti-surveillance advocates, the focus is typically on attempting to rebut claims made by police agencies, which inevitably leads to an inordinate amount of quoting of empirical research. There are two inter-related problems with this approach. First, as I have noted elsewhere (Huey 2010a), no clear-cut answer has emerged as yet to the question of whether CCTV provides either actual or ontological security. Thus, we find both police and privacy advocates cherry-picking the studies that they cite from in support of their respective positions, leading to a mass of contradictory claims that a confused public is expected to make sense of. Second, whereas the message of the police and other CCTV proponents can be parsed to phrases such as 'reduce victimization', counter-claims drawing on the latest study from Britain are not so easily reducible. For example, to counter the frequently employed argument that the general public supports CCTV as a crime-fighting tool, the Vancouver Public Space Network (VPSN 2009), a grassroots anti-surveillance group, released the following statement on their website:

> Webster highlights the considerable variation between different types of CCTV systems, which is at odds with the general perception that systems are constantly monitored and that following an incident an appropriate response will be forthcoming. While some systems are proactive, with live monitoring and immediate response, many are reactive, with recordings that may be accessed after an event has occurred, and some are even nonactive, using fake cameras as a visual deterrent. The Royal Academy notes that the term 'CCTV' itself is increasingly a misnomer, given the increasing number of systems using networked digital cameras, which have much greater flexibility in terms of storing, transmitting and searching for images. As the Royal Academy notes, 'The continued use of the term is an indicator of a general lack of awareness of the nature of contemporary surveillance, and disguises the kinds of purposes, dangers and possibilities of current technologies'.

In the words of Professor Angela Sasse, quoted in the House of Lords' report, 'Very often, where people say they do not actually care about [privacy], it is because people are not very good at assessing risks in the future, because they have not experienced the impact or nobody they know well whom they would understand and empathise with has experienced these bad effects.' The Royal Academy cites a study arguing that CCTV operators in the UK engage in racial and socio-economic profiling, with ethnic minorities being disproportionately targeted for surveillance. This is a reminder that CCTV, like many other forms of technology, is not neutral or impartial but rather is affected by the assumptions and prejudices of individual policy-makers and officials.

Although the paragraphs above were obviously intended for an internet audience with presumably a greater interest in the subject and a longer attention span than the average tabloid reader, it bears noting that the commentary above is intended to persuade an audience to support an anti-surveillance agenda – that is, it's a marketing tool. As such, it is overly complex and analytical, and makes frequent references to reports and experts that readers may not be familiar with. In essence, it is the antithesis of 'punchy'.

Capital and politics

In analysing the rise of public–private security networks, Benoit Dupont (2004) identifies five forms of 'capital' – economic, political, cultural, social and symbolic – that
can be mobilized by institutional actors. In relation to the politics of surveillance, it can
easily be seen that the public police have greater access to some, and depending on the
individual case, all of these forms in comparison to opposing stakeholder groups.

According to Dupont, economic capital refers to the financial resources that
actors have available to them. Developing CCTV proposals and marketing them
to decision-makers and the general public requires resources. For instance, when
the Toronto Police Services implemented their test cameras in the City's downtown core, in order to make the case that the camera network should be retained
and expanded upon, the TPS conducted internal and external reviews aimed at
evaluating the effects of the cameras in both target and buffer areas based on the
number of calls for service before and after implementation. Aside from being able
to commission researchers from the Canadian Police Research Centre to conduct
an external review, the TPS were able to draw on staff, data processing power, and
other resources required to conduct this project because they have a Crime Information Analysis Unit dedicated to such tasks. Indeed, most medium to large police
departments have planning and research sections for similar purposes. Compare this
to the lot of most privacy advocacy organizations that rely on one or two key staff
members to respond to the bulk of privacy threats within their target area, or to that
of grass-roots anti-surveillance groups that draw on ad hoc volunteers. As a frus-
trated privacy advocate once explained to me in relation to discussing the volume
of surveillance work that her organization could be taking on, 'On the NGO [non-
governmental organization] side, there's not enough people, not enough resources.
There's lots of things that we could and should be doing together and separately,
but we can't, we don't have the resources' (Huey 2008: 233).

Cultural capital refers to an actor's unique expertise or knowledge of a particular field. In relation to the field of crime, the police hold a dominant position
in public policy debates because they are uniquely positioned to tap into both
institutional expertise and knowledge of the subject. Indeed, it is police crime
data and analysis that informs and thus shapes both the initial CCTV proposal and
all subsequent discussions of such proposals. After all, the proposal begins with an
identified problem – the existence of levels of crime in a particular area – that is
supported through the use of recorded incidents of crime displayed as statistics or as
colourful GIS maps. Thus, when the VPD sought to implement a camera system in
the Granville Mall, their presentation of the case for CCTV included a GIS map of
the Mall and outlying areas that graphically illustrated a cluster of violent offences
occurring in the area between January and September 2006. The only conclusion
to be drawn from this map is that between 9pm and 6am, the Mall district is a
dangerous area – a conclusion not surprisingly put forward by the police. While anti-
surveillance activists might counter that the analysis is flawed, exaggerated, manipulated or otherwise twisted to suit police goals, they lack comparable access to raw

crime data to support their counter-claims. In short, stakeholder groups that oppose CCTV schemes are almost always playing on a field that is shaped by the advantage of their opponents.

Political capital refers to an actor's relative proximity to or distance from governmental power and the ability to influence this machinery to achieve particular outcomes. Policing is an integral part of the system of modern governance, and in Canada a municipal and provincial responsibility. Thus local governments are the primary sources of police funding, are tasked with providing oversight of police agencies,[4] and routinely seek police expertise on crime-related issues. For such reasons, a local Chief of Police and his or her command staff[5] will be well acquainted with key decision-makers in local government. And, when a CCTV proposal is brought forward to, for example, a City Council meeting for discussion on possible funding, it is very likely that City Council members will already have been subject to low-key lobbying by their 'community partners' in the police department in order to garner support for the project. Certainly Council members will have already read the proposal paper, as such materials are typically circulated with Council agendas. In contrast, stakeholders arrayed against a particular CCTV scheme will have an opportunity to present their arguments to Council in the 10 to 20 minutes typically allotted. A privacy advocate once described for me the experience of appearing at such public hearings in the following terms: 'it completely feels like an exercise in futility' (Huey 2010c).

Social capital can be understood as the strength and direction of an actor's relations in the social field, and their ability to exercise connections to produce outcomes (Dupont 2004). While there are many potential examples that I could draw from, the case of police–media relations illustrates the police advantage most clearly. One of the central themes found in much of the research produced in the field of police–media relations is the view that the police hold a dominant position in relation to the media because they selectively broker access to information, while shaping released information to their advantage (Mawby 1999; Ericson, Baranek and Chan 1989). What appears to be less well discussed is the fact that police hold a privileged position in relation to other stakeholder groups in terms of their ability to access media outlets and to get their message across to a wider audience. This positioning is the result of both institutional privileging, as well as embedded relations between individual police and media outlets. The result can often be that a story is framed to the advantage of the police with little or no input from opposing groups. An excellent example of this can be found in an article produced in 2009 on the Toronto Police Service's (TPS) desire to adopt and expand a public camera system installed on a trial basis. The story, which ran under the headline 'Police Find Trusty Partner in CCTV', contained quotes from three different TPS personnel praising CCTV as a useful police tool.

> 'You will not find an investigation of any consequence today where there isn't some CCTV material', said Toronto Police spokesman Mark Pugash. 'One of the first questions our detectives always ask now is, "What CCTV footage is available?"'

'Videos have assisted in many of our cases – easily half a dozen in the past couple of years', said Staff Inspector Brian Raybould, who heads the homicide squad. 'They've given us images, and people have come forward to identify those responsible.'

Staff Sergeant Kevin Suddes of 52 Division hopes they stay. 'It's all good stuff', he said. 'We haven't had as many shootings, and I think the cameras are an excellent deterrent in that regard'.

(cited in Appleby and Freeman 2009: A1).

In this same article, not one privacy advocate or anti-surveillance activist is cited. Instead, the views of opposed stakeholders are encapsulated within the following two lines: 'Not everybody is cheering. Some privacy advocates still view cameras as intrusive' (ibid). This is an important omission. As Nisbet and Huge (2006: 11) remind us, 'by giving more weight to some dimensions of a controversy over others, the frames in news coverage help guide policy maker and citizen evaluations about the causes and consequences of an issue, and what should be done'.

Lastly, symbolic capital refers to the authority that an actor, organization and/or institution commands by virtue of the honour or prestige conferred upon them through their activities. To the extent that the police remain a trusted institution in Canada – and public opinion polls would seem to suggest that this is the case[6] – we can generally expect that decision-makers and the public at large will afford crime-related claims that police make a greater degree of deference than counter-claims advanced by anti-surveillance groups. Whereas the former can tap into the symbolic capital associated with 'wearing the uniform', representatives among the latter are too easily dismissed as individuals who do not appreciate the 'true' magnitude of the contemporary crime problem, suffer from Big Brother-induced paranoid delusions or simply like to function as rebels without something better to complain about. In a nutshell, privacy advocates can be unfairly denigrated as people more to be annoyed or amused by, than treated as individuals with a serious message. To borrow from those clever pushers of toilet paper and canned spaghetti, privacy advocates and anti-surveillance activists could use a strategic 'rebranding'.

'Fighting against cops is never a fair fight':[7] some concluding thoughts

As I have demonstrated in the preceding paragraphs, when it comes to advocating against a police-endorsed CCTV proposal in Canada, privacy advocates and anti-surveillance activists are painfully aware of the fact that, in the words of an activist quoted above, 'fighting against cops is never a fair fight'. Not only do the police have access to various forms of political, cultural and other capital that can be harnessed in support of a given proposal, but their position is frequently one that lends itself to emotional and/or so-called 'common sense' appeals that resonate with the general public. Thus, their opponents are frequently at enormous disadvantage.

However, it is also the case that anti-surveillance groups, while recognizing these facts, continue blithely to fall into some of the traps laid for them. An excellent example of this is the response to the 'missing child' scenario, which typically involves pointing out how few children are abducted by strangers each year.[8] While that is certainly factually the case, for most people one missing child is one missing child too many, and thus the ends will always justify the means. An alternative strategy might be for such activists to shift the grounds of the debate from the purported investigational utility of cameras, to demanding that police or other government bodies develop alternative means to prevent such incidents in the first place. After all, they might argue, do not most police agencies list crime prevention as part of their mandate? Privacy activists are not obliged always to play on the field prepared by the police or other CCTV proponents.

Although my comments here have been directed to what anti-surveillance activists ought to consider if they want to change the tone and tenor of the debates they engage in, I want to conclude by offering a final thought to surveillance scholars. Although the data presented here is indicative of how the politics of surveillance plays out in Canada, the extent to which police groups are advantaged through the use of symbolic politics, media frames and signal crimes in other countries remain open empirical questions. Indeed, it is very likely that scholarly study on issues related to the politics of surveillance in other nations will yield new empirical and theoretical insights. What I hope is that not only will the issues raised here be picked up by other surveillance scholars across the globe, but that we will continue to see more work that maps out this terrain – on local, national and international levels.

Notes

1 A brief explanation: I don't always sleep well when away from home. The title of this chapter comes from the fact that, being somewhat sleep-deprived, it appeared to me that with all the clicking to link the various terrorists, the heads were dancing.
2 A quote taken from a 2006 interview with an anti-surveillance activist discussing the VPD CCTV proposal.
3 For example, nearly a year prior to Graham's comments, then-President Bush stated in an address that, 'We are fighting against men with blind hatred – and armed with lethal weapons – who are capable of any atrocity. They wear no uniform; they respect no laws of warfare or morality. They take innocent lives to create chaos for the cameras' (BBC 2005).
4 Through municipal police boards and/or appointed Police Complaint Commissioners.
5 Assistant Chiefs and senior line personnel.
6 In a recent Nanos Research (2009) poll of 1,003 Canadians, the police ranked fourth among professions that people view as being highly honest and ethical.
7 Michael Vonn, privacy advocate. Personal communication, 2 November 2009.
8 Having been caught in this one myself, I am keenly sympathetic to how terrible this particular trap is.

References

Appleby, T. and Freeman, J. (2009) 'Police Find Trusty Partner in CCTV', *The Globe and Mail*, 24 January: A13.

BBC News (2005) 'Bush's Iraq Speech, June 2005'. Online. Available HTTP: <http://news.bbc.co.uk> (accessed 14 November 2009).

Brewer, P.R. and Sigelman, L. (2002) 'Political Scientists as Color Commentators', *International Journal of Press/Politics*, 7(1): 23–5.

Dupont, B. (2004) 'Security in the Age of Networks', *Policing & Society*, 14(1): 76–91.

Greater Sudbury Police Services (2009) 'Lions Eye in the Sky'. Online. Available HTTP: <http://www.police.sudbury.on.ca> (accessed 11 November 2009).

Haggerty, K.D. and Ericson, R.V. (eds) (2006) 'The New Politics of Surveillance and Visibility', in *The New Politics of Surveillance and Visibility*, Toronto: University of Toronto Press, 3–34.

Haggerty, K.D., Huey, L. and Ericson, R.V. (2008) 'The Politics of Sight/Site: Locating Cameras in Vancouver's Public Spaces', in M. Deflem (ed.), *Surveillance and Governance: Crime Control Today*, Oxford: Elsevier, pp. 35–56.

Huey, L. (2009) 'Subverting Surveillance Systems: Can Access to Information Mechanisms Be Understood as Counter-surveillance Tools?', in S.P. Hier and J. Greenberg (eds), *Surveillance: Power, Problems, and Politics*, Vancouver: University of British Columbia Press, 219–35.

Huey, L. (2010a) 'False Security or Greater Social Inclusion? Exploring Perceptions of CCTV Use in Public and Private Spaces Accessed by the Homeless', *British Journal of Sociology*, 61(1): 63–82.

Huey, L. (2010b) 'A Social Movement for Privacy/Against Surveillance? The Difficulties in Engendering Mass Resistance in a World of Twitters and Tweets', *Case Western Reserve Journal of International Law*, 42: 699–709.

Huey, L. (2010c) 'When Is a Spade not a Spade? Voluntary Police Associations and Interest Group Work.' Presented at the Canadian Political Science Association Conference, Concordia University, Montreal, June 2010.

Innes, M. (2004) 'Signal Crimes and Signal Disorders: Notes on Deviance as Communicative Action', *British Journal of Sociology*, 55(3): 335–55.

Innes, M. (2005) 'What's Your Problem? Signal Crimes and Citizen-focused Problem Solving', *Criminology and Public Policy*, 4(2): 187–200.

Mason, G. (2006) 'Smile – You're on VPD Camera', *The Globe and Mail*, 18 May: S1.

Nanos Research (2009) 'Canadians Trust Doctors and Pharmacists Most'. Online. Available HTTP: <http://www.nanosresearch.com> (accessed 23 November 2009).

Nisbet, M. and Huge, M. (2006) 'Attention Cycles and Frames in the Plant Biotechnology Debate: Managing Power and Participation through the Press/Policy Connection', *Press/Politics*, 11(2): 3–40.

Toronto Police Service (2009) 'CCTV Pilot Project Evaluation Report'. Online. Available HTTP: <http://www.torontopolice.on.ca.> (accessed 20 November 2009).

Vancouver Police Planning and Research Department (VPD) (2006) 'Closed Circuit Television Project'. PowerPoint presentation. 13 December.

Vancouver Public Space Network (VPSN) (2009) 'Surveillance Cameras – Myths and Realities'. Online. Available HTTP: <http://www.vancouverpublicspace.ca> (accessed 20 November 2009).

Wilton, S. and Dumont, M. (2001) 'Crime Plan Calls for Street Cameras', *Calgary Herald*, 21 June 21: A1.

Winnipeg Police Service (2009) 'CCTV'. Online. Available HTTP: <http://www.winnipeg.ca> (accessed 20 November 2009).

Young, A. (1996) *Imaging Crime: Textual Outlaws and Criminal Conversations*, London: Sage.

15

SURVEILLANCE CAMERAS AND SYNOPTICISM

A case study in Mexico City

Nelson Arteaga Botello

Introduction

The use of surveillance cameras is a phenomenon of global dimensions (Heilmann 2008; Koskela 2006). However, the particular role and impact of the cameras varies depending on individual historic and social contexts. In the specific case of Latin America, the installation of such cameras is linked to the call for 'war against crime', and in general the use of these technologies has had widespread social backing (Barreto and Barreiro 2010). The inhabitants of Latin American cities do not tend to feel threatened by the increased presence of cameras in the streets, notably in financial and commercial districts (Caldeira 2000); on the contrary, there exists a great pressure for government authorities to install such equipment (Mattelart 2007). In Latin America, the increased presence of cameras in urban space is underpinned by 'zero tolerance' public security policies introduced in the last ten years. The goal of such policies has been to reduce the incidence of crime and violence in the cities of the region, and to reduce feelings of insecurity in large sections of the population. The most commonly used surveillance techniques are surveillance cameras. The most important cities of Latin America now feature these cameras; public and private buildings have extended their use, allowing control over the access to these buildings.

Urban space is left divided by electronic walls of surveillance camera protection, identifying and excluding those who, due to a process of categorization and stigmatization by their visible economic and racial characteristics, are considered to be possible instigators of crime and violence. This has had a profound impact in the configuration of cities in Latin America, in that an urban logic has developed which distinguishes between supposed 'secured' and 'dangerous' spaces. Although, as shown throughout this book, these phenomena are also seen in Northern cities around the globe, the Latin American context features some unique facets, particularly when we consider its public security policies. The use of surveillance cameras has been introduced in a context of inequality and poverty, as well as weak democratic institutions, which are particularly prone to permitting the use of authoritarian practices.

However, the use of cameras for monitoring is not only limited to contexts where the few watch the many – that is, to a logic of surveillance that is reminiscent of Bentham's Panopticon (Miller and Rose 2009). In parallel to the global North, in Latin America there also exist processes where the cameras fuel a situation where 'the many watch the few' (Meyrowitz 1985), through different communication media (mainly television) establishing an inverse logic in the establishment of surveillance, through a synoptic process (Mathiesen 1997). Thus, parallel panoptic and synoptic logics of surveillance exist. In panoptic societies, video cameras serve to keep an eye on both public and private spaces, with the apparent goal of guaranteeing security, working to consolidate the normalization of behaviour and the auto-control of persons. In the synoptic logic, the cameras instead allow many to see the life of a few, thanks to a pre-determined framework of surveillance which typifies the behaviour of the people being observed (Mathiesen 1997; Lyon 2006). Documentaries and television reports that refer to the life of criminals or, in general, to the violence in certain neighbourhoods in Latin American cities, are examples of this synoptic process. Nowadays, both surveillance processes develop together and in interaction. Meanwhile, as David Lyon (2006) points out, contemporary cultural tendencies work to foster acceptance of surveillance as more commonplace each day. In Latin America, the relationship between these two surveillance logics, where the few watch the many (panoptic) and where the many watch the few (synoptic), requires a particular examination. On the one hand, the fragility of governmental institutions and the weak recognition of citizens' rights amplify the exclusion process (Arteaga 2009), generated – at certain times – by the use of video cameras in public spaces (parks, avenues, financial and commercial districts) and private spaces (commercial centres and offices, among others). On the other hand, the constant bombardment of images, inscribed in certain narrative frameworks, typifies certain social sectors as potential delinquents (Castells 2009). The images that are transmitted about dangerous neighbourhoods, the stories of criminals' lives, among other visions, inserted within the synoptic logic, construct a particular image of who the criminals are and where they are from (Garland 2001). These images also feed the foundation of a panoptic logic of surveillance – based, particularly but not exclusively, on video surveillance cameras.

But what happens if a reversal takes place? If those people habitually presented as the potential victims of violent crime are now portrayed as the ones who may be perpetrating it? What is the message when those who are protected by sophisticated surveillance camera systems are the ones who apparently commit criminal acts? In other words, how can the synoptic and panoptic logic be understood when members of groups with a certain political and economic power are portrayed as criminal? This question is particularly important in the case of Latin America, where a significant number of people know that the traffic of influence is a generalized practice, above all to the benefit of those social sectors that can mobilize important economic and political resources.

The following chapter tries to respond to these questions. To this end, an analysis is presented of a particular criminal episode which shook Mexican society: the disappearance of, and later discovery of the body of, a four-year-old girl in one of the more exclusive residential zones of Mexico. The disappearance and apparent kidnapping of a child from a wealthy family in Mexico City is examined for the way in which it was linked to both panoptic surveillance devices and synoptic surveillance. As will be discussed, the news of the disappearance of the little girl, whose name was Paulette Gebara Farah, was transmitted from the family's home directly, on national television, and featured in news programmes morning, noon and night. The testimony of the mother in front of the television cameras generated in the viewers feelings of sympathy or dislike towards the parents, fear because apparently a little girl was taken from her own home in front of the most modern and costly surveillance camera equipment, and fury at the attack against the integrity of a little girl with a disability belonging to a 'respectable' family, which seemed to show that crime in the country had got out of control. These feelings play an important role in justifying the installation of video surveillance cameras in residential zones and in the city, as well as in the creation of social networking sites devoted to searching for a minor, making the case even more visible. It was more visible again, although on different terms, when the body of the child appeared, and the mother was suddenly considered a prime suspect, transformed into an object of voyeurism for many sectors of the population, who judged that her voice, look, face, words and attitude gave her away as the murderer of her daughter.

Panoptic and synoptic surveillance

On a global scale, surveillance devices have become an element of everyday life. As is the case elsewhere, concerns about crime and delinquency in Latin America have served to legitimize surveillance, and, in particular, public and private surveillance camera systems. The presence of such cameras in Latin America, as well as an awareness of what happens in the global North, generates the sensation of living in a panoptic society. Michel Foucault (1976) defined in a clear way the organization of discipline in modern societies through the use of Bentham's panoptic model. This model alerts us to the presence of a hierarchy based on viewing, whose end lies in the classification and organization of activities of different individuals in different spaces. In general terms, the panoptic is a form in which the few watch the many, with the objective of modifying the behaviour of the people under view.

For Foucault (1976), this process is linked to a change in the form of punishment. The founding of the panoptic model in modern societies implies the movement away from punishment as a spectacle – as in previous societies – giving way to more subtle forms of control, crystallized in surveillance routines. Foucault states that in this way it disappears '. . . in the beginning of the 19th century, the great spectacle of physical pain; hides the punishment of the body; excluded from punishment the theatrical apparatus of suffering'. However, the perspective of Foucault, as Mathiesen (1997) points out, gives little attention to the growth of the modern mass media and its contribution to making a spectacle of punishment in contemporary societies. This means we are in what Mathiesen called a 'viewer society' or a synoptic society, where in large part social events are experienced through the mass media (Lyon 2006). If the panoptic is the mechanism that allows that the few watch the many, for Mathiesen (1997) the synoptic allows that the many watch the few. Both devices, subtle surveillance, as well as that referred to as 'show business', complement each other, even having a parallel development: they were established in their modern form in the same historical period (from the 18th century), although they had been present in some form from ancient times, and they interact constantly.

Because of this, Mathiesen (1997) suggests that in order to understand surveillance during our time, it is also required that an analysis of the mass media is conducted, so that we can understand the framework in which society sees and understands surveillance. In other words, the synoptic, notably movies and television, guides the interpretation of surveillance for entire societies (Lyon 2007). In this way, the surveillance culture has normalized and been reinforced, thanks to the interaction with the world of media entertainment in particular, although far from exclusively, by the domestication of fear into 'Big Brother' through reality television shows (Lyon 2007). The movies, reality shows, and other television programmes promoting surveillance help make up viewer societies in the global North and are subsequently exported and assimilated on a global scale. Thus, in a contemporary society there exists a constant celebration of and support for surveillance devices, accepted more easily when different types of viewing have been converted into a common place activity. As discussed by Lyon (2007), on the other extreme, lie the dystopian perspectives of the surveillance society – as shown in George Orwell's *Nineteen Eighty-Four*. However, programmes such as *CSI* show a non-critical view of the workings of camera surveillance, highlighting its apparent use in the solving of practically any criminal case. Movies and programmes that project the world of surveillance are relevant, establishing stereotypes that typify the world of crime and delinquency, as well as its main protagonists. Groups and individuals who are found in the categories shown on television screens are the primary objectives of a 'suspect' culture. In this sense, the synoptic serves to classify and categorize groups and individuals (Lyon 2006), while giving impulse to the production of ever more camera surveillance with the objective of watching precisely these groups (Mathiesen 1997). Indubitably, some display themselves voluntarily, and others not, in the same way that in the panoptic model some know that they are being observed and others do not. Surveillance cameras and TV as media are made for each other, and are complementary (Norris and Armstrong 1999). If this is added to the context of criminality and delinquency, it becomes the perfect mix, one which blurs '. . . the distinction between entertainment and the news, between the documentary and the show, between voyeurism and current affairs' (Lyon 2006: 46). These conjunctions are not only a product of the mere process of the articulation of technology. They also respond to an amplified social dynamic, belonging to post-modern times. This dynamic is called, by film theorists, scopophilia (Metz 1982): a kind of voyeurism and love of watching that may make it easy to set aside the rights of those being watched (Lyon 2003).

When the cameras see the many: surveillance private and public

On 24 March 2010, the press and national television in Mexico announced the disappearance of a four-year-old girl named Paulette Gebara Farah. The mother of the girl, Lisette Farah, stated that, on the night of Sunday 21 March, her husband, Mauricio Gebara, dropped off their two daughters in the lobby of one of the exclusive apartment buildings located in the zone of Interlomas, in the municipality of Huixquilucan, in the metropolitan area of Mexico City. She took each of the young girls to their respective rooms to lie down. The next day, Monday 22 March, when she went to wake up Paulette to take her to school, the little girl was not in her room. From this day, the State of Mexico Attorney General (SMAG) initiated a search for the little girl, with the help of search dogs and experts, searching for clues as to how she might have left her room. Due to the fact that Paulette suffered from a motor disability, the first search was directed at determining who could have taken her out of her room.

The building, like all that can be found in that zone, had its own electronic security devices: surveillance cameras, movement detectors, doors that function through the use of RFID cards, as well as doormen and security. It was an environment with a set of control mechanisms that would be very difficult to evade as an adult, and would thus, of course, be even more complicated for a child of four years of age with a disability to slip through. The SMAG established two lines of investigation. The first aimed to determine if the girl could leave under her own power at night, while the electronic security devices – in particular the surveillance cameras – were not working. The second explored if someone close to the girl, such as a family member, took her from her room and the apartment, as there were no broken locks or signs of forced entry in the doors. However, in the media, commentators, experts and the general public, the number of explanations presented for the disappearance continued to multiply: a commando organized the crime and bypassed the building's security measures to kidnap the girl; the nannies kidnapped her because they were part of a criminal gang that is dedicated to kidnapping and murdering children of wealthy families.

In the first week following the disappearance of the girl, the SMAG dispatched 30 investigative agents, with the goal of searching for the girl in every corner of the building, as well as obtaining fingerprints, attempting to detect traces of blood in the girl's apartment, and applying polygraphs to the people living there. The presence of the police in the place generated a feeling of vulnerability in the neighbours, and also in other residential spaces in the municipality. In different gated communities, people demanded that private security companies contract more personnel, and install more cameras and other electronic surveillance devices, as well as maintaining a stricter control of entrances and exits in these gated communities. For their part, the governmental authorities demanded the installation of more efficient urban surveillance camera systems, as well as dispatching more police patrols to make more intensive rounds around the residential zones.[1] In this way, the disappearance of the young girl became a 'signal crime' (see Huey, this volume) leading to calls for ever-more surveillance.

Because the camera system in the building where the little girl disappeared was not working precisely between the night and the morning of the act, this turned the focus to the use of surveillance cameras in gated communities and in other spaces within the municipality. Debate was taken up again concerning the functioning of one of the most expensive surveillance systems in the country, installed in this municipality that for three years has not worked. The municipal surveillance camera system was installed on 10 September 2004, despite the fact that the municipal authorities pointed out that the delinquency rates in the municipality are the lowest in comparison with other municipalities in the metropolitan area of Mexico City (Arteaga 2007). The municipal presidency decided to install camera systems with the objective of establishing a strategy of 'protecting the municipal borders', which were reportedly threatened by a large transient population. According to the data provided by the municipal public security office, 66 per cent of the burglars of the municipality do not inhabit it. The dominant way of thinking was that criminal violence that appeared in the municipality did not originate from there, but rather from neighbouring municipalities. The problem was thus defined as a particular one: 'protecting the border'. The municipality of Huixquilucan can only be accessed by three important routes. This creates a feeling of – as the implementers of the camera system point out – the municipality being a 'type of island'. Likewise, it is considered that the municipality is a space inhabited by people who, independent of their noticeable social and economic differences, do not exhibit deviant behaviours that violate the normal tranquility.

A key problem that faced the municipal government installing the surveillance cameras was a financial one. Because of this, an external agency had to be hired: a private company named Seguritech. In this way a public–private mechanism was created through a decentralized organization that would have the responsibility of controlling the system. Even so, the municipality was obligated to use 17 per cent of its annual budget over three years on the project. Not only did this combined public–private project result in a cost problem, but also it was considered that the municipal police did not have the technical capacity to take charge of the system. There was also concern that the system could be used, in an unethical manner, so that information produced by it could wind up in the hands of organized crime. For these various reasons, the private company was considered to be superior to the city council for running the system. However, the problem of financing a project with these characteristics obliged the administration of the municipality to cancel the project on 6 May 2007. However, the Paulette case activated public opinion again, leading to arguments for the necessity to reinstall a surveillance camera system in the municipality. Social pressure increased when the media spread rumours about the kidnapping of the girl, even though the mother stated that '. . . I only ask the person that has her to please leave her in a shopping center, I don't want reprisals, or in a department store, so that the girl is not in danger and someone might recognize her and bring her into the arms of her mother'.[2] The various residential spaces of the municipality organized a meeting, with the objective of, in the first place, promoting the idea of re-establishing a surveillance camera system that 'takes care of' the streets and avenues; in the second place, they wanted to conduct a diagnosis of the internal security conditions in the buildings and gated communities, looking to detect the key shortcomings and to work to solve them. Although the neighbours accepted that the disappearance of the girl had not occurred in the street: '. . . the Paulette case was in the interior of the building, it would be convenient to analyze what is happening with the internal security',[3] they still argued that installation of a municipal surveillance camera system in the municipality's residential zone was a necessity.

In a few days, the kidnapping of the minor thus provoked a spiral of surveillance camera installations in one of the most exclusive residential zones in Mexico. On 19 May 2010 the municipal government installed an arrangement made up of 50 cameras that are connected to a system with the capacity to record and save up to a month and a half of image streams, which are then saved, for a year, by servers of the state police. In a context marked by the fear of the kidnapping of children, the cameras became seemingly the only possible solution for guaranteeing that the children of these families were safe in gated communities.

When the cameras see the few

The social demand to install surveillance cameras in gated communities and the installation of a new municipal camera surveillance system in public spaces came at the same time as TV cameras and the viewer were also inserted into the situation of the disappearance of the child, in very different ways. This case was presented to the public through interviews, fundamentally by the mother, along with a few by the father. The interviews were recorded with the family's apartment as the backdrop, specifically the missing child's bedroom and the living room. In the first case, the child's room was shown along with her toys and clothes; at times, the mother showed schoolwork and drawings. When the interviews were shot in the living room, a picture of Paulette appeared in the background. The news channels also had reports on the school which the girl attended, with commentary from the teachers who said that the child was '. . . affectionate, always happy [. . .] each morning we prayed, we prayed for her return'.[4] These images served to reinforce the constant call of the mother that Paulette be returned, always stating that her daughter needed therapy and special medicine, and stating that she did not know '. . . if Paulette was being well taken care of, I don't know under whose care she is and I am desperate. I want her back.'[5]

The dramatic presentation in the mass media of a desperate mother showing such concern had significant impact within internet social networks, particularly on Facebook where a group searching for the little girl was formed; also, the father gave access to his email address and telephone number.[6] This information was given at the end of television interviews, as well as in the newspapers, with the objective of it being distributed as widely as possible. The Facebook page showed comments on the case, information and a photograph; this page reached a total of 25,000 confirmed users, variously showing their indignation and presenting speculation on the disappearance of the little girl. From the National Foundation for the Investigation of Kidnapped and Missing Children, a strategy for finding the child was designed for the mass media.[7]

The visibility of the Paulette case reached a media level never before seen in Mexico. During the first two weeks, the disappearance of the child was covered daily by the TV cameras, giving the feeling of a 'reality show' to the newscasts. The parents of the child both asked for support through social media networks to help find their daughter. Numerous opinions circulated on Facebook, in the commentaries in various news media websites, and through Twitter, all trying to explain the disappearance of the girl. Some of the commentaries pointed to the nannies as being guilty or, in other cases, a close family member. The police, in particular the Center for Lost or Missing Persons, ruled out that it was a kidnapping, as there were no calls requesting a ransom for the little girl.[8] The SMAG also considered that the case was not a kidnapping. There were constant calls made to the population to help search for the girl.[9]

However, the case, and the role of visibility in it, took a dramatic turn, when the SMAG obtained an arrest order for the parents and the nannies of the missing girls,[10] particularly when the body of the missing girl was found in her bedroom, in an opening between the floor, the base of the bed and the mattress, only 24 hours after the order was given.[11] The SMAG established then that the mother could be responsible for the death, above all because the body of the child was not there when the investigation took place, '. . . in the same room where the body appeared, interviews were given, searches and technical studies were done, and no body was detected before'.[12] Therefore, it could have been placed there by the mother, because she was the last one who entered the room before the arrest.[13]

The interviews given by the mother in front of the television cameras – shown afterwards on YouTube – began to be the object of meticulous analysis by so-called experts, checking her expressions, her commentaries, the manner of her eye movement, her dress, and the way in which she referred to her daughter, then missing, similarly to what takes place in the American television crime drama *Lie To Me*. The examination of the mother's facial expressions was also linked with the recurring reference to her asking for the interviews to be conducted in the child's own bedroom. For their part, the nannies testified that the mother never showed real concern when the child was not found in her bedroom when she went to wake her up to take her to school. The nannies even mentioned that it was not until after a few hours passed that the parents decided to begin a search.[14]

For their part, the SMAG presented a psychological profile of the mother in a press conference in front of the national television cameras, a few hours after the body of the child was found. In this psychological report, it was shown, among other things, that the mother suffered from deep personality disturbances, and was cold and distant to the situation of her daughter, without attachment, and that she was lying, the conclusion being that she had an 'atypical' personality.[15] The analysis of the mother's personality was also driven by interpretations of her behaviour captured by hidden microphones installed by the SMAG in the house. In these recordings the mother can be heard saying to her older daughter not to ask questions, and that she could be held responsible for the disappearance. It was also recorded when the mother said to the father that 'without evidence there is no crime'.[16] Furthermore, the analysis of information on the mother's Facebook page was used to round out the characterization of her 'atypical' personality. For this analysis, the collaboration of the FBI was requested.[17]

The mother finally gave interviews, outside her house, and in various television studios, with the objective of denying her guilt in the death of her daughter. At the same time, she appeared in one of the most important Mexican 'socialite' magazines to tell her story. Lisette Farah argued that if she appeared cold and without emotions, it was because she had to be strong so that it would not affect her husband and her older daughter. She stated that she had been in shock from the disappearance of her daughter, which kept her from remembering many things that could have been said or done. For his part, her husband, the father of Paulette, was characterized as a responsible person, serene, calm: '. . . a super centered type'.[18] This had the effect of deepening the criticism towards the mother, as it was also said that she was in an extramarital affair.[19] Additionally, it started to be thought that a friend of the mother helped commit the crime and hide the body of the girl; indeed, this friend slept on various days in the bedroom after the child disappeared.[20] The spiral of accusations increased when the nannies, on a national network, showed how they made Paulette's bed when she disappeared, indicating that the body of the girl was not there, and that it was placed there afterwards.

On the Internet, the response was not far behind. At a rate of 13,400 registered commentaries per minute on Twitter, outrage exploded about the death of the child, along with a repudiation of the mother, asking that she should be sentenced to life in prison or given the death penalty; some further suggested that security cameras be placed in the bedrooms of children who have a disability so that family members cannot hurt them.[21] In contrast, the group on Facebook dedicated to the search for Paulette was cancelled. Lisette Farah announced that she was going to bury her daughter; meanwhile, her husband let it be known that he would not attend.[22] Two Facebook groups were formed: one called 'I believe that the parents killed Paulette Gebara', which achieved a total of 15,962 friends, ten days after the discovery of the body of the child; the other, called 'Justice for Paulette', reached, in the same time, 10,107 friends. On the Spanish version of the social network site Twitter, the hashtag #Paulette reached fourth place in popularity.

The case of the disappearance and death of Paulette reached its conclusion on 21 May 2010, when the SMAG announced the cause of death of the child, giving assurances that it was accidental. In the official version, the child rolled down in her bed in such a way that she ended in the place where she was found. The 'reality show' reached an end, with an outraged society that took over the social networks to show their disapproval of the government authority's ruling. The television cameras did not transmit the SMAG judicial ruling nor was there much follow-up. A neighbour in the zone stated: '. . . we are sad that security [the cameras] of the apartments were placed in doubt, to consider that the act is a family problem'. Only one day after the conclusions of the SMAG, the mayor of Huixquilucan launched the installation of a surveillance camera system, and another two neighbouring municipalities announced the installation of theirs.[23]

What is the relation between the panoptic and the synoptic?

For days the Paulette case was followed by television cameras, transmitting interviews with the mother, some of which were re-transmitted on YouTube and other internet spaces. To these images some were added by the SMAG, showing the investigation taking place in the apartment. The case was transformed into a dramatic example of the kind of situation in which it cannot be distinguished whether what is being seen is news or dramatic entertainment, current affairs or a voyeurism show. In general, the case exemplified how the many watch the few. In this case, large sectors of the population were paying attention to Paulette's suffering family, especially the suffering of the mother. As an effect of this synoptic process, an enormous social pressure was generated to install more public and private surveillance camera systems, with the goal of preserving internal security in gated communities. The pressure centred on the point that the private surveillance cameras were not functioning adequately, while the counterpart system, controlled by the municipality, had been abandoned for some time due to financial issues. It was insisted that perhaps if these systems could have functioned, evidence would have existed of who was responsible for the suspected kidnapping of the child. In the first stage, the case of the missing child fuelled the drive to install more surveillance cameras.

However, when the body of the child was found and the mother became the focus, the demand for more camera surveillance lost force, and public opinion was directed towards the observation of the images transmitted by the television cameras. These supposedly showed not only a distressed mother but a monster, classified as a calculating, cold, 'atypical' woman. For those who followed the process, the mother was transformed from a person who reluctantly allowed herself to be watched, since it was believed that she gained some benefit from it in the search for her missing daughter, to a person who enjoyed the spotlight – especially when she appeared in socialite magazines or when it was suspected that her answers and movements during the interviews were rehearsed. In the final stages, her rights as a watched subject had disappeared, and she had been turned into an object of scopophilia. Perhaps the most important element in the case analysed here lies in the very different kinds of social processes that are linked to surveillance devices, by way of which the few watch the many and the many watch the few. The development of the police investigation, and the strange appearance of the body in a location where many people were, generated a mistrust towards the authorities in charge of justice in Mexico. Regularly, the television cameras are directed towards certain social sectors – considered potentially dangerous – that have served to typify who will be monitored through the surveillance cameras installed in shopping centres and outside gated communities. But in the case analysed here, things eventually appeared to be different. In an opposite way, an educated mother was socially typified by using a psychological profile, even though she was in a high social position, as cold, calculated and distant in dealing with the problem she was facing, and then she was displayed by the television cameras. Even so, this typification could not be generalized to the surveillance cameras in the streets, avenues and gated communities, commercial and financial districts. Moreover, as shown in this chapter, between the panoptic and the synoptic mechanisms, sometimes there exist narratives that cannot be transmitted from one to the other. When the narratives are anchored in social sectors that possess economic, political and cultural resources, the bridge between surveillance cameras and television cameras is destroyed. The weakness of the institutions in Latin America means that these groups impede what feeds back between the synoptic cameras and the panoptic cameras. Normally the influence of these groups perpetuates arrangements in which surveillance works in their favour and they avoid being the objects of those watching, thus reinforcing the conditions of social inequality dominant in the Latin American region.

Surveillance cameras are thus distributed in an unequal way according to income level: their protection represents a privilege, from which a large part of the population is excluded, not a right for everybody. This has important implications for understanding how what is public and what is private is being reconfigured: it might be argued that the capacity to have access to surveillance cameras to ensure security is regarded, in a large way, by society, or at least sectors of society, as a precondition for privacy (Zureik 2010). Values of particular cultures play a key role. It is important to point out, in the case of Latin America, the low value placed on individualism, the lack of trust among citizens, and a high tolerance for both social inequality and for the concentration of power within the state. It appears that the use of the cameras, in particular social contexts, not only results in the security for a few, but also the impunity of the few.

Although this is the generalized tendency in Latin America, it is certain that there are differences between the countries that make up the region. In countries that have lived through a past made up of military dictators, countries such as Argentina, Brazil, Uruguay and Chile, they appear to have a weak conscience about the implications of the panoptic and synoptic society; this is practically non-existent in other countries such as Mexico, Colombia or Costa Rica. However, Latin America, as part of the global South, has, through the expanded use of surveillance cameras, a mechanism for amplifying the conditions that deepen inequality in the exercising of citizenship in the context of a weak civil society. In Latin America, institutional supports help guarantee that the surveillance cameras, in their panoptic and synoptic modalities, can serve more for control of those who are considered to be dangerous, a large percentage of the region's population. They are thus directed towards pre-determined social groups, while only a few have the privilege of protection.

Notes

1 'Suben vecinos la guardia por Paulette', *Reforma*, 27 March 2010.
2 'Piden dejar a Paulette en un lugar público', *Reforma*, 28 March 2010.
3 'Extreman vigilancia en condominio donde vive familia de Paulette', *La Prensa*, 30 March 2010.
4 'Es muy tierna, siempre alegre', *Reforma*, 26 March 2010.
5 'Pide madre de Paulette que regresen a su hija', *El Imparcial*, 25 March 2010.
6 'Desaparece niña de su casa', *Reforma*, 24/03/2010.
7 'Crece búsqueda de Paulette en Internet', *Reforma*, 21 March 2010.
8 'Crece búsqueda de Paulette en Internet', *Reforma*, 21 March 2010.
9 'Pide Bazbaz apoyo para buscar a Paulette', *Reforma*, 26 March 2010.
10 'Arraigan a los padres y las nanas de Paulette Gebara', *La Jornada*, 30 March 2010.
11 'Encuentran cuerpo de Paulette en su casa', *Milenio*, 31 March 2010.
12 'Tiene Paulette fin misterioso', *Reforma*, 31 March 2010.
13 'Tiene Paulette fin misterioso', *Reforma*, 31 March 2010.
14 'Dicen nanas que papás no se preocuparon', *Reforma*, 31 March 2010.
15 'Los padres de Paulette son los principales sospechosos del homicidio', *CNNMéxico*, 31 March 2010.
16 'Madre de Paulette, con trastornos psicológicos', *El Universal*, 3 April 2010.
17 'Investigan perfil de Farah en Facebook', *Excelsior*, 5 April 2010.
18 'Consideran a Gebara como tranquilo', *Reforma*, 1 April 2010.
19 'Vinculan más en el caso Paulette', *Reforma*, 1 April 2010.
20 'Usa amiga de Farah cama de la niña', *El Universal*, 1 April 2010.
21 'Indigna a twitteros hallazgo de Paulette', *Reforma*, 1 April 2010.
22 'Dan el último adiós a Paulette', *Milenio*, 6 April 2010.
23 'Relanzan Alcaldías videovigilancia', *Reforma*, 20 May 2010.

References

Arteaga Botello, N. (2007) 'An Orchestration of Electronic Surveillance: A CCTV Experience in Mexico', *International Criminal Justice Review*, 17(4): 325–35.

Arteaga Botello, N. (2009) *Sociedad de la Vigilancia en el Sur-global. Mirando América Latina*, México: Universidad Autónoma del Estado de México and Miguel Ángel Porrua.

Barreto de Castro, R. (2010) 'Redes de vigilância: a experiência da segurança e da visibilidade articuladas às cameras de monitoramento urbano', in F. Bruno, M. Kanashiro and R. Fermino (eds), *Vigilância e Visibilidade. Espaço, Tecnologia, Identificação*, Porto Alegre: Editora Sulina.

Caldeira, T. (2000) *City of Walls: Crime, Segregation and Citizenship in Sao Paulo*, Berkeley: University of California Press.

Castell, M. (2009) *Communication Power*, Oxford: Oxford University Press.

Foucault, M. (1976) *Vigilar y Castigar. Nacimiento de la Prisión*, México: Siglo XXI Editores.

Helimann, E. (2008) 'La vidéosurveillance, un mirage technologique et politique', in L. Mucchielli (ed.), *La Frénésie Sécuritaire*, Paris: La Découverte.

Koskela, H. (2006) 'Cam Era: The contemporary urban Panopticon', *Surveillance & Society*, 1(3): 292–313.

Lyon, D. (2003) *Surveillance after September 11*, Cambridge: Polity Press.

Lyon, D. (2006) '9/11, Synopticon, and Scopophilia: Watching and Being Watched', in K.D. Haggerty and R.V. Ericson (eds), *The New Politics of Surveillance and Visibility*, Toronto: University of Toronto Press, 35–54.

Lyon, D. (2007) *Surveillance Studies. An Overview*, Cambridge: Polity.

Mathiesen, T. (1997) 'The Viewer Society: Michel Foucault's Panopticon Revisited', *Theoretical Criminology*, 1(2): 215–34.

Mattelart, A. (2007) *La Globalisation de la Surveillance. Aux Origenes de l'ordre Sécuritaire*, Paris: La Découverte.

Metz, C. (1982) *The Imaginary Signifier: Psychoanalysis and the Cinema*, Bloomington: Indiana University Press.

Meyrowitz, J. (1985) *No Sense of Place: The Impact of Electronic Media on Social Behavior*, New York and Oxford: Oxford University Press.

Miller, P. and Nikolas, R. (2009) *Governing the Present: Administering Economic, Social and Personal Life*, Cambridge: Polity Press.

Norris, C. and Armstrong, G. (1999) *The Maximum Surveillance Society: The Rise of CCTV*, Oxford and New York: Berg.

Zureik, E. (2010) 'Cross-cultural study of surveillance and privacy: Theoretical and empirical observations', in E. Zureik, L. Harling, E. Smith, D. Lyon and Y. Chan (eds), *Surveillance, Privacy and the Globalization of Personal Information: International Comparisons*, Montreal and Kingston: McGill-Queen's University Press, 348–59.

16

APPROPRIATION AND THE AUTHORING FUNCTION OF CAMERA SURVEILLANCE IN MANU LUKSCH'S *FACELESS*

Martin Zeilinger[1]

In a recent essay, the urban geographer Amy Siciliano recounted a curious anecdote: from the video surveillance control room of a public housing project in Toronto, she observed how two teenagers dismantled and destroyed a surveillance camera – while being recorded by the very device they were in the process of demolishing (Siciliano 2007). Siciliano was not a live witness to this event; what she watched from the safe confines of the housing project's remote control room was, rather, an archival copy that provided an equally safe temporal remove. Yet, despite this spatial and temporal distance, the tape had an oddly visceral effect on the researcher: watching it, Siciliano suddenly felt implicated in the 'narrative' that played out on the screen, and became very conscious of how surveillance technology can distort and invert the social relations and, indeed, the logic of the 'reality' it seeks to control. 'The movements of the youth were methodical and unhurried. They made no effort to conceal their identities . . . I became acutely aware that as the viewer, I, in fact, was what was "represented" and they – the youth – the "reality"' (Siciliano 2007: 53–4). The surveillance camera, then, had not simply recorded reality, but instead had somehow constituted it – '[b]y destroying the instrument that marked my presence as a viewer, the youth effectively made me present, exposing the mediating agent as a determining factor of the event itself' (54). How, then, has this camera served the assumed purposes of surveillance technology, considering that all the device was able to document was its own destruction? Can such a recording be accepted as an authoritative, unbiased document, or must it be acknowledged, rather, that the recording is an effect of the presence of the surveillance apparatus – which in turn prompted the action that was being recorded? Who, by extension, is the 'author' of the recorded act – the youths who performed the destructive event, or the surveillance apparatus that staged it?

This chapter expands on these questions and explores how the authority of control apparatuses can be challenged by exposing their 'authoring' function, or even by wresting this function away from the surveillance machine. In doing so, my primary concern is with an emerging field of 'surveillance art', which is commonly characterized by artists' attempts to appropriate the recorded content and/or the technological infrastructure of the surveillance systems with which they engage. While artists' critical responses to surveillance abound in multiple media, my focus here is on an example that specifically engages camera surveillance. Manu Luksch's *Faceless* (2007) is a film that consists entirely of appropriated surveillance footage, which the artist re-edited in order to construct a dystopian fiction thematizing the negative implications of surveillance on a narrative level. By providing a detailed discussion of Luksch's concrete creative approach, and by drawing connections between her film and the established tradition of creating 'found footage' films, I will argue that appropriative strategies may be particularly useful for the purpose of challenging today's increasingly pervasive surveillance culture. My discussion of Luksch's critical perspective and the narrative strategy she employs in the film will also foreground the authoring function of surveillance, and show how the reshaping of the assumed meaning of surveillance footage through appropriative intervention can successfully problematize the way in which surveillance apparatuses themselves distort the reality which they are designed to control.

By appropriating surveillance footage and surveillance technology, artists are able to challenge larger concepts of surveillance. They turn the surveillance machine's gaze upon itself, and ask what we might see when we look at contemporary societies of control through the very lenses of the surveillance apparatuses such societies have implemented. In this sense, artistic intervention in surveillance processes goes a long way towards raising public awareness of the problematic implications of surveillance. Activist communities as well as cultural organizations have recognized the power of art to complicate and politicize public opinion in this matter. As a consequence, established institutions such as London's Tate Gallery of Modern Art – which hosted a major show on the topic throughout the summer of 2010 – are beginning to thematize surveillance in their programming. Likewise, a film such as *Faceless* must be understood not merely as an aesthetic artifact, but rather as a more performative extension of the critical projects that other scholars of surveillance offer in their respective fields, and in forums such as the present collection.

When artists return the surveillance gaze by way of reusing surveillance footage, their work shares important characteristics with established traditions of 'appropriation art', i.e. art that creatively reuses already existing cultural matter in new work (for a more detailed definition, see, for example, Zeilinger 2009). By repurposing already existing materials, appropriation art (such as, for example, Marcel Duchamp's well-known 'readymade' sculptures of the early twentieth century, or also contemporary sampling music) problematizes conventional notions of authorship, ownership, and the nature of creativity. When surveillance art adopts appropriative practices, it adds to this the critical purpose of raising important issues of authority and individual agency, and asks questions such as the following: who owns the image of a private person, and how is such an image 'authored'? Which discourses negotiate and determine the rights to capture and archive this image? And finally, who has the right to interpret this image, to authoritatively assign it a meaning?

In raising questions such as this, surveillance art shares important strategies with the established practice of found footage filmmaking, i.e. with the creative practice of critically investigating existing film or video footage by re-editing or otherwise transforming it. Throughout this chapter, my discussion of the ways in which artists appropriate the surveillance apparatus in order to turn it upon itself will be framed, therefore, by the context of theories of found footage filmmaking. This context will prove particularly useful for my analysis of the artist and activist Manu Luksch's film *Faceless*, which represents one of the most accomplished and sustained efforts of the critical appropriation of surveillance footage and technology to date. As my reading of the film will suggest, established tactics of appropriation are ideal for transporting the kinds of messages that surveillance art and activism often aim to convey. When artists return the scrutinizing gaze of the surveillance apparatus, in other words, their works' critical effectiveness can be amplified by the subversive reusing of the technology they challenge. Luksch's *Faceless* is an excellent example of this process. Consisting entirely of appropriated surveillance footage, the film is able to instill in its viewers the same uncannily visceral sense of 'being-implicated' experienced by Siciliano in the above-cited anecdote. By hijacking the surveillance machine as an unwitting accomplice, *Faceless* posits the creative repurposing of the surveillance gaze as a complex and immensely provocative political act that goes beyond a general rejection of surveillance, and that instead tests the direct appropriation of 'surveillance culture' as a critically productive practice, rather than as one that is merely antagonistic. In this sense, my discussion of *Faceless* offers a conceptual framework for the more general analysis of appropriative surveillance art – art that often addresses the same questions and problems at issue in sociological and criminological inquiries into surveillance culture (see, for example, Lippert and Wilkinson, this volume).

Manu Luksch, an Austrian, London-based artist and founding member of the progressive media art hub 'Ambient Information Systems', completed *Faceless*, a '50-minute manifesto-driven fiction film' (Luksch 2008c: 1), in 2007. The film, widely screened at festivals and exhibitions as well as in academic contexts dealing with contemporary cultures of control, is constructed entirely from visual material captured by London's network of surveillance cameras (reportedly it is one of the densest networks worldwide; see, for example, Norris and McCahill 2002). Luksch obtained the footage under the UK Data Protection Act (DPA) of 1998, which accorded all individuals the right to request copies of videotaped surveillance footage, as long as they can convincingly demonstrate that their personal image has been recorded at a certain time and place. To make her film, Luksch meticulously documented her everyday activities in publicly accessible spaces that she knew to be covered by surveillance cameras, requested the release of the resulting surveillance footage, and, through compiling and editing it, interpreted the footage for the purposes of assembling the final narrative. The resulting film is a performative piece that took more than five years to finish – a narrativized exercise in 'probing' the Digital Protection Act (Luksch and Patel 2008: §9) and the implications of surveillance culture in general.

Like surveillance regimes almost everywhere in the world, the UK's DPA outlines an absurd double mandate of both erasing and protecting individual privacy. Two concrete consequences emerge from this double mandate: the first is that anyone who wants to recover their image from the surveillance machine must first take it upon themselves to erase all doubts about their identity – they must make themselves known to the authorities and give up the last vestiges of anonymity; the second consequence is that once an individual has successfully reclaimed surveillance footage featuring him or her, this footage is released only in such a form that the identities of all captured individuals except that of the applicant will be rendered unrecognizable. In other words, the individual who has filed the request will only be able to see him- or herself, yet in the process will have had to make him- or herself even more visible to the system that already stores its likeness. Despite such restrictions, the Data Protection Act is curiously imprecise regarding the specific procedure of manipulating the surveillance data that is to be released. Theoretically, this material could take any shape whatsoever, as long as only the applicant's identity is discernible. In practical terms, the necessary manipulation of surveillance footage usually means that black, oval shapes are placed over the heads of all individuals whose identity is to be protected, in each successive still frame of the video footage. This results in footage that is full of figures that are literally faceless – a quality that is alluded to in the title of Luksch's film, and which inevitably also dominates the visual aspects of *Faceless*.

Since Luksch based the story of her film on the retroactive interpretation of the footage she was able to obtain – a strategy that approximates the 'authoring' function of surveillance in general – *Faceless* features a protagonist living in a world full of faceless people. When this protagonist suddenly recovers her face (and thus a vague sense of self), she embarks on a mission to find out about the apparatus responsible for the universal facelessness by which she is surrounded. Thus, the facelessness the DPA forces upon the footage recovered by the artist is not only a visual component – it is furthermore treated as a literalized trope providing the film's narrative premise. As a consequence, viewers will inevitably link the film's narrative to the legal and socio-political reality from which the source material is appropriated, and *Faceless* as a whole comes to function as a direct, critical commentary on UK surveillance policies and the implementation of the DPA.

The fictional protagonist, in this sense, ceases to be faceless when the real-life artist requests the release of the footage. In the narrative, this results in the protagonist's mounting awareness of the facelessness of her peers. The quality of the appropriated footage is thus the real-world premise for the fictional mission on which the protagonist embarks (as noted, Luksch devised the film's narrative by interpreting the available footage, rather than staging specific events to be recorded). In turn, the protagonist's search for identity, meaning and agency in a world of faceless automatons whose every move is controlled (and therefore directed) by an all-knowing machine is a less than thinly veiled analogue to the real-world filmmaker's critical project of exposing the ideologies underlying surveillance regimes. In this way, *Faceless* performs, in effect, its own conceptual premise on a narrative level. The film's narrative literally derives from the 'story' behind the images it uses – i.e. from the real circumstances of the production of these images. As a result, form and content fold in upon each other, the dividing line between diegesis and external reality is blurred, and viewers of *Faceless* will inevitably understand that the questions the work raises on a fictional level are simultaneously relevant on a real, critical level: who creates the images that constitute the reality depicted in the film – who authors, owns and controls them? Does the meaning of these images precede the moment in which they are captured and assimilated as part of the reality created by the surveillance regime, or are they subject to interpretation (perhaps by those they represent)? Is the reality depicted in the film *Faceless* really more fictitious than that of the world that produced the images used?

As a narrative, *Faceless* takes the shape of a futuristic fairy tale. It details the struggle of one individual against an oppressive, overpowering entity, the protagonist's search for answers, and, ultimately, her fight to realize the revolutionary power of love. As such, the film is reminiscent of a large host of dystopian fictions dealing with societies of control, with which it shares not only narrative traits, but also the curious fact that their evocative force emerges from the audience's acknowledgement of the narratives' actual proximity to the reality they fictionalize. As in many such fictions, in *Faceless* the protagonist is faced with an opaque control apparatus that works so well that it is able to hide behind the seemingly perfect world of captured images and information it creates. The control apparatus in *Faceless*, too, has long become quasi-autonomous, and is so sophisticated that it is impossible to imagine a life outside of it. When the protagonist recovers her face and comes to her senses, in a way she emulates the control system's own process of becoming-sentient, and soon she begins to oppose it. Manu Luksch herself summarizes the narrative premise of her film as follows: 'In an eerily familiar city, a "calendar reform" has dispensed with the past and the future, freeing citizens from guilt and regret, anxiety and fear. Without memory or anticipation, faces have become vestigial – the population is literally faceless. Unimaginable happiness abounds – until a woman recovers her face . . .' (Luksch and Patel 2008: §13).

Like all fairy tales, the story told in *Faceless* is thus generic rather than highly specific, a quality which facilitates its viewers' recognition that the film speaks to a broad, contemporary reality, rather than to a fictional diegetic universe. This recognition drastically complicates the film's relatively simple narrative structure – and it is here that the critical potential of appropriative practices becomes most apparent. Since all the materials used are repurposed surveillance footage, the viewers' interpretation of what they see always points beyond the film's fiction. When the protagonist embarks on her mission to discover the control apparatus that constitutes her reality, viewers will, therefore, realize that this mission is not merely recorded by the fictional control apparatus depicted in *Faceless*; instead, it becomes clear that the footage was authored by the real (not the fictional) control apparatus which Luksch's film thematically engages. Thus, viewers of *Faceless* will inevitably recognize the real, material circumstances that determined the creation of the film, and will be acutely aware of the narrative function of surveillance, and of the ways in which it is constitutive of the reality it captures.

Because of the strong extent to which the political reality depicted in *Faceless* is implicated in the actual making of the film, Luksch's critique is felt with extreme immediacy – an effect derived from the aspects that surveillance art shares with creative practices of appropriation. As the film's protagonist begins to recognize and distrust the control system that governs her world, so the audience, in turn, begins to recognize both the protagonist and Luksch-the-artist as individuals who seize up an existing surveillance regime and thoroughly turn it on its head. The resulting work never entirely allows viewers the luxury of perceiving the narrative as a simulation, or the film as mere artifice, and therefore is, as noted in a review in *The Guardian*, 'incredibly uncomfortable' (Hubert 2007: §4).

Faceless, then, is more than a simple story with a political agenda. Instead of simply fictionalizing an existing control system, it directly appropriates the Data Protection Act's concrete application as both thematic and formal premise. In this sense, the filmmaker allowed the footage itself to dictate the narrative of the film. While this is a proposition commonly invoked by collage artists and found footage filmmakers, it is a particularly ingenious twist in a work so strongly concerned with surveillance: *Faceless* performs its own critical premise – the film questions the ethics of surveillance by deriving both its form and its content from the very functionality of the surveillance machine it critiques. More specifically, *Faceless* playfully sub-scribes to the idea of an absolute control society, and in doing so models itself on the practical circumstances of how the DPA is implemented in everyday life. The film is thus a thought experiment that carries the total implementation of surveil-lance technology to its logical conclusion, and then pitches this conclusion against the claim that individual human agents (i.e. both the film's protagonist and the artist herself) will continue to exist even within such a system. The existence of the film itself becomes proof of this claim.

At this point, it becomes clear how appropriative practices can be useful for art-ists and activists who seek to critically engage surveillance technology. The effects of Luksch's creative strategy are so powerful because no critical praxis of appro-priation can be understood as disparate from the spheres on which it comments; instead, appropriation realizes its critical potential in close relation to the issues it engages, through the actual, often physical reuse of already existing materials. As noted, this applies in particular to the cinematic reuse of found or appropriated footage, which has been a relatively widespread practice almost since the inven-tion of moving images. Most basically, the term refers to the reuse of already shot material in new films; this can range from single frames to entire movies. The specific type of creative intervention undertaken by found footage filmmakers can vary greatly: some simply re-edit appropriated material, while others paint over the footage or optically manipulate and re-photograph it in the darkroom. Searching for ways to properly describe the practice, Jay Leyda, one of the first scholars to comprehensively theorize found footage filmmaking, noted that '[t]he proper term would have to indicate that the work begins on the cutting table, with already existing film shots, . . . that the film used originated some time in the past, [and] that [the resulting work] is a film of ideas, for most films made in this form are not content to be mere records or documents . . .' (Leyda 1964: 9). Likewise, the Canadian film scholar William Wees contends that 'the effect of all found footage films [is to] invite us to recognize them as found footage, as recycled images, and due to that self-referentiality, they encourage a more analytical reading' (Wees 1993: 11). In this revisiting of anterior cultural matter, found footage film thus always retains the material proximity between an original image and its appropriated form.

In *Faceless*, too, it is this explicit connection between 'original' and 'copy' that enables the materialization of a critical commentary with the potential of being more effective, immediate and complex than the results of creative processes that simulate reality rather than appropriating it. Like other found footage films, *Faceless* does not comment on reality by recounting or simulating it, but, rather, by using the very recordings that are commonly perceived to constitute this reality. And, again continuing an existing tradition of found footage filmmaking, Luksch's film problematizes the historicity and authenticity of the appropriated footage by treating it as a tangible trace that draws its meanings not so much from the events it depicts, but rather from viewers' interpretations of the contexts it evokes. In doing so, *Faceless* engages the appropriated footage on the level of significations and cultural codes already inscribed in the used materials – again a strategy that facilitates viewers' recognition of real political contexts within the film's fiction.

As in *Faceless*, the specific themes foregrounded in artworks that deal with today's surveillance culture almost always revolve around issues of privacy, civil/human rights, and individual agency. Again, this suggests that appropriative practices are particularly useful for such artworks: when control over one's image and identity is at stake, appropriation becomes an immensely powerful critical device because it inevitably raises issues of the authorship and ownership of the information in question. As noted, the effectiveness of such criticism relies not simply on opposing an existing system – instead, it draws its force directly from the functionality of the technologies and discourses it opposes; these, rather than disabling or weakening it, are its fuel.

During the first stage of making *Faceless*, Luksch mapped parts of London's network of surveillance cameras. Combined with the rights granted her by the DPA, knowledge of the location of the cameras was enough to begin compiling footage by requesting its release, and freed the artists from having to resort to the commonly used practice of 'video sniffing' for obtaining usable footage. The term video sniffing generally describes the practice of using improvised wireless receivers to intercept the images broadcast by surveillance cameras. This allows individuals to map the exact range of the surveillance cameras' field of vision, and to view and record the images they transmit. In practice, activists often employ video sniffing in order to visually expose the range of surveillance cameras. Luksch likely decided against using this method because one of the main purposes of *Faceless* was to test the extent of the right of access that the DPA outlines, and to legally obtain surveillance footage. Under the watchful, presumably all-seeing eye of London's network of surveillance cameras, the artist thus carried out everyday activities that she would later interpret as part of her narrative. At this stage, a record of the time, place and date of her appearances took the place of a conventional film script. Finally, the performed material had to be recovered through the lengthy process of writing detailed 'subject release requests' to the various institutions managing the storage and use of the surveillance material. In the case of *Faceless*, all this constitutes part of the active filmmaking practice – another reason why obtaining the footage through video sniffing practices did not agree with the artist's overall concept.

As noted, found footage filmmaking's potential for effective critical commentary on the documents, ideologies and aesthetics embodied in anterior visual material is heightened because the practice actively negates most of what is commonly understood to be among the manipulative *instrumentarium* of the director, cinema's primary author figure: found footage filmmakers do not use a camera, have no primary influence over the duration, framing or dynamics of any shots being filmed, and likewise cannot manipulate that which the camera captures or the manner by which the camera captures it. As is obvious in *Faceless*, theirs is an art of retrospective creation, of a reworking of already authored material that inevitably makes the appropriative intervention obvious. This tactic finds its direct equivalent in Manu Luksch's 'Manifesto for CCTV Filmmakers', which she distributed in London during the time of her critical intervention (Luksch 2008: n.p.). As outlined in the manifesto, the first and most important rule is that '[t]he filmmaker is not permitted to introduce any cameras or lighting into the location'. In the immediate context of Luksch's commentary on surveillance culture, this is not merely an aesthetic principle. Again, the rule ensures the immediacy of the interaction between the appropriation piece and the reality it comments on. It may be understood to imply that the most powerful way of critically subverting the control sphere of surveillance is to reclaim it as part of the creative process, and thereby to foreground the technological, ideological and 'creative' aspects it implicates.

In this sense, Luksch describes both *Faceless* and the manifesto as 'close readings' of existing surveillance technology, as well as of the legislation governing its application. The manifesto, in fact, heavily cites the Data Protection Act itself, thereby subverting it in much the same way that *Faceless* makes use of the primary products of London's surveillance machine. As Luksch points out, the film's 'scenario . . . derives from the legal properties of CCTV images', which she also describes as 'legal readymades' (Luksch and Patel 2008: §11). Again, such a premise serves to make viewers of *Faceless* acutely aware, at all times, that the film does not simulate the functionality of the surveillance apparatus it critiques, but, rather, that it appropriates it and reworks it from within. In this way, *Faceless* takes on the quality of a multimedia project, rather than simply a film – its making includes not only the public performances outlined above and the post-production process (editing, sound, etc.), but also the interactions with the administrative bodies in charge of the footage. On the whole, *Faceless* thus battles the very real dystopia of seamless surveillance on its own grounds – through reclaiming controlled spaces (whether they are public or merely publicly accessible) as impromptu stages, through recoding public, everyday activities as performed events, and finally through appropriating the materials recorded, and then redistributing the reclaimed materials in altered forms.

As a critical investigation not only of the footage the film appropriates, but also of the formal modes of (re)production that govern surveillance in general and, ultimately, of the realities that surveillance culture thereby creates, *Faceless* calls to mind a number of political theories of tactical appropriation. Among them, the most useful for examining the film's functionality is the French artist and activist Guy Debord's theory and practice of *detournement*. As part of the Marxist Situationist movement (1957 to 1972), Debord was involved in finding ways to counter the alienation that capitalist consumerist societies instill in individuals. He developed simple strategies designed to enable all capitalist subjects to participate in the class struggle, and to revolutionize the everyday by way of reclaiming the mass cultural spheres that are so often instrumentalized for ideological purposes. The practice of *detournement*, in this sense, describes the critical repurposing of everyday situations; it denotes the appropriation and reuse of already circulating media (or, more generally, information) for purposes that expose the ideological bias inherent in the original images, sounds or ideas. In practice, Situationist interventions can take virtually any shape, as long as they demonstrate the critical, subversive use of objects, situations or information.

Debord's theory of *detournement* has resounded most strongly in the context of various types of activism and performance art; it has had a strong appeal for artists and activists working in this field because it essentially encourages its subjects to seize the 'now' and to negate the teleology of traditional, orderly political action (see, for example, Debord and Wolman 1981). Read against Debord's theories and appropriative practices that emerged from it, Luksch's approach adds an interesting level of complication: while *Faceless*, too, practises the repurposing of existing information for critical commentary, in it neither the primary place nor the situation or moment of original actions are *detourned*. Instead, Luksch operates through an important temporal lapse that helps to foreground, firstly, the historicity with which events and images are imbued when they are recorded and stored, and, secondly, the appropriability and malleability of such recordings, thereby emphasizing the artificiality and instability of the 'authored' meanings attached to them.

While Debord's Situationist theories always posit the concrete 'now' (rather than an abstract future) as the moment in which radical, resistant intervention can render the present different from itself, an audio–visual work such as Luksch's *Faceless* complicates the established practice of *detournement* through the added aspect of temporality. Given the potentially infinite storage of captured audio–visual content in today's environment of closed-circuit monitoring, the extent to which the medium-specificities of video bind *Faceless* to the temporal is indeed among the work's most critically important aspects. Undoubtedly, a central implication of surveillance technology is its potential to alter the course of the present by deterring undesirable behaviour/action pre-emptively. Yet, as a work of creative appropriation, the existence of *Faceless* is contingent on the very anteriority of the captured, recorded and reused materials. This emphasizes a contradiction inherent in surveillance culture – while terms such as 'presence' and 'real-time' imply the unaltered, unmediated 'now' and posit surveillance as an effective deterrent, surveillance technology actually stores 'reality' as already authored (or indeed authors it). By extension, surveillance therefore always inevitably reveals its implication in constituting the reality it records. My reading of *Faceless* suggests, then, that surveillance always-already represents an appropriative act, one that actively constitutes the captured individual's image, identity and intent. By adopting the author's perspective and role, the artist emphasizes that surveillance footage is authored already, and consequently challenges surveillance footage's status as 'document'.

As I have argued, cinematic images lend themselves so well to critical appropriative interventions exactly because they forcefully foreground their state of being already authored, and because they explicitly point back to the processual circumstances of their 'original' production. Appropriation thus becomes a useful vehicle for a variety of critical endeavours, regardless of whether what is at stake is the integrity and autonomy of a creative expression, of intellectual or material property, or of an individual's identity and agency. In *Faceless*, the parameters of what is meant by 'authorship', 'ownership' or 'reproduction' may simply have shifted, and now imply the images/identities of all individuals moving through publicly accessible spaces, along with all the actions they produce. It is in this sense that the images reused in *Faceless* serve to reify the various political and ethical relationships represented by the footage. When Luksch pulls the camera surveillance system into her fiction through direct appropriation of the ideological and processual circumstances of the 'creation' of the images she reuses, she in turn also pushes her narrative into the reality she appropriates, and effectively blurs the distinction between the two.

Faceless raises questions not simply about the possibility of author- or ownership claims by those captured on surveillance equipment, but, more importantly, about agency – about the right of image-captured individuals to 'direct' their lives with(out) the automatic and authoritative (yet oddly author-less) creation of records that 'document' their every move. Meanwhile, Manu Luksch's project keeps the status of the surveillance cameras purposefully unclear: does their high concentration at busy urban space-times capture and control the masses, or might they, in fact, establish the visible multitude of individuals as a powerful collective that now indeed needs to be controlled and contained? On the one hand, *Faceless* exposes the ideological problems of this assumption; yet, through its ingenious appropriation of the surveillance apparatus, it simultaneously hints at a utopian potential that may reside in the very appropriability of this same apparatus. Against the background of London's diverse cityscape, and with the city's inhabitants as unwitting and anonymous co-stars in both the diegetic reality of *Faceless* and in the reality the film is staged in, Luksch-the-artist and Luksch-the-protagonist become mediators between the dystopian surveillance machine and its utopian potential.

With an unknown number of surveillance cameras currently holding watch (an early estimate put the number at 4.2 million cameras, see for example Norris and

Armstrong 1999), the UK has one of the densest visual surveillance apparatuses in the world. Yet, reading critical commentary such as the film *Faceless* against the background of the rampant growth of camera surveillance worldwide, the real function of the Benthamian interpellation of individuals through a near-seamless surveillance system becomes doubtful. While the accepted function is, of course, the moderation of criminal activity, Luksch's critical appropriation posits the state's aggregation and extraction of countless images out of the public sphere as an appropriative act in its own right, one that may be understood as productive or creative in the problematic sense that it is constitutive of the dissent it is designed to pre-empt.

Whether or not one agrees that the threat of terrorist attacks (or pickpockets) warrants large-scale surveillance projects, in works such as *Faceless* the state's 'authoring' and storage of surveillance footage is posited, in any case, as the first – not the only – act in a divergent series of possible appropriative interventions. In Luksch's film, the surveillance apparatus's repository of publicly recorded audio-visual material, representing a comprehensive slice of everyday life, is treated as exactly that: a repository of material, an image bank that should be as useful for the artist and activist as it is for the police, and that could be as useful, ultimately, for the collective as it is for the individual. The function of the surveillance apparatus as mediating agent is thus changed from that of 'observation' to that of 'interlocution'. The law governing the creation and circulation of the images in question ceases to be an obstacle and becomes, rather, an arbitrator (its interpretation is itself appropriated) – another node in a larger system of the (re)production and reuse of images that may assume a controlling function in one of its manifestations, a censoring function in another, and a self-critical function in Luksch's variant.

It is in works such as Luksch's *Faceless*, where appropriative intervention so forcefully challenges the restrictive and homogenizing tendencies of current policies regulating matters of the authoring, collection, circulation and reuse of all kinds of information, that the vast political potential of critical appropriation becomes most obvious in all its urgency. Beyond constructing a gripping fiction, the film is able to convey the potentially revolutionary uses of the immense, negative appropriative apparatus that precedes this work, and that has produced the circumstances and possibility of the film's creation. Appropriation art in general, and found footage film in particular, always, as Wees writes, 'open the door to a critical examination of the methods and motives underlying' the use and reuse of the appropriated images (Wees 1993: 32). Accordingly, Luksch herself emphasizes that the critique formulated in and by *Faceless* emerges both from the film's 'mode of coming into being and [from] its plot' (Luksch and Patel 2008: §15). It is in this sense that *Faceless* strikes me as an ideal example of the kind of creative appropriation that may be a viable, productive model for staging critical challenges to surveillance culture. Representative of some of today's most effective appropriation art, what is so strikingly important in Luksch's work is not the disturbing situation her film focuses on thematically, but rather the processes by which the artist is able to do so – processes that show possibilities beyond the restraints they thematize.

Acknowledgements

The author would like to thank Manu Luksch for being so forthcoming with details about her work, and Eric Cazdyn, at the University of Toronto's Centre for Comparative Literature, for invaluable feedback on earlier drafts of this chapter.

Note

1   Banting Postdoctoral Fellow in Law and Culture, York University, Toronto.

References

Debord, G. and Wolman, G.J. (1981) 'Methods of Detournement', in K. Knapp (ed.), *Situationist International Anthology*, Berkeley: Bureau of Public Secrets, 8–14.

Hubert, A. (2007) 'Film stars of CCTV', *The Guardian*. Online. Available HTTP: <http://www.guardian.co.uk/film/2007/oct/13/art.humanrights> (accessed 13 January 2011).

Leyda, J. (1964) *Films Beget Films: A Study of the Compilation Film*, New York: Hill & Wang.

Luksch, M. (2008a) 'Manifesto for CCTV filmmakers', *Vertigo*, 4(1): n.p.

Luksch, M. (2008b) *Faceless* [Film]. London, Amour Fou and Ambient Information Systems.

Luksch, M. (2008c) 'The Faceless Project 2002–2008.' Online. Available HTTP: <http://www.ambienttv.net/pdf/facelessproject.pdf> (accessed 13 January 2011).

Luksch, M. (n.d.) 'Mapping CCTV in Whitehall.' Online. Available HTTP: <http://www.vimeo.com/3802118>.

Luksch, M. and Patel, M. (2008) 'Faceless: Chasing the Data Shadow'. Online. Available HTTP: <http://www.runriot.com/blog?q=node/1545>.

Norris, C. and Armstrong, G. (1999) *The Maximum Surveillance Society: The Rise of CCTV*, Oxford: Berg.

Norris, C. and McCahill, M. (2002) 'CCTV in London'. Urban Eye Working Paper No. 6. Online. Available HTTP: <http://www.urbaneye.net/results/ue_wp6.pdf>.

Siciliano, A. (2007) 'Swinging at the State: Media, Surveillance and Subversion', *Aether: Journal of Media Geography*, 1: 53–5.

Wees, W.C. (1993) *Recycled Images*, New York: Anthology Film Archives.

Zeilinger, M. (2009) *Art and Politics of Appropriation*. PhD thesis, Centre for Comparative Literature, University of Toronto.

17

'WHAT DO *YOU* THINK?'

International public opinion on camera surveillance

Danielle Dawson

Introduction

In 2005, a survey[1] found that an astonishing 90 per cent of Spain's population (based on a sample of 1,200) felt that video surveillance in airports, stations and public transport was desirable. A separate survey in 2006 by the Globalization of Personal Data (GPD) project found that around 75 per cent of the sample Spanish population (based on 1,000 participants) believed that camera surveillance was effective in public places. On the face of it, both questions appear to refer to the same thing, so was this discrepancy in responses due to the broader question ('public places' rather than 'transport sites'), or perhaps to the fact that in March 2004, 191 of Madrid's train commuters died in a bomb attack and a further 1,800 injured?

Knowing about how surveillance cameras work, how effective they are, and whether or not they carry publicly visible signage is one thing; knowing about how ordinary people perceive these things is another. But how does one get at the latter? There are various ways of answering these questions, among which one method is public opinion polling. Of course, statistics are notoriously manipulable – governments may pounce on them for their purposes, interest groups may be involved in funding them and so on – but rigorous, academic surveys do give some sense of on-the-street views of what is happening. Putting the polling dates in the context of other events and the polling data in a context of history, politics and culture also helps to reach a balanced interpretation.

It is with such things in mind that this chapter attempts to provide a quantitative measurement of public opinion of camera surveillance on an international level, though particular attention is paid to the North American perspective. Insight will be offered into some of the factors likely to account for the varying degrees of support. Such an investigation is made possible by the data produced by the

Globalization of Personal Data (GPD) Project Survey (2008) which provides a unique chance to analyse public perceptions of surveillance on an international scale.

Media and market based opinion polling on camera surveillance

Evaluations of public opinion vary widely in method and approach but paint a broad picture of public attitudes towards the use of camera surveillance in public spaces. In North America, media and market research-based opinion polling has consistently demonstrated that the vast majority of the public trusts in the effectiveness of camera surveillance to reduce criminal activity. News outlets including CBC, CNN, MSNBC, the *New York Times* and the *National Post* repeatedly report on a public supportive of camera surveillance due to a belief in its ability to 'solve crimes' (see, for example, Leman-Langlois 2009) and/or prevent possible terrorist attacks (ibid). In both of these examples, 71 per cent of the American public expressed support for the implementation and use of camera surveillance, citing these types of beliefs in their effectiveness (ibid). Similar results were replicated in public polling research in Norway (see, for example, Saetnan, Dahl and Lomell 2004), Berlin (Helten and Fischer 2004), England (Phillips 1999) and Switzerland (Klauser 2004), where public support for camera surveillance is above 70 per cent in all instances.

While these polls provide us with important clues as to the public's general feeling towards camera surveillance in several countries, the reliability of such opinion polling is open to question. Media and market research-based opinion polling of camera surveillance is generally preceded by some heavily publicized tragic event in which camera surveillance is presented to the public in a positive way. In 1993, for example, a blurry image of two-year-old James Bulger being abducted from a shopping centre in Bootle, England was looped in the media and came to be considered by the public as the primary investigatory tool in the search for the missing child. When the Bulger case was solved, camera surveillance was considered a success. As pointed out by Clark (in Davison et al. 2003), mass media often reflect what amounts to little more than propaganda, public relations campaigns and information flows controlled by governments and corporations (345). Such things are likely to have a strong influence when it comes to the outcome of opinion polls.

Subsequent problems arise in media and market research-based opinion polling when the content of the surveys deal with abstract concepts like surveillance and privacy. Haggerty and Gazso (2005) caution us to be cognizant of the fact that people who consider themselves 'anti-surveillance' are less likely to participate in surveys dealing with surveillance and privacy content. As a result, a 'pro-surveillance' public is over-represented and survey results become skewed.

These cautions regarding the mass media and market based opinion polling that dominate popular literature highlight a gap in our knowledge of camera surveillance; the prevalence of the former amplifies the general need for more extensive research that can offer a more comprehensive picture of public perceptions. This chapter will attempt to bridge this gap by analysing the data on public perceptions of camera surveillance produced by the Globalization of Personal Data (GPD) Project Survey (2008).

The GPD Project survey

Colin Bennett (1996) notes the lack of reliable international comparative data on public attitudes towards privacy and surveillance related matters and a pressing need to conduct research from which reliable inferences may be drawn (17). Motivated by this gap in knowledge, the GPD Project[2] (2006) conducted an international survey of nine countries to gain insight into the response of ordinary citizens to the increased flow of personal data. The GPD Project survey is the only major cross-national study to date which deals with issues surrounding surveillance and privacy.

Chosen for their strong differences in history, political climate, culture and socio-economic status, Canada, Brazil, China, France, Hungary, Japan, Mexico, Spain and the USA were selected for international comparison. Initial focus group interviews and intense background research conducted for each country gave shape to a questionnaire designed to reveal public attitudes towards several mechanisms of surveillance. Background research on each of the countries involved in the survey showed increasing implementation of camera surveillance internationally, and so the survey was designed to include questions regarding camera surveillance in relation to subject knowledge of cameras and the effectiveness of both community and in-store cameras.

Due to its scope (with 9,606 respondents between nine countries), design and intentions, the GPD Project survey offers a unique chance to study public perceptions of camera surveillance. A survey of such magnitude provides the opportunity to build a more comprehensive framework for understanding the rise of camera surveillance and the response it elicits across different cultural settings, while providing a unique opportunity to study public perceptions in an academic setting, unbiased by business or government influence.

The language of the survey is indicative of the terminology in use at the time of the survey, which referred to surveillance cameras as 'closed circuit television cameras' or 'CCTVs'. For the remainder of this chapter, these terms will be considered interchangeable, even though the literature has recognized a shift in use as cameras no longer operate primarily on a 'closed-circuit' and the systems have little in common with 'television'.

The following section explores the findings of the international survey's questions regarding camera surveillance, looking at how demographic variables influence perception. The survey also allowed cross-tabulation of questions on camera surveillance with other relevant topics explored by the survey. Such avenues provide a comparative analysis of public opinion on surveillance that was previously unavailable.

Knowledge of camera surveillance

The first step to better understanding public perceptions of camera surveillance is to inquire about individuals' knowledge of surveillance cameras. Question 1.4 of the survey asked: 'In general, how knowledgeable are you about Closed Circuit Television (CCTV) in public spaces? Would you say you are very knowledgeable, somewhat knowledgeable, not very knowledgeable or not at all knowledgeable?' Results show that a considerably large body of respondents believe themselves to be at least somewhat knowledgeable about camera surveillance.[3] A smaller proportion of the respondents from Brazil (26.7 per cent), Japan (25.2 per cent) and Mexico (17 per cent) claimed to be at least somewhat knowledgeable and respondents from Hungary sat somewhere in the middle (34.4 per cent). The claims to least knowledgeability came from Brazil (61 per cent 'not at all knowledgeable' and Mexico (44.8 per cent). An average of the nine countries puts knowledge claims at 39.3 per cent of respondents claiming to be at least somewhat knowledgeable about camera surveillance, with 8.4 per cent of that number claiming to be *very* knowledgeable. Figure 17.1 displays these figures.

The fact that 60 per cent of Chinese respondents felt that they were knowledgeable about camera surveillance is perhaps indicative of the widespread use of cameras in China. Beijing is reportedly home to more than 263,000 systems of camera surveillance located in public spaces (Liang and Huili 2007). Further, the sample population from China was taken from urban areas, which is where most of the cameras are stationed (ibid). China was also the only country involved in the survey from which focus group participants brought up public surveillance cameras without being prompted by a moderator. This suggests that urban Chinese dwellers are more aware of the surveillance of public spaces by CCTV cameras than citizens of the other countries involved in the survey.

While camera surveillance is a prevalent form of surveillance in each of the countries surveyed, we see a pattern of differences in knowledge claims from country to country. Slightly under half of respondents from North America claim to be at least somewhat knowledgeable about camera surveillance.[4] Responses in Europe had a

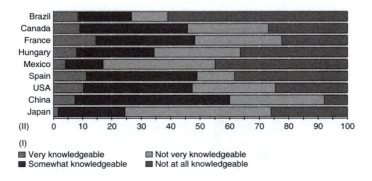

FIGURE 17.1 Knowledge of camera surveillance internationally.

similar pattern.[5] Other research shows a similar response from respondents from England (see, for example, Honess and Charman 1992). Diverging from its European counterparts is Hungary with a comparatively low body of respondents (34.4 per cent) claiming knowledgeability. Again, we find geographical similarities as we travel south, with Mexican (17 per cent) and Brazilian (26.7 per cent) respondents making among the smallest claims of knowledgeability. We see a dramatic difference in claims to knowledgeability in respondents from Asia. While Chinese respondents made the highest claim to being at least somewhat knowledgeable (60 per cent), only 25.2 per cent of Japanese respondents made the same claim.

Demographic variables reveal some trends in response on an international scale. When broken down by gender, males are more likely to claim that they are very knowledgeable and significantly less likely to state that they have no knowledge at all (see Figure 17.2).

Only negligible differences can be garnered from the assessment of the other noted demographic variables. In terms of age the differences were mostly marginal, apart from those belonging to the 65+ age bracket who were more likely to respond that they had no knowledge of camera surveillance at all. This pattern was international (see Figure 17.3).

We can see clearly that, among the nine countries surveyed, a significant body of respondents feel that they are at least somewhat knowledgeable about camera surveillance, with significantly higher claims coming from North America, Europe (excluding Hungary) and China.

Effectiveness of community camera surveillance

GPD survey question 20.1 asked respondents: 'Some communities and private companies are using surveillance cameras, also known as Closed Circuit Television or CCTVs, to monitor public places in order to deter crime and assist in the prosecution of offenders. In your opinion, how effective are community CCTVs (such as outdoor cameras in public places) in reducing crime? Are they very effective, somewhat effective, not very effective, or not at all effective?' Responses to

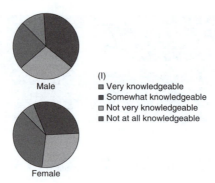

(I)
■ Very knowledgeable
■ Somewhat knowledgeable
▨ Not very knowledgeable
■ Not at all knowledgeable

Male

Female

FIGURE 17.2 Knowledge of camera surveillance by gender.

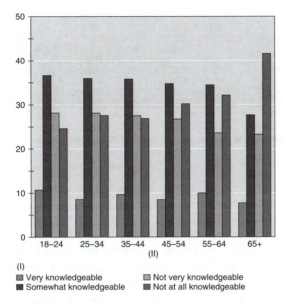

FIGURE 17.3   Knowledge of camera surveillance by age.

this question demonstrate that the overwhelming majority of respondents from the nine countries surveyed believe CCTV to be at least somewhat effective at reducing crime.

Among the countries with responses that stand out the most are Hungary, Brazil and Mexico. Hungary demonstrates the strongest response in favour of community CCTV's ability to reduce crime, with 90.5 per cent of respondents believing it to be at least somewhat effective. In Brazil, 81.9 per cent of respondents believed CCTV to be at least somewhat effective, with 44 per cent believing it to be very effective. This is the highest recorded number of responses in the 'very' category found in all other questions related to camera surveillance. The overwhelming majority of Mexicans (84.3 per cent) also hold the belief that camera surveillance is at least somewhat effective. In fact, the overwhelming majority of respondents globally believe community CCTV to be at least somewhat effective (see Figure 17.4). Hungary, Brazil and Mexico had similar responses in their claims to knowledgeability, being the three countries which claimed to be the least knowledgeable about camera surveillance.

Similar responses have also been replicated by previous academic research on public opinion in the UK, where 80 per cent of respondents believe that camera surveillance would have a significant impact on crime reduction (Spriggs et al. 2005).[6]

When broken down by gender, no significant differences are visible. Women are almost as likely as men to respond that community CCTVs are very effective, somewhat effective, not very effective, or not at all effective. This result is replicated on an international scale. When breaking respondents down by age, a

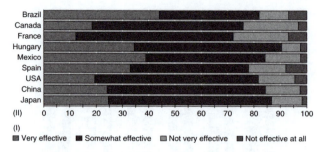

FIGURE 17.4   Internationally perceived effectiveness of community camera surveillance.

slight trend emerges in several of the countries involved. In general, older people believe camera surveillance is effective. In Canada, 68.9 per cent of 18–24 year olds believe community cameras to be at least somewhat effective compared with 80.8 per cent of those over 65. This pattern of positive belief among higher age groups is evident in Canada, France, Spain, USA, and marginally in China where the largest difference between age groups was 5.4 per cent. In an attempt to account for this trend, Stephane Leman-Langlois has suggested that a fundamental difference exists between age groups in matters related to crime, fear and security, where older citizens are likely to feel less secure and answer more favourably towards perceived safety measures like camera surveillance (Leman-Langlois 2008).

Results from question 20.1 were cross-tabulated with the results from question 1.4 in an attempt to understand if knowledge of camera surveillance could be used as an indicator of how effective one believes community camera surveillance to be. The data suggests that those who claimed to be knowledgeable were just as likely to claim the effectiveness of camera surveillance as those who claimed to be not knowledgeable at all. In Canada 78.2 per cent of those claiming to be very knowledgeable about camera surveillance responded that it was at least somewhat effective. 77.4 per cent of people who claimed to have no knowledge at all about community camera surveillance made the same claim about its effectiveness. As such, knowledge of public camera surveillance is not a good indicator of whether the respondent will think it is an effective means of deterring crime.

Responses from question 20.1 were also cross-tabulated with those from question 5, which asked: 'What level of trust do you have that your government is striking the right balance between national security and individual rights?' The idea was to determine whether a respondent's high level of trust in government could be an indicator of how effective they believed community camera surveillance to be at reducing crime. The thought behind this connection was that a citizen who had a high trust in their government to strike the right balance between security and individual rights would also believe that government would not employ a system incapable of performing the service it is designed to provide.

Results reveal a correlation between very high levels of trust in government and the belief that community cameras are very effective. In Canada, 41.8 per cent of the respondents who had a very high level of trust in their government also believed community cameras to be very effective. Correspondingly, only 21.2 per cent of respondents who claimed very high levels of trust in their government believed that community cameras are only somewhat effective. Furthermore, more Europeans than Americans surveyed hold this pairing of beliefs and results were replicated on an international level.[7] This suggests that there may be a positive correlation: those who have higher trust in their government are also more likely to think that the government would not employ a system that is incapable of performing the service it is designed to provide.

Effectiveness of in-store camera surveillance

The perceived effectiveness of in-store camera surveillance is measured by question 20.2 which asked: 'Some communities and private companies are using surveillance cameras, also known as Closed Circuit Television or CCTVs, to monitor public places in order to deter crime and assist in the prosecution of offenders. In your opinion, how effective are in-store CCTVs? Are they very effective, somewhat effective, not very effective, or not effective at all?' An overwhelming majority of respondents believe in-store CCTVs to be at least somewhat effective at reducing crime. Responses indicate that people are more likely to think of in-store CCTVs as being slightly more effective than community cameras. This perception exists on an international scale (see Figure 17.5).

With such extreme response rates demonstrating belief in the effectiveness of in-store camera surveillance, demographics reveal little in terms of differences. All nine countries surveyed, as well as external research on public response rates in England (see, for example, Honess and Charman 1992), show that the majority of the public believes camera surveillance to be an effective means of crime reduction and criminal apprehension.

When comparing question 20.2 with question 1.4 regarding knowledge of public camera surveillance, no strong connection in responses could be made. Those who claimed to be very or somewhat knowledgeable about camera surveillance were as likely to claim that the method was effective as those who claimed to be not very or not at all knowledgeable, a seeming contradiction which will be explored below.

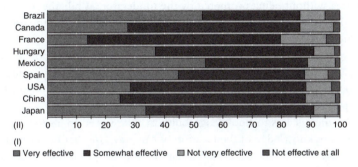

FIGURE 17.5 Internationally perceived effectiveness of in-store camera surveillance.

Limitations of survey design and interpreting the data

There are several problematic aspects of analysing the results of a cross-cultural survey. Cognizant of C. Wright Mills' (1959) assertion that public opinion cannot be separated from the historical and social structural roots from whence it was formed, culture becomes a variable that necessarily has influence on responses. It is difficult to measure responses equally across countries that represent different political climates, histories and socio-economic standings. Experiences of surveillance cannot be expected to be the same cross-culturally so we cannot expect the definition of surveillance to be understood as such. Problems therefore arise in terms of word meaning, language equivalence and the attempt to maintain salience across countries (Worcester, Lagos and Basanez 2000).

The authors of the survey admitted several obstacles in this attempt to conduct global research on public opinion. As they observe, there are challenges to quality, including measurement bias, response bias, non-response bias, proxy sampling frames, unjustified assumptions about Likert scales, situational and cultural relativities, and 'rigour versus relevance to strategy and policy' (Zureik and Stalker 2010: 19). The creators of the GPD survey took care to minimize the identified pitfalls. For example, back-translation was used to ensure that the wording of the questions conveyed the same meaning to respondents in different countries to ensure reliability (ibid 27). Despite its methodological limits, the data remain rich in scope and offer tremendous potential for analysis. Let us consider the content of the questions in some detail.

Understanding knowledgeability

As noted above, the first question in the survey regarding camera surveillance deals with knowledge of these systems. Unfortunately, the parameters of the survey do not allow for an understanding of what the participants consider as knowledge about cameras. Consulting the focus group transcripts which aided in the formation of the GPD survey help make several inferences in this regard.

To begin, China (with the survey's highest claims to knowledgeability) was the only country whose participants referred to the use of public surveillance cameras in their area without being prompted by the moderator. While the second-highest claims to knowledgeability came from North America and Spain, the use of public surveillance cameras was not acknowledged during focus group interviews without a prompt from the moderator. It should be assumed that to have knowledge of surveillance, one must know that some kinds of surveillance and monitoring happen. Apart from China, respondents seem to be largely unaware of the degree to which cameras permeate public spaces.

Perhaps then claims to knowledgeability may be traced to a category different from the mere knowledge of the location of cameras. Another dimension relevant to knowledge of surveillance cameras may be knowledge of their success. While there is no definitive scientific evidence to suggest that camera surveillance has the ability to fulfil its proposed goals, the vast majority of the public from each of the nine countries surveyed believe in the effectiveness of camera surveillance. This replicates public opinion data from the UK (see, for example, Honess and Charman 1992).

Data from the GPD reveals that Canadian respondents who claim to be 'very knowledgeable' about community camera surveillance are more likely to believe that camera surveillance is 'very effective'. Breaking down the Canadian respondents who claimed to be 'very knowledgeable', 32.1 per cent believe camera surveillance to be 'very effective'.[8] This suggests that knowledge of camera surveillance cannot be understood to be an indicator of 'actual' knowledge of the effectiveness of camera surveillance according to current scientific information regarding the success of camera surveillance to achieve its proposed goals. A clear discrepancy between the *proven* and the *perceived* capabilities of surveillance cameras exists, indicating a limited and at least partially inaccurate public knowledge of camera surveillance. Such results may be at least partially explained by the public's reliance on media outlets to form their opinion (Reiner 1997; Norris and Armstrong 1999a; Groombridge 2002).

Popular images, popular perceptions

An examination of popular cultural outlets that incorporate positive uses of CCTV help address the discrepancy between inconclusive research evaluations and positive public opinion. The use of CCTV in popular media has worked to domesticate CCTV and make it appear a natural part of contemporary life. Popular uses of camera surveillance in movies like *The Truman Show*, in computer and video games such as SimCity, and the reliance on reality shows such as *Big Brother* and *Survivor* have worked to neutralize the use of the systems to the public (Groombridge 2002).

This neutralization has been coupled with an ideology of success. Crime shows such as *Cops* demonstrate the apparent ability of camera surveillance to detect crime and focus on stories in which CCTV has led to apprehension and prosecution of criminal offenders (ibid). These types of shows disproportionately portray the function and capabilities of camera surveillance, suggesting that CCTV cameras can be used in inclement weather, always have a pan, tilt and zoom function, and that the pictures provided by CCTV are always clear and distinct (Norris and Armstrong 1999a). Mass media outlets may therefore be said to distort the situation by exaggerating the positive aspects of CCTV, planting positive perceptions in the public mind, and generating commonsense assumptions about (erroneous) capabilities of camera surveillance (ibid; McCahill 2002).

Stories highlighted in news media contribute to an overall picture of success in regard to CCTV's ability to reduce crime by portraying the systems as both a useful investigative instrument and a successful deterrent against criminal activity. In 2007, when Patricia McDermott's murder was caught on camera in the streets of Philadelphia, ABC News published an article entitled 'Catching a Killer, With

Help from a Camera: Surveillance Cameras have become Crucial to Crime Scene Investigations' (Martelli and Adriano 2007) before the footage had even led to an arrest. Media messages like these further contribute to the (mis)conception of camera surveillance as a 'silver bullet' for crime-solving, and work to shape public opinions to be encouraging of a tactic that appears to increase safety in urban areas (Walby 2006).

The range of voices heard in the media is also disproportional. Studies have demonstrated that they belong primarily to those involved in partnerships set up to promote camera surveillance.[9] From police officials to business leaders, the voices resonating in the media are supporters of the camera surveillance initiative (ibid). In Canada, voices of support come from all levels: supported from above by police and state institutions; from the middle by business entrepreneurs; and from below by citizens seeking the safety of their own communities (Walby 2006). Camera surveillance is 'sold' to the public in a way that constructs a positive image and exaggerated idea of success.

Mass media outlets contribute to the positive portrayal of camera surveillance in another way as well: through the production of risk. Footage of the terrorist attacks of 11 September 2001 still resonates clearly in the North American mind. Displayed over and over again, the media use of such images has helped to produce a culture of fear in which surveillance not only seems warranted and justifiable, but is valued (Lyon 2003a). Currently, this culture of fear dominates the mindset of the global North and has created a public willing to trade their right to privacy for feelings of security (Bauman 2000). Of course, September 11th is only one example of an event that has been utilized in the construction of a surveillance society and this example should be considered to be inclusive of areas of the world unaffected by these events. European sociologist Ulrich Beck brings up similar notions in his exploration of risk as the primary organizing principle in modern society (1992). For Beck, contemporary living is saturated by predicting risk and attempting to prevent harm. These types of assessments, coupled with a technologically deterministic attitude that assumes technology will always lead to the greater good, may perhaps explain the qualifying principles under which camera surveillance continues to be implemented and consistently considered successful on an international scale.

The neutralization of camera surveillance in the mind of the public, the exaggeration of the abilities of camera surveillance by popular media outlets and the production of risk are each factors that explain the limited and inaccurate knowledge of camera surveillance demonstrated by the public on an international scale. Such factors should not only be considered a concern in terms of biasing the outcome of public opinion research, but also for the ability of mechanisms of surveillance to have a negative impact on those marginalized groups already at a disadvantage.

Camera surveillance contributes to the perpetuation of social hierarchies by contributing to what sociologists have labelled 'social sorting' (Lyon 2003b). The increasing implementation of camera surveillance has often been justified with reference to the fear of crime and the 'threat of terrorism'. As a result, the increased use of camera surveillance to monitor flows of passengers in airports and public transportation systems is often considered a result of 9/11 in North America, 7/7 in the UK, the subway sarin incident in Japan, etc. In such instances, cameras are used for the purposes of separating those who belong (i.e. consumers and pedestrians) from those who do not (i.e. those judged on the basis of racial profiling, age discrimination and stereotyping) (ibid).

In instances where there is a camera operator, it is his/her subjective discretion that is relied upon to pass judgement on the surveilled subject (Walby 2005). Instances of discrimination have been examined in Norris and Armstrong's empirical studies (1997, 1999b) of camera surveillance operators, which found that 40 per cent of people targeted by the gaze of the operator did 'not fall equally on all users of the street but on those who are stereotypically predefined as potentially deviant . . .' (Norris and Armstrong 1997: 9). Operators have identified 'potentially deviant' groups such as youth, the presence of whom is considered to 'threaten the flow of consumerism' (as quoted in Reeve 1998: 80). Such observations suggest camera surveillance is socially exclusive and contributes to the perpetuation of social hierarchies. The ability to engage in these acts of 'discriminatory policing' facilitated by the use of camera surveillance puts already at risk groups at a further disadvantage.

Discussion

Ditton (2000) suggests that media and market based opinion polling often use leading questions and words to guide responses, as well as conduct surveys immediately following some heavily publicized tragic event which increases positive attitudes towards camera surveillance. The social scientific GPD survey worked to minimize such factors that might skew results one way or the other. A strong belief in the ability of cameras to deter crime and aid in criminal apprehension and prosecution remained prevalent in this academic study. While Ditton was correct in his assertion that positive responses within media and market based opinion polling are up to 35 per cent higher than in social scientific polls, the fact remains that a considerable majority of the public body believes in the effectiveness of camera surveillance. International public opinion shows a strong belief that camera surveillance can achieve its prescribed goals despite the lack of definitive supporting evidence.

While the GPD survey attempts to provide an unbiased and academic account of public perception, and while we may develop informed opinions as to the reasons why the quantitative data appears as it does, there are at least two significant limitations to using the survey method to study public opinion that deserve highlighting. First, surveys fail to capture the various nuances of public opinion. No matter how cleverly the questions are asked, they do little to provide answers to *why* publics hold the opinions they do. The inability to account for the varying subjective experiences which emerge in the process of engaging with camera surveillance calls for a qualitative approach to data-gathering. Qualitative methods like interviewing are much better suited to provide rich data that describes the everyday practices and complex experiences of people (Weiss 1994). Such methods are better able to address citizens' attitudes towards the abstract phenomena like privacy, perceptions of security and public knowledgeability that the GPD attempts to deal with quantitatively. The open-ended forum of qualitative methods allows new and often unexpected variables to emerge (Glaser and Strauss 1999). Such information is always a goal of research into complex issues like surveillance, privacy and control, that are inextricably tied to the culture, values, political orders and institutional systems within which they are embedded.

The second limitation is that surveys only provide a snapshot of the data. Public opinion changes with time as it is heavily influenced by current events. A longitudinal study of public perceptions in relation to camera surveillance is needed in order to bridge this gap in understanding. Without the examination of public opinion longitudinally, it is impossible to be certain of the stability of public attitudes or speak to the research concern that mass media outlets play a role in shaping public opinion by framing public issues in ways that are not neutral (Zureik 2010).

In using the survey method, the GPD has successfully painted a broad picture of the public perceptions in terms of being able to offer specific numbers or statistics to which we can point and say, 'This is what the public thinks.' Further research must revise its methodological approach to be inclusive of the individual's experience of camera surveillance. Scholars must work towards articulating a more productive dialogue that attempts to confront the issues surrounding what shapes the subjective experience. Why are these numbers the way they are? What do we know about the culturally context dependent experience of the individual such that the statistics demonstrate a discrepancy between knowledge and perceived success of surveillance cameras? To answer such questions it is helpful to consider sources of information regarding public opinion towards camera surveillance that have been completed in the UK. This research works to complement and extend existing survey research to be inclusive of more specific questions dealing with public perceptions.

In an attempt to measure the level of support for the installation of surveillance cameras in public spaces, the Home Office survey of the UK (2005) asked how respondents would feel if a new CCTV system were installed in the respondents' area. Response was measured on a scale ranging from 'very happy' to 'very unhappy'. The level of support was positive, with about 82 per cent of people responding that they would be at least 'fairly happy' about installation. The majority in favour has been a consistent response among surveys completed in the UK (see, for example, Bennett and Gelsthorpe 1996; Ditton 2000). A strong relationship has been found between the perceived effectiveness of camera surveillance and attitude towards installation; respondents are more likely to be happy about installation in their area if they believe the technology to be effective at its proposed uses.

To supplement these findings with information from other locations we turn to the GPD focus group interviews conducted prior to the survey. Transcripts from these interviews work both to complement and challenge the notion that attitudes surrounding the implementation of camera surveillance would mimic the quantitative outcome of the survey. The focus groups cannot be said to portray an accurate representation of the public body, with each group containing approximately 25 members. However, they do much in terms of contextualizing the quantitative data. In Canada, for example, a reading of all the available transcripts[10] revealed that people easily point to several ways that surveillance cameras are used, but their examples rarely include police or government operations. The most commonly cited schemes are private systems belonging to apartment buildings, banks, malls, convenience stores and those used by employers to monitor their employees. On only one occasion did a participant speak about cameras in public spaces without being prompted by the moderator and this was in reference to cameras in the UK. Apparently the focus group participant had not noticed the plethora of cameras on his/her own Toronto city streets.

This suggests that people are likely to think of public camera surveillance in terms of private monitoring as opposed to the social monitoring of a public space by government or police officials.[11] The focus group transcripts imply that Canadian citizens are unaware of the extent to which government and police forces are using camera surveillance as a proposed method of crime control, perhaps reflective of earlier discussions exposing the limited and inaccurate information available to the public.

Similar stories were found in a reading of the focus group transcripts from several of the other countries, where camera surveillance was not a topic mentioned by participants during open discussion and was only spoken about when prompted by the moderator. This was not the case for Spain and China, however. At several points during focus group interviews different participants called upon their thoughts of public camera surveillance as examples without being prompted to do so. Recall that the survey told us that Chinese respondents also felt that they were the most knowledgeable about camera surveillance, with 60 per cent of the population indicating moderate to strong levels of knowledgeability. This may be accounted for in the large body of public cameras (estimated at 263,000) in public spaces across Chinese city centres (Liang and Huili 2007). 49 per cent of respondents from Spain claimed to be at least somewhat knowledgeable about camera surveillance, putting Spain's response second only to China's. Focus group respondents spoke of cameras in the city streets of Barcelona without being prompted by a moderator. However, with upwards of 14 cities in Canada deploying extensive camera schemes, and more than 16 municipalities considering or having considered the use of these systems, it is curious why Canadian focus groups, from the city centre of Toronto, didn't have similar examples. This discrepancy is perhaps suggestive that urban Chinese and Spanish dwellers are more aware of camera surveillance in public spaces than the other seven countries involved in the survey.

When discussion shifted to the usefulness of camera surveillance, there was a generally positive consensus, reflecting the data from the GPD survey. When prompted to talk about the widespread implementation of surveillance cameras in the participant's own city, however, responses within the focus groups were rarely supportive. Apart from Brazil, participants from all the countries surveyed expressed unease about being personally monitored in a public place. In France, participants cited infringement of privacy, in Japan a general uneasiness of being monitored, and in Spain the need to balance privacy with security was commented upon. While the responses in the survey indicate that it is commonplace to believe camera surveillance is a successful crime deterrent, the extent to which citizens feel positively about the implementation of camera surveillance in their area is uncertain.

Concluding remarks

Neutralization, exaggeration of ability by media and the production of risk are each factors that attempt to qualify the limited and inaccurate knowledge of camera surveillance demonstrated by the public on an international scale. This view seems to be consistent with the quantitative results of the GPD survey as evidenced by the clear discrepancy (most mentionable in Canada, France, Spain, USA and China) between the public's claims to knowledgeability and the same public's tenuous belief in the system's unproven effectiveness.

The questions addressed in the survey pertaining to knowledge of cameras surveillance, the perceived success of both community and in-store camera surveillance, and the public opinions that surround them, make an important contribution to knowledge of attitudes towards surveillance mechanisms. The current state of liquidity that allows information to flow freely across borders amplifies the need for a richer understanding of the processes that make these systems work. This includes not simply a study of how the technology is having impact, but grapples with the ordinary wo/man's experience of, and interaction with, surveillant mechanisms like camera surveillance. In this sense, public opinion research is crucial to the analysis of the global processes affecting individuals' lives. Discussion of the GPD survey results makes it clear that additional avenues of research are needed to supplement the quantitative data.

There is an urgent need for more innovative research techniques better able to grapple with the subjective experience of camera surveillance. A more qualitative and longitudinally based research method is called for in the study of citizens' attitudes towards being personally affected (or not) by public camera surveillance systems. Such research avenues have a better chance at revealing the complexities of the public's thoughts, feelings and attitudes about mechanisms of surveillance. While the GPD survey provides important insights into the public perceptions of camera surveillance, it should be treated as a stepping-stone to further research opportunities. The unabated growth of camera surveillance on an international scale gives exigency to this method of surveillance as a point of study. The ability of camera surveillance to significantly affect the life chances of social groups already at a disadvantage is extended where camera surveillance is concerned. While the data collected from the GPD survey are rich in scope and cross-national representations, it is clear that the study of such complex phenomena requires inclusion of the subjective experience of surveillance that can only be achieved through a qualitative research forum.

Notes

1 Conducted by an organization called Real Instituto Elcano.
2 Launched in 2003, the GPD Project sought to trace the effects that new uses of personal data, in relation to mobility, globalization and governance, have on ordinary people. This included research into the ways that personal data are being systematically collected to influence, manage, sort, categorize or otherwise process various aspects of social life via the proliferation of surveillance systems in a world that is increasingly mobile.
3 China (60 per cent), Spain (49 per cent), France (48.1 per cent), the USA (47.3 per cent) and Canada (45.7 per cent).
4 45.7 per cent of Canadian respondents and 47.3 per cent of US respondents.
5 48.1 per cent of respondents from France and 49 per cent of Spanish respondents claimed to be 'somewhat knowledgeable'.
6 For examples of similar results, see also Dixon, Levine and McAuley 2003; Honess and Charman 1992; and Phillips 1999, who each report that community response to camera surveillance has been predominantly positive, which is correlated with the public belief that camera surveillance is an effective means of crime deterrence and detection.
7 In China, 37.8 per cent of those who had a very high level of trust in their government thought community cameras to be very effective, whereas only 23.8 per cent of Chinese respondents who had a very low level of trust in their government believed community camera surveillance to be effective. The average of all nine countries in the survey shows 43.7 per cent of respondents with a very high level of trust in their government believed community camera surveillance to be very effective, while only 27.9 per cent of those with very low levels of trust in their government held the same belief.
8 46.1 per cent believed camera surveillance to be 'somewhat effective', with 19.5 per cent believing it is 'not very effective' and only 2.4 per cent stating it is 'not at all effective'. Similar results are demonstrated in France and the USA. In China, those who say they are 'very knowledgeable' are equally as likely to claim that camera surveillance is effective as they are to say it is ineffective.
9 See, for example, Norris and Armstrong (1999a), who found 86 per cent of voices belonged to this group; or McCahill (2002), who found 71 per cent of voices in the media belong to those working to promote camera surveillance initiatives.
10 Four focus groups based in Toronto in May 2004, averaging about seven members per group.
11 There are upwards of 14 systems of camera surveillance currently in use in Canada. Current evaluations tell us Hamilton, London, Peterborough, Sturgeon Falls, Sudbury, Thessalon, Toronto, Thunder Bay and Windsor (ON), Edmonton (AB), Antigonish (NS), Kelowna (BC), Montreal and Baie-Comeau (QC) operate open-street camera surveillance programmes with many more locations having used systems in the past, or are considering/have considered the implementation of a system (Walby, 2006: 6). This estimate is predicted to increase. By 2003, there were more than four million publicly or privately owned cameras in operation in the UK (McCahill and Norris 2003). While Canada is only a tiny echo of the current application of camera surveillance in the UK, this extensive deployment may serve as an indicator of the direction of the Canadian smaller-scale project (Walby 2006).

References

Andrejevic, M. (2007) *iSpy: Surveillance and Power in the Interactive Era*, Kansas: University Press.
Bauman, Z. (2000) *Liquid Modernity*, Cambridge: Polity Press.
Beck, U. (1992) *Risk Society, Towards a New Modernity*, London: Sage.
Bennett, T. (1996) 'Frequently Asked Questions about Privacy: A Comparative Analysis of Privacy Surveys', University of British Columbia, unpublished manuscript.

Bennett, T. and Gelsthorpe, L. (1996) 'Public Attitudes Towards CCTV in Public Places', *Studies on Crime and Crime Prevention*, 5(1): 72–90.

Davison, R., Clarke, R., Smith, H., Langford, D. and Kuo, F. (2003) 'Information Privacy in a Globally Networked Society: Implications for Information Systems Research', *Communications of the Association for Information Systems*, 12: 341–65.

Ditton, J. (2000) 'Crime and the City: Public Attitudes to CCTV in Glasgow', *British Journal of Criminology*, 40: 692–709.

Dixon, J., Levine, M. and McAuley, R. (2003) *Street Drinking Legislation, CCTV and Public Space: Exploring Attitudes Towards Public Order Measures*, Lancaster University. Online. Available HTTP: <http://www.psych.lancs.ac.uk/people/uploads/MarkLevine20041022T115242.pdf> (accessed 10 January 2010).

Gandy Jr, O. (2003) 'Public Opinion Surveys and the Formation of Privacy Policy', *Journal of Social Issues*, 59(2): 293–9.

Glaser, B.G. and Strauss, A.L. (1999) *The Discovery of Grounded Theory: Strategies for Qualitative Research*, New York: Aldine de Gruyter.

Globalization of Personal Data (2008) *An International Survey on Privacy and Surveillance: Summary Report*, The Surveillance Project. Online. Available HTTP: < http://www.surveillanceproject.org/research/intl_survey> (accessed 10 January 2011).

Groombridge, N. (2002) 'Crime Control or Crime Culture TV?', *Surveillance & Society*, 1(1): 30–46.

Haggerty, K.D. and Ericson, R.V. (2006) 'The New Politics of Surveillance and Visibility', in K.D. Haggerty and R.V. Ericson (eds), *The New Politics of Surveillance and Visibility*, Toronto: University of Toronto Press.

Haggerty, K.D and Gazso, A. (2005) 'Seeing Beyond the Ruins: Surveillance as a Response to Terrorist Threats', *Canadian Journal of Sociology*, 30(2):169–87.

Helten, F. and Fischer, B. (2004) 'Reactive Attention: Video Surveillance in Berlin Shopping Malls', *Surveillance & Society*, 2(2/3): 323–45.

Honess, T. and Charman, E. (1992) 'Closed circuit television in public places: its acceptability and perceived effectiveness', Police Research Group Crime Prevention Unit, Paper 35. London: Home Office.

Klauser, F. (2004) 'A Comparison of the Impact of Protective and Preservative Video Surveillance on Urban Territoriality: The Case of Switzerland', *Surveillance & Society*, 2(2/3): 145–60.

Leman-Langlois, S. (2009) 'Public Perceptions of Camera Surveillance', in *A Report on Camera Surveillance in Canada: Part One*, SCAN (2009).

Liang, G. and Huili, C. (2007) 'Surveillance and Privacy in Urban China', in *International Survey on Privacy and Surveillance* by the Globalization of Personal Data Project (2006). Available HTTP: <http://www.sscqueens.org/sites/default/files/China_Report_March_07.pdf>.

Lyon, D. (2003a) *Surveillance after September 11*, Cambridge: Polity.

Lyon, D. (2003b) *Surveillance as Social Sorting: Privacy, Risk, and Digital Discrimination*, London: Routledge.

Lyon, D. (2007) *Surveillance Studies: An Overview*, Cambridge: Polity.

Martelli, J. and Adriano, J. (2007) 'Catching a Killer, With Help from a Camera: Surveillance Cameras Have Become Crucial to Crime Scene Investigations'. Online. Available HTTP: <http://abcnews.go.com/2020/story?id=2755037&page=1> (accessed 10 January 2010).

McCahill, M. (2002) *The Surveillance Web: The Rise of Visual Surveillance in an English City*, Cullompton: Willan.

McCahill, M. and Norris, C. (2003) 'Estimating the Extent, Sophistication and Legality of CCTV in London', in M. Gill (ed.), *CCTV*, Leicester: Perpetuity Press.

Mills, C.W. (1959) *The Sociological Imagination*, New York: Oxford University Press.

Norris, C. and Armstrong, G. (1997). *The Unforgiving Eye: CCTV Surveillance in Public Space*, Hull: University of Hull.

Norris, C. and Armstrong, G. (1999a) 'CCTV and the Social Structuring of Surveillance', in K. Painter and N. Tilley (eds), *Surveillance of Public Space: CCTV, Street Lighting and Crime Prevention*, Monsey, NY: Criminal Justice Press.

Norris, C. and Armstrong, G. (1999b) *The Maximum Surveillance Society: The Rise of CCTV*, Oxford: Berg.

Phillips, C. (1999) 'A Review of CCTV Evaluations: Crime Reduction Effects and Attitudes Towards its Use', in K. Painter and N. Tilley (eds), *Surveillance of Public Space: CCTV, Street Lighting and Crime Prevention*, Crime Prevention Studies Volume 10.

Reeve, A. (1998) 'The panopticisation of shopping: CCTV and leisure consumption', in C. Norris, J. Moran and G. Armstrong (eds), *Surveillance, Closed Circuit Television and Social Control*, Aldershot: Ashgate.

Reiner, R. (1997) 'Media-made Criminality: The Representation of Crime in the Mass Media', in M. Maguire, R. Morgan and R. Reiner (eds), *The Oxford Handbook of Criminology* (2nd edn), Oxford: Oxford University Press.

Saetnan, A., Lomell, M. and Wiecek, C. (2004) 'Controlling CCTV in Public Spaces: Is Privacy the (Only) Issue? Reflections on Norwegian and Danish Observations', *Surveillance & Society*, 2(2/3): 396–414.

Spriggs, A., Argomaniz, J., Gill. M. and Bryan, J. (2005) *Home Office Online Report*. Online. Available HTTP: <http://www.homeoffice.gov.uk/rds/pdfs05/rdsolr1005.pdf >.

Walby, K. (2005) 'How Closed-Circuit Television Surveillance Organizes the Social: An Institutional Ethnography', *The Canadian Journal of Sociology*, 30(2): 189–214.

Walby, K. (2006) 'Little England? The Rise of Open-street Closed Circuit Television Surveillance in Canada', *Surveillance & Society*, 4(1/2): 29–51.

Weiss, R.S. (1994) *Learning from Strangers: The Art and Method of Qualitative Interview Studies*, Free Press: New York.

Wiecek, C. and Saetnan, A. (2002) *Restrictive? Permissive? The Contradictory Framing of Video Surveillance in Norway and Denmark*, Urban Eye Project, Working Paper No.4. Online. Available HTTP: <http://www.urbaneye.net/results/ue_wp4.pdf>.

Worcester, R., Lagos, M. and Basanez, M. (2000) 'Problems and Progress in Cross-National Studies: Lessons Learned the Hard Way'. Paper presented at the World Association for Public Opinion Research (WAPOR)/American Association for Public Opinion Research (AAPOR) annual conference, Portland, OR.

Zureik, E. (2010) 'Methodological Considerations', in Zureik et al. (eds), *Surveillance, Privacy and the Globalization of Personal Information: International Comparisons*, McGill-Queen's Press: Montreal and Kingston.

Zureik, E. and Stalker, L.H. (2010) 'The Cross-Cultural Study of Privacy', in Zureik et al. (eds), *Surveillance, Privacy and the Globalization of Personal Information: International Comparisons*, McGill-Queen's Press: Montreal and Kingston.

PART V

Regulating camera surveillance

Regulating camera surveillance

18

TOWARDS A FRAMEWORK OF CONTEXTUAL INTEGRITY

Legality, trust and compliance of CCTV signage

Mark Lizar and Gary Potter

Introduction

The United Kingdom has long been recognized in camera surveillance research as having the most prolific use of CCTV video surveillance[1] systems in the world (Armitage 2002; McCahill and Norris 2002; House of Lords 2009). McCahill and Norris in 2002 estimated that in the UK there were over 4.2 million CCTV cameras, one for every 14 citizens. The UK CCTV industry grew between 4 and 7 per cent Compound Annual Growth Rate (CAGR) between 2002 and 2009 (Hayfield 2009). These figures indicate a higher camera-to-citizen ratio than any other nation (Carroll-Mayer et al. 2008).

According to forecasts, the world is in a hurry to catch up with the UK as 'The global CCTV market is projected to reach around US$28 billion by the end of 2013, at a CAGR of over 22% from 2010' (RNCOS 2010). In light of the global growth of camera surveillance, the UK, as a world leader in the use of CCTV technology, is a critical country to study.

This high level of CCTV use is presumably due, at least in part, to the British public's acceptance of CCTV systems as a safety and security measure (c.f. Cole 2004). For law enforcement, video surveillance has become something of a panacea. Video surveillance is seen as a cost-effective crime-fighting strategy (Deisman 2003). It has been embraced for its potential in the prevention and detection of crimes, and the identification and prosecution of offenders. In the early days of CCTV, and in much recent debate, its role in combating terrorism also has been trumpeted,[2] although CCTV is more commonly employed for the purposes of combating low-level crime and anti-social behaviour, or for control of particular places and the crowds that frequent them. CCTV, it is claimed, facilitates development of a safer environment, improves police response times, reduces fear, raises property values, lowers insurance premiums, enhances visitor experience and increases workplace efficiency, among other benefits (Deisman 2003). Whether these claims are valid or not, it is clear that CCTV has great appeal politically, publicly and commercially.

Despite this long list of benefits, video surveillance technology is also subject to much criticism. Many claimed advantages, particularly those related to crime prevention and law enforcement, are far from clearly supported by research (see Gill and Spriggs 2005 for a detailed review of the impact of CCTV on crime). More generally, concerns relate to the privacy of those monitored and recorded by camera surveillance and the control of personal data (images) generated by cameras (Rotenburg 2008). In short, there are questions as to whether the public can 'trust' CCTV. Concerns over the misuse of camera surveillance and the data it generates are reflected to some degree in specific laws governing CCTV system use and in general data protection and human rights legislation (see Johnson, this volume). A fundamental element of this legal framework, and a central focus of this chapter, is the legal requirement (in the UK) for organizations to give appropriate notification to the public that CCTV camera surveillance is in operation.

Notification, here, is best understood as the display of signs indicating CCTV system presence to those subject to surveillance. Notification can be understood as a way to elicit informed consent from subjects under surveillance. The fact an individual remains in a location after being informed through signage that it is under surveillance implies the subject consents to be monitored.[3] Even without this somewhat legalistic concept of informed consent, notification can be seen as a way for members of the public to evaluate the appropriateness and trustworthiness of public surveillance (Lippert 2007). In this way notification can be seen not only as a key component of compliance in the UK, but also, regardless of jurisdiction, as a key component in CCTV effectiveness and in building public trust in a given CCTV system. Another (but by no means contradictory) perspective on notification in the form of signage is that signs serve the purpose of increasing the effectiveness of surveillance through (re-)emphasizing both camera presence and purpose (Cole 2004; Lippert 2009b). One particular and peculiar outcome of this perspective is the existence, at times, of signs *without* cameras aimed at influencing behaviour (Lippert 2009b); another is the observation that signage that falls short of legal standards may be more effective in deterring criminal behaviour than that which is legally compliant (Cole 2004; Lippert 2009b). We begin to see here how signage takes on an importance beyond its role of accompanying and legitimizing an active camera surveillance system.

Legality, trust and compliance

Existing regulation for the operation of CCTV in the United Kingdom is found in two pieces of legislation from 1998: the Data Protection Act (DPA) and the Human Rights Act (HRA). The DPA stipulates that a person (data subject) must be notified (1) that personal information is being taken; (2) why that information is being recorded; and (3) to whom this information will be accessible. In the CCTV context this means persons must be informed *when* recording is taking place, *why* that recording is happening, and *who* will control the personal data once recorded. The DPA is in effect an extension of well-established privacy frameworks that can be traced back, in modern times, to the 1948 UN Declaration of Human Rights. Instruments stemming from the UN Declaration include the 1973 American 'Fair Information Practices', which have left a lasting legacy 'as one powerful mechanism for levelling the playing field in a game where participants have unequal starting positions' (Nissenbaum, 2004:110). These are practices designed to balance the power equation in the access, use and control of information and are relevant to the proportional use of public surveillance. The Organization for Economic Co-operation and Development (OECD) included these fair information practices in 'Guidelines on the Protection of Privacy and Transborder Flows of Personal Data' (OECD 1980); the EU incorporated them into law via European Directive 94/95. This EU directive was pivotal to enacting privacy legislation across all European member states (Bennett 1992).

The reasons that such entrenched legal frameworks have evolved and are applied to the use of video surveillance relate to the privacy and security risks presented by the use of public surveillance technology to the persons and communities this technology monitors. The very nature of video surveillance creates a significant power imbalance (House of Lords 2009) because the individual cannot see the watcher and may be unaware of who is watching, what they are watching for and how the data is being recorded, stored and used. They may, of course, not even know they are being watched and recorded in the first place. At the same time, camera operators are anonymous and are in a position of power, accentuated by the fact that no one may be monitoring their use of this technology (Rotenburg 2008), thus making the subjects of surveillance more vulnerable.

It is clear that UK law goes some way to addressing the privacy and trust concerns related to CCTV system uses. However, it should also be clear that the mere existence of relevant laws will not satisfy all these concerns, and that the legality of a system does not necessarily equate to its trustworthiness. The law, for example, allows camera surveillance use by anyone. This may be a concern in itself: video surveillance by official bodies may be more acceptable to some persons than CCTV use by private companies or individuals (Eurobarometer 2008). For others the existence of *any* video surveillance may be deemed intrusive and unacceptable.

The issues of power imbalance are exacerbated by advances in profiling through the development and use of identity management in conjunction with video surveillance technology. The term CCTV – *closed circuit* television – is often no longer adequate to describe the changing nature of video surveillance in contemporary society (Lippert 2009a). This is due, in part, to the rapid increase in the capacity to store, manipulate, analyse, share and distribute an ever-increasing amount of surveillance data. These developments dramatically change the closed circuit context (ibid.), bringing into question whether the law will keep up with technological advances and their implications.

Regardless of whether the law's content is sufficient to counter privacy concerns, there may also be concerns as to how effectively laws are enforced and how sanctions should operate against those breaking the law. The existence of a legal framework around surveillance and data control recognizes the existence of individuals' privacy concerns, but it does not end debate. Even where a legal standard minimum is applied and effectively enforced, there is much room for debate as to whether the legal standard addresses pressing concerns about privacy, and therefore whether legal compliance necessarily renders CCTV systems transparent, trustworthy or useful.

We can illustrate the problem with reference to an empirical study. The legality of CCTV systems in the UK was considered by McCahill and Norris (2002) in a study of a London high-street (main shopping street), where it was found that only 53 per cent[4] of CCTV systems sampled had a sign, and only 22 per cent of the signs that did exist were 'in accordance with national laws' (ibid.: 22). With little over one in ten CCTV systems therefore complying with basic legal requirements under the DPA, it is clear that the mere existence of a law is not enough to ensure even minimum standards of data protection and respect for the right to privacy.[5] Lippert (2007; 2009a; 2009b) makes a similar observation about CCTV and accompanying signage in Canada: notification as provided on signage often falls short of legal requirements. We can assume that similar problems exist in other jurisdictions.

The obvious point to make from this work is that many CCTV systems are not fulfilling their legal obligations of notification.[6] However, observations on legality are only of limited use in discussions about privacy, data protection or 'trust' in relation to CCTV system proliferation, particularly in a comparative context. Legal standards will vary across jurisdictions, and may change within jurisdictions. Legal standards may not match the standards that some members of society would like to see met before considering a system trustworthy. It is also apparent that simply commenting on whether individual systems are legal or not (or on the rate of legal compliance of systems within a single jurisdiction) masks some fundamental differences between systems that are clumped together in one of two binary categories. The data cited above from McCahill and Norris (2002), for example, make it clear that some systems were illegal because their signs were not compliant with the law, while others did not have signs or other notification in place. Some system owners seemingly make some effort (albeit inadequately) to comply with the law; others seemingly make no effort (and may or may not even be aware of the legal requirements). We may well wish to distinguish between these levels of non-compliance or between those systems that *meet* the legal requirements (by providing the bare minimum of information) and those that *exceed* the legal requirements (by providing extra information, for example). Following this discussion we would argue it is more useful to consider 'compliance' as a scale than as a binary concept of legality, albeit a scale where there may be a cut-off point for what constitutes '*legal* compliance' in a given jurisdiction. With a compliance scale approach to assessing camera surveillance[7] we can still comment on the legality of individual systems for specific and general purposes (such as monitoring compliance rates in different parts of the UK or at different points in time). We can compare levels of compliance and/or integrity across jurisdictions where, previously, a binary concept of legal/illegal

would make such comparisons of limited utility (because of different legal requirements, if any, in different jurisdictions). We can use a scale of compliance to inform
discussions where there is no legal standard, or where the legal standard is called into
question; as an objective benchmark where standards applied for measuring compliance can vary. What is more, a compliance scale can be applied not only to camera
surveillance, but to all scenarios where data is collected and potentially shared.

Aims

Keeping the above discussion in mind, the aims of this chapter are twofold. On
the surface level we report on some original research into the extent and legality of
CCTV systems on a busy high-street in London. The methodology and findings
are broadly comparable to those of an early study of CCTV conducted on a similar
London high-street in 2002 (McCahill and Norris 2002). The findings serve as an
interesting study in the legality of CCTV systems in their own right; comparison to
this earlier work adds a dimension to the analysis.

The essay, however, also has a deeper aim. The methodology and findings discussed, and the comparison with earlier research, demonstrate the value of a compliance-scale approach to surveillance research. We hope to illustrate a number of
ways in which a compliance-scale approach to 'privacy' and 'information sharing'
research can contribute to broader academic debates. Finally, we aim to suggest a
number of directions for future research.

Methodology

The research reported here consisted of an audit of CCTV systems on a single
high-street in central London. A central aim was to produce data on CCTV systems that would allow comparison with the earlier research of McCahill and Norris
(2002) and a broadly similar methodology was therefore employed.

McCahill and Norris were attempting to provide a snapshot of CCTV coverage
in the City of London as part of the European Commission-funded Urban-Eye
project reporting on the extent of CCTV use across a number of European countries.[8] They used a range of different methods targeting different sample populations of 'institutions' across London, culminating in descriptions of CCTV usage
on London's public transportation systems, in sports stadiums, at cultural/tourist
attractions and by criminal justice system agencies. They also researched CCTV
usage in the London borough of Wandsworth as an indicator of the scope and
extent of public surveillance by CCTV systems in shopping and business districts
(McCahill and Norris 2002). One element of the Wandsworth research was a survey of businesses around the main business area ('Putney High Street') and their use
of CCTV, including details of signage use and content; it is this particular aspect of
their research that we sought to emulate.

Our own research was conducted on King Street in the London borough of
Hammersmith and Fulham, a London high-street comparable to Putney High

Street based on the number and type of businesses. We conducted an audit covering type of business, whether or not it used CCTV and, if so, details of accompanying signage. The audit was completed through researchers' observations, supplemented, where possible, with face-to-face questioning of institutional staff and, in some cases, photographs of cameras and signs. The initial assumption, or hypothesis, was that the level of use of CCTV by businesses would be greater than that found in 2002, reflecting a general increase in CCTV use.

The research was conducted over separate field trips to King Street. The first of these served as a pilot study: a 20-item survey was tested, the number of institutions and broad extent of CCTV use on the street was assessed, while potential accessibility problems were highlighted. During the pilot visit a number of photographs of CCTV cameras and/or their accompanying signage were taken as data relating to the range of potential legal and privacy issues with which the final audit might need to deal.

The second visit was the main research event. The number of items in the audit was scaled down to cover whether or not the business/institution[9] had CCTV, whether a sign was present, and sign[10] content. Space was also included in the survey for the fieldworker to record anything suspicious, unusual or otherwise interesting in relation to an individual CCTV system. This allowed us to assemble some detailed case studies of problematic use of CCTV and related signage, illustrating how the law is breached and many grey areas where legality is unclear. Finally, details of the type and size of each institution were recorded. In total, data from 140 premises along with eight open-street cameras and one unknown camera system[11] were collected.

It is interesting to note that there was a mixed reception from those business owners and employees encountered during this study. Researchers were met in some cases with very friendly attitudes, but in others by very unreceptive manners. The fieldworker was at one point surrounded by bank managers and asked that photographs taken be deleted, a request we complied with. Interestingly enough, however, there are no laws or signs about taking photographs inside a store, and there is therefore a certain irony around the concerns some CCTV system operators had about surveillance directed at their own surveillance systems!

Findings

One aim of this research was to assess the extent and legality of CCTV usage in King Street and compare it to the situation in Putney High Street, as recorded by McCahill and Norris in 2002.

The Putney High Street sample consisted of 212 premises, compared to 140[11] in the King Street sample. In our study 77 per cent (108) of the premises had a known CCTV system in operation, nearly twice as high as the 40 per cent reported in the earlier study. 59 per cent of the King Street premises with CCTV systems had signs indicating CCTV presence, a slightly higher rate than the 53 per cent reported in earlier work.

In the earlier sample only 22 per cent of CCTV signs were 'in accordance with national laws' (McCahill and Norris 2002: 22). It seems that for the purposes of this earlier study the signs were deemed legally compliant if there was both contact information and 'purpose' provided. In our own research 17 per cent of signs were in accordance with the law in that both contact information and purpose of surveillance were shown on the sign. This means that only about 10 per cent of CCTV systems were legal in the sense of having a sign that included required details, a rate similar to that found in the earlier research (see Table 18.1), while nearly 90 per cent of CCTV systems in both studies were found to be illegal.

Within our sample it was possible to discern which legal requirements signage lacked (Figure 18.1). For those systems with signs, 24 (37 per cent) displayed contact details and 21 (32 per cent) stated the purpose of surveillance. Only 11 systems (17 per cent of those with signs) displayed *both* contact details and purpose.

It was also possible, with our data, to look beyond these basic legal requirements and consider some other legal and non-legal[12] elements of notification that may contribute to the trustworthiness of the information-sharing that occurs with CCTV systems. For example, of the 11 signs that met all legal requirements, only

TABLE 18.1 Comparison of key findings

	King St. (2009)	Putney High St. (2002)
% of businesses operating CCTV	*77%*	*40%*
% of businesses with CCTV displaying signage	*59%*	*53%*
% of signs that meet legal notification requirements	*17%*	*22%*
% of CCTV systems with legally compliant signage	*10%*	*12%*

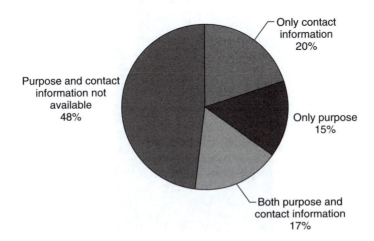

FIGURE 18.1 Availability of contact and purpose information. (% of locations with sign)

two (18 per cent of legal signs, or 3 per cent of all CCTV systems) displayed information relating to a code-of-conduct for the system's operation.[13]

Further examining the concept of *legal* compliance, the criteria we (and McCahill and Norris before us) have employed for assessing 'legality' may not be sufficient to distinguish all compliant and non-compliant systems. One useful aspect to consider here is signage positioning. In the case of CCTV operating in a particular business, it is argued (Lippert 2009a) there needs to be a sign warning persons they are being recorded at the entrance or prior to entering a surveilled area. This is important because without such a sign persons would be unaware of the presence of camera surveillance and therefore have no opportunity to consent. The data subject would also have no information about contacting the data controller or accessing the collected data. In a similar fashion we encountered signs connected to the open-street system in King Street that were three metres off the ground and therefore very difficult to read (Figure 18.2).

These open-street CCTV signs indicated a purpose and identified who was operating the system, but the diminutive text was difficult to see. It is doubtful these signs are readable by vehicle drivers or pedestrians who would be subject to surveillance, and therefore whether the legal duty of notification has been successfully discharged. It is possible to identify other examples where, presence and content of signage aside, contextual issues (such as those relating to the purpose or positioning of the cameras or signs) throw the legality of the system into doubt and undermine the level of trust the system earns. Examples include a camera in a pub

FIGURE 18.2 Open-street CCTV and traffic sign difficult to read from vehicle or pedestrian sidewalk.

FIGURE 18.3   CCTV cameras inside men's washroom over urinals.

FIGURE 18.4   CCTV camera focused into private residence.

positioned inside the men's rest-room (Figure 18.3) and a council-run open-street camera pointed straight into a block of apartments (Figure 18.4).

Discussion

Comparing our research with the previous study conducted by McCahill and Norris (2002), there is a limit to the meaningful conclusions that can be drawn. The two samples are snap-shots of two broadly similar, but separate, London locations. Differences (or similarities) may be due to contextual factors (such as local geographic or social conditions), may reflect changes over the years, or may be there because one or both samples is atypical. Nevertheless the level of CCTV usage by businesses was higher in our study. This is further empirical evidence of a recognized trend that CCTV use in the UK is increasing.[14]

It is also interesting to note the levels of legal compliance of signage found in the two studies. Both report that fewer than 60 per cent of premises with CCTV had any form of CCTV signage. Over 40 per cent of CCTV-using businesses in both research efforts are seemingly not even attempting to comply with the law. Of those premises in each sample with CCTV signage, about four-fifths failed to meet the legal requirements of providing both a reason why surveillance was taking place and the necessary details to identify and contact the data controller. Nearly 90 per cent of CCTV systems in each sample are illegal,[15] which is, in itself, a troubling finding and a major conclusion of this study.

In considering criteria with which systems fail to legally comply and aspects of signage that can be taken as over-compliance, we can apply a more useful analytical framework to the criteria of notification. It is possible, for example, to consider a scale of compliance rather than a simple binary indicator of system legality.

'Scale of compliance'

On one level we can see the scale of compliance as a four-point scale. We can talk about (completely) *non-compliant* systems, *partially compliant* systems, *compliant* systems, and *over-compliant* systems. On another level we can see a more nuanced scale where two of these categories represent ranges rather than points on a scale. The category of partially compliant systems, for example, can be further sub-divided to reflect how many (and which) legal criteria systems lack. In our analysis so far this has included three factors: the presence of signage; whether a sign includes the purpose of surveillance; and whether contact information is provided. Factors such as the positioning of signs or cameras, or the size of signage text, could also be factored into the scale. Similarly, 'over-compliance' may also be further divisible.[16]

One particular example of over-compliance that we did encounter concerned two instances of signs warning of CCTV systems that were not actually present. These examples illustrate how signs themselves can serve a purpose in, for example, deterring crime or otherwise replicating the effects of camera surveillance without a corresponding camera surveillance system (see Lippert 2009b).

In addition to a scale of compliance, a scale of the context of the (CCTV-using) business can also be measured to provide greater insight than through a binary measure of surveillance usage. What has been striking throughout the research conducted here was how a small business with one camera and no recording equipment is treated the same as a large multinational business with high-tech equipment and large databases of aggregated data. Future research could be used to further explore these ideas of compliance within this context; a scale that differentiates a small business from a large business with national or even global reach. The level of compliance can then be examined in relation to the business context, the two scales together (compliance and context) providing a measure of the contextual integrity or trustworthiness of the surveillance. Further research into contextual attributes across jurisdictional boundaries will enable comparative research into the use and effectiveness of regulation.

On a methodological note, more rigorous methods could be applied, for example, cross-checking with surveys distributed to premises owners or managers, Freedom of Information requests, or the use of multiple observers. More importantly, it would be easy to record more variables than we covered in the research, covering both further criteria for legal compliance and indications of size or reach of the business. For example, the positioning of signs and the positioning of cameras, as discussed above, could be added to the compliance scale. As such, this research seeks to extend earlier research by proposing a methodology relevant to and comparable across all contexts and jurisdictions. This is important given the rapid global growth of camera surveillance. With the correct methodological approach, a contextual scale can be created that covers all factors relevant to legal compliance and all factors relevant to contextual integrity: we can compare not only legality (including degrees of compliance and what factors illegal or non-compliant systems lack), we can also compare the contextual integrity of a CCTV system.

Conclusions: towards a framework of contextual integrity

What constitutes legality in relation to public CCTV systems and accompanying notification varies between jurisdictions. Within a given jurisdiction what constitutes legality can also, of course, change over time. Often it may not be clear what the legal standard is, particularly when technology relating to data collection and control evolves more quickly than the laws designed to regulate data and protect privacy (Nissenbaum 2004). This can make direct comparisons on legality difficult and/or meaningless.

Even when legal requirements are met we do not necessarily learn much about standards of notification. In one jurisdiction systems may be legal because legal requirements are minimal or non-existent. In another, a system may be deemed illegal because it falls down on one requirement among many, even though it meets the rest. It is clear that from an objective point of view a system that is illegal because it fails to provide one minor piece of information is better, in terms of what we have here called 'trustworthiness', than a system deemed legal because of minimal legal requirements. Comparisons of legality may well be meaningless when what we are really interested in is the trustworthiness of a system. A methodological approach such as a scale of compliance and a framework of contextual integrity provides methods to evaluate trustworthiness, not only in specific contexts but also for comparison across jurisdictions.

The practices of open-street and business surveillance, which include the monitoring of individuals in public through a variety of media (e.g. video, data monitoring and online tracking), are among the least understood and controversial challenges to privacy and autonomy in an age of information technologies. Research and discussion as to whether or not a legal framework actually reflects the trust concerns surrounding surveillance (not only CCTV systems) are not new. Nissenbaum (2004) extends earlier work on the problem of privacy between public spheres to explain why some of the prominent theoretical approaches to privacy, which were developed over time to meet traditional privacy challenges, yield unsatisfactory conclusions about what is trustworthy in the case of public surveillance.

Ultimately, this research reveals the need for a methodological approach suited to discussions framed around legality, trustworthiness and overall transparency, and that is amenable to comparative and context-specific research. Further research directed at applying and updating these methodologies would be required to understand whether scales of compliance and contextual integrity would address the controversial issues represented by illegal CCTV signage (and in other data protection and privacy situations). Additional research applying this methodology to context-specific discussions of compliance *and* non-context-specific (e.g. comparative) discussions of contextual integrity should, when combined, provide a better indication of 'trustworthiness'. In this way they can be used to extend this research to address issues in data monitoring generally.[17]

Notes

1 Strictly speaking, CCTV is only one form of camera surveillance. The term CCTV is commonly used in the UK and in the literature; the term 'camera surveillance' is used elsewhere in this book. We use the two terms somewhat interchangeably to avoid monotony.

2 After the IRA's terrorist attack on Bishopsgate in central London, a network of cameras known as the 'ring of steel' was assembled to allow the monitoring of all entrances to 'the City', London's central financial district. More recently, and especially in the wake of the 7 July 2005 bombings, CCTV has been touted for its utility in combating terror attacks associated with Islamic fundamentalism.

3 This, of course, assumes that the subject has seen, read and understood the sign, and that the sign provides the necessary information to meet the standard of informed consent.

4 All percentages cited in this chapter are rounded to the nearest whole number.

5 This is assuming that McCahill and Norris were applying the correct legal standards in deciding whether signs in their study were 'in accordance with national laws'.

6 We will shortly report findings of more recent research that shows the situation in the UK has not improved.

7 It can also be applied to other types of surveillance and personal data collection (<http://www.urbaneye.net>).

8 The majority of the institutions were businesses, but there were also council-operated cameras in the sample. We have used the terms 'institution' and 'business' interchangeably from this point onwards.

9 Initially it was hoped that technical data comparable to that recorded by McCahill and Norris would also be collected, but it was more difficult to get these details than information on signage and as such we decided to focus on notification alone.

10 This is unknown in the sense that it could not be ascertained who owned and/or operated the CCTV.

11 Not including the open-street and unknown systems. It is worth noting that although the Putney sample is larger than the King Street sample, the King Street sample has less missing data.

12 Legal and non-legal, that is, in the currently understood legal situation in the UK. What we consider non-legal issues here may be legal issues elsewhere; what we consider legal

issues here may be non-legal issues elsewhere. Further, our interpretation of what is legal or not is based on the interpretation used by McCahill and Norris (2002) – it is possible, as discussed elsewhere, that this interpretation does not do full justice to case-law (see Johnson, this volume). All this demonstrates the utility of a method that goes beyond simple declarations of legality: the comparisons will still be useful even if the law changes.

13 McCahill and Norris produce a table stating that 56 per cent of their CCTV systems had a code-of-conduct, but there is no relevant commentary. It is not clear how this figure is arrived at – it seems likely that this figure reflects the proportion of CCTV system operators who, when asked, claimed the existence of a code of practice rather than the proportion of CCTV systems for which details of a code of practice (and how to consult it) were mentioned on the signage.

14 See, for example, security industry research that reported a compound annual growth rate in video surveillance sales of 4–7 per cent between 2002 and 2009 in the UK (Hayfield 2009).

15 This assumes that the provision of contact information and the reason for surveillance occurring on a sign accompanying the CCTV system are sufficient conditions to ensure legality.

16 It should, of course, be noted that to be *over*-compliant all legal criteria must be met as a minimum requirement – provision of information or consideration that is not legally required does not offset the failure to provide information that is legally required.

17 For example, the same issues observed with illegal CCTV signage are apparent with the online tracking and use of internet protocol (IP) addresses, website cookies and behaviour targeting, where Terms Of Service Agreements and End User Licence Agreements take the place of CCTV signage.

References

Armitage, R. (2002) *To CCTV or Not to CCTV? – A Review of Current Research into the Effectiveness of CCTV Systems in Reducing Crime*, Nacro Community Safety Practice Briefing, London: Nacro.

Bennett, C. (1992) *Regulating Privacy: Data Protection and Public Policy in Europe and the United States*, Cornell: Cornell University Press.

Carroll-Mayer et al. (2008) 'CCTV Identity Management and Implications for Criminal Justice: some considerations', *Surveillance & Society*, 5(1): 33–50.

Cisco (2010) *Cisco Visual Networking Index: Forecast and Methodology, 2009–2014*. Online. Available HTTP: <http://www.cisco.com/en/US/solutions/collateral/ns341/ns525/ns537/ns705/ns827/white_paper_c11-481360_ns827_Networking_Solutions_White_Paper.html>.

Deisman, W. (2003) *CCTV: Literature Review and Bibliography*, Royal Canadian Mounted Police. Online. Available HTTP: <http://dsp-psd.pwgsc.g.ca/Collection/js62-108-2003E.pdf> (accessed 11 November 2009).

Eurobarometer (2008) *Data Protection in the European Union*, T.G. Organization, European Commission, DG Communication – Public Opinion Analysis Sector, 225: 137.

Gill, M. and Spriggs, A. (2005) *Assessing the Impact of CCTV*, Home Office Research Study 292. Online. Available HTTP: <http://www.homeoffice.gov.uk/rds/pdfs05/hors292.pdf> (accessed 11 November 2009).

Gras, M. (2004) 'Legal Regulation of CCTV in Europe', *Surveillance & Society*, 2(2/3): 216–29.

Hayfield, A. (2009) *The EMEA Market for CCTV and Video Surveillance Equipment – 2009 Edition*, email from IMS Research. Sent 29 October 2009.

House of Lords (2009) *Surveillance: Citizens and the State. Constitution Committee Publications Constitution Committee – Second Report.* London: HMSO.

Lippert, R. (2007) 'Open-Street CCTV Canadian Style', *Criminal Justice Matters*, 68(1): 31–2.

Lippert, R. (2009a) 'Camera Surveillance, Privacy Regulation, and 'Informed Consent'', in SCAN, *A Report on Camera Surveillance in Canada: Part One*, Canada: SCAN. Online. Available HTTP: <http://www.surveillanceproject.org/files/SCAN_Report_Phase1_Final_Jan_30_2009.pdf> (accessed 30 December 2009).

Lippert, R. (2009b) 'Signs of the Surveillant Assemblage: Privacy Regulation, Urban CCTV, and Governmentality', *Social & Legal Studies*, 18: 505.

McCahill, M. and Norris, C. (2002) *Working Paper No. 6 CCTV in London: Urban Eye Working Paper Series*, Hull: Centre for Criminology and Criminal Justice, University of Hull. Online. Available HTTP: <http://www.urbaneye.net/results/ue_wp6.pdf> (accessed 30 December 2009).

Nissenbaum, H. (2004) 'Privacy As Contextual Integrity', *Washington Law Review*, 79(1): 119–58.

Organisation for Economic Co-Operation and Development (1980) 'Guidelines on the Protection of Privacy and Transborder Flows of Personal Data. Privacy As Contextual Integrity', *Washington Law Review*. Online. Available HTTP: <http://www.oecd.org/document/53/0,3343,en_2649_34255_15589524_1_1_1_1,00.html> (accessed 11 December 2009).

RNCOS (2010) 'Global CCTV Market Analysis: 2008–2012'. Online. Available HTTP: <http://www.rncos.com/Market-Analysis-Reports/Global-CCTV-Market-Analysis-2008-2012-IM134.htm> (accessed 5 July 2010).

Rotenburg, M. (2008) *Comments of The Electronic Privacy Information Centre To Department of Homeland Security on Docket No. DHS-2007-0076.* Online. Available HTTP: <http://epic.org/privacy/surveillance/epic_cctv_011508.pdf> (accessed 11 December 2009).

SCAN (2009) *Surveillance Camera Awareness Network (SCAN).* Online. Available HTTP: <http://www.surveillanceproject.org/files/SCAN_Report_Phase1_Final_Jan_30_2009.pdf> (accessed 30 December 2009).

19

MITIGATING ASYMMETRIC VISIBILITIES

Towards a signage code for surveillance camera networks

Andrew Clement and Joseph Ferenbok

Introduction

> CCTV signs govern potential surveillant subjects but also CCTV systems themselves.
>
> *(Lippert 2009)*

Conventional practices surrounding the use of video surveillance in public settings pose a significant challenge to established privacy norms and their underlying civil rights principles. For one, video surveillance tends to be shrouded in secrecy. Operators often keep information about their video surveillance schemes away from both the scheme's subjects and the public more generally. Such camera systems enable others to see you, while remaining opaque to external viewers. The result is a dearth of reliable information about how the captured data is used or repurposed. These practices of obscurity prevent subjects and citizens from making reasonable informed decisions about surveilled spaces, about their regulatory and governing practices and about whether such monitoring is appropriate in the first place. The prevailing asymmetric relationships between surveillors and the surveilled undermine the concept of informed consent as well as ideals of democratic transparency. The growing introduction of automated analysis of visual images, rendering the activities of subjects even more highly visible to surveillant authorities while remaining inscrutable in their own operation, exacerbates this asymmetry (Ferenbok and Clement, this volume). Very seldom are there provisions for adequate public oversight and accountability.

This situation has resulted in part because the growth of surveillance camera networks (SCNs) has outpaced regulatory frameworks governing them in both public and publicly accessible private spaces. Where legal frameworks do exist, they generally are constituted through privacy legislation rather than constitutional or criminal law (Gras 2004). In the UK, for example, which, following the 1993 murder of James Bulger, became the most prominent publicly funded 'CCTV state' (Norris and Armstrong 1999), specific protective legislation only came into effect with the 1998 Data Protection Act (Gras 2004).

One means to help redress this unbalanced power dynamic is comprehensive signage systems. Signage plays an important role in regulating a variety of other potentially risky activities, such as vehicular movement, as in the case of traffic signs, and smoking, via cigarette package labels. In the case of SCN regulation, Lippert notes that:

> CCTV signs can govern function creep to the extent signs display a CCTV system's purposes. In so doing, signs limit cameras from being used for other purposes if subjects gain awareness of new functions and their absence from the text of CCTV signs.
>
> *(Lippert 2009: 516)*

Despite these possibilities, however, when it comes to providing surveillance subjects with meaningful information, signage in many jurisdictions, and Canada in particular, falls short, apparently in large part because there is currently little regulation or oversight (Dawson et al. 2009; Deisman et al. 2009; Lippert 2009). Despite strong arguments that signs are a necessary and integral part of the SCN assemblage (Lippert 2009), the sparse research available suggests that signage implementation, design and oversight vary regionally, but are generally inadequate.

This chapter seeks to help fill these gaps in research and regulation by analysing the shortcomings of current signage practices and offering prototypes of signage schemes that address the key privacy and governance issues. The chapter is divided into two parts. The first looks at prevailing practices around video surveillance signage and the regulations and guidelines that govern them. The second part introduces sample prototypes of three signage schemes that are not only designed to enforce compliance with privacy legislation, but also to help to foster an informed, rights-aware citizenry equipped to hold surveilling organizations to public account. While the focus is mainly on Canadian settings, the findings are broadly applicable to the many other jurisdictions with privacy laws similarly based on fair information practice principles.

Part I – Prevailing Signage Practices

1.1 Current SCN signage in Canada

Anyone looking for video surveillance in Canada's major metropolitan centres will have little difficulty finding cameras overseeing stores, office block lobbies and shopping malls, and peering onto public sidewalks and parks.[1] Some cameras are quite visible, placed so that it would be hard not to notice them. Most, however, are more discreet – small black domes dotted across ceilings along with other infrastructural paraphernalia such as lighting, electrical wiring, smoke detectors, sprinklers and ventilation. A first impression is that signs notifying people about the cameras are considerably harder to spot. Most cameras have no signs in their immediate vicinity. Where present, and in contrast to the relatively uniform appearance of the cameras, the signs are varied and far from standardized. Such signs are remarkably uninformative, in that they all give very little indication about what is going on behind the lens. The more fulsome signs tend to be those operated by public bodies. Cameras belonging to private firms appear less likely to be signed and when signs exist, they either exhibit blunt warnings or, less frequently, claim virtues resulting from the cameras such as customer protection and lowered prices. Someone familiar with the Personal Information Privacy and Electronic Documents Act (PIPEDA) could immediately draw the conclusion that many businesses do not comply with Canadian privacy law.

These first impressions are confirmed by other video surveillance researchers in Canada (Deisman et al. 2009; Lippert 2009), as well as preliminary results of a study led by the authors (Clement, Ferenbok and Plataniotis 2010). The following is a sampling of signs displayed at major retail stores in Toronto, Canada. They are part of a much larger corpus of images collected since December 2009 and viewable publicly on the Canadian Surveillance Camera (aka CCTV) Signage Group Flickr page.[2]

In the store from which the photo in Figure 19.1a was taken, the sign(s) are located beside a fire exit – not likely the first place that customers would look for information necessary for informed consent – and one of the signs is obscured by shelving. The stated purposes of the video surveillance in this case are customer protection, 'low prices and efficient customer service'. However, no information is given about how the video actually helps to protect the customer. For example, is there a live agent or analytic algorithm monitoring the video to provide assistance in case of medical emergencies? The smaller text at the bottom reads: '[Tape Recorders] provide the evidence we need to prosecute criminal offenders', suggesting the purpose of capturing forensic evidence, rather than providing a real-time response for customer protection. The language of the sign implies that lower prices and customer service are supported by reduced shoplifting resulting from the prosecution of offenders. The sign in Figure 19.1a does not mention or make clear whether the information is used for any other purposes, how long the information is retained, with whom it may be shared, who is responsible, whom to contact, or any number of other considerations important to fair information practices.

In the store featured in Figure 19.1b, the sign rationalizes video surveillance by claiming that CCTV monitoring, in conjunction with trained associates, provides 'customers with the best possible value and [ensures] a safe and secure shopping environment'. However, parallel to the situation in Figure 19.1a, the mechanisms for achieving the stated purposes are not identified. Similarly, in Figure 19.1c, people at that particular retailer are apparently being monitored because the company 'cares' about the safety and security of its valued customers. Just as with the other

(a)

(b)

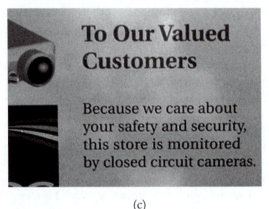

(c)

FIGURE 19.1 Retail video surveillance signs.

two examples, no specific details are provided about the underlying information practices, contrary to the principles of openness and transparency, to established privacy norms and to specific provisions of prevailing privacy law.

The lack of information on existing signs, or the complete absence of signs in many cases, undermines one of the central claims often used to justify video surveillance: that they accomplish deterrence. Although research calls into question arguments about the effectiveness of the cameras as a deterrence measure (Norris, this volume; Deisman et al. 2009), the espoused goal of deterrence should nevertheless provide a strong rationale for visible and effective signage. However, unless individuals know that they are being monitored, the deterrence argument cannot be easily supported. It is ironic then, from a surveillance proponent's perspective, that video surveillance signage is on the whole rare, uninformative, non-compliant with regulations, often located in obscure locations, and mainly text-based and therefore of limited accessibility to non-English-reading populations. The status quo seems to be that informative signs are severely lacking.

1.3 Canadian SCN signage law

In Canada, the collection of information for commercial purposes about identifi-able individuals is governed by the Personal Information Protection and Electronic Documents Act (PIPEDA) 2000, or its provincial counterparts. While PIPEDA makes no explicit reference to video surveillance or related signage, it is clear that all images of a person, regardless of location, if captured with sufficient quality to convey personal information, are subject to PIPEDA. When a video camera captures an image relating to an identifiable 'individual's race, colour, national or ethnic origin, sex, and age' its contents will be 'considered *personal information* under PIPEDA' (2000). PIPEDA obligates companies under Schedule 1, section 5, clause 4.8, the 'Openness Principle', to 'make *readily available to individuals specific information* about its policies and practices relating to the management of personal information' (emphasis added). The first sub-section, 4.8.1, spells out in more detail how this notification is to be provided:

> Organizations *shall* be open about their policies and practices with respect to the management of personal information. Individuals *shall* be able to acquire information about an organization's policies and practices without unreason-able effort. This information *shall* be made available in a form that is generally understandable.
>
> *(2000, emphasis added)*

The use of the word 'shall' in both the statement of the Openness Principle and sub-section 4.8.1 is significant, because it indicates a legally enforceable require-ment. The standard of 'without unreasonable effort' is also significant in the context of video surveillance operations, since individuals often casually walk into surveil-led spaces and thus the information should be easily at hand and quickly understood by people with a diverse range of perceptual and linguistic abilities. People could not reasonably be expected to go to much trouble to seek out information about spaces that they enter casually while going about their everyday affairs.

Further notification requirements are indicated by several other PIPEDA Prin-ciples: principle 9 of PIPEDA – Individual Access – states that every citizen has the right to request their personal information and 'shall be informed of the existence, use, and disclosure of his or her personal information and shall be given access to that information.' Principle 2 – Identifying Purposes – states that, 'The purposes for which personal information is collected shall be identified by the organization at or before the time the information is collected', and Principle 3 – Consent – states that, 'The knowledge and consent of the individual are required for the collection, use, or disclosure of personal information, except where inappropriate.'[3]

Signs posted in the vicinity of cameras represent an obvious way for organiza-tions to inform individuals about video information collection by surveillance cam-eras and make available information about their practices. Lippert (2009) notes that 'Signage is the only relatively permanent form of site-specific notification of 'open-street' CCTV surveillance in Canadian cities' (509). This justifies closer scrutiny of how, where and why surveillance notification is deployed.

1.4 Signage guidelines

As there is no specific reference to camera surveillance in privacy legislation, Canadian privacy commissioners have developed several sets of guidelines for video surveillance in public places. In 2001, the Information and Privacy Commissioner of Ontario (IPC) published *Guidelines for Using Video Surveillance Cameras in Public Places* (IPC 2001). These guidelines are aimed at provincial public sector installations and advocate the placement of signs to notify the public when they are entering a surveilled zone. Lippert (2009) suggests that the requirement for signage is significant 'since it demands CCTV signage be a means of notifying the citizenry not merely of a surveillance camera's presence nearby, but also *why* it is in place, *how* more information about its purposes can be gained, and *how* a complaint can be initiated if necessary' (2009: 509). However, the guidelines are 'intended to assist organizations' with the deployment of their surveillance systems and are not binding or enforceable.

The IPC Guidelines offer public bodies in Ontario this template for a video surveillance sign:

> Attention
> This Area May Be Monitored by Video Surveillance Cameras.
>
> *(CCTV)*
>
> The personal information collected by the use of the CCTV at this site is collected under the authority of (an Act) and (by-law). This information is used for the purpose of promoting public safety and reduction of crime at this site.
>
> Any questions about this collection can be directed to the Manager of (Department) at (phone number), (City Hall address) (e-mail).
>
> *(IPC 2001: Appendix A)*

This template has seen adoption in public organizations such as the Toronto Transit Commission and Toronto City Hall. These signs, however, have several key limitations. As Lippert (2009) has noted, the above example is typical of textual signs that systematically exclude the illiterate, visually impaired, those less likely to be able to read English (or French) like tourists, immigrants, and youth. But perhaps equally as troublesome as the disenfranchisement of various groups is the lack of any mechanism for oversight and regulation. The lack of signage that adequately communicates complaint procedures 'helps explain why from 2001–2007 the Ontario privacy commission received only one complaint about "open-street" CCTV and not a single legal order concerning "open-street" CCTV signage was issued' (Lippert 2009: 514). Although the signage template above superficially informs sign readers that subjects may be monitored, it gives no indication of the type of monitoring employed. Nor are subjects told if the monitoring is live, in real-time, by human agents, or mediated by computers. Furthermore, the template says nothing about system capabilities, storage duration, third-party access, emergency response, and so on. Because the template is silent on any specific capability of the SCN it does not require the organization to update or revise the wording when system practices or technologies change. This means, for example, that there will be nothing to alert subjects when video analytic techniques such as facial recognition are incorporated in the behind-the-lens processing.

The Office of the Privacy Commissioner of Canada (OPC) has also issued three sets of video surveillance guidelines. The first, in 2006, is *Guidelines for the Use of Video Surveillance of Public Places by Police and Law Enforcement Authorities*. Recognizing that 'Video surveillance of public places subjects everyone to scrutiny, regardless of whether they have done anything to arouse suspicion', the OPC stresses in guideline 7:

> The public should be informed with clearly written signs at the perimeter of surveillance areas, which advise that the area is or may be under surveillance, and indicate who is responsible for the surveillance, including who is responsible for compliance with privacy principles, and who can be contacted to answer questions or provide information about the system.
>
> *(OPC 2006)*

Another set of *Guidelines for Overt Video Surveillance in the Private Sector* (OPC 2008), developed jointly with British Columbia and Alberta Commissioners, relates more directly to PIPEDA. In the FAQ section they note:

> **Q**. Should we post signs that there are cameras in operation?
>
> **A**. Yes. Most privacy laws require the organization conducting video surveillance to post a clear and understandable notice about the use of cameras on its premises to individuals whose images might be captured by them, *before* these individuals enter the premises. This gives people the option of not entering the premises if they object to the surveillance. Signs should include a contact in case individuals have questions or if they want access to images related to them.
>
> *(OPC 2008, emphasis in original)*

The emphasis on information that allows citizens to make informed decisions and provide informed consent when entering surveilled spaces is particularly significant to the discussion of signage here. Research findings discussed below suggest that the current practices do not facilitate informed consent.

Finally, in 2009, the OPC published *Guidance on Covert Video Surveillance in the Private Sector* (OPC 2009). Particularly relevant to the present discussion is that the guidelines consider 'video surveillance to be covert when the individual is not made aware of being watched', and that, while justifiable under some circumstances, 'covert video surveillance must be considered only in the most limited cases' (OPC 2009), pointing again to the importance and significance of location-based signage at the point of surveillance. In short, these guidelines all draw on principles of transparency and openness, reinforcing the privacy principles underlining PIPEDA.

1.5 Signage regimes in other jurisdictions

The UK is often used to exemplify the modern surveillance state (Norris and Armstrong 1999). According to Cole (2004), 'the expansion of surveillance in the UK took place with little or no regulation until March 2000, when the Data Protection Act came into force' (2004: 44). The UK code, in keeping with the First Data Protection Principle, requires signs to inform the public that they are entering a surveillance zone. The code also specifies the information that should be contained on the sign. As Cole (2004) reports, a sign should indicate the person or organization responsible for the surveillance, and the purpose of the surveillance, and provide contact information of someone who can provide details about the surveillance scheme. This is essentially just the same information as specified in the IPC guidelines, which, as discussed above, lack many other necessary elements for proper informed consent. However, as research by Lizar and Potter (this volume) indicates, compliance with even this minimal standard is far from universal.

Gras (2004) offers a comparison of CCTV signage across Europe. In 2004, she noted that, 'Denmark certainly has stronger regulation than Britain. CCTV surveillance is generally forbidden there' (Gras 2004). As Norris (this volume) notes, CCTV was slower to penetrate the Scandinavian countries, although some public cameras have been introduced more recently in Denmark and its neighbours. In Germany, significant regulation of CCTV surveillance also exists. German regulations stress proportionality and attempt to weigh the tension between property rights and the rights of individuals. This system of regulation appears to force parties (such as the police) to justify the deployment and continued use of surveillance systems. Gras (2004: 220) notes,

> secret CCTV would be permissible if used to take immediate steps and to prevent crime. Where this purpose is not served, individual privacy is more important. Where CCTV is used more as a form of entrapment to secure evidence, the courts will declare this use unfair and illegal, if no warning of potential surveillance is given.

If this were to occur it might provide corporations the impetus to rethink their video surveillance policies.

Although covert surveillance, without signage or notification, would thus be considered inadmissible or illegal in Germany, legal regulation seems to use *ex-ante* legal thinking by suggesting that 'secret CCTV would be permissible if used to take immediate steps and to prevent crime' (Gras 2004: 220). Signage, therefore, is seen as significantly 'lowering the level of interference with constitutional rights CCTV surveillance is seen as causing' (Gras 2004: 225). This position implies that 'crime prevention' requires live monitoring, to stop an imminent crime from happening. This argument suggests that in order for an operator in Germany to claim crime prevention as a purpose of a SCN, the system must include the possibility of immediate intervention. This argument is even stronger when applied to a stated purpose of 'public safety'. If an operator states the purpose of a SCN installation is, in part, 'public safety' then they have to have real-time (human and/or automated) viewing and a capacity for timely intervention. Extending this to our purposes, any proposed signage scheme, with purposes of either 'public safety' or 'crime prevention' should coincide with real-time monitoring.[4] Conversely, SCN operators cannot adequately justify claims of 'crime prevention' or 'public safety' as purposes with systems that only record.

Similar to the regulation in Germany, 'the law in France, Sweden and the Netherlands requires that attention be drawn to CCTV surveillance by signs placed outside of the surveillance area so that a person be made aware of entering it' (225). The placement of signage outside areas under surveillance speaks to the idea of implied consent, or that a citizen, being made aware of the surveillance, is thereby given the chance to choose whether to enter the space or not. Of course this point remains somewhat contentious, not only because the legal concept of consent is complicated, but also because the cost and inconvenience of avoiding some surveillance zones is arguably unacceptably high: for example, those who need to travel by train for work are given little choice but to enter the surveilled space of a railway station, even if they do not consent to the surveillance there.

1.6 Summary and implications

The above discussion demonstrates that in Canada there is a clear lack of appropriate video surveillance signage, oversight and regulation. This inadequate signage is a serious, publicly visible contravention of fair information practices as well as Canadian privacy guidelines and legislation, particularly that covering the private sector. Other jurisdictions appear to be in a similar position, though in some cases surveillance practices and signage requirements are more rigorously defined and enforced. This situation is exacerbated by the absence of public debate and discussion around surveillance camera issues. The need for more public engagement is clearly evident; as is the need for more open and transparent practices supported by signage that attempts to mitigate the existing asymmetry in the surveillance of public spaces.

Part II – Towards a citizens' rights signage scheme

Supported by the motivations, principles and practices discussed above, the second part of this chapter explores our proposed video surveillance signage schemes. It looks at how other signage practices and domains have informed our design, sketches a basic use scenario that the principal scheme aims to address, outlines the main features of the scheme and presents our sample prototype signs intended for various use contexts.

2.1 Signage regimes in other domains

There are several distinct, although not necessarily mutually exclusive, categories of signs: orientational, informational, directional, identificational, ornamental and statutory or regulatory signage (Sims 1991). Iconic signs are generally more accessible than text-based signs for the greater population. Visual cues offer quick access to information once the icons are commonly recognizable, and with good design, icons are more easily learned. To make images more accessible designers often use icons. Simple icons generally use high contrast to make signs more legible from a distance. But there is a danger with over-simplification, as it can undermine the goals of the signage system leading to vague or muddled readings. Misinterpretation can be mitigated by using combinations of icons and written text. Good design also allows for communication of complex information across cultures, languages and varying levels of literacy.

Signage must take into account target populations, and especially populations that may be in danger of becoming disenfranchised by the systems. For example, signage that is not supplemented by other modes of communication becomes inaccessible for the visually impaired. Signs that are text-based may present challenges for illiterate or non-English/French reading audiences. Commonly, good sign design considers a number of key general and contextual factors. Primary considerations include legibility, colour, material, size, location, positioning, background and ambient lighting (Sims 1991). Legibility often includes concerns such as letterform, contrast and visibility at a distance. Colour has significant symbolic meaning that is often culturally and contextually specific. Further issues include: Is the copy readable? Does the sign answer the design brief? Is it highly legible? Is it appropriate for the target audience? Does it promote the 'right' image? Is the information given a proper degree of visual emphasis? Does it comply with signage legislation? (Sims 1991). These questions are useful not only for the design process but also for subsequent evaluation of the signage. Within Canada, and more generally around the globe, video surveillance signage is varied and far from user-centric, so other, better-developed signage domains can likely offer some valuable lessons.

2.2 Signage characteristics

Cole (2004) classifies signs based, at least in part, on their mode of address. Or, put another way, signs can be analysed according to whom they seem to address or hail. The 'dispassionate' sign attempts to convey the presence of surveillance as simply a matter of fact; the 'inclusionary' sign attempts to hail the 'good' citizenry by including them in promises of safety, security and lower prices; 'exclusionary' signs attempt to repel the other, the criminal or undesirable subset of the population to 'warn' them about the presence and potential repercussions of video surveillance; some signs are double-coded, targeting both desirable and undesirable populations simultaneously. Cole (2004) argues that with its ideological targeting of both the 'public' and the 'other', 'signage now conspires with the surveillance itself to amplify the panoptical effect that many have [been solely] ascribed to CCTV' (2004: 14).

Our aim is to develop a signage scheme that principally hails the surveilled subject as a rightful citizen, in notable contrast to the more typical 'suspicious intruder' (exclusionary) or neo-liberal 'informed consumer' (inclusionary) approaches that Lippert (2009) highlights. We do this in terms of signage content by supplementing the information required for the informed consenting consumer with resources for exercising their rights and for holding the surveillance operators more accountable for their practices. In particular, we provide access to more comprehensive details of the surveillance scheme as a whole, reminders of citizen rights, the procedures for filing complaints and the means for connecting with others who may have similar concerns.

For our visual presentation purposes, we emphasize a few key criteria in our proposed signage scheme: legibility, colour, visibility and location. To promote legibility, we employ high-contrast backgrounds and sans serif fonts that are large enough to be seen from a distance. Following the Vienna Convention on Road Signs and Signals (1968), our signs mainly use black or red text and symbols on yellow or white grounds. We also take into consideration the location and positioning of the signs. If the signs are located by fire exits or obscured by shelving (see Figure 19.1a), they may merely serve as an ironic, theatrical nod towards compliance. Physical signs are best placed at eye level starting just beyond the outer edge of a surveillance zone, and positioned strategically within it.

So we envision two particular types of situational contexts: orientational/informational and statutory/regulatory. The first situation, orientational/informational, requires signage that provides just-in-time information that allows people to determine how to orient themselves in a particular surveillance context. This category, like road signs, requires quick, legible and digestible information at the periphery of a surveillance area that provides useful information to someone about to enter. For those who wish to obtain 'deeper' information about the surveillance system and its compliance and governance, the statutory or regulatory signage includes more extensive information about contacts, policies and capacities of the system. There will be fewer of these signs, but their full content should also be readily available via the web.

2.3 Basic use scenario

We base the design of our surveillance camera network signage scheme on the scenario of a person walking along a public street or a private retail space normally accessible to the public, who encounters a commercially operated video surveillance zone. This provides a good starting point for analysis, as this is the most common site for people to come under video surveillance.

Anyone concerned for their privacy or safety is immediately faced with the decision of whether to proceed into or avoid the surveilled area. She could plausibly ask many of the following questions: Am I safe here? Who is operating the cameras and responsible for this operation? Can they be trusted (i.e. are they a legitimate operator, do they have a legal authority to operate, do they have a good record of legal compliance and civil respect)? What's the purpose of the cameras? What can the cameras see? What is the scope of the surveilled area? When am I inside the area and when am I beyond it?

She may also want to know more about the nature of the surveillance: Is the monitoring live or automated? Is someone watching right now? Who are they? Where are they? Are they trained and competent? Will I get help if something adverse happens to me (e.g. fall down, feel ill, get mugged, etc.)? Whom do they report to? Am I being recorded? Who views the recordings? What is done with them? How might I be affected?

It can be reasonably expected, based on the Openness Principle, that the operator of the SCN should readily provide answers to any of these questions. PIPEDA in particular, as noted above, requires organizations to 'make readily available to individuals specific information about its policies and practices relating to the management of personal information'. Furthermore, 'individuals shall be able to acquire information about an organization's policies and practices without unreasonable effort. This information shall be made available in a form that is generally understandable' (2000).

2.4 Proposed signage schemes

Applying the principles of openness and informed consent to this use scenario helps determine the main features of our proposed signage schemes that, as discussed above, hail the surveillance subject as a rightful citizen. There are two distinct, but consistent, knowledge interests that need to be served. The first is that an individual data subject (e.g. consumer) should be in a position to readily find answers to the questions posed in the scenario above. In particular, such a person should be forewarned of an upcoming surveillance area and its characteristics. Signs should be legible at walking speed and readily provide the individual with sufficient detail to make a rapid, informed decision about whether to enter the space, how to behave within it, and where to turn for assistance. If the individual enters the surveillance zone, she should receive reminders of the basic features of the surveillance while she remains within the zone. If she wants to learn more about the surveillance operation, she should have little difficulty in finding signs that provide full statutorily required details. These signs serve a dual purpose in the sense that they also help regulate the operator by enforcing the public disclosure of video surveillance capacities, purposes and infrastructure as a whole.

A second public interest served by organizational openness and transparency is that of good governance. Citizens seeking to exercise their democratic rights effectively, whether acting individually or collectively through civil society organizations, also need to be well-informed about how organizations process personal (visual) data – the risks, the safeguards, and the opportunities as well as the remedial possibilities. Likely the best way to provide this information is through a website containing the full statutorily required details, and that facilitates the making of formal requests to the responsible organization where further information is required.

While our principal focus is on the signage that an SCN owner/operator should post, there are occasions when the regulator may need to post their own signs to alert (potential) surveillance subjects of the legal status of the operation. Other parties may also post signs in a more ad hoc fashion to draw attention to concerns they have about the surveillance operations. Therefore our proposed scheme includes not only the signage posted by operators, but also signage posted by regulatory enforcement agents as well as signs posted by individual citizens or civil society groups concerned with public policy issues and non-compliant operators. We consider prototypical examples of these three types of sign in turn.

2.5 Operator-posted notification

The principal means to address the two main knowledge interests is to require SCN operators to post a variety of situationally appropriate signs around the periphery of and throughout their surveillance zones. We propose four specific types of location-specific, operator-posted physical signs: surveillance border notification, surveilled area signs, camera labels and full disclosure signs. In addition to these we propose an operator-hosted online portal accessible via a web or smartphone app interface. After enumerating the various icons and their meanings used in the signage scheme, we describe each of these sign types in the order that a surveillance subject will most likely encounter them.

Surveillance camera network signage icons

In order rapidly to convey key information about the purposes and operational characteristics of particular surveillance camera network operations, we have developed a set of high-visibility icons to be used consistently throughout the signage scheme (see Figure 19.2).

This is a partial list covering only some of the more common surveillance scheme characteristics. Other icons in development include those to alert surveillance subjects of various other purposes and video analytics capabilities (e.g. facial/body recognition, facial/body encryption and facial/body blurring).

Surveillance border notification

The first notification of a video surveillance operation that a person encounters should be a border sign like that shown in Figure 19.3. It compactly depicts all the key informational elements on which to make an informed decision about whether

Toronto City University

The area indicated in the accompanying map is monitored by a Video Surveillance Network (VSN, aka CCTV) under the control of the University of Toronto and operated by Chubb, and is in compliance with the relevant regulations of the Office of the Privacy Commissioner.

THIS AREA IS UNDER VIDEO SURVEILLANCE

 Crime Prevention/Prosecution
Criminal investigation and prosecution - In the case of suspected criminal activity, the incident will be reported to law enforcement authorities, who may request access to stored images.

 Public Safety
Emergency response in case of a personal safety incident

 24hr Live Monitoring
The video images are monitored by trained staff 24 hours/day, 7 days a week.

 3 day Image Storage
The stored video images are deleted after 3 days, except when there is duly authorized investigation of an reported incident in which case they are retained only as long as needed for the investigation. All such retentions are logged and reported in the annual audits.

 Face Recognition
No automated facial recognition

 Face Blurring

 Image Encryption
To preserve anonymity, human body images are encrypted before storage, and only de-crypted in case of investigation of serious incident by senior law enforcement authorities. All such de-anonymizations are logged and reported in the annual audits.

To report an incident call 800-555-9999. If an emergency, call 911. To view our privacy and video surveillance policies, request a copy of your personal images, register a complaint, review our annual audits or ask a question, visit: http://organization.ca/videosurveillance. Questions can also be directed to the Chief Privacy Officer, phone 800-555-1000 or PrivacyOffice@organization.com. If this does not produce a satisfactory response, you may register a complaint with the Office of Privacy Commissioner - http://opc.ca

FIGURE 19.2   Index of icons.

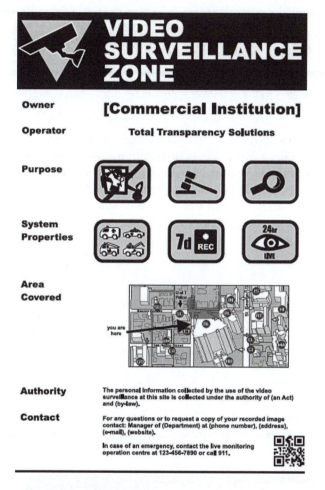

FIGURE 19.3   Sample operator-posted border sign.

or not to enter a surveilled area. In particular, it contains the following elements in text and/or iconic form:

Organization(s) responsible

Purposes/justification for scheme – crime detection, prosecution, forensic analysis?

Properties of the surveillance scheme – emergency response, seven-day recording, 24/7 live monitoring

Area covered by the surveillance scheme

Authority to operate

Responsible person, with contact details

Procedure for accessing or correcting one's personal record

Oversight of scheme – independent third-party oversight

2D barcode providing link to surveillance scheme informational portal website

FIGURE 19.4   Sample operator-posted border stripe.

In our SCN signage scheme, this border sign may be supplemented by yellow stripe with embedded logos and icons that depict the ownership, operator, purposes and properties of the surveillance installation, as shown in Figure 19.4. This strip would be applied to existing surfaces (e.g. sidewalks and walls) along the periphery of the surveilled area. Border and area notification should also be done digitally: for example, a mobile app designed for the purpose tells the subject when approaching a virtual 'yellow stripe'.

Area signs

Small signs scattered throughout the surveilled area would incorporate key icons and contact information. These signs would be placed along trafficked paths and near gathering points within the surveilled area. The image in Figure 19.5 provides a sample of what this type of sign might look like.

Camera labels

Each surveillance camera should have its own identification sign that gives the unique camera ID and key specifications (recording and live monitoring) of the

FIGURE 19.5   Sample operator-posted surveillance area sign.

FIGURE 19.6 Sample operator-posted surveillance camera sign.

camera. The 2D barcode links the camera ID to the portal website where more information about the camera and the SCN is provided (see Figure 19.6).

Full disclosure signs

Placed at prominent points of entrance are larger information signs with full statutorily required details about the surveillance scheme.

These posters incorporate in one place all the information about icons, explanations, coverage map, regulations, authority, access procedures and contact info contained in the various other signs.

Portal website

Integrating all of these forms of signage and ensuring transparent communication will be an online interface that provides full, up-to-date disclosure, including policy documents, annual reports and independent audits about the SCN.

Any such scheme depends on clear, intuitively accessible icons, sensitive to context and culture, that have been tested and iteratively developed. The design of any such system requires incremental refinements based on feedback from the various stakeholders.

2.6 Regulatory enforcement agent-posted signage

In many areas involving public safety or protection, it is common for regulatory or independent certification bodies to require enterprises to post signage of their own creation indicating that the specified operation complies with official standards. Examples include elevators, commercial weight scales, fire extinguishers, and many other devices in common usage, which typically display a certificate of compliance. Often included in the signage is an expiry date, by which time some form of examination and recertification is needed. There is currently no such certification requirement for surveillance camera networks, at least in Canada, but it is not inconceivable that if the widespread non-compliance of current video surveillance with privacy regulations and guidelines becomes better known and public pressure is brought to bear, then the current regulatory bodies will become more active in this area. While this may not be an immediate prospect, it might be helpful to suggest what a model of greater regulatory oversight would involve. One approach is showing samples of the official signage that operators need to display. The signage scheme of the Food Premises Inspection and Disclosure System at the City of Toronto Health Department, better known as DineSafe, provides such an example. The most publicly visible indicator of the inspection and certification programme is the prominent status sign that appears in every restaurant's front window alerting prospective diners of the current state of compliance with the Ontario Food Premises Regulation. A green PASS sign indicates a satisfactory inspection; a yellow CONDITIONAL PASS sign indicates a recent health inspection that found 'Significant Infractions', needing to be corrected within 24–48 hours; and a red CLOSED sign indicates that one or more 'Crucial Infractions' were observed during an inspection, and the establishment ordered to close. An extensive website[5] explains the signage as well as reports on the inspection and compliance history of every restaurant in Toronto.

Taking this as a model and applying it to private sector surveillance camera networks suggests the relevant Privacy Commissioner would make periodic inspections of video surveillance operations and require the prominent posting of one of the following three compliance status indicators (see Figure 19.7):

Pass (green) – meets the relevant privacy law requirements

Probation (yellow) – doesn't meet the relevant privacy law requirements, but is given a certain period to meet the standard before being shut down.

FIGURE 19.7 Sample regulator-posted compliance status signs.

Stopped (red) following a probationary period, or in the case of severe violation of the privacy standards, the scheme is ordered to cease operations.

As with DineSafe, these signs could be integrated with a website that tracks (non)compliance of surveillance camera network operators, enabling relatively easier public oversight that would help mitigate the current asymmetries of visibility.

While the Canadian privacy commissioners currently have audit powers that they could use to conduct inspections of video surveillance operations, they would also need considerable additional resources to carry out inspections on a systematic basis. They could seek an increase in the funding they receive from Parliament, perhaps through a licence fee for video surveillance operations. While such a fee would be a small fraction of the cost of the installation and operation of a surveillance camera network, businesses would certainly actively resist the additional expense, as well as the heightened regulatory oversight more generally. Given the current neo-liberal political climate, it should be expected that they would receive political support in opposing this stiffer form of regulation. It might need major popular resistance to the current video surveillance practices to overcome these obstacles. Suffice to say, such measures are not imminent. However, this does not mean there is nothing that can be done along these lines in terms of greater external compliance monitoring and notification. We turn now to the possibility of a citizen-initiated inspection and signage scheme.

2.7 Citizen-posted signs

While most of any surveillance camera network operation is out of sight, it is often the case that some cameras are visible, at least alerting passersby to the existence of the operation. It is then relatively easy to determine whether there is signage, and if so, whether it meets the standards specified in the privacy commissioners' guidelines. With modest instruction in the requirements of PIPEDA, anyone interested could determine whether the signage associated with a specific video surveillance operation is minimally PIPEDA-compliant or not. This provides the basis for an individual to file a complaint with the appropriate privacy commissioner. To give this more visibility and weight, the complainant could alert others by posting their own sign, as seen in Figure 19.8. Based on the bright yellow parking tickets dreaded by Toronto drivers, this 'Video Surveillance Infraction Notice' identifies the organization responsible, the time, date and place of the infraction, and the specific shortcomings of the signage. Details of the infraction, and preferably a photo of the notice, the issuer and the premises, could be posted to a website similar to the DineSafe site or the Flickr group mentioned above.

The accessibility of an independently maintained website with details of SCN operations and their apparent compliance status by the growing number of smartphones offers a new way of informing people of the proximity to and characteristics of video surveillance zones. Those people with GPS-enabled smartphones with a specially designed application could be automatically alerted by their device as they

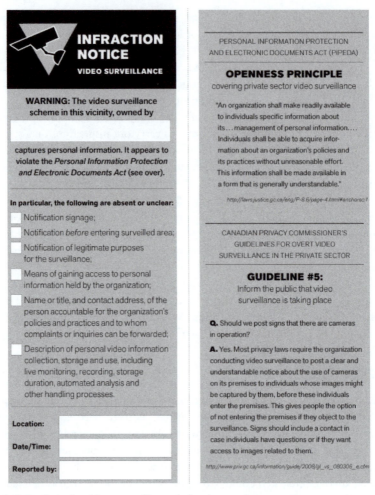

FIGURE 19.8 Sample video surveillance infraction notice.

approach an SCN operation that had previously been registered in the database (see Figure 19.9). Where physical signs have been posted with the 2D barcodes, as shown in the various sample images above, the app could read the barcode and thereby expedite access to the information about the particular installation. The app would also encourage contributions to the database through the uploading of photos and other relevant information. In this way, the signage would become usefully hybridized across physical and digital media and offer a means for public 'crowdsourcing' of (non)compliance reporting data as well as serve as an educational and mobilizing medium.

The specific design features of this hybridized signage scheme will be important factors in attracting and maintaining the active voluntary participation needed to achieve these oversight, educational and political purposes. This will require

FIGURE 19.9   Sample civic alert signs on GPS smartphone.

iterative prototyping with interested individuals, as well as a strategy for wider public involvement.

2.8 Future work

The signage schemes sketched above are still at a rudimentary, conceptual, prototype stage. The images presented here are intended mainly as an illustration of a particular approach to the regulation of SCNs, one that stresses making their presence and operational characteristics more publicly visible. Clearly much work remains to be done to give substance to the proposed approach. A next stage will be to test these prototypes in workshop and field settings. We will be interested to see how people react to the potential value of making SCNs more legible and accountable, as well as to the specific design features, such as the readability of the signs and the icons in particular. We also want to see how retailers and other private sector operators react to the possibility of posting much more explicit signs about their SCN operations. While we anticipate that most will not welcome our approach, based on preliminary findings of fieldwork already underway, we have good reason to believe we will find a few smaller retail operations that would be willing to try out our prototype signs. We will assess how people interact with the signs, and use the feedback to refine the scheme. This will likely require several iterations until we gain a clear sense of what is workable.

It would also be interesting to see how the proposed signage scheme fits in a range of settings and jurisdictions, which, as we have seen above, vary considerably in terms of rules and cultural norms. While the signage scheme has been designed specifically with the Canadian commercial SCNs and legislation in mind, it should be adaptable to other jurisdictions, given that they suffer similar problems of inadequate signage, and that the PIPEDA legislation is considered similar to the EU Data Protection Directive.

Conclusion

The ongoing rapid expansion of video surveillance largely unfettered by effective regulation and public oversight poses a significant challenge to privacy and other civil liberties. The need for action is made more urgent as operators incorporate increasingly powerful digital techniques, such as video analytics (see Ferenbok and Clement, this volume), behind the scenes. This situation calls on those of us concerned with this development to consider the various means to intervene in the process and ameliorate the likely consequences. There may be no turning back the tidal wave of video surveillance systems proliferating across public and quasi-public spaces, but how the surveillance technologies and practices are regulated, and how individuals can learn and exercise their rights in relation to them, still remain to be negotiated between citizens, policy-makers, politicians and surveillors.

Lippert (2009) has identified signage as one aspect of video surveillance assemblages (Haggerty and Ericson 2000) that can help regulate not only surveillance subjects, but also the surveillance assemblages themselves. Signs, both physical and digital, may prove one point of intervention that can inform citizens of their rights as well as bring operators to account.

This chapter has considered what a privacy-oriented, rightful-citizen signage scheme might look like in a Canadian context. We examined how legislation such as the Personal Information Protection and Electronic Documents Act (PIPEDA) and related guidelines can inform video surveillance signage in public spaces. From this analysis we sketched the key elements that a national video surveillance scheme should include and proposed illustrative prototypes to show how such a scheme might appear. Our signage scheme is, at this early conceptual stage, primarily a design probe that we hope will stimulate discussion about signage as a tool for promoting greater transparency and public accountability of video surveillance practices and technologies. The proposed signage code draws on existing conventions of other sign design domains – such as road traffic and food – that have been adapted for displaying key characteristics of surveillance schemes in everyday, street-level situations.

The proposed scheme has a number of advantages. At the very least, signs make surveillance more visible. The increased visibility may make the surveillance more effective in deterrence where deployed legitimately, while raising the profile of surveillance of public spaces as a broader policy issue. The proposed signs provide people with useful, actionable information about surveilled spaces. The operator-posted signs attempt to communicate complex information in a concise and timely way to surveillance subjects, allowing them to know, for example, what type of response they are liable to get in an emergency and how long their information is kept. The signage scheme is designed to be inclusive to multicultural, multilingual and even illiterate audiences. The signage also requires retailers, for example, to be more transparent to their customers, and therefore increases the responsibility of the surveillor for the installation and operation of camera surveillance. The authors understand that the proposed signage scheme may have its own limitations and is bound by the limitations of signage schemes more generally. However, in addition to serving as a public didactic tool, it is a first volley at information design and something for policy-makers to criticize, overhaul and implement.

Of course, no matter how comprehensive and widely implemented a signage scheme may be, it provides no guarantee for what operators actually do and how they affect surveillance subjects. While many operators will likely resist any requirement to post more informative signs, if they are forced to do so, the measure will not be difficult or expensive, at least in comparison to the resources required for SCN installation and operation itself. The more intractable organizational processes could continue largely unchanged, unless the signage scheme is combined with more rigorous independent auditing, reporting and disciplining of internal surveillance operations. In this light, we envision our signage schemes as just one strand of a broader public policy discussion surrounding video surveillance practices. In the absence of any more promising intervention strategy, a citizen-centred video surveillance signage scheme as sketched here may provide an approach to mitigating the current asymmetries of visibility and power.

Notes

1   In Vancouver, volunteers organized by the Vancouver Public Space Network mapped over 2,000 cameras in the central business district and surrounding areas. See: <http://www.vancouverpublicspace.ca/index.php?page=cctv> 'Volunteers map Vancouver's public surveillance cameras' and *Vancouver Sun*, 23 August 2009: <http://www.vancouversun.com/Volunteers+Vancouver+public+surveillance+cameras/1922426/story.html>.

2   See: <http://www.flickr.com/groups/1233129@N25/>.

3   Office of the Privacy Commissioner, Privacy Principles: <http://www.priv.gc.ca/leg_c/p_principle_e.cfm>.

4   Some may argue that the deterrence effect of record-only video surveillance can constitute a form of crime prevention. However, given the very weak evidence for such deterrence effects, the onus should be on the operator to demonstrate convincingly the deterrence effect of their particular SCN.

5   See: <http://app.toronto.ca/food2/DineSafeMain>.

References

Clement, A., Ferenbok, J. and Plataniotis, K. (2010) '"Smart" Private Eyes in Public Places? Video Surveillance Analytics', Toronto: Office of the Privacy Commissioner of Canada.

Cole, M. (2004) 'Signage and Surveillance: Interrogating the Textual Context of CCTV in the UK'. *Surveillance and Society* 2(2/3). Available HTTP: <http://library.queensu.ca/ojs/index.php/surveillance-and-society/article/view/3387> (accessed 10 November 2011).

Dawson, D., Derby, P., Doyle, A., Fonio, C., Huey, L., Johnson, M., Leman Langlois, S., Lippert, R., Lyon, D., Pratte, A. M., Smith, E., Walby, K. and Wilkinson, B. (2009) 'A Report on Camera Surveillance in Canada: Part Two', Kingston: Queens University.

Deisman, W., Derby, P., Doyle, A., Leman Langlois, S., Lippert, R., Lyon, D., Pridmore, J., Smith, E., Walby, K. and Whitson, J. (2009) 'A Report on Camera Surveillance in Canada: Part One', Surveillance Camera Awareness Network (SCAN).

Gras, M.L. (2004) 'The Legal Regulation of CCTV in Europe', *Surveillance & Society*, 2(2/3).

Lippert, R. (2009) 'Signs of the Surveillant Assemblage: Privacy Regulation, Urban CCTV, and Governmentality', *Social & Legal Studies*, (18): 505–22.

Norris, C. and Armstrong, G. (1999) *The Maximum Surveillance Society: The Rise of CCTV*, Oxford: Berg.

Office of the Privacy Commissioner & BC and Alberta Commissioners Guidelines for Overt Video Surveillance in the Private Sector, March 2008.

Peacock, C., Goode, A. and Brett, A. (2004) 'Automatic forensic face recognition from digital images', *Science and Justice*, 44(1): 29–34.

Sims, M. (1991) *Sign Design: Graphics, Materials, Techniques*, London: Thames and Hudson.

Documents cited

'Personal Information Privacy and Electronic Documents Act'. Canada, 2000.

'OPC Guidelines for the Use of Video Surveillance of Public Places by Police and Law Enforcement Authorities (March 2006)'. Online. Available HTTP: <http://www.priv.gc.ca/information/guide/vs_060301_e.cfm> (accessed 23 August 2010).

20

IS IT A 'SEARCH'?

The legal context of camera surveillance in Canada

Mathew Johnson[1]

There are few easy answers to surveillance camera questions; those of the legal variety are no exception. In Canada and around the world, governments have struggled to balance security and law enforcement concerns with civil liberties and privacy rights. The failure to achieve this balance has forced courts to intervene. Given their predisposition towards precedent, courts have generally responded to surveillance issues by applying pre-existing privacy law frameworks. Unfortunately, these frameworks have often proved too unwieldy and inflexible to effectively address the unique challenges posed by increasingly advanced technological surveillance systems.

This chapter describes the early development of legal regimes capable of addressing surveillance, and in particular, camera surveillance. Although this chapter focuses on Canadian law, the legal regimes in the United States, Britain and Europe have developed in similar ways, often using the same legal terminology and tests. These parallel developments in the law of surveillance mean that the Canadian legal approach to surveillance is relevant to a much broader audience. In a similar fashion, foreign developments in this area of law will also guide Canadian courts in the future.

At present, however, Canada's law of public (also commonly called 'open-street') camera surveillance is little more than a legal vacuum. No laws have been written in Canada to specifically address camera surveillance, and no court has yet considered the substantive questions raised by their use. Such a situation is not unusual. Early ambiguity within the law is common for emerging technologies, especially those that do not fit comfortably within traditional legal perspectives or which raise novel human rights issues. Much of our framework for defining the relationship between state and citizen, at least in terms of autonomy and observation, was developed decades, if not centuries, ago. The challenge posed by surveillance is how to adapt that framework from one designed to protect against physical intrusion to one which is capable of regulating digital and virtual intrusion.

In considering how the law should respond to surveillance questions, the underlying issue is the extent to which public camera surveillance is analogous to a physical search. Citizens in Canada, as well as in similar common law or European jurisdictions, enjoy considerable protection from physical searches by the state, absent reasonable cause. The circumstances in which a police officer can, for example, enter an individual's home, or compel them to empty their pockets, are well-defined and prescribed. So too is the use of video cameras when investigating a specific individual suspected of a particular offence. The Canadian Charter of Rights and Freedoms (the Charter) imposes specific requirements on these searches. Thus far, public surveillance has been approached through the same analytical framework, given the similar issues of monitoring, privacy and autonomy raised by its use.

As a result, the question of whether public surveillance is legal is closely tied to the broader question of whether it constitutes a 'search' analogous to physical searches. This question is also fundamentally tied to privacy issues, and specifically whether surveillance violates the privacy of those persons under its gaze. As a result, whether surveillance is conceptualized as a benign public safety tool or an invasive police technology leads to significantly different legal results. Until the courts have an opportunity to weigh the issues raised by public video surveillance, the actual state of the 'law' will continue to be an open question.

This chapter examines the current state of the law of public surveillance, as well as the key legal issues it raises. Identifying the current state of the law for emerging technologies is never easy. This chapter considers the applicability and interpretation of a number of statutes, both federal and provincial, which broadly authorize and limit information-gathering, before turning to how the Courts have ruled on search, privacy and surveillance questions in the past, especially in the context of the Charter. A review of these legal instruments and decisions demonstrates the absence of specific guidance on camera surveillance use. The chapter concludes by examining the voluntary guidelines published by the various Canadian privacy commissioners to fill the legal vacuum left by the absence of specific legislation or jurisprudence. Ultimately, the lack of specific 'law' leads to the conclusion that existing surveillance camera systems are grounded on questionable legal foundations. Absent Parliamentary action, it will likely be the courts which are called upon to mediate the issue.

I. The public–private distinctions

Identifying who is operating a surveillance system, and where that system is located, is the first step in analysing the legal considerations applicable to a particular surveillance system. The two relevant considerations are whether the operators of the system are public or private actors, and whether the system is monitoring public or private space. If the operator is a private actor, it is also relevant whether the surveillance is being conducted for commercial purposes. As this chapter reviews the various legal instruments relevant to surveillance, it will highlight which apply to each set of circumstances.

The Charter is the primary distinction between surveillance by public and private actors. As the Charter only applies to public actors (by virtue of s. 32), its protections only constrain the police or other state agents, as well as any private actors acting on their behalf. The constitutional guarantee against unreasonable searches does not apply to other private actors. As such, the regulation of surveillance by private actors relies on the operation of a variety of information-gathering and privacy statutes, as well as through the common law. Generally, surveillance by private actors is highly context-specific, with the legal result heavily dependent on a variety of factors, including who is conducting the surveillance and who is being surveilled, as well as the location and purpose of the surveillance.

Though it is not intended to be comprehensive, the following summary provides a general sense of the applicable legal instruments for each combination of circumstances:

a. Public surveillance, public actor

The regulation of public surveillance by public actors is primarily dependent on the application of the Charter, but privacy and freedom of information statutes applicable to public institutions will also apply.

b. Public surveillance, private actor

Former Privacy Commissioner George Radwanski has stated that '[t]here is no place in our society for unauthorized surveillance of public places by private sector organizations for commercial reasons' (Radwanski 2001a). Regulating non-commercial surveillance of public space by private actors is also highly problematic, where the private actor was not acting as a state agent, but it is unclear what specific legislation, other than tort law, would directly address such activities.

c. Private surveillance, public actor

The regulation of such surveillance would generally only occur in the context of a criminal investigation, and therefore be subject to the requirements of the Criminal Code (R.S. 1985, c. C-46). In most cases, the Criminal Code will require a warrant or permission if police wish to conduct surveillance of private property.

d. Private surveillance, private commercial actor

Such surveillance is regulated by the Personal Information Protection and Electronic Documents Act, S.C., 2000, c. 5 (PIPEDA), except where provinces have adapted 'substantially similar legislation' (s. 26(2)(b)). Where a province has adopted such similar legislation, the provincial legislation, and not PIPEDA, will apply.

e. Private surveillance, private non-commercial actor

The surveillance of private space by a non-commercial private actor is almost certainly legal, so long as they own that space (i.e. a circumstance where an individual installs cameras in their own home). As with most relationships between private individuals, tort law and some provincial privacy statutes would apply in such circumstances.

		Public	Private
		Charter of Rights and Freedoms Privacy and information gathering statutes applicable to public institutions	Tort Law, *PIPEDA* Highly problematic, though the applicable legal instruments are unclear
		Criminal Code Will generally require a warrant	PIPEDA, if for commercial purposes Tort law and some provincial privacy statutes

Space — Public / Private; Actor — Public / Private

The highly contextual yet still largely undefined nature of this area of law means that legal counsel should be sought in any particular case in order to determine the legal issues for a specific system.

II. Legislation

No Canadian legislature has passed legislation that explicitly addresses or authorizes the use of public camera surveillance in their jurisdiction. Other legislation, however, addresses certain aspects of surveillance or provides for general information-gathering. Part IV.1 of the Criminal Code authorizes video surveillance in the context of criminal investigations. This part of the Criminal Code regulates the surveillance of private space by public actors in the context of a criminal investigation where the surveillance is focused on specific individuals or organizations suspected of having committed an offence. Other federal and provincial statutes regulate privacy and the collection of personal information, which applies to camera surveillance. However, given that they do not directly address the type of general surveillance conducted by camera surveillance systems, these statutes do not provide clear guidance in determining exactly what is and is not acceptable use of this technology. The following section reviews the statutes most relevant to camera surveillance.

a. Federal statutes

The Federal Government has passed two statutes that are relevant to surveillance camera use: the Privacy Act (R.S.C. 1985, c. P–21) and PIPEDA.

i. The Privacy Act

The Privacy Act governs the collection and use of personal information by federal government institutions, as well as providing access to that information. The Privacy Act is relevant because surveillance collects 'personal information' within the meaning of the Act. Its application, however, is limited to the collection of information by federal 'government institutions' (s. 4). In practical terms, this limitation means that the Privacy Act will only apply to surveillance conducted by the RCMP (or other federal agents), and not to municipal or provincial police forces.

Despite its limited applicability, the Privacy Act has served as the backdrop for one of the few administrative rulings on the 'legality' of surveillance. In 2001, George Radwanski, the former Federal Privacy Commissioner, investigated whether an RCMP surveillance programme in Kelowna, British Columbia, complied with the Privacy Act (Radwanski 2001b). Commissioner Radwanski concluded that the system's recording capabilities violated s. 4 of the Act, which states:

> **4**. No personal information shall be collected by a government institution unless it relates directly to an operating program or activity of the institution.

Radwanski interpreted this to mean that government institutions must 'collect only the minimum amount of personal information necessary for the intended purpose' and that any collection requires 'demonstrable need'. The Commissioner found that the Kelowna surveillance system engaged in 'wholesale monitoring' and that, by recording continuously, the system unnecessarily collected the personal information of thousands of innocent citizens engaged in activities unrelated to the mandate of the RCMP. While acknowledging that preventing and deterring crime is an important police objective, Radwanski concluded that the programme did not meet the requirements of s. 4 of the Privacy Act (Radwanski 2001b).

In response to the Commissioner's investigation, the RCMP ceased the practice of continuous recording, and instead began to record only when a violation of the law was detected. Commissioner Radwanski, while acknowledging that this change brought the system into technical compliance with the Privacy Act, argued that even a non-recording camera surveillance system did not respect the spirit of the Act and ordered the cameras removed (Radwanski 2001b).

The RCMP and the Solicitor-General of Canada refused to remove the cameras (Radwanski 2002). In response, Commissioner Radwanski attempted to enforce his finding through the Courts, but his application was dismissed on technical grounds (*Canada (Privacy Commissioner) v. Canada (Attorney General)*, 2003 BCSC 862). As such, the scope of the applicability of the *Privacy Act* remains unclear: the RCMP acknowledged that continuous recording was inconsistent with the Act, but disagreed about whether non-continuous recording was non-compliant. Until the courts conclusively interpret the scope of s. 4, it will continue to be unclear which view is correct. Nevertheless, the investigation into Kelowna's camera surveillance system demonstrated that the Privacy Act imposes some, albeit limited, restrictions on the surveillance activities of the RCMP.

ii. The Personal Information Protection and Electronic Documents Act

PIPEDA was enacted by the federal government to regulate the collection and use of personal information by private actors 'in the course of commercial activities' (s.4). PIPEDA expressly excludes from its ambit any government institutions covered by the *Privacy Act* which means that it is not applicable to the RCMP. The commercial activities requirement also excludes provincial or municipal police forces, or their agents.

PIPEDA applies to all other commercial activities across Canada, other than in provinces that have enacted 'substantially similar' legislation (s. 26(2)(b)), which currently only includes Alberta, Quebec and British Columbia. PIPEDA also applies to information collected by organizations about their employees where the commercial activity is federally regulated. Federally regulated activities mainly include the telecommunications, banking and inter-provincial transportation industries (Levin 2007: 314).

Fundamental to PIPEDA's approach to privacy are ten Fair Information Practice Principles included in Schedule 1 to the *Act*. These principles include the requirements of knowledge and consent, where possible, identifying the purposes of collection, accountability, limiting the use, collection, disclosure and retention of information, where possible, accuracy and openness, and the establishment of safeguards. These principles are outlined in detail, and should provide a starting point for any individual or organization considering using or challenging camera surveillance. Circumstances where the principles are not applicable are also articulated in PIPEDA. Section 7(1)(b), for example, provides that information can only be collected without an individual's knowledge and consent where it is reasonable to believe that obtaining such consent would 'compromise the availability or the accuracy of the information', the decision to collect the information is reasonable, and the collection relates to either the investigation of the breach of an agreement or where a federal or provincial law has been broken.

PIPEDA is interpreted and enforced by the Privacy Commissioner of Canada. The Commissioner can receive and investigate complaints, issue findings and take steps to enforce its decisions. The Commissioner has investigated a number of complaints involving camera surveillance, covering a range of circumstances in which camera surveillance has been used. The decisions in many of those cases have been released, which have helped define the scope of appropriate camera surveillance use by private commercial actors and have established the following criteria for determining whether video surveillance in a particular context meets the requirements of PIPEDA:

> Is the use of video surveillance cameras demonstrably necessary to meet a specific need?

Is video surveillance likely to be effective in meeting these needs?
Is the loss of privacy proportional to the benefit gained?
Is there a less privacy-invasive way of achieving the same end?
        (Office of the Privacy Commissioner, PIPEDA Case Summary #2009–001)

In general, the findings of the Office of the Privacy Commissioner suggest that video surveillance is most likely to be acceptable where its presence and purpose are clear to those being observed, where the purpose is reasonable, and where alternatives are not likely to be successful. In workplaces, cameras for the purposes of safety and the prevention of theft or fraud are acceptable, while those for the purpose of monitoring productivity are inconsistent with PIPEDA (for a cross-section of relevant findings, see PIPEDA Case Summaries #2009–001, #2008–396, #2007–388, #2005–290, #2004–279 and #2004–264. See generally the OPC website at <http://www.priv.gc.ca>).

Compared to its use in commercial or workplace settings, the Office of the Privacy Commissioner has been much less receptive to public camera surveillance. As mentioned earlier, former Commissioner Radwanski was of the view that private sector commercial organizations should not be engaged in public surveillance. Later findings have since clarified, however, that such surveillance is acceptable where there is some form of implied consent. The Commissioner has ruled, for example, that an insurance firm can hire a private investigator to use camera surveillance to record a complainant's public behaviour where litigation has been commenced; the litigation, in such a case, provides the implied consent. Situations where consent can be implied, however, are rare, and generally will not justify general public surveillance. Where there is no actual or implied consent, surveillance of public spaces will contravene PIPEDA (see, for example, PIPEDA Case Summaries #2009–007, #2008–392, #2005–311 and #2004–269).

Taken together, the Privacy Act and PIPEDA provide a federal regulatory framework for camera surveillance conducted by the RCMP and for private actors engaged in commercial activities. The next section addresses the provincial statues that fill some of the gaps left by these federal statutes.

b. Provincial Statutes

i. Freedom of Information and Protection of Privacy Acts

Every province has its own Freedom of Information and Protection of Privacy Act (FIPPA), or something very similar, which impose restrictions on the ability of provincial institutions to collect and use personal information. Ontario has both a *FIPPA* (R.S.O. 1990, c. F.31) and the Municipal Freedom of Information and Protection of Privacy Act (R.S.O. 1990, c. M.56 [MFIPPA]), which contain nearly identical sections on information collection, and are similar to their provincial counterparts. These Acts apply to 'provincial institutions', which include provincial and municipal police forces. Some existing municipal surveillance systems claim to operate under the authority of these statutes. MFIPPA and FIPPA both provide for significant exceptions to the general requirement that information collection only take place with the consent of those whose information is being collected. Section 28(2) of the MFIPPA (and s. 38(2) of the FIPPA, which is identical), for example, provides that:

> **28.** (2) No person shall collect personal information on behalf of an institution unless the collection is expressly authorized by statute, used for the purposes of law enforcement or necessary to the proper administration of a lawfully authorized activity.

On 3 March 2008, Ontario's Information and Privacy Commissioner Ann Cavoukian released a report into whether the use of camera surveillance throughout the Toronto Transport Commission's (TTC) mass transit system complied with the requirements of MFIPPA. The fundamental question for Commissioner Cavoukian was whether the collection of personal information by camera surveillance complied with s. 28(2) of MFIPPA. She confirmed that there are three distinct grounds upon which information can be collected under that section: where the collection is a) authorized by statute; b) necessary to the proper administration of a lawfully authorized activity; or c) for the purposes of law enforcement.

The TTC acknowledged that there was no statutory basis for the collection, leaving the other two grounds as potentially applicable. Turning first to the necessity condition, Commissioner Cavoukian applied the test developed by her office:

> . . . in order to satisfy the necessity condition, the institution must first identify the 'lawfully authorized activity' in question, and second, it must demonstrate how the collection of personal information is 'necessary,' not merely helpful, to the achievement of this objective. In addition, this justification must be provided for all classes of personal information that are collected.
>
> *(Cavoukian 2008: 21)*

Commissioner Cavoukian concluded that the proposed TTC camera system met the requirements of the necessity condition.

With respect to the law enforcement condition, Commissioner Cavoukian concluded that, as TTC 'special constables' engage in 'policing' within the definition of the Police Services Act, they qualified as law enforcement officers. Accordingly, the law enforcement condition was also satisfied.

It is significant that, although MFIPPA and FIPPA contain the necessity condition, which provides for similar requirements as were articulated by Commissioner Radwanski in his interpretation of s. 4 of the federal Privacy Act, there is no similar restrictive language in the MFIPPA or FIPPAs imposing restrictions on the use of the law enforcement condition. It was enough for Commissioner Cavoukian to conclude that the activities of TTC special constables were 'sufficiently similar' to the police in order to satisfy this requirement (Cavoukian 2008: 31). Such an interpretation, applied broadly, would mean that the use of camera surveillance by provincial or municipal police would face few, if any, restrictions on their ability to collect personal information without consent.

In light of Commissioner Cavoukian's conclusion regarding the proposed TTC video surveillance system, provincial FIPPAs appear to provide broad authorization for collecting information through surveillance by provincial institutions where it is done for the purposes of law enforcement or, to a lesser extent, where it is necessary to the administration of a lawfully authorized activity. This authority, however, may be narrowed by the Charter's prohibition of unreasonable search and seizure, especially in circumstances other than for the purposes of monitoring mass transit systems which was a central consideration in Commissioner Cavoukian's analysis (see Section 3-b, which will discuss this in more detail).

It may also be possible to argue that the legislature did not intend to grant unlimited authority for the collection of information in any situation involving law enforcement, and that any such authority should be exercised only when its use is reasonable and effective. The European Court of Human Rights has interpreted s. 8(2) of the European Convention on Human Rights (the right to a 'private and family life') to require that privacy-intrusive technologies be authorized by law, proportional and in furtherance of a legitimate objective (Taylor 2002: 67–9), similar to former Commissioner Radwanski's interpretation of the Privacy Act. If a Court were to agree with Radwanski's characterization of camera surveillance as a programme of 'wholesale monitoring', whose costs outweigh its benefits (Radwanski 2001b), the Court might refuse to endorse Commissioner Cavoukian's broad reading of the law enforcement exception and instead require that any use of surveillance cameras not simply be authorized on the basis that it may further law enforcement, but also that it be proportional and in furtherance of a legitimate objective. Until such an approach is tested before a judge and applied to a particular factual situation, however, it is impossible to predict how such an argument would be received.

ii. Provincial Privacy Acts

British Columbia, Saskatchewan, Manitoba, and Newfoundland and Labrador all have enacted Privacy Acts (R.S.B.C. 1996, c. 373; R.S.S. 1978 c. P-24; C.C.S.M. c. P125; R.S.N. 1990, c. P-22). These Privacy Acts allow individuals to sue for breaches of their privacy. British Columbia's Privacy Act, for example, creates a tort of invasion of privacy, which explicitly applies to surveillance (s. 1(4)). The tort does not require proof of any specific damage (s. 1(1)), which means that it is not necessary to show that harm was caused by surveillance. The lack of a harm requirement is important because it identifies the act of surveillance itself as a wrong that requires compensation. In contrast, the common law tort of invasion of privacy, which will be discussed later, requires an act of communication (the publication or transfer of the information that was collected) which causes harm in order to challenge any surveillance or other violation of privacy.

Despite the benefits of the creation of a statutory tort, provincial Privacy Acts contain law enforcement exceptions similar to those contained in the various

FIPPAs (see, for example, British Columbia's Privacy Act at s. 2). The law enforcement exceptions are more limited compared to the FIPPAs, requiring that any use of surveillance by a peace officer not be 'disproportionate to the gravity of the crime or the matter subject to investigation' (s. 2(2)). Given the lack of individual suspicion in the use of public camera surveillance systems, it may be possible to argue that such systems cannot satisfy this more limited law enforcement exception, other than in exceptional circumstances (e.g. the investigation of a serious crime).

The specific exclusion of 'disproportionate' surveillance in the application of provincial Privacy Acts may therefore resemble the interpretation of s. 4 of the federal Privacy Act or the necessity condition of the FIPPAs. Taken together, these various interpretations may point to an increasing consensus regarding the appropriate balance for the use of surveillance around the issue of proportionality: that camera surveillance should only be used where it can be shown to be demonstrably necessary to meet a specific purpose in light of the circumstances surrounding the proposed installation.

c. The Criminal Code

Section 184(1) of the Criminal Code may also be relevant to the legality of public camera surveillance. The section provides that:

> **184.** (1) Every one who, by means of any electro-magnetic, acoustic, mechanical or other device, wilfully intercepts a private communication is guilty of an indictable offence and liable to imprisonment for a term not exceeding five years.

While this seems to place restriction only on the interception of private communications, two court cases have interpreted this section more broadly: *Druken v. R.G. Fewer and Associates Inc.* (1998), 171 Nfld. & P.E.I.R. 312: para. 43 (Nfld. S.C. (T.D.); *Morgan v. Alta Flights (Charters) Inc.* (2005), 271 F.T.R. 298 (F.C.): para. 22. These two cases suggest that video surveillance in public could intercept private communications within the definition of s. 184(1). As will be discussed, there is an increasingly prevalent view that there are private aspects of public life deserving protection.

Furthermore, given that s. 184(1) covers wiretaps as well as investigative video surveillance, it may be possible to analogously interpret the section also to include public video surveillance. It should be noted that the Supreme Court has already extended the reach of s. 184(1) in a similar fashion: *R. v. Duarte* ([1990] 1 S.C.R. 30).

Interpreting s. 184(1) to include public camera surveillance would require that the police, or agents acting on behalf of the police, obtain a warrant to install surveillance systems and be subject to Part IV.1 of the Criminal Code. While such an interpretation requires some judicial flexibility, it would provide a consistent national standard for camera surveillance use.

III. Jurisprudence

Given the potential rights implications of public camera surveillance use, as well as the need to interpret the various relevant statutes, the courts will likely play a large role in determining the legality and the legal framework for its use. Before turning to the Charter, the following section considers the applicability of the common law. As will be seen, the common law is largely silent both on the issue of surveillance and broader informational privacy issues.

a. Common law

The common law is the body of judge-made law that underpins Canada's legal system by establishing precedent which guides future judicial decisions. Given the recent emergence of public surveillance as a legal issue, there have been few opportunities for the common law to develop on the subject. In one of the few decisions where an appellate court has addressed video surveillance, though only in the context of a targeted criminal investigation, the Ontario Court of Appeal stated that 'nothing at Common Law prohibits a search through use of a video camera and tape' (*R. v. LeBeau* (1988), 62 C.R. (3d) 157 (Ont. C.A.): 181). As a result, it seems as if any legal impediments to public camera surveillance will arise from the Charter and not the common law.

Despite the limitations of the common law, there have been some recent developments that may provide for individual redress. In particular, the emergence of the tort of invasion of privacy in a number of provinces has the potential to be useful. Suits for invasion of privacy would seek monetary damages where privacy has been violated. Unfortunately, there are significant limitations on the capacity of this tort to address public surveillance. The first limitation is that it is unclear whether such a tort in fact exists (it is the nature of the common law to remain uncertain until a number of courts have had the opportunity to consider the same issue: see *Somwar v. McDonald's Restaurants of Canada Ltd.* (2006), 263 D.L.R. (4th) 752 (Ont. Sup. Ct. J.) for a discussion of the existence of the tort in Ontario). The second limitation is that an action for invasion of privacy is quite narrow and is focused on damages resulting from the communication of the private information, not for the act of surveillance itself. As a result, if an individual has their picture taken or image recorded in public, but nothing more, then the tort would be of little use, as there is no harmful communication. However, if an individual were to sell or distribute the picture or footage, then it might be possible to sue. This limitation, unlike the statutory tort of invasion of privacy discussed earlier, means that the tort of invasion of privacy is of no use to those who would argue that the act of surveillance, itself, is the harm that deserves redress.

Given the recent development of the common law tort of invasion of privacy, no definitive conclusions may be drawn other than that any use of the tort will likely only be able to address the most egregious violations of privacy. Nevertheless, this tort may represent a last resort for those opposed to camera surveillance (see also Bezanson 1992; Moreham 2002).

b. The Charter

i. Overview

Despite the existence of various information-gathering statutes, the rights issues at stake suggest that it will be the application and operation of the Charter which will resolve much of the debate over the appropriate use of public camera surveillance. Not only will the courts determine whether any particular surveillance system is Charter-compliant, but they will also consider whether authorization based on the statutes identified earlier, as well as the statutes themselves, is constitutional.

Section 8 is the provision of the Charter relevant to video surveillance:

> **8**. Everyone has the right to be secure against unreasonable search and seizure.

Section 8 has been interpreted by the courts as protecting a 'reasonable expectation of privacy'. Traditionally, protection against unreasonable searches has been primarily concerned with physical searches, and, in particular, with determining when a home, place of business or an individual's person can be searched by the State (see, for example, *Hunter v. Southam*, [1984] 2 S.C.R. 145). With the advent of new forms of technology, the scope of what we consider to be a 'search' has expanded. The Supreme Court has already held that the ambit of s. 8 includes the use of audio and camera surveillance as part of a criminal investigation (*Duarte, supra; R. v. Wong*, [1990] 3 S.C.R. 36; see also generally Boa 2007), drug sniffer dogs (*R. v. Kang-Brown*, [2008] 1 S.C.R. 456; *R. v. A.M.*, [2008] 1 S.C.R. 569), phone taps (*R. v. Garofoli*, [1990] 2 S.C.R. 1421) and GPS tracking devices (*R. v. Wise*, [1992] 1 S.C.R. 527).

To constitute a search within the meaning of s. 8, a particular act must violate an individual's reasonable expectation of privacy. If this expectation is breached, then the government must prove that the search was reasonable. Section 8 presumes that any activity that is determined to be a search and was conducted without a warrant is unreasonable. To prove that a particular search was reasonable, the government must establish that the search was authorized by law, that the law is reasonable, and that the search itself was conducted reasonably (*R. v. Collins*, [1987] 1 S.C.R. 265). If the government is unable to prove reasonability, the search will be found to have contravened the Charter. It should be noted that the reasonable expectation of privacy approach is also used in the United States, the United Kingdom and in Europe (see generally Bickel, Brinkley and White 2003; Moreham 2006; European Commission for Democracy through Law 2007). Although the details of the approach differ, the overlapping approaches between jurisdictions permits them to draw upon each other's experience and decisions in the course of defining the scope and contours of emerging privacy rights.

In Canada, the vital question of the s. 8 analysis is whether a particular activity or technology constitutes a search. If it does, s. 8 will apply and require that the search be reasonable. If the activity is determined not to be a search, then s. 8 does not apply, and there will be no Charter restrictions on the use of the activity or technology in question. The question of whether the activity constitutes a search is complex, context specific, and requires that an individual's reasonable expectation of privacy be breached. This determination is both subjective and objective: an individual must subjectively expect privacy, and this expectation must be objectively reasonable (*R. v. Edwards*, [1996] 1 S.C.R. 128). Surveillance deals with informational privacy, a type of privacy the Supreme Court has identified as deserving protection. A fundamental question of whether an individual's expectation of informational privacy has been breached depends on the meaningfulness of the information collected. The more that the collected information relates to 'intimate details of the lifestyle and personal choices of the individual', the more likely it will be that an individual's reasonable expectation of privacy has been breached (*R. v. Tessling*, [2004] 3 S.C.R. 432: para. 25).

In the case of public camera surveillance, the s. 8 analysis will be complicated by the difficulty in reconciling the idea that an individual has an expectation of privacy while they move about in public, capable of being seen by anybody who should choose to look. In fact, the traditional legal view is that an individual does not have any expectation of privacy while in public (see, for example, *Druken v. R.G. Fewer and Associates Inc.* (1998), 171 Nfld. & P.E.I.R. 312 Nfld. S.C. (T.D.): para. 43). However, recent cases have increasingly concluded that in certain situations, despite being in public, an individual stills enjoys a measure of privacy, though courts have often characterized the result as a 'diminished' expectation of privacy. Legal commentators are also increasingly receptive to public privacy (Paton-Simpson 2000; Nissenbaum 1998; MacKinnon 2007). There have also been a number of recent British and European cases that have acknowledged a public dimension to privacy and concluded that aspects of public lives should be protected (see, for example, *Peck v. The United Kingdom*, [2003] E.C.H.R. 44 (considering the release of a surveillance recording of an individual attempting to commit suicide on a public street); *Douglas v. Hello! Ltd.*, [2005] 4 All ER 128 (identified privacy interests in photographs taken in public, partly because 'a photograph is more than the information you get from it'); see also *von Hannover v. Germany*, [2004] E.C.H.R. 294; *P.G. and J.H. v. The United Kingdom*, [2001] E.C.H.R. 550; *Campbell v. MGN Ltd.*, [2004] 2 A.C. 457 (H.L); *R. v. Loveridge, Lee and Loveridge*, [2001] EWCA Crim 973 (C.A.); Moreham 2006). These cases will be relevant to Canadian courts as they grapple with surveillance questions.

In a legal opinion on the legality of video surveillance written for former Commissioner Radwanski, former Supreme Court Justice Gérard La Forest suggested that it is the continuous nature of surveillance that raises Charter concerns. He argued that while Canadians 'may not have a reasonable expectation that the police will never observe our activities in public spaces . . . surely it is reasonable to expect that they will not always do so' (La Forest 2002). In addition to looking at the effect of surveillance cameras – for instance, whether they create a 'chilling effect' on particular types of activity – Courts will also likely look to the nature of the information collected. Surveillance recordings will likely be of concern to Courts due to their potential to convey intimate details about individuals, especially as computers provide the ability to collate, compare and analyse disparate recordings, allowing for the creation of informational 'human mosaics' from the random bits of electronic information which are left behind as we go about our modern, daily lives (see, for example, Paton-Simpson 2000; Nissenbaum 1998; Steeves 2008; Renke 2006; Bailey 2008). The addition of biometric systems, which provide the capacity to connect and cross-reference what is being seen to informational databases, as has been done in some cities in the United States, will also likely be met with considerable concern (Radwanski 2001b; Phillips 1997; Milligan 1999; Blitz 2004).

Before considering the application of the reasonable expectation of privacy approach to camera surveillance in more detail, it should also be noted that the approach itself has been heavily criticized in Canada, especially in its application to informational privacy and surveillance issues (these issues include the lack of flexibility of the approach, its focus on the privacy interest of the target rather than the actions of investigators, its definition of what constitutes a 'search', and its inability to account for the aggregation of otherwise 'meaningless' information: see, for example, Kerr and McGill 2007; Austin 2003, 2007; Pomerance 2004; Bailey 2008; Steeves 2008; Paton-Simpson 2000). Although the reasonable expectation approach appears well-established, the Supreme Court could choose a novel approach in addressing public privacy issues. Such an occurrence, however, notwithstanding concerns about the reasonable expectation approach, is highly unlikely.

ii. Searches and reasonable expectations of privacy: Stage 1 of the s. 8 analysis

In analysing surveillance technologies, a court is likely to follow one of two recent Supreme Court decisions: *Tessling* or *Kang-Brown*. In *Tessling*, the Court considered whether the use of Forward-Looking Infrared (FLIR) cameras constituted a search. A FLIR camera can take 'pictures' of the heat signatures of a building and that picture can provide insight into the activities inside the building. FLIR images are of particular interest to the police because elevated heat signatures can be indicative of the presence of a marijuana grow operation. In Mr Tessling's case, the police had flown over his house after receiving a tip. The FLIR images enabled the police to obtain a search warrant, and the subsequent search found a grow operation.

In its decision in *Tessling*, the Supreme Court concluded that the image of the heat emanating from Mr Tessling's home was, on it's own, 'meaningless', and that Mr Tessling therefore had no reasonable expectation that the information would not be collected by the State. It then followed that, because the use of the FLIR camera did not violate Mr Tessling's reasonable expectation of privacy, it was not a search and s. 8 offered no protection against it.

In contrast, the Supreme Court found that the use of drug sniffer dogs violated the reasonable expectation of privacy of the two accused in the companion cases of

Kang-Brown and *A.M.* In both cases, the police had used sniffer dogs to find drugs in public locations: in a bus station and a school, respectively. The police did not have any specific suspicion that drugs would be found in either case; instead, the drugs were found as the result of general, random searches. Despite a complicated result due to the fact that four different Justices reached distinct conclusions, the Court unanimously accepted that the use of the dogs violated a reasonable expectation of privacy and thereby constituted a search. Justice Deschamps decided that the odours emanating from the bags containing the drugs were capable of revealing that the individual was likely to have come into contact with a controlled substance either as a user or a trafficker, or to have been in the company of drug users. The nature of this information was 'very personal', and therefore engaged s. 8 of the *Charter* (*Kang-Brown*: para. 175).

In any future video surveillance Charter litigation, a Court will, essentially, choose between following the *Tessling* and *Kang-Brown* precedents. The Court will consider whether video surveillance is more like FLIR technology or sniffer dogs. Both 'technologies' involve situations where information is collected as it emanates publicly, but differ as to their assessment of its informational content. If video surveillance is found to provide as much personal information as sniffer dogs, it will likely qualify as a search, while a conclusion that its information is 'meaningless' would produce the opposite result. Although the full s. 8 analysis is far more complex, recent cases have largely turned on the question of meaningfulness. The analogy chosen by the Court will therefore be highly significant.

The tension between *Tessling* and *Kang-Brown* was fully evident in the Supreme Court's most recent case on informational privacy, *R. v. Gomboc* ([2010] 3 S.C.R.211). Although the deep divisions in the Court in *Gomboc* mean that few, if any, of the fundamental issues left unresolved by the Supreme Court's earlier cases are any more clear, the decision further solidifies meaningfulness as the central consideration of the first stage of the s. 8 analysis. In *Gomboc*, the Court considered whether the use of a Digital Recording Ammeter (DRA) engaged s. 8 of the Charter. A DRA is capable of graphing the flow of electricity into a house. As marijuana grow operations tend to operate on regular day–night cycles, a cyclical flow of energy can suggest that such an operation is present.

The Court was deeply divided over how to approach the use of the DRA. Four Justices, led by Deschamps J., concluded that the information revealed by the DRA was no more revealing than the use of the FLIR camera in *Tessling* or the records of electricity consumption considered in the much earlier case of *R. v. Plant* ([1993] 3 S.C.R. 281). Central to Deschamps J.'s argument was her conclusion that the DRA 'reveals nothing meaningful related to the *Charter*'s protection of biographical core information of an intimate and personal nature'.

McLachlin C.J. and Fish J., writing jointly in dissent, strongly disagreed with Deschamps J., arguing that the effect of the decision was 'to take an incremental but ominous step towards the erosion of the right to privacy guaranteed by s. 8. The two Justices dismissed the comparison to *Tessling* and concluded instead that the DRA instead was capable of providing the capacity to make informed predictions concerning a range of probable activities taking place in the home. As a result they found that the police had breached Mr Gomboc's reasonable expectation of privacy.

Justice Abella, on behalf of the remaining three Judges, agreed with McLachlin C.J. and Fish J. that the information conveyed by the DRA was meaningful, stating that the information was 'undisputably more revealing than what Binnie J. suggested was the "meaningless" information provided by the FLIR data in *Tessling*'. However, Abella J. concluded that a Code of Conduct Regulation made pursuant to Alberta's Electric Utilities Act (which permitted the utility company to share customer information without the customer's consent) undermined Mr Gomboc's objective expectation of privacy, and so agreed with the plurality that the use of the DRA did not constitute a search.

It is vital to note that, although a 7–2 majority of the Court determined that Mr Gomboc had no expectation of privacy, it was only the presence of the Code of Conduct Regulation which precluded the Court dividing 5–4 in favour of Mr Gomboc and finding of a reasonable expectation of privacy. This inconclusive result means that very little useful guidance can be drawn from *Gomboc*, other than to the extent to which it reinforces either *Tessling* or *Kang-Brown*. Until the Court has another opportunity to consider this issue and resolve the different approaches of *Gomboc*'s plurality and dissent, lower Courts will have little choice other than to proceed by analogy between the Supreme Court's earlier judgements.

iii. Reasonable searches: the second stage of the s. 8 analysis

If the Court determines that surveillance constitutes a search, the inquiry does not end there. The second question is whether the search was conducted reasonably. In his legal opinion, Justice La Forest concluded that if surveillance is found to be a search, 'then it follows almost inexorably that it violates section 8 of the Charter' (La Forest 2002). Justice La Forest based his conclusion on the lack of statutory authority which specifically authorizes public video surveillance. Despite the presence of a number of information–collection statutes, none is likely to be specific enough to authorize surveillance if it falls within the ambit of s. 8. The requirements imposed by s. 8 are rigorous, and cannot likely be satisfied by broad information–collection authority, especially if that authorization is engaged by nothing more than the involvement of law enforcement officers, as Commissioner Cavoukian seemed to be suggesting in her discussion of the *MFIPPA* law enforcement exception in her report into the use of camera surveillance by the TTC.

If a Court determines that video surveillance constitutes a search, it may impose a warrant requirement. Such a conclusion is possible because, as mentioned earlier, warrantless searches are presumptively unreasonable under s. 8. Obtaining judicial authorization will almost always justify the resulting search, assuming that reasonable cause exists and that the other requirements for the warrant are satisfied. In the case of public video surveillance, a Judge could ensure that the proposed scheme addresses a specific public safety concern and that other enforcement options have been considered and rejected. Further, such a warrant could limit the surveillance system to an approved geographic location and time. Such an approach would also give the Courts the ability to oversee the collection, retention and use of any footage or images collected by the surveillance system.

Alternatively, a Court could insist that Parliament pass legislation explicitly authorizing surveillance before any searches, other than where the police possess reasonable and probable grounds capable of justifying a traditional warrantless search, are found to be constitutional. A plurality of the Supreme Court resolved the lack of authority for sniffer dogs in *Kang-Brown* in this manner, arguing that legislators are in a better position to balance the various considerations and interests that are relevant to questions of search and seizure. The Judges preferred to allow Parliament to define a legislative scheme for surveillance and then subsequently evaluate that law to evaluate its Charter-compliance.

If the Court were to find that surveillance constitutes a search, there are also a number of other possible outcomes. In addition to imposing a warrant requirement for its use or ruling that it is unconstitutional without legislative authority, the Courts could find authority for the search under traditional police powers, impose a lower standard of suspicion (see, for example, *Kang-Brown*; *R. v. Patrick*, [2009] 1 S.C.R. 579) or craft a uniquely tailored result. Until the Courts have had the opportunity to fully canvass the issue, it is impossible to predict how a Court will rule with any certainty. At the very least, the foregoing should indicate that surveillance raises complex legal issues, none of which will be easily answered.

IV. Non-binding guidelines

The current Privacy Commissioner, Jennifer Stoddart, has turned to non-binding codes of conduct as a means of ensuring that existing surveillance institutions meet certain basic privacy guidelines. This approach has been adopted, in part, because of her predecessor's unsuccessful attempts to directly regulate surveillance. The various provincial information and privacy commissioners have adopted similar approaches.

These codes of conduct tend to adopt a proportional approach to surveillance, by mandating that video surveillance systems should not be used more than necessary in order to regulate prescribed activity. One of the more stringent provincial guidelines in Canada is published by the Commission d'accès à l'information du Québec, which contains 20 'rules of use'. These rules outline strict conditions that must be adhered to for the use of surveillance to be reasonable. A contrasting example is Ontario's guidelines, which are much more permissive. This is evident in the language used in the two documents: where Quebec's rules consistently provide that surveillance operators 'shall' comply with certain limitations, Ontario's guidelines instead use the language of 'should'. This distinction is important, as 'shall' is treated as a mandatory term in law while 'should' is not (Commission d'accès à l'information du Québec 2004; Office of the Information and Privacy Commissioner of Ontario 2001).

The Office of the Federal Privacy Commissioner has also published guidelines for both overt and covert video surveillance by the private sector, as well as for the surveillance of public spaces by police and other law enforcement authorities (Office of the Privacy Commissioner of Canada 2006, 2008, 2009). These, as well as the relevant provincial guidelines, should be consulted both by those intending to install video surveillance systems, as well as by those who wish to challenge them.

Due to the fact that such codes of conduct are non-binding, they are not technically 'legal' as we normally understand the term. There are no sanctions for non-compliance, and such codes permit no basis for judicial oversight. However, non-binding guidelines do fill in the gaps left by law by helping to define what constitutes reasonable surveillance use. They also attempt to strike a balance between concerns over civil liberties and those of law enforcement. Furthermore, such provisions could be of considerable assistance to the Courts in evaluating surveillance. Given that s. 8 of the Charter prohibits only unreasonable searches, it is possible that the various federal and provincial guidelines could provide a starting point for a Court in determining whether any particular search was conducted in a reasonable manner.

V. Conclusion

As a novel technology, public camera surveillance raises issues that the Canadian legal system has not yet had the opportunity to fully consider. Existing surveillance systems operate under the questionable authority of statutes granting broad information collection exceptions such as for law enforcement purposes. Until these claims of authority are challenged, there is no basis to conclude that any such surveillance systems are 'illegal'. If they are challenged, the Courts will have to wrestle with the application of s. 8 of the Charter, a constitutional provision that was designed to deal primarily with physical searches. If s. 8 is found to be applicable, then a range of requirements will be imposed to ensure that technology use is 'reasonable'. If s. 8 is not applicable, then the status quo will be confirmed as 'legal'.

Given the complexity of the legal issues surrounding surveillance, the only certainty is that these questions will not be easily resolved. Although the recent Supreme Court decisions in *Tessling*, *Kang-Brown* and *Gomboc* may point the way forward, they still remain little more than a starting point for the future legal discussion.

Note

1   The views expressed in this chapter are those of the author and do not reflect the position of the Department of Justice or the Public Prosecution Service of Canada.

References

Austin, L. (2003) 'Privacy and the question of technology', *Law and Philosophy*, 22(2): 119–66.

Austin, L. (2007) 'Information Sharing and the "Reasonable" Ambiguities of Section 8 of the Charter', *University of Toronto Law Journal*, 35: 499–523.

Bailey, J. (2008) 'Framed by Section 8: Constitutional Protection of Privacy in Canada', *Canadian Journal of Criminology and Criminal Justice*, 50: 279–306.

Bezanson, R. (1992) 'The Right to Privacy Revisited: Privacy, News, and Social Change, 1890–1990', *California Law Review*, 80(5): 1133–75.

Bickel, R., Brinkley, S. and White, W. (2003) 'Seeing Past Privacy: Will the Development and Application of CCTV and Other Video Security Technology Compromise an Essential Constitutional Right in a Democracy, or will the Courts Strike a Proper Balance?', *Stetson Law Review*, 33: 299–367.

Blitz, M. (2004) 'Video Surveillance and the Constitution of Public Space: Fitting the Fourth Amendment to a World that Tracks Image and Identity', *Texas Law Review*, 82(6): 1349–1481.

Boa, K. (2007) 'Privacy Outside the Castle: Surveillance Technologies and Reasonable Expectations of Privacy in Canadian Judicial Reasoning', *Surveillance & Society*, 4(4): 329–45.

Cavoukian, A. (2008) Privacy and Video Surveillance in Mass Transit Systems: A Special Investigative Report – Privacy Investigation Report MC07-68. March. Online. Available HTTP: <http://www.ipc.on.ca/images/Findings/mc07-68-ttc_592396093750.pdf>.

Commission d'accès à l'information du Québec (2004) Rules For Use of Surveillance Cameras with Recording in Public Places by Public Bodies. June. Online. Available HTTP: <http://www.cai.gouv.qc.ca/06_documentation/01_pdf/new_rules_2004.pdf>.

European Commission for Democracy Through Law (2007) Opinion on Video Surveillance in Public Places by Public Authorities and the Protection of Human Rights. March. Online. Available HTTP: <http://www.venice.coe.int/docs/2007/CDL-AD(2007)014-e.asp>.

Information and Privacy Commissioner (IPC) (2001) *Guidelines for Using Video Surveillance Cameras in Public Places*. Toronto: Information and Privacy Commissioner/Ontario.

Kerr, D. and McGill, J. (2007) 'Emanations, Snoop Dogs and Reasonable Expectations of Privacy', *Criminal Law Quarterly*, 52: 392–432.

Lai, D. (2007) 'Public Video Surveillance by the State: Policy, Privacy Legislation, and the Charter', *Alberta Law Review*, 45: 43–77.

La Forest, G. (2002) *Legal Opinion from Justice Gérard La Forest to George Radwanski*, Federal Privacy Commissioner. April. Online. Available HTTP: <http://www.privcom.gc.ca/media/nr-%20c/opinion_020410_e.asp>.

MacKinnon, W. (2007) '*Tessling, Brown*, and *A.M.*: Towards a Principled Approach to Section 8', *Alberta Law Review*, 45: 79–116.

Milligan, C. (1999) 'Facial Recognition Technology, Video Surveillance, and Privacy', *Southern California Interdisciplinary Law Journal*, 9: 295–333.

Moreham, N. (2006) 'Privacy in Public Places', *Cambridge Law Journal*, 65(3): 606–35.

Nissenbaum, H. (1998) 'Protecting Privacy in an Information Age: The Problem of Privacy in Public, *Law and Philosophy*, 17: 559–96.

Office of the Privacy Commissioner of Canada (2006) OPC Guidelines for the Use of Video Surveillance of Public Places by Police and Law Enforcement Authorities. Ottawa. Online. Available HTTP: <http://www.privcom.gc.ca/information/guide/2008/gl_vs_080306.asp>.

Office of the Privacy Commissioner of Canada (2008) Guidelines for Overt Video Surveillance in the Private Sector. Ottawa. Online. Available HTTP: <http://www.privcom.gc.ca/information/guide/2008/gl_vs_080306.asp>.

Office of the Privacy Commissioner of Canada (2009) Guidelines for Covert Video Surveillance in the Private Sector. Ottawa. Online. Available HTTP: <http://www.privcom.gc.ca/information/guide/2008/gl_vs_080306.asp>.

Paton-Simpson, E. (2000) 'Privacy and the Reasonable Paranoid: The Protection of Privacy in Public Places', *University of Toronto Law Journal*, 50(3): 305–46.

Phillips, B. (1997) 'Privacy in a "Surveillance Society"', *University of New Brunswick Law Journal*, 46: 127–38.

Pomerance, R. (2004) 'Shedding Light on the Nature of Heat: Defining Privacy in the wake of R. v. Tessling', *Criminal Reports*, 23 (6th series): 229.

Radwanski, G. (2001a) *Federal Privacy Commissioner says 'no' to Street Surveillance Cameras.* 15 June. Online. Available HTTP: <http://www.privcom.gc.ca/media/an/nt_010620_e.asp>.

Radwanski, G. (2001b) *Privacy Commissioner's Finding on Video Surveillance by RCMP in Kelowna.* Online. AvailableHTTP: <http://www.privcom. gc.ca/cf-dc/pa/2001-%2002/02_05_b_011004_e.asp>.

Radwanski, G. (2002) *News Release.* 15 March. Online. Available HTTP: <http://www. privcom.gc.ca/media/nr-%20c/02_05_b_020315_e.asp>.

Renke, W. (2006) 'Who Controls the Past Now Controls the Future: Counter-Terrorism, Data Mining and Privacy', *Alberta Law Review*, 43: 779–823.

Steeves, V. (2008) 'If the Supreme Court were on Facebook: Evaluating the Reasonable Expectation of Privacy Test from a Social Perspective', *Canadian Journal of Criminology and Criminal Justice*, 50(3): 331–47.

Taylor, N. (2002) 'State Surveillance and the Right to Privacy', *Surveillance & Society*, 1(1): 66–85.

Legislation

Federal

Canadian Charter of Rights and Freedoms, Part I of the *Constitution Act, 1982*, being Schedule B to the *Canada Act 1982* (U.K.), 1982, c. 11.

Criminal Code, R.S., 1985, c. C-46.

Personal Information Protection and Electronic Documents Act, S.C., 2000, c. 5.

Privacy Act, R.S.C., 1985, c. P-21.

Provincial

Access to Information and Protection of Privacy Act, S.N.L. 2002, c. A-1.1 (Newfoundland and Labrador).

An Act Respecting Access to Documents held by Public Bodies and the Protection of Personal Information, R.S.Q., c. A-2.1, s. 64 (Quebec).

Freedom of Information and Protection of Privacy Act, R.S.A. 2000, c. F-25 (Alberta).

Freedom of Information and Protection of Privacy Act, R.S.B.C. 1996, c. 165 (British Columbia).

Freedom of Information and Protection of Privacy Act, C.C.S.M. c. F175 (Manitoba).

Freedom of Information and Protection of Privacy Act, S.N.S. 1993, c. 5 (Nova Scotia).

Freedom of Information and Protection of Privacy Act, R.S.O. 1990, c. F.31 (Ontario).

Freedom of Information and Protection of Privacy Act, R.S.P.E.I. 1988, c. F-15.01 (Prince Edward Island).

Freedom of Information and Protection of Privacy Act, S.S. 1990–91, c. F-22.01 (Saskatchewan).

Municipal Freedom of Information and Protection of Privacy Act, R.S.O. 1990, c. M.56 (Ontario).

Protection of Personal Information Act, S.N.B. 1998, c. P-19.1 (New Brunswick).

Privacy Act, R.S.B.C. 1996, c. 373 (British Columbia).

Privacy Act, C.C.S.M. c. P125 (Manitoba).
Privacy Act, R.S.N. 1990, c. P-22 (Newfoundland and Labrador).
The Privacy Act, R.S.S. 1978 c. P-24 (Saskatchewan).

Jurisprudence

Campbell v. MGN Ltd., [2004] 2 A.C. 457 (H.L.).
Canada (Combines Investigation Acts, Director of Investigation and Research) v. Southam Inc., [1984] 2 S.C.R. 145.
Canada (Privacy Commissioner) v. Canada (Attorney General), 2003 BCSC 862, [2003] 9 W.W.R. 242, 14 B.C.L.R. (4th) 359.
Douglas v. Hello! Ltd., [2005] All ER (D) 280 (C.A.).
Morgan v. Alta Flights (Charters) Inc., 2005 FC 421, 271 F.T.R. 298.
Peck v. The United Kingdom, no. 44647/98, [2003] E.C.H.R. 44 (Eur. Ct. H.R.).
P.G. and J.H. v. The United Kingdom, no. 44787/98, [2001] E.C.H.R. 550 (Eur. Ct. H.R.).
R. v. A.M., 2008 SCC 19, [2008] 1 S.C.R. 569.
R. v. Collins, [1987] 1 S.C.R. 265.
R. v. Duarte, [1990] 1 S.C.R. 30.
R. v. Edwards, [1996] 1 S.C.R. 128.
R. v. Garofoli, [1990] 2 S.C.R. 1421.
R. v. Gomboc, [2010] 3 S.C.R. 211.
R. v. Kang-Brown, 2008 SCC 18, [2008] 1 S.C.R. 456.
R. v. LeBeau (1988), 62 C.R. (3d) 157 (Ont. C.A.).
R. v. Loveridge, Lee and Loveridge, [2001] EWCA Crim 973 (C.A.).
R. v. Patrick, 2009 SCC 17, [2009] 1 S.C.R. 579.
R. v. Plant, [1993] 3 S.C.R. 281.
R. v. Tessling, [2004] 3 S.C.R. 432.
R. v. Wise, [1992] 1 S.C.R. 527.
R. v. Wong, [1990] 3 S.C.R. 36.
Somwar v. McDonald's Restaurants of Canada Ltd. (2006), 263 D.L.R. (4th) 752 (Ont. Sup. Ct. J.).

Office of the Privacy Commissioner reports

'Mother and Daughter were videotaped during covert surveillance of another individual', *PIPEDA Case Summary #2009–007*, Office of the Privacy Commissioner of Canada.
'Bus terminal video surveillance is challenged by company employee', *PIPEDA Case Summary #2009–001*, Office of the Privacy Commissioner of Canada.
'Identification machines and video cameras in bars examined', *PIPEDA Case Summary #2008–396*, Office of the Privacy Commissioner of Canada.
'Individual objects to being photographed by private investigation', *PIPEDA Case Summary #2008–392*, Office of the Privacy Commissioner of Canada.
'Personal relationship between two employees triggers covert video surveillance by employer and raises consent issues', *PIPEDA Case Summary #2007–388*, Office of the Privacy Commissioner of Canada.
'A woman's activities recorded and videotaped by a private investigator hired by an insurance company', *PIPEDA Case Summary #2005–311*, Office of the Privacy Commissioner of Canada.

'Video surveillance cameras at food processing plant questioning', *PIPEDA Case Summary #2005–290*, Office of the Privacy Commissioner of Canada.

'Surveillance of employees at work', *PIPEDA Case Summary #2004–279*, Office of the Privacy Commissioner of Canada.

'Video cameras and swipe cards in the workplace', *PIPEDA Case Summary #2004–264*, Office of the Privacy Commissioner of Canada.

'Employer hires private investigator to conduct video surveillance on employee', *PIPEDA Case Summary #2004–269*, Office of the Privacy Commissioner of Canada.

21

PRIVACY AS SECURITY

Comparative developments in Canada, the UK and the USA

Christopher Burt

Introduction

We are fast approaching a world in which persistent and absolute identification of the individual is a possibility. In fact, many believe we have already surpassed the technological impediments to such a reality, having only to engender the collective social, economic and political will for its arrival. With absolute identity comes absolute freedom, or so the story goes (Garfinkel 2001). Freedom requires a foundation of trust, however, and trust begins with the opportunity for properly informed consent. This chapter will explore some of the privacy implications concomitant with the continued spread and technological development of global open-street camera surveillance systems. The municipality of Hoboken, New Jersey, USA was used for a city-wide surveillance case study and the data collection effort included 500 voluntary and anonymous pencil and paper public opinion surveys solicited from individuals at various locations and at various times throughout the city. Where appropriate, those survey results are incorporated for comparative purposes and particular focus will be given to discussing the issue of informed consent vis-à-vis the presence or absence of public signage as well as the uncertainty that clouds the decision-making models that govern our daily privacy concerns. The gradual leakage of personal information to our technological environment has not only created a growing security threat, but also an opportunity to recast privacy as a form of security in public debate.

Owing to the developments that have taken place over the past few decades, camera surveillance has assumed an integral part of daily life, but the scope of the system implementations are themselves evolving. Whereas the surveillance efforts of the past were held in check by real physical and technological limitations, the systems being developed today are quite capable of clearing those hurdles. Stunning technological innovations in both computing power and telecommunications capabilities are enabling organic data networks to emerge, at once extending the reach of surveillance efforts by knitting together previously isolated domains and at the same time subjecting the product of that surveillance to machine-driven analysis as a result of digitization. The centrality of the human figure in the conduct of those observations is, to a large extent, receding. Wireless technologies further encroach on spatial protections historically granting privacy. With the pervasive development and deployment of ubiquitous surveillance technologies, we must consider privacy and surveillance in an ever wider and inter-related context.

That same technology also makes it possible to relieve us of the mundane, to connect us to one another, and to improve the quality of our lives. Ever present, but unobtrusive and largely unseen; these are the hallmarks of such enabling and efficient systems and devices. Indeed, today's ubiquitous computing environments are providing us with unprecedented means with which to become informed about, and to interact with, the broader societies that surround us. Yet, such openness and reciprocity cannot flourish without a foundation of trust, accountability and informed consent. Perhaps the not-so-distant future does foretell a time in which the whole of the human race will unite in one effortless, benevolent and technological communicative hum. Until then we are well served to remember that the information exchange is not always reciprocal, and seldom is it directly under our control. These life-enhancing technologies also have the potential to divulge a great deal of personal information to those who stand ready, willing and able to make a note of it (Moncrieff Venkatesh and West 2009).

While it is difficult to advance a set of generalizations with respect to the extent of the impact on privacy resulting from camera surveillance implementations, impact itself is a certainty, and it must be examined in the context of the inter-play among technological, organizational and cultural factors (Hempel and Töpfer 2004). Privacy lacks a universal construct, and individual opinions differ widely when it comes to defining what is personal in nature and what is available for opportunistic public consumption. After all, privacy is not the product of logic, nor is it the product of experience. Rather it is the product of local social anxieties and local ideals (Sullivan 2006). Perceptions, and the effects of messaging, weigh heavily on the decision-making process, as noted for example with the spread of camera surveillance in Canada having been influenced by publicly perceived successes in the UK (Whitson, Doyle and Walby 2009).

As a practical matter, the more we develop systems and devices that communicate seamlessly with one another and the more these systems become embedded and networked within our infrastructure, the further we encroach upon the sanctity of private space; that largely self-defined sphere of anonymity over which an individual holds dominion. While these technological developments herald tremendous advances in efficiency and convenience, they impose an ever-increasing burden of vigilance with respect to the release of personal information. We must be on guard to limit the varied devices we carry to ensure that they are not unwittingly broadcasting our personal secrets, responding to the myriad sensors and pathways that have come to exist throughout our urban and suburban landscapes. This world of technical ubiquity affords us great freedom of movement and information exchange, while at the same time threatening to link us inexorably to the physical and the quotidian.

As active participants in this ubiquity we are helpless to conceal the totality of the personal. The 'always on' nature of camera surveillance technologies leaves us vulnerable to continuous information leakage, as we are unable to exercise full and constant control over every observable aspect of our lives (Moncrieff, Venkatesh and West 2009). Habits that we would consider to be of little interest to others are no longer indistinguishable from the daily flotsam and jetsam. Inexpensive storage capacity has all but eliminated the temporal aspect of our lives. Surveillance technologies are readily and economically available, and what was once ignored can now be the subject of extensive and repetitive study. Our networks no longer need to forget, and much public and private resources have been directed towards the development of anticipatory models and analytic techniques to predict our motivations based on accumulated memory of those behavioural patterns and a host of environmental stimuli (Garfinkel 2001).

Privacy and informed consent

> Canada's electronic surveillance legislation has failed to keep up with advances in wireless and digital communications technologies. In some respects, the current regime unjustifiably impedes efforts to investigate suspects using these technologies; in others, it fails to adequately protect against the novel threats to privacy imposed by those technologies.
>
> *(Penney 2008: 1)*

In the past we could rely on the limitations inherent to the physical world for the preservation of our private space. However, advances in wireless technology have levelled those assumptions. Wireless surveillance cameras can now overcome even the most challenging of spatial constraints, and the acoustic microphones that maintain synchronous communication with those cameras can direct their gaze based on the level of audible activity (Dilworth 2007). The Netherlands have even introduced an audio–visual surveillance system that attempts to ascertain the tone used in conversation, listening for signs of aggression and then directing the camera's gaze accordingly (Bowditch 2009). In many cities around the globe, walking the street may no longer be a private affair. Urban areas that were once considered to be isolated and remote can now be brought to purview with these adaptive surveillance technologies. Whereas we continue to have a reasonable expectation of privacy in our own homes, it is highly questionable as to whether such an expectation continues to be rational when it comes to our open public spaces (Garfinkel 2001). The Hoboken case study reveals that there continues to be strong support for such privacy, with over 69 per cent of survey respondents supporting the belief that they have a right to privacy while outside in an open public place.

These public spaces have historically proven to be a forum for the recognition, if not always the celebration, of societal differences and disorder. They were also conceived as being uniquely democratic, in the sense that access was not dependent on status but guaranteed by virtue of being a citizen (McCahill and Norris 2002). These democratic spaces facilitate disparate human interactions, potentially threatening the status quo via the synthesis of alternative ways of living. As a tool for enhancing the safety of public spaces, however, the effectiveness of camera surveillance systems is hotly debated, with studies supporting a variety of opinion (KPMG 2000; Ratcliffe, Taniguchi and Taylor 2009; Welsh and Farrington 2008; Cameron et al. 2008). Its consistent popularity may perhaps be better understood as a reliance on long-established mental models of scrutiny, and the criminalization of activities of the least powerful inhabitants of urban areas (Coleman 2004). Some argue for the purification of such spaces through the use of audio-visual surveillance technologies. In fact, research suggests that the impact of such surveillance tends to be the straightforward exclusion of disfavoured groups, with the end result being that public spaces are becoming less public (Coleman 2004). Today many argue that public spaces are being reconstituted, not as venues for democratic interaction but as forums for mass consumption (McCahill and Norris 2002).

Absent specific legal protections or legislative mandates that require us to divulge information, individuals are actively engaged in making privacy choices every day. In effect, we are granting or withholding informed consent with every public and private interaction with other individuals, society and the environment. The most troublesome is handling the complexities. We cannot, for example, be fully aware of the processes behind every information exchange. Maintaining adequate control over private information has been made all the more difficult by a networked, digitized and interconnected society. The interplay has become ubiquitous and often invisible (Acquisti and Grossklags 2006).

What then is the meaning of informed consent vis-à-vis this complex and interconnected ubiquitous computing world, and how can the citizenry possibly be expected to grant or to deny it to any meaningful degree? Above all, consent implies full and comprehensive awareness; an awareness not only of environmental facts and circumstances but of the potentialities that go hand in hand with them. Granting informed consent suggests the ability to foretell circumstances or outcomes based on the processing of facts and particulars through the prism of our own decision-making abilities. Of course, there is no such practical reality where one can be in command of a state of perfect information, and our decision-making abilities can be greatly affected by messaging and advertising.

Nevertheless, people continue to make privacy choices. Indeed, people frequently reach those decisions based on incomplete information and they know little about associated consequences. When it comes to privacy issues related to data collection, the subjects providing the information often do not know the extent to which that data will be used or shared. The implications behind the disclosure of personal data can result in a multitude of consequences that individuals are hardly able to grasp. Even with access to complete information and the cognitive power to process it, the vagaries of their decision-making processes could lead individuals to contradictory or inconsistent conclusions with respect to the granting or withholding of informed consent (Acquisti and Grossklags 2006).

The resulting condition is one in which we are unlikely to secure the return of personal information that has been leaked into the environment. The complexity is such that we simply do not know how to purge the systems of our private data. This immediately raises issues from a privacy perspective, since informed consent relies on one's ability to anticipate outcomes based on a set of actions. Of course, the extent to which this becomes a problem is dictated by one's threshold for personal privacy and that is one of the great unknowns when it comes to the privacy debate. There is no universal construct for privacy. We are for the most part free to define our own limits within our respective spheres of anonymity.

After all, the construct of privacy is a uniquely human phenomenon, perhaps the product of centuries of anthropological iterations encompassing both psychological development and the evolutionary social context of tribal and clan based communal living for survival. Under those difficult circumstances being left alone meant more than just a failure to reproduce; isolation may very well have led to death. As a result, our ancestors tended to huddle close to one another out of dire necessity. It is quite easy to imagine the protection of one's individuality and privacy as an outgrowth of humans having lived in such close contact with one another for so long (Pelusi 2007). Out of the communal living of antiquity our modern civil societies have emerged, with many differing views on what constitutes privacy. Jurists, politicians and scholars routinely engage in legal and policy debate in the absence of a shared construct of privacy, and yet, such an articulation is exactly what is necessary for a thorough analysis of these issues (Solove 2007).

To be anonymous is to lack identity, or to be otherwise unrecognizable. The construct of privacy is rooted within an individual's ability to exercise control over their own physical, intellectual or emotional anonymity (Slobogin 2002). Indeed, our public persona is defined by what we choose to reveal to others, relative to what selectively remains concealed. A so-called invasion of privacy can be thought of as an instance or circumstance whereby some aspect of an individual's life that lies within that sphere of private control ceases to be anonymous without their express action and consent. The option to exercise that control is encapsulated within a general expectation of privacy, and surveillance systems tend to penetrate such expectations.

Privacy also has a long association with ownership and property rights. An individual can reasonably expect to enjoy privacy within their own home, for example, whereas once they enter a workplace that expectation begins to deteriorate along the lines of property rights, ownership and control. That being said, where do public places fall in terms of a right to privacy? As outlined, technological advances and legal ambiguities have created a circumstance where the systematic surveillance of public space proceeds largely unchecked. The omnipotent threat lies in the progressive monitoring of public places, where technological ability and legal ambiguity have created something of a surveillance free-for-all. The discussion has moved from one centred on private domiciles to one based on an expansive expectation that our public spaces are in fact anything other than private (Garfinkel 2001).

In an 'always on' ubiquitous computing society, it is the legal protections surrounding individual privacy that establish the boundaries along which the envelope of informed consent is pushed and tested. In absolute terms, that sphere of anonymity is demarcated by those protections. Given the fungible nature of an individual's perception of privacy, it is of little mystery that protections are piecemeal and that major jurisdictional differences abound. Protections in the USA tend to be tightly focused and centred on addressing the potential for governmental intervention in private affairs, whereas European initiatives tend to be broader and more focused on curbing commercial abuses by corporations (Sullivan 2006). Canadian protections have developed along the lines of separate provisions governing the conduct of public or private actors, whether in public or private space (Johnson 2009).

The reality is that individuals often cannot regain control over information once it has been leaked or released into the environment, and privacy protections are often the by-products of unrelated transactions. The Hoboken case study illustrates some of the competing ambiguities with 61 per cent of survey respondents reporting that they would not like to see live data streams from surveillance systems available over the Internet, yet over 75 per cent report that data captured from a surveillance system should be saved for at least a year. When asked if they were concerned about who owns or controls data collected from surveillance systems, 70 per cent affirmed, yet nearly 82 per cent report not knowing where to go or whom to call to review surveillance system data. Whatever privacy benefit accrues over the course of the transaction may be attached to those goods and services indirectly, making comparisons difficult for an individual to manage. Such analysis may be further complicated due to the uncertainties or ambiguities that result from lacking perfect information (Acquisti and Grossklags 2006).

While no explicit constitutional prohibition on public surveillance can be found in the USA, the practice tends to be viewed through the prism of collective judicial interpretations that together have developed into a right to privacy. Similar circumstances may be found in Canada, and no legislation explicitly authorizing the use of public camera surveillance has been adopted. Further variations in protections exist between provinces (Johnson 2009). In contrast, Article 8 of the European Convention for the Protection of Human Rights and Fundamental Freedoms provides a right of respect for a person's 'private and family life, his home and his correspondence', and the use of camera surveillance technology squarely falls within the scope of the landmark EU Directive 95/46/EC, which specified a minimum threshold of care with respect to personal data information-handling. Generally speaking, however, a reasonableness test has come to be applied for any given set of circumstances, based on whether or not the public would have a reasonable expectation of privacy.

Perceptions of surveillance

> A more important achievement [than a reduction in the crime rate] is the change in public perception. A sense of community wellness is replacing exasperations and fears as criminals rethink the cost of committing crimes in East Orange. The added sense of safety has greatly enhanced the city's redevelopment and revitalization efforts, as an increasing number of developers and investors now want to do business in the community.
>
> *(Cordero 2007:1)*

People incorporate any measure of public space into their daily lives, and the experience and interaction they have within that space often plays a significant role in their development of personality and sense of self. The right to privacy incorporates that aspect based on the right of individuals to freely define boundaries, as well as another based on freedom from the imposition of standardized lifestyles. Privacy implies individual control, and surveillance systems can come under fire for obstructing that control through the imposition of conformity over public behaviour. The act of surveillance places pressure on individuals to restrain the public display of what may be perceived to be a socially aberrant demeanour.

Communal living itself has a tendency to reinforce the set of social norms on those who deviate too far from group behavioural practices. Indeed, socially imposed conformity often stands in direct opposition to an individual's need for privacy. This may have the effect of heightening our innate sense of protection with respect to that sphere of anonymity. The paradox of the modern age is that in a world filled with anonymous faces, privacy is readily obtainable. Having obtained it, we then run the 'risk of slipping into detachment, isolation and anxiety' (Pelusi 2007). A sense of community, guidance and support may be closely associated with our mental models of surveillance technologies.

Camera surveillance was thrust to the forefront of public consciousness in Britain in 1993 when cameras in a Merseyside shopping centre captured the moment when two 11-year-old boys, John Venables and Robert Thompson, kidnapped and ultimately murdered two-year-old Jamie Bulger (Gupta 2005). The case generated public outcry, leading Venables and Thompson to become the youngest individuals to be charged with murder in England during the twentieth century. Facts would later show that the little boy suffered extreme violence at the hands of his young killers, and the circumstances of his death still haunt many today. The dialogue on societal security and individual freedom has become contentious, leading to the widespread perception that a trade-off exists between security and surveillance. There is little public discussion as to whether or not additional surveillance contributes directly to security, and less still over what is lost in the way of privacy and civil rights (European Parliamentary Technology Assessment (EPTA) Network 2006).

Witness how quickly surveillance technologies have become an integral part of crime control policy. They have come to be promoted by police and politicians alike, as the primary solution for urban dysfunction. It is not uncommon to see local community groups pleading with local police and administration officials for the resources and support necessary to mount large-scale surveillance camera installations in the commercial streets and on the residential blocks in which those community activists work and live. The success of the grassroots organization, Friends Against Senseless Endings, in bringing public camera surveillance to the streets of downtown London, Ontario, in 2001 is just such an example (Hier et al. 2007). Even though the majority of people have concerns about issues of privacy, there is ample evidence to suggest that they do not see surveillance cameras as a significant factor in formulating those concerns (Leman-Langlois 2009).

In deference to the phrase famously coined by noted media theorist Marshall McLuhan, 'The medium is the message', camera surveillance technologies offer policy-makers a seductive medium. In a public policy domain which is notoriously indeterminate, camera surveillance technology has a sexy and powerful image. The clear message is that surveillance is synonymous with security, and its iconic promotion is almost guaranteed to create a feel-good response within those communities plagued with crime, whether those offences are real or imagined. When people are frightened of criminals, critics of surveillance technologies are often portrayed as enemies of the public interest (Privacy International 1997).

To be certain, there are real security threats fuelling the spread of surveillance. Crime is a loathsome reality and terrorist actions from local cells operating within national borders have caused us to look inwards with less focus on personal liberty and more on communal security and public safety. As an example, the Canadian government and police authorities' surveillance technology responses are based on the premise that Canada is also at risk from domestic and international terror plots (Deisman 2009). In the context of the Hoboken case study, 79 per cent of survey respondents reported that the primary purpose of a surveillance system is personal safety and security, and more than 88 per cent supported the concentration of such systems on areas experiencing higher crime rates. To ignore such public sentiment is simply not a viable policy or sovereign objective. With over 71 per cent of those surveyed reporting feeling safer and more secure in public settings in the presence of a surveillance system, the severity of the potential outcome from a heinous crime or terrorist event is often sufficient to foster support for exceptionally invasive (vis-à-vis privacy) security measures (Deisman 2009).

According to a recent industry analysis report, the worldwide market for camera surveillance is projected to reach US$28 billion by the end of 2013, with governmental initiatives contributing significantly to overall growth (RNCOS E-Services Pvt Ltd 2010). Although Canada is not yet characterized by a propensity for camera surveillance, the spread is steady. Similar to the UK and the USA, unless the proposed location of the technology is particularly sensitive the public tends to be supportive, or at worst, indifferent (Lyon 2009). Perhaps this sentiment reflects the notion that public spaces imply disclosure rather than concealment. As a practical matter, one's presence in, or use of, a public resource or facility is itself an act of revelation, and the courts have been careful to maintain the distinction between physical intrusion and mere observation with respect to law enforcement operatives and their environs. The assertion is that persons in public space have not taken the necessary steps to conceal their activities from the casual observer, and therefore no public expectation of privacy should be applied. Nevertheless, for many people their expectation of privacy does extend into the public purview (Slobogin 2002). Those expectations are not absolute, however, and many have shown a willingness to compromise privacy if justifiable on the basis of enhanced security or efficiency measures (Slobogin 2002).

Research suggests that the conventional policy formation model does not apply when it comes to surveillance installations. Regardless of the setting, surveillance cameras are portrayed as beneficial in, if not vital to, law enforcement and the fight against crime and the public largely presumes it so. The collective mental model anticipates usefulness, even if it is not immediate (Deisman 2009). This type of qualitative decision-making process can be subjected to marketing and communication efforts that may be used to influence public opinion, further altering mental models and influencing collective attitudes. Individuals who do not adopt available data protection technologies or who readily share information with unfamiliar parties may have little appreciation of future risks. Such low valuation of risk could result from a lack of trust of existing privacy protection measures (Acquisti and Grossklags 2006). With respect to the Hoboken case study, for example, the survey responses were equally split when participants were asked if they thought the planning and operation of surveillance systems belonged in public hands with those supporting and those opposing each at 42 per cent.

Philosopher and social theorist Jeremy Bentham is credited with the design of the panopticon, a prison control structure consisting of a central inspection tower surrounded by a ring of cells, each housing an inmate. Those living in the confines around the outer circle could never be sure as to whether or not they were under watch from those in the central tower. This state of constant and pervasive *potential* surveillance, it was believed, would exert a significant level of social control over inmate behaviour, and subject to which would leave them with conformity as the only real option. The architectural design created a state of conscious and permanent visibility, assuring automatic functioning of self-control and self-discipline (McCahill and Norris 2002).

The East Orange New Jersey Police Department's Virtual Community Patrol programme is an interesting twist on the theory that underlies Bentham's panopticon. The programme allows for specially selected individuals to access the department-linked video monitoring system via the Web. Using their home computers, they can instantly alert police to criminal complaint activity and pinpoint problem locales (Dilworth 2007). Public opinion is likely to be most effectively influenced by law enforcement practices that stress crime prevention as their foremost value (Cameron et al. 2008), and one of the challenges facing our leaders is the repackaging of a policing culture that is primarily focused on criminal apprehension into one that is associated with preventative measures (Cordero 2007). Again, such public sentiments may further explain the widespread acceptance of surveillance technologies. In reference to the Hoboken case study, again, over 71 per cent of survey respondents reported feeling safer and more secure in public settings in the presence of a surveillance system, yet only 53 per cent reported a desire to have a surveillance system installed in their own neighbourhood and residential street. Such results suggest that people tend to feel safer in their own neighbourhoods, presumably because they know the area well.

Information and familiarity allow us to stretch our decision-making abilities, and reach those decisions with greater confidence. The feeling of safety is undoubtedly derived from the predictability of the environment, which may further illuminate the popularity of camera surveillance installations in spite of the fact that many of these installations are not actively monitored or even operational. The New York City subway system serves as an example. According to Metropolitan Transportation Authority officials, more than 2,000 of the 4,313 cameras that exist in stations and tunnels are not operational (Rivera and Grynbaum 2010). The cameras themselves have simply become fixed points in the landscape. Perhaps expectedly, ambivalence prevails with respect to surveillance of spaces with which people are more familiar. The 'not-in-my-backyard' argument is in conflict with the potential for benefit. While the public knows that camera systems are not always going to be effective in reducing crime rates, they see a possibility for them to be effective some of the time (Leman–Langlois 2009).

The typical use of surveillance systems does not constitute a physical intrusion, but merely an observation of what would otherwise have been made available to the naked eye. In a public space, however, an individual may still have expectations of a degree of anonymity based on time and place. The presence of a surveillance system may put undue scrutiny on activity that would otherwise go unnoticed or unheeded by passersby. Officers on patrol are able to conduct crime prevention directed patrols in one neighbourhood while virtually monitoring another. The possibility for repetitive analysis and dissemination eliminates the constraints of time and place, and may represent a restriction on personal privacy. As an example, occupants of a patrol car parked at a downtown location can directly observe a crowd assembled in the immediate area and via a dashboard monitor receive a live surveillance feed of activity many blocks away (Dilworth 2007). Surveillance cameras are used to monitor multiple locations simultaneously for signs of disorder, presumably with fewer resources. Law enforcement officials often maintain that random virtual patrols are ineffective, requiring targeted monitoring efforts based on real-time information. Human intelligence, we are told, increases the system's overall effectiveness (Cordero 2007).

The presence of a surveillance system may erode one's expectation of privacy in that it threatens public anonymity, and to that extent it may have a stultifying effect on one's behaviour. This has often been described as the potential chilling effect on public conduct that would otherwise be open and intended for all to see (Solove 2007). Such concerns are often raised in the context of freedom of speech and association, with the presumption often being surveillance followed by retaliation or an enforcement action of some kind. Concerns have also been raised over whether such systems may act on an individual's right to move about freely, causing them to alter routes or destinations in order to avoid any real or imagined ill effects, and individuals with innocent intent wishing to remain in public places may face a psycho-social impediment to doing so (Slobogin 2002).

Some hold the view that surveillance cameras support a normative commercial strategy based on spatial ordering to support socio-economic development. Redevelopment efforts across the city make reference to reuse and reclamation of areas lost to consumption, proposing surveillance installations as a means of restoring consumer, tourist and investor confidence. In the UK such street safety initiatives figure prominently in urban policy (Coleman 2004). There is conflicting evidence that these surveillance systems aid in the actual deterrence and investigation of crime but many cite the increased perception of public safety as a socio-economic good in and of itself (Kaulessar 2009). This becomes an important point for consideration when deciding whether or not to propose open street and mass transit surveillance systems. The argument in support of installation is that feelings of insecurity will lead to lower utilization rates. Heightened public perceptions of safety will increase the flow of pedestrian traffic and correspondent levels of spending, thereby stimulating economic activity and revitalizing areas experiencing urban decline and decay (Whitson, Doyle and Walby 2009).

With respect to notice and disclosure, there are competing positions. In Canada, for example, every province has its own Freedom of Information and Protection of Privacy Act, which presumes to restrict institutions from the collection and use of personal information, but significant exceptions are granted for law enforcement purposes (Johnson 2009). As a tool for crime deterrence, it would seem most logical that perpetrators be made aware of a surveillance system's existence. This would best serve the preventative nature of law enforcement goals, and elevate public perception of safety and security. With respect to the Hoboken case study, this is reflected in public opinion, with over 77 per cent of survey respondents expressing the belief that the public should be informed as to the use and location of surveillance systems and 62 per cent favouring the placement of descriptive signage at areas around the perimeter of surveillance. The prosecutorial and investigative aspect of law enforcement might tend to favour selective or total concealment. Needless to say, such a choice tends to elevate concerns about privacy, further compounded by advances in the development of identity management technologies (Lizar and Potter 2010).

Public signage presents an even more complex set of possibilities. Certainly, for the public, some kind of physical notification must be accessible if we are to be given an opportunity for informed consent. The lack of consistency with respect to signage form and content, and the differences that exist in jurisdictional applicability, mean that anyone who runs across notice of a camera-monitored area would be possessed of imperfect information about the variability in safety and security that can be expected to accrue from such installations (Lippert 2009).

The spread of surveillance systems is approved of not only by policy-makers concerned with safety and security but also by a majority of the citizens who themselves are subject to the surveillance. The conclusion drawn is that the public views security obtained through technologically enhanced forms of control as no less discriminatory than that obtained by traditional social control. In the very physical sense, surveillance cameras are a symbol of scrutiny and omnipresent authority. However, such a mood does not resonate with the general public, whose suspicions have waned (Coleman 2004). Although public opinion reflects the conflict between privacy and security, the majority of those who perceive privacy as a surveillance camera concern seem to favour security. The problem of informed consent is compounded by such perceptions, as the collective decision-making model may be incomplete. Imperfect information may lead us to accept inadvertently the sharing of personal information between private security operatives and the police or the municipal government (Lippert 2009).

Deployment of surveillance systems in public settings inevitably encroaches on the public's expectation of privacy. To address such expectations it is vital that such implementations have clearly communicable and understandable goals and objectives. Furthermore, it is beneficial to keep and maintain well-documented policies and procedures with respect to the sources and uses of surveillance data, and that such information is made available through public disclosure. In the absence of such information the public's ability to give informed consent is compromised, which raises ethical issues that warrant continued research in this area.

Conclusion

> The complexity of the privacy decision environment leads individuals to arrive at highly imprecise estimates of the likelihood and consequences of adverse events, and altogether ignore privacy threats and modes of protection.
>
> *(Acquisti and Grossklags 2006: 3)*

Technological advances are making our lives easier and fulfilling their promise to improve vastly quality of life and the human condition. They enable us to be more productive and efficient at work, to attain ever-higher levels of achievement and to garner more enriching experiences from leisure time pursuits. Communications have become instantaneous, and everyday transactions have lost their anonymity. Society is entering a new era; one of truly ubiquitous, always on, computing. Sensors and machines are attuned to individual characteristics and personalities, making continuous authentication and the micro-delivery of products and services possible. Vast behavioural data stores of the mundane are being interconnected and mined, with patterns of the quotidian emerging. Invisible technologies that function over interconnected networks are increasingly embedded in the environment in ways that are both non-intrusive and supportive. The growth in wireless technologies allows for an unprecedented level of unseen engagement with everyday objects and activities, and these devices are able to communicate seamlessly with one another, with wider structures, data repositories and electronic resources. One of the greatest challenges that lies ahead is in providing users with an effective method of informed consent.

Blending seamless communication with ubiquitous computing devices opens up a whole new world of context-aware technologies. Designed to recede into the periphery, these devices are meant to be unseen and can form an intelligent technological fabric that can take action based on changes to the environment, passive behaviour or specific characteristics of human subjects in the purview. Services running within such a framework can steadily acquire cues from the environment and remote data warehouses, share that information, and based on rules or an intelligent stimulus, adapt accordingly. This interconnectedness of people and place is a positive development for civil discourse. While undoubtedly offering great benefit to individuals and society alike, such context-aware technologies can also befall an erosion of privacy.

Technology has a definite impact on society, but so too does society hold sway over the use of technology. Privacy protection methods should be integrated with the advances in surveillance systems and should aim to maximize privacy while respecting purpose. We need to consider infrastructure that minimizes the outward flow of information from system participants and holds true to the spirit of fair information practices (Moncrieff, Venkatesh and West 2009).

The surveillance of public spaces has seen rapid growth, and advances in digital surveillance technology have changed the rules of the game entirely. Where present, surveillance signage rarely affords the public with the opportunity to grant informed consent. The special needs of persons with visual disabilities and literacy difficulties are systematically ignored, and very often the location of signage has already placed the data subject within the purview of the camera (Lippert 2009). There is no longer a barrier to indefinite storage, and search technology combined with improvements in face and gait recognition is providing us with the tools to consistently and persistently identify individuals. One day soon it may be possible to leverage the growth in organic data networks and connectivity to find the location of a specific person at a particular time on a particular date (The Royal Academy of Engineering 2007).

It is clear that the public is being asked to make decisions regarding surveillance technologies in a state of imperfect information. Protecting one's privacy under such circumstances is a difficult proposition. When it comes to questions of security, many choose to err on the side of privacy loss. To reclaim privacy as a platform for public debate may require us to redefine our notion of security. We may need to develop a new understanding of privacy as a *form* of security. Re-examining the nature of personal information and the growing means by which it can be inadvertently leaked into our ubiquitous computing environments may well engender a new surveillance debate, one that is centred on maintaining absolute privacy as the true measure of security (Leman-Langlois 2009).

Acknowledgements

I would like to take this opportunity to extend a heartfelt thanks to my academic advisor, Dr Susanne Wetzel, for her continued guidance and unfaltering support. She has been a beacon of clarity and resolve without which this project simply would not have been made possible. I would also like to acknowledge the contributions of the following individuals with respect to the development of this chapter: Ms Tista Das and Ms Mary Meladath. Our academic project work together informed my decision to pursue this research.

References

Acquisti, A. and Grossklags, J. (2006) 'What Can Behavioral Economics Teach Us About Privacy?' Presented as Keynote Paper at ETRICS (Emerging Trends in Information and Communication Security) 2006. Freiburg, Germany: Carnegie Mellon University and UC Berkeley: 1–13.

Bowditch, G. (2009) 'Big Brother is not Earning His Keep: A Security Camera Which not Only Films but Records has Been Tried Out in Glasgow, But is it Worth the Money?' *Times Online*, 15 February. Online. Available HTTP: <http://www.timesonline.co.uk> (accessed 24 February 2009).

Cameron, A., Kolodinski, E., May, H. and Williams, N. (2008) 'Measuring the Effects of Video Surveillance on Crime in Los Angeles.' Prepared for the California Research Bureau (CRB-08-007), School of Policy, Planning, and Development, University of Southern California.

Coleman, R. (2004) 'Watching the Degenerate: Street Camera Surveillance and Urban Regeneration', *Local Economy*, 19(3): 199–211.

Cordero, J.M. (2007) 'How Computers Joined the Force', *New Jersey State League of Municipalities*, December. Online. Available HTTP: <http://www.njslom.org> (accessed 17 October 2009).

Deisman, W. (2009) 'Factors Behind the Implementation of Camera Surveillance', *A Report on Camera Surveillance in Canada: Part One*, 21–8.

Dilworth, K.C. (2007) 'East Orange Sees Big Drop in Crime', *The Star-Ledger*, 23 February.

European Parliamentary Technology Assessment (EPTA) Network (2006) *ICT and Privacy in Europe: Experiences from Technology Assessment of ICT and Privacy in Seven Different European Countries*. Research Report, Netherlands: EPTA Privacy Project.

Garfinkel, S. (2001) *Database Nation*, Sebastopol, California: O'Reilly & Associates, Inc.

Gupta, S. (2009) 'A Close Look at Surveillance in Europe', *Deutsche Welle*, 30 April. Online. Available HTTP: <http://www.dw-world.de > (accessed 10 February 2009).

Hempel, L. and Töpfer, E. (2004) *Urban Eye, On the Threshold to Urban Panopticon? Analysing the Employment of CCTV in European Cities and Assessing its Social and Political Impacts, Working Paper No 15: CCTV in Europe*. Final Report, Berlin, Germany: Centre for Technology and Society, Technical University Berlin.

Hier, S.P., Greenberg, J., Walby, K. and Lett, D. (2007) 'Media, Communication and the Establishment of Public Camera Surveillance Programmes in Canada', *Media, Culture and Society*, 29(5): 727–51.

Johnson, M. (2009) 'The "Legality" of Camera Surveillance in Canada', *A Report on Camera Surveillance in Canada: Part Two*, 11–24.

Kaulessar, R. (2009) 'Turning Fear and Anger Into Action', *Jersey City Reporter*, 8 February.

KPMG (2000) Evaluation of the Lion's Eye in the Sky Video Monitoring Project. Sudbury, Ontario: Submitted to the Sudbury Regional Police Service.

Leman-Langlois, S. (2009) 'Public Perceptions of Camera Surveillance', *A Report on Camera Surveillance in Canada: Part One*, 41–52.

Lippert, R. (2009) 'Camera Surveillance, Privacy Regulation, and "Informed Consent", *A Report on Camera Surveillance in Canada: Part One*, 29–40.

Lizar, M. and Potter, G. (2010) 'Legal Compliance, Trust and Contextual Integrity of CCTV Signage: Some Methodological Notes.' Presented at '*Camera Surveillance in Canada' Workshop*, Kingston, Ontario.

Lyon, D. (2009) 'Introduction', *A Report on Camera Surveillance in Canada: Part Two*, 6–8.

McCahill, M. and Norris, C. (2002) *Urban Eye, On the Threshold to Urban Panopticon? Analysing the Employment of CCTV in European Cities and Assessing its Social and Political Impacts, Working Paper No 2: Literature Review*. Hull, United Kingdom: Centre for Criminology and Criminal Justice, School of Comparative and Applied Social Sciences, University of Hull.

Moncrieff, S., Venkatesh, S. and West, G.A.W. (2009) 'Dynamic Privacy in Public Surveillance', *Computer*, September: 22–8.

Pelusi, N. (2007) 'The Privacy Paradox', *Psychology Today Magazine*, November/December. Online. Available HTTP: <http://www.psychologytoday.com > (accessed 24 February 2009).

Penney, S. (2008) 'Updating Canada's Communications Surveillance Laws: Privacy and Security in the Digital Age', *Canadian Criminal Law Review*, 12(115): 1–62.

Privacy International (1997) 'CCTV Frequently Asked Questions', *Privacy International*, 22 July. Online. Available HTTP: <www.privacyinternational.org> (accessed 28 March 2009).

Ratcliffe, J.H., Taniguchi, T. and Taylor, R.B. (2009) 'The Crime Reduction Effects of Public CCTV Cameras: A Multi-Method Spatial Approach', *Justice Quarterly*, 26(4): 746–70.

Rivera, R. and Grynbaum, M.M. (2010) 'Lack of Video Slows Hunt for a Killer in the Subway', *The New York Times*, 30 March, New York edn: A19.

RNCOS E-Services Pvt Ltd (2010) *Global CCTV Market Analysis (2008–2012)*. Market Analysis, Noida, India: RNCOS E-Services Pvt Ltd.

Slobogin, C. (2002) 'Public Privacy: Camera Surveillance of Public Places and the Right to Anonymity', *Mississippi Law Journal*, 72: 213–99.

Solove, D.J. (2007) '"I've Got Nothing to Hide" and Other Misunderstandings of Privacy', *San Diego Law Review* (GWU Law School Publication Law Research Paper No 289), 44: 745–72.

Sullivan, B. (2006) 'Privacy Lost: EU, US Laws Differ Greatly', *MSNBC.com*, 19 October 19. Online. Available HTTP: <http://www.msnbc.msn.com > (accessed 4 February).

The Royal Academy of Engineering (2007) *Dilemmas of Privacy and Surveillance: Challenges of Technological Change*. London: The Royal Academy of Engineering.

Welsh, B.P. and Farrington, D.C. (2008) 'Effects of Closed Circuit Television Surveillance on Crime', *Campbell Systematic Reviews, The Campbell Collaboration*, 73.

Whitson, J., Doyle, A. and Walby, K. (2009) 'Camera Surveillance in Canada', *A Report on Camera Surveillance in Canada: Part One*, 9–20.

22

SOMETIMES WHAT'S PUBLIC IS PRIVATE

Legal rights to privacy in public spaces

Robert Ellis Smith

Introduction

Those interested in a higher level of privacy protection should challenge the notion that the right to privacy protects only that which occurs in private. Certainly in informational privacy, which covers personal information about ourselves, most of what we try to protect has been disclosed previously elsewhere. In communications privacy, which covers correspondence and conversations with others, those communications are exposed to strangers in the normal course of business. However, they are still protected. In physical privacy, which protects our bodies and living space and our present location, we are seeking to protect domains that are visible to the public quite often.

This chapter describes those sensitive parts of our lives that are deserving of privacy protection even though they are observed by others in public or semi-public settings. These aspects of our lives in fact have been recognized by courts in the United States and Canada and by other commentators as covered by traditional privacy protections. If these aspects of our lives are protected by a right to privacy, surely their exposure by unwanted community camera surveillance is an invasion of privacy.

'The accepted wisdom'

It has been conventional wisdom that nothing can be done legally about ubiquitous camera surveillance in our communities, that it does not violate any law or constitutional principle. Part of that accepted wisdom is the mistaken idea that because an activity takes place in public view, it is not protected by any expectation of privacy.

In fact, there are many activities in public that are entitled to privacy protection, according to the clear implications of previous federal court holdings in the US and

Canada. These include: going to and from a house of worship, an abortion clinic, or a medical facility; holding hands or embracing affectionately in public; participating in a political demonstration or wearing political symbols; reading a book or a magazine; mediating or praying, and perhaps chatting on a cell phone in a way that is audible nearby. The right to vote in the US and Canada may be interpreted to prohibit videotaping citizens as they visit a polling place.

'The Fourth Amendment protects people, not places,' said the US Supreme Court in the case of *Katz v. US*, 389 U.S. 347 (1967), in an opinion that restricted law enforcement's use of audio evidence seized from a public phone booth. And the Fourth Amendment to the US constitution protects not merely homes, but also citizens' 'persons, houses, papers, and effects'. The Fourth Amendment is akin to Section 8 of the Charter of Rights and Freedoms in Canada, and the case law under the Fourth Amendment and Section 8 are comparable.

In 1972, the US Supreme Court recognized that certain activities in public 'are historically part of the amenities of life as we have known them. They are not mentioned in the Bill of Rights [the first ten amendments to the US Constitution guaranteeing individual rights]. These unwritten amenities have been in part responsible for giving our people the feeling of independence and self confidence, the feeling of creativity. These amenities have dignified the right of dissent and have honored the right to be nonconformists and the right to defy submissiveness. They have encouraged lives of high spirits rather than hushed, suffocating silence': *Papachristou v. City of Jacksonville*, 405 U.S. 156 (1972). The court said that a state or city may not punish persons engaging in these amenities or 'wandering or strolling around from place to place without any lawful purpose or object'. In 1983, the court cited the *Papachristou* case approvingly: *Kolender v. Lawson*, 461 U.S. 352 (1983). In the *Kolender* case, the high court declared that there was not really any requirement in the US that a person wandering the streets must carry identification or account for what he is doing.

Would the court in 2010 allow a city or state to keep a permanent video record of these wanderings? The personnel of the court has changed significantly (and to the right) over the years, and there may not be a member of the current court who would endorse the opinion in the *Papachristou* case. Still, the case represents the kind of 'building blocks' of precedents that innovative lawyers must use to protect rights in the high-tech age.

What kind of transactions in public are 'private'?

An example of the kind of in-public activities that are entitled to privacy protection is affectionate hand-holding. 'A Day In Hand', a new equal-rights initiative in London, England, that aims to inspire same-sex couples worldwide to hold hands in public, has called on gay persons worldwide to hold hands on the last Saturday of each month so that the public will get used to the idea (see <http://www.adayinhand.com>). The first international Sshh! (same-sex hand-holding) Saturday was held 26 September 2009. David Watkins, the founder of the movement, acknowledged that this simple act of autonomy – and perhaps defiance – may be dangerous. For instance, Daniel Forgie, a photographer, told him, 'I live in downtown Vancouver, arguably one of the most gay-positive cities, in one of the few and first countries to legalize same-sex marriages and it is still really unsafe to hold hands. There have been numerous attacks just in the last year, even in the 'village''.' In an age of pervasive video monitoring, it is increasingly dangerous. Would anyone argue that such a simple public display of affection is any business of law enforcement? Would anyone argue that it is right to keep a permanent video record of this practice? Would anyone argue that the right to privacy, as we understand it in North America and Europe, does not protect this activity? (Watkins' campaign has been co-operating with a scholar at Dalhousie University in Halifax, Nova Scotia, Richard Wassersug, who studies anthropological phenomena.)

At McGill University in Montreal, the Queer McGill organization is said to have staged 'kiss-ins' in which gay couples kiss in public areas on the university's campus, to get passersby accustomed to the behaviour. President Obama, in a speech on 10 October 2009, said, 'Together we can look forward to that day when no one has to fear walking down the street holding the hand of the person they love' (Human Rights Campaign Dinner, Washington, DC, 11 October 2009). Of course, with state-run video cameras in place, there is every reason to believe that there will be persons who fear this for many years to come.

What about videotaping a woman's comings and goings at a clinic that administers abortions? The law of the land in both Canada and the United States protects the right of a woman to have an abortion without governmental intervention, based on the constitutional right to privacy. Would the same right not protect the right of a woman not to be photographed by state agents as she seeks the procedure? Would it protect against having a non-governmental group, like a group adamantly opposed to abortion, capture images outside a clinic and post them on the world wide web?

Legal scholars in the US disagree on the answers to these questions. Eugene Volokh, law professor at the University of California at Los Angeles, presumably referring to photography by private parties, not governmental agents, concludes that posting the photos is constitutionally protected free expression. But Laura Hodes, a writer and attorney in Chicago, argues,

> After all, the Supreme Court has dealt with clashes between asserted First Amendment rights and the constitutional right to obtain an abortion before – and has done so, in particular, in suits on behalf of women who sought not to be intimidated on their way to the abortion clinic. For example, in the 1994 case of *Madsen v. Women's Health Center* [512 U.S. 753 (1994)], the court upheld the constitutionality of a 36-foot buffer zone on a public street around an abortion clinic, as well as limited noise restrictions around the clinic. It remarked that 'The First Amendment does not demand that patients at a medical facility undertake Herculean efforts to escape the cacophony of political protests.'

'It would not be a stretch', continued Hodes, 'to say that the court would find that patients should not have to take Herculean efforts to escape prying cameras outside an abortion clinic, either.'

Actually, it may be a stretch. US Supreme Court Chief Justice William W. Rehnquist said in 1974 that he wasn't sure that an abortion was protected by the right to privacy because, after all, it was a procedure that was observed by others, like a doctor and a nurse! At the same time, in a speech at the University of Kansas Law School, Rehnquist declared there was no constitutional infirmity in the police photographing everybody at a political rally 'because citizens have no right to privacy when they attend a public rally'. 'Is an Expanded Right to Privacy Consistent with Fair and consistent Law enforcement? Or Privacy, You've Come a Long Way, Baby', 23 *University of Kansas Law Review* (1974). John G. Roberts, who became chief justice upon the death of Rehnquist in 2005, is even more hostile to notions of a constitutional right to privacy than was Rehnquist.

Another issue: cameras maintained by a clinic or by police to document harassment of patients may be constitutionally protected whereas cameras intended to deter or harass visitors may not be. Law-enforcement cameras intended to document clients' comings and goings may not be constitutionally permissible as well. Laura Hodes goes on to observe, 'It is worth asking whether we as a society want people posting photos of individuals entering a building for say an Alcoholics Anonymous meeting, or a support group for people with HIV.'

Other places

This notion of protecting privacy in public ought not to shock people, when they think about it. Hotel guests, for example, have a reasonable expectation of privacy in their rooms. *U.S. v. Allen*, 106 F.3d 695 (6th Cir. 1997). This is so even though housemaids enter hotel rooms daily to clean, replace linens and simply turn down the bed. Tenants have a legitimate expectation of privacy in their rental apartments. *U.S. v. Washington*, 573 F.3d 279 (6th Cir. 2009). Landlords and their agents need consent or advance notice to enter rented premises, and no one would argue that what goes on inside an apartment is the public's business because the dweller doesn't own the space and because over the course of a few years several people may come and go to and from the place.

In the nineteenth century, Western Union, the primary carrier of telegraph messages in the US and Canada, zealously proclaimed a strict policy of confidentiality even though scores of its employees routinely perused messages in their routine duties. And the policy gained protection by federal law in the US. Western Union employees are subject to 'strong temptations', said *The New York Times* in 1866 in supporting confidentiality protections. There is strong statutory protection for tax and census information in the US and Canada even though tax and census employees observe personal information routinely in the course of their work. It is the secondary use of this information that threatens privacy; by analogy, this principle extends to photographing, video taping, and live projection of images in public venues.

'Some degree of routine access [by strangers] is hardly dispositive with respect to the privacy question', wrote Danny Boggs, a 25-year veteran as an appeals court judge in the federal court system in the US, in a case decided in late 2010. *U.S. v. Warshak*, 631 F. 3d 266 (6th Cir. 2010).

Recent support for the idea

The US Court of Appeals for the Sixth Circuit, of which Boggs is now Chief Judge, decided in the *Warshak* case that 'a subscriber enjoys a reasonable expectation of privacy in the contents of emails that are stored with, or sent or received through, a commercial ISP [Internet service provider]'. The court, which is one of 12 regional courts adjudicating appeals at a level just below the US Supreme Court, used the same reasoning that justified confidentiality of tax, census and telegraph information, limiting photography without consent in public places, and protecting the privacy of an abortion procedure or of public displays of affection: *It is the attribute of the information or the activity, not whether it is observed by others, that determines the expectation of privacy.* The US Supreme Court has decided to let the Warshak decision stand as is.

Similarly a three-judge panel of the federal appellate court for the District of Columbia circuit ruled in August 2010 that police need a warrant (court approval) to install geographical positioning system (GPS) tracking capability to a vehicle. Jones 615 F. 3d 544 (D.C. Cir. 2010), formerly known as *U.S. v Maynard*.

The US Department of Justice objected to the ruling, saying that Americans should expect no privacy while in public. 'The panel's conclusion that [the drug defendant in the case] had a reasonable expectation of privacy in the public movements of his Jeep rested on the premise that an individual has a reasonable expectation of privacy in the totality of his or her movements in public places.' (Three other circuit courts have said that authorities do *not* need a warrant for GPS vehicle tracking.)

Cameras in public in Canada

The Supreme Court of Canada has ruled that an individual has an expectation of privacy not to be photographed without consent, even in a highly public place. The case involved Pascale Aubry, then a 17-year-old girl, photographed while she innocently sat on the steps of a bank in downtown Montreal in full view of everyone. The photographer claimed a right to snap the photo and to sell it as he wished. When the picture appeared on the cover of a small magazine, Aubry objected and she prevailed at every level of the court system. What was crucial to the majority of the Canadian Supreme Court was not where the photo may have been taken but whether an individual had a right to prevent commercial exploitation of his or her own image and persona. The court ruled in 1998 that the sale of the photograph without consent, if not merely the taking of it, violated the Quebec Charter of Human Rights and Freedoms. *Aubry v. Éditions Vice-Versa Inc.*, [1998] 1 S.C.R. 591.

The photographer, Gilbert Duclos, has conducted a campaign since then to reverse the holding and complains that such an 'imbecilic' policy of asking for permission before snapping a picture of another person in public prevails only in the Province of Quebec. But Canadian lawyers have pointed out that most jurisdictions in North America have essentially the same legal rule. It is called 'misappropriation' in American privacy law.

How are cameras different from human observers?

It is true that each of us, whenever we leave home and enter public spaces, runs the risk that another person will observe our movements, remember them, and tell others about them. That does not mean that we consent to a permanent video record being made of our comings and goings, a video record that may now be stored digitally, searched by date or by location or by characteristics (like time of day, weather conditions, proximity to landmarks in a community, the nature of a public gathering, or even the density of persons within camera view).

Videotape scenes can potentially be reviewed, in an automated way without human intervention, to detect persons with certain characteristics, including the geometrical relationships of the face of a person (biometrics).

It is this new *permanent* and *digital* search capacity that makes video monitoring a far greater threat than the possibility that any stranger will witness our activities in public. The permanent storage of electronic data is far more threatening than the possibility that another person may see us in a public place and even take notes or still photographs about what takes place. It is even more threatening than the possibility that a person may post the images on a website available to millions of persons around the globe.

Therefore, the place to look for Supreme Court precedents on whether governmental video surveillance is constitutional may be the line of cases concerning whether intrusions made possible by new technologies require a search warrant even though a warrant would not be required for surveillance conducted with the naked eye or ear. More about this later.

What is included in the right to privacy?

One reason that scholars and average citizens alike immediately – and erroneously – assume that there can be no privacy claim for things done in public is that they have a narrow view of privacy. Many people believe that privacy is about keeping personal secrets, and no more. But it *is* more. Privacy covers a right of autonomy, or what (in American legal arguments and Supreme Court opinions) has been called 'personhood'. This is akin to a right of autonomy, a right to do that which you desire to do unless it tends to harm others. In fact, the very first recognition of a right to privacy by the US Supreme Court, in the case of *Union Pacific Railway Co. v. Botsford*, 141 U.S. 250 (1891), involved not the right to keep secrets, but the right to control your own person. The court said, 'No right is held more sacred, or is more carefully guarded, by the common law, than the right of every individual to the possession and control of his own person, free from all restraint or interference of others, unless by clear and unquestionable authority of law.' Throughout the United States, Canada and the United Kingdom, there are camera surveillance systems installed without any authority of law at all.

Further, part of the right to privacy, in American jurisprudence, is a right of anonymity (not to be confused with *autonomy*). Repeatedly the US Supreme Court has proclaimed a right of anonymity in political discourse. The state may not ban or punish the circulation of political flyers that do not identify the author, for instance. Alan Westin, the foremost academic expert on privacy in the US, described anonymity as a form of privacy that 'occurs when the individual is in public places or performing public acts but still seeks, and finds, freedom from identification and surveillance'. Would not this right to anonymity argue against pervasive state camera surveillance in public places?

The constitutional right to privacy in the US has been based on several interests, including the constitutionally protected right against government interference with the right to assemble peaceably. This would mean that Rehnquist's acceptance of police cameras at political rallies is misplaced. The First Amendment, the source of the right to assemble, has also been held to include a 'right to read' (in other words, freedom to select reading materials free of undue government censorship or intrusion). If the gaze of the cameras is refined enough, this right to read is threatened by police cameras in public places.

Privacy Act covers federal monitoring

Beyond that, in the US, certain video surveillance *by a federal agency* that becomes part of a system of records in which information may be retrieved by an individual's name or identifiers violates the federal Privacy Act. The same principle would seem to apply to the Privacy Act in Canada and the Data Protection Act in the United Kingdom.

The Privacy Act enacted in the US in 1974 requires collected information to be relevant to a government agency's purpose, prohibits disclosure of personal information for purposes incompatible with the purpose for which it was collected, and requires 'to the greatest extent practicable' that information about a person be collected directly from the individual (same as in Canada). Further, the act says that federal agencies may 'maintain no record describing how any individual exercises rights guaranteed by the First Amendment unless expressly authorized by statute or by the individual'. The First Amendment protects freedom of speech, freedom to petition one's government and to assemble peacefully, and freedom to practise religion unfettered by the government. Thus this prohibition would seem to prohibit the federal government from gathering information – or images – about a person's reading, religious practices, political activities, legislative activism, friendships or associations. The law also permits an individual to inspect any 'records' (as in Canada and England), presumably including videotapes, about himself or herself.

What about video monitoring conducted by *private entities*, like a webcam or video camera in an office lobby or parking lot or overseeing a public sidewalk? Once again it has been assumed erroneously that 'if it's in public, it's not private'. But the monitoring is governed by the common law of torts (which has limited recognition in Canada and very little recognition in England, but is alive and well in the US). This allows for a victim to collect damages for commercial exploitation of any videotaping of a person's image without consent, even in a public space (misappropriation). Other branches of the tort would permit recovery of damages for (1) intrusion upon a person's solitude, (2) disclosing 'private facts' or (3) depicting a person 'in a false light'.

This 'misappropriation' tort is the commercial use of an individual's face, name or personality without consent, usually (but not always) implying endorsement of a product or service (as when a gift shop videotapes customers outside or inside its place of business and uses the images to imply that the individuals depicted endorse the business or its products). The persons depicted could sue for the misappropriation tort that is part of the common-law right to privacy. The misappropriation branch of the tort was implicated when nude photos of a 19-year-old player for the Toronto Maple Leafs were circulated on the Internet in 2007. Threatening possible legal action, a lawyer for the player succeeded in getting the images erased within hours, a miracle in the Internet age.

It is this misappropriation tort that is implicated also in Google's Street View product. Virtually all of the public objections to Street View in Canada and Europe have been based on vehicle registration numbers and individuals possibly being visible on the website, but Google promptly agreed to blur them out. (There have been hardly any objections to Street View in the US.)

What is more alarming than the possible inclusion of individuals or vehicle plates is Google's claim that it may capture images of a personal residence without consent and display the image on a site that is supported by advertising revenue. According to case law developed in the US under the misappropriation tort, the owner of the residence should share in the revenue, by way of royalties, or at least have the right to withhold consent to the display in the first place.

Privacy on Fifth Avenue

It's important to realize that the two most successful invasion-of-privacy (tort) lawsuits in the twentieth century in the US involved snooping *on public streets*. And they involved two of the most famous Americans in the century.

Jacqueline Kennedy Onassis successfully sued an independent paparazzo cameraman who, a federal court ruled, came too close to her and her children on the sidewalks of Fifth Avenue in New York City. Even though the cameraman rightfully claimed a First Amendment right to gather the news, the court in 1973 ordered him to keep his distance, at least 25 feet from her and her two children, and the court made its order stick. *Galella v. Onassis*, 487 F. 2d 986 (2d Cir. 1973).

Three years earlier, the highest court in New York State ruled that Ralph Nader could sue for damages resulting from monitoring of him in public places. *Nader v. General Motors Corp.*, 255 N.E. 2d 765 (Ct. App. N.Y. 1970). After Nader's documented criticism of unsafe automobile manufacturing, General Motors Corp. hired agents to shadow him everywhere he went in Washington. They even looked over Nader's shoulder when the man made personal bank transactions. Nader used the money from an eventual settlement with GM to finance his consumer advocacy over many years.

The New York court said, 'The mere gathering of information about a particular individual does not give rise to a cause of action . . . Privacy is invaded only if the information sought is of a confidential nature and the defendant's conduct was unreasonably intrusive . . . The plaintiff must show that the conduct was truly "intrusive" and that it was designed to elicit information *which would not be available through normal inquiry or observation.*'

Similar to constitutional standard

This implies that observation by a private entity that is enhanced by technology and therefore *abnormal* gives rise to a right to redress. This would closely track the constitutional standard in determining whether a governmental entity violates one's privacy: Is the government using techniques and technology *not in general public use?*

In 2001, in the case of *Kyllo v. U.S.*, 533 U.S. 27, the high court in the US reiterated its standard: 'Where . . . the government uses a ["sense-enhancing" technology] device that is *not in general public use*, to explore details of the home that would previously have been unknowable without physical intrusion, the surveillance is a "search" and is presumptively unreasonable without a warrant.' Would the same standard apply to specialized sense-enhancing technology focused not towards a home but on 'persons, papers, and effects' *in public* that have previously been regarded as constitutionally protected?

The next question is, are ubiquitous and covert TV cameras a type of technology not in general public use? Ten years ago, yes. In 2011? Perhaps not.

But what about use of the so-called 'black screen'? Simon Davies, the director general of Privacy International in London, has identified this as an emerging technology in England. It permits permanent archiving of video images and search capability by time and place, by biometric identifiers like face geometry, or by other criteria supplied by police.

Digital CCTV allows for more substantial archiving, comprehensive wireless networking and the potential for analysis of face, gait and even behaviour. The potential for use of such systems has attracted the interest of private and public sector bodies interested in pursuing 'black screen' technology that would involve less operator scrutiny with, ironically, a presumption of fewer threats of privacy invasion or discrimination. Research has been conducted by EPSRC [Engineering and Physical Sciences Research Council] in the UK on a prototype behaviour-recognition system that has been tested in Liverpool Street and Mile End stations, according to a 2004 study project on 'Privacy and Law Enforcement' by the UK Information Commissioner.

Surely, in an American court of law, civil rights lawyers could cogently argue that this pervasive surveillance is a type of technology *not in general public use*.

Mitigating technologies

If those civil rights lawyers are able to persuade a court that persuasive video surveillance in public places threatens individual rights under the US constitution, the remedy need not be an absolute ban on use of the technology. There is a series of mitigating technologies and administrative precautions that could make the cameras more palatable. The identity of individuals could be masked. The cameras could be programmed not to peer into private residences. The images could be erased after a reasonable period of time if no suspicious activity is detected. The 'dragnet' searching of the images could be prohibited without a warrant. A third-party entity could be created to administer the system and be authorized to search the images. This entity could enforce a ban on capturing images of activities that courts have said are entitled to privacy protection, the kinds of personal activities described here.

The restrictions put into place in the city of Toronto in 2001 form a good prototype, as is the Code of Practice developed by the Data Protection Commissioner in the United Kingdom. See 'Guidelines for the Use of Video Surveillance Cameras in Public Places', 2007, Information and Privacy Commissioner, Province of Ontario, <www.ipc.on.ca/images/Resources/video-e.pdf>. In the US there are no known guidelines for municipal camera surveillance.

Conclusion

We must recognize that privacy must be viewed as a right of personal autonomy, not simply a right to keep secrets. And we must recognize that there is a world of difference between being observed by strangers in the streets who then go about their business and have no capacity to remember all that they have seen, even if they care to, *and* being observed by electronic cameras that can transmit the images to computers for permanent storage and later searching by key words and key characteristics. Not to mention that there is always the possibility that these images will find their way to Internet sites without the consent of the individual involved; this is not a threat when we are observed by random strangers we encounter every day in public.

Simply because the technology has already been deployed everywhere does not mean that a challenge to it could not be successful. Simply because the cameras are in public places does not mean that the right to privacy does not protect many of the activities captured in the millions of images. To concede these points is to default on our birthrights of privacy, autonomy and anonymity, even in 'public' places.

INDEX

Abe, Kiyoshi 95
abortion 372–3
Abu Ghraib prison torture 69–70
accountability 6, 11, 193, 356; 'function creep' 194; signage 319; 'smart' surveillance 227, 230; surveillant assemblages 196
Accra 1
Acquisti, Allesandro 366
Afghanistan 1, 164
Africa 28–9, 110–12, 114
agency 268, 271
Airdrie 30, 32
Alberta 338, 348
Algeria 164
al-Midhar, Khalid 237
analogue signals 219
anonymity, right to 376, 379
anonymization of images 214, 227–8
ANPR see Automated Number Plate Recognition
anti-social behaviour 125, 126, 129, 147, 149, 295
anti-surveillance activists 12–13, 237–48; Canada 128–9; Japan 94; survey participants 275; Turkey 148
appropriation 265, 266, 267–8, 269–70, 262–72
area signs 324
Argentina 259
Armitage, Rachel 25
Armstrong, Gary 38, 157, 285, 289n9
art 14, 263–4, 268, 270, 272

Arteaga Botello, Nelson 13–14, 94, 95–6, 249–61
assemblages, surveillant 11, 140–1, 180, 196–7, 230, 330
AssistUK 57
Athens 10, 127, 179–80, 182
Atick, Joseph 226–7
Aum Shinrikyo 88
Australia: Automated Number Plate Recognition 164; CCTV development 28; Crime Stoppers 204–5, 209; evaluation of CCTV 29, 30, 32; taxi cab cameras 188, 195
Austria 26, 27, 164
Automated Number Plate Recognition (ANPR) 1, 10, 156–73, 223–4; Canada 162–3, 166–7, 168; China 4; description of 156–8; discrimination 169–70; emergence as law enforcement tool 158–9; impact on law enforcement 165–7; Istanbul 142, 144; Lagos 111; political use of 17; privacy issues 167–8, 171; South Africa 104, 106, 112, 116n15; Tokyo 87–8; United Kingdom 159–60, 166–7, 168; United States 160–2
automated vehicle identification (AVI) 156, 158–9, 170
automated vehicle monitoring (AVM) 156, 158–9, 170
automatic teller machines (ATMs) 108–9, 116n21, 226
autonomy, right to 375, 379

AutoVu Technologies 163
AVI *see* automated vehicle identification
AVM *see* automated vehicle monitoring

Baltimore 122
banks: Canada 125; 'smart'
    surveillance 226; South Africa 103,
    108–9; Turkey 139
Barthes, Roland 69, 73
Batchen, Geoffrey 69, 70, 71, 73, 78
Beck, Ulrich 284
Becker, Karin 75
Beijing 28, 127, 180, 188, 277
Bennett, Colin 276
Bentham, Jeremy 140, 250, 251, 363
Berger, John 69
Berlin 37, 275
biometrics 71, 72, 143, 224; privacy
    issues 232, 346; Turkey 139
Birmingham 168–9, 170
Bittner, Egon 38
'black screen' technology 378–9
blurring of video objects 228
Bogard, William 140
Boggs, Danny 374
border security 71, 222
Bosch Security Systems 225, 226
Botswana 117n28
Boyle, Philip 10, 127, 174–84
Brazil: panoptic and synoptic society 259;
    public opinion 276–81, 287; Rio de
    Janeiro 8, 29, 83, 84–7, 90, 91–6
Brisbane 188
British Columbia 163, 168, 188, 337, 338
Budapest 26
Bulgaria 27, 164
Bulger, Jamie 6, 25, 192, 238, 239–40,
    275, 310, 361
Burt, Christopher 15, 355–69
bus transport: alarm systems 159;
    Canada 125, 130; South Africa 113;
    Turkey 139
Bush, George W. 247n3
Butler, O. 115n10

CAD *see* computer-aided dispatch
Cairo 112
Calgary 242
California 28, 161
Calvert, Clay 72
camera labels 324–5
camera positioning 59–60
cameras (photographic) 68, 69, 70
Cameron, A. 32
campus security 107–8

Canada 122–35; abortion rights 372;
    Automated Number Plate
    Recognition 162–3, 166–7, 168;
    camera proposals 130–1; Charter
    of Rights and Freedoms 334, 335,
    336, 341, 344–9, 350, 371; Crime
    Stoppers 202–15; development of
    camera surveillance 9, 28, 123–4;
    evaluation of CCTV 31; lack of
    evidence on effectiveness 129–30;
    legal context of surveillance 15–16,
    333–54; new technologies 357;
    number of camera systems 289n11;
    politics of surveillance 238–47; privacy
    protections 16, 360, 365, 370–1, 373,
    374–5, 376; public opinion 12, 124,
    128–9, 276–81, 283, 287, 288, 362;
    resistance to surveillance 3, 128–9;
    signage 298, 310–16, 317, 318, 327;
    support for surveillance 284; taxi cab
    cameras 11, 185–201; terrorism 362;
    transportation systems 125, 130; UK
    influence on 124, 356; Vancouver
    Olympics 10, 126–8, 163, 174–84;
    violent crime 125–6
Cape Town 104, 115n5, 115n6
capital, types of 244–6
car parks 30–1, 104
case law 342–8, 350, 353, 371–5, 377–8
cash-in-transit vehicles 116n22
casinos 100, 115n3
Çavlin Bozbeyoğlu, Alanur 9–10, 139–55
Cavoukian, Ann 340–1, 348
CBDs *see* central business districts
CCTV *see* Closed Circuit Television
cellphones 8, 76, 77, 78
central business districts (CBDs):
    Nairobi 28; South Africa 9, 100,
    101, 102, 103, 115n5, 115n6;
    Vancouver 127
Central Intelligence Agency (CIA) 162
Charter of Rights and Freedoms 334, 335,
    336, 341, 344–9, 350, 371
Chicago 28, 122, 159
children: Mexican missing child case
    13–14, 251, 253–8, 259; pro-
    surveillance arguments 240–1, 247
Chile 259
China: Beijing Olympics 28, 127, 180,
    188; CCTV 28; police control 144;
    public opinion 3–4, 12, 276–81, 282,
    287, 288, 289n7, 289n8; surveillance
    market 2; taxi cab cameras 188
CIA *see* Central Intelligence Agency
Cisco Systems Inc. 223, 226

citizen activism 125
citizen-posted signs 327–9, 331
City Challenge 6, 25
civil liberties 62, 219, 229, 330, 333; anti-surveillance activists 238; Automated Number Plate Recognition 167; Canada 130; 'smart' surveillance 232; *see also* human rights
Clarke, Roger 139
class 93
Clement, Andrew 11–12, 15, 218–34, 309–32
Closed Circuit Television (CCTV) 5, 6–7, 23–45, 71, 72; Africa 28–9, 110–12, 114; Canada 3, 122–35, 238–47; civil liberties 229; conceptualization of 23–5; conventional model 219–20, 230, 232; criticism of 296; definition of 157; Egypt 117n30; Europe 26–7, 122, 143; evaluation of 29–37; lack of deterrence 190, 211; 'legitimacy discourses' 52–3; marketing of 241–3; Middle East 29; monitoring 224–5; negative media coverage 62–3, 64; operational problems 56–61, 64; 'politics of contraction' 47; politics of implementation 49–55; public opinion 276–88; racial profiling 243; as rhetorical device in film 75; seductive power of 34–5; shift away from 222; signage 295–308, 309–32; South Africa 100–21; South America 29; symbolic functions 49, 51; Tokyo 89; Turkey 139–55; United Kingdom 2, 6–7, 25–6, 46–66, 122, 124, 131n1, 151, 295–308; United States 28; *see also* surveillance
codes of conduct 56, 302, 307n13, 349–50, 379
Cole, 316, 318–19
Coleman, C. 30, 39
Coleman, Roy 94
Colombia 259
common law 341, 343, 377
community safety: public opinion 364; South Africa 102, 107, 114; Tokyo 88–90, 94; Virtual Community Patrol 363; *see also* Crime Stoppers
compliance 295–306
computer-aided dispatch (CAD) 158–9
consent *see* informed consent
context-aware technologies 367
contextual integrity 305–6
control rooms 24, 35, 60; Rio de Janeiro 85; selective targeting 38;

South Africa 103, 105, 113, 114; *see also* monitoring; operators
Copenhagen 26, 27
Corbis 72–4
Cordero, J.M. 361
corporations 73–4
Costa Rica 259
costs: African cities 111; digital recording 220; maintenance 61, 62–3, 64; South Africa 101; taxi cab cameras 194, 195
counter-terrorism 10, 159–60, 169–70
creative images 72–4
Creba, Jane 126, 192
crime: Automated Number Plate Recognition 166–7; Canada 124, 128, 129–30, 336; critique of CCTV use 6–7; dark figure of 165; detection of 32–3, 35; evaluation of CCTV 29–37; failure of deterrence 190–1; fear of 33, 41n7, 240, 362; Istanbul 147–8; Latin America 249; 'legitimacy discourses' 52–3; perceptions of 3, 9; police crime data 244–5; public opinion on camera effectiveness 278–81, 283; punishment of 40; Rio de Janeiro 86; 'signal crimes' 13, 192–3, 239–41, 254; South Africa 101–2, 103, 106, 108–9, 113–14; taxi cabs 185, 187, 190; Tokyo 88, 90; 'trigger events' 5; Turkey 145; United Kingdom 295; Vancouver 174; *see also* property crime; violent crime
crime prevention 34–5, 37; Canada 128; Europe 27; exclusion 39; Istanbul 147; live monitoring 317; Namibia 111; public opinion 363; South Africa 102, 103, 104, 109, 113–14; United Kingdom 25
Crime Stoppers 11, 190, 202–17; deterrence 211–12; errors 207–8, 215; expansion of 210–11; harms and benefits 212–15; increased use of images 208–10; previous research 204; privacy issues 205–8, 211, 214, 215
Criminal Code (Canadian) 335, 336, 342
criminal justice discourse 39–40
Croatia 27
cultural capital 244
culture 5, 149
'culture of fear' 147, 284
Cyprus 164
Czech Republic 27

Dar es Salaam 111

Data Protection Act (DPA, 1998) 14, 264–5, 267–9, 296–7, 310, 316, 376
data protection issues: Automated Number Plate Recognition 168; Crime Stoppers data 206, 211; European Data Protection Directive 330, 360; *Faceless* 264–5; informed consent 358–9; misuse of surveillance 296; signage 298, 330; 'smart' surveillance 228–9, 232; *see also* privacy
databases: Automated Number Plate Recognition 10, 157, 158, 160, 161, 163, 169; biometric 224; facial recognition 231; identification of 9/11 terrorists 237–8; South Africa 107, 109; taxi cab cameras 196; Vancouver Olympics 181–2
dataveillance 139–40, 143, 158
Davies, Simon 378
Dawson, Danielle 12, 124, 132n4, 274–91
Debord, Guy 270
Deisman, Wade 31, 129
Deleuze, Gilles 140, 144
Delhi 28
democracy 11, 194, 196
'democratic deficit' 6, 16–17
demonstrations 148, 152n5, 176, 177–8
Denmark 26, 27, 316
Deol, Pritam 191
Derby, Patrick 10, 156–73
deterrence 2, 331n4; Canada 124, 130; Crime Stoppers 211–12; evaluation of CCTV 31; failure of 190–1; myth of the rational offender 7, 34, 36–7, 191; signage 296, 312, 365; South Africa 102, 103, 109, 113–14; taxi cab cameras 190
detournement 270
Dickson, Gary 189
Digital Recording Ammeters (DRAs) 347–8
digital signage networks (DSN) 226
digital technology 2, 4, 5, 157–8, 220–2; anonymization 227–8; Automated Number Plate Recognition 10, 157; 'black screen' 378–9; open systems 24–5; photography 70–1; social implications for surveillance subjects 229–31; video analytics 11–12, 218, 222–7, 231, 232, 330; *see also* technology
DineSafe 326

Dink, Hrant 152n3
disabled employees 57–8
discrimination 169–70, 285
Ditton, J. 30, 41n7, 285
Doneda, D. 96
Doyle, Aaron 1–19, 185–201
DRAs *see* Digital Recording Ammeters
DSN *see* digital signage networks
Dubbeld, Lynsey 38
Dublin 26
Duchamp, Marcel 263
Dupont, Benoit 244
Durban 115n5, 115n6
Dziekański, Robert 231

East Orange New Jersey Police Department's Virtual Community Patrol 363
Eastern Europe 144
ECoC *see* European Capital of Culture
economic capital 244
economic recession 47, 61, 62
Edmonton 126, 130, 189
e-governmentalization 143–4, 149, 151
Egypt 112, 117n30
Elzinga, A. 187
encryption 227–8
Ericson, Richard 38, 140–1, 144, 180, 196
Europe: CCTV 26–7, 122, 143; Data Protection Directive 330, 360; fair information practices 297; growing camera surveillance 3; privacy protections 360; public opinion 277–8; reasonable expectation of privacy 344; UrbanEye Project 24
European Capital of Culture (ECoC) 9, 10, 140, 149–50
European Convention for the Protection of Human Rights and Fundamental Freedoms 341, 360
Everyday Safety Divisions (SABs) 88–90
evidence 32–3, 34; Canada 124; limits to CCTV 35–6; South Africa 102, 103–4, 108
evidence-based decision-making 63
exclusion 39, 148
expenditure on surveillance 2; Beijing Olympics 180; United Kingdom 25, 63, 122; United States 122; Vancouver Olympics 126, 127, 178, 181; *see also* funding

Facebook 13, 256, 257
Faceless 14, 263, 264–72

facial recognition 4, 157, 221, 224; databases 231; failure of technologies 226–7; Istanbul 143; privacy issues 232; as 'silent technology' 230; South Africa 106, 116n15; Tokyo 88; Toronto 152n4; Vancouver Olympics 127
fair information practices 297, 338, 367
Fantino, Julian 162
Farah, Paulette Gebara 251, 253–8
Farrington, David 31
FASE *see* 'Friends Against Senseless Endings'
favelas 8, 85–6, 87, 91, 94–5
fear 33, 41n7, 147, 240, 284, 362
Ferenbok, Joseph 11–12, 15, 218–34, 309–32
films 74, 75–6, 78, 283; *Faceless* 14, 263, 264–72
Finland 26, 27, 164
Finn, Jonathan 5, 7–8, 67–80
FIPPAs *see* Freedom of Information and Protection of Privacy Acts
First Amendment 372, 376, 377
FLIR *see* Forward-Looking Infrared cameras
focus groups 286–7
Fonio, Chiara 38–9
Forward-Looking Infrared (FLIR) cameras 346, 347
Foucault, Michel 13, 71, 140, 251–2
'found footage' 263, 264, 267–8, 269, 272
Fourth Amendment 371
France: Automated Number Plate Recognition 164; CCTV development 26, 27; public opinion 276–81, 287, 288, 289n5, 289n8; signage 317
Franceville 112
Freedom of Information and Protection of Privacy Acts (FIPPAs) 339–41, 342, 365
freedom of movement 364–5
'Friends Against Senseless Endings' (FASE) 125, 192, 362
Frosh, Paul 73
full disclosure signs 325
'function creep' 16, 162, 170, 194, 310
funding: Africa 110–11; Mexico City 254; South Africa 101; United Kingdom 25; Vancouver Olympics 181; *see also* expenditure on surveillance; investment
Fussey, Pete 49

Gaberone 117n28

Gabon 111–12
gambling industry 100, 115n3
game parks 113, 117n32
Gamso, Jeff 167
gangs 86, 87, 89
Garland, David 39, 40
Garron, Sheldon 95
gated communities: Japan 93; Mexican missing child case 13–14, 253–4, 255, 258; Rio de Janeiro 87; South Africa 105–6, 115n10; Turkey 139; *see also* residential areas
Gates, Bill 74
gay people 371–2
genealogical approach 47–8
Georgetown 161, 165
Germany: Automated Number Plate Recognition 164; CCTV development 26, 27; first use of CCTV 219; public awareness of cameras 37; regulation 316–17
Gerrard, G. 17
Getty Images 72–4
Ghana 1
Gilbert, E. 187
Gill, M. 24, 30–1, 33, 37
Giuliani, Rudy 87
Glasgow 30, 32, 124, 188
Glazso, A. 275
globalization 83, 95, 96, 149–50, 182
Globalization of Personal Data (GPD) project 12, 83, 274, 275–83, 285–8
Goldie-Ryder, Michael 125, 192
Google Street View 228, 377
governance: Brazil 84, 85, 92; e-governmentalization 143–4; Foucauldian notion of 140; neo-liberalism 48; Tokyo 87; Turkey 145
governmentality 83, 96, 140
GPD *see* Globalization of Personal Data project
GPS technology 156, 159, 194, 196, 327, 329, 344, 374
Graham, Stephen 1, 46
Grant, Oscar 76–7
Gras, M.L. 316–17
Greece 10, 27, 179–80, 182
Grossklags, J. 366
Guattari, Felix 140, 144

Haggerty, Kevin 127, 140–1, 144, 180, 196, 275
Halifax, Nova Scotia 189–90
Hamel, Alexandre 125–6, 192
Hamilton 125–6, 192

hand-holding in public 371–2
Helsinki 27
Hier, Sean P. 3, 125, 129, 196
historical sedimentation 56, 60
Hoboken 15, 355, 357, 360, 363, 365
Hodes, Laura 372–3
Holliday, George 77
Honduras 1
Huey, Laura 5, 12–13, 237–48
Huge, M. 241, 246
human rights: Brazil 94; legislation 296; neo-liberal era 142; surveillance art 268; Turkey 151
Human Rights Act (HRA, 1998) (UK) 296
Hungary 27, 151, 276–81
hypercontrol 140

IBM Smart Surveillance Solutions 225, 226
icons 318, 321, 322–4
identification of criminals 102, 109, 144
image archives 72–4
immigrants 88, 93
implied consent 317, 339
'imprescience', organizational 56
impression management 52
India 2, 28, 202
inequalities 93, 259
Information and Privacy Commissioner of Ontario (IPC) 314
informed consent 15, 356, 358–60, 366; Automated Number Plate Recognition 171; Crime Stoppers advertisements 214; signage 296, 311, 313, 315, 320, 365, 367; see also implied consent
Innes, Martin 240
In-Q-Tel 162
inspections 326–7
insurance industry 163, 166
intelligence 160, 161, 237–8
intelligent transportation systems (ITS) 164, 165
integrity see contextual integrity
International Association of Chiefs of Police (IACP) 160
internet 5, 220; see also websites
Introna, Lucas D. 230
investment 50, 54, 61; see also funding
IPC see Information and Privacy Commissioner of Ontario
Iran 29
Iraq 164
Ireland, Republic of 26, 27, 164

Istanbul 2, 9, 10, 139–55
Italy 26, 27, 38–9, 164
ITS see intelligent transportation systems
Ivins, William M. Jr. 68–9

Japan: public opinion 276–81, 287–8; terrorism 285; Tokyo 8, 83, 87–90, 91–6
Johannesburg 102, 103, 112, 115n5, 115n6, 115n7
Johnson, Mathew 15–16, 333–54

Kabul 1
Kanashiro, Marta 85, 92, 94, 96
Kathmandu 1
Kelowna 128, 337–8
Kenya 28, 111
King, J. 30, 32–3
King, Rodney 77
Klein, Naomi 180
Kole, O.J. 109
Koskela, Hille 141
Kozubal, Jerry 189–90
Kurds 150

La Forest, Gérard 345, 348
Lagos 29, 111
Landman, K. 115n10
Latin America 3, 249–51, 259–60
Latour, Bruno 92
Laudon, Kenneth 71
legal issues: abortion 372–3; common law 341, 343; legal context of surveillance in Canada 15–16, 333–54; liability for CCTV maintenance 60–1; privacy 309–10, 360, 370–9; public-private distinctions 334–6; signage and legal compliance 295–308, 325–7; see also case law; regulation
legitimacy 47, 52–3, 61–2, 64
Leman-Langlois, Stephan 129–30, 280
Levin, Thomas 75–6
Leyda, Jay 267–8
liability 60–1
Libreville 112
'lifestyle security' 106
Lion's Eye in the Sky Project 124, 129, 240
Lippert, Randy 1–19, 190, 202–17, 239, 298, 309, 310, 313–14, 319, 330
Lips, Miriam 169
Lithuania 27
Liverpool 147, 149
Lizar, Mark 14–15, 295–308, 316
Lomell, H.M. 39

London: Automated Number Plate
Recognition 87, 159–60; CCTV 24,
25–6, 219; *Faceless* 14, 264, 268–9,
271; Olympics 10, 180; signage and
legal compliance 14–15, 298, 299–303;
street robberies 33; terrorist bombings
(2007) 6, 7, 27, 36, 284–5, 306n2
Los Angeles 30, 161, 165–6
Louisiana 162
Loveday, M. 37
Luksch, Manu 14, 263, 264–72
Lyon, David 1–19, 71, 72, 140, 250, 252

Machin, David 73–4
Madrid bombings (2004) 6, 27, 274
maintenance issues 55, 56, 60–1, 62, 64,
111
Malaguti, Vera 93
'Manifesto for CCTV Filmmakers' 269
Manovich, Lev 69, 70–1
marginalized groups 141–2, 150, 170
market approach 48
marketing 193–4, 241–3
Marx, Gary 71, 186, 197
Mathiesen, Thomas 13, 72, 252
McCahill, Michael 24–6, 39, 122, 196,
289n9, 298–304, 306n5, 307n12,
307n13
McDermott, Patricia 283–4
McGrath, John E. 72
McLuhan, Marshall 69, 362
Measor, L. 40n6, 41n8
media: Canada 129; marketing of
CCTV 241, 242; Mexican missing
child case 13–14, 251, 253, 255–6,
258; negative framing of CCTV 48,
62–3, 64; police access to 245–6;
politics of CCTV implementation 50,
52, 54; public opinion 275, 283–4, 285;
synoptic logic 250, 252; tabloids 75;
United Kingdom 34; 'voyeur nation'
concept 72; *see also* television
'mega-events' 5–6, 10, 16; Rio de
Janeiro 86–7, 91; Tokyo 88; *see also*
Olympics
Menezes, Jean Charles de 231
Mexico: Automated Number Plate
Recognition 164; missing child
case 13–14, 251, 253–8, 259; public
opinion 12, 276–81
Middle East 29, 144
migrants 88, 93, 150
Milan 26, 38–9
Mills, C. Wright 282
mining industry 100, 110

Minnaar, Anthony 8–9, 100–21
minorities 7; CCTV targeted
at 38–9, 168–9; Crime Stoppers
advertisements 214–15, 216; racial
profiling 243; 'smart' surveillance 230
'misappropriation' 16, 375, 377
'mission creep' 16
MOBESE *see* Mobile Electronic System
Integration
mobile ANPR systems 157, 161
Mobile Electronic System Integration
(MOBESE) 2, 9–10, 139, 140, 142–6,
148, 150–1
Monahan, Torin 165
Moncton 189
monitoring 24, 35, 224–5; Germany 317;
Istanbul 142–3; signage 314–15; South
Africa 107; Vancouver Olympics
178–9; *see also* control rooms
Montevideo 1
moral panic 40n2
Moscow 27
Mozambique 164
multiplexing 35–6
Murakami Wood, David 8, 83–99
Muslims 169

Nader, Ralph 378
Nairobi 28, 111
Namibia 111
national security 124, 141, 165
neo-liberalism 6, 7, 8, 17; CCTV 48–9,
51–2; commoditization of culture 149;
decline of social rights 141; destructive
features of 47; globalization 83;
Japan 93, 94, 96; shopping areas 147;
Turkey 140, 142, 145, 146, 148, 150,
151; use of public space 39
Nepal 1
Netherlands: audio-visual surveillance
system 357; CCTV development 26,
27; Crime Stoppers 202; selective
targeting 38; signage 317; violence
against taxi cab drivers 187
networked video recording (NVR)
220
New York City 122, 161, 364
New Zealand 164, 188
news media 75, 145, 275, 283–4; *see also*
media
Nieto, M. 29
Nigeria 29, 111
Nisbet, M. 241, 246
Nissenbaum, H. 306
normative order 38

Norris, Clive 6–7, 23–45, 122, 151, 157, 196, 285, 289n9, 298–304, 306n5, 307n12, 307n13, 316
North America: growing camera surveillance 3; public opinion 275, 277, 282; see also Canada; United States
Norway: Automated Number Plate Recognition 164; CCTV development 26, 27; evaluation of CCTV 145; exclusionary effect of CCTV 39; public opinion 275; taxi cab cameras 195
notification 296–306
NVR see networked video recording

Obama, Barack 372
obsolescence 59–60
OECD see Organization for Economic Co-operation and Development
Office of the Privacy Commissioner of Canada 315–16, 338–9, 349–50
Olympics 6, 9, 149; Athens 179–80, 182; Beijing 28, 180; London 10, 180; Rio de Janeiro 29, 85; Vancouver 10, 126–8, 163, 174–84
Onassis, Jacqueline Kennedy 377
Ontario: Automated Number Plate Recognition 162; camera installations 126; common law 343; Crime Stoppers 203, 205, 208–9, 213–14; databases 231; freedom of information Acts 339–40; 'Friends Against Senseless Endings' 125, 192, 362; guidelines 349; opposition to CCTV 9, 129; signage 314; taxi cab cameras 189
'open street' systems 14–15, 305; Canada 9, 16, 123, 124, 125, 192; Crime Stoppers advertisements 214; diffusion of 196; Europe 26; lack of deterrence 211; marketing of 193; signage 302, 313–14; 'smart' surveillance 219; Turkey 139, 142–3, 144, 148, 150, 151; United Kingdom 25
open systems 24–5
Openness Principle 313, 320
operability issues 59–60
operators 38, 56, 57–8, 104–5, 219, 220, 285, 331; see also control rooms
Organization for Economic Co-operation and Development (OECD) 297
organizational 'imprescience' 56
Orwell, George 252
Oslo 26, 39

Ottawa 11, 186, 192–7, 203–4
outsourcing 101, 105

Pan, Tilt and Zoom (PTZ) cameras 24, 35, 84, 219, 222
Panopticon 13, 71, 140, 363; Istanbul 144; panoptic surveillance 250, 251–2, 259
Paris 27
parking tickets 103, 104
Personal Information Protection and Electronic Documents Act (PIPEDA, 2000) 311, 313, 315–16, 320, 327, 330, 335–6, 338–9
personhood, right to 375
petrol stations 109–10, 116n23–n25
Philadelphia 30
photography 7–8, 68–71, 78; image archives 72–4; tabloids 75
physical searches 334, 344, 350
PIPEDA see Personal Information Protection and Electronic Documents Act
planning issues 53–4
PlateScan Inc. 162
Poland 27
police 3, 37–8; Automated Number Plate Recognition 157, 159, 160–1, 162–3, 165–7, 168, 170–1; Canada 128, 129, 245; computer-aided dispatch 158–9; control rooms 24; Crime Stoppers 11; discriminatory policing 285; Egypt 112; killing of innocent civilians by 231; legal requirements for surveillance 340–1, 342; Muslim communities 169; political summits 176; pro-camera advocacy 13; quality of CCTV footage 36; responsibility for CCTV maintenance 60–1; Rio de Janeiro 84, 85–6, 87; shooting of Oscar Grant 76–7; South Africa 101, 103; symbolic capital 246; Tokyo 87, 89, 90; Toronto 244; transfer of surveillance images to 205–6, 207–8; Turkey 144; Vancouver 174, 175, 177; see also Royal Canadian Mounted Police
political capital 245
political summits 176
politics: CCTV implementation 49–55, 64–5; of criminal justice 39; destructive features of neo-liberalism 47; 'representational' 48, 61–4; Rio de Janeiro 85; Turkey 140, 142, 151; United Kingdom 7
populism 40

Port Gentil 112
portable ANPR systems 157
Portugal 27
positioning of cameras 59–60, 302–3
post-modernism 69
Potter, Gary 14–15, 295–308, 316
power imbalances 297, 310
Prague 27
Pretoria 110, 112, 115n5, 115n6, 115n10, 116n16
prisons 113
privacy 5, 15, 17, 296, 330, 355–69; 'accepted wisdom' 370–1; anti-surveillance activists 238, 242, 243, 244; Automated Number Plate Recognition 167–8, 171; Brazil 95–6; Canada 123, 128–9, 130, 336, 337–50; Crime Stoppers 205–8, 211, 214, 215; guidelines 16, 349–50; legal issues 16, 309–10, 333, 334, 336, 337–50, 370–9; neo-liberal era 142; public opinion 287–8; reasonable expectation of 344–5, 346–8, 357, 360, 373, 374; signage 190, 206–7, 298, 326–7; 'smart' surveillance 12, 227–9, 230, 232; surveillance art 268; taxi cab cameras 195–6; theoretical approaches 306; Turkey 9–10, 144–5, 150, 151; UK Data Protection Act 297
Privacy Act (Canada, 1985) 336, 337–8, 342, 376
Privacy Act (US, 1974) 376–7
Privacy International 378
private sector 6, 16, 17; Africa 110, 111; Canada 123, 125, 127, 131; Crime Stoppers advertisements 213–14, 215; criminal justice driven by 193; neo-liberal transformation 141; public-private distinctions 334–6; Rio de Janeiro 85; South Africa 100–1, 105–7, 113, 116n16; Turkey 139, 142, 146–7, 151; United Kingdom 25
privatization 95, 142
'Project Champion' 168–9, 170
'Project Street Sweeper' 163
property crime 31, 37; Crime Stoppers 213; South Africa 103, 104; see also stolen vehicles
property rights 359
PTZ see Pan, Tilt and Zoom cameras
public, surveillance by the 76–7, 78
public access property 104–5
public opinion 12, 274–91, 363; Canada 124, 128–9, 362; China 3–4; effectiveness of camera surveillance 35,

278–81, 283, 286; fear of crime 33, 41n7; knowledge of camera surveillance 277–8, 280, 281, 282–3, 287; limitations of GPD survey 282, 285–6; media coverage of CCTV 62; Mexican missing child case 254–5; privacy 357, 360; safety 40n6, 364, 365; support for surveillance 145–6, 238, 242, 365–6; Tokyo 89
public order 51
public safety 225–6, 231, 242, 317, 365
public transport: Canada 123, 125, 130; Crime Stoppers 211; New York City subway 364; South Africa 113; Turkey 139
publicity 52
public-private partnerships 6, 7; Africa 110, 114; Lagos 111; Mexico City 254; neo-liberalism 48; South Africa 113; Turkey 9

Qatar 164
qualitative research methods 285–7, 288
Quebec 9, 123, 162, 163, 338, 349, 374–5
Queensland 30
Queer McGill 372

race: Brazil 93; Crime Stoppers advertisements 214–15, 216; racial profiling 243; 'smart' surveillance 230
Radwanski, George 335, 337, 339, 340, 345
Ratcliffe, J. 30, 31
rational offender myth 7, 34, 36–7, 191
RCMP see Royal Canadian Mounted Police
realism 71
regulation 6, 14–16; Canada 128, 336–42; China 4; Japan 93–4; signage 310, 311, 313–14, 315, 316–17, 321, 325–7, 330; 'smart' surveillance 232; United Kingdom 14, 296–9; see also legal issues
Rehnquist, William W. 373, 376
repurposing of security information 229, 230
residential areas: South Africa 105–7, 116n16; Turkey 139; see also gated communities
responsibility 60–1
rhetoric, surveillance as 74–6
rhizomes 140–1, 144
rights 16, 320–1, 330; abortion 372–3; Canadian Charter of Rights and Freedoms 334, 335, 336, 341, 344–9, 350, 371; public activities 371; see also civil liberties; human rights

Rio de Janeiro 8, 10, 29, 83, 84–7, 90, 91–6
riots 4, 175
risk 284, 363
Riyadh 29
Roberts, John G. 373
Rogge, Jacques 10, 127, 179
Romania 164
Royal Academy of Engineers 5
Royal Canadian Mounted Police (RCMP) 162–3, 166, 168, 175, 337–8
Russia 27, 144
Ryan, Peter 179

SABs see Everyday Safety Divisions
'safe shopping' 6
San Diego 161
San Francisco 30, 32–3, 192
Saskatoon 189
Sasse, Angela 243
satellite surveillance 71, 72
Saudi Arabia 29
scale of compliance see compliance
SCAN see Surveillance Camera Awareness Network
schools 108, 116n20
SCNs see surveillance camera networks
scopophilia 253, 258
Scotland 30, 32, 124
searches 334, 344–5, 346, 347, 348–9, 350, 375, 378
secure visual object coding 228, 229
security 141, 149–50, 362, 367; Brazil 95, 96; Canada 124; public opinion 366; Turkey 147–8; Vancouver Olympics 176–7, 179
security guards 147
'security villages/estates' 101, 105–6
'seeing' 5, 67, 68–71, 77–9
selective targeting 38–9
Serbia 164
Shearing, C. 39
Sheffield 188
Sherbrooke 9, 123
Shintaro, Ishihara 88
shopping malls 37, 39, 147; Canada 125; marketing of CCTV 241; police crime data 244; South Africa 101, 104–5; Turkey 139
Short, E. 30
Siciliano, Amy 262
signage 2, 190, 206–7, 309–32, 365, 367; basic use scenario 319–20; Canadian law 313–14, 315; categories of signs 318; characteristics of 318–19;

citizen-posted signs 327–9, 331; guidelines 314–16; Istanbul 143; legal compliance 14–15, 295–308, 325–7; legibility 318, 319; operator-posted notification samples 321–5; proposed schemes 320–9, 330–1; regulatory enforcement agent-posted signage 325–7
'signal crimes' 13, 192–3, 239–41, 254; see also 'trigger events'
signal processing algorithms 218, 220, 222, 223, 227, 230
Singapore 164, 188
Situationists 270
SLPD see St Louis Police Department
small businesses 55, 304
smartphones 327–9
Smith, Emily 9, 122–35
Smith, Gavin 2, 7
Smith, Robert Ellis 16, 370–9
social capital 245–6
social norms 361
social order 8, 63, 65n2, 84, 96
social responsibility 146–7
social services 141, 142
social sorting 140, 284–5
socio-technical system, CCTV as 24, 123
Sontag, Susan 69–70, 71
South Africa 8–9, 100–21; ATMs 108–9, 116n21; Automated Number Plate Recognition 164; campus security 107–8; CCTV development 100–4; Crime Stoppers 202; FIFA World Cup 110, 112; petrol stations 109–10, 116n23–n25; public access property 104; residential areas 105–7, 116n16; schools 108, 116n20; shopping malls 104–5
South America 29
Spain: CCTV development 27; public opinion 12, 274, 276–81, 282, 287, 288, 289n5; terrorism 36
spatial control 176, 177, 181
speed enforcement 164–5
Spriggs, A. 24, 30–1, 33, 37
Squiers, Carol 75
Squires, P. 40n6, 41n8
St Louis Police Department (SLPD) 158–9
staffing issues 56, 57–8, 104–5
stakeholders: politics of CCTV implementation 51–2, 245; proponents of surveillance 242; taxi cab cameras 195–6
state 141, 272

Stenning, P. 187
stock photography 72–4
Stockholm 27
Stoddart, Jennifer 349
stolen vehicles 17, 112, 160, 163, 165–6, 168, 169
suasive surveillance society concept 95
surveillance 67–80; 'accepted wisdom' 370–1; as aesthetic concept 72–4; art 14, 263–4, 268, 270, 272; 'authoring' function 262–3, 265, 271, 272; Crime Stoppers images 202–15; *Faceless* 264–72; industry growth rate 307n14; Latin America 249–51, 259–60; Mexican missing child case 253–8; normalization of 93; panoptic 250, 251–2, 259; as participation in public life 76–7; perceptions of 361–6; politics of 238–47; as rhetoric 74–6; seeing photographically 68–71; 'smart' 11–12, 218–34; as social practice 71–2, 77–9; synoptic 13, 14, 250, 252–3, 258, 259; taxi cab cameras 185–201; Tokyo and Rio de Janeiro 90–6; Vancouver Olympics 174–84; *see also* Closed Circuit Television
surveillance border notification 321–4
Surveillance Camera Awareness Network (SCAN) 2, 123, 131
surveillance camera networks (SCNs) 309, 310, 317, 321, 327–9
'surveillance creep' 194–5, 238
'surveillance societies' 90, 92, 95, 96
Surveillance Studies 71, 190–1, 193, 197, 239
surveillant assemblages 11, 140–1, 180, 196–7, 230, 330
sustainability 56, 64
Sutton, A. 29
Sweden 26, 27, 317
Switzerland 27, 164, 275
symbolic capital 246
synoptic surveillance 13, 14, 250, 252–3, 258, 259

tabloids 75
Tagg, John 69
Tampere 27
Taniguchi, T. 30
Tanzania 111
taxi cabs 10–11, 126, 185–201
technology 6, 141, 355–6, 366–7; 'black screen' 378–9; mitigating technologies 379; photography 70;

South Africa 114; technological reasoning 56, 57; *see also* databases; digital technology
teenagers 39
Tegucigalpa 1
Tehran 29
television: Crime Stoppers advertisements 203, 204–5, 208–9; reality shows 8, 72, 74, 75, 195–6, 252, 283; surveillance as major theme in 74–5, 78; *see also* media
temporality 270–1
terrorism 6, 36, 295; Canada 124, 362; CCTV in London 159–60, 306n2; footage of 9/11 attacks 284; identification of 9/11 terrorists 237–8; proponents of surveillance 13, 241; public opinion 274, 275, 284–5; 'smart' surveillance 226–7; Tokyo 88, 92; United States 28
Texas 222
Thailand 164
Thompson, R. 17
Thompson, Robert 361
time-lapse recording 35–6
Tokyo 8, 83, 87–90, 91–6
Toronto: Automated Number Plate Recognition 162, 166; cameras destroyed by youths 262; Crime Stoppers 203, 209, 210–12, 214–15; focus groups 287; G20 meeting 152n4, 176, 182n2, 183n5; legal requirements for surveillance 340; police research 244; proponents of surveillance 245–6; signage 311, 314, 326; surveillance restrictions 379; taxi cabs 192–3, 197n1; transportation systems 130; violent crime 126
tourism: Egypt 112, 117n30; Istanbul 149
traffic control 3; Egypt 112; Lagos 111; Rio de Janeiro 84–5; South Africa 102, 112, 114; Vancouver 127; *see also* Automated Number Plate Recognition
training 58
transfer of surveillance images 205–6, 207–8
transportation systems: AVI/AVM systems 159; Canada 123, 125, 130; Crime Stoppers 211; intelligent 164, 165; legal requirements for surveillance 340; New York City subway 364; South Africa 113; Turkey 139
'trigger events' 5, 6, 9, 11, 16; *see also* 'signal crimes'

True Beauty (TV show) 8, 74, 75
trust in government 280–1, 289n7
trustworthiness 296–306
truth 5, 76, 219
Turin 127
Turkey 5, 9–10, 139–55; approaches
  to camera surveillance 140–2;
  demand for monitoring 145–6; e-
  governmentalization 143–4, 149,
  151; privacy 144–5; security 147–8;
  support of private sector 146–7; Textile
  Employers' Association 140, 146–7
Twitter 256, 257

United Arab Emirates 164
United Blueline 189
United Kingdom (UK): Automated
  Number Plate Recognition 159–60,
  165, 166–7, 168; 'black screen'
  technology 378–9; CCTV
  development 6, 25–6, 27, 124,
  151; Code of Practice 379;
  counter-terrorism 169–70; Crime
  Stoppers 204–5, 209; Data Protection
  Act 14, 264–5, 267–9, 296–7, 310,
  316, 376; erosion of CCTV use 46–66;
  evaluation of CCTV 2, 7, 29–34,
  36–7, 39; influence on Canada 124,
  356; Jamie Bulger case 6, 25, 192,
  238, 239–40, 275, 310, 361; lack
  of deterrence 190; Liverpool 147;
  London Olympics 10, 180; number of
  cameras 1, 122, 131n1, 271–2, 289n11,
  295; private cameras 17; 'Project
  Champion' controversy 168–9, 170;
  public opinion 275, 278, 279, 283,
  286; racial profiling 243; reasonable
  expectation of privacy 344, 345;
  same-sex hand-holding 371–2;
  signage and legal compliance 295–308,
  316; taxi cab cameras 188; urban
  policy 365
United States (US): abortion
  rights 372; Automated Number
  Plate Recognition 160–2, 170;
  cab cameras 187–8; CCTV
  development 6, 28, 122; Crime
  Stoppers 202; evaluation of CCTV 29,
  30, 32–3; 'misappropriation' 16, 375,
  377; privacy cases 377–8; privacy
  protections 15, 16, 360, 370–1,
  373, 375–7, 379; public opinion 12,
  275, 276–81, 288, 289n8; reasonable
  expectation of privacy 344; surveillance
  market 2; taxi cabs 187, 196

universities 107–8
urban regeneration 94, 365; Istanbul 150;
  South Africa 103; United
  Kingdom 48–9, 51; Vancouver 175
UrbanEye Project 24, 26, 122, 143, 229,
  299
Uruguay 1, 259

VA *see* video analytics
'value for money' 53
Vancouver: anti-surveillance
  activists 243; Automated Number
  Plate Recognition 162–3; CCTV
  proponents 239–41, 244; gay
  people 372; mapping of cameras
  in 331n1; Olympics 10, 126–8, 130,
  174–84; taxi cab cameras 126, 188
Vatican City 164
Venables, John 361
VerifEye Technologies 126, 185, 186, 188,
  189, 193–4
video analytics (VA) 11–12, 218, 222–7,
  231, 232, 330
video internet protocol (VIP) 221
'video sniffing' 268–9
'viewer society' 72
violent crime: Canada 125–6; CCTV
  impact on 30, 31, 37; Crime
  Stoppers 212–13; Latin America 3; taxi
  cab drivers 187, 191, 192–3
VIP *see* video internet protocol
Virtual Community Patrol 363
vision 5, 34, 68–71
Visionics Corporation 226–7
visual content industry 72–4
Volokh, Eugene 372
Von Hirsch, A. 39
Vonn, Michael 10, 174–84
'voyeur nation' concept 72
voyeurism 252–3, 258

Wakefield, Alison 39
Walby, Kevin 10–11, 126, 185–201
warrants, search 348–9, 375, 378
Warsaw 27
Watkins, David 371–2
websites: Crime Stoppers
  advertisements 203, 205, 206, 208–15;
  privacy issues 375, 379; signage 325,
  327
Wees, William 268, 272
Wells, H. 28, 30, 32
Welsh, B. 31
Western culture 5
Westin, Alan 376

Weston, Edward 68, 71
Whitson, Jennifer 192
wildlife protection 113, 117n32
Wilkinson, Blair 11, 190, 202–17, 239
Wilson, Dean 29
Windhoek 111, 117n26
Winnipeg 191, 197n1, 207, 242
wireless technology 5, 356, 357, 366–7
Wood, David 196, 230
workplaces 339
World Cup (FIFA): Rio de Janeiro 29,
85; security measures 149; South
Africa 110, 112; Tokyo 88

YouTube: Crime Stoppers
advertisements 11, 203, 205, 206,
208–15, 216; Mexican missing child
case 256, 258; shooting of Oscar
Grant 76

Zagreb 27
Zeilinger, Martin 14, 262–73